The UK Brewing Industry

Profiles of the leading 2200 companies

John D Blackburn

Editor

dp

First Edition

Spring 2019

ISBN-13: 978-1-912736-11-9

ISBN-10: 1-912736-11-X

All rights reserved. No part of this publication may be reproduced, distributed, or transmitted in any form or by any means, including photocopying, recording, or other electronic or mechanical methods, without our prior written permission, except in the case of brief quotations embodied in critical reviews and certain other non-commercial uses permitted by copyright law. For permission requests, please write to us.

Copyright © 2019 Dellam Publishing Limited

Printed in 8pt Nimbus Sans L

Designed by URW++ Design and Development GmbH

Dellam Publishing Limited

2 Heath Drive, Sutton, Surrey, SM2 5RP

Fax: 020 8770 7478   email: enquiries@dellam.com

SAN: 0177881   EAN/GLN: 5030670177882

Table of Contents

1 Acknowledgements iv

2 Introduction v

3 Total Assets League Table 1
- As a measure of size, total assets is preferable to turnover which is influenced by profit margins and whether companies are capital or labour intensive.

4 Age of Companies 17
- Each company is ranked by its date of incorporation. Newcomers are defined as those registered since 2017.

5 Geographic Distribution 31
- Each company is classed by county.

6 Company Profiles 45
- Full company name, date incorporated, net worth, total assets, registered office, activities, shareholders and parent company, directors (with date of birth, nationality and occupation) and number of employees (if available).

7 Index of Directorships 187
- Alphabetical list of directors showing their directorships. If several directors have identical names then their date of birth is shown.

8 Standard Industrial Classification 245
- These codes are used to classify businesses by the type of economic activity in which they are engaged.

9 *finis* 251

Acknowledgements

This is a long and detailed publication containing thousands of facts and figures. It is only to be expected, despite continuous and repeated editing and checking, that errors may occur. In such cases, once we are aware of any, we publish a correction on our website.

Readers are encouraged to check regularly at www.dellam.com/books for any corrections and updates.

Although we take extreme care to ensure accuracy and being up-to-date, we cannot accept responsibility for any errors or omissions.

Contains public sector information licensed under Open Government Licence v3.0. from The Charity Commission (England and Wales) and The Charity Commission for Northern Ireland. © Crown Copyright and database right (2018).

Contains information from the Scottish Charity Register supplied by the Office of the Scottish Charity Regulator and licensed under the Open Government Licence v.2.0. © Crown Copyright and database right (2018).

Contains OS data © Crown copyright and database right (2018)

Contains Royal Mail data © Royal Mail copyright and database right (2018)

Contains National Statistics data © Crown copyright and database right (2018)

Contains Office for National Statistics © Crown copyright and database right (2018)

Maps based on those produced by the Office for National Statistics Geography GIS & Mapping Unit (2012 and 2018).

Contains HM Land Registry data © Crown copyright and database right (2018).

Contains Parliamentary information licensed under the Open Parliament Licence v3.0.

House of Commons Library Briefing Papers licensed under the Open Parliament Licence v3.0.

Contains Food Standards Agency data © Crown copyright and database right (2018).

Contains Eurostat data, 1995-2018, copyright European Commission by the Decision of 12 December 2011.

Maps based on produced by ONS Geography GIS & Mapping Unit.

Contains Companies House data supplied under section 47 and 50 of the Copyright, Designs and Patents Act 1988 and Schedule 1 of the Database Regulations (SI 1997/3032).

We appreciate your interest in our publications, and your comments and suggestions are always welcome. Please contact us at enquiries@dellam.com.

Introduction

This study looks at all companies registered in the United Kingdom where they identify themselves as manufacturers of beer.

This study includes companies that are dormant or non-trading some of which might be latent while others may operate under their owners' names but are incorporated to protect the business name. In addition, all newly incorporated companies are included.

The study will exclude those companies that do not specifically identify themselves as manufacturers of beer.

The aim of this study is to provide an overview of the key movers and shakers in the UK brewing sector. Only key data has been isolated, particularly the company's net worth and total assets, but also its full name, date incorporated, registered office, other activities, shareholders, directors (with date of birth, occupation and nationality) and number of employees.

Two indicators of size are used: net worth and total assets. These are preferable to turnover which is influenced by profit margins and whether the companies are capital or labour intensive.

In Great Britain, 57% of those aged 16 years and over in 2017 drank alcohol (29 million people of the population) while 20% did not drink alcohol at all.

Burton-on-Trent was the centre of beer making with 30 breweries including Bass, the first company to register its trademark. Beer drinking has been in decline for decades with sales falling and the rise of micro-breweries and craft ales has not halted the downward trend with half of supermarkets' total beer and cider sales accounted for by lager.

The three largest producers of beer are Germany, UK and Spain, which combined produce 42% of the total EU beer production. In the UK, beer has increased by £0.5 billion (15%) from £3.2 billion in 2016 to £3.7 billion in 2017.

Breakdown of beverages in the UK is as follows: soft drinks (28%), beer (27%), whisky (25%), cider (7%), gin (3%), mineral water (3%) and others (2%).

More than 11,000 pubs have closed in the UK in the last decade, a fall of almost a quarter (23%). The number of UK pubs has fallen from around 52,500 in 2001 to some 38,815 in 2018. Although many pubs have closed, the total turnover of pubs and bars has held up, remaining flat since 2008, adjusted for inflation. Around 70% of workers in pubs and bars are paid less than the Living Wage Foundation's living wage.

The Society of Independent Brewers (SIBA) has 800+ brewing members where cask production is now 69% of total production; on average 5.6 full-time and 1.9 part-time staff are employed by members; beer production showed a 1.7% increase in 2017 compared to 2016, confirming the positive trends; 51% of production is supplied to free-trade pubs, with 13% going to controlled pubs; and 69% of beer is sold within 40 miles of the brewery.

The British Beer and Pub Association reported that under the beer duty escalator alone (2008-2013) beer tax rose by 42%, and during that time beer sales fell by 24% in pubs causing 5,000 pubs to close.

Standard cataloguing guidelines for company names in the profile section have been used, but there will be occurrences when the name may not be strictly alphabetical. A certain licence was adopted where it was felt that strictly alphabetical could lead to improper cataloguing. Some company names have been shortened in the league tables for aesthetic reasons.

John D Blackburn
Editor

This page is intentionally left blank

Total Assets League Table

Company	Value	Company	Value
ABI UK Holding 1 Limited	£145,066,819,584	The Innis & Gunn Brewing Company Limited	£12,160,000
ALE Finance Services Limited	£78,933,565,440	The Black Sheep Brewery PLC	£11,888,239
ABI SAB Group Holding Limited	£48,913,764,352	AB InBev UK Investment Company Limited	£11,815,303
Anheuser-Busch Europe Limited	£14,835,154,944	Tynemill Limited	£11,375,271
AB InBev UK Finance Company Limited	£14,650,720,256	The West Berkshire Brewery PLC	£10,169,723
Heineken UK Limited	£6,296,000,000	Thomas Hardy Kendal Limited	£9,162,000
Greene King Brewing and Retailing Limited	£3,969,999,872	Caledonian Brewery Limited	£6,900,321
Marston's PLC	£3,031,200,000	Beavertown Brewery Ltd	£6,666,542
Molson Coors Brewing Company (UK) Limited	£878,267,008	Thomas Hardy Burtonwood Limited	£6,525,000
AB InBev UK Limited	£858,534,016	Wetherells Contracts Limited	£6,314,174
Carlsberg UK Limited	£475,660,992	Felinfoel Brewery Company Limited (The)	£6,146,446
Shepherd Neame Limited	£334,227,008	Holdens Brewery Limited	£6,144,029
Daniel Thwaites Public Limited Company	£308,600,000	Woodforde's BPP Limited	£6,100,000
Belhaven Brewery Company Limited	£288,540,000	Butcombe Brewing Company Limited	£6,020,774
ZX Ventures Limited	£281,748,992	Trumark Properties Limited	£5,902,612
Carlsberg Supply Company UK Limited	£248,720,992	Wye Valley Brewery Limited	£5,867,068
Hall & Woodhouse Limited	£206,032,992	The Wild Beer Co Ltd	£5,741,497
Brewdog PLC	£203,231,008	Elgood & Sons,Limited	£5,674,543
S.A.Brain & Company,Limited	£192,684,992	Moorhouse's Brewery Ltd	£5,641,973
St.Austell Brewery Company Limited	£188,327,008	Purity Brewing Company Limited	£5,428,463
McMullen & Sons, Limited	£171,648,000	True North Brew Co Limited	£5,119,779
Wadworth and Company Limited	£152,864,992	Heather Ale Limited	£5,044,741
Charles Wells,Limited	£141,250,000	T.& R. Theakston Limited	£4,944,000
J.W.Lees & Co.(Brewers) Limited	£115,451,720	Fourpure Limited	£4,675,165
Everards Brewery Limited	£111,340,000	Hepworth & Company Brewers Limited	£4,448,623
Joseph Holt Limited	£111,061,576	Rhymney Brewery Ltd	£4,413,558
Joseph Holt Group Limited	£105,466,624	Higsons 1780 Limited	£4,386,360
Frederic Robinson Limited	£98,526,000	Thornbridge Hall Country House Brewing Co Ltd	£4,227,784
Arkell's Brewery Limited	£70,877,672	LF Brewery Holdings Limited	£4,017,000
Charles Wells Brewery Limited	£65,067,000	The Liverpool Craft Beer Company Limited	£4,015,029
Adnams PLC	£64,708,000	Branded Drinks Ltd	£3,886,575
Camerons Brewery Limited	£60,147,224	Hop Back Brewery Public Limited Company	£3,561,344
Aston Manor Limited	£55,704,092	Hurns Brewing Company Ltd.	£3,508,960
Butcombe Brewery Limited	£48,207,372	Harviestoun Brewery Limited	£3,420,250
Harvey & Son (Lewes) Limited	£47,975,480	St. Peter's Brewery Co. Limited	£3,317,448
Marston's Acquisitions Limited	£44,600,000	Sinclair Breweries Limited	£3,310,000
Camden Town Brewery Limited	£39,531,716	Drygate Brewing Company Ltd	£3,302,378
Hydes' Brewery Limited	£38,585,184	Otter Brewery Limited	£3,135,846
J.C. & R.H. Palmer Limited	£37,139,700	Saltaire Brewery Limited	£3,133,189
Timothy Taylor & Co.,Limited	£35,537,816	Ramsbury Brewing and Distilling Company Limited	£3,085,206
Sharp's Brewery Limited	£29,014,440	Fyne Ales Limited	£3,068,529
George Bateman & Son Limited	£25,884,940	Black Eagle Brewery Ltd	£2,846,247
H.B.Clark & Co.(Successors) Limited	£24,827,042	Magic Rock Brewing Company Ltd	£2,827,454
Meantime Brewing Company Limited	£20,091,000	Crouch Vale Brewery Limited	£2,822,445
Innis & Gunn Holdings Limited	£19,979,000	Freedom Brewery Ltd	£2,787,101
Thomas Hardy Holdings Limited	£19,423,000	Titanic Brewery Co Limited	£2,652,566
Daniel Batham & Son Limited	£15,705,189	Curious Drinks Limited	£2,616,154
Joseph Camm Farms Limited	£15,188,856	Rebellion Beer Company Limited	£2,536,358
Hook Norton Brewery Company,Limited (The)	£15,070,130	St. Peter's Brewery Group Public Limited Company	£2,502,368
French & Jupps Limited	£14,657,962	Ossett Brewing Company Limited	£2,491,694
Joules Brewery Limited	£14,329,697	Bradfield Brewery Limited	£2,475,709
Cobra Beer Partnership Limited	£14,096,065	The Cairngorm Brewery Co. Ltd.	£2,449,294

The UK Brewing Industry — dellam

Black Isle Brewing Co. Ltd.	£2,372,496	Gower Brewery Co Limited	£1,251,866
The Edinburgh Beer Factory Limited	£2,365,710	Cloudwater Brew Co Ltd	£1,249,277
St Andrews Brewers Limited	£2,329,965	Mondo Brewing Company Limited	£1,243,654
Hobsons Brewery and Company Limited	£2,274,040	Wiveliscombe Breweries Limited	£1,241,768
Exmoor Ales Limited	£2,238,827	The Mighty Oak Brewing Co. Limited	£1,241,703
The Dark Star Brewing Company Limited	£2,226,149	German Kraft Brewing Limited	£1,234,867
Brewing and Distilling Company Limited	£2,206,992	Weetwood Ales Limited	£1,200,384
The Innis & Gunn Inveralmond Brewery Limited	£2,129,000	Northern Monk Brewing Co. Ltd	£1,191,657
The Harbour Brewing Company Limited	£2,073,234	Sambrook's Brewery Limited	£1,188,926
Dartmoor Brewery Limited	£2,050,183	Tempest Brewing Co Limited	£1,142,723
Brixton Brewery Limited	£2,030,560	Bays Brewery Limited	£1,134,355
Siren Craft Brew Limited	£2,008,344	Acorn Brewery of Barnsley Limited	£1,099,029
Hogs Back Brewery Limited	£1,992,264	Marble Beers Limited	£1,096,277
Abbeydale Brewery Limited	£1,960,314	Windsor & Eton Brewing Company Limited	£1,096,020
Salopian Brewing Company Ltd.	£1,937,880	The Wimbledon Brewery Company Limited	£1,095,844
The Kernel Brewery Ltd	£1,937,845	Oak Brewing Company Limited	£1,087,852
Skinner's Brewing Co. Limited	£1,923,524	Westerham Brewery Company Limited	£1,073,934
Bristol Brewing Company Limited	£1,921,805	Moncada Brewery Limited	£1,065,707
The Five Points Brewing Company Ltd	£1,918,501	Surrey Hills Brewery Ltd	£1,043,051
Stewart Brewing Limited	£1,899,475	Purple Moose Brewery Ltd	£1,037,016
Bathams (Delph) Limited	£1,857,679	Twickenham Fine Ales Limited	£1,028,140
Wrexham Lager Beer Company Limited	£1,819,298	The Milton Brewery Cambridge Limited	£1,008,562
Cumberland Breweries Limited	£1,803,259	The Staffordshire Brewery Limited	£963,800
Harviestoun Brewery (Holdings) Limited	£1,800,046	Goose Eye Brewery Limited	£956,180
Wold Toppers Limited	£1,794,538	Arbor Ales Ltd	£948,246
Camden Brewing Group Limited	£1,788,777	Wylam Brewery Limited	£928,179
The Leeds Brewery Company Limited	£1,774,296	Vale Brewery Company Ltd.	£921,900
The Great Yorkshire Brewery Limited	£1,766,120	Roosters Brewery Limited	£911,019
Skinnybrands Ltd	£1,702,059	Burton Bridge Brewery Limited	£876,928
Ludlow Brewing Company Limited	£1,654,475	The London Beer Factory Ltd.	£876,032
Morecambe Bay Wines Limited	£1,638,859	Lost and Grounded Brewers Ltd	£869,701
Noah Beers Limited	£1,634,380	Angus Brewing Limited	£843,406
Woodforde's Limited	£1,612,566	Gower Pub Co Ltd	£832,827
Arran Brewery PLC	£1,608,927	Pressure Drop Brewing Limited	£792,590
Lancaster Brewery Company Limited	£1,606,139	Rudgate Brewery Limited	£792,284
Buxton Brewery Company Ltd	£1,549,054	Keith Brewery Limited	£784,487
Beersheba Ltd	£1,530,592	Conwy Brewery Limited	£784,473
The Salcombe Brewery Co. Limited	£1,524,242	Alnwick Ales Limited	£783,708
Vocation Brewery Limited	£1,523,819	Flack Manor Brewery Limited	£782,804
Whitewater Brewing Co. Ltd	£1,493,683	Wood Brewery Limited (The)	£779,520
Scottish Borders Brewery Limited	£1,481,119	Fierce Beer Limited	£777,026
Hawkshead Brewery Limited	£1,481,000	Zymurgorium Ltd	£765,763
John Roberts Brewing Co Ltd	£1,444,884	The Bowland Beer Company Limited	£764,487
Nethergate Brewery Co Ltd	£1,409,286	Andwell Brewing Company Ltd	£749,851
Enville Ales Limited	£1,386,960	Redemption Brewing Company Limited	£747,696
Church End Brewery Limited	£1,354,185	Arran Brew Ltd.	£738,288
The Redchurch Brewery Limited	£1,341,027	Enfield Brewery Limited	£732,708
Windsor Castle Brewery Limited	£1,325,613	The Braybrooke Beer Company Limited	£716,304
Wickwar Wessex Brewing Company Limited	£1,291,132	Old Dairy Brewery Limited	£710,788
Honest Brew Ltd	£1,289,386	The Sussex Beer Company Ltd	£700,807
The Tring Brewery Company Limited	£1,279,175	Nene Valley Brewery Limited	£696,100
Moor Beer Company Limited	£1,256,542	Wiper & True Ltd.	£677,818

Double Maxim Beer Company Limited	£672,995	The Outstanding Brewing Company Ltd	£477,993
The Grainstore Brewery Limited	£666,208	Charlbury Brewing Company Limited	£474,328
Dancing Man Brewery Limited	£665,677	Signature Brew Ltd	£471,671
Highland Brewing Company Limited	£657,957	Shiny Brewing Company Ltd	£469,555
Two Tribes Brewing Ltd	£647,627	Small Beer Brew Co. Ltd	£467,090
Hillside Brewery Limited	£646,493	Dorking Brewery (2016) Limited	£465,775
Strong House Brewery Ltd	£638,400	Hiver Beers Ltd	£457,204
C J Middleton Limited	£637,332	Wooha Brewing Company Ltd	£451,945
Isle of Skye Brewing Company (Leann An Eilein) Ltd	£636,642	Fallen Brewing Company Ltd	£443,385
Cotleigh Brewery Limited	£636,443	Breworks Ltd	£440,747
Green Jack Brewing Company Limited	£632,090	The London Beer Company Limited	£438,913
Great Western Brewing Company Limited	£629,526	Wild Weather Ales Ltd	£437,919
Portobello Brewing Company Ltd	£627,950	Ramsgate Brewery Limited	£433,045
The Ilkley Brewery Company Limited	£623,302	Eden Brewery Limited	£427,756
Irwell Works Brewery Ltd	£616,797	McGrath Davies Public Houses Limited	£427,181
Bedlam Brewery Limited	£609,949	The Whitstable Brewery Company Limited	£426,611
Blue Monkey Brewing Limited	£609,899	Monty's Brewery Limited	£420,498
North East Brewing Company Limited	£605,460	Golcar Brewery Limited	£418,326
Electric Bear Brewing Company Ltd	£604,950	Deeside Brewery Limited	£418,293
Wild Horse Brewing Company Limited	£604,829	B & T Brewery Limited	£412,828
Blackjack Beers Limited	£600,787	Redwillow Brewery Ltd	£400,283
Northern Whisper Brewing Company Limited	£588,992	North Brewing Company Limited	£397,713
Allendale Brew Company Limited	£588,519	Hill House Inns Limited	£396,760
Charles Cooper Limited	£585,543	Harbour Brewery Tenby Limited	£394,236
Brick Brewery Ltd	£585,028	Calvors Brewery Limited	£393,900
Goddards Brewery Limited	£580,178	Spitting Feathers Limited	£393,052
Red Squirrel Brewery Limited	£574,906	Seven Brothers Brewery Limited	£392,828
The Cotswold Brewing Company Limited	£562,589	Colchester Brewery Ltd	£390,121
Hop Stuff Brewery Limited	£558,434	Daleside Brewery Limited	£387,742
Victor's Drinks Limited	£557,301	Badger Ales Limited	£387,421
Keltek Cornish Brewery Limited	£550,492	Four Pillars Brewery Limited	£385,052
Yates Iow Brewery Limited	£545,559	Tyne Bank Brewery Limited	£383,024
Cross Bay Brewery Limited	£542,995	Munro Ventures Limited	£382,261
Agricola Bottling Limited	£540,595	Brew By Numbers Ltd.	£381,595
Lorsho Limited	£535,472	Hoggshead Brewhouse Limited	£375,236
Traditional Scottish Ales Limited	£526,805	London Brewing Company Limited	£373,787
Long Man Brewery Limited	£525,815	Dorset Brewing Company Limited	£371,985
WBC (Norfolk) Limited	£525,378	Kirkstall Brewery Company Limited	£367,555
Mauldon's Limited	£521,032	London Fields Brewery Opco Limited	£365,636
Spey Valley Brewery Limited	£513,372	Brew York Limited	£359,213
Burning Sky Brewery Limited	£508,801	Yellow Hammer Brewing Limited	£349,229
Yorkshire Heart Limited	£508,433	Baltic Beer Company Ltd	£349,130
Branscombe Vale Brewery Limited	£507,271	The Stroud Brewery Limited	£349,108
XT Brewing Company Limited	£507,090	Crate Bars Limited	£347,526
Broughton Ales Limited	£502,688	Hackney Brewery Ltd	£344,649
The Kelham Island Brewery Limited	£502,624	Konigsberg Seven Bridges Breweries Ltd	£342,764
Little Valley Brewery Limited	£498,736	Manning Brewers Ltd	£340,175
71 Brewing Limited	£498,439	Tower Brewery Limited	£339,839
Tintagel Brewery Limited	£497,841	The Eccleshall Brewing Company Limited	£339,054
Phipps Northampton Brewery Company Limited	£485,990	Partizan Brewing Limited	£326,775
The Coniston Brewing Company Limited	£485,223	Vyrnwy Developments Limited	£326,647
Pictish Brewing Co Limited	£481,509	The Flying Monk Brewery Ltd	£324,418

The UK Brewing Industry

Bank Top Brewery Limited	£324,027	Powderkeg Brewery Ltd	£253,112
Reunion Ales Limited	£318,016	Good Chemistry Brewing Limited	£252,899
Langham Brewing Company Limited	£317,991	Arundel Brewery Limited	£251,002
Bellfield Brewery Limited	£315,473	The Great Orme Brewery Limited	£250,346
Heaney Brewing Company Limited	£313,546	Romney Marsh Brewery Limited	£249,197
Cheddar Ales Limited	£313,518	Left Handed Giant Ltd.	£246,169
Wild Card Brewery Limited	£312,674	The Durham Brewery Limited	£240,426
Lymestone Brewery Limited	£309,822	Orbit Brewing Limited	£239,623
Chris O'Connor and Associates Limited	£309,543	Belvoir Brewery Limited	£238,945
Weird Beard Brew Co Ltd	£307,311	The Barrels Hereford Limited	£237,528
The Mobberley Brewhouse Limited	£299,698	The Indian Brewery Company Birmingham Ltd	£237,103
The Belleville Brewing Company Limited	£297,492	Larkins Brewery Limited	£236,863
Tenby Brewing Co. Limited	£293,537	Musket Brewery Limited	£236,270
Anarchy Brew Co. Limited	£293,533	Wensleydale Brewery (2013) Limited	£235,650
Cygnus Brewing Co Limited	£292,447	The Loddon Brewery Ltd	£234,714
Peak Ales Limited	£290,746	Elland Brewery Limited	£231,183
Brentwood Brewing Company Limited	£289,421	Station 119 Ltd	£227,857
Gloucester Brewery Ltd	£287,028	Potbelly Brewery Limited	£227,311
Dancing Duck Beer Ltd	£285,361	W.L.B.C Ltd	£226,640
East London Brewing Company Limited	£284,896	The Backyard Brewhouse Limited	£226,188
Naylor's Brewery Ltd	£284,477	White Horse Brewery Company Limited	£225,353
Windswept Brewing Co Ltd	£283,572	Lake View Country House Ltd	£222,571
Howard Town Brewery Limited	£283,207	Welbeck Abbey Brewery Limited	£219,922
Hammerpot Brewery Limited	£282,749	Southbourne Brewing Limited	£219,633
Church Farm Brewery Ltd	£281,642	Lancar Limited	£218,353
Brewster's Brewing Company Limited	£280,330	Brewsmith Beer Limited	£216,244
The Great Newsome Brewery Limited	£279,828	North Cotswold Brewery Limited	£215,485
Boss Brewing Company Ltd	£278,827	Byatt's Brewery Ltd	£211,745
Batch Brew Ltd	£276,600	LVS Bottling Limited	£211,197
The Exeter Brewery Limited	£275,095	Brass Castle Brewery Limited	£210,892
Gun Brewery Limited	£274,392	Verdant Brewing Company Limited	£210,865
FGW Brewery Limited	£273,684	Deviant and Dandy Brewery Limited	£209,293
The Bridgehouse Pub Company Ltd	£272,867	Earl Soham Brewery Limited	£208,845
Wright & Spillane Limited	£271,617	Red Cat Brewing Limited	£208,840
The Ennerdale Brewery Ltd	£270,772	Ainsty Ales Limited	£208,132
Track Brewing Company Ltd	£267,451	The Bespoke Brewing Co. Limited	£207,313
Farm Yard Ales Ltd	£267,213	Ulverston Brewing Company Limited	£206,688
The Loose Cannon Brewing Company Limited	£266,679	The Cornwall and West Country Craft Brewing Co Ltd	£206,526
Colonsay Beverages Ltd.	£264,888	Mantle Brewery Limited	£206,162
Vibrant Forest Brewery Limited	£264,729	Anspach & Hobday Limited	£205,698
Firebird Brewing Company Ltd	£264,374	Great Heck Brewing Company Ltd	£204,908
Burnt Mill Brewery Ltd	£263,470	Shardlow Brewing Company Limited	£203,741
Steam Town Brewco Limited	£262,723	Loch Lomond Brewery Limited	£203,536
Barney's Beer Limited	£262,055	First Chop Brewing Arm Ltd	£203,375
Grain Brewery Limited	£259,977	The Kinross Brewery Limited	£202,786
Bewdley Brewery Limited	£258,683	1936 Limited	£201,210
Brightside Brewing Company Limited	£258,385	Neepsend Brewery Ltd	£201,173
Cwrw Llyn Cyf	£257,403	The Beer Collective Limited	£201,043
Staneyhill Brewery Limited	£254,406	Christopher Ellis and Son Limited	£200,312
Peerless Brewing Company Limited	£253,807	The Roebuck Brewing Company Limited	£199,694
Tirril Brewery Limited	£253,237	Pilot Beer Limited	£197,592
The Coach House Brewing Company Limited	£253,114	The Pink Ferry Ltd	£197,060

Tatton Brewery Limited	£196,437	The Instant Karma Brewing Company Ltd	£155,918
Stancill Brewery Limited	£196,192	UBrewCC Limited	£154,889
Clarkshaws Brewing Company Ltd.	£194,863	Merchant City Brewing Company Limited	£153,921
Tonbridge Brewery Limited	£193,405	Twisted Barrel Ale Limited	£153,837
North Riding Brewery Limited	£191,911	Penton Park Brewery Limited	£153,757
Stonehenge Ales Limited	£191,539	Artisan Brewing Company Ltd	£153,496
Villages Brewery Limited	£191,112	Kelburn Brewing Company Limited	£152,174
Atom Brewing Co Limited	£190,136	Traquair House Brewery Limited	£150,336
Speyside Craft Brewery Limited	£189,355	Vaux Brewery Ltd	£150,001
Wibblers Brewery (Farms) Limited	£187,463	Geipel Brewing Limited	£149,905
New River Brewery Ltd	£187,083	Wilde Child Brewing Co. Ltd.	£149,548
Myrlex Southend Limited	£186,872	Brewshed Ltd	£149,388
Ashover Brewery Limited	£186,209	Southwark Brewing Company Limited	£149,270
The Great North Eastern Brewing Company Limited	£185,660	Yeovil Ales Limited	£148,679
Kent Brewery Ltd	£184,825	Fine Tuned Brewery Limited	£147,840
Glen Affric Brewery Limited	£181,944	Piddle Brewery Limited	£147,663
The Three Legs Brewing Company Limited	£180,583	Pixie Spring Brewing Company Limited	£147,553
Bishop Nick Limited	£178,876	360 Degree Brewing Company Ltd	£147,076
Time & Tide Brewing Limited	£178,562	Blonde Brothers Limited	£146,209
Khukuri Beer (UK) Limited	£177,859	Wincle Beer Company Limited	£145,957
Recoil Brewing Company Ltd	£177,720	Torrside Brewing Ltd	£145,313
Brew Toon Ltd.	£177,630	Volden Limited	£144,603
Pilot Wharf Limited	£175,625	Signal Brewery Limited	£144,199
Loud Shirt Brewing Co Ltd	£175,436	Legenderry Brewing Company Limited	£143,997
The Downton Brewery Company Ltd	£173,137	The Alnwick Brewery Company Limited	£143,935
Nexus Engineering Limited	£169,527	Clavell & Hind Limited	£143,921
Red Rock Brewery Limited	£168,055	Townes Brewery Limited	£143,197
Vale of Glamorgan Brewery Limited	£167,632	Malt, The Brewery Limited	£143,162
Old School Brewery Limited	£167,079	Bridge House Brewery Limited	£142,661
Exit 33 Brewing Ltd	£167,071	Shetland Refreshments Limited	£142,633
Taddington Brewery Limited	£166,963	Totnes Brewing Co Limited	£141,845
Lincoln Green Brewing Company Limited	£164,382	M Rackstraws Ltd	£141,231
Bowman Ales Limited	£163,757	Almasty Brewing Company Ltd	£139,721
Volden Brewing Limited	£163,706	Teignworthy Brewery Limited	£139,603
Pig and Porter Limited	£163,689	WantsumBrewery Ltd	£139,437
Uley Ales Limited	£162,671	Chantry Brewery Ltd	£138,249
Two Cocks Farm Limited	£162,234	Blewin Trust Limited	£137,259
Whitby Brewery Ltd	£161,533	Jon's Brewery Limited	£136,845
The Filo Brewing Company Limited	£161,497	Brinkburn Street Brewery Ltd	£136,837
Canopy Beer Company Ltd	£159,858	Saffron Brewery (Henham) Limited	£136,747
Devanha Brewery Holdings Limited	£159,812	Brewboard Limited	£136,298
Hercules Brewing & Co. Limited	£159,691	Milltown Brewing Co. Ltd	£136,264
Alphabet Brewing Ltd	£159,341	Hardstate Limited	£136,233
Merlin Brewing Company Ltd	£158,333	Ripple Steam Brewery Limited	£135,355
Small World Beers Ltd	£157,732	Applecross Brewing Company Limited	£135,174
Bollington Brewing Co. Limited	£157,094	Magna Bottling Limited	£134,738
Seven Brothers Ancoats Ltd	£157,003	Roddenloft Brewery Ltd	£134,701
Gustmain Limited	£156,861	Froth Blowers Brewing Company Ltd	£134,571
Alechemy Brewing Ltd	£156,755	The Little Beer Corporation Ltd	£134,567
Ballard's Brewery Limited	£156,208	Bad Seed Brewery Ltd	£134,514
Derby Brewing Company Limited	£156,168	Three Brothers Brewing Company Limited	£134,467
Insight Driven Innovation Limited	£156,039	Magna Brewery Limited	£133,486

The UK Brewing Industry dellam

Company	Amount	Company	Amount
Maldon Brewing Company Limited	£132,765	West By Three Limited	£111,457
The Wobbly Brewing Company Limited	£132,296	The Ridgeside Brewing Company Ltd	£111,189
Dukeries Brewery Ltd.	£132,102	Copper Tun Ltd	£111,000
Frome Brewing Company Limited	£131,666	The Friday Beer Company Limited	£110,054
Dent Brewery Limited	£131,463	Staggeringly Good Ltd	£109,919
Saison 86 Limited	£131,201	Big Smoke Brew Co Limited	£109,790
Sixty Shilling Brewing Ltd	£130,549	Cereal Technology Limited	£109,628
Strands Brewery Ltd	£129,929	Blackpit Brewery Ltd	£109,575
Green Duck Beer Co. Limited	£129,859	Big Hand Brewing Company Limited	£109,102
Bluestone Brewing Company Limited	£129,064	Itchen Valley Brewery Limited	£108,810
Severn Brewing Limited	£128,815	Brighton Bier Limited	£108,751
The Boutique Cellar Limited	£128,656	St Andrews Brewing Company Limited	£108,702
Binghams Brewery Limited	£128,250	Cullercoats Brewery Limited	£108,275
Prospect Brewery Limited	£126,827	Dhillons Brewery Ltd	£108,199
Long Arm Brewing Co Limited	£126,815	Cornish Crown Limited	£107,958
Hardknott UK Ltd	£126,678	The Hop Studio Limited	£107,904
By The Horns Ltd	£125,837	New Bristol Brewery School Ltd	£107,553
Bowness Bay Brewing Limited	£125,784	Watling Street Brewery Limited	£107,534
The Crafty Brewing Co. Limited	£124,656	Frontier Brewing Company Limited	£107,036
The Leighton Buzzard Brewing Company Limited	£124,276	Tillingbourne Brewery Ltd	£106,651
Donkeystone Brewing Co Ltd	£123,249	Taylors Blackbeck Brewery Limited	£106,632
Samuel Webster & Sons Limited	£122,887	Brimstage Brewing Co. Ltd	£106,228
81artisan Limited	£121,711	George's Brewery Limited	£106,189
Towcester Mill Brewery Limited	£121,709	Southbourne Ales Limited	£104,672
Bexley Brewery Limited	£121,475	The Southdown Brewery Limited	£104,529
Jarr Kombucha Ltd	£120,629	Crasi Limited	£102,827
The Borough Brewery Limited	£120,606	Salamander Brewing Company Limited	£102,597
Stealth Brew Co Limited	£120,446	BAA Brewing Limited	£102,475
St Ives Brewery Limited	£120,001	Anglia Pub Company Limited	£102,412
The Inkspot Brewery Limited	£119,119	The Shotover Brewing Company Ltd	£101,947
Wayland's Sixpenny Brewery Ltd	£118,424	Turning Point Brewing Company Limited	£101,334
Firebrick Brewery Limited	£118,220	Wimborne Beer Company Limited	£101,159
Brockley Brewing Company Ltd.	£117,852	Bang-On Brewery Limited	£100,977
Unsworth's Yard Brewery Ltd	£117,766	Dark Tribe Brewery Limited	£100,829
Nelson Brewing Co.Uk Ltd.	£117,719	Westbournia Brewing Company Limited	£100,552
Beermats Brewing Company Limited	£117,056	Brampton Brewery Ltd	£100,267
Wishbone Brewery Limited	£116,977	Meridian Brewery Limited	£100,000
Boxcar Brewery Limited	£116,526	Tollgate Brewery Limited	£99,453
Langton Brewery Ltd	£116,418	Cuillin Brewery Limited	£99,320
Brew Monster Limited	£116,323	Ghost Brewing Co Limited	£98,748
Big Mountain Brewing Company Limited	£116,252	White's Brewery Limited	£98,659
Bizzy Play Limited	£116,240	The Beerblefish Brewing Company Limited	£98,362
Ferry Ales Brewery Limited	£116,179	Somerset Ales Limited	£98,263
Summer Wine Brewery Limited	£115,610	The Dead Crafty Beer Company Limited	£97,936
Umbrella Brewing Limited	£115,512	Don Valley Brewery Limited	£97,566
Cellarhead Brewing Company Ltd	£115,353	Lam Brewing Limited	£97,543
London Beer Lab Ltd	£113,870	Irving & Co. Brewers Limited	£96,810
Grey Trees Brewery Limited	£113,056	Heavy Industry Brewing Limited	£96,619
Overtone Brewing Ltd	£112,528	Tap Social Movement Limited	£96,350
McColl's Brewery Limited	£112,433	Credence Brewing Ltd	£96,026
The Runaway Brewery Limited	£112,340	Penzance Brewing Co Ltd	£95,852
Kingstone Brewery Limited	£112,074	Beer Brothers Ltd	£95,153

The Ham Brewing Company Limited	£94,942	Newcastle Brewing Ltd	£78,333
White Hart Halstead Limited	£94,906	Barngates Brewery Limited	£78,179
Mumbles Brewery Ltd	£93,326	Treen's Brewery Ltd.	£78,090
Two By Two Brewing Ltd	£93,088	The Two Towers Brewery Ltd	£77,854
Silver Street Brewery Limited	£92,683	Quirky Ales Ltd	£77,851
Good Chemistry Apparatus Limited	£92,632	Serious Brewing Company Ltd	£77,774
Goody Ales Limited	£92,553	Turing Complete Solutions Ltd	£77,736
Hadham Brewing Company Limited	£92,229	Whim Ales Limited	£77,598
The Revolutions Brewing Company Limited	£92,091	Utopian Brewing Limited	£77,583
HFBC Ltd	£92,037	Northern Craft Brewers Limited	£77,405
The Bosun's Brewing Company Limited	£91,336	Blue Bee Brewery Ltd	£77,082
Goff's Brewery Limited	£91,322	Black Tor Brewery Ltd	£77,012
Ledbury Real Ales Ltd	£91,310	The Brunswick Brewing Co Ltd	£76,901
Cross Borders Brewing Company Ltd	£90,120	Grasshopper Brewery Limited	£76,848
Boudicca Brewing Company Ltd	£89,938	Selby (Middlebrough) Brewery,Limited	£76,770
Altarnun Brewing Limited	£89,545	Bragdy Nant Cyf	£76,679
Bavarian Gold Limited	£89,370	BC Brewing & Pub Company Ltd	£76,391
Kettlesmith Brewing Company Limited	£89,279	Edinbrew Ltd	£75,926
Martland Mill Brewery Limited	£88,921	Partners Brewery Limited	£75,637
Hattie Brown's Brewery Ltd	£88,605	Sulwath Brewers Limited	£74,525
Hafod Brewing Company Ltd	£88,001	Nailmaker Brewing Company Ltd	£74,478
Squawk Brewing Company Limited	£87,213	The Jaw Brewery Ltd	£73,876
Blackedge Brewing Company Ltd	£87,173	Wilderness Brewery Ltd	£73,586
Bridlington Brewing Co. Limited	£87,050	Amber Ales Limited	£73,304
Cross Inn (Maesteg) Limited	£86,754	Brook House Brewery Limited	£72,138
Fixed Wheel Brewery Limited	£86,543	Recognise Limited	£72,133
The Kinver Brewery Limited	£86,358	Ampersand Brew Co Ltd	£72,051
Scarborough Brewery Limited	£86,113	Crazy Mountain Brewing Company UK Limited	£71,830
Worsthorne Brewing Co Ltd	£85,541	The Margate Brewery Limited	£71,619
Mighty Medicine Brewing Company Ltd	£85,492	The Silverstone Real Ale Company Limited	£71,617
Weltons Limited	£85,450	Cerne Abbas Brewery Ltd	£71,515
Clearwater Brewery Ltd	£85,342	Shipstones Beer Company Ltd	£71,013
Fallen Acorn Brewing Co. Ltd	£85,051	Framework Brewery Limited	£70,589
Oliver Chester Limited	£85,034	Treboom Limited	£70,537
Lyme Bay Brewing Limited	£84,308	Rowton Brewery Ltd	£70,485
Goldmark Craft Beers Ltd	£83,777	Haresfoot Storage & Distribution Company Limited	£70,392
Bay View Brewery Limited	£83,677	Leatherbritches Brewery Limited	£69,998
Yardley Brothers Europe Ltd	£83,196	Papworth Brewery Limited	£69,899
Rockin Robin Brewery Ltd	£83,159	Abbey Ales Limited	£69,783
Epic Beers Limited	£82,604	Derventio Brewery Limited	£69,230
Cwrw Ial Limited	£82,002	The Millis Brewing Company Limited	£69,023
The Untapped Brewing Co Ltd	£81,761	Stardust Brewery Ltd	£68,258
Stratford upon Avon Brewery Limited	£81,727	Bohem Brewery Ltd	£68,255
Nobby's Brewing Company Limited	£81,208	Beeston Brewery Ltd	£68,214
Buffy's Brewery Limited	£81,018	Clouded Minds Limited	£67,881
400 Software Limited	£79,921	Fisher's Brewing Company Ltd.	£67,534
Consett Ale Works Limited	£79,895	Axholme Brewing Company Limited	£66,979
Hornes Brewery Ltd	£79,805	Canterbrew Ltd	£66,748
Half Moon Brewery Ltd	£79,416	Towler and Webb Limited	£66,690
Crystalbrew Limited	£79,133	Eyeball Brewing Ltd	£66,513
Sperrin Brewery Ltd	£78,762	The Campervan Brewery Ltd	£66,179
Red Star Brewery (Formby) Limited	£78,635	Wily Fox Brewery Limited	£66,176

Abernyte Brewery Limited	£65,951	Roam Brewing Company Ltd	£56,364
Fuggle Bunny Brew House Limited	£65,327	SF Brew Co Ltd	£56,118
Big Bog Brewing Company Limited	£65,104	Hybrid Brewing Ltd	£56,096
Hedgedog Brewing Ltd	£65,080	Black Bess Limited	£55,776
Lion Craft Brewery Ltd	£64,914	North Yorkshire Brewing Company Limited	£55,675
Devon Ales Limited	£64,760	Lakehouse Brewing Company Limited	£55,483
Strathaven Ales Limited	£64,401	Elusive Brewing Limited	£55,321
Genius Brewing Limited	£64,366	Vinifera Limited	£55,120
Gun Dog Ales Ltd	£64,281	Mourne Mountains Brewery Limited	£54,829
East Neuk Organic Brewing & Distilling Ltd	£64,209	Birmingham Brewing Company Limited	£54,660
Stubborn Mule Brewery Limited	£64,026	SchoolHouseBrewery Ltd	£54,511
Moonshine Drinks Limited	£63,937	Ards Brewing Company Ltd	£54,486
The Krafty Braumeister Ltd	£63,801	The Burton Old Cottage Beer Company Limited	£54,471
Greyhound Brewery Limited	£63,785	Vendetta Brewing Company Limited	£54,395
Neon Raptor Brewing Company Ltd.	£63,669	Isaac Poad Brewing Ltd	£53,848
Double Barrelled Brewery Ltd.	£63,629	Garden City Brewery Limited	£53,828
Veterans Brewing Ltd	£63,615	The Slaughterhouse Brewery Limited	£53,806
Intrepid Brewing Company Limited	£63,513	Abyss Brewing Ltd	£53,799
Solvay Brewing Ltd	£63,510	Horbury Ales Limited	£53,776
The Jolly Boys Brewery Ltd	£63,265	Halifax Steam Brewing Company Limited	£53,748
Brotherhood Brewery Ltd	£62,554	Croft Ales Ltd	£53,442
Jolly Sailor Brewery Limited	£62,377	Burton Town Brewery Limited	£53,123
Totally Brewed Limited	£62,335	Longhill Garage Limited	£52,672
Hart Family Brewers Limited	£62,164	The 3 Brewers Ltd	£52,450
Little Crosby Village Brewing Company Ltd	£61,785	Unity Brewing Ltd	£52,018
The Millstone Brewery Limited	£61,587	Chorlton Brewing Company Ltd	£51,977
Yorkshire Dales Brewing Company Limited	£61,152	Deva Craft Beer Ltd	£51,761
The Ale Club Ltd	£61,050	Silks Brewery Limited	£51,498
Storm Brewing Company Ltd	£60,967	Blueball Brewery Ltd	£51,363
Nightjar Brew Company Limited	£60,689	West Highland Breweries Limited	£51,343
Plain Ales Brewery Ltd	£60,276	Leadmill Brewery Limited	£51,271
Dark Revolution Ltd	£60,015	Angles Ales Limited	£51,134
Three Castles Brewery Limited	£59,901	Thurstons Horsell Brewery Company Limited	£51,028
Steam Machine Brewing Company Ltd	£59,622	3 Piers Brewery Limited	£50,971
Brewit Microbrewery Ltd	£59,513	Golden Triangle Brewery Limited	£50,730
TwT Lol Cyf	£59,329	The 1648 Brewing Co Limited	£50,720
Butts Brewery Limited	£59,245	Latimer Ales Ltd	£50,251
Big Drop Brewing Company Limited	£58,830	Riverside Brewery Ltd	£50,180
Malvern Hills Brewery Limited	£58,650	The Boat Lane Brewery Limited	£50,171
Argyll Breweries Limited	£58,579	Tunnel Brewery Limited	£50,045
Weatheroak Brewery Ltd	£58,404	Two Thirsty Men Ltd	£49,711
Top Rope Brewing Limited	£57,899	Sibley Brewing Co Ltd.	£49,484
Pentrich Brewing Co. Ltd	£57,517	Ovenstone 109 Limited	£49,303
The Ferry Brewery Co Ltd	£57,464	Glede Brewing Company Limited	£49,116
Compass Brewery Limited	£57,204	Swaddle Micro Brewery Limited	£49,069
Avid Brewing Co. Ltd	£57,185	Old Worthy Brewing Company Ltd	£49,015
Black Lodge Brewery Ltd	£57,016	Little London Brewery Limited	£48,981
Chequers Micropub Limited	£56,663	Campbells Brewery Ltd	£48,707
Islay Ales Company Limited	£56,543	Bute Brew Co Ltd	£48,370
Neptune Brewery Ltd	£56,495	Quartz Brewing Limited	£48,247
Littleover Brewery Limited	£56,453	Bullfinch Brewery Limited	£48,229
Darwin Brewery Limited	£56,398	Empire Brewing Ltd	£47,866

Company	Amount	Company	Amount
Matlock Brewing Company Limited	£47,865	Weal Ales Brewery Limited	£40,025
Sugar Pine Brewing Company Limited	£47,799	GT Ales Limited	£39,527
Broken Bridge Brewing Ltd	£47,787	Brumaison Ltd	£39,504
The Clun Brewery Ltd.	£47,771	Twisted Oak Brewery Ltd	£39,420
Baker's Dozen Brewing Co Limited	£47,525	Staffordshire Spirits Company Limited	£39,271
Red Fox Brewery Limited	£47,155	Metcalfe & Metcalfe Company Ltd	£39,253
Ironstone Brewery Ltd	£46,941	Newark Brewery Ltd	£39,247
Lincolnshire Craft Beers Limited	£46,903	Thirst Class Ale Limited	£39,065
Pokertree Brewing Company Ltd	£46,725	The Icecream Factory Limited	£38,857
Zulu Alpha Brewing Limited	£46,241	Hopjacker Brewery Ltd	£38,411
Oxbrew Ltd	£46,064	The Stockport Brewing Company Ltd	£37,996
Baynhams Brewery Limited	£45,813	John O'Groats Brewery Ltd	£37,889
Star Wing Brewery Ltd	£45,678	Lords Brewing Company Ltd	£37,663
Pin-Up Beers Ltd.	£45,473	Hastings Brewery Ltd	£37,351
Wharfedale Brewery Limited	£45,448	Lions Den Beers Limited	£37,266
Hopshackle Brewery Limited	£45,368	Matthews Brewing Company Ltd	£37,096
Scribbler's Ales Limited	£45,305	Cambridge-Brewery Limited	£36,924
Abstract Jungle Brewing Ltd	£45,172	Mad Cat Brewery Limited	£36,878
Muirhouse Brewery Limited	£44,958	Burning Soul Brewing Ltd	£36,823
Hop King Brewery Ltd	£44,940	Flash House Brewing Company Limited	£36,717
Broxbourne Brewery Ltd.	£44,894	J. Church Brewing Co. Ltd	£35,961
Blindmans Brewery Limited	£44,780	Deeply Vale Brewery Ltd	£35,683
Three Shires Brewery Ltd	£44,763	Three Kings Brewery Limited	£35,619
The Barsham Brewery Limited	£44,665	Corinium Ales Ltd	£35,443
Wingtip Brewing Company Limited	£44,309	EFG International Ltd	£35,378
Odyssey Brew Co Ltd	£43,817	Billericay Brewing Company Ltd	£35,235
Greyhound Drinks Limited	£43,816	Brews of the World Limited	£35,136
Northern Alchemy Limited	£43,717	Bragdy Lleu Cyf	£35,102
The Twisted Brewing Company Limited	£43,689	Temperance Brewing Company Limited	£35,063
Barton House Brewing Company Limited	£43,551	Paradigm Brewery Ltd	£34,842
Fitbeer Ltd.	£43,536	Whitley Bay Brewing Company Ltd	£34,805
Tanners Ales Ltd	£43,383	Hophurst Brewery Ltd	£34,768
Coalition Brewing Company Ltd	£42,864	Encoder Brewery Limited	£33,749
The Sheffield Brewery Company Limited	£42,493	Black Flag Brewery Ltd	£33,643
Wildcraft Brewery Limited	£42,491	Greenfield Real Ale Brewery Ltd	£33,540
Potton Brewing Company Ltd	£42,487	Well Drawn Brewing Company Limited	£33,440
The Fowey Brewery Ltd	£42,393	Mash Brewery Limited	£33,184
Mad Dog Brewing Co Ltd	£42,374	Amwell Springs Brewery Company Limited	£33,156
Richmond Brewing Company Limited	£42,174	Old Pie Factory Brewery Limited	£33,106
Darkplace Brewery Limited	£41,899	Ol Brewery Limited	£33,104
Platform 5 Brewing Company Ltd	£41,661	Bridgnorth Brewing Co. Ltd.	£32,938
Spartan Brewery Ltd	£41,550	Farr Brew Ltd	£32,904
Fosse Way Brewing Company Ltd.	£41,473	The Park Brewery Ltd	£32,834
Chapter Brewing Company Limited	£41,263	Anglesey Ales Ltd	£32,810
Bingley Brewery Limited	£41,220	Hop & Stagger Brewery Ltd	£32,809
Roundhill Brewery Limited	£40,899	Beatnikz Republic Brewing Company Ltd	£32,745
Bond Brews Ltd	£40,612	Barnaby's Brewhouse Ltd	£32,695
Cader Ales Limited	£40,551	Beat Ales Ltd.	£32,514
Lawman Brewing Company, Ltd.	£40,464	Wicked Hathern Brewery Limited	£32,413
Old Spot Brewery Limited	£40,444	Kew Brewery Limited	£32,343
The Cronx Brewery Limited	£40,179	Boutilliers Limited	£32,341
Longdog Brewery Limited	£40,171	Taw Valley Brewery Limited	£31,981

Sloane Home Ltd	£31,948	Mayflower Brewery Ltd	£26,604
Ardgour Ales Ltd	£31,766	Padstow Brewing Company (2013) Ltd	£26,362
Knoydart Brewery Limited	£31,571	3's A Crowd Brewing Ltd	£26,135
Felday Limited	£31,353	Yorkshire Brewing Company Ltd	£26,010
Kathmandu Link Limited	£31,338	Lost Industry Brewing Limited	£25,969
Elmtree Beers Ltd	£31,323	Flipside Brewing Ltd	£25,891
Cold Formd Ltd	£31,230	Little Ox Brewery Limited	£25,722
The Yard of Ale Brewing Company Limited	£31,140	The Pretty Decent Beer Company Ltd	£25,702
The Vine Inn Brewery 2016 Limited	£30,953	Aurora Ales Limited	£25,500
Hopdaemon Brewery Company Limited	£30,881	Grace Land Beer Limited	£25,257
Fermanagh Beer Company Limited	£30,862	Lucky 7 Beer Co Ltd	£25,098
Orchard Road Brewery Limited	£30,730	The Patriot Brewery Limited	£25,053
The Southey Brewing Company Limited	£30,692	Pumphouse Brewing Company Limited	£24,716
Radlett Beer Company Limited	£30,545	The Velvet Owl Brewing Company Ltd.	£24,503
Lincolnshire Brewing Company Limited	£30,289	Bullmastiff Brewery Limited	£24,468
Northern Monkey Brew Co. Ltd	£30,247	Tweed Brewing Ltd	£24,432
Milton and Mortimer Ltd	£30,168	Blackened Sun Brewing Company Limited	£24,387
Brightwater Brewery Limited	£29,801	Nomadic Brewing Company Ltd	£24,342
The Southsea Brewing Company Ltd	£29,791	Sandstone Brewery Ltd	£24,249
Stenroth Limited	£29,719	Cold Bath Brewing Company Limited	£24,107
Ampthill & Woburn Brewery Limited	£29,711	Mid-Cheshire Brewing Ltd	£23,950
Four Kings Brewery Limited	£29,616	The Freewheelin' Brewery Company Limited	£23,881
Muckle Brewing Ltd	£29,574	Black Cat Brewery Limited	£23,795
Bone Machine Brewing Company Limited	£29,508	The East Yorkshire Beer Company Limited	£23,731
Southport Brewery Limited	£29,278	3ABC Ltd	£23,568
Tirindrish Trading Company Limited	£29,274	Genesis Craft Ales Limited	£23,195
Force Brewery Limited	£29,262	Agnate Limited	£23,000
Mile Tree Brewery Limited	£29,142	The Oxted Brewery Ltd	£22,953
Beckstones Brewery Limited	£28,970	Aquila Visum Ltd	£22,813
Blackhill Brewery Limited	£28,763	North Country Ales Limited	£22,718
Ascot Ales Limited	£28,730	The Marlpool Brewing Company Limited	£22,637
Castle Gate Brewery Limited	£28,714	Little Black Dog Beer Company Ltd	£22,637
The Dog and Rabbit Brewery Ltd	£28,618	Brewheadz Limited	£22,469
Shottle Farm Brewery Ltd	£28,545	Fownes Brewing Company Ltd.	£22,387
Windmill Hill Brewing Co. Ltd.	£28,524	Rectory Ales Limited	£22,381
Left Handed Giant Brewing Limited	£28,268	Alpha State Limited	£22,373
Vertical Stack Ltd	£28,225	Lizard Ales Limited	£22,152
Big Shed Brewery Limited	£28,174	Dowr Kammel Brewing Company Limited	£22,107
Humberside Properties [UK] Limited	£28,157	Angel Ales Limited	£21,932
Unbarred Brewery Limited	£28,050	Out of Town Brewing Limited	£21,882
Errant Ltd	£27,943	Granite Rock Brewery and Home Brew Supplies Ltd	£21,864
All Day Brewing Company Limited	£27,583	Caveman Brewing Company Ltd	£21,762
Fuzzy Duck Brewery Limited	£27,461	Brewbox Systems Ltd	£21,500
Chapeau Brewing Limited	£27,403	Bulletproof Brewing Ltd	£21,439
Affinity Brewing Company Limited	£27,306	Peakstones Rock Brewing Co Ltd	£21,384
Tumanny Albion Brewing Company Limited	£27,260	Withnell's Brewing Company Limited	£21,346
Rocket Ales Limited	£27,260	Oddly Limited	£21,097
Little Critters Brewing Company Limited	£27,158	3SB Limited	£21,000
Stamps Brewery Limited	£26,895	Pivo-UK Limited	£20,922
Brew Club Limited	£26,860	AD Hop Brewing Ltd	£20,818
Cwrw Ogwen Cyf	£26,672	Rivington Brewing Co Limited	£20,731
Box Social Ltd	£26,637	Boozy Bods Ltd	£20,669

Lithic Brewing Limited	£20,596	Rockhopper Brewing Company Limited		£15,451
Priest Town Brewing Company Ltd	£20,549	Xtreme Ales Limited		£15,364
Ostlers Ales Ltd	£20,523	Pershore Brewery Limited		£15,356
Hilltop Brewing Company Limited	£20,521	Mill Valley Brewery Limited		£15,323
Cloak and Dagger Brewing Company Ltd	£20,284	The Edenfield Brewery Limited		£15,273
Punchline Brewery Limited	£20,239	Barrell & Sellers Limited		£15,119
Target Brewery Limited	£20,074	Llangollen Brewery Ltd		£15,002
Lecale Brewery Limited	£20,000	Barearts Ltd		£14,933
Isle of Mull Brewing Company Limited	£19,929	Himalayan Traders UK Ltd		£14,819
Caythorpe Brewery Limited	£19,893	Crooked Brewing Limited		£14,777
Clanconnel Brewing Company Limited	£19,795	Zapato Brewery Ltd.		£14,730
Husk Brewing Limited	£19,539	Nightcap Beer Company Limited		£14,717
Crafted Brewing Co. Ltd	£19,524	Hairy Dog Brewery Ltd		£14,514
7 Reasons To Brew Ltd	£19,473	Tinworks Brewing Company Ltd.		£14,462
Beathbrewing Ltd	£19,454	Moody Goose Brewery Limited		£14,306
St Andrews Brewing Company Holdings Limited	£19,406	Sherfield Village Brewery Limited		£14,165
Nameless Brewing Limited	£19,300	Dead End Brew Machine Limited		£14,156
The Kiln Brewery Ltd	£18,737	Watts & Co. Ltd.		£13,868
888 Global Trade Ltd	£18,591	Play Limited		£13,843
Weatheroak Hill Brewery Limited	£18,375	Calverley's Brewery Ltd		£13,813
Bobby Beer Company Limited	£18,354	Island Hamlet Brewing Company Limited		£13,677
Hillfire Limited	£18,276	Toolmakers Brewery Limited		£13,662
Ignition Brewery Limited	£18,136	Devitera Ltd		£13,653
Appleby Brewery Ltd.	£17,937	The Saint Brewing Co Limited		£13,614
Mr Bees Brewery Ltd	£17,885	Jollyboat Brewery (Bideford) Limited		£13,453
Beer Hut Brewing Company Ltd	£17,780	Kall Brand Ltd		£13,121
Kairos Solutions Ltd	£17,630	Copper Fox Brewery Ltd		£13,087
Festival Brewery Ltd.	£17,617	The Hand Brewing Company Limited		£12,945
Cotswold Lion Brewery Ltd	£17,594	Samuels Brewing Company Ltd		£12,933
Tapstone Brewing Company Ltd	£17,580	Little Dragon Brewery Limited		£12,931
Black Metal Brewery Ltd	£17,556	Hairy Brewers Ales Limited		£12,792
Two Beach Brewing Co Limited	£17,515	St Andrews Old Brewing Company Limited		£12,748
Saints Row Brewing Co. Ltd.	£17,490	Isca Ales Limited		£12,573
Harrogate Brewing Company Limited	£17,400	Square Street Distillery Ltd		£12,258
Chelmsford Brewing Company Ltd.	£17,253	Cotton End Brewery Company Limited		£12,084
Hubsters Brewery Ltd	£17,238	K1 Beer PLC		£12,046
Eyes Brewing Limited	£17,154	Loyal City Brewing Company Ltd		£12,013
Woodhalls Brewery Limited	£17,083	Clifford Brothers Brewery Limited		£11,971
Jabru Bevco Ltd	£17,036	Tomos & Lilford Holdings Limited		£11,896
Old Friends Brewery Ltd	£16,907	Ellenberg's Brewery Ltd		£11,744
The Hay Rake Brewery Ltd	£16,881	Violet Cottage Brewing Company Ltd		£11,682
Brightbeer Limited	£16,861	Barlow Brewery Limited		£11,626
Stocklinch Ales Ltd	£16,665	Tombstone Brewery Limited		£11,626
Landlocked Brewing Company Limited	£16,618	Brooks Brewhouse Limited		£11,557
The Shropshire Brewer Limited	£16,597	MC & P Engineering Limited		£11,461
Ralphs Ruin Ltd	£16,039	Missing Link Brewing Ltd		£11,439
Geeves Brewery Limited	£15,947	Bexar County Brewery Ltd		£11,387
Round Tower Brewery Ltd	£15,858	Moogbrew Ltd		£11,315
Norn Iron Brew Company Limited	£15,728	Fearless Brewing Ltd		£11,315
Bartleby's Ltd	£15,711	Hop Fuzz Ltd		£11,266
Duration Brewing Ltd	£15,542	Manchester Union Brewery Limited		£11,241
Yorkshire Brewhouse Limited	£15,522	Bear Brewery Co Ltd		£11,109

The Beer Necessities Limited	£11,039	Turner & Shaw Glasgow Brewing Company Limited	£7,386
Castle Combe Brewery Limited	£10,699	Seal Bay Brewery Sel Bragdy Bae Ltd	£7,224
Bob's Brewing Company Limited	£10,697	Blimey! Brewing Company Limited	£7,222
Kinkell Brewery Ltd	£10,684	Oast House Breweries Cyf	£7,162
Partridge Brewing Company Limited	£10,666	Nine Standards Brewery Limited	£7,141
The Village Inn Pub Company Ltd	£10,337	Plan B Brewing Company Ltd	£7,131
Clearsky Brewing Company Limited	£10,281	Bont Brew Ltd	£6,985
Ashley Down Brewery Limited	£10,259	The Old Prentonian Brewing Company Ltd.	£6,944
Ultimate Maltgold Limited	£10,247	Kendal Brewing Company Limited	£6,878
Beerkat Brewing Company Limited	£10,233	The Pigeon Fishers Craft Brewery Limited	£6,724
Foresight Holdings Limited	£10,212	The Chalk Stone Brewery Limited	£6,651
Merry Miner Brewery Ltd	£10,003	Shed35 Ltd	£6,435
Black Bird Brewery Limited	£10,000	The Draycott Brewing Company Limited	£6,411
Offbeat Brewery Ltd	£9,694	Five Clouds Brewing Company Limited	£6,213
Old Town Brewery Ltd.	£9,611	The Erddig Brewing Company Limited	£6,033
Stannary Brewing Company Ltd.	£9,498	Bubble Works Brew Co Ltd	£6,021
Coul Brewing Company Ltd	£9,418	Market Bosworth Brewery Ltd	£5,964
Chin Chin Brewing Company Ltd	£9,386	The Handyman Brewery Ltd	£5,954
The Engineer Brewery Limited	£9,356	Marchingtons Ltd	£5,931
Spotty Dog Brewery Limited	£9,348	It's Braw Limited	£5,921
Steel Coulson Ltd	£9,333	Clan Brewing Company Limited	£5,777
Trinity Ales Limited	£9,332	Nutbrook Brewery Ltd	£5,622
Tally Ho! Brewery Limited	£9,276	2731 Limited	£5,611
Rival Brewing Co Limited	£9,230	2 Bobs Brewing Company Limited	£5,493
Popes Yard Brewery Limited	£9,199	Born in a Brewery Ltd	£5,481
Woodcote Manor Brewing Company Limited	£9,030	Dockyard Brewery Limited	£5,437
Stag Brewery Ltd	£9,000	Reids Gold Brewing Company Ltd	£5,305
Burner Drinks Limited	£8,999	The Pilot Brewery Limited	£5,255
Winton Brewery Limited	£8,980	Equal Brewkery Community Interest Company	£4,999
Moody Fox Ltd.	£8,975	Mart's Brewing Company Ltd	£4,895
Steel City Brewing Ltd	£8,956	Maregade Brew Co. Ltd.	£4,780
Inner Bay Brewery Limited	£8,856	The Blue Bear Brewery (Worcester) Limited	£4,779
Riviera Brewing Company Limited	£8,854	Holcot Hop-Craft Ltd	£4,737
Fellows Brewery Limited	£8,818	The Kingdom Brewery Limited	£4,725
Brolly Brewing Limited	£8,673	The Three Counties Brewery Limited	£4,713
Black Market Brewery Limited	£8,584	Worfield Brewery Limited	£4,711
Emma J Tilston Ltd	£8,550	Pedal Power Harrogate Limited	£4,608
Uttoxeter Brewing Company Ltd	£8,478	Roath Brewery Ltd	£4,439
Priors Well Brewery Limited	£8,381	Hope Brewery Ltd	£4,434
Morton Collins Brewing Company Ltd	£8,185	Three Engineers Brewery Ltd	£4,388
Stowey Brewery Limited	£8,096	The Meanwood Brewery Ltd	£4,372
Maypole Brewery Limited	£7,988	Little Rotters Limited	£4,370
Posh Boys Brewery Limited	£7,973	Block Brewery Limited	£4,357
Exiled Brewers Limited	£7,920	Moseley Beer Company Limited	£4,356
New Devon Brewing Ltd	£7,838	Dominion Brewery Company Limited	£4,347
Derwent Brewery Ltd	£7,837	Indian Summer Brewing Co. Limited	£4,307
MBH Tap & Shop Limited	£7,790	Buccaneer Brewery Ltd	£4,201
Great Central Brewery Limited	£7,688	St Mary's Brewery Ltd	£4,104
Spencer Panacea Limited	£7,662	Crooked Ship Brewery Ltd	£4,100
Fuddy Duck Limited	£7,655	Upstart Brewing Ltd	£4,003
MBJW Brewing Limited	£7,627	Bowing Hound Brewing Company Limited	£4,001
White Rose Brewery Limited	£7,395	The Craft Brewery Limited	£3,925

Hickbrew Limited	£3,875	Gan Yam Brewing Company Ltd	£1,591
PLS Special Projects Limited	£3,866	Mashdown Brewery Ltd.	£1,577
Hurly Burly Brewery Ltd	£3,708	Thirsty Smile Ltd	£1,554
Archangel Brewing Ltd.	£3,695	Dolphin Brewery Limited	£1,500
Gene Pool Brewing Ltd	£3,660	Two Finches Brewery Ltd.	£1,400
Tiny Vessel Brewing Company Limited	£3,599	Beer Ink Limited	£1,384
Nellyd Limited	£3,526	Linear Brewing Company Limited	£1,364
Peter Laws Brewing Limited	£3,522	Best Brewery Ltd	£1,358
Polarity Brewing Ltd	£3,516	Reds Beer Co Ltd	£1,315
Donzoko Brewing Company Ltd	£3,511	Origami Brewing Company Ltd.	£1,305
Bad Joke Brew Co. Ltd.	£3,462	Lock 34 Brew Co. Limited	£1,285
The GKH Beer Company Ltd	£3,425	Inkerman Ales Limited	£1,123
Great Glen Trading Centre Limited	£3,423	Tidal London Ltd	£1,096
Earth Ale Ltd	£3,401	Rock Solid Brewing Company Limited	£1,090
Iceni Brewery Limited	£3,372	Magee, Marshall and Company, Limited	£1,000
The Lockside Brewery Ltd.	£3,348	The Craft Beer Society Ltd	£991
The Dove Street Brewery Ltd	£3,259	Macclesfield Brewing Company Ltd	£931
Roseland Brewery Limited	£3,237	Colonsay Brewing Co. Ltd.	£900
Whitefaced Ltd	£3,008	Mitchell Ward Limited	£844
Xtraflow Limited	£3,007	Broadway Brewery Ltd	£800
Tarn Hows Brewery Limited	£2,977	Beercraft Brewery Limited	£756
Kentish Town Brewery Limited	£2,961	Beeston Hop Ltd	£617
Modha Ales Ltd	£2,959	Brewers Folly Brewery Ltd.	£593
Ellismuir Limited	£2,938	Lorimers Ales (1919) Limited	£520
Endure Brewing Co Ltd	£2,697	Thomas Dutton Ales Limited	£430
Glasshouse Beer Co Ltd	£2,661	Soul Doubt Brewing Company Ltd	£421
Keep Brewing Ltd	£2,590	Custom Head Brewing Ltd	£395
Pig Iron Brewing Company Limited	£2,563	Elemental Brew House Limited	£381
Rogue Elephant Brewery Limited	£2,502	London Cosmopolitan Drinks Limited	£376
Frisky Bear Brewing Co Ltd	£2,501	Bentley's Yorkshire Breweries (1828) Limited	£350
The Atlantic Craft Soda Company Ltd	£2,472	Devenish & Co (Weymouth) Limited	£350
Strathmore Brewery Limited	£2,400	The Small Beer Brewing Company Limited	£344
Moorside Brewery Ltd	£2,370	Dawkins & Georges Ltd	£247
Urban Island Brewing Co. Limited	£2,286	Alcazar Brewing Company Limited	£240
Wrytree Brewery Limited	£2,270	Tarn51 Brewing Company Limited	£210
Muswell Hillbilly Brewers Ltd	£2,253	Round Corner Brewing Ltd	£200
Brew Shed Beers Limited	£2,226	Melin Tap Brewhouse Limited	£164
Holy Well Brewing Ltd	£2,196	Vaux Beers Ltd	£155
Liquid Light Brewing Company Limited	£2,122	Golden Fox Brewing Ltd	£134
Botley Brewery Ltd	£2,093	The Lingfield Brewing Company Ltd	£130
A Northerly Brewing Ltd	£2,048	Roosters Brewing Company Limited	£100
Hopforge Ltd	£1,965	The Angel Brewery Company Limited	£100
Bishop's Crook Brewery Ltd.	£1,957	Outgang Brewery Ltd	£100
Philsters Limited	£1,943	Dancing Duck Holdings Ltd	£100
Two Drifters Brewery Ltd	£1,863	Dorber Brewing Limited	£100
Connecting Hops Ltd	£1,850	Oldershaw Brewery Ltd	£100
Witch Craft Beers Limited	£1,821	The Flying Fox Brewery Limited	£100
The Brewery Limited	£1,809	The Silverstone Brewing Co Limited	£100
Under The Stairs Brewery Ltd	£1,753	Diamond Dicks Brewing Limited	£100
Hindsight Collective Ltd	£1,711	Great British Breworks Ltd	£100
Rock Springs Brewing Ltd	£1,678	Craft Origins Limited	£100
JP Brew Limited	£1,643	The Glenfinnan Brewing Company Limited	£100

3ways Brewing Co Limited	£90	Bratch Beers Ltd	£10
Tony Clark Enterprises Ltd	£79	Lost Boys Brewery Ltd	£4
Loch Earn Brewery Ltd	£69	St. Peter's Trading Co. Limited	£2
Map Kernow Ltd.	£62	Airborne Ales Ltd	£2
Reality Brewing Limited	£61	TKS Brewing Limited	£2
Two Rabbit Brewing Company Ltd	£58	Pilgrim Brewery (Reigate) Limited	£2
Quad Brewing Company Limited	£55	Doncaster Brewery Limited	£1
East Anglian Brewers Ltd.	£51	Egghead Brewery Limited	£1
XL Brew Ltd	£49	Mybrewpub Limited	£1
Baltic Fleet Brewery Limited	£26	Crafty Leopard Brewing Co Limited	£1
Old Street Brewery Ltd	£20	Rock A Brew Ltd	£1
The East India Company India Pale Ale Limited	£17		

This page is intentionally left blank

Age of Companies

1800s [10]
Adnams PLC
S.A.Brain & Co Ltd
Hall & Woodhouse Limited
Magee,Marshall and Co Ltd
Marston's Acquisitions Limited
Marston's PLC
McMullen & Sons, Limited
Molson Coors Brewing Co (UK) Ltd
Daniel Thwaites PLC
Wadworth and Co Ltd

1900-1909
Carlsberg UK Limited
Elgood & Sons,Limited
Felinfoel Brewery Co Ltd
Hook Norton Brewery Co Ltd

1910-1919 [5]
H.B.Clark & Co.(Successors) Ltd
Hydes' Brewery Limited
Shepherd Neame Limited
St.Austell Brewery Co Ltd
Charles Wells,Limited

1920-1929 [9]
Arkell's Brewery Limited
George Bateman & Son Limited
French & Jupps Limited
Harvey & Son (Lewes) Limited
Joseph Holt Limited
Frederic Robinson Limited
Samuel Smith Old Brewery (Tadcaster)
Timothy Taylor & Co.,Limited
Wetherells Contracts Limited

1930-1939
Everards Brewery Limited

1940-1949 [5]
Daniel Batham & Son Limited
Belhaven Brewery Co Ltd
Blewin Trust Limited
Mansfield Brewery Trading Ltd
Selby (Middlebrough) Brewery,Limited

1950-1959
J.W.Lees & Co.(Brewers) Ltd

1960-1969
Joseph Camm Farms Limited
Holdens Brewery Limited

1970-1979 [6]
Badger Ales Limited
Butcombe Pubco Limited
Gustmain Limited
Heineken UK Limited
J.C. & R.H. Palmer Limited
Tynemill Limited

1980-1989 [16]
Anheuser-Busch Europe Limited
Aston Manor Limited
Ballard's Brewery Limited
Bathams (Delph) Limited
Big Shed Brewery Limited
Caledonian Brewery Limited
Crouch Vale Brewery Limited
Dobbins Guiltless Stout Co Ltd
Exmoor Ales Limited
Goddards Brewery Limited
Golcar Brewery Limited
Harviestoun Brewery Limited
Larkins Brewery Limited
Moorhouse's Brewery Ltd
Wood Brewery Limited
Woodforde's Norfolk Ales Ltd

1990-1994 [23]
Adshead's Ales Ltd
Arundel Brewery Limited
B & T Brewery Limited
Black Sheep Brewery PLC
Butts Brewery Limited
Cereal Technology Limited
Church End Brewery Limited
Coach House Brewing Co Ltd
Coniston Brewing Co Ltd
Charles Cooper Limited
Dartmoor Brewery Limited
Dorset Brewing Co Ltd
Goff's Brewery Limited
Heather Ale Limited
Hop Back Brewery PLC
London Beer Co Ltd
Nexus Engineering Limited
Oak Brewing Co Ltd
Rudgate Brewery Limited
Shefford Brewery Co. Limited
Tring Brewery Co Ltd
Weetwood Ales Limited
Wye Valley Brewery Limited

1995 [10]
Belvoir Brewery Limited
Broughton Ales Limited
Dark Star Brewing Co Ltd
Hogs Back Brewery Limited
Marble Beers Limited
Mighty Oak Brewing Co. Limited
Rectory Ales Limited
St. Peter's Brewery Co. Ltd
Weltons Limited
ZX Ventures Limited

1996 [6]
Devon Ales Limited
Thomas Hardy Holdings Limited
Hawkshead Brewery Limited
Innis & Gunn Inveralmond Brewery Ltd
Murree Breweries (UK) Limited
Sulwath Brewers Limited

1997 [17]
Abbey Ales Limited
Anglia Pub Co Ltd
Arran Brew Ltd.
Brewster's Brewing Co Ltd
Darwin Brewery Limited
Durham Brewery Limited
Greene King Brewing and Retailing
Hobsons Brewery and Co Ltd
Kelham Island Brewery Limited
Keltek Cornish Brewery Limited
Ossett Brewing Co Ltd
Rebellion Beer Co Ltd
Salopian Brewing Co Ltd.
Sherborne Brewery Limited
St. Peter's Brewery Group PLC
St. Peter's Trading Co. Ltd
Traquair House Brewery Limited

1998 [16]
ABI SAB Group Holding Limited
Black Isle Brewing Co Ltd
Camerons Brewery Limited
Daleside Brewery Limited
Dodd's Brewery Co. Limited
Enville Ales Limited
Thomas Hardy Burtonwood Ltd
Thomas Hardy Kendal Limited
Inkerman Ales Limited
Isle of Skye Brewing Company (Leann An Eilein)
Malvern Hills Brewery Limited
Otter Brewery Limited
Shetland Refreshments Limited
Stonehenge Ales Limited
Strathaven Ales Limited
West Berkshire Brewery PLC

1999 [15]
Barngates Brewery Limited
Branded Drinks Ltd
Cairngorm Brewery Co Ltd
Double Maxim Beer Co Ltd
Itchen Valley Brewery Limited
Meantime Brewing Co Ltd
Milton Brewery Cambridge Ltd
Padstow Brewing Company (2013) Ltd
Salamander Brewing Co Ltd
Shardlow Brewing Co Ltd
Two Tribes Brewing Ltd
Whim Ales Limited
Wicked Hathern Brewery Limited
Woodforde's Limited
Yeovil Ales Limited

2000 [12]
AB InBev UK Limited
Battersea Brewery Co Ltd
Hepworth & Company Brewers Ltd
Joseph Holt Group Limited
Hopdaemon Brewery Co Ltd
Jollyboat Brewery (Bideford) Ltd
Mauldon's Limited
C J Middleton Limited
Roosters Brewing Co Ltd
Wessex Brewery Limited
Wold Toppers Limited
Wylam Brewery Limited

2001 [9]
Alcazar Brewing Co Ltd
Festival Brewery Ltd.
Fyne Ales Limited
Kelburn Brewing Co Ltd
Lizard Ales Limited
Chris O'Connor and Associates Ltd
Tirril Brewery Limited
Whitewater Brewing Co. Ltd
Wickwar Wessex Brewing Co Ltd

2002 [31]
Abbeydale Brewery Limited
Branscombe Vale Brewery Ltd
Bristol Brewing Co Ltd
Buffy's Brewery Limited
Burton Bridge Brewery Limited
Cardiff Brewing Co Ltd
Curious Drinks Limited
Downton Brewery Co Ltd
East Anglian Brewers Ltd.
Eccleshall Brewing Co Ltd
Elland Brewery Limited
Goose Eye Brewery Limited
Halifax Steam Brewing Co Ltd
Hurns Brewing Co Ltd.
Innis & Gunn Brewing Co Ltd
Loddon Brewery Ltd
Maldon Brewing Co Ltd
Map Kernow Ltd.
Millis Brewing Co Ltd
Millstone Brewery Limited
Oakhill Brewery Limited
Pictish Brewing Co Limited
Purple Moose Brewery Ltd
Rhymney Brewery Ltd
John Roberts Brewing Co Ltd
Skinner's Brewing Co. Limited
Staffordshire Brewery Limited
Sugar Pine Brewing Co Ltd
Teller Lager Co Ltd
True North Brew Co Limited
Weatheroak Brewery Ltd

2003 [28]
1648 Brewing Co Limited
360 Degree Brewing Co Ltd
Acorn Brewery of Barnsley Ltd
Alnwick Ales Limited
Black Country Brewery Limited
Bob's Brewing Co Ltd
Bowland Beer Co Ltd
Butcombe Brewery Limited
Butcombe Brewing Co Ltd
Conwy Brewery Limited
Cotleigh Brewery Limited
Cross Inn (Maesteg) Limited
Earl Soham Brewery Limited
Hardstate Limited
Insight Driven Innovation Ltd
Islay Ales Co Ltd
Leadmill Brewery Limited
Loch Earn Brewery Ltd
London Cosmopolitan Drinks Ltd
Purity Brewing Co Ltd
Saltaire Brewery Limited
Sharp's Brewery Limited
Slaughterhouse Brewery Limited
Summer Wine Brewery Limited
Teignworthy Brewery Limited
T.& R. Theakston Limited
Titanic Brewery Co Limited
Westerham Brewery Co Ltd

2004 [38]
Allendale Brew Co Ltd
Baltic Beer Co Ltd
Bank Top Brewery Limited
Bizzy Play Limited
Blindmans Brewery Limited
Brancaster Brewery Limited
Brimstage Brewing Co. Ltd
Charlbury Brewing Co Ltd
Consett Ale Works Limited
Cotswold Brewing Co Ltd
Cuillin Brewery Limited
Dent Brewery Limited
Derby Brewing Co Ltd
Filo Brewing Co Ltd
Freedom Brewery Ltd
Great Orme Brewery Limited
Greenfield Real Ale Brewery Ltd
Highland Brewing Co Ltd
Isle of Mull Brewing Co Ltd
Little Valley Brewery Limited
Long Ashton Cider Co Ltd
Magna Bottling Limited
Magna Brewery Limited
Midmart Limited
Phipps Northampton Brewery Co Ltd
Potbelly Brewery Limited
Ramsgate Brewery Limited
Stewart Brewing Limited
Stroud Brewery Limited
Surrey Hills Brewery Ltd
Thornbridge Hall Country House Brewing Co
Tunnel Brewery Limited
Twickenham Fine Ales Limited
Vale of Glamorgan Brewery Ltd
Vinifera Limited
Vyrnwy Developments Limited
White Horse Brewery Co Ltd
Windsor Castle Brewery Limited

2005 [20]
Alnwick Brewery Co Ltd
Amber Ales Limited
Beeston Brewery Ltd
Caythorpe Brewery Limited
Derventio Brewery Limited
Hammerpot Brewery Limited
Howard Town Brewery Limited
Lancaster Brewery Co Ltd
Matthews Brewing Co Ltd
Maypole Brewery Limited
Moor Beer Co Ltd
Old Spot Brewery Limited
Quartz Brewing Limited
Stowey Brewery Limited
Tomson & Wotton Limited
Traditional Scottish Ales Ltd
Ulverston Brewing Co Ltd
WBC (Norfolk) Limited
Yates low Brewery Limited
Yorkshire Dales Brewing Co Ltd

2006 [36]
Arbor Ales Ltd
Atlas Brewery Limited
Bays Brewery Limited
Bowman Ales Limited
Brentwood Brewing Co Ltd
Brewdog PLC
Bridgnorth Brewing Co Ltd
Cheltenham Brewery Limited
Colonsay Brewing Co Ltd
Christopher Ellis and Son Ltd
Great Heck Brewing Co Ltd
Great Newsome Brewery Limited
Great Western Brewing Co Ltd
Hopshackle Brewery Limited
Peter Laws Brewing Limited
Leeds Brewery Co Ltd
Lincolnshire Brewing Co Ltd
Ludlow Brewing Co Ltd
Metcalfe & Metcalfe Co Ltd
Mourne Mountains Brewery Ltd
Nelson Brewing Co.Uk Ltd.
Red Rock Brewery Limited
Sheffield Brewery Co Ltd
Sinclair Breweries Limited
Sixty Shilling Brewing Ltd
Storm Brewing Co Ltd
Taddington Brewery Limited
Tatton Brewery Limited
Three Castles Brewery Limited
Tintagel Brewery Limited
Tiny Vessel Brewing Co Ltd
Tower Brewery Limited
Vaux Beers Ltd
Samuel Webster & Sons Limited
Charles Wells Brewery Limited
Wiveliscombe Breweries Limited

2007 [30]
Angel Brewery Co Ltd
Ascot Ales Limited
Barlow Brewery Limited
Beverley Brewery Co Ltd
Bewdley Brewery Limited
Binghams Brewery Limited
Brampton Brewery Ltd
Bromtec Limited
Bucket Brewing Co Ltd
Daleside Holdings (Harrogate) Ltd
Exeter Brewery Limited
Exit 33 Brewing Ltd
Harviestoun Brewery (Holdings) Ltd
Innis & Gunn Holdings Limited
Irving & Co. Brewers Limited
Khukuri Beer (UK) Limited
Leatherbritches Brewery Ltd
Loose Cannon Brewing Co Ltd
Lyme Bay Brewing Limited
Noah Beers Limited
Outstanding Brewing Co Ltd
PLS Special Projects Limited
Prospect Brewery Limited
Richmond Brewing Co Ltd
Spey Valley Brewery Limited
Uley Ales Limited
White Rose Brewery Limited
Whitstable Brewery Co Ltd
Woodhalls Brewery Limited
Yeast Pod Ltd

2008 [36]
Abbey Grange Brewing Limited
Artisan Brewing Co Ltd
Blue Monkey Brewing Limited
Bollington Brewing Co. Limited
Buxton Brewery Co Ltd
Calside Brewery and Taste Room Ltd
Calvors Brewery Limited
Castle Combe Brewery Limited
Cheddar Ales Limited
Oliver Chester Limited
Clanconnel Brewing Co Ltd
Cornish Crown Limited
Cumberland Breweries Limited
Dood and Frinks Ltd
Engineer Brewery Limited
Finns (UK) Limited
Green Jack Brewing Co Ltd

Joules Brewery Limited
Lymestone Brewery Limited
Monty's Brewery Limited
North East Brewing Co Ltd
Nutbrook Brewery Ltd
Offbeat Brewery Ltd
Penzance Brewing Co Ltd
Red Fox Brewery Limited
Rowton Brewery Ltd
Sambrook's Brewery Limited
Scottish Borders Brewery Ltd
Sherwood Forest Brewing Co Ltd
Spencer Panacea Limited
Square Street Distillery Ltd
St Andrews Old Brewing Co Ltd
Trumark Properties Limited
Weatheroak Hill Brewery Ltd
Wincle Beer Co Ltd
Yard of Ale Brewing Co Ltd

2009 [50]
Antic Brewing Limited
Ashley Down Brewery Limited
Barearts Ltd
Black Eagle Brewery Ltd
Blackedge Brewing Co Ltd
Blue Bear Brewery (Worcester) Ltd
Bradfield Brewery Limited
Bragdy Nant Cyf
Brightside Brewing Co Ltd
CFS Castus Test 001 Ltd
Cains Limited
Camden Town Brewery Limited
Clearwater Brewery Ltd
Cobra Beer Partnership Limited
Dancing Duck Beer Ltd
Dove Street Brewery Ltd
Fellows Brewery Limited
Flack Manor Brewery Limited
Grace Land Beer Limited
Himalayan Traders UK Ltd
Icecream Factory Limited
Iceni Brewery Limited
Ilkley Brewery Co Ltd
Irwell Works Brewery Ltd
Isca Ales Limited
Kinver Brewery Limited
Kirkstall Brewery Co Ltd
Lancar Limited
Loch Lomond Brewery Limited
Merlin Brewing Co Ltd
Munro Ventures Limited
Old Dairy Brewery Limited
Outgang Brewery Ltd
Patriot Brewery Limited
Peerless Brewing Co Ltd
Reality Brewing Limited
Recognise Limited
Redchurch Brewery Limited
Redemption Brewing Co Ltd
Roseland Brewery Limited
Shotover Brewing Co Ltd
Sly Fox Brewery Ltd
Spitting Feathers Limited
Towcester Mill Brewery Limited
WantsumBrewery Ltd
Wayland's Sixpenny Brewery Ltd
Welbeck Abbey Brewery Limited
Windsor & Eton Brewing Co Ltd
Wrexham Lager Beer Co Ltd
X-Ray Brewing Co Ltd

January-June 2010 [24]
Agricola Bottling Limited
Angel Ales Limited
Baltic Fleet Brewery Limited
Bridge House Brewery Limited
Canterbrew Ltd
Fuzzy Duck Brewery Limited
George's Brewery Limited
Grainstore Brewery Limited
Great Yorkshire Brewery Ltd
Isle-of-Cumbrae Brewing Co Ltd
Kent Brewery Ltd
London Brewing Co Ltd
Marlpool Brewing Co Ltd
Maxim Brewery Limited
Ridgeside Brewing Co Ltd
Scarborough Brewery Limited
Steel City Brewing Ltd
Sussex Beer Co Ltd
Two Towers Brewery Ltd
Verulam Brewery Limited
Victor's Drinks Limited
White's Brewery Limited
Wibblers Brewery (Farms) Ltd
Windermere Brewery Ltd

July-December 2010 [28]
Argyll Breweries Limited
Backyard Brewhouse Limited
Barton House Brewing Co Ltd
Blue Bee Brewery Ltd
Byatt's Brewery Ltd
Cwrw Llyn Cyf
Dow Bridge Brewery Limited
Ennerdale Brewery Ltd
Golden Triangle Brewery Ltd
Great Glen Brewing Co Ltd
Hastings Brewery Ltd
Liverpool Craft Beer Co Ltd
Magic Rock Brewing Co Ltd
Merry Miner Brewery Ltd
Moncada Brewery Limited
Octagon Brewery Limited
Red Squirrel Brewery Limited
Redwillow Brewery Ltd
Revolutions Brewing Co Ltd
Sherfield Village Brewery Ltd
St Ives Brewery Limited
Strands Brewery Ltd
Turing Complete Solutions Ltd
Twisted Oak Brewery Ltd
Two Roses Brewery Ltd
Winchester Brewery Ltd
Worsthorne Brewing Co Ltd
Yellow Hammer Brewing Limited

January-June 2011 [51]
1936 Limited
2 Bobs Brewing Co Ltd
Anchor Brewery Ltd
Ards Brewing Co Ltd
Bedlam Brewery Limited
Bishop's Stortford Brewery Ltd
Blackjack Beers Limited
Broxbourne Brewery Ltd.
By The Horns Ltd
Cirencester Brewery Ltd
Dhillons Brewery Ltd
Duffstar Brewing Limited
East India Company India Pale Ale
East London Brewing Co Ltd
FGW Brewery Limited
Geeves Brewery Limited
Geipel Brewing Limited
Goody Ales Limited
Hafod Brewing Co Ltd
Heavy Industry Brewing Limited
Hop Fuzz Ltd
Hop Monster Brewing Co. Ltd.
Hull Brewing Co Ltd
Humber Brewery Ltd
Long Man Brewery Limited
Longdog Brewery Limited
Melville's Fruit Beers Limited
Middle Earth Brewing Co Ltd
Milltown Brewing Co. Ltd
Mobberley Brewhouse Limited
Moonshine Drinks Limited
Nine Standards Brewery Limited
North Brewing Co Ltd
Old Pie Factory Brewery Ltd
Old School Brewery Limited
Partners Brewery Limited
Pin-Up Beers Ltd.
Shottle Farm Brewery Ltd
Smith and Jones Brewery Ltd
Staneyhill Brewery Limited
Three Counties Brewery Limited
Treboom Limited
Tyne Bank Brewery Limited
Unsworth's Yard Brewery Ltd
Village Inn Pub Co Ltd
W.L.B.C Ltd
Wombourne Brewing Co Ltd
Wright & Spillane Limited
XT Brewing Co Ltd
Yorkshire Brewing Co Ltd
Yorkshire Heart Limited

July-December 2011 [56]
Abbey Ford Brewery Ltd
Alechemy Brewing Ltd
Anarchy Brew Co. Limited
Annuity Ales Limited
Aquila Visum Ltd
Barrell & Sellers Limited
Batch Brew Ltd
Beavertown Brewery Ltd
Bishop Nick Limited
Blackhill Brewery Limited
Blueball Brewery Ltd
Bowness Bay Brewing Limited
Chantry Brewery Ltd
Colchester Brewery Ltd
Compass Brewery Limited
Cullercoats Brewery Limited
Dancing Man Brewery Limited
Eden Brewery Limited
Ellenberg's Brewery Ltd
Fourpure Limited
Friday Beer Co Ltd
Gloucester Brewery Ltd
Gower Brewery Co Limited
Grain Brewery Limited
Gun Dog Ales Ltd
Hackney Brewery Ltd
Harbour Brewing Co Ltd
Hart Family Brewers Limited
Hop Studio Limited
Indian Summer Brewing Co. Ltd
Ledbury Real Ales Ltd
Lincoln Green Brewing Co Ltd
Lingfield Brewing Co Ltd

The UK Brewing Industry

Little Beer Corporation Ltd
Lockside Brewery Ltd.
London Beer Factory Ltd.
Malt, The Brewery Limited
Mantle Brewery Limited
Mile Tree Brewery Limited
Mumbles Brewery Ltd
Nene Valley Brewery Limited
North Cotswold Brewery Limited
Old Worthy Brewing Co Ltd
Peakstones Rock Brewing Co Ltd
Portobello Brewing Co Ltd
Ripple Steam Brewery Limited
Rock & Roll Brewhouse Ltd
Roosters Brewery Limited
Saint Brewing Co Limited
Shere Brewery Ltd
Signature Brew Ltd
Southdown Brewery Limited
Sperrin Brewery Ltd
Tillingbourne Brewery Ltd
Tollgate Brewery Limited
Weird Beard Brew Co Ltd

January-March 2012 [33]
Affinity Brewing Co Ltd
Ashover Brewery Limited
Barney's Beer Limited
Bespoke Brewing Co. Limited
Bexar County Brewery Ltd
Billericay Brewing Co Ltd
Boozy Bods Ltd
Brew By Numbers Ltd.
Cader Ales Limited
Cambridge-Brewery Limited
Cotswold Lion Brewery Ltd
Cronx Brewery Limited
Deeside Brewery Limited
Force Brewery Limited
Fosse Way Brewing Co Ltd.
Green Duck Beer Co. Limited
Hardknott UK Ltd
Hop & Stagger Brewery Ltd
Kernel Brewery Ltd
Langton Brewery Ltd
Llangollen Brewery Ltd
Longhill Garage Limited
Newark Brewery Ltd
Pixie Spring Brewing Co Ltd
Shiny Brewing Co Ltd
Southport Brewery Limited
Speyside Craft Brewery Limited
St Andrews Brewers Limited
Summerhall Brewing Limited
Violet Cottage Brewing Co Ltd
White Boar Brewing Co Ltd
Wild Weather Ales Ltd
Windswept Brewing Co Ltd

April-June 2012 [29]
3 Brewers Ltd
Anspach & Hobday Limited
Atom Brewing Co Limited
Bartleby's Ltd
Botley Brewery Ltd
Boutique Cellar Limited
Brockley Brewing Co Ltd.
Corinium Ales Ltd
Dominion Brewery Co Ltd
Fallen Brewing Co Ltd
Farm Yard Ales Ltd

Firebrick Brewery Limited
Froth Blowers Brewing Co Ltd
Hay Rake Brewery Ltd
John O'Groats Brewery Ltd
Keith Brewery Limited
Latimer Ales Ltd
Lions Den Beers Limited
London Beer Lab Ltd
Mad Cat Brewery Limited
Muirhouse Brewery Limited
Pilot Beer Limited
Proper Beer Co Ltd
Stocklinch Ales Ltd
Three Kings Brewery Limited
Toolmakers Brewery Limited
Vaux Brewery Ltd
Whitby Brewery Ltd
Wild Beer Co Ltd

July-September 2012 [30]
Arran Brewery PLC
Big Hand Brewing Co Ltd
Black Cat Brewery Limited
Black Metal Brewery Ltd
Brick Brewery Ltd
Brightbeer Limited
Brighton Bier Limited
Brightwater Brewery Limited
Caveman Brewing Co Ltd
Deeply Vale Brewery Ltd
Dukeries Brewery Ltd.
First Chop Brewing Arm Ltd
Instant Karma Brewing Co Ltd
Jon's Brewery Limited
K1 Beer PLC
Kathmandu Link Limited
Kimberley Brewery Limited
Kimberley Brewing Co Ltd
L1 Brewer Ltd
Little Dragon Brewery Limited
Mash Brewery Limited
Partizan Brewing Limited
Pig and Porter Limited
Pokertree Brewing Co Ltd
Popes Yard Brewery Limited
Saffron Brewery (Henham) Ltd
Siren Craft Brew Limited
Tumanny Albion Brewing Co Ltd
Wild Card Brewery Limited
Worfield Brewery Limited

October-December 2012 [33]
Samuel Adams (Beer) Ltd
Alpha State Limited
Anley Ales Limited
Ardgour Ales Ltd
Belfast Brewing Co Ltd
Belleville Brewing Co Ltd
Bosun's Brewing Co Ltd
Brighton Brewery Ltd
Clearsky Brewing Co Ltd
Derwent Brewery Ltd
Five Points Brewing Co Ltd
Freewheelin' Brewery Co Ltd
Granite Rock Brewery and Home Brew Supplies
Greyhound Drinks Limited
Hercules Brewing & Co. Limited
Hillfire Limited
Honest Brew Ltd
Langford Brewing Co. Limited

Naylor's Brewery Ltd
Oast House Breweries Cyf
Pressure Drop Brewing Limited
Rosebank Brewery Camelon Ltd
Rosebank Brewery Limited
Shropshire Brewer Limited
Stealth Brew Co Limited
Thurstons Horsell Brewery Co Ltd
Totally Brewed Limited
Two Beach Brewing Co Limited
UK Camra Beer Co., Ltd
West Belfast Real Ale Limited
Wharfedale Brewery Limited
White Hart Halstead Limited
Wiper & True Ltd.

January-March 2013 [36]
4 Ladies Brewery Ltd
Bad Seed Brewery Ltd
Black Flag Brewery Ltd
Black Tor Brewery Ltd
Bluestone Brewing Co Ltd
Borough Brewery Limited
Bullfinch Brewery Limited
Burning Sky Brewery Limited
Campion Ale Limited
Cross Bay Brewery Limited
Cwrw Ial Limited
Dolphin Brewery Poole Ltd
Firebird Brewing Co Ltd
Flying Monk Brewery Ltd
Gales Brewery Limited
Garretts Green Garage Mikro Brewery Ltd
Goldmark Craft Beers Ltd
Half Moon Brewery Ltd
Humberside Properties [UK] Ltd
Kendal Brewing Co Ltd
LVS Bottling Limited
Lion Craft Brewery Ltd
Lorimers Ales (1919) Limited
Lorsho Limited
Morecambe Bay Wines Limited
Mortlake Brewery Ltd
Ostlers Ales Ltd
Platform 5 Brewing Co Ltd
Ramsbury Brewing and Distilling Co Ltd
Red Cat Brewing Limited
Tapstone Brewing Co Ltd
Tonbridge Brewery Limited
Untapped Brewing Co Ltd
Wensleydale Brewery (2013) Ltd
Wimbledon Brewery Co Ltd
XL Brew Ltd

April-June 2013 [32]
All Day Brewing Co Ltd
Arlingham Ales Limited
Bingley Brewery Limited
Brass Castle Brewery Limited
Brixton Brewery Limited
Brook House Brewery Limited
Brunswick Brewing Co Ltd
Calverley's Brewery Ltd
Clarkshaws Brewing Co Ltd.
Clouded Minds Limited
Crystalbrew Limited
Deverell's Brewing Co Ltd
Doncaster Brewery Limited
East Riding Brewery Ltd
Empire Brewing Ltd
Grey Trees Brewery Limited

Hillside Brewery Limited
Hiver Beers Ltd
Hop Stuff Brewery Limited
Left Handed Giant Ltd.
Mayflower Brewery Ltd
Mitchell Ward Limited
Musket Brewery Limited
Old Town Brewery Ltd.
Range Ales Brewery Limited
Red Rose Brewery Ltd
SchoolHouseBrewery Ltd
Shipstones Beer Co Ltd
Squawk Brewing Co Ltd
Upstart Brewing Ltd
Wobbly Brewing Co Ltd
Xtraflow Limited

July-September 2013 [35]
Ainsty Ales Limited
Axholme Brewing Co Ltd
Big Lamp Brewers Limited
Bobby Beer Co Ltd
Bridgehouse Pub Co Ltd
Carlsberg Supply Company UK Ltd
Darlington Brewing and Distilling Co Ltd
Dawkins & Georges Ltd
EFG International Ltd
Fremlins Limited
Fuggle Bunny Brew House Ltd
Hedgedog Brewing Ltd
Lerwick Brewery Limited
Lost Industry Brewing Limited
Manning Brewers Ltd
McGrath Davies Public Houses Ltd
Northern Monk Brewing Co. Ltd
Pedal Power Harrogate Limited
Round Tower Brewery Ltd
Salcombe Brewery Co. Limited
Sandstone Brewery Ltd
Slow Beer Ltd
Small World Beers Ltd
Soho Brewing Ltd
Southbourne Ales Limited
Southbourne Brewing Limited
Stancill Brewery Limited
Tarn Hows Brewery Limited
Tempest Brewing Co Limited
Time & Tide Brewing Limited
Twisted Barrel Ale Limited
Vale Brewery Co Ltd.
Vibrant Forest Brewery Limited
Westbournia Brewing Co Ltd
Xtreme Ales Limited

October-December 2013 [28]
Bavarian Gold Limited
Bishop's Crook Brewery Ltd.
Black Dragon Brewery Limited
Bragdy Lleu Cyf
Brew Toon Ltd.
Brewing and Distilling Co Ltd
Copper Tun Ltd
Don Valley Brewery Limited
Dore Brewery Limited
Gun Brewery Limited
Hadham Brewing Co Ltd
Hyde & Wills Limited
Nevis Brewery Ltd
Orbit Brewing Limited
Paddy's Clover Ltd
Pigeon Fishers Craft Brewery Ltd

Rockin Robin Brewery Ltd
Runaway Brewery Limited
Seven Brothers Brewery Limited
Sloane Home Ltd
Southwark Brewing Co Ltd
Tewkesbury Brewery Ltd
Townes Brewery Limited
Twisted Brewing Co Ltd
Two By Two Brewing Ltd
Under The Stairs Brewery Ltd
Wimborne Beer Co Ltd
Zulu Alpha Brewing Limited

January-March 2014 [57]
Airborne Ales Ltd
Almasty Brewing Co Ltd
Archangel Brewing Ltd.
BC Brewing & Pub Co Ltd
Beardyman Brewery Limited
Bentley's Yorkshire Breweries (1828)
Bexley Brewery Limited
Big Smoke Brew Co Limited
Black Bess Limited
Black Hole Brewery Limited
Black Wolf Brewery Limited
Born in a Brewery Ltd
Brewsmith Beer Limited
Bridlington Brewing Co. Ltd
Broadway Brewery Ltd
Chequers Micropub Limited
Cloudwater Brew Co Ltd
Cornwall and West Country Craft Brewing Co
Cotton End Brewery Co Ltd
Dead End Brew Machine Limited
Drygate Brewing Co Ltd
Thomas Dutton Ales Limited
Electric Bear Brewing Co Ltd
Fixed Wheel Brewery Limited
Fownes Brewing Co Ltd.
Gower Pub Co Ltd
Growler Swap Ltd
Haresfoot Storage & Distribution Co Ltd
Harrogate Brewing Co Ltd
Hill House Inns Limited
Hopforge Ltd
Hophurst Brewery Ltd
Inkspot Brewery Limited
Intrepid Brewing Co Ltd
Jaw Brewery Ltd
Kiln Brewery Ltd
Landlocked Brewing Co Ltd
Leighton Buzzard Brewing Co Ltd
Lucky 7 Beer Co Ltd
Martland Mill Brewery Limited
Mashdown Brewery Ltd.
Mumbles Brewing Co Ltd
Northern Alchemy Limited
Pig Iron Brewing Co Ltd
Plain Ales Brewery Ltd
Proper Brewing Co Ltd
Proud Peacock Limited
Pryor Reid & Co Limited
Roddenloft Brewery Ltd
Sevenoaks Brewery Limited
Severn Brewing Limited
Station 119 Ltd
Stockport Brewing Co Ltd
Target Brewery Limited
Track Brewing Co Ltd
Vocation Brewery Limited
Weal Ales Brewery Ltd

April-June 2014 [45]
3SB Limited
Alphabet Brewing Ltd
Bay View Brewery Limited
Bear Brewery Co Ltd
Beer Engineer Ltd
Black Bird Brewery Limited
Chorlton Brewing Co Ltd
Clun Brewery Ltd.
Crafty Brewing Co. Limited
Deva Craft Beer Ltd
Edenfield Brewery Limited
Edinburgh Brewing Co Ltd
Eldridge, Pope & Co Ltd
Erddig Brewing Co Ltd
Exile Brewing Co Ltd
Frisky Bear Brewing Co Ltd
GKH Beer Co Ltd
Inner Bay Brewery Limited
Jaw Brew Ltd
Laid Back Brewing Limited
Legenderry Brewing Co Ltd
Mad Dog Brewing Co Ltd
Modha Ales Ltd
Moorside Brewery Ltd
Moseley Beer Co Ltd
Nethergate Brewery Co Ltd
North Country Ales Limited
North Riding Brewery Limited
Paradigm Brewery Ltd
Park Brewery Ltd
Penton Park Brewery Limited
Philsters Limited
Pig Iron Brewing Limited
Pilot Brewery Limited
Pinnora Ltd
Powderkeg Brewery Ltd
Reds Beer Co Ltd
Seal Bay Brewery Sel Bragdy Bae Ltd
Silktown Brewery Ltd
Stratford upon Avon Brewery Ltd
Three Legs Brewing Co Ltd
Wessex Brewing & Pub Co Ltd
Wickwar Craft Taverns Limited
Wickwar Town Taverns Ltd
Wooha Brewing Co Ltd

July-September 2014 [37]
2731 Limited
AD Hop Brewing Ltd
Anglesey Ales Ltd
Appleby Brewery Ltd.
Boutilliers Limited
Box Social Ltd
Breworks Ltd
Bushey Brewery Co Ltd
Canopy Beer Co Ltd
Cerne Abbas Brewery Ltd
Clan Brewing Co Ltd
Dead Crafty Beer Co Ltd
Greyhound Brewery Limited
Inadequate Brewery Limited
Island Hamlet Brewing Co Ltd
Jarrow Innovations Ltd
Kellentay Beers Ltd
Konigsberg Seven Bridges Breweries Ltd
Mondo Brewing Co Ltd
Moogbrew Ltd
New River Brewery Ltd
Piddle Brewery Limited
Portpatrick Brewery Ltd

The UK Brewing Industry

Priest Town Brewing Co Ltd
Renegade Pub Co 2 Limited
Riviera Brewing Co Ltd
Signal Brewery Limited
Spotty Dog Brewery Limited
Stenroth Limited
Thirst Class Ale Limited
UBrewCC Limited
Unity Brewing Ltd
Urban Island Brewing Co. Ltd
Verdant Brewing Co Ltd
Wild Horse Brewing Co Ltd
Wishbone Brewery Limited
Wrytree Brewery Limited

October-December 2014 [49]
81artisan Limited
Agnate Limited
Ale Club Ltd
Bellfield Brewery Limited
Boss Brewing Co Ltd
Campervan Brewery Ltd
Dancing Duck Holdings Ltd
Dorber Brewing Limited
Earth Ale Ltd
Edinbrew Ltd
Edinburgh Beer Factory Limited
Egghead Brewery Limited
Enfield Brewery Limited
Frome Brewing Co Ltd
Frontier Brewing Co Ltd
Glen Affric Brewery Limited
Grasshopper Brewery Limited
HFBC Ltd
Harbour Brewery Tenby Limited
Hoggshead Brewhouse Limited
Holy Well Brewing Ltd
Hope Brewery Ltd
Hurly Burly Brewery Ltd
Indian Brewery Company Birmingham Ltd
Isle of Ely Brewing Co Ltd.
Jolly Boys Brewery Ltd
Kew Brewery Limited
Lam Brewing Limited
Long Arm Brewing Co Limited
Mart's Brewing Co Ltd
Microcosm Brewing Ltd.
Monks Bridge Brewery Ltd
Moody Goose Brewery Limited
Nobby's Brewing Co Ltd
Over The Hill Brewery Ltd
Papworth Brewery Limited
Rivington Brewing Co Limited
Romney Marsh Brewery Limited
Silverstone Real Ale Co Ltd
Southsea Brewing Co Ltd
Taylors Blackbeck Brewery Ltd
Tenby Brewing Co. Limited
Three Shires Brewery Ltd
Tombstone Brewery Limited
Torrside Brewing Ltd
TwT Lol Cyf
Veterans Brewing Ltd
Volden Limited
Youngs Beers Limited

January 2015 [22]
Abernyte Brewery Limited
Baker's Dozen Brewing Co Ltd
Beatnikz Republic Brewing Co Ltd
Beer Brothers Ltd

Brewit Microbrewery Ltd
Brinkburn Street Brewery Ltd
Coalition Brewing Co Ltd
Crafty Pales Ltd
Dark Revolution Ltd
GT Ales Limited
Great Central Brewery Limited
Ham Brewing Co Ltd
Holcot Hop-Craft Ltd
Hornes Brewery Ltd
Left Handed Giant Brewing Ltd
Marches Brewery Limited
Quad Brewing Co Ltd
Red Star Brewery (Formby) Ltd
Steam Machine Brewing Co Ltd
Tankley's Brewery Limited
Valve Brewing Co Ltd.
Wily Fox Brewery Limited

February 2015 [15]
Beckstones Brewery Limited
Beerkat Brewing Co Ltd
Big Brewing Co Ltd
Bohem Brewery Ltd
Camden Brewing Group Limited
Colonsay Beverages Ltd.
Encoder Brewery Limited
Jordan's Car Review Ltd
Little Crosby Village Brewing Co Ltd
Nightcap Beer Co Ltd
Oldershaw Brewery Ltd
Sociable Beer Co Ltd.
Tarn51 Brewing Co Ltd
Trinity Ales Limited
Wingtip Brewing Co Ltd

March 2015 [22]
AB InBev UK Finance Co Ltd
AB InBev UK Investment Co Ltd
Beer Collective Limited
Brumaison Ltd
Bullmastiff Brewery Limited
Company of Dead Brewers Ltd
Craft Beer Society Ltd
Elemental Brew House Limited
Errant Ltd
Fierce Beer Limited
Foresight Holdings Limited
Gemstone Ales Ltd.
Hopsmith Brewing Co Ltd
Little Ox Brewery Limited
Matlock Brewing Co Ltd
Old Friends Brewery Ltd
Oxbrew Ltd
Peak Ales Limited
Seven Brothers Ancoats Ltd
Silks Brewery Limited
Tally Ho! Brewery Limited
Woodcote Manor Brewing Co Ltd

April 2015 [16]
Beeston Hop Ltd
Bent Iron Brewing Co Ltd
Craft Brewery Limited
Devenish & Co (Weymouth) Ltd
Fine Tuned Brewery Limited
Glesga Brewery Ltd.
Merrimans Brewery Ltd
Mighty Medicine Brewing Co Ltd
Neepsend Brewery Ltd
Neptune Brewery Ltd

Newcastle Brewing Ltd
Old Prentonian Brewing Co Ltd.
Radlett Beer Co Ltd
Serious Brewing Co Ltd
Staggeringly Good Ltd
Zapato Brewery Ltd.

May 2015 [22]
Abstract Jungle Brewing Ltd
Brew Club Limited
Brew York Limited
Church Farm Brewery Ltd
Cross Borders Brewing Co Ltd
Dog and Rabbit Brewery Ltd
Double Tap Brewery Ltd
Good Chemistry Apparatus Ltd
Good Chemistry Brewing Limited
Hattie Brown's Brewery Ltd
Jarr Kombucha Ltd
Kettlesmith Brewing Co Ltd
Kingstone Brewery Limited
Littleover Brewery Limited
Loane Brothers Limited
Nightjar Brew Co Ltd
Project X Brewing Co Ltd
Quirky Ales Ltd
RPM Brewery Ltd
George Samuel Brewing Co. Ltd.
St Andrews Brewing Co Holdings Ltd
St Andrews Brewing Co Ltd

June 2015 [21]
71 Brewing Limited
Ampthill & Woburn Brewery Ltd
Bond Brews Ltd
Brooks Brewhouse Limited
Cocktails and Craft Beers Ltd
Credence Brewing Ltd
Endure Brewing Co Ltd
Fisher's Brewing Co Ltd.
Ghost Brewing Co Limited
Golden Fox Brewing Ltd
Hopjacker Brewery Ltd
Kall Brand Ltd
Maregade Brew Co Ltd
Nightowl Brewing Co Ltd
Oddly Limited
Pershore Brewery Limited
Pink Ferry Ltd
Reunion Ales Limited
Scribbler's Ales Limited
Star Wing Brewery Ltd
Totnes Brewing Co Limited

July 2015 [11]
Big Bog Brewing Co Ltd
Black Lodge Brewery Ltd
Burton Town Brewery Limited
Elusive Brewing Limited
Little London Brewery Limited
Macclesfield Brewing Co Ltd
Margate Brewery Limited
Riverside Brewery Ltd
Roam Brewing Co Ltd
Tanners Ales Ltd
Umbrella Brewing Limited

August 2015 [18]
After The Harvest Brewing Ltd
Avid Brewing Co. Ltd
Beerblefish Brewing Co Ltd
Boudicca Brewing Co Ltd
Boxcar Brewery Limited
Crasi Limited
Crate Bars Limited
Crate Brewery Limited
Damnation Breweries Limited
Damnation Limited
Ferry Brewery Co Ltd
Hairy Brewers Ales Limited
Hilltop Brewing Co Ltd
Ignition Brewery Limited
Linear Brewing Co Ltd
Little Critters Brewing Co Ltd
Nauticales Ltd
Rockhopper Brewing Co Ltd

September 2015 [16]
400 Software Limited
Bespoke Beer Co Ltd
Bestens Brewery Limited
Bubble Works Brew Co Ltd
Cartmel Valley Brewery Ltd
Cwrw Mon Cyf
Dockyard Brewery Limited
Great North Eastern Brewing Co Ltd
Husk Brewing Limited
Lords Brewing Co Ltd
Morton Collins Brewing Co Ltd
Mybrewpub Limited
Skinnybrands Ltd
Temperance Brewing Co Ltd
Three Engineers Brewery Ltd
Wye Brewing Co Ltd

October 2015 [25]
BAA Brewing Limited
Beercraft Brewery Limited
Black Market Brewery Limited
Brewery Limited
Burford Brewery Co Ltd
Chin Chin Brewing Co Ltd
Dowr Kammel Brewing Co Ltd
Farr Brew Ltd
Feisty Caribbean Ltd
Flash House Brewing Co Ltd
Higsons 1780 Limited
Horbury Ales Limited
Lawman Brewing Company, Ltd.
Lost and Grounded Brewers Ltd
Mid-Cheshire Brewing Ltd
Moo Brewing Co Ltd
Nameless Brewing Limited
Neon Raptor Brewing Co Ltd.
Oxted Brewery Ltd
Priors Well Brewery Limited
SF Brew Co Ltd
Soul Doubt Brewing Co Ltd
Stannary Brewing Co Ltd.
Tealby Brewing Co Ltd
Westley Brewing Co Ltd.

November 2015 [11]
Boat Lane Brewery Limited
Brews Brothers Brewery Ltd
Craft Beer Cab Co Ltd
Crafted Brewing Co. Ltd
Crazy Mountain Brewing Co UK Ltd
Double Barrelled Brewery Ltd.
Four Pillars Brewery Limited
Knoydart Brewery Limited
Pentrich Brewing Co. Ltd
Silver Street Brewery Limited
Solvay Brewing Ltd

December 2015 [16]
Another Brewery Limited
Block Brewery Limited
Brewheadz Limited
Cloak and Dagger Brewing Co Ltd
Etrusca Brewery & Distillery in St. Andrews
Five Clouds Brewing Co Ltd
Flying Fox Brewery Limited
Melin Tap Brewhouse Limited
Plan B Brewing Co Ltd
Rock Springs Brewing Ltd
Tipsy Angel Brewery Ltd
Tomos & Lilford Holdings Ltd
Two Finches Brewery Ltd.
Two Thirsty Men Ltd
Vine Inn Brewery 2016 Limited
Watling Street Brewery Limited

January 2016 [20]
Bang-On Brewery Limited
Barnaby's Brewhouse Ltd
Bears Den Brewery Limited
Beathbrewing Ltd
Brew Shed Beers Limited
Broken Bridge Brewing Ltd
Eyeball Brewing Ltd
Garden City Brewery Limited
Greyfriars Brewery Ltd
Kingdom Brewery Limited
Mill Valley Brewery Limited
Odyssey Brew Co Ltd
Original Goole Brewery Co Ltd
Republic of Beer Ltd
Rocket Ales Limited
Seren Brewing Co Ltd
Silverstone Brewing Co Limited
Temple Road Brewing Co Ltd
Villages Brewery Limited
Websters Brewery Ltd.

February 2016 [28]
Abbey Brewery Ltd
Burning Soul Brewing Ltd
J. Church Brewing Co. Ltd
Cwrw Ogwen Cyf
Dorking Brewery (2016) Limited
Fit Like Beer Limited
Fitbeer Ltd.
Four Kings Brewery Limited
Hand Brewing Co Ltd
Headstocks Brewery Ltd Ltd
Konigsberg Limited
Langham Brewing Co Ltd
Loud Shirt Brewing Co Ltd
Madchester Brewing Co Ltd
Myrlex Southend Limited
New Wharf Brewing Co Ltd
Isaac Poad Brewing Ltd
Prussia 1701 Limited
Prussia Bier Limited
Rufford Abbey Brewery Ltd
Tamar Valley Brewing Co Ltd
Treen's Brewery Ltd.

Tweed Brewing Ltd
Watts & Co Ltd
Wildcraft Brewery Limited
Winton Brewery Limited
Woodbridge Brewing Co Ltd
Yardley Brothers Europe Ltd

March 2016 [30]
Angles Ales Limited
Atlantic Craft Soda Co Ltd
Beat Ales Ltd.
Beer Ink Limited
Blackpit Brewery Ltd
Brewbox Systems Ltd
Brucehaven Brewery Ltd.
Bulletproof Brewing Ltd
Bute Brew Co Ltd
Buzz Brewing Co Ltd
Christchurch Brewing Co. Ltd
Elmtree Beers Ltd
Eyes Brewing Limited
Foxhat Beer Limited
Frome Brewery Limited
Fuddy Duck Limited
Interstate Craft Brewing Co Ltd
Lakehouse Brewing Co Ltd
Lock 34 Brew Co. Limited
Meridian Brewery Limited
New Devon Brewing Ltd
Northern Craft Brewers Limited
Out of Town Brewing Limited
Partridge Brewing Co Ltd
Small Beer Brewing Co Ltd
St Mary's Brewery Ltd
Three Brothers Brewing Co Ltd
Two Happy Captains Ltd
Withnell's Brewing Co Ltd
Woodforde's BPP Limited

April 2016 [24]
A Northerly Brewing Ltd
J.B. Almond Ltd
Bratch Beers Ltd
Brewboard Limited
Buccaneer Brewery Ltd
Crafty Brewing Co Ltd
Dark Tribe Brewery Limited
Exiled Brewers Limited
Felday Limited
Ferry Ales Brewery Limited
Fowey Brewery Ltd
Hybrid Brewing Ltd
Muckle Brewing Ltd
Pink Moon Brewery Limited
Pumphouse Brewing Co Ltd
M Rackstraws Ltd
Real Crafty Brewing Co Ltd
Roath Brewery Ltd
Stardust Brewery Ltd
Strong House Brewery Ltd
Uttoxeter Brewing Co Ltd
Velvet Owl Brewing Co Ltd.
West By Three Limited
Whitley Bay Brewing Co Ltd

May 2016 [16]
Beckenham Brewery Ltd.
Chalk Stone Brewery Limited
Chapeau Brewing Limited
Keep Brewing Ltd
Kinross Brewery Limited
Lake View Country House Ltd
Lithic Brewing Limited
Luddites Revenge Ltd
Old Windsor Brewery Ltd
Saison 86 Limited
Salisbury Brewery Limited
Small Beer Brew Co. Ltd
Stubborn Mule Brewery Limited
Ticketytap Ltd
Volden Brewing Limited
Wharf Brewing Co Ltd

June 2016 [18]
7 Reasons To Brew Ltd
Bidwell Brewery Co Ltd
Black Squirrel Brewing Limited
Bostin Brews Ltd
Brazen Brewing Co. Ltd
Brotherhood Brewery Ltd
Crooked Brewing Limited
Donzoko Brewing Co Ltd
Framework Brewery Limited
Genesis Craft Ales Limited
Heaney Brewing Co Ltd
Heathen Brewers Limited
Hilden Brewery Limited
Mad Scientists Pty. Ltd
Norn Iron Brew Co Ltd
Polarity Brewing Ltd
Pretty Decent Beer Co Ltd
Roebuck Brewing Co Ltd

July 2016 [23]
3ways Brewing Co Limited
Andwell Brewing Co Ltd
Chapter Brewing Co Ltd
Clifford Brothers Brewery Ltd
Cold Formd Ltd
Eskdale Brewery Ltd
Gene Pool Brewing Ltd
Genius Brewing Limited
Hickbrew Limited
Hubsters Brewery Ltd
Ironstone Brewery Ltd
Little Black Dog Beer Co Ltd
MBJW Brewing Limited
Milton and Mortimer Ltd
Origami Brewing Co Ltd.
Ralphs Ruin Ltd
Ride Industrys Limited
Roundhill Brewery Limited
Staffordshire Spirits Co Ltd
Tap Social Movement Limited
Test Brewing Ltd
Ullage Ale Ltd
Vision Brewing Co Ltd

August 2016 [17]
Aurora Ales Limited
Big Drop Brewing Co Ltd
Birmingham Brewing Co Ltd
Brewshed Ltd
Brolly Brewing Limited
Burnt Mill Brewery Ltd
Craft Origins Limited
Diamond Dicks Brewing Limited
Fallen Acorn Brewing Co. Ltd
Glede Brewing Co Ltd
It's Braw Limited
Krafty Braumeister Ltd
Little Rotters Limited
Sibley Brewing Co Ltd.
Southey Brewing Co Ltd
Tuckers Ales Limited
Wriggly Monkey Brewery Limited

September 2016 [14]
ABI UK Holding 1 Limited
ALE Finance Services Limited
Angry Coot Fermentation Co Ltd.
Applecross Brewing Co Ltd
Draycott Brewing Co Ltd
Eagles Crag Brewery Ltd
Fermanagh Beer Co Ltd
Hop King Brewery Ltd
Kentish Town Brewery Limited
McColl's Brewery Limited
Medieval Bread and Ale Co Ltd
Muswell Hillbilly Brewers Ltd
Old Street Brewery Ltd
Zymurgorium Ltd

October 2016 [17]
3's A Crowd Brewing Ltd
Abyss Brewing Ltd
Altarnun Brewing Limited
Boothtown Brewery Co Ltd
Chelmsford Brewing Co Ltd.
Copper Dragon Brewery Limited
Dartmouth Brewing Co Ltd
Glasshouse Beer Co Ltd
Great British Breworks Ltd
Recoil Brewing Co Ltd
Sonnet 43 Brewery Ltd
Stamps Brewery Limited
Steel Coulson Ltd
Tiptree Brewing Co Ltd
Turner & Shaw Glasgow Brewing Co Ltd
Vertical Stack Ltd
World Bier Huis Limited

November 2016 [23]
7grains Limited
Chichester Brewery Limited
Chubby Seal Ltd
Croft Ales Ltd
Custom Head Brewing Ltd
East Yorkshire Beer Co Ltd
Fallen Angel Brewery Ltd
Garagebrew Ltd
Jabru Bevco Ltd
Kinkell Brewery Ltd
Liquid Light Brewing Co Ltd
Manchester Union Brewery Ltd
Merchant City Brewing Co Ltd
Thomas Paine Brewery Limited
Pivo-UK Limited
Play Limited
Saints Row Brewing Co Ltd
Shed35 Ltd
Somerset Ales Limited
Spartan Brewery Ltd
Stamford Ales Limited
Strathmore Brewery Limited
Two Cocks Farm Limited

December 2016 [12]
Beermats Brewing Co Ltd
Best Brewery Ltd
Black Angus Brewing Ltd
Crafty Beer Seller Limited
Darkplace Brewery Limited
Dogtag Beer Co. Ltd
Meanwood Brewery Ltd
Moody Fox Ltd.
Mr Bees Brewery Ltd
Nomadic Brewing Co Ltd
Redruth Brewery Limited
Towler and Webb Limited

January 2017 [31]
Allbeer Limited
Ampersand Brew Co Ltd
Beer Hut Brewing Co Ltd
Blimey! Brewing Co Ltd
Bone Machine Brewing Co Ltd
Bont Brew Ltd
Brews of the World Limited
Campbells Brewery Ltd
Coastal Brewing Co Ltd
Crankshaft Brewery Limited
Devitera Ltd
Dolphin Brewery Limited
Donnington Brewery Limited
East Neuk Organic Brewing & Distilling
Floff UK Limited
Gentleman Bear Brewing Co Ltd
Handyman Brewery Ltd
Hindsight Collective Ltd
Kintyre Ales Limited
Lion Brewery Co. Limited
Lost Boys Brewery Ltd
Lost Roots Limited
Marourde Limited
Reids Gold Brewing Co Ltd
River Widow Brewery Ltd
Space Trash Brewing Ltd
Stag Brewery Ltd
Steam Town Brewco Limited
Tirindrish Trading Co Ltd
Turning Point Brewing Co Ltd
Well Drawn Brewing Co Ltd

February 2017 [26]
3ABC Ltd
Baynhams Brewery Limited
Beer Necessities Limited
Black Fen Brewery Ltd
Blackened Sun Brewing Co Ltd
Blonde Brothers Limited
Bowing Hound Brewing Co Ltd
Chevin Brew Co Ltd
Craft Soft Drinks Community Ltd
Deviant and Dandy Brewery Ltd
Ellismuir Limited
Glenfinnan Brewing Co Ltd
Hopsox Brewing Co Ltd
LF Brewery Holdings Limited
Lecale Brewery Limited
Loopland Brewing Co Ltd
Luddite Brewing Co Ltd
Miswell Brewery Ltd
Nellyd Limited
Ovenstone 109 Limited
Overtone Brewing Ltd
Rogue Elephant Brewery Limited
TKS Brewing Limited

Taw Valley Brewery Limited
West Highland Breweries Ltd
Windmill Hill Brewing Co Ltd

March 2017 [28]
3 Piers Brewery Limited
Samuel Allsopp & Sons Ltd
Arnold and Hancock Limited
Aussie Brewing Co Ltd
Brew Monster Limited
Cellarhead Brewing Co Ltd
Clavell & Hind Limited
Equal Brewkery CIC
Hairy Dog Brewery Ltd
Kairos Solutions Ltd
MBH Tap & Shop Limited
Market Bosworth Brewery Ltd
Newquay Brewing Co Ltd
Northern Whisper Brewing Co Ltd
Piglove Brewing Co Limited
Pilot Wharf Limited
Rival Brewing Co Limited
Romford Brewery Co Ltd
Sheffield Brewers Collective
David Sheriff Brewing Services Ltd
Thirsty Smile Ltd
Emma J Tilston Ltd
Two Bears Brewery Ltd
Two Rabbit Brewing Co Ltd
Vendetta Brewing Co Ltd
Wilderness Brewery Ltd
Witch Craft Beers Limited
Yorkshire Brewhouse Limited

April 2017 [41]
888 Global Trade Ltd
Angus Brewing Limited
Bad Joke Brew Co Ltd
Bear's Head Brewery Limited
Beersheba Ltd
Blighty Brewery Limited
Brute Brewing Co Ltd
Burner Drinks Limited
Cheshire Brewhouse Ltd
Cornish Brewery Limited
Craft Life Brewing Ltd.
Crafty Leopard Brewing Co Ltd
Cygnus Brewing Co Limited
Donkeystone Brewing Co Ltd
Duration Brewing Ltd
Emperor's Brewery Ltd.
Epic Beers Limited
Fat Boi Brewery & Sauce Co Ltd
Gan Yam Brewing Co Ltd
Great Glen Trading Centre Ltd
JP Brew Limited
Jolly Sailor Brewery Limited
Lancaster Brewery Holdings Ltd
Liquid Revolution Ltd
Loyal City Brewing Co Ltd
MC & P Engineering Limited
Nailmaker Brewing Co Ltd
New Bristol Brewery School Ltd
Northern Monkey Brew Co. Ltd
Nuglyfe Ltd
Orchard Road Brewery Limited
Pilgrim Brewery (Reigate) Ltd
Punchline Brewery Limited
Rock Solid Brewing Co Ltd
Sentinel Brewery Holdings Ltd
South Hams Brewery Ltd
Swaddle Micro Brewery Limited
Tinworks Brewing Co Ltd.
Top Rope Brewing Limited
Ultimate Maltgold Limited
Unbarred Brewery Limited

May 2017 [32]
1533 Brewery Limited
Ar Suil Brewing Project Ltd
Barrels Hereford Limited
Barsham Brewery Limited
Beer Monkey Brew Co. Limited
Beta Pilot Brewing Ltd
Brewers Folly Brewery Ltd.
Burton Old Cottage Beer Co Ltd
Collyfobble Brewery Limited
Connecting Hops Ltd
Copper Fox Brewery Ltd
Devanha Brewery Holdings Ltd
Devanha Brewery Limited
Flipside Brewing Ltd
Gloucestershire Old Cottage Beer Co Ltd
Greenwich Old Cottage Beer Co Ltd
Korca Brewery St Andrews Ltd
Lincolnshire Craft Beers Ltd
Maestro Brew Ltd
Mill Lane Brewing Co Ltd
Missing Link Brewing Ltd
Old Vault Brewing Co Ltd
Penistone Brewers Limited
Potton Brewing Co Ltd
Silvertown Brewery and Distillery Co Ltd
Steel River Drinks Ltd
Swift Half Collective Ltd
Thetford Brewery Limited
Tidal London Ltd
Two Drifters Brewery Ltd
Utopian Brewing Limited
Whitefaced Ltd

June 2017 [18]
Beerfisch Brewery Limited
Boody Brewery Ltd.
Braybrooke Beer Co Ltd
Brockenhurst Brewery Limited
Foggie Beer Co Ltd
German Kraft Brewing Limited
Good Things Brewing Co Ltd
Leith Brewing Co Ltd
London Fields Brewery Opco Ltd
Marchingtons Ltd
Monkey Shed Estate Brewing Co Ltd
Phaded World Ltd
Project Brewery Ltd
Round Corner Brewing Ltd
Samuels Brewing Co Ltd
Session Brewing Co. Limited
Summershed Brewery Limited
Two Fools Brewery Ltd

July 2017 [24]
Amwell Springs Brewery Co Ltd
Andys' Ales Limited
Boozehound Ltd
Coul Brewing Co Ltd
Earth Station Beers Ltd
Faultline Brew Co. Ltd
Grumpy Git Brewery Limited
Horse Box Brewing Ltd
Hurst Brewery Ltd
Kirton Fen Brewery Limited
Liverpool Brewery Limited
New Cross Ales Ltd
New Forest Beer Co Ltd
North Yorkshire Brewing Co Ltd
Pomona Island Brew Co Ltd
Posh Boys Brewery Limited
SK Brew Ltd
Stoatcraft Revolutionary Beers Ltd
Thistlerock Enterprises UK Ltd
Uncanny Valley Brewing Co Ltd
WeBrew4U Ltd
Webru4u Ltd
Wetherby Brew Co Limited
Woodruff Brewing Ltd

August 2017 [13]
BeerHug Ltd
Blackdown Brewery Ltd
Castle Gate Brewery Limited
Cold Bath Brewing Co Ltd
Fearless Brewing Ltd
Ipbridge Limited
Kimbland Distillery Ltd
Monks Well Brewing Co Ltd
Oaks Brewing Co Ltd
Oxford Brewing Co Ltd
Rock Leopard Brewing Co Ltd
Tres Bien Brewery Ltd
Whitechapel Industries Ltd

September 2017 [27]
4 Mice Brewery Limited
Bang The Elephant Brewing Co Ltd
Barefaced Brewing Ltd
Br3wery Ltd
Brithop Brewing Co Ltd
Carnival Brewing Co Ltd
Chain House Brewing Co Ltd
Crafty Monkey Brewing Co Ltd
Degrees Plato Brewing Ltd.
Elemental Brewing Ltd
Galldachd Na H-Alba Brewing Ltd
Hexad Brewing Ltd
Holley Paquette Brewers Ltd
Hoptimistic Brewery Limited
Kendal Brewery Ltd
Makeshift Brewing Co Ltd
Nicol Brewery Ltd.
Ol Brewery Limited
Omnebonum Ltd
Outhouse Brewing Ltd
Penistone Brewing (Penistone) Ltd
Scot Brew Limited
Sheeptown Brewery Limited
Stod Fold Brewing Limited
White Wolf Brewery Ltd
Wigan Brew House Ltd
Wizard Brewing Company Combe Ltd

October 2017 [33]
23-7 Brewing Ltd
Anthology Brewing Co Ltd
Asylum Harbour Brewing Co Ltd
Beauty and The Beer Limited
Beer Belly Brewery Limited
Beltane Brewing Co Ltd
Big Mountain Brewing Co Ltd
Brothers of Ale Limited
Candid Brewing Co. Limited
Tony Clark Enterprises Ltd
Fire Rock Brewing Co Ltd.

Four Bulls Brewing Co Ltd
Gibberish Brewing Ltd
Ground Hammer Beer Co Ltd
Hale Brewing Limited
Hildenborough Brewery Ltd
Hitchin Brewery Ltd
Inlaw Brewing Co Ltd
Lekker Days Ltd
London Ale UK Ltd
Luxbev Limited
Many Hands Brewery Ltd
Nansen Street Holdings Ltd
Overworks Limited
Radio City Beer Works Limited
Sneaky Peacock Ltd
Soul Brewing Co Ltd
Spotlight Brewing Ltd
Staff Beer Ltd
Stroud Brewery Development Ltd
Wanderlust Bar Limited
Wilde Child Brewing Co Ltd
Workshy Brewing Ltd

November 2017 [29]
3 Cities Brewing Co Ltd
Arcadian Brewing Co Ltd
Bad Girls Brew Limited
Bullhouse Brewing Co Ltd
Burnt Hill Brewery Limited
By The River Brewery Ltd
Cheviot Brewery Ltd
City Vaults Real Ale Ltd
Cosmic Brewing Co Ltd
Dovedale Brewing Co Ltd
Grafham Brewing Co Ltd
Infinite Session Ltd
Kelchner Ltd
Koomor Brewing Co Ltd
Lewanbrew Limited
Lion-Beer, Spirits & Wine (UK) Ltd
Little Eaton Brewery Co Ltd
Matterdale Brewery Limited
Phantom Brewing Co. Limited
Three Arches Brewing Limited
Twinshock Brewery Ltd
Two Fathoms Distillery Ltd.
Unicorn Craft Brewing Co Ltd
Uppingham Brewery Limited
Uppingham Brewhouse Limited
Vovin Ltd
Walsall Brewing Co Ltd
Witchcraft Brewery Limited
Wylde Sky Brewing Ltd

December 2017 [13]
Alex Barlow Brewing Consulting Ltd
Beer Smiths Limited
Bigla Brewing Co Ltd
Box Brewery Ltd
Farmageddon Brewing Limited
Holler Brewery Limited
Lennox Brewery Limited
Loomshed Hebrides Ltd
Mad Yank Brewery Ltd
Moot Oak Brewing Co Ltd
Mudlark Investments Ltd
Sonder Brewing Co Ltd.
Yellow Top Brewing Co Ltd

January 2018 [32]
Alter Ego Brewing Co Ltd
Badwells Brewery Ltd
Baronscourt Brewing Co Ltd
Battle Brewery Limited
Big Bear Brewery Limited
Big Hop Brewing Co Ltd
Crooked Ship Brewery Ltd
Dead Parrot Beer Co Ltd
Epic Brewing Limited
Gravity Well Brewing Co Ltd
Green Times Brewing Limited
Hawkins Drinks Limited
Hunter Brewing Co Ltd
Leviathan Brewing Ltd
Littondale Brewing Co Ltd
Mashionistas Brewing Co Ltd
McGrath's Brewing Limited
Mechanic Brewing Co Ltd
Mortimer Brewing Co Ltd
No Abode Brew Co Ltd
Sandbanks Brewery Limited
Silver Rocket Brewing Ltd
Stokesley Brewing Co Ltd
Titsey Brewing Co. Limited
Topcat Brewery Limited
Topsham Brewery Ltd
Van Pur UK Ltd
Vault City Brewing Ltd.
Veterans Brewing Sussex Ltd
Wharf Beers Ltd
Whyte BR Brewing Co Ltd
Whyte Bar Brewing Co Ltd

February 2018 [34]
Another Beer Ltd
Bason Bridge Brewing Co Ltd
Bert and Chris Brew Beer Ltd
Black Horse Brewery Ltd
Bog Brew Beers Limited
Boot Town Brewery Ltd
Brechin Park Brewing Co Ltd
Brew & Bottle Limited
Crosby Beverages Ltd
Cullach Brewing Ltd
Deutschlond Brewery Limited
Docks Beers Limited
Egan & Martin Limited
Fairy Glen Brewery Ltd
Foghorn Brew Co Ltd
Fokof Limited
Forest Hill Brewing Co Ltd
Forth Bridge Brewery and Distillery
Good Kombucha Drinks Ltd
Harr Engineering Limited
I.T's Brewing Co Ltd
Last Sign Brewing Co Ltd
Laughing Ass Brewery Ltd
Little Monster Brewing Co Ltd
Lock 81 Brewery Limited
MB Collective Limited
Malts & Hops Brewing Limited
Old Tree Brewery Ltd
One Swan Ltd
Paper Fort Brew Co Ltd.
Rock A Brew Ltd
Shoreditch Brewing Co Ltd
Ten Tors Brewery Ltd
Trale Brewing Co Ltd

March 2018 [34]
BL Drinks Ltd
Bad Boy Brewing Ltd
Brewsmith Limited
Cains Brewing Co Ltd
Creative Juices Brewing Co Ltd
Darkland Brewery Limited
Dunfermline Brewery Limited
Eden Mill Brewers Ltd
Elements Brewing Co Ltd
Good Living Brew Co Limited
Got 2 Bee Clean Ltd
Halton Turner Brewing Co Ltd
Harvey Elizabeth Limited
Hopscotch Craft Brewers Ltd
Icon Brewery Limited
Inverbrewery Limited
Jacobite Brewery Limited
Laiho Limited
Lake District Brewery Limited
Lost Skulls Brewing Co Ltd
Lucky Shaman Limited
Makemake Beer Ltd
Mister A's Beer Co Ltd
Mousehole Brewery Limited
O'Neill's Brewing Co Ltd
Owlcrab Limited
Raven Hill Brewery Limited
Steam Brewing Co Limited
Stokes Brewing Co Ltd
Taylor Illingworth Brewing Co Ltd
Tom's Tap and Brewhouse Ltd
Top-Notch Brewing Co Ltd
Veterans Brewing (South East) Ltd
Yarm Brewing and Distilling Co Ltd

April 2018 [36]
1st Icon Ltd
Ascent Location Solutions Ltd
Askham Brewery Limited
Attic Brew Co. Ltd
Beer in the Blood Ltd
Bomb Shelter Brewing Limited
Bowtie Brewers Limited
Brewkeepers Limited
Crossroads Brewery Limited
Dead Fridge Farm Limited
Dynamite Valley Brewery Ltd
Flat Cap Holding Co Ltd
Fresh Beer Co Ltd
Head Thirst Ltd
Hollow Tree Brewing Co. Ltd
Inferno Brewery Limited
K L Brewery Limited
Killer Hop Brew Co Ltd
Lazy Bay Brewery Ltd
Lazy Turtle Brewing Co Ltd
Letterpress Brewery Ltd
Little Wolf Brewing Limited
Liverpool Craft Holdings Ltd
Liverpool Craft Limited
Loka Polly Ltd
Merrimen Brewery Limited
OM Food Corp Ltd
Portishead Brewing Co Ltd
Punchbowl Brewery Limited
Shady Shed Brewery Limited
Stannington Brewery Ltd
Stoney Ford Brew Co. Ltd
Three Geezers Brewing Limited
Urbeer Ltd
Vandal Brewing Co Ltd
York Brewery Limited

May 2018 [28]
Bad Moon Brewery Ltd
Brewery Z Ltd
Decagram Art and Craft CIC
Delphic Brewing Co Ltd
Doromomo & Sons Ltd
Fingerprint Brewing Co Ltd
Foamology Limited
Howe Capital Limited
Live Brew Co Ltd
Mersea Island Brewery & Vineyard Ltd
Moody Stag Limited
Newcastle Eden Bottling Co Ltd
Newt Brew Ltd
Postlethwaites Brewery Ltd
Punjabi Ltd
Robel Pawlos Ltd
Rude Mechanicals Limited
Saltdean Brewing Co Ltd
Shropshire Beers Limited
Soham Brewery Ltd
Solway Spirits Ltd
Stocks Brewing Co Ltd
Stone Cold Brewery Limited
To The Moon Brewery Ltd
Universal Robo Innovations Ltd
Urban Alchemy Brewing Co Ltd
Wentworth Brewery Ltd
Weymouth Brewery Limited

June 2018 [27]
Alcohol Beverages Co Ltd
Bellrock Brew Co. Ltd
Blithe Nook Brewery Ltd
Bold Brewing Ltd
Chasing Everest Brew Co Ltd
Comet Brewery Ltd
Dog Falls Brewing Co. Ltd
Hops and Dots Brewing Co Ltd
Humber Doucy Brewing Co Ltd
Impavive Ltd
Keswick Brewing Co Ltd
Lost at Sea Brewing Limited
Luckie Drinks Ltd
Nothing Bound Brewing Co Ltd
Nungate Brewery Co Ltd
Original Brewers Limited
Pivo Beverages Ltd
Religious Ales Ltd
Second Wave Brewing Ltd
Serpent Brew Co Ltd
Shadow Brewing Ltd
Silver Brewhouse Limited
Snakestorm Limited
Splott Brewery Ltd
Thirsty Pioneers Brewing Co Ltd
Upper Harglodd Farm Ltd
Wedmore Ales Ltd

July 2018 [24]
Brixworth Brewery Co Ltd
Broadtown Brewery Ltd
Casorho Ltd
Craftwater Brewing Co Ltd
Eko Brewery Limited
Ethical Ales Limited
Fishponds Brewery Ltd
Getset Brew Co Ltd
Imaginary Friends Brewing Ltd
Jocks and Peers Brewing Co Ltd
Lastonser Ltd

London Brewery Limited
Onebeer Brewing Ltd
Organic Laundry Limited
Parbold Bottle Limited
Red Bay Brewing Co Ltd
Round Tower Brewery (Chelmsford) Ltd
Smokin Barrels Brewery Ltd
Southbrew Co Ltd
TW@ Limited
Vadum Brewery Ltd
Vodaso Limited
Welland Brewery Ltd
Wicked Hog Brewery Ltd

August 2018 [30]
A-Zero Energy Beer Limited
Bakewell Road Brewery Ltd
Battery Brewing Ltd
Blackened Abbey Ltd
Calarta Ltd
Cillenx Ltd
Devil's Pleasure Limited
Dowdeswell Brewery Limited
Emprise Brewery Limited
Evensong Brewing Limited
Gargiulo's Production Ltd
Gil's Brewery Ltd
Howardian Hills Brewing Co Ltd
Lord Randalls Brewery Ltd
Lucky Cat Brewery Limited
Narugelia Ltd
Near Beer Brewing Co. Ltd
Out of the Woods Brew Co Ltd
Phonymick Ltd
Rocksnarl Ltd
Scariosa Ltd
Sea Brewing Co Ltd
Shandy Shack Ltd
Slopemeister Brewing Co Ltd
Stag Ales Ltd
Symmetry Brewing Co Ltd
Three Hills Brewing Ltd
Three Lions Brewery Ltd
Urban Brewery Ltd
Via Academia Vocatus Ltd

September 2018 [31]
Adriyel Ltd
Alonaoracle Ltd
Birkenhead Brewery Co Ltd
Conferta Ltd
Crai Cider Co Ltd
Crooked Fish Ltd
DHBeers Ltd
Deil's Heid Brewing Co Ltd
Droylsden Craft Limited
Ferox and Noble Limited
Fleabag Brewing Co Ltd
Gilt & Flint Ltd
HU Caret 4 Limited
Hartlebury Brewing Co Ltd
Hop and Pray Ltd
Kettle Green Brewing Ltd
Little Teapot Ltd
Midshires Brewery Limited
Now Then Brewery Ltd
OTL Brew Co Ltd
Old Thistle Co Ltd
Pastore Brewing and Blending Ltd
Pointeer Ltd
Pongolo Ltd

Revelry Brewing & Distilling Ltd
Signpost Brewery Ltd
Skelpers Ltd
Sky Pirate Ltd
Stay Gold Beer Co Ltd
Three Acre Brewery Limited
Xylo Brewing Ltd

October 2018 [26]
3 Bru's Brewing Co Ltd
32 Islands Brewery Ltd
Ale Factory Ltd
Avocet Ales Limited
Beermondsey Limited
Biercafe Ltd
Bullards Beers Limited
JD Campbell Brewing Limited
Common Rioters Beer Limited
Ealing Brewing Ltd
Glastonbury Brewing Co Ltd
Hair of The Frog Brewing Ltd
Hop Forward Ltd
Hush Brewing Co. Ltd
Jimbrew Ltd
Laughing Pug Ltd
Legless Brewing Ltd
New Lion Totnes Ltd
Oakland Brewing Co Ltd
Parkway Brewing Co Ltd
Rough Brothers Brewing Limited
Sativa Brewing Co Ltd
Six Towns Brewery Limited
Snowdon Craft Beer Limited
Spyglass Brewing Co Ltd
Team Toxic Ltd

November 2018 [24]
5hop Limited
Avitas Craft Beer Ltd
Baird Brewing Co Ltd
Blue Armadillo Brewing Co Ltd
Bragdy Mona Cyf
Brew Locker Ltd
Cataclysm Brewing Limited
Dingbat Beer Ltd
Evolution Brewing Ltd
Faking Bad Brewery Limited
Fulham Brewery Ltd
Gander Brewing Co Ltd
A & C Green Food and Beverage Ltd
Hip Hop Brewery Limited
Incapico Inc Limited
Lough Neagh Distillers - 1837 Ltd
Matheson Brewers Ltd
Motley Hog Brewery Limited
New Invention Brewery Ltd
Quantock Brewery Limited
Southport Brewing Limited
Triple Point Brewing Ltd
Westmoor Botanicals Limited
YB Ventures (2018) Ltd

December 2018 [19]
4 Acre Brewing Co. Ltd
Beak Brewery Limited
Beer Station Brewery Ltd
Brewis Beer Co Ltd
Clandestine Distillery Limited
Craft Beer Collective Limited
Crank Beers Limited
Gleneagles Distillery Limited

Ivybridge Brewing Co Ltd
Lads & Dads Brewing Limited
Mersey Gin Co Ltd
Moon Cartel Limited
Oxford Brewery Limited
Saeburh Brewery Ltd
Smoky Dragon Brewery & Preservas
Southside Brewing Ltd
Twin Barrel Brewery Limited
White Park Brewery Limited
YSTY Limited

January 2019 [30]
Ashen Clough Ales Ltd
Bib Brewing Ltd
Braemar Brewery Ltd
Brewhouse Brewery Limited
Bridgnorth Brewery Limited
Bruin Beer Co Ltd
Camden Beer Ltd
Coast Beer Co Limited
Crossover Blendery Limited
Epochal Barrel-Fermented Ales Ltd
Frank and Otis Brewing Ltd

Groovy Grains Brewery Limited
Harrison's Brewery Ltd
Heroic Brew Co Ltd
Hopper House Brew Farm Ltd
Ironstone Brewery JVW Ltd
Jackrabbit Brewing Co. Ltd
Jawbone Brewing Ltd
Monachis Ltd
New Union Brewing Co Ltd
Oast & Tread Brewing Ltd
Padlock Brewery Ltd.
SRA Brewery Limited
Saltrock Brewing Co Ltd
Shelsley Brewing Co Ltd
Stratton Lane Ltd
Thesis Brewing Co. Ltd
Thunder and Little Ltd
Vitosha Wine Ltd
W & W Drinks Ltd

February 2019 [27]
BCM Brewing Co Ltd
Blackstar Brewery Ltd
Bucklebury Brewers Ltd

Dark Tower Brewery Ltd
Dovik Bast Ltd
Drumgaw Holdings Ltd
Fearnought Brewery Ltd
Hambleton Brewery Limited
Kindeace Ales Limited
Kuwa Trading Ltd
Law and Disorder Brew Co Ltd
Los Perros Sueltos Brewing Co Ltd
Maverick Brewing Co Ltd
No Comply Ltd
Old Farmhouse Brewery Ltd.
Pawed Brewery Ltd
Queer Brewing Project Ltd
Red Moon Brewery Limited
Rossendale Brew Co Ltd
Seafire Brewing Co. Ltd
Slice & Brew Ltd
St Davids Farm Brewery Ltd
Stornoway Brewers Limited
Tantum Brewing Limited
Trailhead Brew Co Ltd
Two Bob Brewing Co Ltd
Two Towns Down Brewing Ltd

This page is intentionally left blank

Geographic Distribution by County

Co Antrim [11]
Belfast Brewing Co Ltd
HFBC Ltd
Hercules Brewing & Co. Limited
Hilden Brewery Limited
McGrath's Brewing Limited
Nansen Street Holdings Ltd
Norn Iron Brew Co Ltd
Paddy's Clover Ltd
Red Bay Brewing Co Ltd
Samuels Brewing Co Ltd
West Belfast Real Ale Limited

Co Armagh
Clanconnel Brewing Co Ltd
Drumgaw Holdings Ltd
Lough Neagh Distillers - 1837 Ltd

Co Down [11]
Ards Brewing Co Ltd
Beer Hut Brewing Co Ltd
Brute Brewing Co Ltd
Bullhouse Brewing Co Ltd
Farmageddon Brewing Limited
Horse Box Brewing Ltd
Lecale Brewery Limited
Loopland Brewing Co Ltd
Mashdown Brewery Ltd.
Mourne Mountains Brewery Ltd
Whitewater Brewing Co. Ltd

Co Fermanagh
Fermanagh Beer Co Ltd
Loane Brothers Limited

Co Londonderry
Heaney Brewing Co Ltd
Legenderry Brewing Co Ltd
One Swan Ltd
Rough Brothers Brewing Limited

Co Tyrone
Baronscourt Brewing Co Ltd
Clearsky Brewing Co Ltd
Pokertree Brewing Co Ltd

Aberdeenshire [21]
Battery Brewing Ltd
Bold Brewing Ltd
Braemar Brewery Ltd
Brew Toon Ltd.
Brewdog PLC
Copper Fox Brewery Ltd
Deeside Brewery Limited
Devanha Brewery Holdings Ltd
Devanha Brewery Limited
Duffstar Brewing Limited
Fierce Beer Limited
Fit Like Beer Limited
Foggie Beer Co Ltd
Inverbrewery Limited
Lewanbrew Limited
Matheson Brewers Ltd
Metcalfe & Metcalfe Co Ltd
Overworks Limited
Reids Gold Brewing Co Ltd
Scot Brew Limited
Stoatcraft Revolutionary Beers Ltd

Angus [13]
71 Brewing Limited
Alechemy Brewing Ltd
Angus Brewing Limited
Brechin Park Brewing Co Ltd
DHBeers Ltd
Deil's Heid Brewing Co Ltd
Harvey Elizabeth Limited
Keith Brewery Limited
Shed35 Ltd
Spey Valley Brewery Limited
Strathmore Brewery Limited
Two Thirsty Men Ltd
Wooha Brewing Co Ltd

Argyll [5]
Colonsay Beverages Ltd.
Colonsay Brewing Co Ltd
Fyne Ales Limited
Islay Ales Co Ltd
Kintyre Ales Limited

Argyll & Bute
Loch Lomond Brewery Limited

Ayrshire [5]
Baird Brewing Co Ltd
Tony Clark Enterprises Ltd
Ethical Ales Limited
Isle-of-Cumbrae Brewing Co Ltd
Roddenloft Brewery Ltd

Clackmannanshire
Devon Ales Limited
Harviestoun Brewery (Holdings) Ltd
Harviestoun Brewery Limited
Heather Ale Limited

Dumfries & Galloway
Galldachd Na H-Alba Brewing Ltd
Portpatrick Brewery Ltd
Solway Spirits Ltd

Dunbartonshire
Lennox Brewery Limited
Turner & Shaw Glasgow Brewing Co Ltd

Fife [23]
A-Zero Energy Beer Limited
Beathbrewing Ltd
Brew Shed Beers Limited
Brucehaven Brewery Ltd.
Coul Brewing Co Ltd
Craft Origins Limited
Dunfermline Brewery Limited
East Neuk Organic Brewing & Distilling
Etrusca Brewery & Distillery in St. Andrews
A & C Green Food and Beverage Ltd
Inner Bay Brewery Limited
Kingdom Brewery Limited
Kinkell Brewery Ltd
Korca Brewery St Andrews Ltd
Luckie Drinks Ltd
Ovenstone 109 Limited
Saltrock Brewing Co Ltd
Seafire Brewing Co. Ltd
St Andrews Brewers Limited
St Andrews Brewing Co Holdings Ltd
St Andrews Brewing Co Ltd
WeBrew4U Ltd
Webru4u Ltd

Highland
Applecross Brewing Co Ltd
Ardgour Ales Ltd
Glenfinnan Brewing Co Ltd

Inverness-shire [6]
Cairngorm Brewery Co Ltd
Cuillin Brewery Limited
Dog Falls Brewing Co. Ltd
Great Glen Trading Centre Ltd
Tirindrish Trading Co Ltd
West Highland Breweries Ltd

Isle of Bute
Bute Brew Co Ltd

Isle of Lewis
Loomshed Hebrides Ltd
Stornoway Brewers Limited

Isle of Mull
Argyll Breweries Limited
Isle of Mull Brewing Co Ltd

Isle of Skye
Isle of Skye Brewing Company (Leann An Eilein)

Kincardineshire
7 Reasons To Brew Ltd

Kinross-shire
Kinross Brewery Limited

Kirkcudbrightshire
Sulwath Brewers Limited

Lanarkshire [29]
7grains Limited
Arran Brew Ltd.
Arran Brewery PLC
Broughton Ales Limited
Clan Brewing Co Ltd
Dead End Brew Machine Limited
Drygate Brewing Co Ltd
Eden Mill Brewers Ltd
Ellismuir Limited
Epochal Barrel-Fermented Ales Ltd
Genius Brewing Limited
Glesga Brewery Ltd.
Jaw Brew Ltd
Jaw Brewery Ltd
Kelburn Brewing Co Ltd
Lawman Brewing Company, Ltd.
Loch Earn Brewery Ltd
Merchant City Brewing Co Ltd
Moody Stag Limited
Myrlex Southend Limited
Noah Beers Limited
Organic Laundry Limited
Out of Town Brewing Limited
Overtone Brewing Ltd
Ride Industrys Limited
Strathaven Ales Limited
Veterans Brewing Ltd
Veterans Brewing Sussex Ltd
Via Academia Vocatus Ltd

The UK Brewing Industry — dellam

Moray
Dark Tower Brewery Ltd
Monks Well Brewing Co Ltd
Speyside Craft Brewery Limited
Windswept Brewing Co Ltd

Orkney
Highland Brewing Co Ltd

Peebles-shire
Campbells Brewery Ltd
Freewheelin' Brewery Co Ltd
Traquair House Brewery Limited

Perthshire [6]
888 Global Trade Ltd
Abernyte Brewery Limited
Black Angus Brewing Ltd
Cullach Brewing Ltd
Gleneagles Distillery Limited
It's Braw Limited

Perth & Kinross
Laiho Limited

Renfrewshire
Calside Brewery and Taste Room Ltd
Craft Soft Drinks Community Ltd
Two Towns Down Brewing Ltd

Ross-shire
Black Isle Brewing Co Ltd
Great Glen Brewing Co Ltd
Kindeace Ales Limited
C J Middleton Limited

Roxburghshire
Scottish Borders Brewery Ltd

Selkirkshire
Tempest Brewing Co Limited
Valve Brewing Co Ltd.

Shetland
Lerwick Brewery Limited
Shetland Refreshments Limited
Staneyhill Brewery Limited

Stirlingshire [9]
Barney's Beer Limited
Black Wolf Brewery Limited
Hybrid Brewing Ltd
Nicol Brewery Ltd.
Rosebank Brewery Camelon Ltd
Rosebank Brewery Limited
Slopemeister Brewing Co Ltd
Summerhall Brewing Limited
Traditional Scottish Ales Ltd

Sutherland
A Northerly Brewing Ltd
John O'Groats Brewery Ltd

Anglesey
Cwrw Mon Cyf
Marches Brewery Limited

Bedfordshire [18]
AB InBev UK Limited
Ampthill & Woburn Brewery Ltd
Bert and Chris Brew Beer Ltd
Brewery Z Ltd
Camden Brewing Group Limited
Damnation Breweries Limited
Damnation Limited
Kelchner Ltd
Leighton Buzzard Brewing Co Ltd
Nellyd Limited
Potton Brewing Co Ltd
Quad Brewing Co Ltd
Rockhopper Brewing Co Ltd
Turing Complete Solutions Ltd
Verulam Brewery Limited
Charles Wells Brewery Limited
Charles Wells,Limited
White Park Brewery Limited

Berkshire [31]
Bellrock Brew Co. Ltd
Binghams Brewery Limited
Bond Brews Ltd
Brew Locker Ltd
Bucklebury Brewers Ltd
Butts Brewery Limited
Delphic Brewing Co Ltd
Dolphin Brewery Limited
Double Barrelled Brewery Ltd.
Elusive Brewing Limited
Hillfire Limited
Killer Hop Brew Co Ltd
Loddon Brewery Ltd
Longhill Garage Limited
Moogbrew Ltd
Nameless Brewing Limited
New Wharf Brewing Co Ltd
Old Windsor Brewery Ltd
Phantom Brewing Co. Limited
Pivo-UK Limited
Renegade Pub Co 2 Limited
Stardust Brewery Ltd
Three Geezers Brewing Limited
Trale Brewing Co Ltd
Two Cocks Farm Limited
Uppingham Brewery Limited
Uppingham Brewhouse Limited
W & W Drinks Ltd
West Berkshire Brewery PLC
Wild Weather Ales Ltd
Windsor & Eton Brewing Co Ltd

Buckinghamshire [19]
Ascot Ales Limited
Bad Joke Brew Co Ltd
Blackened Sun Brewing Co Ltd
Blackpit Brewery Ltd
Bucket Brewing Co Ltd
Chalk Stone Brewery Limited
Fat Boi Brewery & Sauce Co Ltd
Fisher's Brewing Co Ltd.
Getset Brew Co Ltd
Growler Swap Ltd
Hornes Brewery Ltd
Lock 81 Brewery Limited
Malt, The Brewery Limited
Mile Tree Brewery Limited
Monks Bridge Brewery Ltd
Rebellion Beer Co Ltd
Recognise Limited

Vale Brewery Co Ltd.
XT Brewing Co Ltd

Cambridgeshire [34]
5hop Limited
Angel Brewery Co Ltd
Angles Ales Limited
Archangel Brewing Ltd.
Badwells Brewery Ltd
Bexar County Brewery Ltd
Black Fen Brewery Ltd
Calverley's Brewery Ltd
Elgood & Sons,Limited
Fellows Brewery Limited
Garagebrew Ltd
Grafham Brewing Co Ltd
Hardstate Limited
Interstate Craft Brewing Co Ltd
Island Hamlet Brewing Co Ltd
Isle of Ely Brewing Co Ltd.
Little Rotters Limited
Magna Bottling Limited
Magna Brewery Limited
Microcosm Brewing Ltd.
Milton Brewery Cambridge Ltd
Nene Valley Brewery Limited
OM Food Corp Ltd
Old Friends Brewery Ltd
Over The Hill Brewery Ltd
Papworth Brewery Limited
Pastore Brewing and Blending Ltd
Rocket Ales Limited
Sneaky Peacock Ltd
Soham Brewery Ltd
Star Wing Brewery Ltd
White Wolf Brewery Ltd
Wylde Sky Brewing Ltd
Xtreme Ales Limited

Cardiganshire
Castle Gate Brewery Limited
Hopforge Ltd
Oast House Breweries Cyf
Seal Bay Brewery Sel Bragdy Bae Ltd

Carmarthenshire
Felinfoel Brewery Co Ltd
Omnebonum Ltd

Cheshire [54]
Adshead's Ales Ltd
Blueball Brewery Ltd
Bollington Brewing Co. Limited
Born in a Brewery Ltd
Bromtec Limited
Buccaneer Brewery Ltd
Chapter Brewing Co Ltd
Cheshire Brewhouse Ltd
Coach House Brewing Co Ltd
Charles Cooper Limited
Deva Craft Beer Ltd
Devenish & Co (Weymouth) Ltd
Dockyard Brewery Limited
Thomas Dutton Ales Limited
Five Clouds Brewing Co Ltd
Four Kings Brewery Limited
Thomas Hardy Burtonwood Ltd
Thomas Hardy Holdings Limited
Thomas Hardy Kendal Limited
Howe Capital Limited
Hush Brewing Co. Ltd
Laid Back Brewing Limited
MBH Tap & Shop Limited
Macclesfield Brewing Co Ltd
Manning Brewers Ltd
Merlin Brewing Co Ltd
Mersey Gin Co Ltd
Mid-Cheshire Brewing Ltd
Mitchell Ward Limited
Mobberley Brewhouse Limited
Monachis Ltd
Oaks Brewing Co Ltd
Offbeat Brewery Ltd
Redwillow Brewery Ltd
Frederic Robinson Limited
Rossendale Brew Co Ltd
Rude Mechanicals Limited
Silktown Brewery Ltd
Soul Brewing Co Ltd
Spitting Feathers Limited
Stockport Brewing Co Ltd
Storm Brewing Co Ltd
Stubborn Mule Brewery Limited
Symmetry Brewing Co Ltd
Tantum Brewing Limited
Tatton Brewery Limited
Thirst Class Ale Limited
Ticketytap Ltd
Tipsy Angel Brewery Ltd
To The Moon Brewery Ltd
Tom's Tap and Brewhouse Ltd
Tweed Brewing Co Ltd
Weetwood Ales Limited
Wincle Beer Co Ltd

Cleveland [12]
Camerons Brewery Limited
Consett Ale Works Limited
Crafty Monkey Brewing Co Ltd
Donzoko Brewing Co Ltd
Hops and Dots Brewing Co Ltd
Lions Den Beers Limited
North Yorkshire Brewing Co Ltd
Roundhill Brewery Limited
Steel River Drinks Ltd
Taylor Illingworth Brewing Co Ltd
Three Brothers Brewing Co Ltd
Yarm Brewing and Distilling Co Ltd

Clwyd [10]
Big Hand Brewing Co Ltd
Bragdy Nant Cyf
Conwy Brewery Limited
Erddig Brewing Co Ltd
Great Orme Brewery Limited
Heavy Industry Brewing Limited
Sandstone Brewery Ltd
Snowdon Craft Beer Limited
Wild Horse Brewing Co Ltd
Wrexham Lager Beer Co Ltd

Co Durham [15]
Blackhill Brewery Limited
Brewing and Distilling Co Ltd
Durham Brewery Limited
Hopper House Brew Farm Ltd
Maxim Brewery Limited
McColl's Brewery Limited
Orchard Road Brewery Limited
Richmond Brewing Co Ltd
Saints Row Brewing Co Ltd
George Samuel Brewing Co Ltd.
SchoolHouseBrewery Ltd
Sea Brewing Co Ltd
Stag Ales Ltd
Steam Machine Brewing Co Ltd
Yard of Ale Brewing Co Ltd

Cornwall [29]
Agnate Limited
Altarnun Brewing Limited
Black Flag Brewery Ltd
Boody Brewery Ltd.
Cornish Brewery Limited
Cornish Crown Limited
Cornwall and West Country Craft Brewing Co
Crafty Beer Seller Limited
Dowr Kammel Brewing Co Ltd
Dynamite Valley Brewery Ltd
Christopher Ellis and Son Ltd
Fowey Brewery Ltd
Granite Rock Brewery and Home Brew Supplies
Keltek Cornish Brewery Limited
Liquid Revolution Ltd
Little Monster Brewing Co Ltd
Lizard Ales Limited
Marchingtons Ltd
Mousehole Brewery Limited
Penzance Brewing Co Ltd
Redruth Brewery Limited
Roseland Brewery Limited
Sharp's Brewery Limited
Skinner's Brewing Co. Limited
St Ives Brewery Limited
St.Austell Brewery Co Ltd
Tamar Valley Brewing Co Ltd
Treen's Brewery Ltd.
Verdant Brewing Co Ltd

Cumbria [29]
Barngates Brewery Limited
Beckstones Brewery Limited
Bowness Bay Brewing Limited
Cartmel Valley Brewery Ltd
Oliver Chester Limited
Coniston Brewing Co Ltd
Derwent Brewery Ltd
Eden Brewery Limited
Ennerdale Brewery Ltd
Hardknott UK Ltd
Hawkshead Brewery Limited
Kendal Brewery Ltd
Kendal Brewing Co Ltd
Keswick Brewing Co Ltd
LVS Bottling Limited
Lake View Country House Ltd
Peter Laws Brewing Limited
Matterdale Brewery Limited
New Union Brewing Co Ltd
North Country Ales Limited
M Rackstraws Ltd
Strands Brewery Ltd
Tarn Hows Brewery Limited
Taylors Blackbeck Brewery Ltd
Tirril Brewery Limited
Ulverston Brewing Co Ltd
Unsworth's Yard Brewery Ltd
Windermere Brewery Ltd
Wrytree Brewery Limited

Denbighshire
Abbey Grange Brewing Limited
Llangollen Brewery Ltd

Derbyshire [54]
Alter Ego Brewing Co Ltd
Amber Ales Limited
Ashen Clough Ales Ltd
Ashover Brewery Limited
Aurora Ales Limited
Bakewell Road Brewery Ltd
Barlow Brewery Limited
Beermats Brewing Co Ltd
Black Hole Brewery Limited
Brampton Brewery Ltd
Burton Town Brewery Limited
Buxton Brewery Co Ltd
Calarta Ltd
Collyfobble Brewery Limited
Dancing Duck Beer Ltd
Dancing Duck Holdings Ltd
Derby Brewing Co Ltd
Derventio Brewery Limited
Dovedale Brewing Co Ltd
Endure Brewing Co Ltd
Hairy Brewers Ales Limited
Hickbrew Limited
Hollow Tree Brewing Co. Ltd
Hopjacker Brewery Ltd
Howard Town Brewery Limited
Inkerman Ales Limited
Instant Karma Brewing Co Ltd
Kellentay Beers Ltd
Landlocked Brewing Co Ltd
Leadmill Brewery Limited
Leatherbritches Brewery Ltd
Little Eaton Brewery Co Ltd
Littleover Brewery Limited
MBJW Brewing Limited
Marlpool Brewing Co Ltd
Matlock Brewing Co Ltd
Middle Earth Brewing Co Ltd
Midshires Brewery Limited
Moody Fox Ltd.
Moot Oak Brewing Co Ltd
Muirhouse Brewery Limited
Nutbrook Brewery Ltd
Peak Ales Limited
Pentrich Brewing Co. Ltd
Pigeon Fishers Craft Brewery Ltd
Roebuck Brewing Co Ltd
Shiny Brewing Co Ltd

Shottle Farm Brewery Ltd
Silver Brewhouse Limited
Taddington Brewery Limited
Thornbridge Hall Country House Brewing Co
Torrside Brewing Ltd
Townes Brewery Limited
Villages Brewery Limited

Devon [50]
2731 Limited
Avocet Ales Limited
Barnaby's Brewhouse Ltd
Barton House Brewing Co Ltd
Bays Brewery Limited
Best Brewery Ltd
Black Tor Brewery Ltd
Branscombe Vale Brewery Ltd
Bulletproof Brewing Ltd
Clearwater Brewery Ltd
Craftwater Brewing Co Ltd
Darkplace Brewery Limited
Dartmoor Brewery Limited
Devil's Pleasure Limited
Exeter Brewery Limited
GT Ales Limited
Gilt & Flint Ltd
Isca Ales Limited
Ivybridge Brewing Co Ltd
Jollyboat Brewery (Bideford) Ltd
Jon's Brewery Limited
Lion Craft Brewery Ltd
Many Hands Brewery Ltd
New Devon Brewing Ltd
New Lion Totnes Ltd
Octagon Brewery Limited
Otter Brewery Limited
Patriot Brewery Limited
Platform 5 Brewing Co Ltd
Powderkeg Brewery Ltd
Red Rock Brewery Limited
Riviera Brewing Co Ltd
Roam Brewing Co Ltd
Salcombe Brewery Co. Limited
South Hams Brewery Ltd
Stannary Brewing Co Ltd.
Tally Ho! Brewery Limited
Taw Valley Brewery Limited
Teignworthy Brewery Limited
Temple Road Brewing Co Ltd
Tintagel Brewery Limited
Topsham Brewery Ltd
Totnes Brewing Co Limited
Two Beach Brewing Co Limited
Two Drifters Brewery Ltd
Wickwar Wessex Brewing Co Ltd
Wizard Brewing Company Combe Ltd
YSTY Limited
Yellow Hammer Brewing Limited
Yellow Top Brewing Co Ltd

Dorset [21]
Ascent Location Solutions Ltd
Atlantic Craft Soda Co Ltd
Badger Ales Limited
Barefaced Brewing Ltd
Brewers Folly Brewery Ltd.
Cerne Abbas Brewery Ltd
Christchurch Brewing Co. Ltd
Company of Dead Brewers Ltd
Dodd's Brewery Co. Limited
Dolphin Brewery Poole Ltd

Dorset Brewing Co Ltd
Eldridge, Pope & Co Ltd
Hall & Woodhouse Limited
Hattie Brown's Brewery Ltd
Lyme Bay Brewing Limited
J.C. & R.H. Palmer Limited
Piddle Brewery Limited
Sandbanks Brewery Limited
Sly Fox Brewery Ltd
Wayland's Sixpenny Brewery Ltd
Wimborne Beer Co Ltd

Dyfed [7]
Bay View Brewery Limited
Blewin Trust Limited
Gustmain Limited
Little Dragon Brewery Limited
Mantle Brewery Limited
Seren Brewing Co Ltd
Tinworks Brewing Co Ltd.

Essex [52]
4 Acre Brewing Co. Ltd
Beer Belly Brewery Limited
BeerHug Ltd
Big Bear Brewery Limited
Billericay Brewing Co Ltd
Bishop Nick Limited
Brentwood Brewing Co Ltd
Brewboard Limited
Brews Brothers Brewery Ltd
Broxbourne Brewery Ltd.
Camden Beer Ltd
Chelmsford Brewing Co Ltd.
Colchester Brewery Ltd
Crouch Vale Brewery Limited
Deverell's Brewing Co Ltd
Dhillons Brewery Ltd
Dominion Brewery Co Ltd
Fallen Angel Brewery Ltd
Flying Fox Brewery Limited
George's Brewery Limited
Hop Monster Brewing Co Ltd.
Hope Brewery Ltd
Jackrabbit Brewing Co. Ltd
London Beer Co Ltd
Lucky Cat Brewery Limited
Maldon Brewing Co Ltd
Mersea Island Brewery & Vineyard Ltd
Mighty Oak Brewing Co. Limited
Mill Lane Brewing Co Ltd
Moody Goose Brewery Limited
Oast & Tread Brewing Co Ltd
Posh Boys Brewery Limited
Radio City Beer Works Limited
Red Fox Brewery Limited
Rock A Brew Ltd
Romford Brewery Co Ltd
Round Tower Brewery (Chelmsford) Ltd
Round Tower Brewery Ltd
Saeburh Brewery Ltd
Serpent Brew Co Ltd
Silks Brewery Limited
Small Beer Brew Co. Ltd
Three Counties Brewery Limited
Tiptree Brewing Co Ltd
Two Fathoms Distillery Ltd.
Two Fools Brewery Ltd
Vendetta Brewing Co Ltd
Westley Brewing Co Ltd.
White Hart Halstead Limited

Whyte BR Brewing Co Ltd
Whyte Bar Brewing Co Ltd
Wibblers Brewery (Farms) Ltd

Flintshire [5]
Blackened Abbey Ltd
Cwrw Ial Limited
Exile Brewing Co Ltd
Hafod Brewing Co Ltd
Loka Polly Ltd

Glamorgan [33]
Airborne Ales Ltd
Arcadian Brewing Co Ltd
Artisan Brewing Co Ltd
Bang-On Brewery Limited
Bont Brew Ltd
Boss Brewing Co Ltd
S.A.Brain & Co Ltd
Bullmastiff Brewery Limited
Cardiff Brewing Co Ltd
Cross Inn (Maesteg) Limited
Fairy Glen Brewery Ltd
Floff UK Limited
Frank and Otis Brewing Ltd
Gil's Brewery Ltd
Gower Brewery Co Limited
Gower Pub Co Ltd
Hurns Brewing Co Ltd.
Kairos Solutions Ltd
Mumbles Brewery Ltd
Mumbles Brewing Co Ltd
No Comply Ltd
Piglove Brewing Co Limited
Pilot Brewery Limited
Pilot Wharf Limited
Rival Brewing Co Limited
Roath Brewery Ltd
Sloane Home Ltd
Smoky Dragon Brewery & Preservas
Splott Brewery Ltd
Tomos & Lilford Holdings Ltd
Vale of Glamorgan Brewery Ltd
Violet Cottage Brewing Co Ltd
West By Three Limited

Gloucestershire [27]
Arlingham Ales Limited
Bespoke Brewing Co. Limited
Black Horse Brewery Ltd
Branded Drinks Ltd
Cheltenham Brewery Limited
Cirencester Brewery Ltd
Corinium Ales Ltd
Cotswold Lion Brewery Ltd
Donnington Brewery Limited
Double Tap Brewery Ltd
Dowdeswell Brewery Limited
Egghead Brewery Limited
Elements Brewing Co Ltd
Festival Brewery Ltd.
Force Brewery Limited
Gloucester Brewery Ltd
Goff's Brewery Limited
Ham Brewing Co Ltd
Inferno Brewery Limited
Jordan's Car Review Ltd
Keep Brewing Ltd
Queer Brewing Project Ltd
Severn Brewing Limited
Stroud Brewery Development Ltd

Stroud Brewery Limited
Tewkesbury Brewery Ltd
Uley Ales Limited

Gwent [5]
Boozy Bods Ltd
Gentleman Bear Brewing Co Ltd
Kingstone Brewery Limited
Pixie Spring Brewing Co Ltd
Well Drawn Brewing Co Ltd

Gwynedd [8]
Anglesey Ales Ltd
Bragdy Lleu Cyf
Bragdy Mona Cyf
Cader Ales Limited
Cwrw Llyn Cyf
Cwrw Ogwen Cyf
Purple Moose Brewery Ltd
Religious Ales Ltd

Hampshire [48]
Anley Ales Limited
BL Drinks Ltd
Ballard's Brewery Limited
Battersea Brewery Co Ltd
Baynhams Brewery Limited
Black Dragon Brewery Limited
Botley Brewery Ltd
Bowman Ales Limited
Brewkeepers Limited
Brockenhurst Brewery Limited
Bruin Beer Co Ltd
Burnt Hill Brewery Limited
Cronx Brewery Limited
Dancing Man Brewery Limited
Fallen Acorn Brewing Co. Ltd
Flack Manor Brewery Limited
Flat Cap Holding Co Ltd
Four Bulls Brewing Co Ltd
Irving & Co. Brewers Limited
Itchen Valley Brewery Limited
Kew Brewery Limited
Little London Brewery Limited
Longdog Brewery Limited
Mash Brewery Limited
Maverick Brewing Co Ltd
Mister A's Beer Co Ltd
New Forest Beer Co Ltd
Penton Park Brewery Limited
Pig and Porter Limited
Red Cat Brewing Limited
Republic of Beer Ltd
Shady Shed Brewery Limited
Shandy Shack Ltd
Sherfield Village Brewery Ltd
Siren Craft Brew Limited
Southbourne Ales Limited
Southbourne Brewing Limited
Southsea Brewing Co Ltd
Steam Town Brewco Limited
Stratton Lane Ltd
Test Brewing Ltd
Thistlerock Enterprises UK Ltd
Unity Brewing Ltd
Urban Island Brewing Co. Ltd
Vibrant Forest Brewery Limited
Vitosha Wine Ltd
Weymouth Brewery Limited
Winchester Brewery Ltd

Herefordshire [9]
After The Harvest Brewing Ltd
Ground Hammer Beer Co Ltd
Ledbury Real Ales Ltd
Lucky 7 Beer Co Ltd
Motley Hog Brewery Limited
Odyssey Brew Co Ltd
Untapped Brewing Co Ltd
Wobbly Brewing Co Ltd
Wye Valley Brewery Limited

Hertfordshire [46]
3 Brewers Ltd
Bears Den Brewery Limited
Beta Pilot Brewing Ltd
Bishop's Stortford Brewery Ltd
Black Squirrel Brewing Limited
Bog Brew Beers Limited
Bowtie Brewers Limited
Brancaster Brewery Limited
Bubble Works Brew Co Ltd
Bushey Brewery Co Ltd
Craft Beer Collective Limited
Craft Beer Society Ltd
Creative Juices Brewing Co Ltd
Farr Brew Ltd
Foamology Limited
French & Jupps Limited
Garden City Brewery Limited
Hadham Brewing Co Ltd
Haresfoot Storage & Distribution Co Ltd
Hitchin Brewery Ltd
Hop King Brewery Ltd
Ipbridge Limited
K L Brewery Limited
Kettle Green Brewing Ltd
Kimbland Distillery Ltd
Los Perros Sueltos Brewing Co Ltd
Lost Boys Brewery Ltd
Lucky Shaman Limited
McMullen & Sons, Limited
Miswell Brewery Ltd
Murree Breweries (UK) Limited
New River Brewery Ltd
Paradigm Brewery Ltd
Pawed Brewery Ltd
Popes Yard Brewery Limited
Pryor Reid & Co Limited
Radlett Beer Co Ltd
Red Squirrel Brewery Limited
Saffron Brewery (Henham) Ltd
Southey Brewing Co Ltd
Space Trash Brewing Ltd
Summershed Brewery Limited
Tring Brewery Co Ltd
Two Bob Brewing Co Ltd
Urban Alchemy Brewing Co Ltd
Wharf Brewing Co Ltd

Humberside
Crystalbrew Limited

Isle of Anglesey
Coastal Brewing Co Ltd

Isle of Wight
Goddards Brewery Limited
Laughing Pug Ltd
Yates Iow Brewery Limited

Kent [58]
Alpha State Limited
Battle Brewery Limited
Beckenham Brewery Ltd.
Bexley Brewery Limited
Blighty Brewery Limited
Boutilliers Limited
Br3wery Ltd
Brithop Brewing Co Ltd
Brumaison Ltd
Canterbrew Ltd
Caveman Brewing Co Ltd
Cellarhead Brewing Co Ltd
Curious Drinks Limited
Doromomo & Sons Ltd
Engineer Brewery Limited
Finns (UK) Limited
Gemstone Ales Ltd.
Goody Ales Limited
Grumpy Git Brewery Limited
Hildenborough Brewery Ltd
Hop Fuzz Ltd
Hopdaemon Brewery Co Ltd
Hyde & Wills Limited
Koomor Brewing Co Ltd
Lads & Dads Brewing Limited
Larkins Brewery Limited
London Cosmopolitan Drinks Ltd
Mad Cat Brewery Limited
Margate Brewery Limited
Marourde Limited
Meridian Brewery Limited
Millis Brewing Co Ltd
Moo Brewing Co Ltd
Musket Brewery Limited
Nauticales Ltd
Nelson Brewing Co.Uk Ltd.
Old Dairy Brewery Limited
Quantock Brewery Limited
Ramsgate Brewery Limited
Range Ales Brewery Limited
Revelry Brewing & Distilling Ltd
Rockin Robin Brewery Ltd
Romney Marsh Brewery Limited
Sevenoaks Brewery Limited
Shepherd Neame Limited
Spartan Brewery Ltd
Stag Brewery Ltd
TW@ Limited
Tankley's Brewery Limited
Thesis Brewing Co. Ltd
Time & Tide Brewing Limited
Tonbridge Brewery Limited
WantsumBrewery Ltd
Westerham Brewery Co Ltd
Whitstable Brewery Limited
Wye Brewing Co Ltd
Xtraflow Limited
Youngs Beers Limited

The UK Brewing Industry

Lancashire [130]
23-7 Brewing Ltd
3 Piers Brewery Limited
3's A Crowd Brewing Ltd
4 Mice Brewery Limited
Allendale Brew Co Ltd
J.B. Almond Ltd
Alphabet Brewing Ltd
Appleby Brewery Ltd.
Askham Brewery Limited
Avid Brewing Co. Ltd
Bank Top Brewery Limited
Barearts Ltd
Batch Brew Ltd
Beatnikz Republic Brewing Co Ltd
Beer Brothers Ltd
Big Bog Brewing Co Ltd
Big Brewing Co Ltd
Bishop's Crook Brewery Ltd.
Blackedge Brewing Co Ltd
Blackjack Beers Limited
Borough Brewery Limited
Bowland Beer Co Ltd
Brewsmith Beer Limited
Brightside Brewing Co Ltd
JD Campbell Brewing Limited
Casorho Ltd
Chain House Brewing Co Ltd
Chorlton Brewing Co Ltd
Cillenx Ltd
Cloudwater Brew Co Ltd
Copper Dragon Brewery Limited
Crankshaft Brewery Limited
Crate Bars Limited
Crate Brewery Limited
Cross Bay Brewery Limited
Deeply Vale Brewery Ltd
Dobbins Guiltless Stout Co Ltd
Donkeystone Brewing Co Ltd
Droylsden Craft Limited
Eagles Crag Brewery Ltd
Edenfield Brewery Limited
Egan & Martin Limited
Farm Yard Ales Ltd
First Chop Brewing Arm Ltd
Fuzzy Duck Brewery Limited
Geipel Brewing Limited
Glen Affric Brewery Limited
Greenfield Real Ale Brewery Ltd
Hay Rake Brewery Ltd
Hindsight Collective Ltd
Joseph Holt Group Limited
Joseph Holt Limited
Holy Well Brewing Ltd
Hophurst Brewery Ltd
Hubsters Brewery Ltd
Hydes' Brewery Limited
Icon Brewery Limited
Impavive Ltd
Ironstone Brewery JVW Ltd
Irwell Works Brewery Ltd
Jarr Kombucha Ltd
Jimbrew Ltd
Lancaster Brewery Co Ltd
Lancaster Brewery Holdings Ltd
Lastonser Ltd
J.W.Lees & Co.(Brewers) Ltd
Letterpress Brewery Ltd
Little Teapot Ltd
Lorimers Ales (1919) Limited
Lorsho Limited
MB Collective Limited

Madchester Brewing Co Ltd
Magee,Marshall and Co Ltd
Makeshift Brewing Co Ltd
Manchester Union Brewery Ltd
Marble Beers Limited
Martland Mill Brewery Limited
Mayflower Brewery Ltd
Mighty Medicine Brewing Co Ltd
Millstone Brewery Limited
Milton and Mortimer Ltd
Moon Cartel Limited
Moorhouse's Brewery Ltd
Morecambe Bay Wines Limited
Nightcap Beer Co Ltd
Nine Standards Brewery Limited
Northern Monkey Brew Co. Ltd
Northern Whisper Brewing Co Ltd
Chris O'Connor and Associates Ltd
Oak Brewing Co Ltd
Ol Brewery Limited
Old School Brewery Limited
Origami Brewing Co Ltd.
Outstanding Brewing Co Ltd
Padlock Brewery Ltd.
Parbold Bottle Limited
Partridge Brewing Co Ltd
Pictish Brewing Co Limited
Postlethwaites Brewery Ltd
Priest Town Brewing Co Ltd
Prospect Brewery Limited
Punchbowl Brewery Limited
Recoil Brewing Co Ltd
Red Rose Brewery Ltd
Rivington Brewing Co Limited
Rock Solid Brewing Co Ltd
Rock Springs Brewing Ltd
Saint Brewing Co Limited
Serious Brewing Co Ltd
Seven Brothers Ancoats Ltd
Seven Brothers Brewery Limited
Silver Street Brewery Limited
Skelpers Ltd
Skinnybrands Ltd
Smith and Jones Brewery Ltd
Soul Doubt Brewing Co Ltd
Southport Brewery Limited
Square Street Distillery Ltd
Temperance Brewing Co Ltd
Daniel Thwaites PLC
Track Brewing Co Ltd
Twinshock Brewery Ltd
Vaux Beers Ltd
Velvet Owl Brewing Co Ltd.
Vodaso Limited
Wigan Brew House Ltd
Wily Fox Brewery Limited
Withnell's Brewing Co Ltd
Worsthorne Brewing Co Ltd
Zymurgorium Ltd

Leicestershire [22]
3 Cities Brewing Co Ltd
Beat Ales Ltd.
Belvoir Brewery Limited
Brew & Bottle Limited
Brunswick Brewing Co Ltd
EFG International Ltd
Emperor's Brewery Ltd.
Everards Brewery Limited
Framework Brewery Limited
Grainstore Brewery Limited
Great Central Brewery Limited

Inlaw Brewing Co Ltd
Langton Brewery Ltd
Market Bosworth Brewery Ltd
Modha Ales Ltd
Shardlow Brewing Co Ltd
Stoney Ford Brew Co. Ltd
Target Brewery Limited
Tollgate Brewery Limited
Topcat Brewery Limited
Tres Bien Brewery Ltd
Wicked Hathern Brewery Limited

Lincolnshire [25]
Alcazar Brewing Co Ltd
Axholme Brewing Co Ltd
Baker's Dozen Brewing Co Ltd
George Bateman & Son Limited
Brewster's Brewing Co Ltd
Cumberland Breweries Limited
Dark Tribe Brewery Limited
Docks Beers Limited
Eskdale Brewery Ltd
Ferry Ales Brewery Limited
Fuddy Duck Limited
Hopshackle Brewery Limited
Kirton Fen Brewery Limited
Lincolnshire Brewing Co Ltd
Lincolnshire Craft Beers Ltd
Oldershaw Brewery Ltd
Thomas Paine Brewery Limited
Proper Brewing Co Ltd
Proud Peacock Limited
SF Brew Co Ltd
Sherwood Forest Brewing Co Ltd
Stamford Ales Limited
Tealby Brewing Co Ltd
Tomson & Wotton Limited
Welland Brewery Ltd

London [222]
1936 Limited
1st Icon Ltd
3ABC Ltd
AB InBev UK Finance Co Ltd
AB InBev UK Investment Co Ltd
ABI SAB Group Holding Limited
ABI UK Holding 1 Limited
ALE Finance Services Limited
Samuel Adams (Beer) Ltd
Affinity Brewing Co Ltd
Alcohol Beverages Co Ltd
Ale Factory Ltd
Samuel Allsopp & Sons Ltd
Andwell Brewing Co Ltd
Angry Coot Fermentation Co Ltd.
Anheuser-Busch Europe Limited
Anspach & Hobday Limited
Antic Brewing Limited
Aussie Brewing Co Ltd
Avitas Craft Beer Ltd
B & T Brewery Limited
Bad Girls Brew Limited
Baltic Beer Co Ltd
Bavarian Gold Limited
Bear's Head Brewery Limited
Beardyman Brewery Limited
Beauty and The Beer Limited
Beavertown Brewery Ltd
Beerblefish Brewing Co Ltd
Beermondsey Limited
Beersheba Ltd

Belleville Brewing Co Ltd
Beltane Brewing Co Ltd
Bidwell Brewery Co Ltd
Biercafe Ltd
Big Mountain Brewing Co Ltd
Black Eagle Brewery Ltd
Blackstar Brewery Ltd
Blithe Nook Brewery Ltd
Block Brewery Limited
Blonde Brothers Limited
Bohem Brewery Ltd
Bomb Shelter Brewing Limited
Boxcar Brewery Limited
Brazen Brewing Co. Ltd
Brew By Numbers Ltd.
Brew Club Limited
Brewheadz Limited
Brewhouse Brewery Limited
Brewit Microbrewery Ltd
Brick Brewery Ltd
Brixton Brewery Limited
Brockley Brewing Co Ltd.
Bullfinch Brewery Limited
Burner Drinks Limited
By The Horns Ltd
CFS Castus Test 001 Ltd
Camden Town Brewery Limited
Canopy Beer Co Ltd
Chapeau Brewing Limited
Clarkshaws Brewing Co Ltd.
Cold Formd Ltd
Comet Brewery Ltd
Common Rioters Beer Limited
Connecting Hops Ltd
Copper Tun Ltd
Craft Life Brewing Ltd.
Crafty Leopard Brewing Co Ltd
Crosby Beverages Ltd
Crossover Blendery Limited
Dark Star Brewing Co Ltd
Degrees Plato Brewing Ltd.
Deutschlond Brewery Limited
Deviant and Dandy Brewery Ltd
Diamond Dicks Brewing Limited
Earth Station Beers Ltd
East India Company India Pale Ale
East London Brewing Co Ltd
Eko Brewery Limited
Elemental Brew House Limited
Encoder Brewery Limited
Enfield Brewery Limited
Epic Brewing Limited
Fallen Brewing Co Ltd
Fearnought Brewery Ltd
Feisty Caribbean Ltd
Fitbeer Ltd.
Five Points Brewing Co Ltd
Fokof Limited
Forest Hill Brewing Co Ltd
Four Pillars Brewery Limited
Fourpure Limited
Fremlins Limited
Gan Yam Brewing Co Ltd
German Kraft Brewing Limited
Golden Fox Brewing Ltd
Good Kombucha Drinks Ltd
Good Things Brewing Co Ltd
Got 2 Bee Clean Ltd
Grace Land Beer Limited
Gravity Well Brewing Co Ltd
Green Times Brewing Limited
Hackney Brewery Ltd

Hale Brewing Limited
Harr Engineering Limited
Heroic Brew Co Ltd
Hip Hop Brewery Limited
Hiver Beers Ltd
Honest Brew Ltd
Hop Stuff Brewery Limited
Hopsmith Brewing Co Ltd
Husk Brewing Limited
Ignition Brewery Limited
Infinite Session Ltd
Inkspot Brewery Limited
JP Brew Limited
Jocks and Peers Brewing Co Ltd
K1 Beer PLC
Kathmandu Link Limited
Kent Brewery Ltd
Kentish Town Brewery Limited
Kernel Brewery Ltd
Langford Brewing Co. Limited
Lion Brewery Co. Limited
Lion-Beer, Spirits & Wine (UK) Ltd
Lockside Brewery Ltd.
London Ale UK Ltd
London Beer Factory Ltd.
London Beer Lab Ltd
London Brewery Limited
London Brewing Co Ltd
London Fields Brewery Opco Ltd
Long Arm Brewing Co Limited
Lord Randalls Brewery Ltd
Lost Roots Limited
Lost Skulls Brewing Co Ltd
Luxbev Limited
Mad Scientists Pty. Ltd
Maestro Brew Ltd
Malts & Hops Brewing Limited
Map Kernow Ltd.
Maregade Brew Co Ltd
Mechanic Brewing Co Ltd
Medieval Bread and Ale Co Ltd
Moncada Brewery Limited
Mondo Brewing Co Ltd
Mortlake Brewery Ltd
Muswell Hillbilly Brewers Ltd
Mybrewpub Limited
Near Beer Brewing Co. Ltd
No Abode Brew Co Ltd
Nuglyfe Ltd
OTL Brew Co Ltd
Oddly Limited
Old Street Brewery Ltd
Onebeer Brewing Ltd
Orbit Brewing Limited
Owlcrab Limited
Padstow Brewing Company (2013) Ltd
Partizan Brewing Limited
Phaded World Ltd
Pongolo Ltd
Portobello Brewing Co Ltd
Pressure Drop Brewing Limited
Pretty Decent Beer Co Ltd
Project Brewery Ltd
Project X Brewing Co Ltd
Punjabi Ltd
Redchurch Brewery Limited
Redemption Brewing Co Ltd
Reunion Ales Limited
Ripple Steam Brewery Limited
River Widow Brewery Ltd
Rock Leopard Brewing Co Ltd
Round Corner Brewing Ltd

SK Brew Ltd
Saison 86 Limited
Sambrook's Brewery Limited
Second Wave Brewing Ltd
Shefford Brewery Co. Limited
Shoreditch Brewing Co Ltd
Signature Brew Ltd
Signpost Brewery Ltd
Silvertown Brewery and Distillery Co Ltd
Sky Pirate Ltd
Small Beer Brewing Co Ltd
Soho Brewing Ltd
Solvay Brewing Ltd
Southport Brewing Limited
St Mary's Brewery Ltd
Staff Beer Ltd
Stay Gold Beer Co Ltd
TKS Brewing Limited
Ten Tors Brewery Ltd
Thetford Brewery Limited
Thirsty Smile Ltd
Tidal London Ltd
Tumanny Albion Brewing Co Ltd
Two Finches Brewery Ltd.
Two Rabbit Brewing Co Ltd
UBrewCC Limited
UK Camra Beer Co., Ltd
Umbrella Brewing Limited
Universal Robo Innovations Ltd
Upstart Brewing Ltd
Urbeer Ltd
Utopian Brewing Limited
Van Pur UK Ltd
Vandal Brewing Co Ltd
Victor's Drinks Limited
Volden Brewing Limited
Volden Limited
Watling Street Brewery Limited
Weird Beard Brew Co Ltd
Wharf Beers Ltd
Whitechapel Industries Ltd
Wild Card Brewery Limited
Wimbledon Brewery Co Ltd
Woodforde's Norfolk Ales Ltd
Workshy Brewing Ltd
Xylo Brewing Ltd
ZX Ventures Limited

Lothian [8]
Belhaven Brewery Co Ltd
Edinbrew Ltd
Eyeball Brewing Ltd
Faking Bad Brewery Limited
Ferry Brewery Co Ltd
Foxhat Beer Limited
Hurly Burly Brewery Ltd
Winton Brewery Limited

Merseyside [44]
AD Hop Brewing Ltd
Baltic Fleet Brewery Limited
Beer Station Brewery Ltd
Birkenhead Brewery Co Ltd
Black Lodge Brewery Ltd
Brimstage Brewing Co. Ltd
Brooks Brewhouse Limited
Cains Brewing Co Ltd
Cains Limited
Carnival Brewing Co Ltd
Craft Brewery Limited
Dead Crafty Beer Co Ltd

Dogtag Beer Co. Ltd
Emprise Brewery Limited
Gibberish Brewing Ltd
Handyman Brewery Ltd
Hexad Brewing Ltd
Higsons 1780 Limited
Humberside Properties [UK] Ltd
Incapico Inc Limited
L1 Brewer Ltd
Lekker Days Ltd
Little Crosby Village Brewing Co Ltd
Liverpool Brewery Limited
Liverpool Craft Beer Co Ltd
Liverpool Craft Holdings Ltd
Liverpool Craft Limited
Mudlark Investments Ltd
Neptune Brewery Ltd
Nexus Engineering Limited
Original Brewers Limited
Peerless Brewing Co Ltd
Red Star Brewery (Formby) Ltd
Scariosa Ltd
Slice & Brew Ltd
Stamps Brewery Limited
Swift Half Collective Ltd
Team Toxic Ltd
Teller Lager Co Ltd
Top Rope Brewing Limited
Uncanny Valley Brewing Co Ltd
Urban Brewery Ltd
Vovin Ltd
World Bier Huis Limited

Middlesex [19]
3 Bru's Brewing Co Ltd
Beerfisch Brewery Limited
Brewery Limited
Clavell & Hind Limited
Crooked Fish Ltd
Ealing Brewing Ltd
Ellenberg's Brewery Ltd
Fulham Brewery Ltd
Himalayan Traders UK Ltd
Indian Summer Brewing Co. Ltd
Khukuri Beer (UK) Limited
Mad Yank Brewery Ltd
Pinnora Ltd
Proper Beer Co Ltd
Robel Pawlos Ltd
Shere Brewery Ltd
Stokesley Brewing Co Ltd
Tillingbourne Brewery Ltd
Twickenham Fine Ales Limited

Midlothian [35]
Bellfield Brewery Limited
Black Metal Brewery Ltd
Caledonian Brewery Limited
Campervan Brewery Ltd
Coast Beer Co Limited
Cross Borders Brewing Co Ltd
Decagram Art and Craft CIC
Dovik Bast Ltd
Edinburgh Beer Factory Limited
Edinburgh Brewing Co Ltd
Exiled Brewers Limited
Forth Bridge Brewery and Distillery
Greyhound Drinks Limited
Heineken UK Limited
Innis & Gunn Brewing Co Ltd
Innis & Gunn Holdings Limited

Innis & Gunn Inveralmond Brewery Ltd
Jacobite Brewery Limited
Kall Brand Ltd
Leith Brewing Co Ltd
Little Wolf Brewing Limited
Melville's Fruit Beers Limited
Midmart Limited
Newt Brew Ltd
Nungate Brewery Co Ltd
Old Thistle Co Ltd
Old Worthy Brewing Co Ltd
Pilot Beer Limited
Southside Brewing Ltd
Stewart Brewing Limited
Sugar Pine Brewing Co Ltd
Vault City Brewing Ltd.
Samuel Webster & Sons Limited
Witchcraft Brewery Limited
Yeast Pod Ltd

Monmouthshire [12]
Arbor Ales Ltd
BAA Brewing Limited
Bent Iron Brewing Co Ltd
Boutique Cellar Limited
Brew Monster Limited
Clandestine Distillery Limited
Lithic Brewing Limited
Mad Dog Brewing Co Ltd
Melin Tap Brewhouse Limited
Oakland Brewing Co Ltd
Rhymney Brewery Ltd
Zulu Alpha Brewing Limited

Nairnshire
Atlas Brewery Limited
Crasi Limited
Nevis Brewery Ltd
Sinclair Breweries Limited

Norfolk [26]
All Day Brewing Co Ltd
Ampersand Brew Co Ltd
Barrell & Sellers Limited
Beeston Brewery Ltd
Blimey! Brewing Co Ltd
Boudicca Brewing Co Ltd
Buffy's Brewery Limited
Bullards Beers Limited
Cambridge-Brewery Limited
Chubby Seal Ltd
Duration Brewing Ltd
Earl Soham Brewery Limited
Elmtree Beers Ltd
Equal Brewkery CIC
Evolution Brewing Ltd
GKH Beer Co Ltd
Golden Triangle Brewery Ltd
Grain Brewery Limited
Hill House Inns Limited
Three Arches Brewing Limited
Tombstone Brewery Limited
Unicorn Craft Brewing Co Ltd
WBC (Norfolk) Limited
Wildcraft Brewery Limited
Woodforde's BPP Limited
Woodforde's Limited

Northamptonshire [27]
Adriyel Ltd
Allbeer Limited
Black Bess Limited
Blue Armadillo Brewing Co Ltd
Boot Town Brewery Ltd
Brixworth Brewery Co Ltd
Carlsberg Supply Company UK Ltd
Carlsberg UK Limited
J. Church Brewing Co. Ltd
Cotton End Brewery Co Ltd
Gun Dog Ales Ltd
Hart Family Brewers Limited
Holcot Hop-Craft Ltd
LF Brewery Holdings Limited
Latimer Ales Ltd
Merrimen Brewery Limited
Nobby's Brewing Co Ltd
Phipps Northampton Brewery Co Ltd
Potbelly Brewery Limited
Runaway Brewery Limited
SRA Brewery Limited
Silverstone Brewing Co Limited
Silverstone Real Ale Co Ltd
Spotty Dog Brewery Limited
Three Hills Brewing Ltd
Towcester Mill Brewery Limited
Westbournia Brewing Co Ltd

Northumberland [11]
Alnwick Brewery Co Ltd
Anarchy Brew Co. Limited
Brewis Beer Co Ltd
Chasing Everest Brew Co Ltd
Cheviot Brewery Ltd
Credence Brewing Ltd
Fearless Brewing Ltd
Jarrow Innovations Ltd
Muckle Brewing Ltd
Rocksnarl Ltd
Village Inn Pub Co Ltd

Nottinghamshire [51]
Abbey Brewery Ltd
Abstract Jungle Brewing Ltd
Bang The Elephant Brewing Co Ltd
Beeston Hop Ltd
Black Market Brewery Limited
Blue Monkey Brewing Limited
Brewsmith Limited
Brook House Brewery Limited
Joseph Camm Farms Limited
Caythorpe Brewery Limited
Cereal Technology Limited
Draycott Brewing Co Ltd
Dukeries Brewery Ltd.
Fire Rock Brewing Co Ltd.
Flipside Brewing Ltd
Frontier Brewing Co Ltd
Gales Brewery Limited
Grasshopper Brewery Limited
Harrison's Brewery Ltd
Headstocks Brewery Ltd Ltd
Kimberley Brewery Limited
Kimberley Brewing Co Ltd
Konigsberg Limited
Konigsberg Seven Bridges Breweries Ltd
Lazy Bay Brewery Ltd
Lincoln Green Brewing Co Ltd
Linear Brewing Co Ltd
Liquid Light Brewing Co Ltd

Lost Industry Brewing Limited
Maypole Brewery Limited
Moonshine Drinks Limited
Munro Ventures Limited
Neon Raptor Brewing Co Ltd.
Newark Brewery Ltd
Phonymick Ltd
Priors Well Brewery Limited
Prussia 1701 Limited
Prussia Bier Limited
Reality Brewing Limited
Rufford Abbey Brewery Ltd
Scribbler's Ales Limited
Shipstones Beer Co Ltd
Sixty Shilling Brewing Ltd
Strong House Brewery Ltd
Emma J Tilston Ltd
Totally Brewed Limited
Tynemill Limited
W.L.B.C Ltd
Welbeck Abbey Brewery Limited
Wicked Hog Brewery Ltd
Yardley Brothers Europe Ltd

Oxfordshire [25]

Amwell Springs Brewery Co Ltd
Aquila Visum Ltd
Beer Smiths Limited
Beerkat Brewing Co Ltd
Bobby Beer Co Ltd
Charlbury Brewing Co Ltd
Clouded Minds Limited
Compass Brewery Limited
Cotswold Brewing Co Ltd
Earth Ale Ltd
Froth Blowers Brewing Co Ltd
Harbour Brewing Co Ltd
Hook Norton Brewery Co Ltd
Lam Brewing Limited
Little Ox Brewery Limited
Loose Cannon Brewing Co Ltd
Mortimer Brewing Co Ltd
Oxbrew Ltd
Philsters Limited
Stenroth Limited
Tap Social Movement Limited
Vertical Stack Ltd
White Horse Brewery Co Ltd
Wriggly Monkey Brewery Limited
XL Brew Ltd

Pembrokeshire [7]

Bizzy Play Limited
Bluestone Brewing Co Ltd
Harbour Brewery Tenby Limited
Old Farmhouse Brewery Ltd.
St Davids Farm Brewery Ltd
Tenby Brewing Co. Limited
Upper Harglodd Farm Ltd

Powys

Crai Cider Co Ltd
Monty's Brewery Limited
Wilderness Brewery Ltd

Rhondda Cynon Taf

Grey Trees Brewery Limited
TwT Lol Cyf

Shropshire [18]

BC Brewing & Pub Co Ltd
Big Shed Brewery Limited
Bridgnorth Brewing Co Ltd
Broadway Brewery Ltd
Clun Brewery Ltd.
Hair of The Frog Brewing Ltd
Hop & Stagger Brewery Ltd
Joules Brewery Limited
Ludlow Brewing Co Ltd
Plan B Brewing Co Ltd
John Roberts Brewing Co Ltd
Rowton Brewery Ltd
Salopian Brewing Co Ltd.
Shropshire Beers Limited
Shropshire Brewer Limited
Vyrnwy Developments Limited
Woodhalls Brewery Limited
Worfield Brewery Limited

Somerset [76]

Abbey Ales Limited
Another Brewery Limited
Arnold and Hancock Limited
Ashley Down Brewery Limited
Bason Bridge Brewing Co Ltd
Beer Engineer Ltd
Beer Necessities Limited
Bespoke Beer Co Ltd
Bigla Brewing Co Ltd
Blackdown Brewery Ltd
Blindmans Brewery Limited
Brewbox Systems Ltd
Bristol Brewing Co Ltd
Butcombe Brewery Limited
Butcombe Brewing Co Ltd
Butcombe Pubco Limited
Cheddar Ales Limited
Cosmic Brewing Co Ltd
Cotleigh Brewery Limited
Croft Ales Ltd
Dartmouth Brewing Co Ltd
Dawkins & Georges Ltd
Electric Bear Brewing Co Ltd
Epic Beers Limited
Evensong Brewing Limited
Exmoor Ales Limited
Ferox and Noble Limited
Fine Tuned Brewery Limited
Fishponds Brewery Ltd
Frome Brewery Limited
Frome Brewing Co Ltd
Glastonbury Brewing Co Ltd
Glede Brewing Co Ltd
Good Chemistry Apparatus Ltd
Good Chemistry Brewing Limited
Great Western Brewing Co Ltd
Imaginary Friends Brewing Ltd
Insight Driven Innovation Ltd
Left Handed Giant Brewing Ltd
Left Handed Giant Ltd.
Long Ashton Cider Co Ltd
Lost and Grounded Brewers Ltd
Matthews Brewing Co Ltd
McGrath Davies Public Houses Ltd
Moor Beer Co Ltd
New Bristol Brewery School Ltd
New Cross Ales Ltd
Newquay Brewing Co Ltd
Oakhill Brewery Ltd
Parkway Brewing Co Ltd
Portishead Brewing Co Ltd
RPM Brewery Ltd
Ralphs Ruin Ltd
Sherborne Brewery Limited
Snakestorm Limited
Somerset Ales Limited
Spyglass Brewing Co Ltd
Stealth Brew Co Limited
Steel Coulson Ltd
Stocklinch Ales Ltd
Stokes Brewing Co Ltd
Stowey Brewery Limited
Tanners Ales Ltd
Tapstone Brewing Co Ltd
Three Engineers Brewery Ltd
Tuckers Ales Limited
Twin Barrel Brewery Limited
Twisted Oak Brewery Ltd
Wedmore Ales Ltd
Wessex Brewing & Pub Co Ltd
Wickwar Craft Taverns Limited
Wickwar Town Taverns Ltd
Wild Beer Co Ltd
Wiper & True Ltd.
Wiveliscombe Breweries Limited
Yeovil Ales Limited

Staffordshire [33]

Brews of the World Limited
Burton Bridge Brewery Limited
Burton Old Cottage Beer Co Ltd
Candid Brewing Co. Limited
Cobra Beer Partnership Limited
Custom Head Brewing Ltd
Eccleshall Brewing Co Ltd
Fleabag Brewing Co Ltd
Freedom Brewery Ltd
Gloucestershire Old Cottage Beer Co Ltd
Greenwich Old Cottage Beer Co Ltd
Halton Turner Brewing Co Ltd
Hawkins Drinks Limited
Hoptimistic Brewery Limited
Inadequate Brewery Limited
Lymestone Brewery Limited
Mart's Brewing Co Ltd
Molson Coors Brewing Co (UK) Ltd
Narugelia Ltd
Peakstones Rock Brewing Co Ltd
Quartz Brewing Limited
Rogue Elephant Brewery Limited
Six Towns Brewery Limited
Staffordshire Brewery Limited
Staffordshire Spirits Co Ltd
Titanic Brewery Co Limited
Tower Brewery Limited
Uttoxeter Brewing Co Ltd
Vine Inn Brewery 2016 Limited
Weal Ales Brewery Limited
Whim Ales Limited
Wombourne Brewing Co Ltd
Wood Brewery Limited

The UK Brewing Industry — dellam

Suffolk [35]
Adnams PLC
Anglia Pub Co Ltd
Barsham Brewery Limited
Big Drop Brewing Co Ltd
Black Bird Brewery Limited
Box Brewery Ltd
Brewshed Ltd
Burnt Mill Brewery Ltd
Calvors Brewery Limited
Clifford Brothers Brewery Ltd
Cygnus Brewing Co Limited
Dead Fridge Farm Limited
Dorber Brewing Limited
Dove Street Brewery Ltd
East Anglian Brewers Ltd.
Green Jack Brewing Co Ltd
Greene King Brewing and Retailing
Humber Doucy Brewing Co Ltd
Iceni Brewery Limited
Krafty Braumeister Ltd
Last Sign Brewing Co Ltd
Mauldon's Limited
Mr Bees Brewery Ltd
Nethergate Brewery Co Ltd
St. Peter's Brewery Co. Ltd
St. Peter's Brewery Group PLC
St. Peter's Trading Co. Ltd
Station 119 Ltd
Trinity Ales Limited
Two Happy Captains Ltd
Vinifera Limited
Watts & Co Ltd
Woodbridge Brewing Co Ltd
Wright & Spillane Limited
YB Ventures (2018) Ltd

Surrey [45]
1533 Brewery Limited
3SB Limited
3ways Brewing Co Limited
Abbey Ford Brewery Ltd
BCM Brewing Co Ltd
Bad Boy Brewing Ltd
Bear Brewery Co Ltd
Big Smoke Brew Co Limited
Brightwater Brewery Limited
Buzz Brewing Co Ltd
Campion Ale Limited
Coalition Brewing Co Ltd
Crafty Brewing Co. Limited
Crafty Brewing Co Ltd
Faultline Brew Co. Ltd
Felday Limited
Gargiulo's Production Ltd
Genesis Craft Ales Limited
Good Living Brew Co Limited
Groovy Grains Brewery Limited
Hedgedog Brewing Ltd
Hogs Back Brewery Limited
Jabru Bevco Ltd
Jawbone Brewing Ltd
Knoydart Brewery Limited
Kuwa Trading Ltd
Lingfield Brewing Co Ltd
Little Beer Corporation Ltd
Meantime Brewing Co Ltd
Out of the Woods Brew Co Ltd
Oxford Brewery Limited
Oxford Brewing Co Ltd
Oxted Brewery Ltd
Park Brewery Ltd
Pilgrim Brewery (Reigate) Ltd
Real Crafty Brewing Co Ltd
Shotover Brewing Co Ltd
Signal Brewery Limited
Surrey Hills Brewery Ltd
Three Lions Brewery Ltd
Thunder and Little Ltd
Thurstons Horsell Brewery Co Ltd
Tiny Vessel Brewing Co Ltd
Trailhead Brew Co Ltd
Ultimate Maltgold Limited

Sussex [72]
1648 Brewing Co Limited
360 Degree Brewing Co Ltd
81artisan Limited
Abyss Brewing Ltd
Arundel Brewery Limited
Bartleby's Ltd
Beak Brewery Limited
Bedlam Brewery Limited
Beer Collective Limited
Beer in the Blood Ltd
Beercraft Brewery Limited
Bestens Brewery Limited
Black Cat Brewery Limited
Boozehound Ltd
Braybrooke Beer Co Ltd
Brighton Bier Limited
Brighton Brewery Ltd
Broken Bridge Brewing Ltd
Brolly Brewing Limited
Cataclysm Brewing Limited
Chichester Brewery Limited
Cloak and Dagger Brewing Co Ltd
Craft Beer Cab Co Ltd
Filo Brewing Co Ltd
Firebird Brewing Co Ltd
Foghorn Brew Co Ltd
Fresh Beer Co Ltd
Goldmark Craft Beers Ltd
Greyhound Brewery Limited
Gun Brewery Limited
Hairy Dog Brewery Ltd
Hammerpot Brewery Limited
Hand Brewing Co Ltd
Harvey & Son (Lewes) Limited
Hastings Brewery Ltd
Heathen Brewers Limited
Hepworth & Company Brewers Ltd
Holler Brewery Limited
Hurst Brewery Ltd
Ironstone Brewery Ltd
Kiln Brewery Ltd
Langham Brewing Co Ltd
Long Man Brewery Limited
Loud Shirt Brewing Co Ltd
MC & P Engineering Limited
Makemake Beer Ltd
Missing Link Brewing Ltd
Old Prentonian Brewing Co Ltd.
Old Tree Brewery Ltd
Pin-Up Beers Ltd.
Pink Ferry Ltd
Polarity Brewing Ltd
Rectory Ales Limited
Riverside Brewery Ltd
Saltdean Brewing Co Ltd
Sativa Brewing Co Ltd
Session Brewing Co. Limited
Silver Rocket Brewing Ltd
Southbrew Co Ltd
Southdown Brewery Limited
Staggeringly Good Ltd
Sussex Beer Co Ltd
Three Acre Brewery Limited
Three Legs Brewing Co Ltd
Titsey Brewing Co. Limited
Top-Notch Brewing Co Ltd
Two Tribes Brewing Ltd
Unbarred Brewery Limited
Veterans Brewing (South East) Ltd
Weltons Limited
White's Brewery Limited
Wingtip Brewing Co Ltd

Tyne & Wear [35]
400 Software Limited
Almasty Brewing Co Ltd
Alnwick Ales Limited
Bad Moon Brewery Ltd
Big Lamp Brewers Limited
Box Social Ltd
Brinkburn Street Brewery Ltd
By The River Brewery Ltd
H.B.Clark & Co.(Successors) Ltd
Crossroads Brewery Limited
Cullercoats Brewery Limited
Darwin Brewery Limited
Dog and Rabbit Brewery Ltd
Double Maxim Beer Co Ltd
Errant Ltd
Firebrick Brewery Limited
Flash House Brewing Co Ltd
Great North Eastern Brewing Co Ltd
Head Thirst Ltd
Hunter Brewing Co Ltd
Lake District Brewery Limited
Newcastle Brewing Ltd
Newcastle Eden Bottling Co Ltd
North East Brewing Co Ltd
Northern Alchemy Limited
Sibley Brewing Co Ltd.
Sonnet 43 Brewery Ltd
Swaddle Micro Brewery Limited
Three Kings Brewery Limited
Trumark Properties Limited
Two By Two Brewing Ltd
Tyne Bank Brewery Limited
Vaux Brewery Ltd
Whitley Bay Brewing Co Ltd
Wylam Brewery Limited

Warwickshire [27]
Bib Brewing Ltd
Black Country Brewery Limited
Byatt's Brewery Ltd
Church End Brewery Limited
Church Farm Brewery Ltd
Crank Beers Limited
Dow Bridge Brewery Limited
Fingerprint Brewing Co Ltd
Fosse Way Brewing Co Ltd.
Law and Disorder Brew Co Ltd
Lock 34 Brew Co. Limited
Mashionistas Brewing Co Ltd
Merry Miner Brewery Ltd
North Cotswold Brewery Limited
O'Neill's Brewing Co Ltd
Old Pie Factory Brewery Ltd
Purity Brewing Co Ltd
Slaughterhouse Brewery Limited

Smokin Barrels Brewery Ltd
Southwark Brewing Co Ltd
Sperrin Brewery Ltd
Stratford upon Avon Brewery Ltd
Thirsty Pioneers Brewing Co Ltd
Tunnel Brewery Limited
Twisted Barrel Ale Limited
Weatheroak Brewery Ltd
Windmill Hill Brewing Co Ltd

West Midlands [48]
Andys' Ales Limited
Angel Ales Limited
Ar Suil Brewing Project Ltd
Aston Manor Limited
Attic Brew Co. Ltd
Backyard Brewhouse Limited
Daniel Batham & Son Limited
Bathams (Delph) Limited
Birmingham Brewing Co Ltd
Blue Bear Brewery (Worcester) Ltd
Bostin Brews Ltd
Bowing Hound Brewing Co Ltd
Bratch Beers Ltd
Burning Soul Brewing Ltd
Conferta Ltd
Crazy Mountain Brewing Co UK Ltd
Dingbat Beer Ltd
Dorking Brewery (2016) Limited
Enville Ales Limited
Fixed Wheel Brewery Limited
Fownes Brewing Co. Ltd.
Garretts Green Garage Mikro Brewery Ltd
Glasshouse Beer Co Ltd
Green Duck Beer Co. Limited
Greyfriars Brewery Ltd
Holdens Brewery Limited
Indian Brewery Company Birmingham Ltd
Leviathan Brewing Ltd
Mansfield Brewery Trading Ltd
Marston's Acquisitions Limited
Marston's PLC
Moseley Beer Co Ltd
New Invention Brewery Ltd
Ostlers Ales Ltd
Pig Iron Brewing Co Ltd
Pig Iron Brewing Limited
Pink Moon Brewery Limited
Punchline Brewery Limited
Red Moon Brewery Limited
Reds Beer Co Ltd
Rock & Roll Brewhouse Ltd
Spencer Panacea Limited
Towler and Webb Limited
Two Bears Brewery Ltd
Two Towers Brewery Ltd
Walsall Brewing Co Ltd
Weatheroak Hill Brewery Ltd
Windsor Castle Brewery Limited

Wiltshire [23]
32 Islands Brewery Ltd
Arkell's Brewery Limited
Brightbeer Limited
Broadtown Brewery Ltd
Brotherhood Brewery Ltd
Burning Sky Brewery Limited
Castle Combe Brewery Limited
Dark Revolution Ltd
Devitera Ltd
Downton Brewery Co Ltd

Flying Monk Brewery Ltd
Hop Back Brewery PLC
I.T's Brewing Co Ltd
Kettlesmith Brewing Co Ltd
Old Town Brewery Ltd.
Plain Ales Brewery Ltd
Ramsbury Brewing and Distilling Co Ltd
Salisbury Brewery Limited
Stonehenge Ales Limited
Three Castles Brewery Limited
Twisted Brewing Co Ltd
Wadworth and Co Ltd
Wessex Brewery Limited

Worcestershire [27]
Alonaoracle Ltd
Barrels Hereford Limited
Bewdley Brewery Limited
Boat Lane Brewery Limited
Bridgnorth Brewery Limited
Brothers of Ale Limited
Burford Brewery Co Ltd
Crafted Brewing Co. Ltd
Dood and Frinks Ltd
Friday Beer Co Ltd
Gander Brewing Co Ltd
Hartlebury Brewing Co Ltd
Hillside Brewery Limited
Hobsons Brewery and Co Ltd
Hopsox Brewing Co Ltd
Kinver Brewery Limited
Lakehouse Brewing Co Ltd
Loyal City Brewing Co Ltd
Malvern Hills Brewery Limited
Monkey Shed Estate Brewing Co Ltd
Nothing Bound Brewing Co Ltd
Pershore Brewery Limited
Shelsley Brewing Co Ltd
Sociable Beer Co Ltd.
Sonder Brewing Co Ltd.
Three Shires Brewery Ltd
Woodcote Manor Brewing Co Ltd

Yorkshire [215]
2 Bobs Brewing Co Ltd
4 Ladies Brewery Ltd
Abbeydale Brewery Limited
Acorn Brewery of Barnsley Ltd
Agricola Bottling Limited
Ainsty Ales Limited
Ale Club Ltd
Anchor Brewery Ltd
Annuity Ales Limited
Another Beer Ltd
Anthology Brewing Co Ltd
Asylum Harbour Brewing Co Ltd
Atom Brewing Co Limited
Bad Seed Brewery Ltd
Alex Barlow Brewing Consulting Ltd
Beer Ink Limited
Beer Monkey Brew Co. Limited
Bentley's Yorkshire Breweries (1828)
Beverley Brewery Co Ltd
Big Hop Brewing Co Ltd
Bingley Brewery Limited
Black Sheep Brewery PLC
Blue Bee Brewery Ltd
Bob's Brewing Co Ltd
Bone Machine Brewing Co Ltd
Boothtown Brewery Co Ltd
Bosun's Brewing Co Ltd

Bradfield Brewery Limited
Brass Castle Brewery Limited
Brew York Limited
Breworks Ltd
Bridge House Brewery Limited
Bridgehouse Pub Co Ltd
Bridlington Brewing Co. Ltd
Chantry Brewery Ltd
Chequers Micropub Limited
Chevin Brew Co Ltd
Chin Chin Brewing Co Ltd
City Vaults Real Ale Ltd
Cocktails and Craft Beers Ltd
Cold Bath Brewing Co Ltd
Crafty Pales Ltd
Crooked Brewing Limited
Crooked Ship Brewery Ltd
Daleside Brewery Limited
Daleside Holdings (Harrogate) Ltd
Darkland Brewery Limited
Darlington Brewing and Distilling Co Ltd
Dead Parrot Beer Co Ltd
Dent Brewery Limited
Don Valley Brewery Limited
Doncaster Brewery Limited
Dore Brewery Limited
East Riding Brewery Ltd
East Yorkshire Beer Co Ltd
Elemental Brewing Ltd
Elland Brewery Limited
Empire Brewing Ltd
Exit 33 Brewing Ltd
Eyes Brewing Limited
FGW Brewery Limited
Foresight Holdings Limited
Frisky Bear Brewing Co Ltd
Fuggle Bunny Brew House Ltd
Geeves Brewery Limited
Gene Pool Brewing Ltd
Ghost Brewing Co Limited
Golcar Brewery Limited
Goose Eye Brewery Limited
Great British Breworks Ltd
Great Heck Brewing Co Ltd
Great Newsome Brewery Limited
Great Yorkshire Brewery Ltd
HU Caret 4 Limited
Half Moon Brewery Ltd
Halifax Steam Brewing Co Ltd
Hambleton Brewery Limited
Harrogate Brewing Co Ltd
Hilltop Brewing Co Ltd
Hoggshead Brewhouse Limited
Holley Paquette Brewers Ltd
Hop Forward Ltd
Hop Studio Limited
Hop and Pray Ltd
Hopscotch Craft Brewers Ltd
Horbury Ales Limited
Howardian Hills Brewing Co Ltd
Hull Brewing Co Ltd
Humber Brewery Ltd
Icecream Factory Limited
Ilkley Brewery Co Ltd
Intrepid Brewing Co Ltd
Jolly Boys Brewery Ltd
Jolly Sailor Brewery Limited
Kelham Island Brewery Limited
Kirkstall Brewery Co Ltd
Lancar Limited
Laughing Ass Brewery Ltd
Lazy Turtle Brewing Co Ltd

Leeds Brewery Co Ltd
Legless Brewing Ltd
Little Black Dog Beer Co Ltd
Little Critters Brewing Co Ltd
Little Valley Brewery Limited
Littondale Brewing Co Ltd
Live Brew Co Ltd
Lords Brewing Co Ltd
Lost at Sea Brewing Limited
Luddite Brewing Co Ltd
Luddites Revenge Ltd
Magic Rock Brewing Co Ltd
Meanwood Brewery Ltd
Merrimans Brewery Ltd
Mill Valley Brewery Limited
Milltown Brewing Co. Ltd
Moorside Brewery Ltd
Morton Collins Brewing Co Ltd
Nailmaker Brewing Co Ltd
Naylor's Brewery Ltd
Neepsend Brewery Ltd
Nightjar Brew Co Ltd
Nightowl Brewing Co Ltd
Nomadic Brewing Co Ltd
North Brewing Co Ltd
North Riding Brewery Limited
Northern Craft Brewers Limited
Northern Monk Brewing Co. Ltd
Now Then Brewery Ltd
Old Spot Brewery Limited
Old Vault Brewing Co Ltd
Original Goole Brewery Co Ltd
Ossett Brewing Co Ltd
Outgang Brewery Ltd
Outhouse Brewing Ltd
PLS Special Projects Limited
Paper Fort Brew Co Ltd.
Partners Brewery Limited
Pedal Power Harrogate Limited

Penistone Brewers Limited
Penistone Brewing (Penistone) Ltd
Pivo Beverages Ltd
Play Limited
Isaac Poad Brewing Ltd
Pointeer Ltd
Pomona Island Brew Co Ltd
Pumphouse Brewing Co Ltd
Quirky Ales Ltd
Raven Hill Brewery Limited
Revolutions Brewing Co Ltd
Ridgeside Brewing Co Ltd
Roosters Brewery Limited
Roosters Brewing Co Ltd
Rudgate Brewery Limited
Salamander Brewing Co Ltd
Saltaire Brewery Limited
Scarborough Brewery Limited
Selby (Middlebrough) Brewery,Limited
Sentinel Brewery Holdings Ltd
Shadow Brewing Ltd
Sheeptown Brewery Limited
Sheffield Brewers Collective
Sheffield Brewery Co Ltd
David Sheriff Brewing Services Ltd
Slow Beer Ltd
Small World Beers Ltd
Samuel Smith Old Brewery (Tadcaster)
Spotlight Brewing Ltd
Squawk Brewing Co Ltd
St Andrews Old Brewing Co Ltd
Stancill Brewery Limited
Stannington Brewery Ltd
Steam Brewing Co Limited
Steel City Brewing Ltd
Stocks Brewing Co Ltd
Stod Fold Brewing Limited
Stone Cold Brewery Limited
Summer Wine Brewery Limited

Tarn51 Brewing Co Ltd
Timothy Taylor & Co.,Limited
T.& R. Theakston Limited
Toolmakers Brewery Limited
Treboom Limited
Triple Point Brewing Ltd
True North Brew Co Limited
Turning Point Brewing Co Ltd
Two Roses Brewery Ltd
Ullage Ale Ltd
Under The Stairs Brewery Ltd
Vadum Brewery Ltd
Vision Brewing Co Ltd
Vocation Brewery Limited
Wanderlust Bar Limited
Websters Brewery Ltd.
Wensleydale Brewery (2013) Ltd
Wentworth Brewery Ltd
Westmoor Botanicals Limited
Wetherby Brew Co Limited
Wetherells Contracts Limited
Wharfedale Brewery Limited
Whitby Brewery Ltd
White Boar Brewing Co Ltd
White Rose Brewery Limited
Whitefaced Ltd
Wilde Child Brewing Co Ltd
Wishbone Brewery Limited
Witch Craft Beers Limited
Wold Toppers Limited
Woodruff Brewing Ltd
X-Ray Brewing Co Ltd
York Brewery Limited
Yorkshire Brewhouse Limited
Yorkshire Brewing Co Ltd
Yorkshire Dales Brewing Co Ltd
Yorkshire Heart Limited
Zapato Brewery Ltd.

This page is intentionally left blank

Company Profiles

1533 Brewery Limited
Incorporated: 26 May 2017
Registered Office: 28 Chipstead Station Parade, Chipstead, Coulsdon, Surrey, CR5 3TF
Shareholders: John Vincent Hatch; Michael Hardman
Officers: Michael Hardman [1946] Director/Journalist; John Vincent Hatch [1966] Director/Brewer

The 1648 Brewing Co Limited
Incorporated: 11 February 2003 *Employees:* 3
Net Worth: £18,918 *Total Assets:* £50,720
Registered Office: The 1648 Brewing Co Ltd, Inn House, 1 High Street, East Hoathly, Lewes, E Sussex, BN8 6DR
Shareholder: Robert Wallace
Officers: Robert Wallace, Secretary/Publican; Robert Wallace [1945] Director/Publican

1936 Limited
Incorporated: 24 March 2011
Net Worth Deficit: £74,163 *Total Assets:* £201,210
Registered Office: Office 166, 8 Shepherd Market, London, W1J 7JY
Officers: Scott Haspineall [1971] Managing Director

1st Icon Ltd
Incorporated: 30 April 2018
Registered Office: 5 Thaxted Lodge, Victoria Road, London, E18 1LL
Shareholder: Preeti Rana
Officers: Tarun Ghulati [1960] Director; Preeti Rana [1983] Director

2 Bobs Brewing Company Limited
Incorporated: 10 January 2011
Net Worth Deficit: £3,012 *Total Assets:* £5,493
Registered Office: 145 Holmsley Lane, Woodlesford, Leeds, LS26 8SB
Shareholders: Ian Robert Walker; Robert John Bradley
Officers: Robert John Bradley, Secretary; Ian Robert Walker [1963] Director

23-7 Brewing Ltd
Incorporated: 25 October 2017
Registered Office: 5 Marsett Close, Norden, Rochdale, Lancs, OL12 7QT
Major Shareholder: Alexander David O'Mahony
Officers: Alexander David O'Mahony [1975] Director/Teacher

2731 Limited
Incorporated: 18 August 2014
Net Worth Deficit: £13,006 *Total Assets:* £5,611
Registered Office: Main Building, 2 College Road, Newton Abbot, Devon, TQ12 1EF
Major Shareholder: Nicholas John Perkovic
Officers: Nicholas John Perkovic [1962] Director

The 3 Brewers Ltd
Incorporated: 15 June 2012 *Employees:* 3
Net Worth: £8,771 *Total Assets:* £52,450
Registered Office: The Potato Shed Symondshyde Farm, Symondshyde Lane, Hatfield, Herts, AL10 9BB
Shareholder: Mark Ashley Fanner
Officers: Mark Ashley Fanner [1965] Director/Brewer; Petar Zivkovic [1966] Director/Brewer

3 Bru's Brewing Company Ltd
Incorporated: 17 October 2018
Registered Office: 19 Frayslea, Uxbridge, Middlesex, UB8 2AT
Shareholders: Anthony Michael Delport; Frank Wurzbach; Stephen Martin Pio Michael
Officers: Frank Wurzbach, Secretary; Anthony Michael Delport [1972] Director/Operations Manager; Stephen Martin Pio Michael [1966] Director/Operations Manager [South African]

3 Cities Brewing Company Ltd
Incorporated: 15 November 2017
Registered Office: 42 Hogarth Road, Whitwick, Coalville, Leics, LE67 5GF
Major Shareholder: Marcus Garry Edward Goddard
Officers: Marcus Garry Edward Goddard [1980] Director

3 Piers Brewery Limited
Incorporated: 29 March 2017 *Employees:* 2
Net Worth Deficit: £17,080 *Total Assets:* £50,971
Registered Office: Unit 19 Cocker Avenue, Poulton Industrial Estate, Poulton-le-Fylde, Lancs, FY6 8JU
Major Shareholder: Michael Gainford Henry
Officers: Michael Gainford Henry [1979] Director

3's A Crowd Brewing Ltd
Incorporated: 31 October 2016 *Employees:* 2
Net Worth: £443 *Total Assets:* £26,135
Registered Office: Capital House, 272 Manchester Road, Droylsden, Manchester, M43 6PW
Shareholders: Christopher Ashley; Liam Whitehead
Officers: Christopher Ashley [1979] Director/Gas Engineer; Liam Whitehead [1979] Director/Personal Advisor

32 Islands Brewery Ltd
Incorporated: 22 October 2018
Registered Office: Bakers Ground, 7 Church Street, Sherston, Malmesbury, Wilts, SN16 0LR
Shareholders: James Leslie Archibald; Nicola Jane Lucy Archibald
Officers: James Leslie Archibald [1962] Director/Chairman

360 Degree Brewing Company Ltd
Incorporated: 26 June 2003
Net Worth: £26,156 *Total Assets:* £147,076
Registered Office: Unit 24B, Bluebell Business Estate, Sheffield Park, Uckfield, E Sussex, TN22 3HQ
Shareholders: John David Shepherd; Mark David Grady
Officers: Mark David Grady [1970] Director; Stephen Norris Hunt [1987] Director/Head Brewer [Irish]; Christopher Mark McClune [1969] Finance Director; Chris Nicholas Paul [1965] Commercial Director; John David Shepherd [1969] Commercial Director; Philip David Shepherd [1969] Director

3ABC Ltd
Incorporated: 14 February 2017
Net Worth: £5,617 *Total Assets:* £23,568
Registered Office: Flat 1, 180 St Pauls Road, London, N1 2LL
Shareholders: Akshit Raj Gupta; Ashwin Balivada; Aditya Nigudkar
Officers: Ashwin Balivada [1988] Director [Indian]; Akshit Raj Gupta [1988] Director/Operations [Indian]; Aditya Nigudkar [1983] Director/Cofounder [Indian]

3SB Limited
Incorporated: 28 May 2014 *Employees:* 3
Net Worth: £7,914 *Total Assets:* £21,000
Registered Office: 48 Smallfield Road, Horley, Surrey, RH6 9AT
Shareholder: Adam Paul Foster
Officers: Adam Paul Foster, Secretary; Wilson Digby [1987] Sales Director; Adam Paul Foster [1979] Director/Hop Chief [South African]; David Jonsson-Buttery [1983] Director/Head Brewer; Jordan Kirrane [1982] Director/Chief Taster

3ways Brewing Co Limited
Incorporated: 18 July 2016
Net Worth Deficit: £546 *Total Assets:* £90
Registered Office: 1 High Street, Guildford, Surrey, GU2 4HP
Officers: Duncan Butchart [1980] Director; James Butchart [1980] Director; Matthew Simon Hodges [1977] Director; Timothy Philip Hodges [1980] Director; Timothy Martin John Mortimer [1977] Director; James Edgar Leigh Vickery [1977] Director; Thomas Jan Wehmeier [1980] Director; James Andrew Thomas Williamson [1982] Director

4 Acre Brewing Co. Ltd
Incorporated: 31 December 2018
Registered Office: 198 Berechurch Hall Road, Colchester, Essex, CO2 9PN
Shareholders: Spencer Aaron Gilbert; Amir William Anbouche; Jack William James Snell
Officers: Amir William Anbouche [1992] Director

4 Ladies Brewery Ltd
Incorporated: 19 February 2013
Registered Office: Unit 8a The Sidings Industrial Estate, Settle, N Yorks, BD24 9RP
Officers: Ian Daniel Simkins [1976] Director/Brewer

4 Mice Brewery Limited
Incorporated: 1 September 2017
Registered Office: The Coach and Horses Public House, Bolton by Bowland, Clitheroe, Lancs, BB7 4NW
Parent: Pangolin Holding Limited
Officers: Jacobus Labeij [1946] Director [Dutch]; Susan Margaret Lord [1964] Director

400 Software Limited
Incorporated: 1 September 2015 *Employees:* 2
Previous: Autumn Brewing Company Limited
Net Worth Deficit: £89,599 *Total Assets:* £79,921
Registered Office: P O Box 305, Shibdon Cottage, Shibdon Bank, Blaydon on Tyne, Tyne & Wear, NE21 9AN
Major Shareholder: Peter Briggs
Officers: Peter Briggs [1966] Director

5hop Limited
Incorporated: 1 November 2018
Registered Office: 6 Crawford Gardens, Crowland, Peterborough, PE6 0AZ
Major Shareholder: Andy Philip Neal
Officers: Andy Philip Neal [1980] Director

7 Reasons To Brew Ltd
Incorporated: 14 June 2016
Net Worth Deficit: £4,227 *Total Assets:* £19,473
Registered Office: 16 Woodlands Park, Durris, Banchory, Kincardineshire, AB31 6BF
Shareholder: Stephen Christopher Newman
Officers: Claire Louise Hesketh-Crafts [1972] Director; Angela Mary Catherine Rooksby [1973] Director

71 Brewing Limited
Incorporated: 30 June 2015 *Employees:* 5
Net Worth Deficit: £55,017 *Total Assets:* £498,439
Registered Office: 36-40 Bellfield Street, Dundee, DD1 5HZ
Shareholder: Duncan George Alexander
Officers: Duncan George Alexander [1971] Director/IT Consultant; Dr Mark Garry Fowlestone [1964] Director; Mark John Griffiths [1973] Director; Alasdair Iain McGill [1969] Director/Accountant; John Wesley Nelms [1971] Director [American]; Alan Ian Warnock [1971] Director

7grains Limited
Incorporated: 7 November 2016
Registered Office: 1 Witcutt Way, Wishaw, N Lanarks, ML2 0AP
Major Shareholder: Russell McCoull
Officers: Russell McCoull [1981] Director/Business Analyst

81artisan Limited
Incorporated: 17 November 2014
Net Worth Deficit: £73,318 *Total Assets:* £121,711
Registered Office: c/o Evans Weir, The Victoria, 25 St Pancras, Chichester, W Sussex, PO19 7LT
Major Shareholder: Adrian Kingsbury
Officers: Adrian Kingsbury [1981] Director/Oil and Gas Engineer

888 Global Trade Ltd
Incorporated: 21 April 2017
Net Worth Deficit: £3,152 *Total Assets:* £18,591
Registered Office: 10 Main Street, Doune, Perthshire, FK16 6BJ
Officers: LEA Cunningham [1977] Director/Property Manager; Stephen Cunningham [1976] Director/Cost Engineer

A Northerly Brewing Ltd
Incorporated: 13 April 2016
Net Worth Deficit: £1,453 *Total Assets:* £2,048
Registered Office: Corner House, Sutherland Street, Helmsdale, Sutherland, KW8 6LQ
Major Shareholder: David Andrew Shaw
Officers: David Andrew Shaw [1979] Director

A-Zero Energy Beer Limited
Incorporated: 9 August 2018
Registered Office: 146 South Street, St Andrews, Fife, KY16 9EQ
Parent: Afrodysia Beverage Group Ltd
Officers: Giorgio Cozzolino Cozzolino [1964] Director [Italian]

AB InBev UK Finance Company Limited
Incorporated: 16 March 2015
Net Worth: £14,650,677,248 *Total Assets:* £14,650,720,256
Registered Office: Bureau, 90 Fetter Lane, London, EC4A 1EN
Parent: Anheuser-Busch Europe Limited
Officers: Kevin Jean-Frederic Douws [1982] Director [Belgian]; Sibil Jiang [1990] Director [Australian]; Stephen John Turner [1966] Director/Accountant

AB InBev UK Investment Company Limited
Incorporated: 16 March 2015
Net Worth: £11,789,528 *Total Assets:* £11,815,303
Registered Office: Bureau, 90 Fetter Lane, London, EC4A 1EN
Parent: ABI Southern Holding Ltd
Officers: Kevin Jean-Frederic Douws [1982] Director [Belgian]; Sibil Jiang [1990] Director [Australian]; Stephen John Turner [1966] Director/Accountant

AB InBev UK Limited
Incorporated: 27 April 2000 *Employees:* 991
Net Worth: £111,152,000 *Total Assets:* £858,534,016
Registered Office: Porter Tun House, 500 Capability Green, Luton, Beds, LU1 3LS
Parent: Nimbuspath Limited
Officers: Kayleigh Anne Wilshaw, Secretary; Oliver James Devon [1989] Finance Director; Jens Hoffmann [1975] Supply Director Germany & UK [German]; Martin Evert Ijntema [1981] Sales Director [Dutch]; Paula Nogueira Lindenberg [1975] Director/President BU West [Brazilian]; Rory McLellan [1978] Commercial Director; Claire Louise Richardson [1983] People Director; James Malcom Rowe [1978] UK Operations Director; Tatiana Stadukhina [1982] Marketing Director [American]; Andrew George Whiting [1982] Legal Director

Abbey Ales Limited
Incorporated: 13 February 1997 *Employees:* 5
Net Worth: £54,352 *Total Assets:* £69,783
Registered Office: 49a Goose Street, Beckington, Somerset, BA11 6SS
Major Shareholder: Alan Richard Morgan
Officers: Susan Elizabeth Morgan, Secretary; Alan Richard Morgan [1947] Director; Simon Lewis Morgan [1972] Director; Susan Elizabeth Morgan [1947] Director

Abbey Brewery Ltd
Incorporated: 16 February 2016
Previous: Konigsberg Food and Beverages Limited
Registered Office: Konigsberg Food and Beverages Limited Meden Road, Boughton, Newark, Notts, NG22 9ZD

Abbey Ford Brewery Ltd
Incorporated: 6 September 2011
Registered Office: 6 Ford Road, Chertsey, Surrey, KT16 8HD
Major Shareholder: Daniel Anthony Crowley
Officers: Daniel Crowley, Secretary; Daniel Anthony Crowley [1972] Director/Security Systems

Abbey Grange Brewing Limited
Incorporated: 17 July 2008
Net Worth Deficit: £8,451
Registered Office: Abbey Grange Hotel, Llangollen, Denbighshire, LL20 8DD
Major Shareholder: Steven Vaughan Evans
Officers: Steven Vaughan Evans [1957] Director

Abbeydale Brewery Limited
Incorporated: 11 November 2002 *Employees:* 24
Net Worth: £659,845 *Total Assets:* £1,960,314
Registered Office: Unit 8 Aizlewood Road, Sheffield, S8 0YX
Shareholders: Patrick Hugh Morton; Susan Ann Morton
Officers: Dawn Milton, Secretary; Daniel James Baxter [1986] Director/Sales Manager; Jonathan Michael Conroy [1962] Director/Engineer; Toby David Grattidge [1978] Director; Patrick Hugh Morton [1953] Director/Brewer; Susan Ann Morton [1955] Director; John Parkinson [1969] Director

Abernyte Brewery Limited
Incorporated: 8 January 2015
Net Worth Deficit: £32,623 *Total Assets:* £65,951
Registered Office: South Latch Farm, Abernyte, Perth, PH14 9SU
Shareholders: Ian St Clair Campbell; Stuart Donald Meldrum
Officers: Ian Campbell, Secretary; Ian St Clair Campbell [1972] Director/Brewer; Stuart Donald Meldrum [1980] Director/Brewer

ABI SAB Group Holding Limited
Incorporated: 17 March 1998 *Employees:* 177
Previous: Sabmiller Limited
Net Worth: £48,800,354,304 *Total Assets:* £48,913,764,352
Registered Office: Bureau, 90 Fetter Lane, London, EC4A 1EN
Parent: ABI UK Holding 2 Limited
Officers: Kevin Jean-Frederic Douws [1982] Director [Belgian]; Sibil Jiang [1990] Director [Australian]; Stephen John Turner [1966] Director/Accountant

ABI UK Holding 1 Limited
Incorporated: 15 September 2016
Net Worth: £85,742,592,000 *Total Assets:* £145,066,819,584
Registered Office: Bureau, 90 Fetter Lane, London, EC4A 1EN
Parent: Anheuser-Busch InBev SA/NV
Officers: Kevin Jean-Frederic Douws [1982] Director [Belgian]; Sibil Jiang [1990] Director [Australian]; Stephen John Turner [1966] Director/Accountant

Abstract Jungle Brewing Ltd
Incorporated: 8 May 2015
Net Worth Deficit: £35,641 *Total Assets:* £45,172
Registered Office: Unit 14 Baileybrook Industrial Estate Amber Drive, Langley Mill, Nottingham, NG16 4BE
Shareholder: Simon King
Officers: Simon King [1972] Director

Abyss Brewing Ltd
Incorporated: 6 October 2016
Net Worth Deficit: £18,155 *Total Assets:* £53,799
Registered Office: Pelham Arms, High Street, Lewes, E Sussex, BN7 1XL
Officers: Andrew Daniel Bridge [1975] Director/Marketing; Andrew Peter Mellor [1971] Director/Publican & Brewing

Acorn Brewery of Barnsley Limited
Incorporated: 18 May 2003 *Employees:* 11
Net Worth: £959,989 *Total Assets:* £1,099,029
Registered Office: Unit 3 Aldham Industrial Estate, Mitchell Road, Wombwell, Barnsley, S Yorks, S73 8HA
Shareholders: Christy Hughes; David Stewart Hughes
Officers: Christy Hughes [1979] Director; David Stewart Hughes [1968] Director/Brewer

AD Hop Brewing Ltd
Incorporated: 1 July 2014
Net Worth Deficit: £73,452 *Total Assets:* £20,818
Registered Office: Flat 7, Derwent House, 24a Aigburth Drive, Liverpool, L17 4JH
Major Shareholder: Anders Aqulin
Officers: Anders Aqulin [1968] Director [Swedish]

Samuel Adams (Beer) Ltd
Incorporated: 31 December 2012
Registered Office: Premier Business Centre, 47-49 Park Royal Road, Park Royal, London, NW10 7LQ
Major Shareholder: Everoy Johnson
Officers: Everoy Johnson [1959] Director/Businessman

Adnams PLC
Incorporated: 24 March 1890 *Employees:* 203
Net Worth: £28,642,000 *Total Assets:* £64,708,000
Registered Office: East Green, Southwold, Suffolk, IP18 6JW
Officers: Elizabeth Sarah Cantwell, Secretary; Jonathan Adnams [1956] Director; Nicola Joy Dulieu [1963] Director; Michael Guy Hilliard Heald [1950] Director; Karen Hester [1962] Director; Bridget Fiona McIntyre [1961] Director; Stephen Crommelin Pugh [1958] Director; Dr Steven Michael Sharp [1950] Marketing Director; Andrew Charles Wood [1960] Director

The UK Brewing Industry

Adriyel Ltd
Incorporated: 18 September 2018
Registered Office: 12a Market Place, Kettering, Northants, NN16 0AJ
Major Shareholder: Kyle Chadwick
Officers: Jovelle Javinal [1987] Director [Filipino]

Adshead's Ales Ltd
Incorporated: 30 November 1992
Registered Office: Hollin Old Hall, East Grimshaw Lane, Bollington, Macclesfield, Cheshire, SK10 5LY
Major Shareholder: Ruth Mary Inskip
Officers: Geoffrey Stuart Inskip, Secretary/Director; Ruth Mary Inskip [1955] Director

Affinity Brewing Company Limited
Incorporated: 23 March 2012 *Employees:* 1
Net Worth: £9,390 *Total Assets:* £27,306
Registered Office: Railway Arch 7, Almond Road, London, SE16 3LR
Shareholders: Benjamin Joseph Duckworth; Steven Phillip Grae
Officers: Steven Phillip Grae [1983] Director

After The Harvest Brewing Ltd
Incorporated: 11 August 2015
Registered Office: 65 West Street, Hereford, HR4 0BX
Shareholders: Jonathan Bright; Amelie Jeannine Marcelle Varin
Officers: Jonathan Bright [1984] Director; Amelie Jeannine Marcelle Varin [1987] Director [French]

Agnate Limited
Incorporated: 20 October 2014
Net Worth Deficit: £14,073 *Total Assets:* £23,000
Registered Office: Tremethick, Grampound, Truro, Cornwall, TR2 4QY
Major Shareholder: Richard Dean Jenkins
Officers: Dr Richard Dean Jenkins, Secretary; Richard Dean Jenkins [1966] Director/Consultant

Agricola Bottling Limited
Incorporated: 23 April 2010 *Employees:* 4
Net Worth: £242,202 *Total Assets:* £540,595
Registered Office: Humanby Grange, Wold Newton, Driffield, E Yorks, YO25 3HS
Shareholders: Thomas Leslie Mellor; Gillian Mary Mellor
Officers: Alex Balchin [1988] Director; Kate Balchin [1987] Director; Gillian Mary Mellor [1960] Director; Thomas Leslie Mellor [1959] Director

Ainsty Ales Limited
Incorporated: 6 September 2013
Net Worth Deficit: £49,203 *Total Assets:* £208,132
Registered Office: Manor Farm Buildings, Mill Lane, Acaster Malbis, York, YO23 2TY
Shareholders: Neil Antony Hopkinson; Andrew Mark Herrington
Officers: Andrew Mark Herrington [1977] Director/Taxi Driver; Neil Antony Hopkinson [1966] Director

Airborne Ales Ltd
Incorporated: 4 February 2014
Net Worth: £2 *Total Assets:* £2
Registered Office: 12 Clos Brynach, Brynmenyn, Bridgend, Mid Glamorgan, CF32 9QD
Officers: Patricia Jean Smiles, Secretary; Alan Smiles [1961] Marketing and Development Director

Alcazar Brewing Company Limited
Incorporated: 15 August 2001
Net Worth Deficit: £120,928 *Total Assets:* £240
Registered Office: Avocet House, Bittern Way, Riverside Industrial Estate, Boston, Lincs, PE21 7NX
Parent: Turnstone Taverns Limited
Officers: Kym Christopher Ellington, Secretary; John Nicholas Gorensweigh [1964] Director

Alcohol Beverages Company Ltd
Incorporated: 15 June 2018
Registered Office: Pitts and Seeus, Omnibus Business Centre, 39-41 North Road, London, N7 9DP
Major Shareholder: James Gerald McMackin
Officers: James Generanl McMackin [1961] Director [Irish]

The Ale Club Ltd
Incorporated: 8 December 2014 *Employees:* 1
Net Worth Deficit: £24,753 *Total Assets:* £61,050
Registered Office: 18 Jarrow Road, Sheffield, S11 8YB
Shareholders: James Robert Eardley; Robert Carter Eardley
Officers: James Robert Eardley [1982] Director; Robert Carter Eardley [1951] Director

The Ale Factory Ltd
Incorporated: 10 October 2018
Registered Office: 252 Higham Hill Road, London, E17 5RQ
Major Shareholder: Harry Napier
Officers: Harry Napier [1986] Director

ALE Finance Services Limited
Incorporated: 16 September 2016
Net Worth: £19,155,951,616 *Total Assets:* £78,933,565,440
Registered Office: Bureau, 90 Fetter Lane, London, EC4A 1EN
Parent: ABI UK Holding 2 Limited
Officers: Kevin Jean-Frederic Douws [1982] Director [Belgian]; Sibil Jiang [1990] Director [Australian]; Stephen John Turner [1966] Director/Accountant

Alechemy Brewing Ltd
Incorporated: 18 October 2011 *Employees:* 5
Net Worth Deficit: £65,235 *Total Assets:* £156,755
Registered Office: Spalding House, 90-92 Queen Street, Broughty Ferry, Dundee, DD5 1AJ
Major Shareholder: James William Davies
Officers: James Derek Scott Carnegie [1961] Director; Dr James William Davies [1977] Director/Owner & Head Brewer; Anthony Schofield [1959] Director; Donald John Smith [1968] Director

All Day Brewing Company Limited
Incorporated: 12 June 2013
Net Worth: £27,573 *Total Assets:* £27,583
Registered Office: Salle Brewery, Barns 14, 15 & 16, Salle Moor Farm, Wood Dalling Road, Salle, Norfolk, NR10 4SB
Major Shareholder: Simon Stanley Barker
Officers: Dr Simon Stanley Barker [1957] Director/Brewer

Allbeer Limited
Incorporated: 10 January 2017
Registered Office: 4 Vicarage Lane, Mears Ashby, Northampton, NN6 0EE
Major Shareholder: Jake Laurance Gordon-Leaf
Officers: Jake Laurance Gordon-Leaf [1993] Director

Allendale Brew Company Limited
Incorporated: 27 October 2004 *Employees:* 12
Net Worth: £185,182 *Total Assets:* £588,519
Registered Office: 95 King Street, Lancaster, LA1 1RH
Shareholders: Lucy Claire Hick; Thomas James Augustine Hick
Officers: Thomas James Augustine Hick, Secretary; Lucy Claire Hick [1980] Director; Thomas James Augustine Hick [1980] Director/Company Secretary; Neil John Allan Thomas [1980] Director

Samuel Allsopp & Sons Ltd
Incorporated: 14 March 2017
Registered Office: 16 Leamington Road Villas, London, W11 1HS
Major Shareholder: James Leonard Allsopp
Officers: James Leonard Allsopp [1978] Director/Brewer

Almasty Brewing Company Ltd
Incorporated: 21 January 2014
Net Worth: £66,246 *Total Assets:* £139,721
Registered Office: Unit 11 Algernon Industrial Estate, New York Road, Shiremoor, Tyne & Wear, NE27 0NB
Major Shareholder: Mark McGarry
Officers: Mark McGarry [1977] Director/Founder

J.B. Almond Ltd
Incorporated: 11 April 2016
Registered Office: 13 Moores Lane, Standish, Wigan, Lancs, WN6 0JD
Officers: Ian Anthony Norris [1971] Director

Alnwick Ales Limited
Incorporated: 3 January 2003 *Employees:* 14
Net Worth: £116,737 *Total Assets:* £783,708
Registered Office: Unit 5 The Preserving Works, Shelley Road, Newburn Industrial Estate, Newcastle upon Tyne, NE15 9RT
Shareholders: Andrew Stuart Burrows; Shona Patrine Jean Burrows
Officers: Shona Patrine Jean Burrows, Secretary/Brewer; Andrew Stuart Burrows [1962] Director/Brewer; Shona Patrine Jean Burrows [1967] Director/Brewer

The Alnwick Brewery Company Limited
Incorporated: 4 November 2005 *Employees:* 3
Net Worth Deficit: £69,006 *Total Assets:* £143,935
Registered Office: 6 Market Place, Alnwick, Northumberland, NE66 1HS
Parent: Spirit of Northumberland
Officers: Ian Booth Robinson [1947] Director/Manager; Keith Caville Stephenson [1954] Director/Retired; Christopher Darryl Walwyn-James [1952] Director/Manager

Alonaoracle Ltd
Incorporated: 11 September 2018
Registered Office: Office 2, Crown House, Church Row, Pershore, Worcs, WR10 1BH
Major Shareholder: Claire McNally
Officers: Precious Anne Ersando [1997] Director [Filipino]

Alpha State Limited
Incorporated: 9 November 2012
Net Worth Deficit: £79,513 *Total Assets:* £22,373
Registered Office: Crowhursts, The Heath, Horsmonden, Tonbridge, Kent, TN12 8HT
Officers: Joan Rosemary Queally [1951] Director; Jonathan Patrick Queally [1979] Director

Alphabet Brewing Ltd
Incorporated: 20 June 2014 *Employees:* 6
Net Worth Deficit: £329,616 *Total Assets:* £159,341
Registered Office: 99 North Western Street, Manchester, M12 6JL
Shareholders: Daniel Patrick Sudbury; Joseph Thomas Fearnhead
Officers: Joseph Thomas Fearnhead [1981] Director; Alex Johnson [1981] Sales Director; Daniel Patrick Sudbury [1972] Director

Altarnun Brewing Limited
Incorporated: 18 October 2016
Net Worth: £38,234 *Total Assets:* £89,545
Registered Office: Inner Trenarrett, Altarnun, Launceston, Cornwall, PL15 7SY
Shareholder: Joseph Thomson
Officers: Stephen Anthony Medlicott [1964] Director/Farmer; Joseph Thomson [1986] Director/Brewer

Alter Ego Brewing Co Ltd
Incorporated: 26 January 2018
Registered Office: 3 Rays Avenue, Heanor, Derbys, DE75 7GN
Major Shareholder: Matthew Makins
Officers: Matthew Makins [1983] Director

Amber Ales Limited
Incorporated: 9 May 2005
Net Worth Deficit: £54,727 *Total Assets:* £73,304
Registered Office: The Mill, Pentrich Lane End, Ripley, Derbys, DE5 3RH
Major Shareholder: Peter Neil Hounsell
Officers: Elizabeth Jane Hounsell [1965] Director; Peter Neil Hounsell [1966] Director

Ampersand Brew Co Ltd
Incorporated: 17 January 2017
Net Worth Deficit: £18,290 *Total Assets:* £72,051
Registered Office: Great Green Farm, Norwich Road, Denton, Harleston, Norfolk, IP20 0BB
Shareholders: Andrew James Hipwell; Adrian Paul Hipwell
Officers: Adrian Paul Hipwell [1958] Director/Farmer; Andrew James Hipwell [1985] Director/Estimator

Ampthill & Woburn Brewery Limited
Incorporated: 10 June 2015
Net Worth: £25,023 *Total Assets:* £29,711
Registered Office: Unit D, The Sidings, Station Road, Ampthill, Beds, MK45 2QY
Officers: Christopher John Kelly [1976] Director; Marisa Riette Kirchner [1978] Director [British/South African]

Amwell Springs Brewery Company Limited
Incorporated: 19 July 2017
Net Worth Deficit: £6,347 *Total Assets:* £33,156
Registered Office: Westfield Farm House, Westfield Road, Cholsey, Wallingford, Oxon, OX10 9LS
Officers: Andrew William Gibbons [1982] Director; David Ernest Gibbons [1951] Director; Michael David Gibbons [1979] Director; Thomas James Hammond [1982] Director; Darren Rudkin Pavitt [1967] Director

Anarchy Brew Co. Limited
Incorporated: 17 August 2011 *Employees:* 14
Net Worth: £38,269 *Total Assets:* £293,533
Registered Office: Unit 5 A & B, The Whitehouse Farm Centre Stannington, Morpeth, Northumberland, NE61 6AW
Shareholders: Simon Miles; Dawn Miles
Officers: Dawn Miles, Secretary; Dawn Miles [1967] Director; Simon Miles [1966] Managing Director

Anchor Brewery Ltd
Incorporated: 28 February 2011
Registered Office: 23 North Bar Without, Beverley, E Yorks, HU17 7AG
Major Shareholder: Guy Stuart Falkingham
Officers: Susan Falkingham, Secretary; Guy Stuart Falkingham [1960] Director/Consultant; Susan Falkingham [1953] Director/Teacher

Andwell Brewing Company Ltd
Incorporated: 29 July 2016
Net Worth: £585,554 *Total Assets:* £749,851
Registered Office: Global House, 303 Ballards Lane, London, N12 8NP
Parent: Gandhi Wine Suppliers Limited
Officers: Richard Geoffrey Martin [1954] Director/Consultant; Kaushik Amritlal Mody [1957] Director

Andys' Ales Limited
Incorporated: 31 July 2017
Registered Office: First Floor, Black Country House, Rounds Green Road, Oldbury, W Midlands, B69 2DG
Officers: Andrew Ince [1979] Director; Andrew Lee Williams [1975] Director; Michael John Williams [1947] Director

Angel Ales Limited
Incorporated: 17 June 2010 *Employees:* 1
Net Worth: £14,990 *Total Assets:* £21,932
Registered Office: Old Bank Buildings, Upper High Street, Cradley Heath, W Midlands, B64 5HY
Major Shareholder: Andrew John Kirk
Officers: Andrew John Kirk [1957] Director

The Angel Brewery Company Limited
Incorporated: 7 September 2007
Net Worth: £100 *Total Assets:* £100
Registered Office: The Chapel, Silver Street, Witcham, Ely, Cambs, CB6 2LF
Parent: Craft and Artisan Group Limited
Officers: Charles Henry Fairpo [1968] Director/Consultant

Angles Ales Limited
Incorporated: 24 March 2016
Net Worth Deficit: £14,158 *Total Assets:* £51,134
Registered Office: 22 Annesley Close, Sawtry, Huntingdon, Cambs, PE28 5RN
Shareholders: Paul Kenneth Dickinson; Nicholas Vaughan Ashley
Officers: Dr Nicholas Vaughan Ashley [1953] Director/Consultant; Paul Kenneth Dickinson [1956] Director/Marketing Consultant

Anglesey Ales Ltd
Incorporated: 16 September 2014
Net Worth Deficit: £17,190 *Total Assets:* £32,810
Registered Office: 12c Ash Court, Ffordd Y Llyn, Parc Menai, Bangor, Gwynedd, LL57 4DF
Major Shareholder: Karen Elizabeth Chadwick
Officers: Karen Elizabeth Chadwick [1955] Director/Housewife

Anglia Pub Company Limited
Incorporated: 18 April 1997 *Employees:* 30
Net Worth Deficit: £95,091 *Total Assets:* £102,412
Registered Office: Bear Inn, Tostock Road, Beyton, Bury St Edmunds, Suffolk, IP30 9AG
Major Shareholder: Garry John Clark
Officers: Garry John Clark [1956] Director

Angry Coot Fermentation Company Ltd.
Incorporated: 22 September 2016
Registered Office: Flat 35, Tequila Wharf, 681 Commercial Road, London, E14 7LG
Major Shareholder: Samuel Fraser Thomas
Officers: Samuel Fraser Thomas [1990] Director/Brewer

Angus Brewing Limited
Incorporated: 20 April 2017 *Employees:* 34
Net Worth: £712,974 *Total Assets:* £843,406
Registered Office: Dalhousie Estate Office, Brechin Castle, Brechin, Angus, DD9 6SG
Major Shareholder: Simon David Ramsay
Officers: Lord Simon David Ramsay [1981] Director/Farm Partner

Anheuser-Busch Europe Limited
Incorporated: 28 June 1989
Net Worth: £14,270,832,640 *Total Assets:* £14,835,154,944
Registered Office: Bureau, 90 Fetter Lane, London, EC4A 1EN
Parent: Anheuser-Busch InBev SA/NV
Officers: Kevin Jean-Frederic Douws [1982] Director [Belgian]; Sibil Jiang [1990] Director [Australian]; Stephen John Turner [1966] Director/Accountant

Anley Ales Limited
Incorporated: 13 December 2012
Previous: Siren Craft Brew Limited
Registered Office: 12-14 Carlton Place, Southampton, SO15 2EA
Parent: Siren Craft Brew Limited
Officers: Darron Anley [1970] Director; Joanne Anley [1974] Director

Annuity Ales Limited
Incorporated: 13 July 2011
Registered Office: 20 Woodland Drive, Wakefield, W Yorks, WF2 6DD
Major Shareholder: Matthew James Rippon
Officers: Matthew James Rippon [1980] Director

Another Beer Ltd
Incorporated: 19 February 2018
Registered Office: Flat 2, 2 Driffield Terrace, York, YO24 1EJ
Major Shareholder: James Fawcett
Officers: James Fawcett [1988] Director

Another Brewery Limited
Incorporated: 2 December 2015
Registered Office: 16 Cotham Road South, Bristol, BS6 5TZ
Parent: Fermenter Limited
Officers: Ross David French [1974] Director; Sarah Elisabeth Mildenhall [1982] Director

Anspach & Hobday Limited
Incorporated: 26 April 2012
Net Worth: £76,376 *Total Assets:* £205,698
Registered Office: 118 Druid Street, London, SE1 2HH
Shareholders: John Henly Hobday; Paul James Anspach
Officers: Paul James Anspach [1988] Director/Brewer; John Henly Hobday [1988] Director/Brewer

Anthology Brewing Company Ltd
Incorporated: 12 October 2017
Registered Office: 6 Bankfield Terrace, Leeds, LS4 2RE
Major Shareholder: Liam James Kane
Officers: Liam James Kane [1989] Director

Antic Brewing Limited
Incorporated: 11 November 2009
Registered Office: 77 Malham Road, Forest Hill, London, SE23 1AH
Major Shareholder: Anthony James Thomas
Officers: Anthony James Thomas [1970] Director

Appleby Brewery Ltd.
Incorporated: 21 July 2014 Employees: 2
Net Worth Deficit: £82,998 Total Assets: £17,937
Registered Office: Alex House, 260-268 Chapel Street, Salford, M3 5JZ
Officers: Richard Henry Charles Husbands [1969] Director

Applecross Brewing Company Limited
Incorporated: 16 September 2016
Net Worth: £134,774 Total Assets: £135,174
Registered Office: 5 Camusterrach Place, Camusterrach, Applecross, Strathcarron, Wester Ross, Highland, IV54 8LQ
Officers: Mark Robert Horsley, Secretary; Phil Buckley [1953] Director/Retired; Ewen Alexander Gillies [1964] Director/Engineer; Mark Robert Horsley [1959] Director/Bar Manager

Aquila Visum Ltd
Incorporated: 14 July 2011
Net Worth: £1,063 Total Assets: £22,813
Registered Office: Tithe Barn South, Church Hanborough, Witney, Oxon, OX29 8AA
Shareholders: Christian Matyas Gyuricza; Luciana Asson Sartorelli Gyuricza
Officers: Luciana Asson Sartorelli Gyuricza, Secretary; Christian Matyas Gyuricza [1975] Director/Business Analyst [Hungarian]

Ar Suil Brewing Project Limited
Incorporated: 24 May 2017
Registered Office: 14 Hillaries Road, Birmingham, B23 7QP
Major Shareholder: Donncha Burke
Officers: Donncha Burke [1988] Director/Founder/Head Brewer [Irish]

Arbor Ales Ltd
Incorporated: 2 August 2006 Employees: 12
Net Worth: £467,042 Total Assets: £948,246
Registered Office: Roadside Cottage, Caerwent, Caldicot, Monmouthshire, NP26 5AZ
Major Shareholder: Jonathan Hugh Comer
Officers: Ishka Megan Oliver, Secretary; Jonathan Hugh Comer [1973] Director/Brewer; Ishka Megan Oliver [1974] Director/Company Secretary

Arcadian Brewing Company Ltd
Incorporated: 17 November 2017
Registered Office: Arcadian Brewing Co The Bridge Studios, 454 Western Avenue, Cardiff, CF5 3BL
Shareholders: Kristy Durbridge; Bethan Millett
Officers: Kristy Durbridge [1981] Director/Brewer; Bethan Millett [1980] Director/Brewer

Archangel Brewing Ltd.
Incorporated: 19 March 2014
Net Worth: £363 Total Assets: £3,695
Registered Office: 8 Enniskillen Road, Cambridge, CB4 1SQ
Major Shareholder: Andrew James Edward Cleland
Officers: Andrew James Edward Cleland [1972] Director/Brewer

Ardgour Ales Ltd
Incorporated: 9 November 2012
Net Worth Deficit: £293 Total Assets: £31,766
Registered Office: The Old Manse, Ardgour, Fort William, Highland, PH33 7AH
Shareholders: Fergus Findlay Stokes; Elizabeth Stokes
Officers: Elizabeth Stokes [1962] Director/Housewife; Fergus Findlay Stokes [1959] Director/Chief Executive

Ards Brewing Company Ltd
Incorporated: 10 March 2011
Net Worth Deficit: £35,652 Total Assets: £54,486
Registered Office: 34b Carrowdore Road, Greyabbey, Newtownards, Co Down, BT22 2LX
Officers: Andrew Charles Ballantyne [1960] Director

Argyll Breweries Limited
Incorporated: 29 December 2010
Net Worth: £52,293 Total Assets: £58,579
Registered Office: Unit 8a Baliscate Industrial Estate, Tobermory, Isle of Mull, PA75 6QA
Officers: Derwyn Hewitt [1978] Director; Calum Eoghann MacLachlainn [1963] Director; Allan MacLean [1953] Director; Roderick Scott [1960] Director; Paul Gerard Sloan [1967] Director

Arkell's Brewery Limited
Incorporated: 28 December 1927 Employees: 251
Net Worth: £44,568,540 Total Assets: £70,877,672
Registered Office: Kingsdown, Upper Stratton, Swindon, Wilts, SN2 7RU
Officers: Emma Louise Defty, Secretary; Alexander Thomas Arkell [1985] Director/Head Brewer; George James Arkell [1978] Brewery Director; James Rixon Arkell [1951] Director/Chairman; Nicholas Henry Arkell [1955] Director of Brewery Co; Barry John Russell [1961] Director/Chartered Accountant

Arlingham Ales Limited
Incorporated: 27 June 2013
Registered Office: The Old Dairy, Church Road, Arlingham, Glos, GL2 7JL
Major Shareholder: Jonathan Mark Wilkinson
Officers: Michael James Lamerton [1975] Director/Surveyor; Jonathan Mark Wilkinson [1975] Director/Solicitor

Arnold and Hancock Limited
Incorporated: 20 March 2017
Registered Office: First Floor Office Suite, 1 The Crescent, Taunton, Somerset, TA1 4EA
Major Shareholder: Alison Louise Simpson
Officers: Alison Louise Simpson [1969] Director

Arran Brew Ltd.
Incorporated: 18 July 1997 Employees: 17
Net Worth: £32,714 Total Assets: £738,288
Registered Office: 100 Wellington Street, Glasgow, G2 6DH
Shareholder: Gerald Robert Michaluk
Officers: Generald Robert Michaluk, Secretary; Teresa Ballota [1958] Finance Director; Generald Robert Michaluk [1960] Director/Consultant; Malcolm Douglas Michaluk [1990] Director/Student; Veronica Michaluk [1989] Director/Student

Arran Brewery PLC
Incorporated: 13 August 2012 *Employees:* 17
Net Worth: £898,388 *Total Assets:* £1,608,927
Registered Office: 100 Wellington Street, Glasgow, G2 6DH
Major Shareholder: Gerald Robert Michaluk
Officers: Generall Michaluk, Secretary; Generall Robert Michaluk [1960] Managing Director; Veronica Michaluk [1989] Director/Brewery Manager; Nick Simon Pyne [1961] Director/Head of Engineering

Artisan Brewing Company Ltd
Incorporated: 19 April 2008
Net Worth: £111,245 *Total Assets:* £153,496
Registered Office: Ground Rear, 44b Clive Street, Cardiff, CF11 7JB
Major Shareholder: Simon Thomas Doherty
Officers: Simon Thomas Doherty [1979] Director

Arundel Brewery Limited
Incorporated: 19 November 1992 *Employees:* 8
Net Worth Deficit: £33,812 *Total Assets:* £251,002
Registered Office: Unit C7, Ford Airfield Estate, Arundel, W Sussex, BN18 0HY
Major Shareholder: Stuart Daniel Walker
Officers: Stuart Daniel Walker, Secretary; Jeremy Owen [1960] Director; Stuart Daniel Walker [1967] Director

Ascent Location Solutions Ltd
Incorporated: 3 April 2018
Registered Office: Meadow Lodge, Mampitts Road, Shaftesbury, Dorset, SP7 8PG
Officers: Michael Eric John Crockett [1983] Director

Ascot Ales Limited
Incorporated: 19 January 2007
Net Worth Deficit: £14,634 *Total Assets:* £28,730
Registered Office: Sterling House, 5 Buckingham Place, Bellfield Road West, High Wycombe, Bucks, HP13 5HQ
Officers: Timothy Steven Bittleston [1958] Director; Christopher Davies [1952] Commercial Director; Michael John Neame [1961] Director/Accountant; Stephen Wells [1978] Director

Ashen Clough Ales Ltd
Incorporated: 4 January 2019
Registered Office: Ashen Clough, Maynestone Road, Chinley, High Peak, Derbys, SK23 6AH
Major Shareholder: Adrian Brian Porteous
Officers: Adrian Brian Porteous [1965] Director/Brewer

Ashley Down Brewery Limited
Incorporated: 17 September 2009
Net Worth: £1,498 *Total Assets:* £10,259
Registered Office: 15 Wathen Road, Bristol, BS6 5BY
Major Shareholder: Vincent Crocker
Officers: Vincent Crocker [1962] Director

Ashover Brewery Limited
Incorporated: 16 February 2012 *Employees:* 5
Net Worth: £47,072 *Total Assets:* £186,209
Registered Office: Unit 1 Kershaw Building, Derby Road Business Park, Clay Cross, Chesterfield, Derbys, S45 9AG
Officers: Jacqueline Jane Beresford, Secretary; Jacqueline Jane Beresford [1963] Director/Public Houses & Bar Owner; Kim Shaun Beresford [1960] Director/Public Houses & Bar Owner; Janine Shorrock [1981] Director/Brewery Owner; Roy David Alan Shorrock [1953] Director/Brewery Owner

Askham Brewery Limited
Incorporated: 16 April 2018
Registered Office: 453 Blackburn Road, Turton, Bolton, Lancs, BL7 0PW
Major Shareholder: Ian Brown
Officers: Eileen Brown [1952] Director/Retired; Ian Brown [1953] Director/Retired

Aston Manor Limited
Incorporated: 15 February 1983 *Employees:* 299
Previous: Aston Manor Brewery Company Limited
Net Worth: £28,624,414 *Total Assets:* £55,704,092
Registered Office: Deykin Avenue, Birmingham, B6 7BH
Officers: James Douglas Ellis, Secretary; James Douglas Ellis [1978] Director; Yves Jacobs [1963] Director [French]; Gordon Paul Hazell Johncox [1961] Managing Director; Marc Roubaud [1958] Director/General Manager [French]; Ludovic Spiers [1960] Director [French]

Asylum Harbour Brewing Co Limited
Incorporated: 6 October 2017
Registered Office: Holly Rise, 7 Raincliffe Avenue, Scarborough, N Yorks, YO12 5BU
Shareholders: Julian Edward Holloway; Roger Smith
Officers: Julian Edward Holloway [1973] Director/Head Landfill Commercials; Dr Roger Smith [1969] Director/Doctor

The Atlantic Craft Soda Company Ltd
Incorporated: 15 March 2016
Net Worth Deficit: £11,670 *Total Assets:* £2,472
Registered Office: 38 Middlehill Road, Colehill, Wimborne, Dorset, BH21 2SE
Major Shareholder: Gerard Brendan Gaughan
Officers: Felicity Jane Gaughan [1965] Finance Director; Gerard Brendan Gaughan [1966] Director/Management Consultant

Atlas Brewery Limited
Incorporated: 5 June 2006
Registered Office: Sinclair Breweries Ltd, Cawdor, Nairn, IV12 5XP
Major Shareholder: Norman Sinclair
Officers: Christine Sinclair, Secretary; Norman James Anderson Sinclair [1961] Director/Brewery Owner

Atom Brewing Co Limited
Incorporated: 25 June 2012
Net Worth: £25,019 *Total Assets:* £190,136
Registered Office: Unit 4 Food & Drink Park, Malmo Road, Sutton Fields Industrial Estate West, Hull, HU7 0YF
Shareholders: Allan Edward Rice; Sarah Jill Thackray
Officers: Allan Edward Rice [1980] Director; Dr Sarah Thackray [1982] Director

Attic Brew Co. Ltd
Incorporated: 11 April 2018
Registered Office: Unit 3r2 Maryvale Road Business Park, 29b Maryvale Road, Stirchley, Birmingham, B30 2DA
Major Shareholder: Samuel Back
Officers: Samuel Back [1991] Director/Brewer; Oliver James Hurlow [1991] Director/Brewer

Aurora Ales Limited
Incorporated: 11 August 2016
Net Worth: £24,409 *Total Assets:* £25,500
Registered Office: 98 Church Street, Ilkeston, Derbys, DE7 8QG
Officers: Gillian Derbyshire, Secretary; Trevor James Bishop [1952] Director/Brewing; Mark Wayne Derbyshire [1963] Director/Brewing

Aussie Brewing Company Ltd
Incorporated: 13 March 2017
Registered Office: 31c Richmond Avenue, London, N1 0NB
Shareholders: Russell David Watson; Anmol Bedi
Officers: Russell David Watson [1984] Director/Brewer [Australian]

Avid Brewing Co. Ltd
Incorporated: 26 August 2015 *Employees:* 2
Net Worth Deficit: £17,944 *Total Assets:* £57,185
Registered Office: 29 Jepps Avenue, Barton, Preston, Lancs, PR3 5AS
Shareholders: David Coss; Alan Thomas Rainford
Officers: David Cross [1970] Director/IT Consultant; Alan Rainford [1971] Director/Headmaster

Avitas Craft Beer Ltd
Incorporated: 29 November 2018
Registered Office: Unit 9, 109 East Street, London, SE17 2SB
Major Shareholder: Stuart David Morgan
Officers: Stuart David Morgan [1990] Director

Avocet Ales Limited
Incorporated: 31 October 2018
Registered Office: The Exeter Brewery, Cowley Bridge Road, Exeter, EX4 5AD
Major Shareholder: Alan Anthony Collyer
Officers: Alan Anthony Collyer [1957] Director/Brewer

Axholme Brewing Company Limited
Incorporated: 13 September 2013
Net Worth: £5,637 *Total Assets:* £66,979
Registered Office: 26 South St Marys Gate, Grimsby, N E Lincs, DN31 1LW
Officers: William Douglas [1972] Director; Charles Lumley [1980] Director/Shop Owner and Analyst; Julie Richards [1975] Director/Brewer; Michael Richards [1982] Director/Brewer; Shahram Paul Shadan [1987] Director

B & T Brewery Limited
Incorporated: 16 December 1993 *Employees:* 18
Net Worth Deficit: £17,466 *Total Assets:* £412,828
Registered Office: 43 Manchester Street, London, W1U 7LP
Shareholders: Martin Leigh Ayres; Michel Andre Desquesnes
Officers: Lesley Cheryl Follington, Secretary; Martin Leigh Ayres [1949] Director/Brewer; Michel Andre Desquesnes [1948] Director/Brewer

BAA Brewing Limited
Incorporated: 8 October 2015
Net Worth Deficit: £16,941 *Total Assets:* £102,475
Registered Office: Unit 4 Station Yard Industrial Estate, Station Road, Chepstow, Monmouthshire, NP16 5PF
Officers: Charles Lewin Heaven [1977] Director/Manager; Sian Elizabeth Heaven [1978] Director/PA; James Howard Langworth [1973] Director/Manager; Juliette Langworth [1973] Director/PA; Julian Robert Powell [1973] Director/Business Manager; Victoria Powell [1975] Director/Nurse

The Backyard Brewhouse Limited
Incorporated: 13 September 2010 *Employees:* 5
Net Worth: £75,597 *Total Assets:* £226,188
Registered Office: Unit 8a Gatehouse Trading Estate, Lichfield Road, Brownhills, Walsall, W Midlands, WS8 6JZ
Major Shareholder: Austen James Morgan
Officers: Austen James Morgan [1972] Director

Bad Boy Brewing Ltd
Incorporated: 9 March 2018
Registered Office: Twelve Thirty, Taggs Island, Hampton, Surrey, TW12 2HA
Shareholders: Paul Haslam; Connor Declan Earley
Officers: Connor Declan Earley [1976] Director [Irish]; Paul Haslam [1980] Director

Bad Girls Brew Limited
Incorporated: 7 November 2017
Registered Office: 22a Thorney Crescent, London, SW11 3TT
Major Shareholder: Barbara Elizabeth Gorna
Officers: Barbara Elizabeth Gorna, Secretary; Barbara Elizabeth Gorna [1955] Director

Bad Joke Brew Co. Ltd.
Incorporated: 13 April 2017
Net Worth: £3,462 *Total Assets:* £3,462
Registered Office: Unit 2C(A) Penn Street Works, Penn Street, Amersham, Bucks, HP7 0PX
Shareholders: Jessica Lucy Bailey; James Phillip Cross
Officers: Jessica Lucy Bailey [1992] Director/Brewer; James Phillip Cross [1993] Director/Brewer

Bad Moon Brewery Ltd
Incorporated: 17 May 2018
Registered Office: 12 Hoyle Fold, Sunderland, Tyne & Wear, SR3 2TT
Officers: Josh Paul Moon [1997] Director/Student

Bad Seed Brewery Ltd
Incorporated: 12 March 2013
Net Worth: £34,103 *Total Assets:* £134,514
Registered Office: 17a Yorkersgate, Malton, N Yorks, YO17 7AA
Shareholders: Christopher Michael Waplington; James Cameron Broad
Officers: James Cameron Broad [1986] Director; Christopher Michael Waplington [1983] Director

Badger Ales Limited
Incorporated: 31 October 1974
Net Worth: £365,699 *Total Assets:* £387,421
Registered Office: The Brewery, Blandford St Mary, Dorset, DT11 9LS
Parent: Hall & Woodhouse Limited
Officers: Marianne Susie Jarvis, Secretary; Michael James Owen [1970] Finance Director; Anthony William Woodhouse [1965] Director; Mark John Michael Woodhouse [1955] Director

Badwells Brewery Ltd
Incorporated: 16 January 2018
Registered Office: 7 Manchester Way, St Ives, Cambs, PE27 3DG
Major Shareholder: Lee Badwell
Officers: Lee Badwell [1996] Director/Owner

Baird Brewing Company Ltd
Incorporated: 15 November 2018
Registered Office: The Byre, Halket Holm, Halket Road, Lugton, Kilmarnock, E Ayrshire, KA3 4EE
Major Shareholder: Kevin Paul Brown
Officers: Kevin Paul Brown [1957] Director/Quantity Surveyor

Baker's Dozen Brewing Co Limited
Incorporated: 20 January 2015
Net Worth Deficit: £20,478 *Total Assets:* £47,525
Registered Office: 69 Main Road, Collyweston, Stamford, Lincs, PE9 3PQ
Shareholders: Jill Frances Perkins; Dean Matthew Baker
Officers: Dean Matthew Baker [1975] Director/Publican; Jill Frances Perkins [1980] Director/Publican

Bakewell Road Brewery Ltd
Incorporated: 24 August 2018
Registered Office: The Woodlands, Bakewell Road, Matlock, Derbys, DE4 3AU
Shareholders: David Stuart Walsh; Cathy Walsh
Officers: Cathy Walsh [1978] Director; David Stuart Walsh [1978] Director

Ballard's Brewery Limited
Incorporated: 10 June 1980 *Employees:* 3
Net Worth: £89,722 *Total Assets:* £156,208
Registered Office: Cumbers Farm, Rogate, Petersfield, Hants, GU31 5DB
Major Shareholder: Harriet Lindsay Brown
Officers: Carola Jane Brown [1951] Managing Director

Baltic Beer Company Ltd
Incorporated: 19 January 2004
Net Worth: £4,834 *Total Assets:* £349,130
Registered Office: 62 Wilson Street, London, EC2A 2BU
Shareholders: Paul Baxendale; Baltic Brand Development Corporation
Officers: Paul Baxendale, Secretary/Director; Paul Baxendale [1962] Director; Alex Klaos [1965] Director [Estonian]

Baltic Fleet Brewery Limited
Incorporated: 15 June 2010 *Employees:* 1
Net Worth Deficit: £474 *Total Assets:* £26
Registered Office: 1 Mortimer Street, Birkenhead, Merseyside, CH41 5EU
Officers: Julie Ann Broome, Secretary; Simon Nicholas Holt [1967] Director/Brewer

Bang The Elephant Brewing Co Ltd
Incorporated: 1 September 2017
Registered Office: 17 Craig Street, Long Eaton, Nottingham, NG10 1ET
Shareholders: Nigel Patton; Michael Shipman
Officers: Nigel Patton, Secretary; Michael Shipman, Secretary; Nigel Patton [1978] Director/Master Brewer; Michael Shipman [1982] Director/Master Brewer

Bang-On Brewery Limited
Incorporated: 11 January 2016 *Employees:* 2
Net Worth Deficit: £86,453 *Total Assets:* £100,977
Registered Office: Unit 3 George Street, Bridgend, Industrial Estate, Bridgend, Mid Glamorgan, CF31 3TS
Major Shareholder: Neil Peter Randle
Officers: Neil Peter Randle [1974] Director

Bank Top Brewery Limited
Incorporated: 5 February 2004 *Employees:* 12
Net Worth: £242,437 *Total Assets:* £324,027
Registered Office: The Pavilion, Ashworth Lane, Bank Top, Bolton, Lancs, BL1 8RA
Shareholders: Sharn David Sweeney; Angela Sweeney
Officers: Angela Sweeney, Secretary; Angela Sweeney [1964] Director; Sharn David Sweeney [1964] Director/Brewer

Barearts Ltd
Incorporated: 9 February 2009
Net Worth Deficit: £140,345 *Total Assets:* £14,933
Registered Office: 110 Rochdale Road, Todmorden, Lancs, OL14 7LP
Major Shareholder: Kathryn Cook
Officers: Kathryn Cook [1966] Director

Barefaced Brewing Ltd
Incorporated: 20 September 2017
Registered Office: 48 West Borough, Wimborne, Dorset, BH21 1NQ
Shareholders: Thomas Albert Cooper; Nicholas James Horne
Officers: Thomas Albert Cooper [1989] Managing Director; Laura Aileen Green [1984] Director; Nicholas James Horne [1990] Director

Barlow Brewery Limited
Incorporated: 9 May 2007 *Employees:* 1
Net Worth: £4,810 *Total Assets:* £11,626
Registered Office: 41 Clarence Road, Chesterfield, Derbys, S40 1LH
Major Shareholder: Glyn Paul Sanderson
Officers: Glyn Paul Sanderson [1960] Director

Alex Barlow Brewing Consulting Ltd
Incorporated: 22 December 2017
Registered Office: 95 Harcourt Road, Sheffield, S10 1DH
Officers: Alex Gavin Barlow [1965] Director/Brewer

Barnaby's Brewhouse Ltd
Incorporated: 13 January 2016
Net Worth Deficit: £59,653 *Total Assets:* £32,695
Registered Office: The Old Stable, Hole Farm, Staverton, Devon, TQ11 0LA
Shareholders: Tim Stacey; Edward Barnaby Harris
Officers: Edward Barnaby Harris [1963] Director/Brewer; Tim Stacey [1964] Director/Brewer

Barney's Beer Limited
Incorporated: 28 February 2012
Net Worth: £111,589 *Total Assets:* £262,055
Registered Office: Springfield House, Laurelhill Business Park, Stirling, FK7 9JQ
Major Shareholder: Andrew Roger Barnett
Officers: Andrew Roger Barnett [1966] Director/Brewer

Barngates Brewery Limited
Incorporated: 5 July 1999 *Employees:* 3
Net Worth: £60,424 *Total Assets:* £78,179
Registered Office: Birbeck House, Duke Street, Penrith, Cumbria, CA11 7NA
Parent: The Duck at Barngates Limited
Officers: Stephanie Jane Henderson Barton [1955] Director/Buyer

Baronscourt Brewing Company Ltd
Incorporated: 22 January 2018
Registered Office: 38 Baronscourt Road, Newtownstewart, Omagh, Co Tyrone, BT78 4EY
Major Shareholder: Matthew John Wauchob
Officers: Matthew John Wauchob, Secretary; Adam Colhoun [1993] Director/Building Supervisor; Matthew John Wauchob [1983] Director/Farmer

Barrell & Sellers Limited
Incorporated: 5 September 2011
Net Worth Deficit: £72,784 *Total Assets:* £15,119
Registered Office: Spring Farm Mendham Lane, St Cross South Elmham, Harleston, Norfolk, IP20 0NZ
Shareholder: Martin Barrell
Officers: Martin Barrell [1960] Director/Brewer; Margaret Amanda Sellers [1959] Director

The Barrels Hereford Limited
Incorporated: 15 May 2017 *Employees:* 20
Net Worth: £47,788 *Total Assets:* £237,528
Registered Office: The Oakley, Kidderminster Road, Droitwich, Worcs, WR9 9AY
Shareholders: Francesca Amor; Peter William Amor
Officers: Peter William Amor [1946] Director

The Barsham Brewery Limited
Incorporated: 8 May 2017
Net Worth Deficit: £15,935 *Total Assets:* £44,665
Registered Office: Greenwood House, Greenwood Court, Bury St Edmunds, Suffolk, IP32 7GY
Shareholders: Susanna Soames; Archibald Christopher Winston Soames
Officers: James Prideaux [1954] Director; Archibald Christopher Winston Soames [1988] Director; Susanna Soames [1952] Director

Bartleby's Ltd
Incorporated: 1 June 2012
Net Worth Deficit: £24,892 *Total Assets:* £15,711
Registered Office: 9 Islingword Road, Brighton, BN2 9SE
Officers: Matthew Charles Naish [1976] Director/Pay and Reward Manager; Matthew James Wilson [1977] Director/Brewer

Barton House Brewing Company Limited
Incorporated: 25 November 2010
Net Worth: £39,370 *Total Assets:* £43,551
Registered Office: Barton House, Stowford, Lewdown, Okehampton, Devon, EX20 4BZ
Shareholders: David John Slocombe; Sarah Louise Slocombe
Officers: Sarah Slocombe, Secretary; David John Slocombe [1974] Director

Bason Bridge Brewing Company Ltd
Incorporated: 7 February 2018
Registered Office: Unit 2 Church Road, Bason Bridge, Highbridge, Somerset, TA9 4RG
Major Shareholder: Timothy Edward Cullum
Officers: Timothy Edward Cullum [1969] Director

Batch Brew Ltd
Incorporated: 7 November 2011 *Employees:* 6
Net Worth: £110,013 *Total Assets:* £276,600
Registered Office: Batch Brew, Coal Clough Lane, Unit 10 Habgerham Mill, Burnley, Lancs, BB11 5BS
Shareholders: Philip Whitwell; Philip Whitwell
Officers: Paul Anthony Hancock, Secretary; Philip Whitwell [1971] Director of Product Strategy

George Bateman & Son Limited
Incorporated: 23 July 1928 *Employees:* 101
Net Worth: £18,917,072 *Total Assets:* £25,884,940
Registered Office: Salem Bridge Brewery, Mill Lane, Wainfleet, Lincs, PE24 4JE
Officers: Jaclyn Carol Bateman [1957] Marketing Director; Stuart George Carson Bateman [1960] Managing Director (Trading); Haydn Biddle [1946] Director/Chairman; John Derek Else [1944] Director/Consultant; Ian William Furniss [1962] Finance Director; Jeffrey Philip Moore [1954] Director; Stephen John Oliver [1958] Director

Daniel Batham & Son Limited
Incorporated: 14 May 1942 *Employees:* 111
Net Worth: £14,150,298 *Total Assets:* £15,705,189
Registered Office: 10a The Delph, Brierley Hill, W Midlands, DY5 2TN
Shareholders: Timothy Arthur Joseph Batham; Matthew Daniel Batham
Officers: Dorothy Jean Batham, Secretary; Dorothy Jean Batham [1932] Director/Company Secretary; Matthew Daniel Batham [1969] Director; Timothy Arthur Joseph Batham [1958] Director/Brewer

Bathams (Delph) Limited
Incorporated: 11 June 1980 *Employees:* 111
Net Worth: £980,281 *Total Assets:* £1,857,679
Registered Office: The Delph, Brierley Hill, W Midlands, DY5 2TN
Shareholders: Timothy Arthur Joseph Batham; Matthew Daniel Batham
Officers: Dorothy Jean Batham, Secretary; Dorothy Jean Batham [1932] Director/Company Secretary; Matthew Daniel Batham [1969] Director/Manager; Timothy Arthur Joseph Batham [1958] Director/Brewer

The Battersea Brewery Company Limited
Incorporated: 8 December 2000
Registered Office: Spencer Cottage, Upham, Southampton, SO32 1JD
Major Shareholder: Stephen Lindsay Nockolds
Officers: Stephen Lindsay Nockolds [1964] Director/Accountant

Battery Brewing Ltd
Incorporated: 21 August 2018
Registered Office: 6 Lochnagar Road, Torry, Aberdeen, AB11 8SX
Shareholders: James Iain Moir; Iain Alexander Moir
Officers: Iain Alexander Moir [1963] Director/Mechanic; James Iain Moir [1993] Director/Retail

Battle Brewery Limited
Incorporated: 24 January 2018
Registered Office: Linden House, Linden Close, Tunbridge Wells, Kent, TN4 8HH
Officers: Joanna Dudman [1972] Director; Robert William Dudman [1973] Director; Greg Templeman [1977] Director; Rachel Templeman [1976] Director

Bavarian Gold Limited
Incorporated: 7 November 2013 *Employees:* 2
Net Worth: £59,035 *Total Assets:* £89,370
Registered Office: 303 Global House, Ballards Lane, London, N12 8NP
Shareholders: Kaushik Amritlal Mody; Patrick Greier
Officers: Patrick Greier [1984] Director [Dutch]; Kaushik Amritlal Mody [1957] Director

Bay View Brewery Limited
Incorporated: 23 June 2014 *Employees:* 5
Net Worth: £2,257 *Total Assets:* £83,677
Registered Office: Panteg Farm, Maenygroes, New Quay, Dyfed, SA45 9TL
Shareholders: John Jason Howarth; Lisa Jane Angela Howarth
Officers: John Jason Howarth, Secretary; John Jason Howarth [1970] Director; Lisa Jane Angela Howarth [1973] Director

Baynhams Brewery Limited
Incorporated: 6 February 2017
Net Worth: £20,000 *Total Assets:* £45,813
Registered Office: Hops House, Lymington Road, Brockenhurst, Hants, SO42 7UF
Shareholders: Thomas Roland James Baynham; Lawrence Peter Stewart Baynham; Henry Roland Atton Baynham
Officers: Thomas Roland James Baynham, Secretary; Henry Roland Atton Baynham [1992] Director; Lawrence Peter Stewart Baynham [1989] Director; Thomas Roland James Baynham [1983] Director

Bays Brewery Limited
Incorporated: 14 August 2006 *Employees:* 17
Net Worth: £461,849 *Total Assets:* £1,134,355
Registered Office: Sigma House, Oak View Close, Edginswell Park, Torquay, Devon, TQ2 7FF
Shareholder: Mark Stephen Salmon
Officers: Melanie Anne Freeland, Secretary; William James Henry Freeland [1972] Director/Brewer; Mark Stephen Salmon [1975] Director; Peter David James Salmon [1981] Sales Director

BC Brewing & Pub Company Ltd
Incorporated: 8 January 2014
Net Worth Deficit: £115,696 *Total Assets:* £76,391
Registered Office: Six Bells Pub & Brewery, Church Street, Bishops Castle, Salop, SY9 5AA
Shareholders: John David Stradling; Mary Stradling
Officers: John David Stradling [1956] Director/Brewery Operator; Mary Stradling [1961] Director/Publican & IT Program Manager

BCM Brewing Company Ltd
Incorporated: 15 February 2019
Registered Office: Hayles Bridge Offices, 228 Mulgrave Road, Cheam, Surrey, SM2 6JT
Officers: David Richard Johnson [1972] Director; Lesley Edna Meeson [1977] Director; Rosalyn Porter [1957] Director; Stephen John Porter [1955] Director

The Beak Brewery Limited
Incorporated: 17 December 2018
Registered Office: 16 Priory Street, Lewes, E Sussex, BN7 1HH
Major Shareholder: Daniel Alexander Tapper
Officers: Daniel Alexander Tapper [1984] Director

Bear Brewery Co Ltd
Incorporated: 4 April 2014
Net Worth: £11,009 *Total Assets:* £11,109
Registered Office: The Ridge, 3 Shadyhanger, Godalming, Surrey, GU7 2HR
Shareholders: Hemaxi Natu; Nimmitha de Silva
Officers: Nimmitha de Silva [1963] Director/Operations Manager [Czech]

Bear's Head Brewery Limited
Incorporated: 27 April 2017
Registered Office: 17 Fransfield Grove, Sydenham, London, SE26 6BA
Major Shareholder: Phillip John Goode
Officers: Phillip John Goode [1960] Director/Self Employed

Beardyman Brewery Limited
Incorporated: 20 March 2014
Registered Office: 80 Onslow Gardens, London, E18 1NB
Major Shareholder: Arjun Fyron Mahendran
Officers: Arjun Fyron Mahendran [1988] Director

The Bears Den Brewery Limited
Incorporated: 20 January 2016
Registered Office: 136 Queens Avenue, Watford, Herts, WD18 7NT
Shareholders: Richard Mark Elliott; Gareth James Cobley
Officers: Gareth Cobley [1985] Director/Micro Brewery; Richard Mark Elliott [1985] Director/Micro Brewery

Beat Ales Ltd.
Incorporated: 14 March 2016 *Employees:* 1
Net Worth: £1 *Total Assets:* £32,514
Registered Office: 42 Glebe Street, Loughborough, Leics, LE11 1JR
Major Shareholder: Jack Pike
Officers: Rachel Hunt [1991] Director; Ricky John Hunt [1959] Director/Engineer; Michael William Rogers [1960] Director/Operations Manager; Christopher Willacy [1988] Director

Beathbrewing Ltd
Incorporated: 7 January 2016
Net Worth Deficit: £4,714 *Total Assets:* £19,454
Registered Office: The Rectory, Foulford Road, Cowdenbeath, Fife, KY4 9AP
Major Shareholder: Ian Denis McGrath
Officers: Ian Denis McGrath [1974] Director/Brewer [Irish]

Beatnikz Republic Brewing Company Ltd
Incorporated: 5 January 2015 *Employees:* 8
Net Worth: £3,033 *Total Assets:* £32,745
Registered Office: Unit 15 Red Bank Court, Manchester, M4 4HF
Major Shareholder: Paul Greetham
Officers: Paul William Greetham [1983] Director

The Beauty and The Beer Limited
Incorporated: 23 October 2017
Registered Office: 27 Balfour Avenue, London, W7 3HS
Officers: Anna Katherine McCarthy [1992] Business Director

Beavertown Brewery Ltd
Incorporated: 14 July 2011 *Employees:* 91
Net Worth: £3,024,902 *Total Assets:* £6,666,542
Registered Office: Unit 17 & 18 Lockwood Industrial Estate, Mill Mead Road, London, N17 9PQ
Parent: TP & Munch Limited
Officers: Adam David Gregory [1978] Finance Director; Logan Romero Plant [1979] Director/Food and Beverage

Beckenham Brewery Ltd.
Incorporated: 31 May 2016
Registered Office: 38 Oakwood Avenue, Beckenham, Kent, BR3 6PJ
Officers: Peter McKay [1952] Director/Publisher; Thomas Simpson [1961] Director/Civil Servant

Beckstones Brewery Limited
Incorporated: 24 February 2015
Net Worth: £13,239 *Total Assets:* £28,970
Registered Office: Upper Beckstones Mill, The Green, Millom, Cumbria, LA18 5HL
Shareholders: Adrian Paul Smith; Jill Smith
Officers: Holly Faye Smith [1995] Director/Administrator; David Taylor [1947] Director/Brewer

Bedlam Brewery Limited
Incorporated: 18 February 2011 *Employees:* 6
Net Worth: £519,115 *Total Assets:* £609,949
Registered Office: The Brewery, St Helena Farm, St Helena Lane, Plumpton, E Sussex, BN7 3DH
Officers: Dr Nicholas John Cooper [1967] Director; Robert Andrew Emms [1967] Director; Ian Mark Hawkins [1962] Director/Accounts Manager; James O'Connor [1969] Director; Tom Oakley Robinson [1971] Director; Robert James Shepherd [1966] Director; Dominic Christian Worrall [1971] Director

The Beer Belly Brewery Limited
Incorporated: 18 October 2017
Registered Office: 12 Devereux Road, Southend on Sea, Essex, SS1 1DR
Major Shareholder: James Michael Paul Parry
Officers: James Michael Paul Parry [1978] Director

Beer Brothers Ltd
Incorporated: 19 January 2015
Net Worth: £78,248 *Total Assets:* £95,153
Registered Office: 335 Ranglet Road, Walton Summit Centre, Preston, Lancs, PR5 8AR
Shareholders: Neil Richards; Caroline Leyland; David Elliot Reece
Officers: David Elliot Reece [1983] Director/HSE Manager

The Beer Collective Limited
Incorporated: 5 March 2015 *Employees:* 3
Net Worth Deficit: £136,121 *Total Assets:* £201,043
Registered Office: The Old Casino, 28 Fourth Avenue, Hove, E Sussex, BN3 2PJ
Parent: The Pink Ferry Ltd
Officers: Justin Lance Deighton [1970] Director; Nicola Ruth Deighton [1970] Director; Paul William Frederick Kempe [1957] Director; Michael James Penkethman [1964] Director

The Beer Engineer Ltd
Incorporated: 30 June 2014
Registered Office: 186 Dundridge Lane, Bristol, BS5 8SX
Major Shareholder: Christopher Payze
Officers: Christopher Payze [1980] Director/Chartered Engineer

Beer Hut Brewing Company Ltd
Incorporated: 9 January 2017
Net Worth: £17,780 *Total Assets:* £17,780
Registered Office: 6 Riverside Park, Kilkeel, Co Down, BT34 4NA
Shareholder: Neil Chambers
Officers: Neil Chambers, Secretary; Andrew Alan McBride [1985] Director/Joiner

Beer in the Blood Ltd
Incorporated: 27 April 2018
Registered Office: 1 Diamond Cottages, Green Road, Wivelsfield Green, Haywards Heath, W Sussex, RH17 7QA
Shareholders: Richard James Mathews; Thomas Charles Mathews
Officers: Richard James Mathews [1977] Director/Driver; Thomas Charles Mathews [1983] Director/Barman

Beer Ink Limited
Incorporated: 16 March 2016
Net Worth Deficit: £19,588 *Total Assets:* £1,384
Registered Office: Plover Road Garage, Plover Road, Lindley, Huddersfield, W Yorks, HD3 3PJ
Major Shareholder: Ryan Stoppard
Officers: Diane Lesley Stoppard [1962] Director/Brewery; Ryan Stoppard [1990] Director/Brewer

Beer Monkey Brew Co. Limited
Incorporated: 10 May 2017
Registered Office: Units 3 & 4 Enterprise Way, Airedale Business Centre, Skipton, N Yorks, BD23 2TZ
Officers: Ian Terence Vart [1964] Director/General Manager; Vivienne Gail Wilson [1955] Director/Office Manager

The Beer Necessities Limited
Incorporated: 9 February 2017
Net Worth Deficit: £23,594 *Total Assets:* £11,039
Registered Office: Unit 22 Cargo 2, Museum Street, Bristol, BS1 6ZA
Major Shareholder: Henry Wallis Revell
Officers: Henry Wallis Revell [1987] Director

Beer Smiths Limited
Incorporated: 15 December 2017
Registered Office: 63 Marlborough Road, Oxford, OX1 4LW
Major Shareholder: Aaron Smith
Officers: Aaron Smith [1994] Director/Hotelier

Beer Station Brewery Ltd
Incorporated: 6 December 2018
Registered Office: 3b Victoria Buildings, Victoria Road, Formby, Merseyside, L37 7DB
Shareholders: Ian Walsh; Michael John Bell; Keir Edward Walsh
Officers: Michael John Bell [1957] Director/Retired; Ian Walsh [1955] Director; Keir Edward Walsh [1985] Director

The Beerblefish Brewing Company Limited
Incorporated: 3 August 2015 *Employees:* 1
Net Worth Deficit: £25,278 *Total Assets:* £98,362
Registered Office: 47 Pemberton Road, London, N4 1AX
Major Shareholder: James Peter Atherton
Officers: James Peter Atherton [1981] Director/Entrepreneur

Beercraft Brewery Limited
Incorporated: 3 October 2015
Net Worth Deficit: £13,656 *Total Assets:* £756
Registered Office: c/o Partners in Enterprise, First Floor Office, 5 Bartholomews, Brighton, BN1 1HG
Major Shareholder: Jack Tavare
Officers: Jack Tavare [1990] Director

Beerfisch Brewery Limited
Incorporated: 13 June 2017
Registered Office: 4-6 Peterborough Road, Harrow, Middlesex, HA1 2BQ
Major Shareholder: Janet Ann Nichole Fischer
Officers: Janet Ann Nichole Fischer [1982] Director [Canadian]

BeerHug Ltd
Incorporated: 10 August 2017
Registered Office: 6 Barnardo Village Walk, Barkingside, Ilford, Essex, IG6 1FU
Officers: Guy Belchier, Secretary; Guy Belchier [1982] Director/Accountant; Joel Hughes [1987] Director/Marketing Manager

Beerkat Brewing Company Limited
Incorporated: 6 February 2015
Net Worth: £4,329 *Total Assets:* £10,233
Registered Office: The Old Chapel, Union Way, Witney, Oxon, OX28 6HD
Shareholders: Desmond John Warne; Paul Ingham
Officers: Robert William Jacob Ingham [1985] Director; Desmond John Warne [1962] Director/Property Developer & Landlord

Beermats Brewing Company Limited
Incorporated: 22 December 2016
Net Worth Deficit: £66,202   Total Assets: £117,056
Registered Office: 77-77a High Street, South Normanton, Derbys, DE55 2BP
Officers: Crichton Peter Brauer [1977] Director; Andrew James Kendrick [1983] Director/Brewer; Gregg Ivan McDermott [1976] Director/Brewer

Beermondsey Limited
Incorporated: 8 October 2018
Registered Office: Flat 503, Lascar Wharf Building, 21 Parnham Street, Limehouse, London, E14 7FN
Major Shareholder: Michael Elliott Marks
Officers: Michael Elliott Marks [1984] Director/Project Manager

Beersheba Ltd
Incorporated: 4 April 2017   Employees: 2
Net Worth: £1,454,411   Total Assets: £1,530,592
Registered Office: 22 Chancery Lane, London, WC2A 1LS
Shareholders: Markus Christof Hottenrott; Reginald Reeves Bradford
Officers: Reggie Bradford [1966] Director [American]; Christian Wilhelm Walter Harnischfeger [1978] Director/Investor [German]; Ryan Robbins [1980] Director/Manager [American]; Luke Stephen Scanlon [1982] Director/Manager

Beeston Brewery Ltd
Incorporated: 31 March 2005   Employees: 5
Net Worth: £43,169   Total Assets: £68,214
Registered Office: Fransham Road Farm, Beeston, Kings Lynn, Norfolk, PE32 2LZ
Officers: Mark Stephen Riches [1967] Director

Beeston Hop Ltd
Incorporated: 20 April 2015
Net Worth Deficit: £760   Total Assets: £617
Registered Office: 28 Windmill Lane, Sneinton, Nottingham, NG9 4BA
Officers: Dr John Edward Richardson [1974] Director/Lecturer

Belfast Brewing Company Ltd
Incorporated: 25 October 2012
Registered Office: 4 Belmont Park, Belfast, BT4 3DU
Major Shareholder: Alexandra Sara Tennant
Officers: Alexandra Sara Tennant, Secretary; Alexandra Sara Tennant [1968] Director/Manager

Belhaven Brewery Company Limited
Incorporated: 4 July 1944
Net Worth: £248,730,000   Total Assets: £288,540,000
Registered Office: Belhaven Brewery, Dunbar, E Lothian, EH42 1PE
Parent: Belhaven Pubs Limited
Officers: Lindsay Anne Keswick, Secretary; Richard Smothers [1967] Director

The Belleville Brewing Company Limited
Incorporated: 12 October 2012
Net Worth: £203,925   Total Assets: £297,492
Registered Office: 29 Ravenslea Road, London, SW12 8SL
Shareholder: Adrian Thomas
Officers: Mark Rowley McGuinness-Smith [1968] Director/Accountant; Adrian Thomas [1962] Director/Musician

Bellfield Brewery Limited
Incorporated: 2 December 2014
Net Worth: £240,738   Total Assets: £315,473
Registered Office: 46 Stanley Place, Edinburgh, EH7 5TB
Shareholder: Alistair Sandford Burns Brown
Officers: Marie Brown, Secretary; Alistair Sandford Burns Brown [1966] Director; Marie Brown [1965] Director; Giselle Jane Therese Dye [1960] PR Director

Bellrock Brew Co. Ltd
Incorporated: 5 June 2018
Registered Office: 48 Perigee, Shinfield, Reading, Berks, RG2 9FT
Shareholders: Daren Fearon; Russell Purves
Officers: Dr Daren Fearon [1987] Director/Research Scientist; Dr Russell Purves [1986] Director/Scientist

Beltane Brewing Co Ltd
Incorporated: 24 October 2017
Registered Office: 20-22 Wenlock Road, London, N1 7GU
Officers: Alexander Dunlop [1980] Director/Software Engineer; Ross Robert Hamilton [1978] Director/Business Analyst

Belvoir Brewery Limited
Incorporated: 23 March 1995
Net Worth: £195,942   Total Assets: £238,945
Registered Office: Crown Park, Station Road, Old Dalby, Melton Mowbray, Leics, LE14 3NQ
Major Shareholder: Colin William Brown
Officers: Margaret Ruth Griffiths, Secretary; Colin William Brown [1959] Director/Businessman

Bent Iron Brewing Company Ltd
Incorporated: 23 April 2015
Registered Office: Swn Yr Afon, 7 Old Brewery Lane, Rhymney, Caerphilly, NP22 5HT
Major Shareholder: Michael Evans
Officers: Michael Evans, Secretary; Michael Evans [1957] Director/IT Manager

Bentley's Yorkshire Breweries (1828) Limited
Incorporated: 27 February 2014
Net Worth: £300   Total Assets: £350
Registered Office: Suite 158, 33 Great George Street, Leeds, LS1 3AJ
Major Shareholder: Hassan Webb
Officers: Hassan Webb [1973] Director/Accountant

Bert and Chris Brew Beer Limited
Incorporated: 8 February 2018
Registered Office: Orchard House, The Brache, Maulden, Bedford, MK45 2DS
Officers: Robert Alexander John Crowther [1964] Director; Christopher Samuel Harrop [1992] Director

The Bespoke Beer Company Limited
Incorporated: 10 September 2015
Registered Office: 19 Orchard Street, Weston-Super-Mare, Somerset, BS23 1RG
Shareholder: Christopher Cureton
Officers: Christopher Cureton [1952] Director/Publican; Cureton Samuel [1990] Director/Publican

The Bespoke Brewing Co. Limited
Incorporated: 13 January 2012 *Employees:* 5
Net Worth Deficit: £18,379 *Total Assets:* £207,313
Registered Office: Unit 5, Building 6, First Floor, The Mews, Brook Street, Mitcheldean, Glos, GL17 0SL
Major Shareholder: Michael John Bayliss
Officers: Ian Henderson [1958] Director; Sandra Louise Hague Henderson [1964] Director; Rowan Hill [1959] Director/Estate Agent; Sharon Hill [1966] Director/Estate Agent; Amelia Hughes [1995] Director; Matthew Hughes [1995] Director; Rhys Hughes [1965] Director; Susan Hughes [1964] Director

Best Brewery Ltd
Incorporated: 2 December 2016
Net Worth Deficit: £2,359 *Total Assets:* £1,358
Registered Office: Yetson Hayes, Ashprington, Devon, TQ9 7EG
Major Shareholder: Andrew Gregory Best
Officers: Andrew Gregory Best [1956] Director

Bestens Brewery Limited
Incorporated: 2 September 2015
Registered Office: Unit 17 Church Lane Estate, Plummers Plain, Horsham, W Sussex, RH13 6LU
Major Shareholder: Paul Michael Swaffield
Officers: Andrew John Burton [1980] Director/Learning Support Coordinator; Gail Joanna Dampney-Jay [1981] Director/Psychologist; Steven Mark Dampney-Jay [1979] Director/Managing Partner; Paul Michael Swaffield [1980] Director/Consultant; William James Swaffield [1947] Director/Retired

Beta Pilot Brewing Ltd
Incorporated: 26 May 2017
Registered Office: 77 Tilehouse Street, Hitchin, Herts, SG5 2DY
Major Shareholder: Tobias Bror Lekman
Officers: Tobias Bror Lekman [1978] Director/IT Consultant [Swedish]

Beverley Brewery Company Limited
Incorporated: 12 January 2007
Registered Office: 23 North Bar Without, Beverley, E Yorks, HU17 7AG
Shareholders: Guy Stuart Falkingham; Susan Falkingham
Officers: Guy Stuart Falkingham, Secretary; Guy Stuart Falkingham [1960] Director; Susan Falkingham [1953] Director

Bewdley Brewery Limited
Incorporated: 31 December 2007
Net Worth: £141,228 *Total Assets:* £258,683
Registered Office: Unit 7-8 Bewdley Craft Centre, Lax Lane, Bewdley, Worcs, DY12 2DZ
Shareholders: Christine Carr; David Edward Carr; Timothy Edward Wilkins
Officers: Christine Carr, Secretary; David Edward Carr [1945] Director; Timothy Edward Wilkins [1973] Director

Bexar County Brewery Ltd
Incorporated: 20 January 2012
Net Worth Deficit: £88,676 *Total Assets:* £11,387
Registered Office: 8 Belgic Square, Peterborough, Cambs, PE1 5XF
Major Shareholder: Steven Saldana
Officers: Matthew Anthony Mace [1971] Director; Steven Saldana [1975] Director

Bexley Brewery Limited
Incorporated: 10 March 2014
Net Worth Deficit: £82,897 *Total Assets:* £121,475
Registered Office: 124 Parkhill Road, Bexley, Kent, DA5 1JA
Shareholders: Clifford Russell David Murphy; Jane Elizabeth Murphy
Officers: Clifford Russell David Murphy [1965] Director/Brewer

Bib Brewing Ltd
Incorporated: 21 January 2019
Registered Office: 69 John McGuire Crescent, Binley, Coventry, Warwicks, CV3 2QH
Shareholders: Bradley Charles Hemple; Qifen Bi
Officers: Qifen Bi [1990] Product Development Director [Chinese]; Bradley Charles Hemple [1980] Managing Director

The Bidwell Brewery Company Ltd
Incorporated: 3 June 2016
Registered Office: 9 Brighton Terrace, London, SW9 8DJ
Major Shareholder: Tobias Thomas Bidwell
Officers: Dominic Edward Charles Bidwell [1965] Director; Stephen James John Bidwell [1964] Director; Tobias Bidwell [1971] Director

Biercafe Ltd
Incorporated: 22 October 2018
Registered Office: 29 Flat 3, 29 Shore Road, London, E9 7TA
Major Shareholder: Roman Hochuli
Officers: Dr. Roman Hochuli [1989] Director [Dutch]

The Big Bear Brewery Limited
Incorporated: 10 January 2018
Registered Office: The Barn, Tumblers Green, Braintree, Essex, CM77 8AZ
Major Shareholder: Mark Hughes
Officers: Mark Hughes [1963] Director

Big Bog Brewing Company Limited
Incorporated: 6 July 2015 *Employees:* 3
Net Worth Deficit: £40,799 *Total Assets:* £65,104
Registered Office: 164 Walkden Road, Worsley, Manchester, M28 7DP
Major Shareholder: Paul David Jefferies
Officers: Paul David Jefferies [1965] Director/Brewer

The Big Brewing Company Ltd
Incorporated: 27 February 2015
Registered Office: 1 Larch Avenue, Swinton, Manchester, M27 0DQ
Major Shareholder: Liam James Doherty
Officers: Liam James Doherty [1982] Director

Big Drop Brewing Company Limited
Incorporated: 1 August 2016
Net Worth: £11,278 *Total Assets:* £58,830
Registered Office: Cardinal House, 46 St Nicholas Street, Ipswich, Suffolk, IP1 1TT
Major Shareholder: Robert Fink
Officers: Robert Fink [1978] Director/Solicitor; James Kindred [1977] Director/Designer

Big Hand Brewing Company Limited
Incorporated: 31 August 2012
Net Worth Deficit: £54,938 *Total Assets:* £109,102
Registered Office: Unit A1, Abbey Close, Redwither Business Park, Wrexham, Clwyd, LL13 9XG
Major Shareholder: David Ian Shaw
Officers: Martin Jeffrey Benson, Secretary; Andrew James Benson [1983] Director/Brewer; David Ian Shaw [1964] Director

Big Hop Brewing Company Ltd
Incorporated: 4 January 2018
Registered Office: 13 Powell Street, Harrogate, N Yorks, HG1 4BY
Major Shareholder: Thomas Kirkham
Officers: Thomas Kirkham [1988] Director/Brewer

Big Lamp Brewers Limited
Incorporated: 18 July 2013
Registered Office: 178 Sandyford Road, Newcastle upon Tyne, NE2 1RN
Shareholders: George Kenneth Storey; Lee Goulding
Officers: Lee Goulding [1957] Director; George Kenneth Storey [1964] Director

Big Mountain Brewing Company Limited
Incorporated: 30 October 2017
Net Worth: £113,885 Total Assets: £116,252
Registered Office: Found Studios, 1 Lindsey Street, London, EC1A 9HP
Shareholder: Jack Geldard
Officers: Jack Geldard [1981] Director/Brewer; Misha Gopaul [1980] Director; Timothy Pearce [1968] Director/Landlord

Big Shed Brewery Limited
Incorporated: 30 October 1987
Net Worth Deficit: £130,040 Total Assets: £28,174
Registered Office: 2 Muckleton Lane, Shawbury, Shrewsbury, Salop, SY4 4HF
Officers: John Paulson [1952] Director

Big Smoke Brew Co Limited
Incorporated: 13 March 2014 Employees: 4
Net Worth Deficit: £7,647 Total Assets: £109,790
Registered Office: The Antelope, 87 Maple Road, Surbiton, Surrey, KT6 4AW
Shareholder: Richard Andrew Craig
Officers: Richard Andrew Craig [1976] Director [New Zealander]; James Laurence Morgan [1981] Director

Bigla Brewing Company Ltd
Incorporated: 18 December 2017
Registered Office: 1 St Marys Park Road, Portishead, Bristol, BS20 6SN
Major Shareholder: Yavor Kostadinchev
Officers: Yavor Kostadinchev [1981] Director [Bulgarian]

Billericay Brewing Company Ltd
Incorporated: 16 March 2012
Net Worth Deficit: £181,482 Total Assets: £35,235
Registered Office: 55 Crown Street, Brentwood, Essex, CM14 4BD
Shareholders: Anne Mairi Jeffery; Trevor Lawrence Jeffery
Officers: Anne Mairi Jeffery [1960] Director/Health Visitor; Trevor Lawrence Jeffery [1964] Director/Teacher

Binghams Brewery Limited
Incorporated: 29 March 2007 Employees: 5
Net Worth Deficit: £20,814 Total Assets: £128,250
Registered Office: Unit 10 Tavistock Industrial Estate, Ruscombe Lane, Ruscombe, Reading, Berks, RG10 9NJ
Shareholders: Christopher Bingham; Michelle Ann Joyce Bingham; Delia Robina Allott
Officers: Michelle Ann Joyce Bingham, Secretary; Delia Robina Allott [1971] Director/Accountant; Christopher Bingham [1973] Director; Michelle Ann Joyce Bingham [1974] Director/Accountant

Bingley Brewery Limited
Incorporated: 23 May 2013 Employees: 4
Net Worth Deficit: £77,299 Total Assets: £41,220
Registered Office: Weald House, Otley Road, Bingley, W Yorks, BD16 3DA
Officers: Darren Paul Marks [1965] Director

Birkenhead Brewery Company Ltd
Incorporated: 3 September 2018
Registered Office: 17 Dodd Avenue, Greasy, Wirral, Merseyside, CH49 1RR
Shareholders: Rhys Bland; Simon Andrew Doyle
Officers: Rhys Bland [1983] Director/Engineer; Simon Andrew Doyle [1975] Director/Management Information Manager

Birmingham Brewing Company Limited
Incorporated: 4 August 2016
Net Worth Deficit: £38,404 Total Assets: £54,660
Registered Office: 15 Stirchley Trading Estate, Hazelwell Road, Birmingham, B30 2PF
Major Shareholder: Paul Harwood
Officers: Paul Harwood [1987] Director

Bishop Nick Limited
Incorporated: 26 July 2011
Net Worth Deficit: £118,127 Total Assets: £178,876
Registered Office: 33 East Street, Braintree, Essex, CM7 3JJ
Shareholders: Nelion Lorimer Edward Ridley; Elizabeth Anne Ridley
Officers: Nelion Ridley, Secretary; Elizabeth Anne Ridley [1974] Director/Marketing Manager; Nelion Lorimer Edward Ridley [1972] Director/Brewer

Bishop's Crook Brewery Ltd.
Incorporated: 18 October 2013
Net Worth: £1,669 Total Assets: £1,957
Registered Office: 51 Woodcroft Close, Penwortham, Preston, Lancs, PR1 9BX
Officers: David James Bishop [1972] Director; Ian David Grant [1970] Director

Bishop's Stortford Brewery Limited
Incorporated: 23 May 2011
Registered Office: 24 Trinity Street, Bishop's Stortford, Herts, CM23 3TJ
Officers: Darren Lawrence [1985] Director/Beer Maker

Bizzy Play Limited
Incorporated: 31 March 2004 Employees: 2
Net Worth: £80,135 Total Assets: £116,240
Registered Office: Park View House, Ropewalk, Fishguard, Pembrokeshire, SA65 9BT
Shareholders: Christopher Peter Bannister; Sharon Jayne Galliers Bannister
Officers: Christopher Peter Bannister [1962] Director/Playground Constructor; Sharon Jayne Galliers Bannister [1961] Director

BL Drinks Ltd
Incorporated: 22 March 2018
Registered Office: 16a The Parade, Yately, Hants, GU46 7UN
Shareholders: Paul Robert Lockhart; Darren Welch
Officers: Paul Robert Lockhart [1967] Director/Business Development; Darren Welch [1975] Director/Sales Manager

Black Angus Brewing Ltd
Incorporated: 9 December 2016
Registered Office: Keillor Farm, Kettins, Blairgowrie, Perthshire, PH13 9JT
Officers: Andrew Dunn [1986] Director/Data Manager; Paul McLean [1986] Director/Farmer

Black Bess Limited
Incorporated: 27 March 2014
Net Worth Deficit: £73,830 *Total Assets:* £55,776
Registered Office: 165a Mill Road, Wellingborough, Northants, NN8 1PR
Major Shareholder: Marcus Turpin
Officers: Marcus Turpin [1971] Director/Manager

Black Bird Brewery Limited
Incorporated: 24 June 2014
Net Worth: £10,000 *Total Assets:* £10,000
Registered Office: Pantiles, Ashfield Road, Norton, Bury St Edmunds, Suffolk, IP31 3NN
Major Shareholder: Christopher Thompson
Officers: Christopher Thompson [1991] Director/Founder; Michael Thompson [1963] Director

Black Cat Brewery Limited
Incorporated: 11 July 2012
Net Worth Deficit: £55,830 *Total Assets:* £23,795
Registered Office: Twitten Cottage, Southview Road, Crowborough, E Sussex, TN6 1HF
Shareholders: Kathryn Margaret Mary Wratten; Paul Wratten
Officers: Kathryn Margaret Mary Wratten [1962] Director/Brewery Owner; Paul Wratten [1964] Director/Brewery Owner

Black Country Brewery Limited
Incorporated: 28 October 2003
Registered Office: Sovereign House, 12 Warwick Street, Coventry, Warwicks, CV5 6ET
Officers: John Michael McMeeking, Company Secretary; Angus Gilchrist McMeeking [1962] Director

Black Dragon Brewery Limited
Incorporated: 11 November 2013
Registered Office: 16 Verona Avenue, Bournemouth, BH6 3JW
Major Shareholder: Stewart Michael Bell
Officers: Stewart Michael Bell [1967] Director/Bookkeeper

Black Eagle Brewery Ltd
Incorporated: 4 December 2009 *Employees:* 30
Net Worth: £1,010,479 *Total Assets:* £2,846,247
Registered Office: The Eyrie, Truman's, 2-3 Stour Road, Hackney Wick, London, E3 2NT
Officers: David Jonathan Goodwin [1950] Director/Retired; Malcolm Stuart Joseph Heap [1971] Director/Businessman; Emma Hearle [1979] Director/Accountant; Michael-George Carwardine Hemus [1980] Director/Entrepreneur; Andrew James Minter [1966] Director/Chartered Accountant; James William Heudebourck Morgan [1980] Director; Geoff Richard Smith [1976] Director/Businessman; Robert Bruce Taylor [1960] Director/Businessman

Black Fen Brewery Ltd
Incorporated: 7 February 2017
Registered Office: 29b North Street, Burwell, Cambs, CB25 0BA
Major Shareholder: Michael Taylor
Officers: Michael Taylor, Secretary; Michael Taylor [1959] Director/Heating Engineer

Black Flag Brewery Ltd
Incorporated: 2 January 2013
Net Worth Deficit: £93,706 *Total Assets:* £33,643
Registered Office: Unit 1D, New Road, Perranporth, Cornwall, TR6 0DL
Shareholder: Nick Sales
Officers: Benedict Sales [1978] Director/Brewer; Nicholas Sales [1981] Director/Brewer

Black Hole Brewery Limited
Incorporated: 14 January 2014
Registered Office: The Mills, Canal Street, Derby, DE1 2RJ
Shareholders: Mark David Edmond; Carl Andrew Haspel
Officers: Mark David Edmond [1961] Director; Carl Andrew Haspel [1959] Director

Black Horse Brewery Ltd
Incorporated: 1 February 2018
Registered Office: 13 Union Street, Cheltenham, Glos, GL52 2JN
Major Shareholder: Adam Tugwell
Officers: Adam Tugwell [1973] Director

Black Isle Brewing Co. Ltd.
Incorporated: 2 April 1998 *Employees:* 32
Net Worth: £1,144,461 *Total Assets:* £2,372,496
Registered Office: Taeblair, Munlochy, Ross-shire, IV8 8NZ
Shareholders: David John Gladwin; Julia-Jane Kristen Gladwin
Officers: Julia-Jane Kristen Gladwin, Secretary/Furniture Restorer; David John Gladwin [1962] Director/Sporting Agent; Julia-Jane Kristen Gladwin [1965] Director/Furniture Restorer

Black Lodge Brewery Ltd
Incorporated: 29 July 2015
Net Worth Deficit: £5,085 *Total Assets:* £57,016
Registered Office: 3 Kings Dock Street, Liverpool, L1 8JU
Officers: Paul Michael Seiffert [1983] Director

Black Market Brewery Limited
Incorporated: 28 October 2015
Net Worth Deficit: £9,249 *Total Assets:* £8,584
Registered Office: 43 High Street, Warsop, Mansfield, Notts, NG20 0AB
Shareholders: David Drury; Kenneth Ward
Officers: David Drury [1964] Director/Pub Landlord; Kenneth Ward [1958] Director/Carpenter

Black Metal Brewery Ltd
Incorporated: 27 July 2012
Net Worth Deficit: £3,202 *Total Assets:* £17,556
Registered Office: Unit 4 6b Dryden Road, Bilston Glen Industrial Estate, Loanhead, Midlothian, EH20 9LZ
Officers: Jaan Ratsep [1983] Director [Estonian]

The Black Sheep Brewery PLC
Incorporated: 7 February 1992 *Employees:* 102
Net Worth: £5,656,933 *Total Assets:* £11,888,239
Registered Office: Wellgarth, Masham, Ripon, N Yorks, HG4 4EN
Officers: Stephen John Constable, Secretary; Stephen John Constable [1964] Finance Director; Charlene Lyons [1978] Director/Management Consultant; Paul Richard Nolan [1968] Director; Andrew Peter Slee [1965] Director; Jonathan Francis Theakson [1976] Director; Robert Joseph Theakston [1973] Director

Black Squirrel Brewing Limited
Incorporated: 12 June 2016
Registered Office: 123 Marmet Avenue, Letchworth Garden City, Herts, SG6 4QF
Major Shareholder: Andrew Peter Finlay
Officers: Andrew Peter Finlay [1986] Director/Brewer [Irish]

Black Tor Brewery Ltd
Incorporated: 28 March 2013
Net Worth Deficit: £62,888 *Total Assets:* £77,012
Registered Office: Unit 5 Gidleys Meadow, Christow, Exeter, Devon, EX6 7QB
Major Shareholder: Jonathon Henry Crump
Officers: Jonathon Henry Crump [1984] Director/Brewer

Black Wolf Brewery Limited
Incorporated: 7 February 2014
Registered Office: 7c Bandeath Industrial Estate Bandeath Industrial Estate, Throsk, Stirling, FK7 7NP
Officers: Alexander Douglas Moffat [1941] Director/Writer to The Signet; Andrew John Richardson [1962] Director; Carlo Louis Valente [1962] Director

Blackdown Brewery Ltd
Incorporated: 1 August 2017
Registered Office: 15 Whirligig Lane, Taunton, Somerset, TA1 1SQ
Major Shareholder: Frederick James Farnworth
Officers: Frederick James Farnworth [1987] Director

Blackedge Brewing Company Ltd
Incorporated: 30 November 2009 *Employees:* 5
Net Worth: £4 *Total Assets:* £87,173
Registered Office: Moreton Mill, Hampson Street, Horwich, Bolton, Lancs, BL6 7JH
Shareholder: Wayne Roper
Officers: Shaun Reynolds [1974] Director/Civil Servant; Rowena Rose Roper [1980] Director/Brewery Administrator; Wayne Roper [1975] Brewery Director

Blackened Abbey Ltd
Incorporated: 6 August 2018
Registered Office: 3 Llys Saron, Brynford, Holywell, Flintshire, CH8 8AS
Shareholders: Andrew Vincent Southall; Michael John Minion
Officers: Michael John Minion [1986] Director; Andrew Vincent Southall [1989] Director

Blackened Sun Brewing Company Limited
Incorporated: 6 February 2017 *Employees:* 2
Net Worth Deficit: £24,694 *Total Assets:* £24,387
Registered Office: 3 Heathfield, Stacey Bushes, Milton Keynes, Bucks, MK12 6HP
Shareholders: Gary David Morse; Sharon Elaine Morse
Officers: Gary David Morse [1972] Director/Brewer; Sharon Elaine Morse [1973] Director/Brewer

Blackhill Brewery Limited
Incorporated: 6 July 2011
Net Worth Deficit: £104,112 *Total Assets:* £28,763
Registered Office: 14 Stella Gill Industrial Estate, Pelton Fell, Chester-le-Street, Co Durham, DH2 2RG
Major Shareholder: Christopher Graham
Officers: Christopher Graham [1965] Director/Consultant

Blackjack Beers Limited
Incorporated: 21 February 2011
Net Worth: £146,963 *Total Assets:* £600,787
Registered Office: 31 Barlow Road, Levenshulme, Manchester, M19 3DB
Shareholder: Robert Hamilton
Officers: Matthew Williams, Secretary; Joseph Bird [1986] Director/Brewer; Robert Hamilton [1979] Director; Jonathan Hartley [1988] Director/Brewer

Blackpit Brewery Ltd
Incorporated: 18 March 2016 *Employees:* 3
Net Worth Deficit: £29,827 *Total Assets:* £109,575
Registered Office: Blackpit Farm, Silverstone Road, Stowe, Buckingham, MK18 5LJ
Shareholders: Ben John Williams; Duncan Charles Wheeler; Oliver Richard Whiteley
Officers: Duncan Charles Wheeler [1984] Director; Oliver Richard Whiteley [1983] Director; Benjamin John Williams [1983] Director

Blackstar Brewery Ltd
Incorporated: 28 February 2019
Registered Office: 20-22 Wenlock Road, London, N1 7GU
Shareholders: Mark David Stephens; Adam Nicholas Ruffinato; Harry George Pitt
Officers: Harry George Pitt [1973] Director; Adam Nicholas Ruffinato [1974] Director; Mark David Stephens [1973] Director

Blewin Trust Limited
Incorporated: 2 November 1944
Net Worth: £132,241 *Total Assets:* £137,259
Registered Office: Gosport House, Laugharne, Dyfed, SA33 4TA
Major Shareholder: Beryn Charles Martin Lewis
Officers: Philip John Lewis, Secretary; Captain Beryn Charles Martin Lewis [1958] Director

The Blighty Brewery Limited
Incorporated: 18 April 2017
Registered Office: Britannia House, 16 Broad Street, Ramsgate, Kent, CT11 8QY
Major Shareholder: Graham Dougal Young
Officers: Graham Dougal Young [1943] Director/Brewer

Blimey! Brewing Company Limited
Incorporated: 27 January 2017
Net Worth: £1,072 *Total Assets:* £7,222
Registered Office: First Floor, 24e Norwich Street, Dereham, Norfolk, NR19 1BX
Shareholders: John Michael Moriarty; Adrian Keith Bryan
Officers: Adrian Keith Bryan [1954] Director/IT Consultant; John Michael Moriarty [1966] Director/Entrepreneur [American]

Blindmans Brewery Limited
Incorporated: 26 April 2004 *Employees:* 2
Net Worth: £1,432 *Total Assets:* £44,780
Registered Office: 7a King Street, Frome, Somerset, BA11 1BH
Shareholders: Lloyd Francis Chamberlain; Paul Edney
Officers: Lloyd Francis Chamberlain, Secretary; Lloyd Francis Chamberlain [1972] Director; Paul Edney [1971] Director

Blithe Nook Brewery Ltd
Incorporated: 11 June 2018
Registered Office: 289 Hackney Road, London, E2 8NA
Major Shareholder: Arber Pacarada
Officers: Arber Pacarada [1972] Director

Block Brewery Limited
Incorporated: 14 December 2015
Net Worth: £123 Total Assets: £4,357
Registered Office: 137 Cropley Street, London, N1 7HJ
Shareholders: Eugene Pacelli Broderick; Hannah Elizabeth Runcie
Officers: Eugene Pacelli Broderick [1974] Director [Irish]; Hannah Elizabeth Runcie [1983] Director

Blonde Brothers Limited
Incorporated: 9 February 2017
Net Worth Deficit: £3,791 Total Assets: £146,209
Registered Office: 20 Knivet Road, London, SW6 1JH
Shareholders: Samuel James Maitland-Robinson; Joseph Charles Maitland-Robinson
Officers: Joseph Charles Maitland-Robinson [1989] Director; Samuel James Maitland-Robinson [1994] Director

Blue Armadillo Brewing Co Ltd
Incorporated: 9 November 2018
Registered Office: 3 Southfields Drive, Crick, Northampton, NN6 7TQ
Shareholders: Paul Graham Preece; Kieran James McLoughney
Officers: Kieran James McLoughney [1975] Director/Chef; Paul Graham Preece [1969] Director/Operations Manager

The Blue Bear Brewery (Worcester) Limited
Incorporated: 2 December 2009 Employees: 2
Net Worth Deficit: £181,999 Total Assets: £4,779
Registered Office: 19 Hereward Rise, Halesowen, W Midlands, B62 8AN
Major Shareholder: Ian Edward Robinson
Officers: Ian Edward Robinson [1974] Director/Accountant; Paran Singh Sandhu [1966] Director/Head Brewer

Blue Bee Brewery Ltd
Incorporated: 28 July 2010 Employees: 3
Net Worth Deficit: £44,886 Total Assets: £77,082
Registered Office: 29-30 Hoyland Road, Sheffield, S3 8AB
Major Shareholder: Philip John Garner
Officers: Philip John Garner [1987] Director/Lead DevOps Engineer; Joshua Michael Jepson [1991] Director/Brewer

Blue Monkey Brewing Limited
Incorporated: 31 March 2008 Employees: 12
Net Worth: £458,283 Total Assets: £609,899
Registered Office: White House, Wollaton Street, corner of Clarendon Street, Nottingham, NG1 5GF
Major Shareholder: Trevor Vickers
Officers: Elizabeth Ann Vickers [1979] Director; Thomas William Vickers [1982] Director; Trevor John Vickers [1947] Director/Manager

Blueball Brewery Ltd
Incorporated: 7 November 2011 Employees: 1
Net Worth: £50,097 Total Assets: £51,363
Registered Office: 31 Ashridge Street, Runcorn, Cheshire, WA7 1HU
Officers: Alexander Richard Haycraft [1969] Managing Director

Bluestone Brewing Company Limited
Incorporated: 19 March 2013 Employees: 4
Net Worth: £1,512 Total Assets: £129,064
Registered Office: Tyriet, Cilgwyn, Newport, Pembrokeshire, SA42 0QW
Shareholders: Simon Robert Turner; Kerry Patricia Turner
Officers: Neil Harper Burchell [1958] Director; Amy Ffion Evans [1987] Director; Tony Gartland [1956] Director; Kerry Patricia Turner [1960] Director; Simon Robert Turner [1958] Director

The Boat Lane Brewery Limited
Incorporated: 19 November 2015
Net Worth Deficit: £38,669 Total Assets: £50,171
Registered Office: Unit 3 Streamside Business Park Boat Lane, Offenham, Evesham, Worcs, WR11 8RS
Major Shareholder: Ian Hazeldene
Officers: Elizabeth Jane Hazeldene [1970] Director; Ian Hazeldene [1967] Director

Bob's Brewing Company Limited
Incorporated: 18 March 2003
Net Worth: £5,697 Total Assets: £10,697
Registered Office: 589 The Brew House, Halifax Road, Liversedge, W Yorks, WF15 8HQ
Major Shareholder: Richard Dean Sharp
Officers: Richard Dean Sharp [1985] Director

Bobby Beer Company Limited
Incorporated: 5 August 2013
Net Worth Deficit: £113,287 Total Assets: £18,354
Registered Office: c/o Bronsens, Albion Street, Chipping Norton, Oxon, OX7 5BH
Shareholders: Georgina Elizabeth Pearman; Sam Murray Pearman
Officers: Georgina Elizabeth Pearman [1973] Director; Pearman Sam [1978] Director

Bog Brew Beers Limited
Incorporated: 5 February 2018
Registered Office: 11 High Street, Stevenage, Herts, SG1 3BG
Shareholders: Paul Clinton; Marie-Claire Clinton
Officers: Marie-Claire Clinton [1972] Director; Paul Clinton [1964] Director

Bohem Brewery Ltd
Incorporated: 26 February 2015 Employees: 4
Net Worth: £33,610 Total Assets: £68,255
Registered Office: Unit 5 Littleline House, 43 West Road, London, N17 0RE
Shareholders: Petr Skocek; Zdenek Kudr
Officers: Neil William Edmonds [1972] Director/Banker; Zdenek Kudr [1974] Director [Czech]; Petr Skocek [1986] Director/Headbrewer [Czech]

Bold Brewing Ltd
Incorporated: 22 June 2018
Registered Office: 11 Lea Rig Road, Peterhead, Aberdeenshire, AB42 3NP
Major Shareholder: George Ritchie Cordiner
Officers: George Ritchie Cordiner [1976] Director/Policeman

Bollington Brewing Co. Limited
Incorporated: 30 July 2008
Net Worth: £46,896 Total Assets: £157,094
Registered Office: Unit 2 & 3 Adlington Road, Bollington, Macclesfield, Cheshire, SK10 5JT
Parent: Wainwright Group Limited
Officers: Kirsten Wainwright [1980] Director/Sales; Lee Owen Wainwright [1973] Director

Bomb Shelter Brewing Limited
Incorporated: 4 April 2018
Registered Office: 25 Mitford Road, London, N19 4HJ
Officers: Richard Allen [1988] Director/Technology; Thomas Beresford [1982] Director/Technology

Bond Brews Ltd
Incorporated: 15 June 2015
Net Worth Deficit: £21,863 *Total Assets:* £40,612
Registered Office: 2 Mays Road, Wokingham, Berks, RG40 1RW
Major Shareholder: Dean Earl Bond
Officers: Dean Earl Bond [1970] Director/Solutions Architect

Bone Machine Brewing Company Limited
Incorporated: 24 January 2017
Net Worth Deficit: £9,189 *Total Assets:* £29,508
Registered Office: Unit 1e Hampden Road, Pocklington Industrial Estate, York, YO42 1NR
Shareholders: Marko Antero Karjalainen; Kimmo Eerik Karjalainen
Officers: Kimmo Eerik Karjalainen [1984] Sales Director [Finnish]; Marko Antero Karjalainen [1987] Director/Brewer and Brewing Consultant [Finnish]

Bont Brew Ltd
Incorporated: 30 January 2017
Net Worth: £785 *Total Assets:* £6,985
Registered Office: 7 Maes Y Piod, Bridgend, CF31 5FJ
Shareholders: Jan Andreas Kletta; Charlotte Kletta
Officers: Dr Jan Andreas Kletta [1984] Director/General Practitioner

Boody Brewery Ltd.
Incorporated: 28 June 2017
Registered Office: The Beeches, Egloshayle, Wadebridge, Cornwall, PL27 6HJ
Officers: George Albert James Biggs [1995] Director/Aquaculturist; Tom Cox [1995] Director/Sales Assistant; Dominic Eddison [1995] Director/Bartender; Joseph David Slack [1995] Director/Sales Assistant

Boot Town Brewery Ltd
Incorporated: 15 February 2018
Registered Office: 110 Finedon Road, c/o Bosworth's Garden Centre, Burton Latimer, Northants, NN15 5QA
Shareholders: Ian Leslie Bosworth; Lee Arthur Kellett
Officers: Ian Leslie Bosworth [1969] Director/Brewer; Lee Arthur Kellett [1979] Director/Brewer

Boothtown Brewery Co Ltd
Incorporated: 25 October 2016
Registered Office: 48-50 Wakefield Road, Ackworth, Pontefract, W Yorks, WF7 7AB
Major Shareholder: Howard Marsh
Officers: Howard Marsh, Secretary; Howard Marsh [1972] Director

Boozehound Ltd
Incorporated: 28 July 2017
Registered Office: 5 Glenleigh Walk, Robertsbridge, E Sussex, TN32 5DQ
Major Shareholder: Aaron Thomas Rowsell
Officers: Aaron Thomas Rowsell [1986] Director

Boozy Bods Ltd
Incorporated: 27 February 2012
Net Worth Deficit: £41,223 *Total Assets:* £20,669
Registered Office: Unit A, Llanhilleth Industrial Estate, Llanhilleth, Abertillery, Gwent, NP13 2RX
Major Shareholder: Jaime Clifford Devine
Officers: Jaime Clifford Devine [1972] Director/Teacher/Lecturer

Born in a Brewery Ltd
Incorporated: 20 March 2014
Net Worth: £3,349 *Total Assets:* £5,481
Registered Office: Tin Shed, Chapel Court, Wervin, Chester, CH2 4BT
Officers: Andrew Robert Taylor [1983] Brewery Director

The Borough Brewery Limited
Incorporated: 4 February 2013
Net Worth: £3,581 *Total Assets:* £120,606
Registered Office: The Borough, 3 Dalton Square, Lancaster, LA1 1PP
Officers: Martin Richard Horner, Secretary; Martin Richard Horner [1968] Director/Restaurateur; Rory Walker [1986] Director/Beer Brewer

Boss Brewing Company Ltd
Incorporated: 16 December 2014
Net Worth Deficit: £202,479 *Total Assets:* £278,827
Registered Office: 176 Neath Road, Landore, Swansea, SA1 2JT
Officers: Roy John George Allkin [1975] Director; Sarah John [1986] Director

Bostin Brews Ltd
Incorporated: 29 June 2016
Registered Office: 19 Parkgate Mews, Shirley, Solihull, W Midlands, B90 3GF
Officers: Mark Antony Windridge [1967] Director/FLT Driver

The Bosun's Brewing Company Limited
Incorporated: 21 November 2012 *Employees:* 6
Net Worth Deficit: £63,036 *Total Assets:* £91,336
Registered Office: c/o D & A Hill Chartered Accountants, No 18 T8/9, Brooke's Mill, Armitage Bridge, Huddersfield, W Yorks, HD4 7NR
Shareholder: Grahame Francis Andrews
Officers: Eileen Andrews [1954] Director; Grahame Francis Andrews [1954] Director; Emma Sarah Lund [1977] Sales Director

Botley Brewery Ltd
Incorporated: 1 June 2012
Net Worth Deficit: £57,462 *Total Assets:* £2,093
Registered Office: Botley Brewery, Mill Hill, Botley, Southampton, SO30 2GB
Shareholders: Meg Harris; Robert Steven Sanderson
Officers: Meg Harris [1966] Finance Director; Martin David Luther Phelps [1987] Director; Robert Steven Sanderson [1977] Director/Head Brewer

Boudicca Brewing Company Ltd
Incorporated: 16 August 2015
Net Worth Deficit: £15,018 *Total Assets:* £89,938
Registered Office: 34 Clabon Road, Norwich, NR3 4HF
Shareholders: Simon St Ruth; Emma Pinder
Officers: Emma Pinder [1970] Director/Wholesaler; Helen St Ruth [1973] Director/IT Consultant; Simon St Ruth [1971] Director/IT Consultant

Boutilliers Limited
Incorporated: 14 August 2014
Net Worth Deficit: £359 *Total Assets:* £32,341
Registered Office: The Hop Shed Macknade Fine Foods, Selling Road, Faversham, Kent, ME13 8XF
Shareholders: Philip Dodd; Richard Peter Bennett
Officers: Richard Peter Bennett [1978] Director/Teacher; Philip Dodd [1979] Director/Civil Servant

The Boutique Cellar Limited
Incorporated: 7 June 2012
Net Worth Deficit: £30,394 *Total Assets:* £128,656
Registered Office: Low Barn, Gwehelog, Usk, Monmouthshire, NP15 1HY
Officers: Sarah Thompson [1976] Director

Bowing Hound Brewing Company Limited
Incorporated: 20 February 2017
Net Worth: £1 *Total Assets:* £4,001
Registered Office: 49 Barrows Lane, Birmingham, B26 1RZ
Major Shareholder: Joseph James Howell
Officers: Joseph James Howell [1987] Director/Brewer

The Bowland Beer Company Limited
Incorporated: 6 February 2003 *Employees:* 12
Net Worth: £105,777 *Total Assets:* £764,487
Registered Office: The Station House, Station Road, Whalley, Clitheroe, Lancs, BB7 9RT
Parent: Bowland Enterprises Limited
Officers: Andrew Robert Warburton [1966] Director/Publican; James Peter Warburton [1965] Director/Hotelier

Bowman Ales Limited
Incorporated: 28 June 2006 *Employees:* 7
Net Worth: £194 *Total Assets:* £163,757
Registered Office: Clock Offices, High Street, Bishops Waltham, Southampton, SO32 1AA
Shareholders: Raymond Clifford Page; Martin Gilman Roberts
Officers: Martin Gilman Roberts, Secretary/Brewer; Raymond Clifford Page [1965] Director/Brewer; Martin Gilman Roberts [1957] Director/Brewers

Bowness Bay Brewing Limited
Incorporated: 27 October 2011 *Employees:* 6
Net Worth: £24,728 *Total Assets:* £125,784
Registered Office: Unit 10 Castle Mills, Kendal, Cumbria, LA9 7DE
Major Shareholder: Richard Henry Charles Husbands
Officers: Richard Henry Charles Husbands [1969] Director

Bowtie Brewers Limited
Incorporated: 30 April 2018
Registered Office: 78 Church Road, Watford, Herts, WD17 4PU
Shareholders: Matthew Juggins; Peter Robert Hodge
Officers: Peter Robert Hodge [1992] Director/Customer Service Advisor; Matthew Juggins [1990] Director/Administrator

Box Brewery Ltd
Incorporated: 20 December 2017
Registered Office: 15 Red House Walk, Levington, Ipswich, Suffolk, IP10 0LY
Major Shareholder: Nicholas Gray
Officers: Nicholas Gray [1984] Managing Director

Box Social Ltd
Incorporated: 14 August 2014
Net Worth Deficit: £9,190 *Total Assets:* £26,637
Registered Office: 18 Riversdale Court, Newcastle upon Tyne, NE15 8SG
Shareholder: Stephen Holland
Officers: Ross Holland, Secretary; Nicola Joy Holland [1960] Director/Sales Person; Stephen Holland [1959] Director/Fire Safety Consultant

Boxcar Brewery Limited
Incorporated: 3 August 2015 *Employees:* 2
Previous: Leake Street Brewery Limited
Net Worth: £30,804 *Total Assets:* £116,526
Registered Office: Flat 3, 44-46 Belsize Lane, London, NW3 5AR
Major Shareholder: Stephen William Finch
Officers: Stephen William Finch [1975] Director; Simon Gold [1980] Director/Banker

Br3wery Ltd
Incorporated: 11 September 2017
Registered Office: 57 MacKenzie Road, Beckenham, Kent, BR3 4RY
Major Shareholder: Carlos Eduardo Santos Gomes
Officers: Carlos Eduardo Santos Gomes [1980] Director [Portuguese]

Bradfield Brewery Limited
Incorporated: 27 July 2009 *Employees:* 22
Net Worth: £1,842,790 *Total Assets:* £2,475,709
Registered Office: Watt House Farm, High Bradfield, Sheffield, S6 6LG
Shareholders: Lisa Moat; Richard William Gill
Officers: Susan Gill, Secretary; John Richard Gill [1959] Director; Richard William Gill [1983] Director; Susan Gill [1961] Director and Secretary; Lisa Moat [1985] Director

Braemar Brewery Ltd
Incorporated: 4 January 2019
Registered Office: 8 Canmore Road, Braemar, Ballater, Aberdeenshire, AB35 5XG
Major Shareholder: Robert Joseph McCabe
Officers: Robert Joseph McCabe [1988] Director/Head Brewer

Bragdy Lleu Cyf
Incorporated: 16 October 2013 *Employees:* 9
Net Worth: £12,806 *Total Assets:* £35,102
Registered Office: Uned A9 Ystad Ddiwydiannol Penygroes, Ffordd Llanllyfni, Penygroes, Gwynedd, LL54 6DB
Officers: Elwyn Jones [1955] Director/Hunan Gyflogedig; Robat Eifion Jones [1980] Director/Cyflogedig; Iwan Gwyn Morris [1987] Director; Kelvin Roberts [1972] Director/Cyflogedig; Rhys Roberts [1967] Director/Cyflogedig; Myrddin Williams [1949] Director/Cyflogedig

Bragdy Mona Cyf
Incorporated: 27 November 2018
Registered Office: Uned 6 Stad Ddiwydianol, Gaerwen, Gwynedd, LL60 6HR
Major Shareholder: Huw Gethin Jones
Officers: Robat Rhys Evans, Secretary; Gwyn Anwyl [1981] Director/Teacher; Sion Morgan Edwards [1987] Director/Teacher; Robat Rhys Evans [1980] Director/Self Employed; Huw Gethin Jones [1986] Director/Editor; Meurig Rhys Jones [1987] Director/Administrator; Rhys Lloyd Jones [1981] Director/Farmer/Contractor; Thomas Daniel Williams [1987] Director/Teacher

Bragdy Nant Cyf
Incorporated: 23 December 2009 *Employees:* 1
Net Worth: £69,693 *Total Assets:* £76,679
Registered Office: 3 Pen Y Bryn, Llanrwst, Conwy, LL26 0DT
Officers: Nerys Dobson [1966] Director/Language Officer; Dewi Arfon Jones [1962] Director/Engineer; Gareth Wyn Jones [1961] Director/Local Government Officer; Sion Wyn [1962] Director

S.A.Brain & Company,Limited
Incorporated: 12 April 1897 *Employees:* 2,520
Net Worth: £74,859,000 *Total Assets:* £192,684,992
Registered Office: Dragon Brewery, Pacific Road, Cardiff, CF24 5HJ
Officers: Charles Nicholas Brain, Company Secretary; Alistair Grant Arkley [1947] Director; Charles Nicholas Brain [1971] Director/Company Secretary; Jonathan Bridge [1978] Operations Director; Alistair William Darby [1966] Director/Chief Executive; Martin Stuart Reed [1960] Director/Accountant; John Frederick William Rhys [1958] Director/Marketing Consultant; Peter John Wilson [1958] Director

Brampton Brewery Ltd
Incorporated: 8 February 2007
Net Worth: £56,182 *Total Assets:* £100,267
Registered Office: Unit 5 Chatsworth Business Park, Chatsworth Road, Chesterfield, Derbys, S40 2AR
Officers: Jon Paul Leeming, Secretary; John Mario Frederick [1959] Director; David John Hattersley [1955] Director; John Hirst [1952] Director/Senior Architectural Assistant; Jon Paul Leeming [1965] Director/Business Analyst; Christopher Mark Radford [1968] Director

Brancaster Brewery Limited
Incorporated: 5 October 2004
Net Worth Deficit: £436
Registered Office: Fox Barn, Willian, Letchworth Garden City, Herts, SG6 2AE
Major Shareholder: James Owen Bradley Nye
Officers: Robert James Ness, Secretary; James Owen Bradley Nye [1981] Restaurant Group Director

Branded Drinks Ltd
Incorporated: 16 September 1999 *Employees:* 24
Net Worth: £1,041,037 *Total Assets:* £3,886,575
Registered Office: The Bottling Works, Unit 1 The Business Park, Tufthorn Avenue, Coleford, Glos, GL16 8PN
Major Shareholder: Jonathan Charles Calver
Officers: Gray Bensted Olliver, Secretary; Jonathan Charles Calver [1970] Managing Director; Gray Bensted Olliver [1949] Sales & Marketing Director

Branscombe Vale Brewery Limited
Incorporated: 25 November 2002
Net Worth: £438,958 *Total Assets:* £507,271
Registered Office: Branscombe Vale Brewery, Great Seaside Farm, Branscombe, Seaton, Devon, EX12 3DP
Major Shareholder: Paul Christopher Dimond
Officers: Paul Christopher Dimond, Secretary/Chairman; Paul Christopher Dimond [1965] Director/Chairman

Brass Castle Brewery Limited
Incorporated: 2 April 2013 *Employees:* 21
Net Worth: £26,277 *Total Assets:* £210,892
Registered Office: 10 Yorkersgate, Malton, N Yorks, YO17 7AB
Shareholders: Ian Charles Goodall; Philip James Rous Saltonstall
Officers: Philip James Rous Saltonstall [1975] Director

Bratch Beers Ltd
Incorporated: 27 April 2016
Net Worth: £10 *Total Assets:* £10
Registered Office: 100 Planks Lane, Wombourne, Wolverhampton, W Midlands, WV5 8DU
Major Shareholder: James Peter Rushton
Officers: Margaret Rushton, Secretary; James Peter Rushton [1980] Director/Head Brewer

The Braybrooke Beer Company Limited
Incorporated: 23 June 2017 *Employees:* 2
Net Worth: £68,510 *Total Assets:* £716,304
Registered Office: Ground Floor, Afon House, Worthing Road, Horsham, W Sussex, RH12 1TL
Shareholder: Luke Adam Wilson
Officers: Cameron James Emirali [1980] Director/Restaurateur [New Zealander]; Nicholas James Trower [1978] Director/Beer Importer/Wholesaler; Luke Adam Wilson [1981] Director/Restaurateur

Brazen Brewing Co. Ltd
Incorporated: 20 June 2016
Registered Office: 34 Nightingale Lane, London, E11 2HE
Major Shareholder: Alexander Daniel Wing
Officers: Alexander Daniel Wing [1975] Director/Graphic Designer

The Brechin Park Brewing Company Ltd
Incorporated: 13 February 2018
Registered Office: Unit 10 Brechin Business Centre, 10 Southesk Street, Brechin, Angus, DD9 6DY
Officers: John Leatherbarrow [1972] Director/Software Engineer

Brentwood Brewing Company Limited
Incorporated: 4 July 2006
Net Worth Deficit: £34,807 *Total Assets:* £289,421
Registered Office: Calcott Hall, Ongar Road, Pilgrims Hatch, Brentwood, Essex, CM15 9HS
Shareholders: Roland Henry Kannor; Jason Barry Jopson
Officers: Jason Barry Jopson [1967] Director/Builder; Roland Henry Kannor [1961] Director/Brewer [American]

Brew & Bottle Limited
Incorporated: 8 February 2018
Registered Office: Park House, 37 Clarence Street, Leicester, LE1 3RW
Shareholders: Ben Harrison; Lee Thomas John Jeffries; Maurice Newton
Officers: Ben Harrison [1980] Director; Lee Thomas Jeffries [1981] Director; Maurice Newton [1965] Director

Brew By Numbers Ltd.
Incorporated: 12 March 2012 *Employees:* 17
Net Worth: £115,717 *Total Assets:* £381,595
Registered Office: 79 Enid Street, London, SE16 3RA
Shareholders: Tom Hutchings; David Seymour
Officers: Tom Hutchings [1982] Director; David Seymour [1982] Director

Brew Club Limited
Incorporated: 8 May 2015 *Employees:* 2
Net Worth Deficit: £69,854 *Total Assets:* £26,860
Registered Office: 7-8 Bohemia Place, London, E8 1DU
Officers: Robert John Berezowski [1977] Director/IT Consultant; Jonathan Llewellyn-Jones [1984] Director/Contracts Manager

Brew Locker Ltd
Incorporated: 13 November 2018
Registered Office: 15 Brattain Court, Bracknell, Berks, RG12 9ED
Major Shareholder: Zak Joshua Atte La Crouche
Officers: Zak Joshua Atte La Crouche [1995] Director/Head Brewer

Brew Monster Limited
Incorporated: 20 March 2017 *Employees:* 3
Net Worth: £61,118 *Total Assets:* £116,323
Registered Office: Unit C, Avondale Way, Pontrhydyrun, Cwmbran, NP44 1XE
Officers: Jason Paginton [1974] Director; Stephen Glenn White [1985] Director

Brew Shed Beers Limited
Incorporated: 25 January 2016
Net Worth: £2,226 *Total Assets:* £2,226
Registered Office: Wellheads House, Sandilands, Limekilns, Dunfermline, Fife, KY11 3JD
Major Shareholder: Steven Hope
Officers: Steven Hope [1963] Director/Owner

Brew Toon Ltd.
Incorporated: 5 December 2013 *Employees:* 5
Net Worth Deficit: £131,702 *Total Assets:* £177,630
Registered Office: 17 Queens Den, Aberdeen, AB15 8BW
Shareholder: Shirley Ann Gerrard Bowden
Officers: Frederick James Bowden [1964] Managing Director; Shirley-Ann Gerrard Bowden [1964] Director/Accounts Manager

Brew York Limited
Incorporated: 26 May 2015
Net Worth: £111,403 *Total Assets:* £359,213
Registered Office: Unit 6 Enterprise Complex, Walmgate, York, YO1 9TT
Shareholders: Wayne Steven Smith; Lee David Grabham
Officers: Lee David Grabham [1978] Director; Wayne Steven Smith [1981] Director

Brewboard Limited
Incorporated: 28 April 2016
Net Worth Deficit: £1,300 *Total Assets:* £136,298
Registered Office: Mar Lodge, High Street, Little Chesterford, Essex, CB10 1TS
Officers: Paul Duncan Archer, Secretary; Paul Duncan Archer [1957] Director/Chartered Accountant; Raymond Stuart Chambers [1962] Director/Brewer; Nicholas Paul Davis [1960] Director/Consultant; Oliver Peter Pugh [1974] Director/Graphic Designer

Brewbox Systems Ltd
Incorporated: 23 March 2016
Net Worth: £21,500 *Total Assets:* £21,500
Registered Office: 15 Whirligig Lane, Taunton, Somerset, TA1 1SQ
Major Shareholder: Frederick James Farnworth
Officers: Frederick James Farnworth [1987] Director/Beer Brewery Systems

Brewdog PLC
Incorporated: 7 November 2006 *Employees:* 777
Net Worth: £149,023,008 *Total Assets:* £203,231,008
Registered Office: Brewdog, Balmacassie Commercial Park, Ellon, Aberdeenshire, AB41 8BX
Shareholders: James Bruce Watt; Alan Martin Dickie
Officers: Alan Martin Dickie, Secretary; Alan Martin Dickie [1982] Director; Allison Dawn Green [1970] Director; Charles Keith Greggor [1954] Director [American]; Frances Blythe Jack [1974] Director/Private Equity - Finance [American]; Jason Keith Marshall [1969] Director; David McDowall [1978] Director; James Lewis O'Hara [1966] Director/Private Equity - Finance [American]; Andrew Shaw [1974] Director; Neil Allan Simpson [1971] Finance Director; Jamie Bruce Watt [1982] Director

Brewers Folly Brewery Ltd.
Incorporated: 12 May 2017
Net Worth: £506 *Total Assets:* £593
Registered Office: Ashton Farm House, Stanbridge, Wimborne, Dorset, BH21 4JD
Officers: Richard Rufus Francis Glyn [1971] Director/Charity Trustee; Dean Patrick Harris [1988] Director/Mechanic; Eric Frank Nelson [1968] Director/IT Consultant [American]

The Brewery Limited
Incorporated: 13 October 2015
Net Worth Deficit: £8,175 *Total Assets:* £1,809
Registered Office: 27a Maxwell Road, Northwood, Middlesex, HA6 2XY
Major Shareholder: Nicholas Zivkovic
Officers: Nicholas Zivkovic [1963] Director/Brewer

Brewery Z Ltd
Incorporated: 21 May 2018
Registered Office: c/o Zoedale, Stannard Way, Priory Business Park, Bedford, MK44 3WG
Shareholders: Timothy Lawrence Peter Guest; Katie Jayne Guest
Officers: Katie Jayne Guest [1981] Director; Timothy Lawrence Peter Guest [1977] Director

Brewheadz Limited
Incorporated: 16 December 2015
Net Worth Deficit: £71,742 *Total Assets:* £22,469
Registered Office: Unit 16a Rosebery Industrial Park, Rosebery Avenue, London, N17 9SR
Shareholders: Vincenzo Conte; Giovanni Massa; Rotunno Gianni; Stefano Rotunno
Officers: Vincenzo Conte [1988] Director/Chef [Italian]; Giovanni Massa [1984] Director/Waiter [Italian]; Gianni Rotunno [1987] Director/Accountant [Italian]; Stefano Rotunno [1982] Director/Waiter [Italian]

Brewhouse Brewery Limited
Incorporated: 15 January 2019
Registered Office: Flat 506, John Harrison Way, London, SE10 0BL
Major Shareholder: Nicholas Paul Harkin
Officers: Nicholas Paul Harkin [1986] Director/Consultant

Brewing and Distilling Company Limited
Incorporated: 23 October 2013 *Employees:* 18
Net Worth Deficit: £1,864,158 *Total Assets:* £2,206,992
Registered Office: Rowlands House, Portobello Road, Birtley, Chester-le-Street, Co Durham, DH3 2RY
Major Shareholder: David Patrick Brown
Officers: David Patrick Brown [1955] Director

Brewis Beer Co Ltd
Incorporated: 11 December 2018
Registered Office: 3 West Close, Warkworth, Morpeth, Northumberland, NE65 0JZ
Shareholders: Christopher Brewis; Maxine Brewis
Officers: Christopher Brewis [1967] Director; Maxine Brewis [1964] Director

Brewit Microbrewery Ltd
Incorporated: 28 January 2015
Net Worth Deficit: £31,905 *Total Assets:* £59,513
Registered Office: 151 Cleveland Street, London, W1T 6QN
Shareholders: Raymond Jonathan Corner; Marie Jones
Officers: Raymond Jonathan Corner [1969] Director/Sales

Brewkeepers Limited
Incorporated: 17 April 2018
Registered Office: The Incuhive Space, Mayflower Close, Chandler's Ford, Eastleigh, Hants, SO53 4AR
Major Shareholder: Steven John Northam
Officers: Steven John Northam [1984] Director

Breworks Ltd
Incorporated: 15 July 2014 *Employees:* 23
Net Worth Deficit: £144,811 *Total Assets:* £440,747
Registered Office: Black Swan Hotel, 18 Birdgate, Pickering, N Yorks, YO18 7AL
Shareholders: Philip Robert Hall; Jill Hall
Officers: Jill Hall, Secretary; Jill Hall [1967] Director/Publican; Philip Robert Hall [1964] Director/Brewer

Brews Brothers Brewery Ltd
Incorporated: 12 November 2015
Registered Office: 5 Common Road, Ingrave, Brentwood, Essex, CM13 3QL
Shareholders: Joshua Whyatt; Christopher John Pascoe; Richard Pascoe
Officers: Christopher John Pascoe [1984] Director; Richard Pascoe [1986] Director; Joshua Whyatt [1990] Director

Brews of the World Limited
Incorporated: 17 January 2017
Net Worth Deficit: £18,663 *Total Assets:* £35,136
Registered Office: 159 Station Street, Burton on Trent, Staffs, DE14 1BN
Shareholders: Robin Anthony Ludlow; Christopher McCormack
Officers: Robin Anthony Ludlow [1976] Director; Christopher McCormack [1975] Director

Brewshed Ltd
Incorporated: 17 August 2016 *Employees:* 1
Net Worth Deficit: £21,114 *Total Assets:* £149,388
Registered Office: The One Bull, 25 Angel Hill, Bury St Edmunds, Suffolk, IP33 1UZ
Shareholders: Roxane Elizabeth Marjoram; David Marjoram
Officers: Roxane Elizabeth Marjoram, Secretary; David Marjoram [1976] Director/Publican

Brewsmith Beer Limited
Incorporated: 20 January 2014
Net Worth Deficit: £99,698 *Total Assets:* £216,244
Registered Office: 8-10 Bolton Street, Ramsbottom, Bury, Lancs, BL0 9HX
Shareholders: James Edward Smith; Jennifer Ellen Smith
Officers: James Edward Smith [1978] Director; Jennifer Ellen Smith [1978] Director

Brewsmith Limited
Incorporated: 9 March 2018
Registered Office: 96 Welham Road, Retford, Notts, DN22 6UG
Major Shareholder: Dorothy Smith
Officers: Dorothy Smith [1946] Director

Brewster's Brewing Company Limited
Incorporated: 26 June 1997 *Employees:* 5
Net Worth: £167,783 *Total Assets:* £280,330
Registered Office: The Hollies, Main Street, Woolsthorpe, Grantham, Lincs, NG32 1LT
Shareholder: Sara Louise McArdle
Officers: Sean Peter McArdle, Secretary/Accountant; Sara Louise McArdle [1965] Director/Brewer; Sean Peter McArdle [1965] Director/Accountant

Brick Brewery Ltd
Incorporated: 29 August 2012 *Employees:* 14
Net Worth: £284,294 *Total Assets:* £585,028
Registered Office: Units 13-14 Deptford Industrial Estate, Blackhorse Road, London, SE8 5HY
Shareholders: Ian Donald Robertson Stewart; Sally Lorraine Stewart
Officers: Ian Donald Robertson Stewart [1970] Managing Director; Sally Lorraine Stewart [1976] Director

Bridge House Brewery Limited
Incorporated: 22 January 2010 *Employees:* 3
Net Worth: £8,729 *Total Assets:* £142,661
Registered Office: Wilkinson and Partners, Fairfax House, 6a Mill Field Road, Cottingley Business Park, Cottingley, Bingley, W Yorks, BD16 1PY
Shareholder: Mark Anthony Kelly
Officers: Andrew Clough [1957] Director; David Jonathan Halliday [1970] Director; Mark Anthony Kelly [1964] Director; David Ayrton Stocks [1964] Director

The Bridgehouse Pub Company Ltd
Incorporated: 16 August 2013 *Employees:* 64
Net Worth: £35,911 *Total Assets:* £272,867
Registered Office: 6a Mill Field Road, Cottingley Business Park, Cottingley, W Yorks, BD16 1PY
Shareholders: Mark Anthony Kelly; Andrew Clough; David John Halliday
Officers: Andrew Clough [1957] Managing Director; David John Halliday [1958] Managing Director; Mark Anthony Kelly [1964] Managing Director; David Ayrton Stocks [1964] Director

Bridgnorth Brewery Limited
Incorporated: 22 January 2019
Registered Office: 41 Wardle Way, Kidderminster, Worcs, DY11 5UJ
Officers: Andrea Dayus, Secretary; Christopher Jon Dayus [1968] Director

Bridgnorth Brewing Co. Ltd.
Incorporated: 5 January 2006
Net Worth: £19,172 *Total Assets:* £32,938
Registered Office: 46 High Street, Bridgnorth, Salop, WV16 4DX
Major Shareholder: Annabelle Beaman
Officers: Richard Edward Beaman, Secretary; Annabelle Beaman [1996] Director

Bridlington Brewing Co. Limited
Incorporated: 15 January 2014
Net Worth Deficit: £2,753 *Total Assets:* £87,050
Registered Office: 34-35 Queen Street, Bridlington, N Yorks, YO15 2SP
Shareholders: Robert Daykin; Helen Lesley Norman
Officers: Robert Daykin [1960] Director/Brewer; Helen Lesley Norman [1964] Director/Licensee

Brightbeer Limited
Incorporated: 9 July 2012
Net Worth Deficit: £1,422 *Total Assets:* £16,861
Registered Office: 38 Andrews Way, Salisbury, Wilts, SP2 8QR
Major Shareholder: Roderick Read MacDonald
Officers: Roderick Read MacDonald [1958] Director/Brewer & Software Developer

Brighton Bier Limited
Incorporated: 18 September 2012 *Employees:* 3
Net Worth Deficit: £32,744 *Total Assets:* £108,751
Registered Office: Unit 10 Bell Tower Industrial Estate, Roedean Road, Brighton, BN2 5RU
Shareholders: Oliver John Fisher; Gary James Sillence; Stephen Whitehurst
Officers: Stephen Whitehurst, Secretary; Oliver Fisher [1976] Director; Gary James Sillence [1975] Director - Brewer; Stephen Whitehurst [1973] Director

Brighton Brewery Ltd
Incorporated: 5 November 2012
Registered Office: 8 Sillwood Place, Brighton, BN1 2LH
Officers: Richard Moore [1964] Director; Stephen Oliver [1969] Director

Brightside Brewing Company Limited
Incorporated: 28 April 2009 *Employees:* 6
Net Worth: £71,130 *Total Assets:* £258,385
Registered Office: 41 Knowsley Street, Bury, Lancs, BL9 0ST
Shareholder: Neil Friedrich
Officers: Maxine Louise Friedrich, Secretary; Carley Friedrich [1981] Director; Lance Friedrich [1984] Director; Maxine Louise Friedrich [1948] Director; Neil Friedrich [1956] Director

Brightwater Brewery Limited
Incorporated: 22 August 2012 *Employees:* 2
Net Worth Deficit: £73,003 *Total Assets:* £29,801
Registered Office: 8-10 South Street, Epsom, Surrey, KT18 7PF
Major Shareholder: Edward Alexander Coomes
Officers: Edward Alexander Coomes [1966] Director/Brewer

Brimstage Brewing Co. Ltd
Incorporated: 9 December 2004
Net Worth: £71,343 *Total Assets:* £106,228
Registered Office: 26 Thingwall Road, Irby, Wirral, Merseyside, CH61 3UE
Officers: Graham Edward Tomkins, Secretary; Benjamin John Matthew Young [1983] Director; Nathanial Joseph Young [1986] Director

Brinkburn Street Brewery Ltd
Incorporated: 20 January 2015 *Employees:* 5
Net Worth Deficit: £256,380 *Total Assets:* £136,837
Registered Office: Unit 1a, Ford Street, Ouseburn Valley, Byker, Newcastle upon Tyne, NE6 1LN
Major Shareholder: Lee Andrew Renforth
Officers: Dr Lee Andrew Renforth [1968] Managing Director

Bristol Brewing Company Limited
Incorporated: 14 June 2002 *Employees:* 16
Net Worth: £1,019,485 *Total Assets:* £1,921,805
Registered Office: Bristol Beer Factory Tap Room, 291 North Street, Bedminster, Bristol, BS3 1JP
Major Shareholder: George Robin Paget Ferguson
Officers: Simon John Bartlett [1966] Director/Brewing; Sam Burrows [1979] Sales Director; George Robin Paget Ferguson [1947] Director/Architect; Natasha Clare Arabella Elsbeth Miller [1974] Finance Director; Guy Barrington Newell [1948] Director; Rebecca Anne Newell [1963] Director

Brithop Brewing Company Limited
Incorporated: 1 September 2017
Registered Office: 133 Parsonage Manorway, Belvedere, Kent, DA17 6NG
Major Shareholder: Stuart James Holland
Officers: Stuart James Holland [1978] Director/Brewer

Brixton Brewery Limited
Incorporated: 3 June 2013 *Employees:* 19
Net Worth: £18,158 *Total Assets:* £2,030,560
Registered Office: Unit 1 & 2 Dylan Road, London, SE24 0HL
Shareholder: Heineken UK Limited
Officers: Jeremy Daniel Galaun [1976] Managing Director, Brixton Brewery; David Michael Ross [1976] Director [Canadian/British]; Johannes Henricus Adrianus Van Esch [1974] Director/Brewing and Operations Manager [Dutch]

Brixworth Brewery Company Ltd
Incorporated: 16 July 2018
Registered Office: 88a Northampton Road, Brixworth, Northampton, NN6 9DY
Major Shareholder: Jason Tear
Officers: Jason Tear [1968] Director

Broadtown Brewery Ltd
Incorporated: 24 July 2018
Registered Office: 29 Broad Town Road, Swindon, Wilts, SN4 7RB
Officers: Jason Bayliffe [1969] Director; Anthony Raymond Davies [1967] Director/Engineer

Broadway Brewery Ltd
Incorporated: 10 January 2014
Net Worth Deficit: £5,637 *Total Assets:* £800
Registered Office: 21 Eltham Drive, Priorslee, Telford, Salop, TF2 9NQ
Major Shareholder: Peter George Giles
Officers: Christopher Morris, Secretary; Peter George Giles [1960] Director/Engineer

Brockenhurst Brewery Limited
Incorporated: 20 June 2017
Registered Office: Balmer Lawn Hotel, Lyndhurst Road, Brockenhurst, Hants, SO42 7ZB
Shareholders: Trevor Victor Madden; Christopher Edwin Wilson
Officers: Christopher Edwin Wilson [1960] Director

Brockley Brewing Company Ltd.
Incorporated: 1 May 2012 *Employees:* 3
Net Worth: £70,977 *Total Assets:* £117,852
Registered Office: 31 Harcourt Road, London, SE4 2AJ
Officers: Michael Avis [1964] Director/Procurement Manager; Michael Gerard John Basquill [1956] Director/Retired [Irish]; Deborah Anne Canavan [1960] Director/Business Adviser; Rachel Lucy Gretton [1964] Director/Solicitor

Broken Bridge Brewing Ltd
Incorporated: 12 January 2016
Net Worth Deficit: £5,335 *Total Assets:* £47,787
Registered Office: A2 Yeoman Gate, Yeoman Way, Worthing, W Sussex, BN13 3QZ
Officers: Caroline McGeever [1964] Director; Katie McGeever [1991] Director; Michael Dermot Patrick McGeever [1962] Director; Richard Warman [1984] Director

Brolly Brewing Limited
Incorporated: 16 August 2016
Net Worth Deficit: £6,656 *Total Assets:* £8,673
Registered Office: 17 Madeira Avenue, Horsham, W Sussex, RH12 1AB
Major Shareholder: Brook Saunders
Officers: Brook Saunders [1975] Trading Director

Bromtec Limited
Incorporated: 11 April 2007
Registered Office: 23 Ashford Drive, Appleton, Warrington, Cheshire, WA4 5GG
Major Shareholder: Ian Bromley
Officers: Ruth Helen Bromley, Secretary; Ian Bromley [1967] Director/Project Engineer

The UK Brewing Industry

Brook House Brewery Limited
Incorporated: 17 May 2013
Net Worth Deficit: £5,267 *Total Assets:* £72,138
Registered Office: 12 Besthorpe Road, Collingham, Newark, Notts, NG23 7NP
Major Shareholder: Henry John Bealby
Officers: Henry John Bealby [1957] Director

Brooks Brewhouse Limited
Incorporated: 23 June 2015
Net Worth Deficit: £9,162 *Total Assets:* £11,557
Registered Office: 17 Birkenhead Road, Hoylake, Meols, Wirral, Merseyside, CH47 5AE
Major Shareholder: Robert Charles Brooks
Officers: Robert Charles Brooks [1955] Director/Graphic Designer

Brotherhood Brewery Ltd
Incorporated: 27 June 2016
Net Worth Deficit: £42,376 *Total Assets:* £62,554
Registered Office: Unit 20 Northacre Industrial Park, Westbury, Wilts, BA13 4WF
Major Shareholder: Joseph Brian Lewis
Officers: Joseph Brian Lewis [1987] Director/Accountant

Brothers of Ale Limited
Incorporated: 17 October 2017
Registered Office: Unit 3 Anglo Buildings, Baldwin Road, Stourport on Severn, Worcs, DY13 9AX
Shareholders: Alexander Vale; Sebastian Vale
Officers: Sebastian Vale [1992] Director

Broughton Ales Limited
Incorporated: 14 August 1995 *Employees:* 9
Net Worth: £269,366 *Total Assets:* £502,688
Registered Office: Main Street, Broughton Village, Biggar, S Lanarks, ML12 6HQ
Shareholders: Stephen Lawrence McCarney; David Andrew McGowan; John Simon Hunt
Officers: John Simon Hunt [1963] Director; Stephen Lawrence McCarney [1961] Director; David Andrew McGowan [1963] Director

Broxbourne Brewery Ltd.
Incorporated: 18 May 2011 *Employees:* 2
Previous: Chameleon By Design Ltd
Net Worth Deficit: £38,642 *Total Assets:* £44,894
Registered Office: 6 St Marys Mead, Broomfield, Chelmsford, Essex, CM1 7ZT
Shareholders: Martin William Smith; Gillian Margaret Burgis-Smith
Officers: Gillian Burgis [1968] Director/Architect; Martin William Smith [1966] Director/Brewer

Brucehaven Brewery Ltd.
Incorporated: 7 March 2016
Registered Office: Wellheads House, Sandilands, Limekilns, Dunfermline, Fife, KY11 3JD
Major Shareholder: Steven Hope
Officers: Steven Hope [1963] Director

Bruin Beer Company Ltd
Incorporated: 22 January 2019
Registered Office: 65 Southbourne Grove, Bournemouth, BH6 3QU
Major Shareholder: David Graham Holland
Officers: David Graham Holland [1965] Director

Brumaison Ltd
Incorporated: 31 March 2015
Net Worth Deficit: £31,853 *Total Assets:* £39,504
Registered Office: The Stables, Goblands Farm Business Centre, Cemetery Lane, Hadlow, Kent, TN11 0LT
Shareholders: Peter James Alldis; Caroline Alldis
Officers: Caroline Alldis [1962] Director/GP Receptionist; Peter James Alldis [1962] Director/IT Manager

The Brunswick Brewing Co Ltd
Incorporated: 3 April 2013
Net Worth: £26,569 *Total Assets:* £76,901
Registered Office: 22a Burton Street, Melton Mowbray, Leics, LE13 1AF
Major Shareholder: James Salmon
Officers: James Peter Salmon [1979] Director/Local Brewer

Brute Brewing Company Ltd
Incorporated: 5 April 2017
Registered Office: 9 Slievecorragh Avenue, Newcastle, Co Down, BT33 0JA
Major Shareholder: David Andrew Irvine
Officers: David Andrew Irvine [1983] Director/Chef

Bubble Works Brew Co Ltd
Incorporated: 21 September 2015 *Employees:* 2
Net Worth Deficit: £3,924 *Total Assets:* £6,021
Registered Office: 71 London Road, St Albans, Herts, AL1 1LN
Shareholders: John Gudgin; Benjamin Hudson
Officers: John Gudgin [1984] Director; Benjamin Hudson [1984] Director

Buccaneer Brewery Ltd
Incorporated: 21 April 2016
Net Worth Deficit: £16,350 *Total Assets:* £4,201
Registered Office: Sycamore House, Sutton Quays Business Park, Sutton Weaver, Runcorn, Cheshire, WA7 3EH
Shareholders: Manuela Alice Simpson; Michelle Louise Bryan
Officers: Michelle Louise Bryan [1982] Director; Manuela Alice Simpson [1961] Director

Bucket Brewing Company Limited
Incorporated: 17 December 2007
Registered Office: 1 Stratton Road, Princes Risborough, Bucks, HP27 9BH
Major Shareholder: Ian Frederick Coventry
Officers: Ian Coventry, Secretary; Ian Frederick Coventry [1956] Director/General Manager

Bucklebury Brewers Ltd
Incorporated: 18 February 2019
Registered Office: Highgates, Broad Lane, Upper Bucklebury, Reading, Berks, RG7 6QJ
Officers: Stephen Harris [1966] Director; Raymond Peter Herbert [1956] Director/Engineer

Buffy's Brewery Limited
Incorporated: 2 October 2002 *Employees:* 2
Net Worth Deficit: £215,413 *Total Assets:* £81,018
Registered Office: Mardle Hall, Rectory Road, Tivetshall St Mary, Norwich, NR15 2DD
Shareholders: Roger William Abrahams; Julie Savory
Officers: Julie Savory, Secretary; Roger William Abrahams [1951] Director/Head Brewer; Julie Savory [1960] Director/Office Manager

Bullards Beers Limited
Incorporated: 19 October 2018
Registered Office: 2 Chestnut Cottage, Bunwell Road, Spooner Row, Wymondham, Norfolk, NR18 9LH
Parent: Bullards Holding Company Limited
Officers: Clare Evans [1969] Director; Russel Barrie Evans [1962] Director

Bulletproof Brewing Ltd
Incorporated: 22 March 2016
Net Worth Deficit: £6,894 *Total Assets:* £21,439
Registered Office: Highlands, Queens Road, Lipson, Plymouth, PL4 7PJ
Major Shareholder: Philip Patrick Lawrence
Officers: Connor William David Johnson [1990] Director/Brewer; Benjamin James Lawrence [1981] Director; Philip Patrick Lawrence [1979] Director/Owner

Bullfinch Brewery Limited
Incorporated: 19 February 2013
Net Worth: £1,583 *Total Assets:* £48,229
Registered Office: 2 Sinclair Place, Brockley, London, SE4 1RS
Shareholders: Carly Ann Morris; Ryan Francis McLean
Officers: Ryan Francis McLean [1976] Director/Sound Engineer; Carly Ann Morris [1980] Director/Dog Groomer

Bullhouse Brewing Company Limited
Incorporated: 22 November 2017
Registered Office: 10 Greengraves Road, Newtownards, Co Down, BT23 5AG
Major Shareholder: William David Mayne
Officers: William David Mayne [1992] Managing Director

Bullmastiff Brewery Limited
Incorporated: 10 March 2015
Net Worth Deficit: £69,185 *Total Assets:* £24,468
Registered Office: 14 Bessemer Close, Cardiff, CF11 8DL
Major Shareholder: Andrew James Mackie
Officers: Andrew James Mackie [1963] Director

The Burford Brewery Company Limited
Incorporated: 8 October 2015
Registered Office: Orchard House, Crab Apple Way, Vale Business Park, Evesham, Worcs, WR11 1GE
Major Shareholder: Geoffrey John Cleaver
Officers: Geoffrey John Cleaver [1962] Director

Burner Drinks Limited
Incorporated: 18 April 2017
Net Worth Deficit: £2,365 *Total Assets:* £8,999
Registered Office: 27 Old Gloucester Street, London, WC1N 3AX
Shareholders: Gregory James Nutt; Adam John Sisson
Officers: Gregory James Nutt [1981] Director/Financial Analyst; Adam John Sisson [1982] Director/Structural Engineer

Burning Sky Brewery Limited
Incorporated: 22 March 2013
Net Worth: £209,241 *Total Assets:* £508,801
Registered Office: 1st Floor, 11 Church Street, Melksham, Wilts, SN12 6LS
Major Shareholder: Mark Crispin Tranter
Officers: Mark Crispin Tranter [1972] Director/Brewer

Burning Soul Brewing Ltd
Incorporated: 15 February 2016
Net Worth Deficit: £8,136 *Total Assets:* £36,823
Registered Office: 51 Mott Street, Unit 1, Mott Street Industrial Estate, Birmingham, B19 3HE
Shareholders: Richard James Murphy; Christopher Richard Marvin Small
Officers: Richard James Murphy [1987] Director/Brewer; Christopher Richard Marvin Small [1987] Director/Brewer

Burnt Hill Brewery Limited
Incorporated: 13 November 2017
Registered Office: Minstead Manor Farm Minstead Manor Farm, Emery Down, Lyndhurst, Hants, SO43 7GA
Major Shareholder: Harry Rupert Green
Officers: Harry Rupert Green [1989] Director

Burnt Mill Brewery Ltd
Incorporated: 1 August 2016
Net Worth Deficit: £19,244 *Total Assets:* £263,470
Registered Office: Unit 10 The Woodlands, Badley, Ipswich, Suffolk, IP6 8RS
Major Shareholder: Charles Hugo Claude O'Reilly
Officers: Eric Charles Morton [1955] Director; Sally Anne Morton [1958] Director; Charles O'Reilly [1986] Director/Founder; Dr David Terence O'Reilly [1956] Director; Olivia O'Reilly [1987] Director

Burton Bridge Brewery Limited
Incorporated: 18 July 2002 *Employees:* 13
Net Worth: £697,584 *Total Assets:* £876,928
Registered Office: Burton Bridge Brewery, 24 Bridge Street, Burton on Trent, Staffs, DE14 1SY
Shareholders: Geoffrey Charles Mumford; James Bruce Wilkinson
Officers: James Bruce Wilkinson, Secretary; Geoffrey Charles Mumford [1942] Director/Brewer; James Bruce Wilkinson [1948] Director/Brewer

The Burton Old Cottage Beer Company Limited
Incorporated: 23 May 2017 *Employees:* 4
Net Worth Deficit: £45,851 *Total Assets:* £54,471
Registered Office: Unit 10 Eccleshall Business Park, Hawkins Lane, Burton on Trent, Staffs, DE14 1PT
Shareholders: Jeffrey Stephen Denton Alden; Roger Barry Shone
Officers: Jeffrey Stephen Denton Alden [1968] Director; Roger Barry Shone [1969] Director

Burton Town Brewery Limited
Incorporated: 23 July 2015
Net Worth Deficit: £20,040 *Total Assets:* £53,123
Registered Office: 81 Burton Road, Derby, DE1 1TJ
Major Shareholder: Richard Cully
Officers: Richard Lewis Cully [1961] Director/Specialist Orthodontist

The Bushey Brewery Company Limited
Incorporated: 1 July 2014
Registered Office: 34 King Street, Tring, Herts, HP23 6BJ
Officers: Julian Kendall Evans [1958] Director; Rachel Dawn Osnowska-Evans [1961] Director

Butcombe Brewery Limited
Incorporated: 8 January 2003 *Employees:* 395
Net Worth: £5,004,378 *Total Assets:* £48,207,372
Registered Office: Cox's Green, Wrington, Bristol, BS40 5PA
Parent: Butcombe Brewing Company Limited
Officers: Richard Stuart Grainger [1960] Director; Timothy Hubert [1962] Director; Nigel Richard Osborne [1966] Director; Jayson Peter Perfect [1979] Director

Butcombe Brewing Company Limited
Incorporated: 8 January 2003
Net Worth: £3,855,656 *Total Assets:* £6,020,774
Registered Office: Cox's Green, Wrington, Bristol, BS40 5PA
Parent: The Liberation Group UK Limited
Officers: Richard Stuart Grainger [1960] Director; Timothy Hubert [1962] Director; Nigel Richard Osborne [1966] Director

Butcombe Pubco Limited
Incorporated: 14 August 1978
Registered Office: Cox's Green, Wrington, Bristol, BS40 5PA
Parent: Butcombe Brewing Company Limited
Officers: Richard Stuart Grainger [1960] Director; Timothy Hubert [1962] Director; Nigel Richard Osborne [1966] Director

Bute Brew Co Ltd
Incorporated: 14 March 2016
Net Worth: £3,453 *Total Assets:* £48,370
Registered Office: 15-17 Columshill Street, Rothesay, Isle of Bute, PA20 0DN
Major Shareholder: Aidan Canavan
Officers: Aidan Canavan [1978] Director/Brewer

Butts Brewery Limited
Incorporated: 15 June 1994
Net Worth: £7,080 *Total Assets:* £59,245
Registered Office: Unit 6A Northfield Farm, Wantage Road, Great Shefford, Hungerford, Berks, RG17 7BY
Major Shareholder: Christopher Geoffrey Butt
Officers: Richard Bosley, Secretary/Business Consultant; Christopher Geoffrey Butt [1962] Director/Brewer

Buxton Brewery Company Ltd
Incorporated: 11 April 2008 *Employees:* 11
Net Worth: £793,708 *Total Assets:* £1,549,054
Registered Office: Unit 4b Staden Business Park, Buxton, Derbys, SK17 9RZ
Shareholders: Deborah Kathleen Quinn; Geoff Quinn
Officers: Deborah Kathleen Quinn, Secretary; Denis Andrew Johnstone [1986] Director; Deborah Kathleen Quinn [1972] Director; Geoff Quinn [1971] Director/Brewer

Buzz Brewing Company Limited
Incorporated: 2 March 2016
Registered Office: 43 Cobham Road, Kingston upon Thames, Surrey, KT1 3AE
Shareholder: Conor Gerard O'Reilly
Officers: Conor O'Reilly, Secretary; Conor O'Reilly [1966] Director/Management Consultant [Irish]; Petr Tischler [1985] Director/Bar Manager [Czech]

By The Horns Ltd
Incorporated: 14 April 2011
Net Worth Deficit: £67,871 *Total Assets:* £125,837
Registered Office: 25 Summerstown, London, SW17 0BQ
Shareholder: Alex Bull
Officers: Alex Bull [1986] Director/Brewery Manager; Christopher Mills [1984] Director/Brewery Manager

By The River Brewery Ltd
Incorporated: 1 November 2017
Registered Office: Tait Walker LLP Bulman House, Regent Centre, Gosforth, Newcastle upon Tyne, NE3 3LS
Shareholders: David Jonathan Stone; Robert Cameron
Officers: Robert Cameron [1968] Director; David Jonathan Stone [1963] Director

Byatt's Brewery Ltd
Incorporated: 15 July 2010
Net Worth Deficit: £65,657 *Total Assets:* £211,745
Registered Office: Units 7 & 8 Lythalls Lane Industrial Estate, Lythalls Lane, Coventry, Warwicks, CV6 6FL
Major Shareholder: Lee Anthony Byatt
Officers: Lee Anthony Byatt [1971] Director; Shelley Ann Chamley-Byatt [1978] Director

Cader Ales Limited
Incorporated: 3 January 2012 *Employees:* 1
Net Worth: £30,551 *Total Assets:* £40,551
Registered Office: Tan Y Coed, Arthog New Barns, Arthog, Dolgellau, Gwynedd, LL39 1YU
Major Shareholder: Sean St John Meagher
Officers: Sean St John Meagher [1964] Director

The Cains Brewing Company Limited
Incorporated: 13 March 2018
Registered Office: Eccleston Arms Bar and Grill, 156 Prescott Road, St Helens, Merseyside, WA10 3TU
Parent: Mikhail Hotels and Leisure Limited
Officers: Robert Ashcroft [1983] Director; Andrew Mikhail [1974] Director

Cains Limited
Incorporated: 22 January 2009
Registered Office: Robert Cain Brewery, Stanhope Street, Liverpool, L8 5XJ
Shareholders: Balginder Kaur Dusanj; Sudarghara Singh Dusanj
Officers: Balginder Kaur Dusanj, Secretary; Sudarghara Singh Dusanj [1965] Director

The Cairngorm Brewery Co. Ltd.
Incorporated: 16 September 1999 *Employees:* 41
Net Worth: £429,895 *Total Assets:* £2,449,294
Registered Office: 12 Dalfaber Industrial Estate, Dalfaber Drive, Aviemore, Inverness-shire, PH22 1ST
Shareholder: Martin John Riley
Officers: Samantha Jane Faircliff [1964] Managing Director; Martin John Riley [1952] Director/Manager; Merlin Sandbach [1970] Sales Director; Colin Douglas Richardson Whittle [1947] Director/Solicitor

Calarta Ltd
Incorporated: 14 August 2018
Registered Office: 7 Palm Court, Green Lane, Hadfield, Glossop, Derbys, SK13 2DB
Major Shareholder: Holly Beth Cassin
Officers: Holly Beth Cassin [1993] Director/Consultant

Caledonian Brewery Limited
Incorporated: 5 May 1987 *Employees:* 3
Net Worth: £6,628,848 *Total Assets:* £6,900,321
Registered Office: 3-4 Broadway Park, South Gyle Broadway, Edinburgh, EH12 9JZ
Parent: Heineken UK Limited
Officers: David Michael Forde [1968] Managing Director [Irish]; Lynsey Jane Nicoll [1980] Director/Senior Commercial Lawyer; Radovan Sikorsky [1967] Finance Director [Slovak]

Calside Brewery and Taste Room Limited
Incorporated: 7 March 2008
Registered Office: 31 Stanely Avenue, Paisley, Renfrewshire, PA2 9LB
Major Shareholder: David Simpson
Officers: Carole Simpson, Secretary; David Simpson [1971] Managing Director

Calverley's Brewery Ltd
Incorporated: 19 April 2013 Employees: 6
Net Worth Deficit: £18,627 Total Assets: £13,813
Registered Office: 87 Scholars Walk, Cambridge, CB4 1DW
Major Shareholder: Samuel Thomas Calverley
Officers: Samuel Thomas Calverley [1983] Director; Thomas George Calverley [1985] Director

Calvors Brewery Limited
Incorporated: 18 February 2008 Employees: 5
Net Worth: £213,413 Total Assets: £393,900
Registered Office: The Gables, Coddenham Green, Ipswich, Suffolk, IP6 9UN
Shareholders: Alec Philip Williamson; Andrew Williamson
Officers: Alec Philip Williamson [1983] Director/Brewer

Cambridge-Brewery Limited
Incorporated: 9 January 2012
Net Worth Deficit: £11,399 Total Assets: £36,924
Registered Office: 24e Norwich Street, Dereham, Norfolk, NR19 1BX
Major Shareholder: Kay Diane Edwards
Officers: Kay Diane Edwards [1960] Director/Publican; William George Edwards [1992] Director/Brewer

Camden Beer Ltd
Incorporated: 31 January 2019
Registered Office: 94 Parsloes Avenue, Dagenham, Essex, RM9 5NU
Major Shareholder: Tulsi Das Rajbahak
Officers: Tulsi Das Rajbahak [1976] Director/Self Employed

Camden Brewing Group Limited
Incorporated: 4 February 2015
Net Worth: £1,758,826 Total Assets: £1,788,777
Registered Office: Porter Tun House, 500 Capability Green, Luton, Beds, LU1 3LS
Parent: Pioneer Brewing Company
Officers: Terri Francis, Secretary; Jasper George Cuppaidge [1975] Director [Australian]; Oliver James Devon [1989] Finance Director; Claire Louise Richardson [1983] People Director

Camden Town Brewery Limited
Incorporated: 19 March 2009 Employees: 101
Net Worth Deficit: £5,222,359 Total Assets: £39,531,716
Registered Office: Bureau, Fetter Lane, London, EC4A 1EN
Parent: Camden Brewing Group Limited
Officers: Terri Francis, Secretary; Rory Batt [1986] Managing Director; Jasper George Cuppaidge [1975] Director/Brewer [Australian]; Terri Nicole Francis [1986] Director/Lawyer [Australian]; Adrien Mahieu [1985] Director [Belgian]

Camerons Brewery Limited
Incorporated: 27 May 1998 Employees: 450
Net Worth: £16,119,376 Total Assets: £60,147,224
Registered Office: Main Gate House, Waldon Street, Hartlepool, Cleveland, TS24 7QS
Shareholders: David John Soley; Ramscove Ltd
Officers: John Richard Foots, Secretary; John Richard Foots [1968] Director/Chartered Accountant; Christopher David Soley [1975] Commercial Director; David John Soley [1949] Director/Management Consultant

Joseph Camm Farms Limited
Incorporated: 21 March 1962 Employees: 18
Net Worth: £14,311,667 Total Assets: £15,188,856
Registered Office: Upper Morton, Babworth, Retford, Notts, DN22 8HG
Shareholders: Ruth Margaret Girdham; Beatrix Mary Easterbrook
Officers: Mark Pickard, Secretary; Beatrix Mary Easterbrook [1966] Director/Chartered Accountant; Mark Easterbrook [1966] Director/Brewer; Ruth Margaret Girdham [1959] Director; Margaret Emily Morrell [1931] Director/Farmer

JD Campbell Brewing Limited
Incorporated: 4 October 2018
Registered Office: 3 Railton Avenue, Manchester, M16 8AU
Major Shareholder: James Douglas Campbell
Officers: James Douglas Campbell [1971] Director

Campbells Brewery Ltd
Incorporated: 25 January 2017 Employees: 2
Net Worth: £528 Total Assets: £48,707
Registered Office: Windylaws, Peebles, EH45 8PJ
Shareholders: Murray Alasdair Lister Campbell; Mark Simon Harrison
Officers: Murray Alasdair Lister Campbell [1979] Director

The Campervan Brewery Ltd
Incorporated: 3 October 2014
Net Worth Deficit: £61,409 Total Assets: £66,179
Registered Office: Unit 4 Bonnington Business Centre, 112 Jane Street, Edinburgh, EH6 5HG
Major Shareholder: Paul Andrew Gibson
Officers: Paul Andrew Gibson [1977] Director/Brewery and Food Production

Campion Ale Limited
Incorporated: 11 January 2013
Registered Office: 5 College Close, Lingfield, Surrey, RH7 6HG
Major Shareholder: James Edward Campion Williams
Officers: James Edward Campion Williams [1981] Director

Candid Brewing Co. Limited
Incorporated: 16 October 2017
Registered Office: 14 Yelverton Avenue, Stafford, ST17 0HE
Major Shareholder: Mark Christopher Carlton Bamping
Officers: Jessica Anne Bamping [1987] Director; Mark Christopher Carlton Bamping [1985] Director

Canopy Beer Company Ltd
Incorporated: 28 July 2014 Employees: 7
Net Worth: £24,013 Total Assets: £159,858
Registered Office: Arch 1127, 41 Norwood Road, London, SE24 9AJ
Shareholders: Matthew James Theobalds; Estelle Theobalds
Officers: Estelle Theobalds [1982] Director; Matthew James Theobalds [1984] Director/Head Brewer

Canterbrew Ltd
Incorporated: 14 June 2010 Employees: 4
Net Worth Deficit: £19,274 Total Assets: £66,748
Registered Office: Unit 7 Stour Valley Business Park, Ashford Road, Canterbury, Kent, CT4 7HF
Officers: Martin Richard Guy [1960] Director; Vanessa Ann Kent [1963] Director

The Cardiff Brewing Company Limited
Incorporated: 10 January 2002
Registered Office: 58 Mount Stuart Square, Cardiff Bay, CF10 5LR
Shareholders: Anwen Thomas; Pamela Dando
Officers: Pamela Dando, Secretary; Anwen Thomas [1963] Director

Carlsberg Supply Company UK Limited
Incorporated: 26 July 2013 *Employees:* 899
Net Worth: £124,421,000 *Total Assets:* £248,720,992
Registered Office: Jacobsen House, 140 Bridge Street, Northampton, NN1 1PZ
Parent: Carlsberg UK Limited
Officers: Jeremy Robert Brown, Secretary; Paul Benedict Armstrong [1957] Director [Irish]; Peter Clark Hammond [1979] Director/Vice President Production

Carlsberg UK Limited
Incorporated: 28 August 1903 *Employees:* 431
Net Worth: £151,572,992 *Total Assets:* £475,660,992
Registered Office: 140 Bridge Street, Northampton, NN1 1PZ
Parent: Carlsberg UK Holdings Limited
Officers: Jeremy Robert Brown, Secretary; Anna Cecilia Gunnarsson Lundgren [1973] Director/CFO Western Europe [Swedish]; Andreas Bernhard Kirk [1974] Director [Danish]; Julian Akhtar Karim Momen [1963] Director/Chief Financial Officer; Stephen Stringer [1967] Director; Adam Stubbs [1972] Director

Carnival Brewing Company Limited
Incorporated: 6 September 2017
Registered Office: 6 Hillingdon Road, Liverpool, L15 9ES
Shareholders: Dominic Stefan Hope-Smith; Samantha Jane Burke
Officers: Samantha Jane Burke [1974] Director/Researcher; Dominic Stefan Hope-Smith [1978] Director

Cartmel Valley Brewery Ltd
Incorporated: 8 September 2015
Registered Office: Stony Dale, Egg Pudding Stone Lane, Field Broughton, Grange Over Sands, Cumbria, LA11 6HN
Shareholder: Ian Armstrong Burden
Officers: Angela Margaret Constantine Burden [1948] Director; Ian Armstrong Burden [1946] Director

Casorho Ltd
Incorporated: 18 July 2018
Registered Office: Suite 6, First Floor, Wadsworth Mill, Wordsworth Street, Bolton, Lancs, BL1 3ND
Major Shareholder: Arron Lee Chaloner
Officers: Richard Bumagat [1994] Director [Filipino]

Castle Combe Brewery Limited
Incorporated: 5 August 2008
Net Worth Deficit: £35,197 *Total Assets:* £10,699
Registered Office: 2 New Road, Chippenham, Wilts, SN15 1EJ
Parent: Flying Monk Brewery Limited
Officers: Alison Jane Hender, Secretary; Alison Jane Hender [1962] Director; Martin William Hender [1971] Director; William Thomas Hender [1930] Director

Castle Gate Brewery Limited
Incorporated: 8 August 2017
Net Worth: £1,179 *Total Assets:* £28,714
Registered Office: 6 Well Street, Llandysul, Ceredigion, SA44 4LA
Major Shareholder: Andrew Philip Meese
Officers: Andrew Philip Meese [1960] Director

Cataclysm Brewing Limited
Incorporated: 30 November 2018
Registered Office: 42 Upperton Gardens, Eastbourne, E Sussex, BN21 2AQ
Major Shareholder: Mark Daniel Colin Potter
Officers: Mark Daniel Colin Potter [1984] Director/Brewer

Caveman Brewing Company Ltd
Incorporated: 31 July 2012 *Employees:* 1
Net Worth Deficit: £49,167 *Total Assets:* £21,762
Registered Office: 3 Enterprise House, 8 Essex Road, Dartford, Kent, DA1 2AU
Major Shareholder: Nicholas Byram
Officers: Nick Byram, Secretary; Nicholas Byram [1968] Director/Brewing

Caythorpe Brewery Limited
Incorporated: 18 August 2005
Net Worth Deficit: £17,690 *Total Assets:* £19,893
Registered Office: Trentham Cottage, Boat Lane, Hoveringham, Nottingham, NG14 7JP
Major Shareholder: John Stachura
Officers: Sandra Collings, Secretary; Sandra Collings [1956] Director/Accountant; John Stachura [1953] Director/Brewer

Cellarhead Brewing Company Ltd
Incorporated: 16 March 2017 *Employees:* 5
Net Worth: £88,928 *Total Assets:* £115,353
Registered Office: Hollybank, Cryals Road, Matfield, Tonbridge, Kent, TN12 7HL
Officers: Nigel James Bent [1956] Director; Christopher Cromar McKenzie [1967] Director; Julia Caroline McKenzie [1976] Director; Ian Peter Solley [1960] Director of Property Development

Cereal Technology Limited
Incorporated: 22 August 1991
Net Worth: £107,349 *Total Assets:* £109,628
Registered Office: Jubilee House, Nottingham Road, Basford, Nottingham, NG7 7BT
Officers: David Reynolds, Secretary; Jan Peter Palewicz [1950] Director/Biochemist

Cerne Abbas Brewery Ltd
Incorporated: 21 August 2014 *Employees:* 2
Net Worth: £204 *Total Assets:* £71,515
Registered Office: 2 Mill Lane, Cerne Abbas, Dorset, DT2 7LB
Shareholders: Jodie Robert Moore; Victor Michael Irvine
Officers: Victor Michael Irvine [1970] Director/Brewer; Jodie Robert Moore [1974] Director/Brewer

CFS Castus Test 001 Ltd
Incorporated: 10 August 2009
Previous: CFS Castest Shelf Ltd
Registered Office: Dept 1794, 196 High Road, Wood Green, London, N22 8HH
Officers: Christalla Kirkillari [1978] Director/Economist [Australian]

Chain House Brewing Company Ltd
Incorporated: 23 September 2017
Registered Office: 20 Brookdale, New Longton, Preston, Lancs, PR4 4XL
Major Shareholder: Ryan Hayes
Officers: Ryan Hayes [1991] Director

The Chalk Stone Brewery Limited
Incorporated: 11 May 2016
Net Worth Deficit: £1,290 *Total Assets:* £6,651
Registered Office: 19-21 Chapel Street, Marlow, Bucks, SL7 3HN
Officers: Russell White, Secretary; Fiona White [1966] Director/Training Consultant; Russell White [1964] Director

Chantry Brewery Ltd
Incorporated: 8 December 2011 *Employees:* 1
Net Worth: £12,954 *Total Assets:* £138,249
Registered Office: Unit 1 Callum Court, Gateway Industrial Estate, Parkgate, Rotherham, S Yorks, S62 6NR
Shareholders: Michael Warburton; Kevin Waburton; Sean Thomas Page
Officers: Sean Thomas Page [1954] Director/Sales Person; Kevin Warburton [1965] Director/Brewer; Michael Warburton [1968] Director

Chapeau Brewing Limited
Incorporated: 6 May 2016
Net Worth: £19,394 *Total Assets:* £27,403
Registered Office: 55 Church Lane, London, SW19 3HQ
Shareholders: Michael John Nugent; Katharine Ann Dennes Lee
Officers: Katharine Ann Dennes Lee, Secretary; Katharine Ann Dennes Lee [1978] Director; Michael John Nugent [1980] Director

Chapter Brewing Company Limited
Incorporated: 7 July 2016
Net Worth Deficit: £29,668 *Total Assets:* £41,263
Registered Office: 38 Swanlow Lane, Winsford, Cheshire, CW7 1JE
Shareholder: Alan Keith McClellan
Officers: Sophie Claire McClellan, Secretary; Daniel John Brown [1987] Director; Dr Alan Keith McClellan [1961] Director; David Peter Stuart [1954] Director; Noah Torn [1987] Director/Brewer

Charlbury Brewing Company Limited
Incorporated: 25 March 2004
Net Worth Deficit: £51,181 *Total Assets:* £474,328
Registered Office: Three Horseshoes, Sheep Street, Charlbury, Chipping Norton, Oxon, OX7 3RR
Parent: Barry Dodman-Edwards
Officers: Matthew Dodman-Edwards, Secretary; Barry Dodman-Edwards [1955] Director/Chartered Civil Engineer

Chasing Everest Brew Co Limited
Incorporated: 27 June 2018
Registered Office: 15 Ponteland Square, Blyth, Northumberland, NE24 4SH
Officers: Isaac Nolan [1988] Director/Brewer

Cheddar Ales Limited
Incorporated: 4 March 2008
Net Worth: £177,767 *Total Assets:* £313,518
Registered Office: Winchester Farm, Draycott Road, Cheddar, Somerset, BS27 3RP
Major Shareholder: Jeremy Robert Ham
Officers: Jeremy Robert Ham, Secretary; Jeremy Robert Ham [1967] Director; Lucy Ham [1971] Director

Chelmsford Brewing Company Ltd.
Incorporated: 5 October 2016 *Employees:* 1
Net Worth Deficit: £6,178 *Total Assets:* £17,253
Registered Office: 85 Bramley Way, Mayland, Chelmsford, Essex, CM3 6ES
Major Shareholder: Johannes Stephanus Albertus Oelofse
Officers: Johannes Stephanus Albertus Oelofse [1983] Director/Brewer

Cheltenham Brewery Limited
Incorporated: 12 May 2006
Registered Office: Swinley Court, Swinley Lane, Corse Lawn, Gloucester, GL19 4PF
Officers: Kenneth Robert Pickering, Secretary; John Robert Pickering [1968] Director/General Manager

Chequers Micropub Limited
Incorporated: 13 January 2014 *Employees:* 2
Net Worth: £11,499 *Total Assets:* £56,663
Registered Office: 15 Swabys Yard, Beverley, E Yorks, HU17 9BZ
Officers: Ian David Allott [1959] Director/Publican; Maria Yolanda Allott [1961] Director/Teacher

The Cheshire Brewhouse Ltd
Incorporated: 25 April 2017
Registered Office: Unit 13 Daneside Business Park, Riverdane Road, Congleton, Cheshire, CW12 1UN
Major Shareholder: Shane Robert Swindells
Officers: Shane Swindells, Secretary; Shane Robert Swindells [1970] Director

Oliver Chester Limited
Incorporated: 10 November 2008
Net Worth Deficit: £75,943 *Total Assets:* £85,034
Registered Office: Unit 1B Townfoot Industrial Estate, Brampton, Cumbria, CA8 1SW
Major Shareholder: James Kent
Officers: Navinder Gill, Secretary; James Kent [1948] Director/Accountant

Chevin Brew Co Ltd
Incorporated: 9 February 2017
Registered Office: 4 Mill Avenue, Otley, W Yorks, LS21 1FJ
Officers: David Tindall, Secretary; Stephen Boddy [1980] Director/Brewer; David Cridland [1979] Director/Brewer; Ian Michael Shutt [1978] Director/Accountant; David Tindall [1978] Director/Brewing

Cheviot Brewery Ltd
Incorporated: 16 November 2017
Registered Office: Slainsfield, Cornhill on Tweed, Northumberland, TD12 4TP
Parent: NHB Group Ltd
Officers: Neil Adam Baker [1984] Director; Jonathan Philip Hodgson [1984] Director; Peter Charles Nash [1961] Director

Chichester Brewery Limited
Incorporated: 7 November 2016
Registered Office: St John's House, St John's Street, Chichester, W Sussex, PO19 1UU
Officers: Laurence James Creamer [1973] Director/Brewer

Chin Chin Brewing Company Ltd
Incorporated: 1 October 2015
Net Worth: £6,343 *Total Assets:* £9,386
Registered Office: Unit 53f Lidgate Crescent, South Kirkby, Pontefract, W Yorks, WF9 3NR
Shareholders: David Currie; Andrew Currie
Officers: Andrew Currie [1980] Director; David Currie [1975] Director

Chorlton Brewing Company Ltd
Incorporated: 9 May 2014
Net Worth Deficit: £68,575 *Total Assets:* £51,977
Registered Office: 69 North Western Street, Manchester, M12 6DX
Major Shareholder: Mike Marcus
Officers: Mike Marcus [1972] Director/Brewer

Christchurch Brewing Co. Limited
Incorporated: 24 March 2016
Registered Office: 23 Seafield Road, Christchurch, Dorset, BH23 4ET
Major Shareholder: Steven Robert Lee
Officers: Steven Robert Lee [1975] Director

Chubby Seal Ltd
Incorporated: 16 November 2016
Registered Office: 8-10 Shirehall Plain, Holt, Norfolk, NR25 6HT
Officers: Luke Joseph Spackman [1988] Director; Roger William Spackman [1945] Director; Hayley Louise Tullberg [1983] Director

J. Church Brewing Co. Ltd
Incorporated: 26 February 2016
Net Worth Deficit: £22,812 *Total Assets:* £35,961
Registered Office: 199a Kettering Road, Northampton, NN1 4BP
Major Shareholder: Paul Anthony Charles Hepworth
Officers: Paul Anthony Charles Hepworth [1962] Director/Accountant

Church End Brewery Limited
Incorporated: 9 February 1994 *Employees:* 45
Net Worth: £774,194 *Total Assets:* £1,354,185
Registered Office: Ridge Lane, Nuneaton, Warwicks, CV10 0RD
Shareholders: Stewart Martin Elliott; Rosemary Anne Elliott
Officers: Rosemary Ann Elliott, Secretary; Rosemary Ann Elliott [1956] Director; Stewart Martin Elliott [1956] Director/M D of Brewery

Church Farm Brewery Ltd
Incorporated: 14 May 2015
Net Worth: £36,143 *Total Assets:* £281,642
Registered Office: Church Farm, Church Lane, Budbrooke, Warwick, CV35 8QL
Officers: Michael Dennis Brown [1949] Director; Sam Brown [1987] Director; Andrew Paul Reynolds [1962] Director; Joanna Lorraine Reynolds [1961] Director

Cillenx Ltd
Incorporated: 20 August 2018
Registered Office: 25 St Georges Gardens, Denton, Manchester, M34 7TB
Major Shareholder: Kevin Challoner
Officers: Kevin Challoner [1988] Director/Manager

Cirencester Brewery Ltd
Incorporated: 26 May 2011
Registered Office: 12b Wilkinson Road, Love Lane Industrial Estate, Cirencester, Glos, GL7 1YT
Major Shareholder: Dino Sebastian Mussell
Officers: Dino Sebastian Mussell [1977] Director/Hotelier

City Vaults Real Ale Ltd
Incorporated: 9 November 2017
Registered Office: c/o Tiffin, 20 Commondale Way, Euroway Industrial Estate, Bradford, W Yorks, BD4 6SF
Shareholders: Lisa Marie Mahoney; Paul Timothy Blann
Officers: Lisa Marie Mahoney [1988] Director/Accounts Administrator

Clan Brewing Company Limited
Incorporated: 5 September 2014
Net Worth Deficit: £295 *Total Assets:* £5,777
Registered Office: Filshill International Limited Ainslie Avenue, Hillington Park, Glasgow, G52 4HE
Shareholders: J.W. Filshill Limited; Heather Ale Limited
Officers: Simon John Hannah [1977] Director; Christopher Stuart Miller [1971] Director; David Neill Moore [1970] Director; Scott John Williams [1964] Director

Clanconnel Brewing Company Limited
Incorporated: 24 June 2008
Net Worth Deficit: £12,368 *Total Assets:* £19,795
Registered Office: Quaker Buildings, High Street, Lurgan, Craigavon, Co Armagh, BT66 8BB
Shareholders: Quintessential Brands Ireland Beverages Ltd; Norman Mark Pearson
Officers: Steven Pattison [1979] Director; Norman Mark Pearson [1974] Director/Procurement Manager; Richard Henderson Ryan [1977] Director

The Clandestine Distillery Limited
Incorporated: 21 December 2018
Registered Office: Low Barn, Llancayo Business Park, Usk, Monmouthshire, NP15 1HY
Shareholders: Nathan Edward Thompson; Sarah Thompson
Officers: Nathan Edward Thompson [1978] Director

H.B.Clark & Co.(Successors) Limited
Incorporated: 31 July 1913 *Employees:* 281
Net Worth: £6,754,456 *Total Assets:* £24,827,042
Registered Office: Unit S3, Narvik Way, Tyne Tunnel Trading Estate, North Shields, Tyne & Wear, NE29 7XJ
Officers: Patricia Ada Rice, Secretary; David Leonard Brind [1972] Director; John Frederick Hope [1969] Group Operations Director; Jay MacKay [1966] Managing Director; Patricia Ada Rice [1957] Director; Paul Victor Young [1957] Director

Tony Clark Enterprises Ltd
Incorporated: 16 October 2017
Net Worth Deficit: £2,090 *Total Assets:* £79
Registered Office: 12 Longcraigs Avenue, Ardrossan, N Ayrshire, KA22 7PU
Major Shareholder: Tony Clark
Officers: Tony Clark [1993] Managing Director

Clarkshaws Brewing Company Ltd.
Incorporated: 9 May 2013
Net Worth: £90,030 *Total Assets:* £194,863
Registered Office: 34 Surrey Road, London, SE15 3AT
Shareholders: Ian Clark; Lucinda Celia Grimshaw
Officers: Ian Clark [1978] Director; Dr Lucinda Celia Grimshaw [1978] Director

Clavell & Hind Limited
Incorporated: 8 March 2017
Net Worth Deficit: £69,561 *Total Assets:* £143,921
Registered Office: 166 Northwood Way, Northwood, Middlesex, HA6 1RB
Officers: William John Bennett [1975] Director; James Warren Diamond Dobson [1973] Director/Brewery Consultant; Timothy Hieghton-Jackson [1979] Director/Head Brewer; Richard Carl Shorting [1966] Director/Estate Agent

Clearsky Brewing Company Limited
Incorporated: 21 December 2012
Net Worth Deficit: £9,269 *Total Assets:* £10,281
Registered Office: 48 Lisnagowan Road, Dungannon, Co Tyrone, BT70 3LH
Officers: Stephen Charles McKenna [1965] Director

Clearwater Brewery Ltd
Incorporated: 6 July 2009 *Employees:* 2
Net Worth Deficit: £122,911 *Total Assets:* £85,342
Registered Office: Unit 1 Little Court, Manteo Way, Bideford, Devon, EX39 4FG
Shareholders: Jennifer Ann Raynes; Barry Raynes; Barry Raynes
Officers: Barry George Raynes [1959] Director

Clifford Brothers Brewery Limited
Incorporated: 21 July 2016
Net Worth Deficit: £8,035 *Total Assets:* £11,971
Registered Office: 22 Earsham Street, Bungay, Suffolk, NR35 1AG
Shareholders: Rory Clifford; Seamus Clifford
Officers: Rory Clifford [1973] Director; Seamus Clifford [1971] Director

Cloak and Dagger Brewing Company Ltd
Incorporated: 7 December 2015
Net Worth Deficit: £6,804 *Total Assets:* £20,284
Registered Office: 35a Preston Road, Brighton, BN1 4QE
Shareholders: Ben David Hucker; Leigh James Pearce; David John Seward
Officers: Ben David Hucker [1978] Director/Consultant; Leigh James Pearce [1975] Director/Graphic Designer; David John Seward [1984] Director/Brewer

Clouded Minds Limited
Incorporated: 13 May 2013
Net Worth Deficit: £32,041 *Total Assets:* £67,881
Registered Office: Unit 5b Brailes Industrial Estate, Winderton Road, Lower Brailes, Banbury, Oxon, OX15 5JW
Officers: Peter John Hutchinson [1985] Director/Brewer; Riccardo Pulcinelli [1987] Director/Brewer [Italian]

Cloudwater Brew Co Ltd
Incorporated: 13 January 2014
Net Worth Deficit: £579,055 *Total Assets:* £1,249,277
Registered Office: Unit 7 & 8 Piccadilly Trading Estate, Manchester, M1 2NP
Major Shareholder: Paul Jones
Officers: Paul Jones [1979] Director

The Clun Brewery Ltd.
Incorporated: 9 April 2014
Net Worth: £12,159 *Total Assets:* £47,771
Registered Office: The White Horse Inn, The Square, Clun, Craven Arms, Salop, SY7 8JA
Shareholders: Matthew James Ian Williamson; John Michael Toby Clifford Limond
Officers: John Michael Toby Clifford Limond [1967] Director/Publican; Dr Matthew James Ian Williamson [1974] Director/Scientist

The Coach House Brewing Company Limited
Incorporated: 27 February 1991 *Employees:* 9
Net Worth: £150,674 *Total Assets:* £253,114
Registered Office: Wharf Street, Howley, Warrington, Cheshire, WA1 2DQ
Parent: Shawbrook Holdings Ltd
Officers: Annabel Joanna Bailey, Secretary; Martin Bryan Bailey [1973] Director

Coalition Brewing Company Ltd
Incorporated: 23 January 2015 *Employees:* 3
Net Worth Deficit: £995 *Total Assets:* £42,864
Registered Office: 15 Hillview Close, Purley, Surrey, CR8 1AU
Officers: Matthew Jon Clark [1964] Director/Food and Beverages [New Zealander]; William Roger Parkes [1984] Director/Food and Beverages

Coast Beer Co Limited
Incorporated: 7 January 2019
Registered Office: 65 Haymarket Terrace, Edinburgh, EH12 5HD
Major Shareholder: James Ronald Brown
Officers: James Ronald Brown [1989] Director/Entrepreneur

Coastal Brewing Company Limited
Incorporated: 3 January 2017
Registered Office: Shamal, Saith Llathen, Ty Croes, Isle of Anglesey, LL63 5SW
Major Shareholder: Carl Hudson
Officers: Carl Hudson [1974] Director

Cobra Beer Partnership Limited
Incorporated: 28 January 2009 *Employees:* 5
Net Worth: £12,104,656 *Total Assets:* £14,096,065
Registered Office: 137 High Street, Burton on Trent, Staffs, DE14 1JZ
Shareholders: Karan Faridoon Bilimoria; Molson Coors Brewing Company (UK) Limited
Officers: Gemma Louise Wisniewski, Secretary; Lord Karan Faridoon Bilimoria [1961] Director; Simon John Cox [1967] Director; Dynshaw Fareed Italia [1970] Director; James Christian Shearer [1980] Marketing Director; Philip Mark Whitehead [1977] Director

Cocktails and Craft Beers Ltd
Incorporated: 1 June 2015
Registered Office: 99 Dore Road, Sheffield, S17 3NF
Shareholder: Kane Steven Yeardley
Officers: Kane Yeardley [1954] Director

Colchester Brewery Ltd
Incorporated: 10 August 2011 *Employees:* 6
Net Worth: £188,612 *Total Assets:* £390,121
Registered Office: Unit 16 Wakes Hall Business Centre, Colchester Road, Wakes Colne, Colchester, Essex, CO6 2DY
Shareholders: Roger John Clark; Thomas Kenyon Knox
Officers: Anthony Charles Watney Bone, Secretary; Anthony Charles Watney Bone [1941] Director/Engineer; Roger John Clark [1950] Sales Director; Thomas Kenyon Knox [1971] Director/Brewer

Cold Bath Brewing Company Limited
Incorporated: 3 August 2017
Net Worth Deficit: £20,720 *Total Assets:* £24,107
Registered Office: 2nd Floor, Woodside House, 261 Low Lane, Horsforth, Leeds, LS18 5NY
Major Shareholder: James Raymond Mossman
Officers: James Raymond Mossman [1966] Director; Roger Timothy Moxham [1963] Director; Michael Wren [1976] Director

Cold Formd Ltd
Incorporated: 19 July 2016
Net Worth Deficit: £1,509 *Total Assets:* £31,230
Registered Office: 52 Berkeley Square, London, W1J 5BT
Shareholder: Andrew George Michael
Officers: Andrew George Michael [1983] Director

The Collyfobble Brewery Limited
Incorporated: 4 May 2017
Registered Office: Sudbrook Hall, Nesfield, Dronfield, Derbys, S18 7TB
Major Shareholder: Derek Mapp
Officers: Derek Mapp, Secretary; Derek Mapp [1950] Director

Colonsay Beverages Ltd.
Incorporated: 13 February 2015 *Employees:* 6
Net Worth: £91,704 *Total Assets:* £264,888
Registered Office: The Brew House, Dun Oran Park, Scalasaig, Isle of Colonsay, Argyll, PA61 7YW
Officers: Keith Bonnington [1976] Director/Senior Brand Manager; Allan Robert Erskine [1979] Director/Chartered Accountant; David Melville Steele Johnston [1954] Director; Christopher William Nisbet [1958] Director/Self Employed

Colonsay Brewing Co. Ltd.
Incorporated: 7 June 2006
Net Worth: £100 *Total Assets:* £900
Registered Office: The Brew House, Dun Oran Park, Scalasaig, Isle of Colonsay, Argyll, PA61 7YW
Officers: David Melville Steele Johnston [1954] Director; Christopher William Nisbet [1958] Director/Development Officer

Comet Brewery Ltd
Incorporated: 28 June 2018
Registered Office: 3rd Floor, 6-8 Bonhill Street, London, EC2A 4BX
Officers: Richard Mahoney [1986] Director/Accountant

Common Rioters Beer Limited
Incorporated: 29 October 2018
Registered Office: 19 Irwin Avenue, Plumstead, London, SE18 2HP
Shareholders: Stephen James Granville O'Connor; Maryann O'Connor
Officers: Maryann O'Connor [1980] Director/Brand Ambassador [Irish]; Stephen James Granville O'Connor [1979] Director/Brewer

The Company of Dead Brewers Limited
Incorporated: 2 March 2015
Registered Office: Vineyard Farm, Bucknowle, Norden, Corfe Castle, Wareham, Dorset, BH20 5DY
Shareholder: Alastair Wyllie Wallace
Officers: Andrew Parsons, Secretary; Paul Henry Oswald Astal Stain [1950] Director/Retired; Andrew Philip Parsons [1954] Director; Dr Alastair Wyllie Wallace [1951] Director

Compass Brewery Limited
Incorporated: 12 August 2011
Previous: Topferment Limited
Net Worth Deficit: £254,033 *Total Assets:* £57,204
Registered Office: Box 125, 94 London Road, Oxford, OX3 9FN
Major Shareholder: Gregory Michael Fish
Officers: Gregory Michael Fish [1964] Director

Conferta Ltd
Incorporated: 13 September 2018
Registered Office: Suite 4, 43 Hagley Road, Stourbridge, W Midlands, DY8 1QR
Major Shareholder: Amy Plummer
Officers: Anthony Sace [1980] Director [Filipino]

The Coniston Brewing Company Limited
Incorporated: 31 May 1994 *Employees:* 7
Net Worth: £439,763 *Total Assets:* £485,223
Registered Office: Hollin Brow, High Hollin Bank, Coniston, Cumbria, LA21 8AG
Shareholders: Ian Stewart Bradley; Susan Mary Bradley
Officers: Susan Mary Bradley, Secretary/Director; Ian Stewart Bradley [1969] Director; Susan Mary Bradley [1946] Director

Connecting Hops Ltd
Incorporated: 26 May 2017
Net Worth Deficit: £158 *Total Assets:* £1,850
Registered Office: 71-75 Shelton Street, Covent Garden, London, WC2H 9JQ
Shareholder: Edoardo Tosca
Officers: Giuseppe D'Elia [1983] Director/Software Developer [Italian]; Renata Smocowisk Miranda [1982] Director/Lodging Content Associate [Brazilian]; Edoardo Tosca [1982] Director/Software Engineer [Italian]

Consett Ale Works Limited
Incorporated: 12 March 2004 *Employees:* 3
Net Worth: £38,659 *Total Assets:* £79,895
Registered Office: Dairy Cottage, The Avenue, Wynyard, Billingham, Cleveland, TS22 5SH
Shareholders: Jeffrey John Hind; Lynn Hind
Officers: Jeffrey John Hind [1954] Director; Lynn Hind [1956] Director

Conwy Brewery Limited
Incorporated: 17 February 2003 *Employees:* 9
Net Worth: £588,127 *Total Assets:* £784,473
Registered Office: Unit 2 Ty Mawr Enterprise Park, Tan Y Graig Road, Llysfaen, Conwy, LL29 8UE
Shareholders: Gwynne Thomas; Adele Thomas
Officers: Adele Thomas, Secretary/Administrator; Adele Thomas [1971] Director/Administrator; Gwynne Byron Thomas [1969] Director/Brewer

Charles Cooper Limited
Incorporated: 5 April 1991 *Employees:* 2
Net Worth: £389,535 *Total Assets:* £585,543
Registered Office: Kenann House, Unit 32 Newby Road Industrial Estate, Newby Road, Hazel Grove, Stockport, Cheshire, SK7 5DA
Major Shareholder: David John Ware
Officers: Adele Anne Ware, Secretary; David John Ware [1957] Director

Copper Dragon Brewery Limited
Incorporated: 4 October 2016
Registered Office: Ivy Mill, Crown Street, Failsworth, Manchester, M35 9BG
Major Shareholder: Steven Taylor
Officers: Darran Hancock [1963] Director; Steven Taylor [1954] Director/Engineer

Copper Fox Brewery Ltd
Incorporated: 3 May 2017
Net Worth Deficit: £5,970 *Total Assets:* £13,087
Registered Office: 26 Aspen Grove, Westhill, Aberdeenshire, AB32 6QE
Shareholder: Kevin Cameron
Officers: Kevin Cameron [1962] Director/Police Officer

Copper Tun Ltd
Incorporated: 20 November 2013
Net Worth: £99,805 *Total Assets:* £111,000
Registered Office: Unit T6, Leyton Industrial Village, Argall Avenue, London, E10 7QP
Shareholders: Susan Patricia Kean; Shubh Dass
Officers: Rebecca Lucy Anne Kean [1990] Director/Self Employed

Corinium Ales Ltd
Incorporated: 5 April 2012
Net Worth: £3,946 *Total Assets:* £35,443
Registered Office: 22 Bowling Green Avenue, Cirencester, Glos, GL7 2HB
Shareholders: Colin Knight; Lucy Catherine Cordrey
Officers: Lucy Catherine Cordrey [1964] Director; Colin Knight [1973] Director

Cornish Brewery Limited
Incorporated: 3 April 2017
Registered Office: 17 Fettling Lane, Charlestown, St Austell, Cornwall, PL25 3FS
Officers: Kelly Shaun Fegan [1968] Director/Business Owner

Cornish Crown Limited
Incorporated: 2 October 2008 *Employees:* 2
Net Worth Deficit: £21,595 *Total Assets:* £107,958
Registered Office: The Crown, 1 Victoria Square, Penzance, Cornwall, TR18 2EP
Major Shareholder: Joshua Christian Dunkley
Officers: Joshua Christian Dunkley [1972] Director/Publican

The Cornwall and West Country Craft Brewing Company Limited
Incorporated: 25 March 2014
Net Worth Deficit: £412 *Total Assets:* £206,526
Registered Office: Kernow House, Gas Hill, Newham, Truro, Cornwall, TR1 2XP
Officers: Rolf Hugo Munding [1953] Director

Cosmic Brewing Company Ltd
Incorporated: 21 November 2017
Registered Office: 13 Glaisdale Road, Bristol, BS16 2HY
Major Shareholder: Peter Livingstone
Officers: Peter Livingstone, Secretary; Peter Livingstone [1982] Director/Engineer

Cotleigh Brewery Limited
Incorporated: 9 May 2003 *Employees:* 9
Net Worth Deficit: £21,259 *Total Assets:* £636,443
Registered Office: Cotleigh Brewery, Ford Road, Wiveliscombe, Somerset, TA4 2RE
Major Shareholder: Stephen Barry Heptinstall
Officers: Stephen Barry Heptinstall, Secretary/Director; Stephen Barry Heptinstall [1960] Director

The Cotswold Brewing Company Limited
Incorporated: 6 October 2004 *Employees:* 9
Net Worth: £62,042 *Total Assets:* £562,589
Registered Office: Hillside, Albion Street, Chipping Norton, Oxon, OX7 5BH
Shareholder: Emma Keene
Officers: Emma Keene, Secretary/Sales Manager; Emma Keene [1972] Managing Director; Richard Thomas Keene [1967] Director/Brewer

Cotswold Lion Brewery Ltd
Incorporated: 13 January 2012 *Employees:* 2
Net Worth Deficit: £340 *Total Assets:* £17,594
Registered Office: Grain Store 5, Dowmans Farm Coberley Road, Coberley, Cheltenham, Glos, GL53 9QY
Officers: Andrew Forbes [1959] Director

Cotton End Brewery Company Limited
Incorporated: 27 February 2014
Net Worth Deficit: £17,785 *Total Assets:* £12,084
Registered Office: 10 Cotton End, Northampton, NN4 8BS
Officers: Matthew John Walmsley Felce [1965] Director/Manager; Benjamin David Hall [1977] Director/Manager; Robert Hart [1971] Director/Brewer; Steven Ward [1968] Director/Retailer

Coul Brewing Company Ltd
Incorporated: 5 July 2017
Net Worth Deficit: £5,932 *Total Assets:* £9,418
Registered Office: 22 Laggan Crescent, Glenrothes, Fife, KY7 6FY
Officers: Andrew Christopher Dean [1975] Director; Sandra Rowan Duncan [1964] Director; Robyn Christina Janet Duncan - Dean [1990] Director

The Craft Beer Cab Company Limited
Incorporated: 23 November 2015
Net Worth Deficit: £9,158
Registered Office: Anova House, Wickhurst Lane, Broadbridge Heath, Horsham, W Sussex, RH12 3LZ
Officers: Joanne Leigh Coetser [1983] Director; Nicholas David Thomas [1979] Director

Craft Beer Collective Limited
Incorporated: 6 December 2018
Registered Office: 89 Coleridge Way, Borehamwood, Herts, WD6 2AE
Major Shareholder: Nicholas Simon Marsh
Officers: Nicholas Simon Marsh [1968] Director

The Craft Beer Society Ltd
Incorporated: 24 March 2015
Net Worth Deficit: £4,041 *Total Assets:* £991
Registered Office: The Firs House, Homefield Road, Chorleywood, Herts, WD3 5QJ
Officers: Michael Shaw [1963] Director

The Craft Brewery Limited
Incorporated: 8 April 2015
Net Worth Deficit: £7,500 *Total Assets:* £3,925
Registered Office: 29a Part Street, Southport, Merseyside, PR8 1HY
Major Shareholder: Robert Thornton-Davidson
Officers: Robert Thornton-Davidson [1968] Director/Owner

Craft Life Brewing Ltd.
Incorporated: 13 April 2017
Registered Office: 202 Fletching Apartments, 3 Siyah Gardens, London, E3 4TR
Major Shareholder: Cameron Alan Atkinson
Officers: Cameron Alan Atkinson [1983] Director/Chief Executive Officer

Craft Origins Limited
Incorporated: 31 August 2016
Net Worth: £100 *Total Assets:* £100
Registered Office: 1 Tofthill, Markinch, Glenrothes, Fife, KY7 6NX
Major Shareholder: John Reade
Officers: John Reade [1953] Director

The Craft Soft Drinks Community Ltd
Incorporated: 21 February 2017
Registered Office: Unit D5, Kelburn Business Park, Port Glasgow, Inverclyde, PA14 6BL
Officers: Hannah Magdaline Fisher [1983] Director; Craig Robert Strachan [1988] Director

Crafted Brewing Co. Ltd
Incorporated: 5 November 2015 *Employees:* 1
Net Worth Deficit: £42,343 *Total Assets:* £19,524
Registered Office: Ground Floor, Hallow Park, Hallow, Worcester, WR2 6PG
Shareholders: Matthew Phillip Soper; David Albert Tabberer; Phillip Soper
Officers: Matthew Philip Soper [1990] Director/Car Sales Executive; Philip Soper [1965] Director/Engineer

Craftwater Brewing Company Limited
Incorporated: 23 July 2018
Registered Office: 11 Moorsend, Kingsteignton, Newton Abbot, Devon, TQ12 3JY
Shareholders: Russell Stanley Nixon; Christopher James Thackray; Christopher Andrew Ward
Officers: Christopher James Thackray [1983] Managing Director

Crafty Beer Seller Limited
Incorporated: 14 December 2016
Registered Office: Kernow House, Gas Hill, Newham, Truro, Cornwall, TR1 2XP
Major Shareholder: Rolf Hugo Munding
Officers: Rolf Hugo Munding [1953] Director

The Crafty Brewing Co. Limited
Incorporated: 11 April 2014 Employees: 1
Net Worth Deficit: £115,802 Total Assets: £124,656
Registered Office: Thatched House Farm, Dunsfold Road, Loxhill, Godalming, Surrey, GU8 4BW
Officers: Ashley John Herman [1954] Director/Chairman; Luke Arthur John Herman [1988] Director

The Crafty Brewing Company Ltd
Incorporated: 11 April 2016
Registered Office: Thatched House Farm, Dunsfold Road, Loxhill, Godalming, Surrey, GU8 4BW
Major Shareholder: Luke Arthur John Herman
Officers: Luke Arthur John Herman [1988] Director

Crafty Leopard Brewing Co Limited
Incorporated: 8 April 2017
Net Worth: £1 Total Assets: £1
Registered Office: 1 Kingfisher Close, London, SE28 8ES
Officers: Stacey Ayeh [1972] Director/Catalyst

Crafty Monkey Brewing Co Limited
Incorporated: 26 September 2017
Registered Office: Benknowle Farm, Elwick, Hartlepool, Cleveland, TS27 3HF
Officers: Paul Garrett [1967] Director/Brewer; Gary Olvanhill [1965] Director/Brewer

Crafty Pales Ltd
Incorporated: 5 January 2015
Registered Office: Nether Farm, The Sands, Low Bradfield, Sheffield, S6 6LB
Major Shareholder: James Michael Muirhead
Officers: James Michael Muirhead [1965] Director

Crai Cider Company Limited
Incorporated: 19 September 2018
Registered Office: Pentwyn Uchaf, Crai, Brecon, Powys, LD3 8YN
Shareholders: Stephen Kinghan; Anneka Kinghan
Officers: Anneka Kinghan [1985] Director; Stephen Kinghan [1983] Director

Crank Beers Limited
Incorporated: 18 December 2018
Registered Office: 58 Barbridge Road, Bulkington, Bedworth, Warwicks, CV12 9PD
Shareholders: Damien Keith Bracey; Kyle Russell Barlow
Officers: Kyle Russell Barlow [1988] Director/Head Brewer

Crankshaft Brewery Limited
Incorporated: 24 January 2017
Registered Office: 22 Willow Tree Crescent, Leyland, Lancs, PR25 1YA
Major Shareholder: Haydn David Williams
Officers: Haydn David Williams [1973] Director

Crasi Limited
Incorporated: 3 August 2015
Net Worth: £75,719 Total Assets: £102,827
Registered Office: Heaton House, 4 Gordon Street, Nairn, IV12 4DQ
Shareholders: David Orr; Wilma Orr
Officers: David William Orr [1961] Director; Wilma Margaret Orr [1964] Director

Crate Bars Limited
Incorporated: 3 August 2015 Employees: 44
Previous: Crate Bar Limited
Net Worth: £39,648 Total Assets: £347,526
Registered Office: 1 Worsley Court, High Street, Worsley, Manchester, M28 3NJ
Parent: Crate Group (London) Limited
Officers: Neil Robert Hinchley [1973] Director; Jessica Holly Seaton [1984] Director; Thomas Roger Seaton [1981] Director

Crate Brewery Limited
Incorporated: 3 August 2015
Registered Office: 1 Worsley Court, High Street, Worsley, Manchester, M28 3NJ
Parent: Crate Group (London) Limited
Officers: Neil Robert Hinchley [1973] Director; Jessica Holly Seaton [1984] Director; Thomas Roger Seaton [1981] Director

Crazy Mountain Brewing Company UK Limited
Incorporated: 26 November 2015 Employees: 2
Net Worth Deficit: £243,273 Total Assets: £71,830
Registered Office: 1st Floor, New Road, Stourbridge, W Midlands, DY8 1PH
Shareholders: Graham Henry Burton; Kevin Thomas Selvy
Officers: Edward Firth [1967] Director; Mark Edward Charles Smith [1974] Director

Creative Juices Brewing Company Ltd
Incorporated: 19 March 2018
Registered Office: 72 Parkside Drive, Watford, Herts, WD17 3AZ
Shareholders: Ben Janaway; Sarah Jane Chiappi; Stuart Wallace
Officers: Sarah Jane Chiappi [1973] Director; Ben Janaway [1975] Director; Stuart Wallace [1978] Director

Credence Brewing Ltd
Incorporated: 25 June 2015
Net Worth: £78,233 Total Assets: £96,026
Registered Office: Unit 16b Coquet Enterprise Park, Amble, Morpeth, Northumberland, NE65 0PE
Officers: Michael Graham [1983] Director

Croft Ales Ltd
Incorporated: 4 November 2016
Net Worth Deficit: £23,475 Total Assets: £53,442
Registered Office: 32 Upper York Street, Bristol, BS2 8QN
Major Shareholder: Brendan James O'Reilly
Officers: Brendan James Oreilly [1965] Director

The Cronx Brewery Limited
Incorporated: 30 March 2012 Employees: 3
Net Worth Deficit: £90,248 Total Assets: £40,179
Registered Office: 5 Poole Road, Bournemouth, BH2 5QL
Shareholders: Simon Christopher Dale; Mark David Russell
Officers: Simon Christopher Dale [1982] Director; Mark David Russell [1983] Director

Crooked Brewing Limited
Incorporated: 15 June 2016
Net Worth Deficit: £32,720 *Total Assets:* £14,777
Registered Office: 530 Huntington Road, Huntington, York, YO32 9QA
Officers: Hudson John Aschmann [1969] Director/Chartered Accountant; Steven Joseph Dawson [1978] Director/Registered Nurse; Andrew John Evans [1969] Director/Radio Producer; Mark William Field-Gibson [1969] Director/Registered Nurse [Irish]

Crooked Fish Ltd
Incorporated: 7 September 2018
Registered Office: 17 Albany Rd Brentford, 17 Albany Road, Brentford, Hounslow, Middlesex, TW8 0NF
Major Shareholder: Peter Louis Brew
Officers: Peter Louis Brew [1973] Director [Australian]

Crooked Ship Brewery Ltd
Incorporated: 19 January 2018
Net Worth: £4 *Total Assets:* £4,100
Registered Office: Unit 6 Byron Street Mills, Millwright Street, Leeds, LS2 7QG
Shareholder: Simon Micklewright
Officers: Ian Leck [1968] Director; Simon Micklewright [1968] Director and Company Secretary; Simon Walker [1982] Director

Crosby Beverages Ltd
Incorporated: 19 February 2018
Registered Office: 193 Drayton Bridge Road, London, W13 0JH
Major Shareholder: Odi Olali
Officers: Rhys Johnson [1991] Director; Odi Olali [1990] Director

Cross Bay Brewery Limited
Incorporated: 9 January 2013
Net Worth: £4,147 *Total Assets:* £542,995
Registered Office: 46 Broadway, Morcambe, Lancs, LA4 5BJ
Major Shareholder: Peter Michael Cross
Officers: Peter Michael Cross [1958] Director/Wholesale Drinks Consultant; Malcolm John Savage [1955] Director

Cross Borders Brewing Company Ltd
Incorporated: 6 May 2015 *Employees:* 1
Net Worth Deficit: £15,019 *Total Assets:* £90,120
Registered Office: 1 Iona Street Lane, Edinburgh, EH6 8SX
Major Shareholder: Gary Daniel Munckton
Officers: Gary Daniel Munckton [1981] Director/Manager; Jonathan William Edward Wilson [1981] Director/Brewer

Cross Inn (Maesteg) Limited
Incorporated: 8 May 2003 *Employees:* 6
Net Worth: £44,921 *Total Assets:* £86,754
Registered Office: Cross Inn, Maesteg Road, Bridgend, Mid Glamorgan, CF34 9LB
Shareholders: David Morgan; Gillian Scott-Morgan
Officers: Gillian Christine Scott Morgan, Secretary; David Paul Morgan [1963] Director/Licensee; Gillian Christine Scott Morgan [1964] Director/Licensee

Crossover Blendery Limited
Incorporated: 16 January 2019
Registered Office: 56 Bonham Road, London, SW2 5HG
Shareholders: George Randle William Stagg; Charles William Wood
Officers: George Randle William Stagg [1990] Managing Director; Charles William Wood [1989] Managing Director

The Crossroads Brewery Limited
Incorporated: 7 April 2018
Registered Office: 70 Park Avenue, Washington, Tyne & Wear, NE37 2QS
Major Shareholder: Christopher Thomas Mitchinson
Officers: Christopher Thomas Mitchinson [1987] Director

Crouch Vale Brewery Limited
Incorporated: 27 October 1980 *Employees:* 18
Net Worth: £2,504,246 *Total Assets:* £2,822,445
Registered Office: 23 Haltwhistle Road, South Woodham Ferrers, Chelmsford, Essex, CM3 5ZA
Shareholder: Colin John Bocking
Officers: Fiona Michelle Bocking, Secretary; Colin John Bocking [1954] Director; Fiona Michelle Bocking [1959] Director

Crystalbrew Limited
Incorporated: 26 April 2013 *Employees:* 8
Net Worth Deficit: £62,801 *Total Assets:* £79,133
Registered Office: Unit 40 Humber Enterprise Park, Brough, N Humbers, HU15 1EQ
Officers: David Andrew Snaith [1966] Director; Nicholas James Thomas Snaith Tyldsley [1986] Director

Cuillin Brewery Limited
Incorporated: 8 March 2004
Net Worth: £49,437 *Total Assets:* £99,320
Registered Office: Forbes House, 36 Huntly Street, Inverness, IV3 5PR
Officers: Alexander James Coghill [1953] Director/Campsite Operator; Rachael MacLeod Coghill [1986] Director

Cullach Brewing Ltd
Incorporated: 12 February 2018
Registered Office: 26 Lapwing Drive, Perth, PH1 5FW
Major Shareholder: William Bond
Officers: William Bond [1989] Director/Brewer

Cullercoats Brewery Limited
Incorporated: 23 August 2011 *Employees:* 3
Net Worth: £25,985 *Total Assets:* £108,275
Registered Office: 17 St Oswins Avenue, Cullercoats, North Shields, Tyne & Wear, NE30 4PH
Shareholders: Jason William Jesse Scantlebury; Anna Ruth Scantlebury
Officers: Anna Ruth Scantlebury [1968] Director; Jason William Jesse Scantlebury [1967] Director

Cumberland Breweries Limited
Incorporated: 10 September 2008 *Employees:* 16
Net Worth: £934,778 *Total Assets:* £1,803,259
Registered Office: Alltech House, Ryhall Road, Stamford, Lincs, PE9 1TZ
Shareholders: Alltech Beverage Division Ireland Limited; Alltech Worldwide Holdings LLC
Officers: Alric Anthony Blake, Secretary; Alric Anthony Blake [1964] Director; Earl Michael Castle II [1979] Director [American]; Mark Pearse Lyons [1976] Director/President [American]; Nigel Quentin Tidbury [1969] Director/Accountant [Irish]

Curious Drinks Limited
Incorporated: 6 June 2002
Net Worth: £1,076,317 Total Assets: £2,616,154
Registered Office: Chapel Down Winery, Small Hythe Road, Tenterden, Kent, TN30 7NG
Officers: Richard Alexander Bruce Woodhouse, Secretary/Chartered Accountant; Gareth Bath [1978] Managing Director; Stewart Charles Gilliland [1957] Director; Rachel Montague-Ebbs [1982] Director; Frazer Douglas Thompson [1959] Managing Director; Richard Alexander Bruce Woodhouse [1973] Director/Chartered Accountant

Custom Head Brewing Ltd
Incorporated: 8 November 2016
Net Worth Deficit: £1,441 Total Assets: £395
Registered Office: 8 Rocklands Crescent, Lichfield, Staffs, WS13 6DH
Shareholder: Paul Samual Hudson
Officers: Paul Samual Hudson [1963] Director

Cwrw Ial Limited
Incorporated: 5 March 2013
Net Worth: £6,870 Total Assets: £82,002
Registered Office: Bryn Tirion Cottage, Ffordd Rhiw Ial, Llanarmon-Yn-Ial, Mold, Flintshire, CH7 4QD
Officers: Dr Meirion Tudor Jones [1942] Director/Retired Scientist; Douglas Rory Macpherson [1974] Director; David Willis [1950] Director

Cwrw Llyn Cyf
Incorporated: 10 September 2010 Employees: 5
Net Worth: £80,701 Total Assets: £257,403
Registered Office: 1 Parc Eithin, Ffordd Dewi Sant, Nefyn, Pwllheli, Gwynedd, LL53 6EG
Officers: Myrddin Ap Dafydd [1956] Director; Iwan Ap Llyfnwy [1972] Director; Robert Gwilym Edwards [1950] Director; Dyfed Wyn Griffith [1963] Director; Euron Wyn Griffiths [1967] Director; Gareth Hughes-Jones [1947] Director; Bleddyn Prys Jones [1967] Director; Dylan Jones [1967] Director; John Llyfnwy Jones [1943] Director; Nic Reed [1959] Director; Dafydd Peredur Williams [1959] Director; Iorwerth Llywelyn Williams [1982] Director/Accountant

Cwrw Mon Cyf
Incorporated: 8 September 2015
Registered Office: Llwydiarth Fawr, Llanerchymedd, Sir Ynys Mon, LL71 8DF
Major Shareholder: Ffion Haf Hughes
Officers: Ffion Haf Hughes [1982] Director/Businesswoman

Cwrw Ogwen Cyf
Incorporated: 3 February 2016
Net Worth: £3,922 Total Assets: £26,672
Registered Office: Moreia, South Penralt, Caernarfon, Gwynedd, LL55 1NS
Major Shareholder: John Tudur Owen
Officers: Robin Wyn Evans [1960] Director/Brewer; John Tudur Owen [1960] Director/Solicitor; Gwynedd Roberts [1970] Director/Estate Manager

Cygnus Brewing Co Limited
Incorporated: 27 April 2017
Net Worth Deficit: £3,844 Total Assets: £292,447
Registered Office: 11 Poppy Close, Ditchingham, Bungay, Suffolk, NR35 2SG
Shareholder: Warren Candler
Officers: Warren Candler [1971] Director; Melanie Rush [1964] Director

Daleside Brewery Limited
Incorporated: 24 February 1998 Employees: 11
Net Worth: £95,731 Total Assets: £387,742
Registered Office: Unit 1 Camwal Road, Starbeck, Harrogate, N Yorks, HG1 4PT
Shareholders: Alan Douglas Barker; Elizabeth Ann Barker; Cheryl Wilkins
Officers: Alan Douglas Barker, Secretary; Alan Douglas Barker [1941] Director/Accountant; Eric Lucas [1939] Director

Daleside Holdings (Harrogate) Limited
Incorporated: 12 February 2007
Registered Office: Camwal Road, Starbeck, Harrogate, N Yorks, HG1 4PT
Shareholders: Alan Douglas Barker; Eric Lucas
Officers: Alan Douglas Barker, Secretary/Chartered Accountant; Alan Douglas Barker [1941] Director/Chartered Accountant; Eric Lucas [1939] Director

Damnation Breweries Limited
Incorporated: 3 August 2015
Registered Office: 25 Flitwick Road, Ampthill, Bedford, MK45 2NS
Major Shareholder: Adam Harrison
Officers: Adam Oliver Harrison [1968] Director

Damnation Limited
Incorporated: 4 August 2015
Registered Office: 25 Flitwick Road, Ampthill, Bedford, MK45 2NS
Major Shareholder: Adam Harrison
Officers: Adam Oliver Harrison [1968] Director

Dancing Duck Beer Ltd
Incorporated: 17 April 2009 Employees: 8
Net Worth: £76,079 Total Assets: £285,361
Registered Office: Dancing Duck Brewery, 1 John Cooper Buildings, Payne Street, Derby, DE22 3AZ
Parent: Dancing Duck Holdings Ltd
Officers: Rachel Claire Matthews, Secretary; Rachel Claire Matthews [1973] Director/Brewer; Ian James Murfin [1974] Director/Engineer

Dancing Duck Holdings Ltd
Incorporated: 11 November 2014
Net Worth: £100 Total Assets: £100
Registered Office: Unit 1 John Cooper Buildings, Payne Street, Derby, DE22 3AZ
Shareholders: Ian James Murfin; Rachel Claire Matthews
Officers: Rachel Claire Matthews [1973] Director; Ian Murfin [1974] Director

Dancing Man Brewery Limited
Incorporated: 26 October 2011 Employees: 31
Net Worth: £454,471 Total Assets: £665,677
Registered Office: The Wool House, Town Quay, Southampton, SO14 2AR
Shareholders: Mandy Lacey-Cross; Aidan Lavin
Officers: Sarah Hopper [1965] Director; Mandy Lacey-Cross [1965] Director/Consultant; Aidan Lavin [1979] Director/Brewer

Dark Revolution Ltd
Incorporated: 22 January 2015 Employees: 1
Net Worth: £11,331 Total Assets: £60,015
Registered Office: Unit 9 Lancaster Road, Sarum Business Park, Salisbury, Wilts, SP4 6FB
Shareholders: Gregory Hughes; Tanya Hughes
Officers: Gregory Hughes [1973] Director; Tanya Hughes [1974] Director

The Dark Star Brewing Company Limited
Incorporated: 3 May 1995 *Employees:* 72
Net Worth: £277,025 *Total Assets:* £2,226,149
Registered Office: Griffin Brewery, Chiswick Lane South, Chiswick, London, W4 2QB
Parent: Fuller Smith & Turner P.L.C
Officers: Severine Pascale Bequin, Secretary; James Richard Cuthbertson [1974] Director/Marketing Manager; Simon Ray Dodd [1974] Director; Simon Emeny [1965] Director; Richard Hamilton Fleetwood Fuller [1960] Director; Jonathon David Swaine [1971] Director

Dark Tower Brewery Ltd
Incorporated: 25 February 2019
Registered Office: Brackenbrae, Wardend, Birnie, Elgin, Moray, IV30 8RW
Shareholders: Maria McLean; Raymond McLean
Officers: Maria McLean, Secretary; Raymond McLean, Secretary; Maria McLean [1980] Director/Councillor; Raymond McLean [1981] Director/Engineer

Dark Tribe Brewery Limited
Incorporated: 15 April 2016 *Employees:* 3
Net Worth Deficit: £21,386 *Total Assets:* £100,829
Registered Office: The Dog & Gun, High Street, East Butterwick, Scunthorpe, N Lincs, DN17 3AJ
Major Shareholder: Andrew Clarke
Officers: Andrew Clarke [1961] Director

Darkland Brewery Limited
Incorporated: 10 March 2018
Registered Office: Unit 4c, Ladyship Business Park Mill Lane, Boothtown, Halifax, W Yorks, HX3 6TA
Major Shareholder: Gavin Duncan Riach
Officers: Gavin Duncan Riach, Secretary; Gavin Duncan Riach [1968] Director

Darkplace Brewery Limited
Incorporated: 2 December 2016
Net Worth: £39,260 *Total Assets:* £41,899
Registered Office: Musbury Barn, Axminster Road, Musbury, Axminster, Devon, EX13 8AE
Shareholders: David Paul Sadler; Roger Penny Kinsella; Susi Elizabeth Sadler
Officers: Roger Kinsella [1970] Director; Dr David Paul Sadler [1981] Director; Susi Elizabeth Sadler [1982] Director

Darlington Brewing and Distilling Company Ltd
Incorporated: 26 July 2013
Registered Office: 2 Park View, Middleton Tyas, Richmond, N Yorks, DL10 6SG
Shareholder: Ralph English Wilkinson
Officers: Gillian Margaret Wilkinson [1969] Director/Designer; Ralph English Wilkinson [1955] Director

Dartmoor Brewery Limited
Incorporated: 17 March 1994 *Employees:* 19
Net Worth: £884,505 *Total Assets:* £2,050,183
Registered Office: 9 Lady Park Road, Livermead, Torquay, Devon, TQ2 6UA
Parent: Warm Welcome Management Limited
Officers: Peter Brian Maurice Cliff [1951] Director/Chartered Accountant; Ian Cobham [1972] Director/Head Brewer; Philip Glyn Davies [1945] Director; Richard John Hutchings [1949] Director/Solicitor; Richard William Smith [1969] Sales Director

The Dartmouth Brewing Company Limited
Incorporated: 12 October 2016
Registered Office: The Anvil, Chard Junction, Chard, Somerset, TA20 4QJ
Parent: Westcountry Access Ltd
Officers: Christopher John Craven [1970] Managing Director

Darwin Brewery Limited
Incorporated: 1 May 1997 *Employees:* 2
Net Worth Deficit: £87,145 *Total Assets:* £56,398
Registered Office: 1 West Quay Court, Sunderland Enterprise Park, Sunderland, Tyne & Wear, SR5 2TE
Major Shareholder: Keith Robert Thomas
Officers: Dr Keith Robert Thomas, Secretary; Dr Keith Robert Thomas [1951] Director/Lecturer

Dawkins & Georges Ltd
Incorporated: 31 July 2013
Net Worth: £247 *Total Assets:* £247
Registered Office: 2 Lawnwood Road Industrial Estate, Lawnwood Road, Bristol, BS5 0EF
Shareholders: Glen Dawkins; Antony Arnese
Officers: Antony Arnese [1971] Director/Broadcaster; Glen Dawkins [1971] Director; Laurence Orchard Williams [1955] Director

The Dead Crafty Beer Company Limited
Incorporated: 23 July 2014 *Employees:* 5
Net Worth: £18,598 *Total Assets:* £97,936
Registered Office: Seymour Chambers, 92 London Road, Liverpool, L3 5NW
Officers: Gareth Edward Morgan [1979] Director/Rigger; Victoria Morgan [1977] Director/Administrator

Dead End Brew Machine Limited
Incorporated: 9 January 2014
Net Worth: £3,360 *Total Assets:* £14,156
Registered Office: Flat 1-2, 10 Lawrence Street, Glasgow, G11 5HQ
Shareholder: Chris Lewis
Officers: Christopher Lewis [1984] Director/Auditor [Irish]

Dead Fridge Farm Limited
Incorporated: 18 April 2018
Registered Office: The Red Lion, High Street, Brinkley, Newmarket, Suffolk, CB8 0RA
Major Shareholder: Morris Hunter Fenton
Officers: Morris Hunter Fenton [1960] Director/Chef; Gwynth Alise Manney [1981] Director/Chef [American]

Dead Parrot Beer Company Ltd
Incorporated: 22 January 2018
Registered Office: 44 Garden Street, Sheffield, S1 4BJ
Officers: Nicholas Brian Simmonite [1968] Managing Director

Decagram Art and Craft CIC
Incorporated: 31 May 2018
Registered Office: 112/3 Polwarth Gardens, Edinburgh, EH11 1LH
Officers: Edward Charles Rowan Stack [1981] Director/Producer; Radomir Veverka [1980] Director/Brewer [Czech]

Deeply Vale Brewery Ltd
Incorporated: 24 July 2012
Net Worth Deficit: £16,582 *Total Assets:* £35,683
Registered Office: 5 Weaver Drive, Bury, Lancs, BL9 6QY
Shareholder: George Michael Stewart
Officers: George Michael Stewart, Secretary; Anne Stewart [1957] Director/Cleaner; George Michael Stewart [1955] Director/BT Analyst; James Michael Stewart [1981] Director/Warehouse Operative

Deeside Brewery Limited
Incorporated: 13 January 2012 *Employees:* 3
Previous: Deeside Brewery & Distillery Limited
Net Worth Deficit: £15,510 *Total Assets:* £418,293
Registered Office: 22 Dee Street, Banchory, Aberdeenshire, AB31 5ST
Major Shareholder: Michael Bain
Officers: Michael Alexander Bain [1973] Director

Degrees Plato Brewing Ltd.
Incorporated: 14 September 2017
Registered Office: Adam Khedheri, Flat 5, 67 Mare Street, London, E8 4RG
Major Shareholder: Adam Al-Khedheri
Officers: Adam Al-Khedheri [1970] Director/Brewer

Deil's Heid Brewing Company Limited
Incorporated: 27 September 2018
Registered Office: Flat 2b, 2 Commerce Street, Arbroath, Angus, DD11 1NB
Shareholders: Christopher Randall Hall; Operations Integrated Solutions Ltd
Officers: Christopher Randall Hall [1979] Director/Deil's Heid Brewing Company [American]

Delphic Brewing Company Ltd
Incorporated: 14 May 2018
Registered Office: 7 The Henrys, Thatcham, Berks, RG18 4LR
Officers: Thomas Broadbank [1995] Director/Brewer; Caoimhe Haynes [1991] Director/Inside Sales Representative

Dent Brewery Limited
Incorporated: 8 November 2004 *Employees:* 4
Net Worth Deficit: £167,858 *Total Assets:* £131,463
Registered Office: Stoneleigh, Ferncliffe Drive, Keighley, W Yorks, BD20 6HN
Shareholders: Paul Beeley; Judith de Quincey Beeley
Officers: Dr Paul Beeley, Secretary; Judith de Quincey Beeley [1953] Director/Chartered Accountant; Dr Paul Beeley [1951] Director/Consultant Scientist

Derby Brewing Company Limited
Incorporated: 15 January 2004
Net Worth: £6,000 *Total Assets:* £156,168
Registered Office: 1 College Place, Derby, DE1 3DY
Shareholders: Trevor Andrew Harris; Linda Ann Harris; Leanne Harris; Paul Andrew Harris
Officers: Linda Ann Harris, Secretary; Leanne Harris [1981] Director; Linda Ann Harris [1952] Director; Paul Andrew Harris [1982] Director; Trevor Andrew Harris [1950] Director

Derventio Brewery Limited
Incorporated: 7 June 2005
Net Worth: £13,220 *Total Assets:* £69,230
Registered Office: The Brewshed, Darley Abbey Mills, Darley Abbey, Derby, DE22 1DZ
Shareholder: Peter Nash
Officers: John Baldock [1956] Director/Engineer; Peter David Nash [1955] Director/Construction Manager

Derwent Brewery Ltd
Incorporated: 21 December 2012
Net Worth Deficit: £44,628 *Total Assets:* £7,837
Registered Office: Greyholme, Skinburness, Wigton, Cumbria, CA7 4QY
Shareholders: Mark Anthony Johnston; Alison Patricia Johnston
Officers: Alison Johnston [1969] Director/Manager; Mark Johnston [1964] Director/Brewer

Deutschlond Brewery Limited
Incorporated: 14 February 2018
Registered Office: 71-75 Shelton Street, Covent Garden, London, WC2H 9JQ
Major Shareholder: Marc-Oliver Lesch
Officers: Marc-Oliver Lesch [1984] Director [German]

Deva Craft Beer Ltd
Incorporated: 18 June 2014
Net Worth Deficit: £47,016 *Total Assets:* £51,761
Registered Office: 82 Saddlery Way, Chester, CH1 4LW
Shareholder: Neil Adrian Gilbody
Officers: Lindsey Ann Gilbody, Secretary; Lindsey Ann Gilbody [1958] Director; Neil Adrian Gilbody [1956] Director/Brewer

Devanha Brewery Holdings Limited
Incorporated: 25 May 2017 *Employees:* 3
Net Worth Deficit: £10,978 *Total Assets:* £159,812
Registered Office: Unit 5 Insch Business Park, Insch, Garioch, Aberdeenshire, AB52 6TA
Officers: Graeme Forbes Coutts [1959] Director; Colin Smith [1955] Director

Devanha Brewery Limited
Incorporated: 25 May 2017
Registered Office: Unit 5 Insch Business Park, Insch, Garioch, Aberdeenshire, AB52 6TA
Parent: Devanha Brewery Holdings Limited
Officers: Graeme Forbes Coutts [1959] Director; Colin Smith [1955] Director

Devenish & Co (Weymouth) Limited
Incorporated: 13 April 2015
Net Worth: £100 *Total Assets:* £350
Registered Office: Suite 9, Peel House, 30 The Downs, Altrincham, Cheshire, WA14 2PX
Major Shareholder: Hassan Webb
Officers: Hassan Webb [1973] Director/Accountant

Deverell's Brewing Company Ltd
Incorporated: 24 May 2013
Registered Office: Unit 16 Globe Industrial Estate, Towers Road, Grays, Essex, RM17 6ST
Shareholders: Benjamin Robert Deverell; Michael Robert Deverell
Officers: Benjamin Robert Deverell [1984] Director; Michael Robert Deverell [1954] Director

Deviant and Dandy Brewery Limited
Incorporated: 16 February 2017 *Employees:* 2
Net Worth Deficit: £93,191 *Total Assets:* £209,293
Registered Office: 71-75 Shelton Street, Covent Garden, London, WC2H 9JQ
Shareholder: Benjamin Ari Taub
Officers: Benjamin Ari Taub [1976] Director [Finnish]

The Devil's Pleasure Limited
Incorporated: 23 August 2018
Registered Office: Higher Sigford Farm Higher Sigford Farm, Bickington, Newton Abbot, Devon, TQ12 6LD
Shareholders: Alistair Richard Pollard; Oliver Hely-Hutchinson Graves
Officers: Oliver Hely-Hutchinson Graves [1979] Director/Manager; Alistair Richard Pollard [1979] Director/Brewer

Devitera Ltd
Incorporated: 6 January 2017 *Employees:* 1
Net Worth Deficit: £12,430 *Total Assets:* £13,653
Registered Office: 17 The Market Place, Devizes, Wilts, SN10 1HT
Major Shareholder: Glen Upward
Officers: Glen Upward [1978] Director

Devon Ales Limited
Incorporated: 25 January 1996
Net Worth: £57,768 *Total Assets:* £64,760
Registered Office: Mansfield Arms, Main Street, Sauchie, Alloa, Clackmannanshire, FK10 3JR
Officers: Lorna Graham, Secretary; Catherine Gibson [1948] Director; John Gibson [1946] Director; Derrick John Graham [1970] Director/Publican

DHBeers Ltd
Incorporated: 24 September 2018
Registered Office: Old Mill, Kellas, Dundee, DD5 3PD
Major Shareholder: Dominic Michael Hughes
Officers: Dominic Michael Hughes [1984] Director

Dhillons Brewery Ltd
Incorporated: 6 May 2011 *Employees:* 3
Previous: Lion Heart Brewery Ltd
Net Worth: £21,911 *Total Assets:* £108,199
Registered Office: Suite 302 EW, Sterling House, Langston Road, Loughton, Essex, IG10 3TS
Major Shareholder: Dalvinder Singh Dhillon
Officers: Dalvinder Singh Dhillon [1978] Director

Diamond Dicks Brewing Limited
Incorporated: 8 August 2016
Net Worth: £100 *Total Assets:* £100
Registered Office: 5 White Rose Court, Widegate Street, London, E1 7ES
Officers: Paul Diamond [1983] Marketing Director; Richard Derby Williams [1981] Director/Consultant [American]

Dingbat Beer Ltd
Incorporated: 27 November 2018
Registered Office: 60 Bryanston Road, Solihull, W Midlands, B91 1EN
Shareholders: Scott Wakefield; Simon Ieuan Evans
Officers: Simon Ieuan Evans [1977] Director; Scott Wakefield [1972] Director [Australian]

The Dobbins Guiltless Stout Co. Ltd.
Incorporated: 14 February 1989
Registered Office: 1 Worsley Court, High Street, Worsley, Manchester, M28 3NJ
Major Shareholder: Brendon Dobbin
Officers: Anita Omoera Dobbin, Secretary [Nigerian]; Brendan Patrick Dobbin [1958] Director/Banana Grower [Irish]

Docks Beers Limited
Incorporated: 7 February 2018
Registered Office: 33 Park Drive, Grimsby, N E Lincs, DN32 0EG
Major Shareholder: William Douglas
Officers: William Douglas [1972] Director

Dockyard Brewery Limited
Incorporated: 24 September 2015 *Employees:* 2
Net Worth Deficit: £381 *Total Assets:* £5,437
Registered Office: 1 Levens Road, Hazel Grove, Stockport, Cheshire, SK7 5DL
Officers: Steven Pilling [1956] Director/Restaurateur

Dodd's Brewery Co. Limited
Incorporated: 23 January 1998
Registered Office: Gaines House, Church Hill, Kington Magna, Gillingham, Dorset, SP8 5EG
Major Shareholder: Helen Louise Dodd
Officers: Irwin Peter Sarif, Secretary/Consultant; Helen Louise Dodd [1966] Director/Housewife

The Dog and Rabbit Brewery Ltd
Incorporated: 18 May 2015 *Employees:* 4
Net Worth: £8,405 *Total Assets:* £28,618
Registered Office: 41 Norham Close, Wideopen, Newcastle upon Tyne, NE13 7HS
Shareholders: Julie Patton; Antony David Patton
Officers: Antony David Patton [1964] Director/Brewery/Micro Pub; Julie Patton [1968] Director

Dog Falls Brewing Co. Ltd
Incorporated: 13 June 2018
Registered Office: Chlumas, Scaniport, Inverness, IV2 6DL
Shareholder: Robert Dougal Masson
Officers: Robert Dougal Masson [1980] Director/Brewer

Dogtag Beer Co. Ltd
Incorporated: 19 December 2016
Registered Office: 3 Hartismere Road, Wallasey, Merseyside, CH44 9DT
Shareholder: Jonathan Charlesworth
Officers: Jonathan Charlesworth [1984] Managing Director; Michael New [1979] Director/Chief Executive Officer

Dolphin Brewery Limited
Incorporated: 18 January 2017
Net Worth: £1,500 *Total Assets:* £1,500
Registered Office: 8 Corby Close, Woodley, Reading, Berks, RG5 4TL
Major Shareholder: Andrew Barnes
Officers: Andrew Barnes [1980] Director; Laura Dolphin [1984] Director

Dolphin Brewery Poole Ltd
Incorporated: 7 March 2013
Registered Office: Suite 2, 7 The Square, Wimborne, Dorset, BH21 1JA
Major Shareholder: Richard David Pride
Officers: Michael William Garrett [1968] Director; Richard David Pride [1971] Director/Video Editing & Streaming

Dominion Brewery Company Limited
Incorporated: 29 June 2012
Net Worth Deficit: £94,387 *Total Assets:* £4,347
Registered Office: 3 Warners Mill, Silks Way, Braintree, Essex, CM7 3GB
Major Shareholder: Andrew Elliott Skene
Officers: Andrew Elliott Skene, Secretary; Andrew Elliott Skene [1963] Director/Brewer

Don Valley Brewery Limited
Incorporated: 3 October 2013 *Employees:* 3
Net Worth: £29,753 *Total Assets:* £97,566
Registered Office: Unit 3 Canalside Industrial Estate, off Cliff Street, Mexborough, S Yorks, S64 9HU
Major Shareholder: Gordon Jones

Doncaster Brewery Limited
Incorporated: 16 May 2013
Net Worth: £1 *Total Assets:* £1
Registered Office: 51 St Marys Road, Wheatley, Doncaster, S Yorks, DN1 2NR
Major Shareholder: Ian Blaylock
Officers: Ian Blaylock [1969] Director/Brewer

Donkeystone Brewing Co Ltd
Incorporated: 7 April 2017
Net Worth Deficit: £54,830 *Total Assets:* £123,249
Registered Office: Units 17-18 Boarshurst Business Park, Greenfield, Oldham, Saddleworth, Lancs, OL3 7ER
Shareholder: Stephen Michael James
Officers: Leslie Allan Gill [1966] Director/Landlord; David Stuart Halford [1977] Director/Landlord; Stephen Michael James [1977] Director/Property Developer

Donnington Brewery Limited
Incorporated: 20 January 2017
Registered Office: Donnington Brewery, Upper Swell, Stow on-the-Wold, Cheltenham, Glos, GL54 1EP
Major Shareholder: James Rixon Arkell
Officers: John Peter Arkell, Secretary; James Rixon Arkell [1951] Director/Brewer

Donzoko Brewing Company Ltd
Incorporated: 6 June 2016
Net Worth Deficit: £8,218 *Total Assets:* £3,511
Registered Office: 34 Comfrey, Coulby Newham, Middlesbrough, Cleveland, TS8 0XT
Major Shareholder: Reece Hugill
Officers: Reece Hugill [1994] Director; Robert Hugill [1964] Director

Dood and Frinks Ltd
Incorporated: 2 January 2008
Registered Office: Summerhill, Bath Road, Broomhall, Worcester, WR5 3HR
Officers: Andrew James Tull, Secretary; Andrew James Tull [1955] Director/Secretary

Dorber Brewing Limited
Incorporated: 1 December 2014
Net Worth: £100 *Total Assets:* £100
Registered Office: The Anchor, Main Street, Walberswick, Suffolk, IP18 6UA
Shareholders: Mark Lindsay Dorber; Sophie Mellor
Officers: Mark Lindsay Dorber [1957] Director; Sophie Mellor [1963] Director

Dore Brewery Limited
Incorporated: 28 November 2013
Registered Office: No 1 Velocity, 2 Tenter Street, Sheffield, S1 4BY
Major Shareholder: Steven Robert Ford
Officers: Steven Robert Ford [1976] Director/IT Professional

Dorking Brewery (2016) Limited
Incorporated: 9 February 2016 *Employees:* 2
Net Worth Deficit: £35,924 *Total Assets:* £465,775
Registered Office: 24 Bittell Road, Barnt Green, Birmingham, B45 8LT
Major Shareholder: Neel Singh
Officers: Daman Raj Singh, Secretary; Daman Raj Singh [1948] Director; Neel Singh [1981] Director

Doromomo & Sons Ltd
Incorporated: 8 May 2018
Registered Office: 198 High Street, Tonbridge, Kent, TN9 1BE
Shareholders: Winston Rainer Cuthbert; Aidan Julius Lethem
Officers: Aidan Julius Lethem [1994] Director

Dorset Brewing Company Limited
Incorporated: 18 October 1994 *Employees:* 9
Net Worth: £84,803 *Total Assets:* £371,985
Registered Office: Unit 7 Hybris Business Park, Warmwell Road, Crossways, Dorset, DT2 8BF
Shareholders: Giles Nicholas Smeath; Susan Valerie Thornton
Officers: Giles Nicholas Smeath, Secretary; Giles Nicholas Smeath [1946] Director/Retired Solicitor; Michael Edward Charles Thornton [1974] Director/Film Producer; Susan Valerie Thornton [1949] Director/Property Landlord

Double Barrelled Brewery Ltd.
Incorporated: 24 November 2015
Net Worth Deficit: £28,815 *Total Assets:* £63,629
Registered Office: Unit 20 Stadium Way, Tilehurst, Reading, Berks, RG30 6BX
Shareholders: Lucy Alice Clayton-Jones; Michael Alan Clayton-Jones
Officers: Lucy Alice Clayton-Jones [1988] Marketing Director; Michael Alan Clayton-Jones [1987] Operations Director

Double Maxim Beer Company Limited
Incorporated: 23 November 1999
Net Worth: £300,943 *Total Assets:* £672,995
Registered Office: c/o Muckle LLP, Time Central, 32 Gallowgate, Newcastle upon Tyne, NE1 4BF
Shareholders: Douglas Joseph Trotman; Mark Anderson
Officers: Mark Anderson, Secretary/Director; Mark Anderson [1962] Director; Susan Anderson [1958] Director; Douglas Joseph Trotman [1962] Director; Glen Andrew Whale [1974] Director

Double Tap Brewery Ltd
Incorporated: 8 May 2015
Registered Office: 39 Brooklands Park, Longlevens, Gloucester, GL2 0DN
Officers: Martin Anthony Coles [1972] Director; Kevin Russell Peters [1969] Director

The Dove Street Brewery Ltd
Incorporated: 9 September 2009
Net Worth Deficit: £74,274 *Total Assets:* £3,259
Registered Office: The Dove Inn, 76 St Helens Street, Ipswich, Suffolk, IP4 2LA
Major Shareholder: Adrian Nigel Smith
Officers: Karen Linda Beaumont [1968] Director/Publican; Adrian Nigel Smith [1966] Director/Publican

Dovedale Brewing Company Limited
Incorporated: 6 November 2017
Registered Office: Damgate Farm, Stanshope, Ashbourne, Derbys, DE6 2AD
Major Shareholder: Andrea Clarke
Officers: Andrea Clarke [1966] Director/Business Owner

Dovik Bast Ltd
Incorporated: 25 February 2019
Registered Office: 7-8 Brighton Street, Edinburgh, EH1 1HD
Shareholder: Luke Ashley Dobinson
Officers: Luke Ashley Dobinson [1990] Director/Software Engineer

Dow Bridge Brewery Limited
Incorporated: 12 August 2010
Registered Office: 2 Rugby Road, Catthorpe, Warwicks, LE17 6DA
Major Shareholder: Russell Webb
Officers: Russell Webb [1958] Director/Brewer

Dowdeswell Brewery Limited
Incorporated: 21 August 2018
Registered Office: 93 London Road, Cheltenham, Glos, GL52 6HL
Officers: Clarice Bijou Elliott-Berry [1993] Director

The Downton Brewery Company Ltd
Incorporated: 22 May 2002 *Employees:* 6
Net Worth: £88,890 *Total Assets:* £173,137
Registered Office: Unit 11 Batten Road Industrial Estate, Downton, Salisbury, Wilts, SP5 3HU
Shareholders: Martin David Strawbridge; Katie Elizabeth Strawbridge
Officers: Martin David Strawbridge, Secretary/Brewer; Martin Howard [1939] Director; Brian Patrick O'Kane [1946] Director; Mark Andrew Rowlinson [1950] Director/Accountant; Katie Elizabeth Strawbridge [1980] Director/Administrator; Martin David Strawbridge [1979] Director/Brewer

Dowr Kammel Brewing Company Limited
Incorporated: 22 October 2015
Net Worth Deficit: £19,815 *Total Assets:* £22,107
Registered Office: 9 Tregarne Terrace, St Austell, Cornwall, PL25 4DD
Major Shareholder: Simon James Corruthers
Officers: Justine Louise Carruthers [1969] Director; Simon James Carruthers [1974] Director

The Draycott Brewing Company Limited
Incorporated: 13 September 2016
Net Worth Deficit: £3,426 *Total Assets:* £6,411
Registered Office: 22 Eldon Business Park Eldon Road, Attenborough, Beeston, Nottingham, NG9 6DZ
Major Shareholder: Gregory Kenneth Maskalick
Officers: Gail Maskalick [1961] Director; Gregory Kenneth Maskalick [1959] Director

Droylsden Craft Limited
Incorporated: 3 September 2018
Registered Office: 50 Clough Road, Droylsden, Manchester, M43 7NG
Major Shareholder: Anthony Thomas Conway
Officers: Anthony Thomas Conway [1990] Director/Manager

Drumgaw Holdings Ltd
Incorporated: 26 February 2019
Registered Office: 27 Drumgaw Road, Armagh, BT60 2AD
Major Shareholder: Gareth William John Megaw
Officers: Gareth William John Megaw [1988] Director/Engineer

Drygate Brewing Company Ltd
Incorporated: 22 January 2014 *Employees:* 12
Net Worth: £360,861 *Total Assets:* £3,302,378
Registered Office: 85 Drygate, Glasgow, G4 0UT
Shareholders: Tennent Caledonian Breweries; Heather Ale Ltd
Officers: Shona Shannon, Secretary; Matthew James Corden [1987] Operations Director; John Gilligan [1952] Director; Scott John Williams [1964] Director

Duffstar Brewing Limited
Incorporated: 24 March 2011
Registered Office: 60 Union Grove, Aberdeen, AB10 6RX
Major Shareholder: Steven Duffy
Officers: Steven Duffy [1979] Director/Software Engineer

Dukeries Brewery Ltd.
Incorporated: 31 July 2012 *Employees:* 4
Net Worth: £2,280 *Total Assets:* £132,102
Registered Office: 18 Newcastle Avenue, Worksop, Notts, S80 1ET
Shareholder: George Phillip Longley
Officers: George Phillip Longley [1973] Director/Brewery Technician

Dunfermline Brewery Limited
Incorporated: 7 March 2018
Registered Office: Dunfermline Brewery, Lynburn Industrial Estate, Halbeath Place, Dunfermline, Fife, KY11 4JT
Major Shareholder: Jonathan Lewis Sharman
Officers: Jonathan Lewis Sharman [1993] Director/Brewer

Duration Brewing Ltd
Incorporated: 5 April 2017 *Employees:* 2
Net Worth Deficit: £62,283 *Total Assets:* £15,542
Registered Office: Westacre Estate Office, Church Green, West Acre, King's Lynn, Norfolk, PE32 1TS
Officers: Derek Seth Bates [1981] Director [American]; Miranda Lilian Hudson [1975] Director; Lewis Benedict Sinclair Marten [1976] Director/Business Executive

The Durham Brewery Limited
Incorporated: 23 May 1997 *Employees:* 4
Net Worth: £23,198 *Total Assets:* £240,426
Registered Office: 18 Lingdale, Belmont, Durham, DH1 2AN
Shareholders: Eleanor Jayne Bell; Steven Gibbs
Officers: Eleanor Jayne Bell, Secretary; Eleanor Jayne Bell [1979] Director; Steven Gibbs [1956] Director/Brewer

Thomas Dutton Ales Limited
Incorporated: 28 February 2014
Net Worth Deficit: £350 *Total Assets:* £430
Registered Office: Suite 9, Peel House, 30 The Downs, Altrincham, Cheshire, WA14 2PX
Major Shareholder: Hassan Webb
Officers: Hassan Webb [1973] Director/Accountant

Dynamite Valley Brewery Limited
Incorporated: 6 April 2018
Registered Office: 30 Pentire Avenue, Newquay, Cornwall, TR7 1PD
Shareholders: Keith John Baker; Gareth Edward Jenkins
Officers: Keith John Baker [1951] Director; Gareth Edward Jenkins [1975] Director

Eagles Crag Brewery Ltd
Incorporated: 12 September 2016
Registered Office: Hillside House East, Church Road, Todmorden, Lancs, OL14 8HP
Shareholders: Christopher Paul Milton; David Mortimer
Officers: Christopher Milton, Secretary; Christopher Paul Milton [1959] Director/IT Consultant; David Mortimer [1961] Director/University Lecturer

Ealing Brewing Ltd
Incorporated: 17 October 2018
Registered Office: 48 Paddington Close, Yeading, Hayes, Middlesex, UB4 9QH
Shareholders: Paul Stuart Nock; Mark David Yarnell
Officers: Paul Stuart Nock [1970] Director; Mark David Yarnell [1972] Director

Earl Soham Brewery Limited
Incorporated: 28 March 2003
Net Worth: £102,625 Total Assets: £208,845
Registered Office: Wyndham House, The Street, Market Weston, Diss, Norfolk, IP22 2NZ
Shareholders: John Stephen Bjornson; Jeremy Moss
Officers: Charles Andrew St. John Bagnall, Secretary; John Stephen Bjornson [1953] Director/Brewer; Jeremy Moss [1964] Director/Brewer

Earth Ale Ltd
Incorporated: 19 November 2014
Net Worth Deficit: £7,415 Total Assets: £3,401
Registered Office: 1 Badswell Lane, Appleton, Abingdon, Oxon, OX13 5JN
Major Shareholder: Alexander Charles Fraser Lewis
Officers: Barbara Fraser, Secretary; Alex Lewis [1989] Director/Chef

Earth Station Beers Ltd
Incorporated: 21 July 2017
Registered Office: 128 Haldane Road, London, E6 3JP
Major Shareholder: Jenn Merrick
Officers: Jenn Merrick [1977] Director [American]

East Anglian Brewers Ltd.
Incorporated: 13 November 2002
Total Assets: £51
Registered Office: 70 Risbygate Street, Bury St Edmunds, Suffolk, IP33 3AZ
Officers: Brendan Joseph Moore, Secretary; Brendan Joseph Moore [1954] Director/Brewer

The East India Company India Pale Ale Limited
Incorporated: 19 May 2011
Net Worth: £17 Total Assets: £17
Registered Office: 39 St James's Street, London, SW1A 1JD
Major Shareholder: Robin Chapman
Officers: Robin Chapman [1947] Director

East London Brewing Company Limited
Incorporated: 9 May 2011 Employees: 9
Net Worth: £12,081 Total Assets: £284,896
Registered Office: Units 44-45 Fairways Business Park, Lammas Road, London, E10 7QB
Shareholders: Claire Ashbridge-Thomlinson; Stuart Francis Lascelles
Officers: Claire Ashbridge-Thomlinson [1970] Director; Stuart Francis Lascelles [1969] Director

East Neuk Organic Brewing & Distilling Ltd
Incorporated: 16 January 2017
Net Worth Deficit: £20,242 Total Assets: £64,209
Registered Office: Unit 2 The Bowhouse, St Monans, Fife, KY10 2FB
Shareholders: Stephen Joseph Marshall; Lucy Catherine Hine
Officers: Lucy Catherine Hine [1983] Director; Stephen Joseph Marshall [1976] Director

East Riding Brewery Ltd
Incorporated: 10 June 2013
Registered Office: Royal Mail Cottage, Main Road, Thorngumbald, E Yorks, HU12 9NF
Major Shareholder: Michael Anthony Ferrier
Officers: Michael Anthony Ferrier [1958] Director

The East Yorkshire Beer Company Limited
Incorporated: 15 November 2016
Net Worth Deficit: £32,861 Total Assets: £23,731
Registered Office: 2a Tokenspire Park, Beverley, E Yorks, HU17 0TB
Officers: Stephen Aitcheson [1959] Director/Shopfitter; David Wilkinson [1973] Director/Engineer

The Eccleshall Brewing Company Limited
Incorporated: 11 October 2002 Employees: 11
Net Worth: £101,198 Total Assets: £339,054
Registered Office: St Albans Road, Stafford, ST16 3DR
Shareholders: Andrew Philip Slater; Moyra Jennifer Slater; Victoria Slater
Officers: Moyra Jennifer Slater, Secretary; Andrew Philip Slater [1974] Director/Brewer; Moyra Jennifer Slater [1949] Director/Hotelier; Victoria Slater [1977] Director

Eden Brewery Limited
Incorporated: 3 October 2011 Employees: 3
Net Worth Deficit: £69,599 Total Assets: £427,756
Registered Office: Unit 3 Hartness Road, Gilwilly Industrial Estate, Penrith, Cumbria, CA11 9BD
Major Shareholder: Jason Craig Hill
Officers: Anthony Gerard Kelly, Secretary; Anthony Gerard Kelly [1991] Director; Tony Kelly [1963] Director [Irish]; Paul Miller [1961] Director

Eden Mill Brewers Ltd
Incorporated: 23 March 2018
Registered Office: Eden Mill, Glasgow Business Park, Glasgow, G69 6GA
Major Shareholder: Anthony Kelly
Officers: Anthony Gerard Kelly, Secretary; Anthony Gerard Kelly [1991] Director; Anthony Kelly [1963] Director [Irish]; Paul Miller [1961] Director

The Edenfield Brewery Limited
Incorporated: 25 April 2014
Net Worth Deficit: £9,420 Total Assets: £15,273
Registered Office: 1 Market Place, Edenfield, Bury, Lancs, BL0 0JZ
Shareholders: David Francis Swarbrick; David Francis Swarbrick
Officers: David Francis Swarbrick [1977] Director

Edinbrew Ltd
Incorporated: 9 October 2014
Net Worth: £502 Total Assets: £75,926
Registered Office: Unit 5 Knightsridge Industrial Estate, Knightsridge East, Livingston, W Lothian, EH54 8RA
Major Shareholder: Ross William Hamilton
Officers: Ross William Hamilton [1982] Director/Brewery

The Edinburgh Beer Factory Limited
Incorporated: 24 November 2014 Employees: 18
Net Worth: £2,097,473 Total Assets: £2,365,710
Registered Office: Unit 15, 32 Bankhead Drive, Edinburgh, EH11 4EQ
Major Shareholder: John Michael Dunsmore
Officers: John Michael Dunsmore [1959] Director; Lynne Dunsmore [1961] Director

The Edinburgh Brewing Company Limited
Incorporated: 2 May 2014
Registered Office: 6 Randolph Crescent, Edinburgh, EH3 7TH
Parent: Innis & Gunn Holdings Limited
Officers: Anthony Leonard Hunt [1946] Director/Consultant; Dougal Gunn Sharp [1972] Director

EFG International Ltd
Incorporated: 2 September 2013
Previous: D. O'Brien Brewery Limited
Net Worth: £35,378 *Total Assets:* £35,378
Registered Office: 19 Wilnicott Road, Leicester, LE3 2TE
Major Shareholder: Daniel Ryan O'Brien
Officers: Daniel Ryan O'Brien [1974] Director

Egan & Martin Limited
Incorporated: 13 February 2018
Registered Office: Office 1+2 Buildman Bus Centre Laburnum Street, Atherton, Manchester, M46 9FP
Officers: Craig William Egan [1986] Director/Brewer; James William George Martin [1986] Director/Brewer

Egghead Brewery Limited
Incorporated: 2 December 2014
Net Worth Deficit: £11,099 *Total Assets:* £1
Registered Office: Barton End Barn, Barton End, Horsley, Stroud, Glos, GL6 0QF
Major Shareholder: Giles Sinclair Davey
Officers: Karen Annette Davey, Secretary; Giles Sinclair Davey [1966] Director

Eko Brewery Limited
Incorporated: 18 July 2018
Registered Office: 130 Old Street, London, EC1V 9BD
Officers: Helena-Aude Adedipe, Secretary; Anthony Adedipe [1982] Director/Consultant; Helena-Aude Adedipe [1987] Director/Consultant

Eldridge, Pope & Company Limited
Incorporated: 17 April 2014
Registered Office: Vineyard Farm, Bucknowle, Norden, Corfe Castle, Wareham, Dorset, BH20 5DY
Major Shareholder: Alastair Wyllie Wallace
Officers: Andrew Philip Parsons, Secretary; Andrew Philip Parsons [1954] Director; Dr Alastair Wyllie Wallace [1951] Director

Electric Bear Brewing Company Ltd
Incorporated: 15 January 2014
Net Worth: £91,562 *Total Assets:* £604,950
Registered Office: 6 Bloomfield Avenue, Bath, BA2 3AB
Major Shareholder: Christopher Adrian Rees Lewis
Officers: Christopher Adrian Rees Lewis [1967] Director; Jacqueline Ann Lewis [1965] Director

Elemental Brew House Limited
Incorporated: 30 March 2015
Net Worth: £381 *Total Assets:* £381
Registered Office: Flat 1 Alverton Court, Tonsley Street, London, SW18 1BN
Shareholders: Christopher Matthew Mortensen; James Cartwright
Officers: James Cartwright [1972] Director & Chief of Staff; Christopher Matthew Mortensen [1977] Director

Elemental Brewing Ltd
Incorporated: 22 September 2017
Registered Office: 44 Holgate Road, York, YO24 4AB
Major Shareholder: Alistair Martin Crockford
Officers: Alistair Martin Crockford [1983] Director/Student

Elements Brewing Co Ltd
Incorporated: 5 March 2018
Registered Office: Amphlett House, Pancake Hill, Chedworth, Cheltenham, Glos, GL54 4AW
Major Shareholder: Jamie Masters Cowell
Officers: Jamie Masters Cowell [1973] Managing Director

Elgood & Sons, Limited
Incorporated: 2 October 1905 *Employees:* 35
Net Worth: £4,240,517 *Total Assets:* £5,674,543
Registered Office: North Brink Brewery, Wisbech, Cambs, PE13 1LN
Shareholder: Nigel Stewart Elgood
Officers: Jennifer Anne Everall, Secretary; Anne Mary Elgood [1941] Director; Nigel Stewart Elgood [1937] Director/Chairman; Jennifer Anne Everall [1968] Director/Buyer; Claire Jane Simpson [1966] Director/Landscape Designer; Belinda Mary Sutton [1964] Managing Director

Elland Brewery Limited
Incorporated: 16 April 2002 *Employees:* 10
Net Worth: £170,300 *Total Assets:* £231,183
Registered Office: 7 Henry Street, Keighley, W Yorks, BD21 3DR
Shareholders: Stephen Edwin Francis; Stephen Edwin Francis
Officers: Stephen Edwin Francis [1962] Director; Michael George Hiscock [1962] Director/Brewery Manager

Ellenberg's Brewery Ltd
Incorporated: 23 September 2011
Net Worth Deficit: £82,130 *Total Assets:* £11,744
Registered Office: 199 Sudbury Heights Avenue, Greenford, Middlesex, UB6 0LR
Major Shareholder: Michael Jonathan Ellenberg
Officers: Michael Ellenberg [1961] Director

Christopher Ellis and Son Limited
Incorporated: 29 August 2006
Net Worth: £76,599 *Total Assets:* £200,312
Registered Office: Prospect Villa, Greenbank Road, Devoran, Truro, Cornwall, TR3 6PH
Officers: Anthony Paul Fleming Stephens, Secretary; Anthony Paul Fleming Stephens [1948] Director; Christopher George Stephens [1978] Director/Solicitor; Claire Louise Stephens [1982] Director/PA at Fashion House; Elaine Mary Stephens [1953] Director

Ellismuir Limited
Incorporated: 6 February 2017
Net Worth Deficit: £12,782 *Total Assets:* £2,938
Registered Office: 9 Royal Crescent, Glasgow, G3 7SP
Major Shareholder: Sebajeevan Sebaratnam
Officers: John David Atkings [1948] Director; Robert Donald [1950] Director; Sebajeevan Sebaratnam [1976] Director [German]

Elmtree Beers Ltd
Incorporated: 4 March 2016 *Employees:* 2
Net Worth: £4,016 *Total Assets:* £31,323
Registered Office: Unit 10 Oakwood Industrial Estate Harling Road, Snetterton, Norwich, NR16 2JU
Shareholders: Allan Roy Cooper; Jacqueline Claire Nelmes
Officers: Allan Roy Cooper [1962] Director; Jacqueline Claire Nelmes [1956] Director

Elusive Brewing Limited
Incorporated: 8 July 2015
Net Worth Deficit: £9,585 *Total Assets:* £55,321
Registered Office: Unit 5 Marino Way, Finchampstead, Wokingham, Berks, RG40 4RF
Major Shareholder: Andrew Parker
Officers: Andrew Parker [1973] Director/Consultant

Emperor's Brewery Ltd.
Incorporated: 12 April 2017
Registered Office: 2 Worthington Lane, Newbold Coleorton, Coalville, Leics, LE67 8PH
Major Shareholder: Damian John Doherty
Officers: Damian John Doherty [1972] Director/General Manager

Empire Brewing Ltd
Incorporated: 2 April 2013
Net Worth: £5,740 *Total Assets:* £47,866
Registered Office: Unit 33 The Old Boiler House, Slaithwaite, Huddersfield, W Yorks, HD7 5HA
Shareholders: Russell Beverley; Lorraine Beverley
Officers: Lorraine Beverley, Secretary; Russell Beverley [1956] Director

Emprise Brewery Limited
Incorporated: 28 August 2018
Registered Office: 3 Gormley Drive, St Helens, Merseyside, WA10 2UL
Officers: Robin Twist [2002] Director/Electrician

Encoder Brewery Limited
Incorporated: 24 February 2015
Net Worth Deficit: £22,844 *Total Assets:* £33,749
Registered Office: 43a Altenburg Gardens, London, SW11 1JH
Major Shareholder: William Peter Fleming Strange
Officers: Tom Charles Fleming Strange [1986] Director; William Peter Fleming Strange [1984] Director/Business Consultant

Endure Brewing Co Ltd
Incorporated: 15 June 2015
Net Worth: £388 *Total Assets:* £2,697
Registered Office: Bank House, Market Street, Whaley Bridge, High Peak, Derbys, SK23 7AA
Shareholder: Gareth Syms
Officers: Nicholas Kirk [1955] Director; Christa Jane Syms [1979] Director; Gareth Syms [1978] Director

Enfield Brewery Limited
Incorporated: 1 October 2014 *Employees:* 8
Net Worth Deficit: £382,758 *Total Assets:* £732,708
Registered Office: 18 Eley Road, Edmonton, London, N18 3BB
Major Shareholder: Rahul Mulchandani
Officers: Rahul Mulchandani [1986] Director

The Engineer Brewery Limited
Incorporated: 24 January 2008
Previous: John E Packer Limited
Net Worth Deficit: £14,847 *Total Assets:* £9,356
Registered Office: 1 The Old Stables, Eridge Park, Tunbridge Wells, Kent, TN3 9JT
Shareholders: John Edward Packer; Ann Packer
Officers: Ann Packer, Secretary; John Edward Packer [1957] Director/Chartered Engineer

The Ennerdale Brewery Ltd
Incorporated: 18 October 2010 *Employees:* 11
Net Worth Deficit: £143,639 *Total Assets:* £270,772
Registered Office: Chapel Row, Rowrah, Frizington, Cumbria, CA26 3XS
Major Shareholder: Barrie Roberts
Officers: Jodi Parke, Secretary; Jodi Ann Parke [1979] Director/Company Secretary; Barrie Roberts [1952] Director/Project Engineer; Emily Jane Zanacchi [1983] Director/Junior Procurement Manager; Paul Zanacchi [1983] Director/Lead Training Officer

Enville Ales Limited
Incorporated: 3 November 1998 *Employees:* 14
Net Worth: £1,216,037 *Total Assets:* £1,386,960
Registered Office: Enville Brewery, Cox Green, Hollies Lane, Stourbridge, W Midlands, DY7 5LG
Parent: Enville Brewery Limited
Officers: Malcolm Ernest Elihood Braham [1959] Director

Epic Beers Limited
Incorporated: 13 April 2017
Net Worth: £17,452 *Total Assets:* £82,604
Registered Office: The Brewery, West Hewish, Weston-Super-Mare, Somerset, BS24 6RR
Shareholders: Graham Dunbavan; Mark Charles Davey
Officers: Mark Charles Davey [1966] Director/Manager; Graham Dunbavan [1959] Director/Brewer; David Allen Turner [1974] Director

Epic Brewing Limited
Incorporated: 8 January 2018
Registered Office: Devonshire House, 60 Goswell Road, London, EC1M 7AD
Shareholders: David Benjamin Green; Ian James
Officers: David Benjamin Green [1981] Director; Ian James [1989] Director

Epochal Barrel-Fermented Ales Ltd
Incorporated: 31 January 2019
Registered Office: 2/1, 3 Belmont Street, Glasgow, G12 8EP
Major Shareholder: Gareth Young
Officers: Dr Gareth Young [1985] Director/Brewer

Equal Brewkery Community Interest Company
Incorporated: 31 March 2017
Net Worth: £4,287 *Total Assets:* £4,999
Registered Office: 120 Ipswich Road, Norwich, NR4 6QS
Officers: Susan Farrell, Secretary; Lucy Ann Arkell [1967] Director/Teacher; Susan Farrell [1957] Director/Administrator; Garry Hollett [1971] Director/Hair Stylist; Joel Charles Robert Hull [1968] Director/Local Council Officer; William Russell [1951] Director; Peter David Walker [1957] Director/Retired

The Erddig Brewing Company Limited
Incorporated: 16 April 2014
Net Worth Deficit: £28,731 *Total Assets:* £6,033
Registered Office: 27 Valley Way, Hermitage Park, Wrexham, Clwyd, LL13 7GW
Major Shareholder: Antoni Sznerch
Officers: Antoni Sznerch, Secretary; Antoni Sznerch [1956] Director

Errant Ltd
Incorporated: 2 March 2015
Net Worth: £603 *Total Assets:* £27,943
Registered Office: Arch 19 Forth Street, Newcastle upon Tyne, NE1 3PG
Shareholders: Martyn Eric Stockley; Thomas Oliver Meads
Officers: Thomas Oliver Meads [1988] Managing Director; Martyn Eric Stockley [1988] Managing Director

Eskdale Brewery Ltd
Incorporated: 25 July 2016
Registered Office: 39 Albert Street, Brigg, Lincs, DN20 8HU
Shareholder: Thomas Smith
Officers: Thomas Smith [1985] Director/Manager

Ethical Ales Limited
Incorporated: 23 July 2018
Registered Office: Rodenloft House, Roddenloft, Mauchline, E Ayrshire, KA5 5HH
Officers: George Douglas Hammersley [1952] Director

Etrusca Brewery & Distillery in St. Andrews Ltd
Incorporated: 31 December 2015
Registered Office: 59 Bonnygate, Cupar, Fife, KY15 4BY
Major Shareholder: Giorgio Cozzolino
Officers: Giorgio Cozzolino [1964] Director [Italian]

Evensong Brewing Limited
Incorporated: 3 August 2018
Registered Office: 6b Hill Avenue, Bristol, BS3 4SF
Shareholders: Andrew John Sherlock; Rachel Louise Cartwright
Officers: Rachel Louise Cartwright [1984] Director/Project Manager; Andrew John Sherlock [1984] Director/Brewer

Everards Brewery Limited
Incorporated: 7 October 1936 *Employees:* 75
Net Worth: £81,160,000 *Total Assets:* £111,340,000
Registered Office: Devana Avenue, Optimus Point, Glenfield, Leicester, LE3 8JS
Major Shareholder: Richard Anthony Spencer Everard
Officers: Nigel Geoffrey Allen, Secretary; Nigel Geoffrey Allen [1975] Finance Director; Julian William Spencer Everard [1988] Director; Richard Anthony Spencer Everard [1954] Director; Stephen Gould [1968] Director; John Nicholas Lloyd [1948] Director; Serena Anne Richards [1952] Director; Charlotte Ione Vowles [1985] Director; Adrian Robert Weston [1935] Director

Evolution Brewing Ltd
Incorporated: 28 November 2018
Registered Office: Sixty Six North Quay, Great Yarmouth, Norfolk, NR30 1HE
Shareholders: Pilson Group Limited; Samantha Jane Elliott; Gordon Fisher
Officers: Samantha Jane Elliott [1986] Director; Kenneth John Turner [1949] Director

The Exeter Brewery Limited
Incorporated: 19 November 2007 *Employees:* 9
Net Worth: £43,088 *Total Assets:* £275,095
Registered Office: 1 Cowley Bridge Road, Exeter, Devon, EX4 4NX
Major Shareholder: Alan Anthony Collyer
Officers: Alan Anthony Collyer, Secretary; Alan Anthony Collyer [1957] Director/Brewer

Exile Brewing Company Ltd
Incorporated: 9 April 2014
Registered Office: Gorwel, Hafod Road, Pant Glas, Gwernaffield, Mold, Flintshire, CH7 5ES
Officers: Phillip Blanchard [1980] Director

Exiled Brewers Limited
Incorporated: 22 April 2016
Net Worth: £7,920 *Total Assets:* £7,920
Registered Office: 12-14 Jeffrey Street, Edinburgh, EH1 1DT
Shareholders: Vladimir Jason Stamenkovic; Daniel Alberto Chavez Santiago; Joanna Malgorzata Marczuk-Santiago
Officers: Joanna Malgorzata Marczuk-Santiago [1985] Director [Polish]; Daniel Alberto Chavez Santiago [1986] Director [Mexican]

Exit 33 Brewing Ltd
Incorporated: 19 March 2007
Net Worth: £140,655 *Total Assets:* £167,071
Registered Office: Unit 7, 106 Fitzwalter Road, Sheffield, S2 2SP
Major Shareholder: Peter John Roberts
Officers: Peter John Roberts [1969] Director

Exmoor Ales Limited
Incorporated: 9 June 1988 *Employees:* 21
Net Worth: £498,483 *Total Assets:* £2,238,827
Registered Office: Golden Hill Brewery, Old Brewery Road, Wiveliscombe, Somerset, TA4 2PW
Major Shareholder: Jonathan Price
Officers: Penelope Jane Price, Secretary; Jonathan Price [1951] Director; Robin Mark Dodgson Price [1956] Director/Chartered Accountant

Eyeball Brewing Ltd
Incorporated: 12 January 2016 *Employees:* 1
Net Worth Deficit: £50,422 *Total Assets:* £66,513
Registered Office: The Works, Implement Road, West Barns, Dunbar, E Lothian, EH42 1UN
Major Shareholder: James Dempsey
Officers: Dr James Dempsey [1977] Director

Eyes Brewing Limited
Incorporated: 22 March 2016 *Employees:* 3
Net Worth: £3,491 *Total Assets:* £17,154
Registered Office: 22 Rawson Road, Bradford, BD1 3SQ
Major Shareholder: Daniel Jon Logan
Officers: Philippa Alexis Hardy [1984] Director; Daniel Jon Logan [1984] Director/Teacher

Fairy Glen Brewery Ltd
Incorporated: 6 February 2018
Registered Office: 60 Oaklands Avenue, Bridgend, CF31 4ST
Shareholders: Kelvin Johns; Simon Johns
Officers: Kelvin Johns [1959] Director; Simon Johns [1988] Director

Faking Bad Brewery Limited
Incorporated: 30 November 2018
Registered Office: 32 Woodhall Road, Pencaitland, Tranent, E Lothian, EH34 5AR
Shareholders: Gareth Alun Evans; Gordon George Kidd
Officers: Gareth Alun Evans [1973] Director; Gordon George Kidd [1974] Director

Fallen Acorn Brewing Co. Ltd
Incorporated: 27 August 2016 *Employees:* 4
Net Worth Deficit: £175,400 *Total Assets:* £85,051
Registered Office: Larch House, Parklands Business Park, Denmead, Hants, PO7 6XP
Parent: Just Develop It Limited
Officers: Matthew Curd [1986] Director; Daniel Peter Richards [1987] Director

Fallen Angel Brewery Ltd
Incorporated: 21 November 2016
Registered Office: 6 St Marys Mead, Broomfield, Chelmsford, Essex, CM1 7ZT
Officers: Gillian Margaret Burgis-Smith [1968] Director/Architect; Martin William Smith [1966] Director/Master Brewer

Fallen Brewing Company Ltd
Incorporated: 18 April 2012 *Employees:* 8
Net Worth: £130,533 *Total Assets:* £443,385
Registered Office: 20-22 Wenlock Road, London, N1 7GU
Major Shareholder: Paul Raymond Fallen
Officers: Karen Belinda Fallen [1970] Director/Sales & Business Development; Dr Paul Raymond Fallen [1974] Director/Brewer

Farm Yard Ales Ltd
Incorporated: 10 May 2012
Previous: Wingman Beers Ltd
Net Worth: £14,359 *Total Assets:* £267,213
Registered Office: c/o Tower S & Gornall, Abacus House, The Ropewalk, Garstang, Preston, Lancs, PR3 1NS
Major Shareholder: Steven James Holmes
Officers: Steven James Holmes [1988] Director/Labourer

Farmageddon Brewing Limited
Incorporated: 12 December 2017
Registered Office: Farmageddon Brewery 25 Ballykeigle Road, Comber, Newtownards, Co Down, BT23 5SD
Officers: Susan Jackson [1966] Director/Brewery Administration; Mark Uprichard [1976] Director/Surveyor; Eoin Wilson [1980] Director/Fireman

Farr Brew Ltd
Incorporated: 22 October 2015 *Employees:* 2
Net Worth Deficit: £111 *Total Assets:* £32,904
Registered Office: Unit 7 The Courtyard, Samuels Farm, Coleman Green Lane, Wheathampstead, St Albans, Herts, AL4 8ER
Shareholder: Nick John Farr
Officers: Nick John Farr, Secretary; Matthew Elvidge [1976] Director; Nick John Farr [1977] Director

Fat Boi Brewery & Sauce Company Limited
Incorporated: 19 April 2017
Registered Office: 3 Norman Crescent, Middleton, Milton Keynes, Bucks, MK10 9JN
Major Shareholder: Mark Ridel
Officers: Mark Ridel, Secretary; Mark Ridel [1969] Director

Faultline Brew Co. Ltd
Incorporated: 7 July 2017
Registered Office: 25 Ashley Road, Westcott, Dorking, Surrey, RH4 3QJ
Officers: Matthew John Gillam [1966] Director; Antoine Josserand [1980] Director

Fearless Brewing Ltd
Incorporated: 14 August 2017
Net Worth Deficit: £21,436 *Total Assets:* £11,315
Registered Office: 6 Rear Battle Hill, Hexham, Northumberland, NE46 1BB
Major Shareholder: Eldon Robson
Officers: Craig Whitfield, Secretary; Jamie Robson [1990] Director

Fearnought Brewery Ltd
Incorporated: 1 February 2019
Registered Office: 20-22 Wenlock Road, London, N1 7GU
Major Shareholder: Leonard Anthony Johnson
Officers: Leonard Anthony Johnson [1958] Director

Feisty Caribbean Ltd
Incorporated: 5 October 2015
Registered Office: 16 Louisa House, Medici Close, London, IG3 8FG
Major Shareholder: Yvonne Mae Raynor
Officers: Yvonne Raynor [1965] Director/Entrepreneur

Felday Limited
Incorporated: 21 April 2016
Net Worth Deficit: £9,230 *Total Assets:* £31,353
Registered Office: Aissela, 46 High Street, Esher, Surrey, KT10 9QY
Major Shareholder: Richard Froude Newman
Officers: Richard Froude Newman [1959] Director

Felinfoel Brewery Company Limited (The)
Incorporated: 28 September 1906 *Employees:* 38
Net Worth: £3,941,312 *Total Assets:* £6,146,446
Registered Office: Felinfoel Brewery, Llanelli, Carmarthenshire, SA14 8LB
Major Shareholder: Beryn Charles Martin Lewis
Officers: Charles Edward Hardy Coombes [1976] Director/Chartered Surveyor; Beryn Charles Martin Lewis [1958] Director; Jeremy John Cayley Lewis [1993] Director/Brewer; Philip John Lewis [1959] Director/Manager

Fellows Brewery Limited
Incorporated: 14 July 2009
Net Worth Deficit: £5,087 *Total Assets:* £8,818
Registered Office: 2 Leopold Walk, Cottenham, Cambridge, CB24 8XS
Major Shareholder: Mark Jonathan Burton
Officers: Mark Jonathan Burton [1972] Director

Fermanagh Beer Company Limited
Incorporated: 5 September 2016
Net Worth Deficit: £29,636 *Total Assets:* £30,862
Registered Office: 374 Lough Shore Road, Drummenagh More, Derrygonnelly, Co Fermanagh, BT93 6HX
Shareholder: Norman James Donaldson
Officers: Norman James Donaldson, Secretary; Norman James Donaldson [1988] Director

Ferox and Noble Limited
Incorporated: 11 September 2018
Registered Office: 1st Floor, 283 Church Road, Redfield, Bristol, BS5 9HT
Major Shareholder: Tobie William Holbrook
Officers: Tobie William Holbrook [1970] Director

Ferry Ales Brewery Limited
Incorporated: 7 April 2016 *Employees:* 3
Net Worth Deficit: £29,037 *Total Assets:* £116,179
Registered Office: Ferry Hill Farm, Ferry Road, Fiskerton, Lincoln, LN3 4HU
Shareholders: William John Cussons; Michael Holman
Officers: William John Cussons [1975] Director; Michael Stuart Holman [1964] Director

The Ferry Brewery Co Ltd
Incorporated: 12 August 2015 *Employees:* 2
Net Worth Deficit: £52,168 *Total Assets:* £57,464
Registered Office: Bankhead Farm Steading, Bankhead Road, South Queensferry, W Lothian, EH30 9TF
Shareholders: Jan Moran; Mark Moran
Officers: Mark Moran [1967] Director

Festival Brewery Ltd.
Incorporated: 1 May 2001 *Employees:* 1
Net Worth Deficit: £93,294 *Total Assets:* £17,617
Registered Office: 4 Meadow Lane, Up Hatherley, Cheltenham, Gloucester, GL51 3NP
Shareholder: Andrew Forbes
Officers: Caron Tracey Forbes, Secretary; Andrew Forbes [1959] Director

FGW Brewery Limited
Incorporated: 27 April 2011
Net Worth: £61,448 *Total Assets:* £273,684
Registered Office: Horizon House, 2, Whiting Street, Sheffield, S8 9QR
Shareholders: Alexander David Wilson; Nicholas John Folkard
Officers: Nicholas John Folkard [1985] Director/Businessman; Alexander David Wilson [1987] Director/Businessman

Fierce Beer Limited
Incorporated: 23 March 2015 Employees: 5
Net Worth: £205,708 Total Assets: £777,026
Registered Office: 175 Great Western Road, Aberdeen, AB10 6PS
Shareholder: David Grant
Officers: David Grant, Secretary; Russell James Boltman [1973] Director [South African]; David Grant [1965] Director/Engineer; David Charles McHardy [1980] Director/Brewer; Derek William Szabo [1977] Director [Dutch]

The Filo Brewing Company Limited
Incorporated: 20 July 2004 Employees: 13
Net Worth: £74,435 Total Assets: £161,497
Registered Office: 8 Old London Road, Hastings, E Sussex, TN34 3HA
Shareholders: Michael Bigg; Sharon Ann Bigg
Officers: Sharon Ann Bigg, Secretary; Michael Bigg [1944] Director/Publican; Sharon Ann Bigg [1964] Director/Administrator

Fine Tuned Brewery Limited
Incorporated: 9 April 2015 Employees: 4
Net Worth Deficit: £103,937 Total Assets: £147,840
Registered Office: Unit 16 Wessex Park, Somerton Business Park, Bancombe Road, Somerton, Somerset, TA11 6SB
Major Shareholder: Pawel Michal Kubinski
Officers: Pawel Michal Kubinski [1983] Director/Brewer [Polish]

Fingerprint Brewing Company Ltd
Incorporated: 8 May 2018
Registered Office: 2 Wasperton Lane, Barford, Warwick, CV35 8DT
Major Shareholder: Robert Bayliss
Officers: Robert Bayliss [1965] Director/Brewer

Finns (UK) Limited
Incorporated: 2 June 2008
Registered Office: 4 Stirling House, Sunderland Quay, Culpeper Close, Medway City Estate, Rochester, Kent, ME2 4HN
Shareholders: Antony Patrick Finnerty; Anthony Nicholson
Officers: Antony Patrick Finnerty [1958] Director; Anthony Nicholson [1943] Director

Fire Rock Brewing Company Ltd.
Incorporated: 3 October 2017
Registered Office: 32 Sotheby Avenue, Sutton in Ashfield, Notts, NG17 5JX
Officers: Neil Beaver [1985] Director/Training Manager; Daniel Hallam [1986] Director/Ground Technician

Firebird Brewing Company Ltd
Incorporated: 21 January 2013 Employees: 11
Net Worth Deficit: £36,366 Total Assets: £264,374
Registered Office: Rudgwick Brickworks, Lynwick Street, Rudgwick, W Sussex, RH12 3DH
Shareholders: William James King; Richard David Peters
Officers: William James King [1960] Director; Richard David Peters [1960] Director

Firebrick Brewery Limited
Incorporated: 24 May 2012
Net Worth Deficit: £204,036 Total Assets: £118,220
Registered Office: Units 10 & 11, Cowen Road, Blaydon on Tyne, Tyne & Wear, NE21 5TW
Shareholders: Alistair William Lawrence; Alistair William Lawrence
Officers: Alistair William Lawrence [1964] Director

First Chop Brewing Arm Ltd
Incorporated: 27 July 2012
Net Worth: £72,802 Total Assets: £203,375
Registered Office: Station Chambers, 36 Bolton Street, Bury, Lancs, BL9 0LL
Major Shareholder: Richard Garner
Officers: Richard Garner [1971] Director/Bar Owner

Fisher's Brewing Company Ltd.
Incorporated: 29 June 2015 Employees: 1
Net Worth Deficit: £52,137 Total Assets: £67,534
Registered Office: Unit 8 Central Park Business Centre, Bellfield Road, High Wycombe, Bucks, HP13 5HG
Major Shareholder: Mike Fisher
Officers: Roland William Taplin, Secretary; Mike Fisher [1983] Director; Leslie Peter Fraser [1957] Director/Sales and Marketing - IT; David Michael Hooper [1962] Director/Chartered Accountant; Nicholas Richard Jones [1961] Director/Retired Banker, Property Developer; Graeme Christopher Iain Smith [1984] Director/Business Analyst

Fishponds Brewery Ltd
Incorporated: 27 July 2018
Registered Office: The Star, 539 Fishponds Road, Fishponds, Bristol, BS16 3AF
Shareholders: Oisin Senan Hawes; Eimear Anthony Hawes
Officers: Eimear Anthony Hawes [1958] Director/Barman [Irish]; Oisin Senan Hawes [1962] Director/Carpenter [Irish]

Fit Like Beer Limited
Incorporated: 5 February 2016
Registered Office: 1 Grieves Cottage, Deer Park Farm, Banff, Aberdeenshire, AB45 3TJ
Major Shareholder: Tiernan Chillingworth
Officers: Tiernan Alexis Chillingworth [1982] Director/Brewer

Fitbeer Ltd.
Incorporated: 18 February 2016
Net Worth: £42,018 Total Assets: £43,536
Registered Office: Unit T6, Leyton Industrial Village, Argall Avenue, London, E10 7QP
Shareholders: Susan Patricia Kean; James Joseph Anthony Kean
Officers: James Joseph Anthony Kean [1961] Director/Investment Manager; Rebecca Lucy Anne Kean [1990] Director; Susan Patricia Kean [1962] Director/Chartered Accountant

Five Clouds Brewing Company Limited
Incorporated: 14 December 2015
Net Worth: £74 Total Assets: £6,213
Registered Office: 59 Pitt Street, Macclesfield, Cheshire, SK11 7PX
Shareholders: Thomas Owen Rhys Lewis; Joshua Mark Alan Sharples
Officers: Thomas Owen Rhys Lewis [1990] Director; Joshua Mark Alan Sharples [1993] Director/Retail Staff

The Five Points Brewing Company Ltd
Incorporated: 11 December 2012 Employees: 26
Net Worth: £7,530 Total Assets: £1,918,501
Registered Office: 3 Institute Place, London, E8 1JE
Major Shareholder: Edward Mason
Officers: Steven Allison [1969] Director; Edward Mason [1970] Director; Michael John Nicholas [1969] Director/Publican

Fixed Wheel Brewery Limited
Incorporated: 27 March 2014 *Employees:* 4
Net Worth: £3,812 *Total Assets:* £86,543
Registered Office: Unit 9 Long Lane Trading Estate Long Lane, Blackheath, Halesowen, W Midlands, B62 9LD
Shareholder: Scott Kristian Povey
Officers: Sharon Ann Bryant [1967] Director/Cleaning Supervisor; Scott Kristian Povey [1978] Director/Service Technician

Flack Manor Brewery Limited
Incorporated: 14 October 2009 *Employees:* 11
Net Worth: £584,123 *Total Assets:* £782,804
Registered Office: Midland House, 2 Poole Road, Bournemouth, BH2 5QY
Shareholder: Nigel Stead Welsh
Officers: Sandra Welsh, Secretary; Terence Baker [1964] Director; Ann Marie Stantiford [1956] Director; Nigel Stead Welsh [1955] Director

Flash House Brewing Company Limited
Incorporated: 27 October 2015
Net Worth Deficit: £19,175 *Total Assets:* £36,717
Registered Office: Unit 1a Northumberland Street, North Shields, Tyne & Wear, NE30 1DS
Major Shareholder: Jack Okeefe
Officers: Jack Okeefe [1991] Director/Brewery

Flat Cap Holding Company Limited
Incorporated: 13 April 2018
Registered Office: The Wool House, Town Quay, Southampton, SO14 2AR
Shareholders: Aidan Lavin; Mandy Lacey-Cross
Officers: Sarah Hopper [1965] Director; Mandy Lacey-Cross [1965] Director; Aidan Lavin [1979] Head Brewer & Director

Fleabag Brewing Company Ltd
Incorporated: 6 September 2018
Registered Office: 39 New Street, Chase Terrace, Burntwood, Staffs, WS7 1BT
Shareholders: Robert Alexander Brasher; Deborah Jayne Brasher
Officers: Deborah Jayne Brasher [1964] Director/Teacher; Robert Alexander Brasher [1964] Director/Chartered Surveyor

Flipside Brewing Ltd
Incorporated: 11 May 2017
Net Worth Deficit: £2,290 *Total Assets:* £25,891
Registered Office: 550 Valley Road, Basford, Nottingham, NG5 1JJ
Officers: Margaret Susan Dunkin [1954] Director

Floff UK Limited
Incorporated: 25 January 2017
Registered Office: 40 St Johns Drive, Newton, Porthcawl, Mid Glamorgan, CF36 3BB
Shareholder: David Fussell
Officers: David Fussell [1969] Director/Beer Sales

The Flying Fox Brewery Limited
Incorporated: 30 December 2015
Net Worth: £100 *Total Assets:* £100
Registered Office: 34 Marlborough Road, Southend on Sea, Essex, SS1 2UA
Major Shareholder: James Frederick Durritt
Officers: James Frederick Durritt [1983] Director

The Flying Monk Brewery Ltd
Incorporated: 18 March 2013 *Employees:* 14
Net Worth Deficit: £128,926 *Total Assets:* £324,418
Registered Office: 2 New Road, Chippenham, Wilts, SN15 1EJ
Shareholders: Martin William Hender; Iain Cameron Morrison; Anthony David Hibbard
Officers: Martin William Hender [1961] Director; Anthony David Hibbard [1960] Director; Iain Cameron Morrison [1949] Director

Foamology Limited
Incorporated: 1 May 2018
Registered Office: Cart Lodge, Harps Farm, Bedlars Green, Great Hallingbury, Bishop's Stortford, Herts, CM22 7TL
Officers: Nik Leontine Maurice Lemmens [1973] Director/Business Consultant [Belgian]

Foggie Beer Company Ltd
Incorporated: 1 June 2017
Registered Office: Foggie Farm, South Brownhills, Turriff, Aberdeenshire, AB53 4GZ
Major Shareholder: Karl James Scott
Officers: Karl James Scott [1969] Director/Farmer

Foghorn Brew Co Ltd
Incorporated: 27 February 2018
Registered Office: 91-93 Bohemia Road, St Leonards on Sea, E Sussex, TN37 6RJ
Shareholders: Niall Richard Buckler; Thomas Wyndham Bowen; Timothy James Harrow
Officers: Katya Rosalind Harrow, Secretary; Thomas Wyndham Bowen [1984] Director/Barman; Niall Richard Buckler [1985] Director/Barman; Timothy James Harrow [1978] Director/Barman

Fokof Limited
Incorporated: 23 February 2018
Registered Office: 179 Lambeth Walk, London, SE11 6EJ
Major Shareholder: Keith Allingham
Officers: Keith Allingham [1952] Director/Building

Force Brewery Limited
Incorporated: 20 February 2012
Net Worth: £29,262 *Total Assets:* £29,262
Registered Office: Unit 2 Bulley Poultry Farm, Bulley, Gloucester, GL2 8BJ
Major Shareholder: Charles Neville Wyndham Malet
Officers: Charles Neville Wyndham Malet [1976] Director

Foresight Holdings Limited
Incorporated: 2 March 2015 *Employees:* 2
Previous: Foresight Energy Solutions Ltd
Net Worth Deficit: £813 *Total Assets:* £10,212
Registered Office: New Dunsley Farm, Brow Lane, Holmfirth, W Yorks, HD9 2SW
Shareholder: Morri Consult Ltd.
Officers: Neal Mortimer [1960] Director; Paul Riley [1960] Director/Engineer

Forest Hill Brewing Company Limited
Incorporated: 12 February 2018
Registered Office: 14b Ryecroft Road, Lewisham, London, SE13 6EZ
Major Shareholder: Thomas Dennis
Officers: Thomas Dennis [1991] Director/Self Employed Musician

Forth Bridge Brewery and Distillery Limited
Incorporated: 6 February 2018
Registered Office: 43 Christiemiller Avenue, Edinburgh, EH7 6TB
Shareholders: James Stephen Brady; Carolyn Jayne Brady
Officers: Carolyn Jayne Brady [1964] Director; James Stephen Brady [1963] Director

Fosse Way Brewing Company Ltd.
Incorporated: 26 March 2012
Previous: Long Itch Brewery Ltd
Net Worth: £34,973 *Total Assets:* £41,473
Registered Office: Unit 5 Manor Farm Hunningham Road, Offchurch, Leamington Spa, Warwicks, CV33 9AG
Officers: Anthony Alexander Hobson [1958] Director/Brewer

The Four Bulls Brewing Company Limited
Incorporated: 13 October 2017
Registered Office: Flat 5 The Beeches, Church Road West, Farnborough, Hants, GU14 6QG
Officers: Scott Judd [1988] Director/Sales Manager; Lewis Marsh [1993] Director/Assistant Underwriter

Four Kings Brewery Limited
Incorporated: 12 February 2016
Net Worth Deficit: £46,240 *Total Assets:* £29,616
Registered Office: 225 Market Street, Hyde, Cheshire, SK14 1HF
Shareholders: Paul Michael Ashworth; Toby Colbourne
Officers: Paul Michael Ashworth [1972] Director/Brewer; Toby Colbourne [1974] Director/Brewer

Four Pillars Brewery Limited
Incorporated: 3 November 2015 *Employees:* 2
Net Worth Deficit: £138,567 *Total Assets:* £385,052
Registered Office: Unit 2 Ravenswood Industrial Estate, Walthamstow, London, E17 9HQ
Shareholder: Gavin Matthew Litton
Officers: Gavin Matthew Litton [1988] Director; Eamonn Muhammed Razaq [1989] Director; Omar Andrew Razaq [1988] Director; Samie Heider Razaq [1992] Director

Fourpure Limited
Incorporated: 16 September 2011
Net Worth Deficit: £521,572 *Total Assets:* £4,675,165
Registered Office: 22 Bermondsey Trading Estate, Rotherhithe New Road, London, SE16 3LL
Parent: Fourpure Holdco Limited
Officers: Toby Jason Kelly Knowles [1974] Director; Luke Anthony Solomons [1979] Finance Director [Australian]

The Fowey Brewery Ltd
Incorporated: 26 April 2016
Net Worth Deficit: £4,374 *Total Assets:* £42,393
Registered Office: Pawton Mill, St Breock, Wadebridge, Cornwall, PL27 7LH
Shareholders: Dominic Sheridan Austell Comonte; Geoff Troup
Officers: Dominic Sheridan Austell Comonte [1970] Director/Brewer; Geoff Troup [1958] Director/Brewer

Fownes Brewing Company Ltd.
Incorporated: 17 March 2014
Net Worth: £11,856 *Total Assets:* £22,387
Registered Office: 42 The Ridgeway, Sedgley, Dudley, W Midlands, DY3 3UR
Shareholder: Thomas David Fownes
Officers: David Reginald Fownes [1958] Director/Brewer; James David Fownes [1980] Director/Brewer; Thomas David Fownes [1984] Director/Brewer

Foxhat Beer Limited
Incorporated: 2 March 2016
Registered Office: 56 High Street, Tranent, E Lothian, EH33 1HH
Parent: Craigvinean Outdoor Centre Trust
Officers: Stephen Boyle [1980] Director/Head of Service; Niall Gordon Forrest Grant [1990] Director; Eliot James Stark [1969] Director

Framework Brewery Limited
Incorporated: 20 June 2016 *Employees:* 6
Net Worth: £25,124 *Total Assets:* £70,589
Registered Office: The Old City Depot, 72-74 Friday Street, Leicester, LE1 3BW
Shareholder: Bulb Studios Limited
Officers: Michael Martin Willis, Secretary; Andrew Duncan Goodliffe [1964] Director/Manager; Matthew Philip Mabe [1977] Director/Manager; James Thomas Willis [1974] Director/Manager; Michael Martin Willis [1951] Director/Management Consultant

Frank and Otis Brewing Ltd
Incorporated: 17 January 2019
Registered Office: The Coach House, Dock Street, Penarth, Vale of Glamorgan, CF64 2LA
Shareholders: Robert James Parker; Stephen Paul McDonald
Officers: Stephen Paul McDonald [1979] Director; Robert James Parker [1984] Director

Freedom Brewery Ltd
Incorporated: 18 November 2004 *Employees:* 27
Net Worth Deficit: £1,257,994 *Total Assets:* £2,787,101
Registered Office: Freedom Brewery, Bagots Park, Abbots Bromley, Rugeley, Staffs, WS15 3ER
Officers: Matthew William Willson [1972] Director

The Freewheelin' Brewery Company Limited
Incorporated: 8 November 2012
Net Worth: £5,283 *Total Assets:* £23,881
Registered Office: 15 Lyne Park, West Linton, Peebles-shire, EH46 7HP
Officers: Alastair Mouat [1945] Director/Retired; Michael Edwin Pearson [1943] Director/Retired; Linda White [1956] Director/Teacher; Richard Charles White [1954] Director/Programme Manager

Fremlins Limited
Incorporated: 27 August 2013
Registered Office: 13 Kestrel Avenue, London, SE24 0ED
Major Shareholder: William George Fremlin-Key
Officers: Mark Ross Telfer, Secretary; William George Fremlin-Key [1985] Director/Insurance Broker

French & Jupps Limited
Incorporated: 11 March 1920 *Employees:* 23
Net Worth: £13,642,729 *Total Assets:* £14,657,962
Registered Office: The Maltings, Roydon Road, Stanstead Abbotts, Herts, SG12 8HG
Shareholders: David Holroyd Jupp; Jennifer Jupp
Officers: David Holroyd Jupp [1959] Director/Malster; David Frank Watson [1964] Director

The Fresh Beer Company Ltd
Incorporated: 18 April 2018
Registered Office: 5 Glenleigh Walk, Robertsbridge, E Sussex, TN32 5DQ
Major Shareholder: Aaron Thomas Rowsell
Officers: Aaron Thomas Rowsell [1986] Director

The Friday Beer Company Limited
Incorporated: 6 July 2011
Net Worth Deficit: £159,625 *Total Assets:* £110,054
Registered Office: 28a Avenue Road, Malvern, Worcs, WR14 3BG
Officers: Peregrine Orr Jackson [1973] Director; Andrew Keir [1959] Director; Generald Martin Williams [1951] Director

Frisky Bear Brewing Co Ltd
Incorporated: 23 April 2014
Net Worth Deficit: £2,619 *Total Assets:* £2,501
Registered Office: 2a Queen Street, Morley, Leeds, LS27 9DG
Major Shareholder: Carl David Saint
Officers: Carl David Saint [1984] Managing Director

Frome Brewery Limited
Incorporated: 2 March 2016
Registered Office: The Griffin, Milk Street, Frome, Somerset, BA11 3DB
Major Shareholder: Richard John Lyall
Officers: Richard John Lyall [1969] Director/Licensee

Frome Brewing Company Limited
Incorporated: 12 December 2014 *Employees:* 30
Net Worth Deficit: £33,582 *Total Assets:* £131,666
Registered Office: Unit L, 13 Marshall Way, Commerce Park, Frome, Somerset, BA11 2FB
Major Shareholder: Keith Edward Hewett
Officers: Keith Edward Hewett [1971] Director/Licensee

Frontier Brewing Company Limited
Incorporated: 21 October 2014
Net Worth Deficit: £45,445 *Total Assets:* £107,036
Registered Office: Unit 5G The Midway, Lenton, Nottingham, NG7 2TS
Shareholders: David George Garland; John William Russell
Officers: David George Garland [1974] Director; John William Russell [1974] Director

Froth Blowers Brewing Company Ltd
Incorporated: 25 May 2012
Net Worth Deficit: £119,943 *Total Assets:* £134,571
Registered Office: 4 Fitzcount Way, Wallingford, Oxon, OX10 8JP
Officers: William James Hunt [1981] Sales Director; Andrew James Williams [1969] Director/Brewer; Neil Alan Williams [1965] Director/Sales Manager; David Leonard Woodhead [1940] Director/Retired

Fuddy Duck Limited
Incorporated: 30 March 2016 *Employees:* 1
Net Worth Deficit: £9,161 *Total Assets:* £7,655
Registered Office: 3 Arcott Drive, Boston, Lincs, PE21 7QJ
Major Shareholder: Jason Shaun Marshall
Officers: Jason Shaun Marshall [1970] Director/Microbrewery

Fuggle Bunny Brew House Limited
Incorporated: 5 August 2013 *Employees:* 1
Net Worth Deficit: £18,139 *Total Assets:* £65,327
Registered Office: Cedar House, 63 Napier Street, Sheffield, S11 8HA
Shareholders: David Steeple; Wendy Steeple
Officers: David Steeple [1955] Director/Master Brewer

Fulham Brewery Ltd
Incorporated: 27 November 2018
Registered Office: 8 Old Lodge Place, Twickenham, Middlesex, TW1 1RQ
Major Shareholder: Nicholas Joseph Dolan
Officers: Nicholas Joseph Dolan [1976] Director

Fuzzy Duck Brewery Limited
Incorporated: 9 June 2010
Net Worth Deficit: £71,262 *Total Assets:* £27,461
Registered Office: 11 Hillside Avenue, Preesall, Poulton-le-Fylde, Lancs, FY6 0ES
Major Shareholder: Benjamin Thomas Croston
Officers: Benjamin Thomas Croston, Secretary; Benjamin Thomas Croston [1978] Director

Fyne Ales Limited
Incorporated: 12 March 2001 *Employees:* 21
Net Worth: £602,581 *Total Assets:* £3,068,529
Registered Office: Achadunan, Cairndow, Argyll, PA26 8BJ
Shareholders: Michael Jonathan Sinclair Delap; James Robert Onslow Delap
Officers: Anastasia Diana Delap [1948] Director; James Robert Onslow Delap [1969] Director; Michael Jonathan Sinclair Delap [1972] Director

Gales Brewery Limited
Incorporated: 25 March 2013
Registered Office: Stonecroft, Main Road, Hawksworth, Nottingham, NG13 9DD
Major Shareholder: Paul Antony Gale
Officers: Paul Antony Gale [1956] Director/Entrepreneur

Galldachd Na H-Alba Brewing Ltd
Incorporated: 22 September 2017
Registered Office: Sunnybrae, Old Well Road, Moffat, Dumfries & Galloway, DG10 9AP
Major Shareholder: Michael Stuart Tough
Officers: Thomas Joseph Barr, Secretary; Michael Stuart Tough [1965] Managing Director

Gan Yam Brewing Company Ltd
Incorporated: 21 April 2017
Net Worth Deficit: £214 *Total Assets:* £1,591
Registered Office: 149 Hillingdon Street, London, SE17 3JH
Officers: John Seymour Batteson [1985] Director; William Burgess [1985] Director; Nicolas Kyle Graves [1985] Director; Jonathan Le Mare [1985] Director; Christopher Robert Talbot [1985] Director; William Wilkinson [1985] Director

Gander Brewing Company Ltd
Incorporated: 28 November 2018
Registered Office: Unit 16b, Top Barn Business Centre, Worcester Road, Holt Heath, Worcester, WR6 6NH
Shareholders: Aaron Michael Bushell; Lee Anthony Bushell
Officers: Aaron Michael Bushell [1984] Director/Diver; Lee Anthony Bushell [1995] Director/Brewer

Garagebrew Ltd
Incorporated: 17 November 2016
Registered Office: 21a Kelvin Close, Cambridge, CB1 8DN
Officers: Roger Rich [1964] Director/Homebrewing

Garden City Brewery Limited
Incorporated: 18 January 2016
Net Worth: £28,826 *Total Assets:* £53,828
Registered Office: 108 Ridge Road, Letchworth Garden City, Herts, SG6 1PT
Shareholders: Nicholas Laurits Price; Holly-Anne Katherine Lydia Rolfe
Officers: Holly-Anne Katherine Lydia Rolfe [1980] Director

Gargiulo's Production Ltd
Incorporated: 10 August 2018
Registered Office: 7 Greenwood Road, Mitcham, Surrey, CR4 1PF
Major Shareholder: Pasquale Gargiulo
Officers: Pasquale Gargiulo [1987] Director/Dog Handler [Italian]

Garretts Green Garage Mikro Brewery Ltd
Incorporated: 13 March 2013
Registered Office: 19 Westcott Road, Garretts Green, Birmingham, B26 2EX
Major Shareholder: Mike Ward
Officers: Mike Ward [1985] Director/Accountant

Geeves Brewery Limited
Incorporated: 18 February 2011 *Employees:* 2
Net Worth Deficit: £49,302 *Total Assets:* £15,947
Registered Office: 36-40 Doncaster Road, Barnsley, S Yorks, S70 1TL
Shareholders: Peter Michael Geeves; Henry Hugo Geeves
Officers: Henry Hugo Geeves [1990] Director/Student; Peter Michael Geeves [1955] Director/Actor

Geipel Brewing Limited
Incorporated: 2 March 2011
Net Worth Deficit: £281,488 *Total Assets:* £149,905
Registered Office: 48 Barlow Moor Road, Manchester, M20 2GJ
Shareholder: Erik Arnold Geupel
Officers: Erik Arnold Geupel [1966] Director [American]; Amanda Rooth-Geupel [1965] Director

Gemstone Ales Ltd.
Incorporated: 23 March 2015
Registered Office: 473 Willington Street, Maidstone, Kent, ME15 8HA
Shareholders: Martin Moss; Valerie Gillingham
Officers: Valerie Gillingham [1969] Director/Brewer

Gene Pool Brewing Ltd
Incorporated: 8 July 2016
Net Worth Deficit: £4,458 *Total Assets:* £3,660
Registered Office: Unit 6, 23 Arthur Street, Hull, HU3 6BH
Shareholders: Lindsey Michael Simpson; Ian Andrew Simpson
Officers: Ian Andrew Simpson [1967] Director; Lindsey Michael Simpson [1991] Director

Genesis Craft Ales Limited
Incorporated: 9 June 2016
Net Worth Deficit: £6,859 *Total Assets:* £23,195
Registered Office: The Duke of Cambridge Public House, Tilford Road, Tilford, Surrey, GU10 2DD
Shareholder: Mark Ainley Collins
Officers: Mark Ainley Collins [1969] Director; Paul David Griffiths [1985] Director; Mark Fairfax Robson [1977] Director

Genius Brewing Limited
Incorporated: 7 July 2016
Net Worth: £53,424 *Total Assets:* £64,366
Registered Office: 168 Bath Street, Glasgow, G2 4TP
Shareholders: Jason Paul Sansom Clarke; Charles Thomas Garrioch Craig
Officers: Jason Paul Sansom Clarke [1969] Director; Charles Thomas Garrioch Craig [1968] Director

The Gentleman Bear Brewing Company Ltd
Incorporated: 31 January 2017
Registered Office: 63 Pen Y Cae, Caerphilly, Gwent, CF83 3BX
Officers: Christopher Gurner [1983] Director/Brewer of Beer; Michael Hall [1983] Director/Brewer of Beer

George's Brewery Limited
Incorporated: 8 January 2010
Net Worth: £54,442 *Total Assets:* £106,189
Registered Office: 11 Redhills Road, South Woodham Ferrers, Chelmsford, Essex, CM3 5UL
Major Shareholder: Mark Adam Mawson
Officers: Mark Adam Mawson [1963] Director/Brewer

German Kraft Brewing Limited
Incorporated: 1 June 2017 *Employees:* 25
Net Worth: £67,651 *Total Assets:* £1,234,867
Registered Office: 34 Kay Road, London, SW9 9DE
Major Shareholder: Felix Bollen
Officers: Felix Bollen [1995] Director [German]; Anton Borkmann [1994] Director [German]; Michele Tieghi [1995] Director [Italian]

Getset Brew Co Ltd
Incorporated: 30 July 2018
Registered Office: 73 Townsend Grove, New Bradwell, Milton Keynes, Bucks, MK13 0DS
Major Shareholder: David Vaughn Alan Williams
Officers: Sarah-Ann Bedford, Secretary; David Vaughn Alan Williams [1987] Managing Director

Ghost Brewing Co Limited
Incorporated: 17 June 2015 *Employees:* 2
Net Worth: £60,584 *Total Assets:* £98,748
Registered Office: 13a South Hawksworth Street, Ilkley, W Yorks, LS29 9DX
Shareholders: Champagne Warehouse Ltd; James Thompson; Steven Crump
Officers: Steve Crump [1981] Director/Brewer; James Thompson [1972] Sales Director

Gibberish Brewing Ltd
Incorporated: 4 October 2017
Registered Office: Unit 1, 15 Caryl Street, Liverpool, L8 5AA
Major Shareholder: Gareth Michael John Kershaw Matthews
Officers: Dr Gareth Michael John Kershaw Matthews [1976] Director/Brewer

Gil's Brewery Ltd
Incorporated: 8 August 2018
Registered Office: 9 Ashcroft Crescent, Cardiff, CF5 3RJ
Shareholders: Kyle Edward Foat; Michael John Smith
Officers: Kyle Edward Foat [1992] Director/Electrician; Michael John Smith [1993] Director/Electrician

Gilt & Flint Ltd
Incorporated: 19 September 2018
Registered Office: Haye Farm, Musbury, Axminster, Devon, EX13 8ST
Shareholders: Daniel Paul Fitzpatrick; Harry Luca Boglione; Jason Samuel Slade
Officers: Harry Luca Boglione [1990] Director [Australian/Italian]; Daniel Paul Fitzpatrick [1974] Director; Jason Samuel Slade [1972] Director

The GKH Beer Company Ltd
Incorporated: 14 April 2014
Net Worth: £3,412 *Total Assets:* £3,425
Registered Office: Old Chimneys, The Street, Market Weston, Diss, Norfolk, IP22 2NZ
Major Shareholder: Alan Rodger Thomson
Officers: Alan Rodger Thomson [1955] Director/Brewer

Glasshouse Beer Co Ltd
Incorporated: 21 October 2016 *Employees:* 2
Net Worth Deficit: £2,745 *Total Assets:* £2,661
Registered Office: Unit 6b Waterside Business Park, 1649-1652 Pershore Road, Kings Norton, Birmingham, B30 3DR
Officers: Joshua Andrew Hughes [1991] Director/Brewer; Calum Robert Marnock [1989] Director/Brewer

The Glastonbury Brewing Company Ltd
Incorporated: 25 October 2018
Registered Office: 14 Queen Square, Bath, BA1 2HN
Shareholders: Paul Geoffrey Nash; David Tucker
Officers: Paul Geoffrey Nash [1964] Director; David Tucker [1976] Director

Glede Brewing Company Limited
Incorporated: 24 August 2016
Net Worth Deficit: £30,244 *Total Assets:* £49,116
Registered Office: Unit 1 Tweed Road Industrial Estate, Tweed Road, Clevedon, Somerset, BS21 6RR
Major Shareholder: Howard James Tucker
Officers: Dawn Tucker [1955] Director; Howard James Tucker [1964] Director

Glen Affric Brewery Limited
Incorporated: 20 November 2014 *Employees:* 1
Net Worth Deficit: £88,465 *Total Assets:* £181,944
Registered Office: 53 Wood Street, Ashton under Lyne, Lancs, OL6 7NB
Major Shareholder: Calum McCormick
Officers: Calum McCormick [1993] Director

Gleneagles Distillery Limited
Incorporated: 20 December 2018
Registered Office: Briven House, Main Road, Aberuthven, Auchterarder, Perthshire, PH3 1HB
Major Shareholder: Graham Charles Bennett
Officers: Graham Charles Bennett [1958] Director

The Glenfinnan Brewing Company Limited
Incorporated: 3 February 2017
Net Worth: £100 *Total Assets:* £100
Registered Office: Tirindrish House, Tirindrish, Spean Bridge, Highland, PH34 4EU
Officers: Lucy Alexandra Hicks [1976] Director/B & B Proprietor; James Fraser Leggett [1970] Director/B & B Proprietor; Ian Peter MacDonald [1961] Director

Glesga Brewery Ltd.
Incorporated: 14 April 2015
Registered Office: 1/1, 3 Lloyd Street, Glasgow, G31 2PE
Major Shareholder: Reuben Cameron
Officers: Reuben Cameron [1991] Director

Gloucester Brewery Ltd
Incorporated: 15 September 2011 *Employees:* 6
Net Worth: £70,230 *Total Assets:* £287,028
Registered Office: Llanthony Warehouse, The Docks, Gloucester, GL1 2EH
Major Shareholder: Jared Jared Brown
Officers: Jared Brown [1979] Director/Owner

Gloucestershire Old Cottage Beer Company Limited
Incorporated: 23 May 2017
Registered Office: Unit 10 Eccleshall Business Park, Hawkins Lane, Burton on Trent, Staffs, DE14 1PT
Shareholders: Jeffrey Stephen Denton Alden; Roger Barry Shone
Officers: Jeffrey Stephen Denton Alden [1968] Director; Roger Barry Shone [1969] Director

Goddards Brewery Limited
Incorporated: 24 January 1989 *Employees:* 8
Net Worth: £200,893 *Total Assets:* £580,178
Registered Office: Barnsley Farm, Bullen Road, Ryde, Isle of Wight, PO33 1QF
Officers: Anthony Howard Goddard, Secretary/Brewer; Xavier Lee Baker [1977] Director/Brewer; Alix Ormond Goddard [1945] Director/Brewer; Anthony Howard Goddard [1945] Director/Brewer; Janet Margaret Goddard [1946] Director; Richard Charles Harvey [1954] Director/Brewer

Goff's Brewery Limited
Incorporated: 4 May 1993
Net Worth Deficit: £161,480 *Total Assets:* £91,322
Registered Office: 9 Isbourne Way, Winchcombe, Glos, GL54 5NS
Shareholders: Marcus James Goff; Alison Robertson-Goff
Officers: Marcus James Goff, Secretary; Marcus James Goff [1968] Director/Accountant; Alison Robertson Goff [1968] Director/Office Manager

Golcar Brewery Limited
Incorporated: 4 August 1986 *Employees:* 2
Net Worth: £348,553 *Total Assets:* £418,326
Registered Office: Swallow Lane, Golcar, Huddersfield, W Yorks, HD7 4NB
Major Shareholder: John Edward Broadbent
Officers: John Edward Broadbent, Secretary; John Edward Broadbent [1951] Director/Service Manager; Peter Howard Broadbent [1949] Director/Engineer

Golden Fox Brewing Ltd
Incorporated: 15 June 2015
Net Worth Deficit: £2,404 *Total Assets:* £134
Registered Office: 13b Broadway Parade, Harringay, London, N8 9DE
Shareholder: Edward Murray Sheens
Officers: Anne-Cecile Schmidt, Secretary; Edward Murray Sheens [1985] Director/Teacher Brewer [Australian]

Golden Triangle Brewery Limited
Incorporated: 13 September 2010 *Employees:* 2
Net Worth Deficit: £8,431 *Total Assets:* £50,730
Registered Office: Unit 9 Watton Road, Barford, Norwich, NR9 4BG
Major Shareholder: Kevin Alexander Tweedy
Officers: Kevin Tweedy, Secretary; Kevin Tweedy [1958] Director/Brewer

Goldmark Craft Beers Ltd
Incorporated: 18 January 2013 *Employees:* 2
Net Worth Deficit: £14,202 *Total Assets:* £83,777
Registered Office: 43 Tideway, Littlehampton, W Sussex, BN17 6PP
Shareholder: Nicholas Hart
Officers: Mark Wolfram Lehmann [1970] Director/Brewer

Good Chemistry Apparatus Limited
Incorporated: 21 May 2015
Net Worth: £1,888 *Total Assets:* £92,632
Registered Office: 6 Beaconsfield Road, Clifton, Bristol, BS8 2TS
Shareholders: Robert James Cary; Kelly Anna Sidgwick
Officers: Robert James Cary [1979] Director; Kelly Anna Sidgwick [1981] Director

Good Chemistry Brewing Limited
Incorporated: 21 May 2015 *Employees:* 4
Net Worth: £6,096 *Total Assets:* £252,899
Registered Office: 6 Beaconsfield Road, Clifton, Bristol, BS8 2TS
Shareholders: Robert James Cary; Kelly Anna Sidgwick
Officers: Robert James Cary [1979] Director; Kelly Anna Sidgwick [1981] Director

Good Kombucha Drinks Ltd
Incorporated: 23 February 2018
Registered Office: 144 East Carriage House, Royal Carriage Mews, London, SE18 6GL
Major Shareholder: Christopher Robert Crocker
Officers: Christopher Robert Crocker [1980] Director

Good Living Brew Co Limited
Incorporated: 16 March 2018
Registered Office: Sundial House, High Street, Horsell, Woking, Surrey, GU21 4SU
Major Shareholder: Brett Jason Venter
Officers: Danielle Bekker [1976] Director/Engineer [South African]; Brett Jason Venter [1976] Director [South African]

Good Things Brewing Company Ltd
Incorporated: 9 June 2017
Registered Office: 119 The Hub, 300 Kensal Road, London, W10 5BE
Shareholders: Christopher Drummond; Sam Pallach Robinson
Officers: Christopher Drummond [1983] Director; Sam Pallach Robinson [1979] Director

Goody Ales Limited
Incorporated: 14 March 2011 *Employees:* 7
Net Worth Deficit: £60,461 *Total Assets:* £92,553
Registered Office: 7 The Broadway, Broadstairs, Kent, CT10 2AD
Shareholders: Karen Goody; Peter McCabe
Officers: Karen Goody [1960] Director; Peter McCabe [1958] Director

Goose Eye Brewery Limited
Incorporated: 13 September 2002 *Employees:* 5
Net Worth: £407,546 *Total Assets:* £956,180
Registered Office: Unit S, Castlefields Road, Bingley, W Yorks, BD16 2AF
Shareholder: David Atkinson
Officers: Linda Atkinson, Secretary; David Atkinson [1969] Director/Brewer; Jack Atkinson [1944] Director/Brewer

Got 2 Bee Clean Ltd
Incorporated: 21 March 2018
Registered Office: 71-75 Shelton Street, London, WC2H 9JQ
Major Shareholder: Janice Smith
Officers: Janice Smith [1970] Director/Property Professional

Gower Brewery Co Limited
Incorporated: 30 September 2011 *Employees:* 13
Net Worth: £383,703 *Total Assets:* £1,251,866
Registered Office: Unit 25 Crofty Industrial Estate, Penclawdd, Swansea, SA4 3RS
Shareholders: Christopher John Mabbett; Christopher Paul Stevens
Officers: Paul Graham Chiverton [1967] Director/Self Employed Haulier; Leigh Andrew John Dineen [1965] Director; Keith Robert Jones [1967] Director; Matthew Richard Lewis Joslin [1983] Director/Software Engineer; Christopher John Mabbett [1975] Director; Stephen John Rees [1963] Commercial Director; Christopher Paul Stevens [1982] Director

Gower Pub Co Ltd
Incorporated: 17 January 2014 *Employees:* 21
Net Worth Deficit: £41,076 *Total Assets:* £832,827
Registered Office: Kings Head, Llangennith, Gower, Swansea, SA3 1HX
Officers: Richard Knox [1976] Director; Sarah Gwen Knox [1979] Director/Prison Officer; Christopher Paul Stevens [1982] Director/Publican

Grace Land Beer Limited
Incorporated: 16 March 2009
Net Worth Deficit: £59,224 *Total Assets:* £25,257
Registered Office: 23 Exmouth Market, London, EC1R 4QL
Parent: Grace Land Group Ltd
Officers: Andreas Akerlund, Secretary; Jon Andreas Akerlund [1971] Director [Swedish]; Anselm Chatwin [1979] Director/Finance Manager; Marc Francis-Baum [1971] Director

Grafham Brewing Company Ltd
Incorporated: 29 November 2017
Registered Office: 30 Breach Road, Grafham, Cambs, PE28 0BA
Major Shareholder: Paul Robinson
Officers: Paul Robinson [1974] Director/Designer

Grain Brewery Limited
Incorporated: 26 July 2011 *Employees:* 8
Net Worth: £19,967 *Total Assets:* £259,977
Registered Office: 124 Thorpe Road, Norwich, NR1 1RS
Shareholders: Phil Halls; Geoff Wright
Officers: Hilary Anne Halls [1972] Director; Phil Halls [1969] Director; Geoff Wright [1972] Director; Victoria Kate Wright [1971] Director

The Grainstore Brewery Limited
Incorporated: 4 May 2010 *Employees:* 28
Net Worth: £415,695 *Total Assets:* £666,208
Registered Office: 110 Regent Road, Leicester, LE1 7LT
Parent: Spidercrab Limited
Officers: Peter David Atkinson [1972] Director; William Anthony Davis [1974] Director

Granite Rock Brewery and Home Brew Supplies Ltd
Incorporated: 5 November 2012 *Employees:* 2
Net Worth Deficit: £117,340 *Total Assets:* £21,864
Registered Office: Unit 19 Kernick Road Industrial Estate, Penryn, Cornwall, TR10 9EP
Shareholders: David Willmot; Frances Williams
Officers: Frances Williams [1964] Director/Registered Mental Health Nurse; David Richard Willmot [1957] Director

Grasshopper Brewery Limited
Incorporated: 6 November 2014
Net Worth Deficit: £43,292 *Total Assets:* £76,848
Registered Office: Unit F2, Langley Bridge Industrial Estate, Linkmel Road, Eastwood, Notts, NG16 3RZ
Shareholders: Antony Marriott; Beau O'Dowd
Officers: Nicola Stacey Marriott, Secretary; Zoe Yi Zhang, Secretary; Antony Marriott [1975] Director; Beau O'Dowd [1974] Director

Gravity Well Brewing Company Limited
Incorporated: 16 January 2018
Registered Office: Arch 142 Tilbury Road, London, E10 6RE
Major Shareholder: Ben Duck
Officers: Ben Duck [1984] Director/Brewer

Great British Breworks Ltd
Incorporated: 25 October 2016
Net Worth: £100 *Total Assets:* £100
Registered Office: The Black Swan, Birdgate, Pickering, N Yorks, YO18 7AL
Shareholder: Tristan Philip Hall
Officers: Jill Hall [1967] Director; Philip Robert Hall [1964] Director/Breworks Ltd; Tristan Hall [1993] Director/Brewer

Great Central Brewery Limited
Incorporated: 12 January 2015
Net Worth: £7,688 *Total Assets:* £7,688
Registered Office: Unit B, Marlow Road, Leicester, LE3 2BQ
Major Shareholder: Neil Charles Leonard Rowley
Officers: Neil Charles Leonard Rowley [1967] Director/Telecommunications Project Engineer

The Great Glen Brewing Company Limited
Incorporated: 9 July 2010
Registered Office: 18 Wards Drive, Muir of Ord, Ross-shire, IV6 7PX
Shareholder: John Davidson
Officers: John Davidson [1954] Director/Consultant; Brian Wright [1960] Director/Commercial Manager

Great Glen Trading Centre Limited
Incorporated: 12 April 2017
Net Worth: £2,091 *Total Assets:* £3,423
Registered Office: Westoaks, Fort William Road, Fort Augustus, Inverness-shire, PH32 4BH
Shareholders: George Wilson Girvan; Robbie James Macpherson Girvan
Officers: Catriona Girvan [1950] Director; George Wilson Girvan [1948] Director; Robbie James Macpherson Girvan [1987] Director

Great Heck Brewing Company Ltd
Incorporated: 16 October 2006 *Employees:* 5
Net Worth: £88,942 *Total Assets:* £204,908
Registered Office: Harwinn House, Main Street, Great Heck, Goole, N Yorks, DN14 0BQ
Major Shareholder: Denzil William Vallance
Officers: Denzil William Vallance, Secretary; Denzil William Vallance [1970] Director

The Great Newsome Brewery Limited
Incorporated: 7 September 2006 *Employees:* 9
Net Worth: £109,907 *Total Assets:* £279,828
Registered Office: Great Newsome Farm, South Frodingham, Hull, HU12 0NR
Parent: I M Hodgson & Son Limited
Officers: Matthew Hodgson, Secretary; Jonathan Hodgson [1976] Director/Farmer; Laurence Hodgson [1950] Director/Farmer; Matthew Hodson [1973] Director/Farmer

The Great North Eastern Brewing Company Limited
Incorporated: 15 September 2015
Net Worth Deficit: £66,430 *Total Assets:* £185,660
Registered Office: Unit E, Contract House, Wellington Road West, Dunston, Gateshead, Tyne & Wear, NE11 9HS
Major Shareholder: Paul Minnikin
Officers: Paul Minnikin [1957] Director

The Great Orme Brewery Limited
Incorporated: 25 March 2004
Net Worth Deficit: £26,437 *Total Assets:* £250,346
Registered Office: The Great Orme Brewery Limited, Builder Street, Llandudno, Conwy, LL30 1DR
Major Shareholder: Jonathan Roger Hughes
Officers: Lorna Hughes, Secretary; Jonathan Roger Hughes [1972] Director/Management Consultant-Engineer

Great Western Brewing Company Limited
Incorporated: 17 November 2006 *Employees:* 27
Net Worth: £206,531 *Total Assets:* £629,526
Registered Office: Great Western Brewing Company Ltd, Bristol Road, Hambrook, Bristol, BS16 1RF
Officers: Sandra Stone, Secretary; Ashley Craig Stone [1989] Director/Brewery Manager; Kevin Paul Stone [1959] Director/Licensee; Leanne Jane Stone [1991] Director; Sandra Stone [1963] Director/Licensee

The Great Yorkshire Brewery Limited
Incorporated: 18 June 2010 *Employees:* 10
Net Worth: £136,297 *Total Assets:* £1,766,120
Registered Office: W H Prior, Railway Court, Doncaster, S Yorks, DN4 5FB
Parent: The Spirit Beer Company Limited
Officers: Craig Butler [1969] Director; Philip Craig Lee [1970] Director; Christopher James Spencer [1974] Director

Green Duck Beer Co. Limited
Incorporated: 17 February 2012
Net Worth Deficit: £7,521 *Total Assets:* £129,859
Registered Office: Unit 13 Gainsborough Trading Estate, Rufford Road, Stourbridge, W Midlands, DY9 7ND
Shareholder: Alan James Preece
Officers: Alex Edward Hill [1992] Director; Curt Nathan Kiszka [1971] Director; Alan James Preece [1971] Director; John Preece [1943] Director/Retired

A & C Green Food and Beverage Limited
Incorporated: 21 November 2018
Registered Office: 59 Bonnygate, Cupar, Fife, KY15 4BY
Officers: Giorgio Cozzolino Cozzolino [1964] Director [Italian]

Green Jack Brewing Company Limited
Incorporated: 25 February 2008 *Employees:* 20
Net Worth: £296,220 *Total Assets:* £632,090
Registered Office: Argyle Place, Love Road, Lowestoft, Suffolk, NR32 2NZ
Major Shareholder: Timothy Richard Dunford
Officers: Timothy Richard Dunford [1964] Director/Brewer

Green Times Brewing Limited
Incorporated: 5 January 2018
Registered Office: 170 Southstand Apartments, Highbury Stadium Square, London, N5 1FB
Major Shareholder: Thierry Florit
Officers: Carl Daniel Boon [1978] Business Development Director; Thierry Florit [1979] Director/Senior Designer [French]

Greene King Brewing and Retailing Limited
Incorporated: 6 January 1997 *Employees:* 39,168
Net Worth: £1,954,000,000 *Total Assets:* £3,969,999,872
Registered Office: Westgate Brewery, Bury St Edmunds, Suffolk, IP33 1QT
Parent: Greene King Pubs Limited
Officers: Lindsay Anne Keswick, Secretary; Rooney Anand [1964] Director; Nicholas Robertson Elliot [1966] Director; Richard Lewis [1970] Director; Wayne Shurvinton [1978] Director; Richard Smothers [1967] Director; Matthew Anthony Starbuck [1969] Director; Philip Andrew Thomas [1969] Director

Greenfield Real Ale Brewery Ltd
Incorporated: 23 November 2004 *Employees:* 1
Net Worth Deficit: £37,462 *Total Assets:* £33,540
Registered Office: Unit 8 Waterside Mills, Greenfield, Oldham, Lancs, OL3 7NH
Major Shareholder: Anthony Brian Harratt
Officers: Anthony Joseph Pye [1957] Director/Civil Servant; Patricia Georgina Pye [1961] Director/Bursar

Greenwich Old Cottage Beer Company Limited
Incorporated: 23 May 2017
Registered Office: Unit 10 Eccleshall Business Park, Hawkins Lane, Burton on Trent, Staffs, DE14 1PT
Shareholders: Jeffrey Stephen Denton Alden; Roger Barry Shone
Officers: Jeffrey Stephen Denton Alden [1968] Director; Roger Barry Shone [1969] Director

Grey Trees Brewery Limited
Incorporated: 14 June 2013 *Employees:* 6
Net Worth: £6,289 *Total Assets:* £113,056
Registered Office: 5 The Willows, Aberdare, Rhondda Cynon Taf, CF44 8BX
Shareholder: Raymond Thomas Davies
Officers: Raymond Thomas Davies [1969] Director; Tracey Kerslake-Davies [1973] Director

Greyfriars Brewery Ltd
Incorporated: 7 January 2016
Registered Office: Featherstone Hall Farm New Road, Featherstone, Wolverhampton, W Midlands, WV10 7NW
Major Shareholder: Steven Mann
Officers: Steven Mann [1971] Director/Mechanic

Greyhound Brewery Limited
Incorporated: 26 September 2014
Net Worth Deficit: £73,807 *Total Assets:* £63,785
Registered Office: Watershed, Smock Alley, West Chiltington, Pulborough, W Sussex, RH20 2QX
Shareholders: Sarah Rebecca Allen; Nick Eric Leonard Allen
Officers: Nick Eric Leonard Allen [1952] Director/Designer; Sarah Rebecca Allen [1975] Director/Glass Maker; Lars Klawitter [1970] Managing Director [German]

Greyhound Drinks Limited
Incorporated: 13 November 2012 *Employees:* 2
Net Worth Deficit: £17,339 *Total Assets:* £43,816
Registered Office: 6 Logie Mill, Beaverbank Business Park, Edinburgh, EH7 4HG
Major Shareholder: John Simon Hunt
Officers: John Simon Hunt [1963] Director; Linda Hunt [1962] Director

Groovy Grains Brewery Limited
Incorporated: 31 January 2019
Registered Office: Parker House, 44 Stafford Road, Wallington, Surrey, SM6 9AA
Major Shareholder: Andrew Stephen North
Officers: Andrew Stephen North [1966] Director/Business Analyst/Brewery Owner

Ground Hammer Beer Company Limited
Incorporated: 23 October 2017
Registered Office: 12a Thorn Business Park, Rotherwas, Hereford, HR2 6JT
Shareholders: Ben Garwood; David Michael Richardson
Officers: Ben Garwood [1977] Director; David Michael Richardson [1985] Finance Director

Growler Swap Ltd
Incorporated: 3 January 2014
Previous: Bucks Star Ltd
Registered Office: 23 Twizel Close, Stonebridge, Milton Keynes, Bucks, MK13 0DX
Shareholder: Datis Gol-Shecan
Officers: Datis Gol-Shecan [1981] Director/Businessman

The Grumpy Git Brewery Limited
Incorporated: 6 July 2017
Registered Office: 2 Bewlies Cottage, Three Elm Lane, Tonbridge, Kent, TN11 0AD
Officers: Maria Rose McKenzie, Secretary; Peter John Twort [1947] Director/Accountant

GT Ales Limited
Incorporated: 5 January 2015
Net Worth Deficit: £5,656 *Total Assets:* £39,527
Registered Office: Unit 5 Chivenor, Barnstaple, Devon, EX31 4AY
Shareholder: Gary Jarvis
Officers: Gary Jarvis [1970] Director; Toby Marsh [1970] Director

Gun Brewery Limited
Incorporated: 22 November 2013
Net Worth: £176,364 *Total Assets:* £274,392
Registered Office: Hawthbush Farm, Gun Hill, Heathfield, E Sussex, TN21 0JY
Shareholders: Toby John Smallpeice; Mark Dominic Loxham Berry
Officers: Mark Dominic Loxham Berry [1969] Director/Gentleman; Toby John Smallpeice [1972] Director/Farmer

Gun Dog Ales Ltd
Incorporated: 1 November 2011 *Employees:* 6
Net Worth: £1,138 *Total Assets:* £64,281
Registered Office: Unit 5b Great Central Way, Woodford Halse, Daventry, Northants, NN11 3PZ
Shareholders: James Pickering; Sarah Pickering
Officers: James Pickering [1980] Director; Sarah Pickering [1987] Director

Gustmain Limited
Incorporated: 1 March 1973
Net Worth: £156,861 *Total Assets:* £156,861
Registered Office: c/o The Felinfoel Brewery Co Ltd, Farmers Row, Felinfoel, Llanelli, Dyfed, SA14 8LB
Parent: Beryn Charles Martyn Lewis
Officers: Tracey Jenkins, Secretary; Charles Edward Hardy Coombs [1976] Director/Chartered Surveyor; Beryn Charles Martin Lewis [1958] Director; Philip John Lewis [1959] Director/Company Secretary

Hackney Brewery Ltd
Incorporated: 7 July 2011 *Employees:* 9
Net Worth: £18,634 *Total Assets:* £344,649
Registered Office: Arch 358 Laburnum Street, London, E2 8BB
Shareholders: Peter John Hills; Jonathan Michael Swain
Officers: Peter John Hills [1977] Director/Brewer; Jonathan Swain [1985] Director/Brewer

Hadham Brewing Company Limited
Incorporated: 22 October 2013
Net Worth Deficit: £136,255 *Total Assets:* £92,229
Registered Office: 4a Hadham Industrial Estates, Church End, Little Hadham, Herts, SG11 2DY
Major Shareholder: David John Collins
Officers: David John Collins [1966] Director

Hafod Brewing Company Ltd
Incorporated: 23 May 2011 *Employees:* 1
Net Worth Deficit: £90,058 *Total Assets:* £88,001
Registered Office: Gorwel, Hafod Road, Pant Glas, Gwernaffield, Mold, Flintshire, CH7 5ES
Major Shareholder: Phillip Blanchard
Officers: Phillip Blanchard [1980] Director

Hair of The Frog Brewing Ltd
Incorporated: 9 October 2018
Registered Office: 49 Underdale Road, Shrewsbury, Salop, SY2 5DT
Officers: Edward Holloway [1989] Director/Electrical Engineer

Hairy Brewers Ales Limited
Incorporated: 28 August 2015
Net Worth Deficit: £17,864 *Total Assets:* £12,792
Registered Office: Venture Garage, Belper Road, Holbrook, Belper, Derbys, DE56 0SX
Officers: David Bacon [1987] Director/Mechanic

Hairy Dog Brewery Ltd
Incorporated: 31 March 2017
Net Worth Deficit: £6,485 *Total Assets:* £14,514
Registered Office: 30-34 North Street, Hailsham, E Sussex, BN27 1DW
Shareholders: Paul David Cohen; James Peter Nolan
Officers: Paul David Cohen [1957] Director; James Peter Nolan [1968] Director

Hale Brewing Limited
Incorporated: 16 October 2017
Registered Office: 13 Woodend Road, London, E17 4JS
Major Shareholder: Mark Hislop
Officers: Mark Hislop [1983] Director; Dean Stratos Joannides [1986] Director

Half Moon Brewery Ltd
Incorporated: 5 February 2013 *Employees:* 3
Net Worth: £50,594 *Total Assets:* £79,416
Registered Office: Forge House, Main Street, Ellerton, E Yorks, YO42 4PB
Shareholders: Anthony George Rogers; Jacqueline Rogers
Officers: Anthony George Rogers [1969] Director/Brewer; Jacqueline Rogers [1962] Director/Brewer

Halifax Steam Brewing Company Limited
Incorporated: 22 October 2002 *Employees:* 10
Net Worth Deficit: £53,467 *Total Assets:* £53,748
Registered Office: Halifax Steam Brewing Company Limited, The Conclave, South Edge Works, Halifax Road, Halifax, W Yorks, HX3 8EF
Major Shareholder: Samuel Davidson
Officers: Julie Earnshaw, Secretary; Samuel Davidson [1990] Director; Paul David Earnshaw [1961] Director

Hall & Woodhouse Limited
Incorporated: 8 June 1898 *Employees:* 1,419
Net Worth: £118,890,000 *Total Assets:* £206,032,992
Registered Office: The Brewery, Blandford St Mary, Dorset, DT11 9LS
Officers: Marianne Susie Jarvis, Secretary; Timothy Clarke [1957] Director; Lucinda Rachel Gray [1979] Director; David Harry Christopher Hoare [1964] Director; Mark James [1972] Director/Solicitor; Matthew Richard Kearsey [1972] Director; Dean James Livesey [1977] Director; Michael James Owen [1970] Finance Director; James Martin Scott [1959] Director; Michael Anthony Street [1947] Director; Anthony William Woodhouse [1965] Director; Mark John Michael Woodhouse [1955] Director

Halton Turner Brewing Company Ltd
Incorporated: 26 March 2018
Registered Office: 11 Whitley Avenue, Amington, Tamworth, Staffs, B77 3QU
Shareholders: Christopher Paul Turner; Giles Halton
Officers: Christopher Paul Turner [1983] Director

The Ham Brewing Company Limited
Incorporated: 19 January 2015
Net Worth: £62,368 *Total Assets:* £94,942
Registered Office: The Salutation Inn, Ham, Berkeley, Glos, GL13 9QH
Major Shareholder: Peter Robert Tiley
Officers: Peter Robert Tiley, Secretary; Peter Robert Tiley [1983] Director/Landlord

Hambleton Brewery Limited
Incorporated: 12 February 2019
Registered Office: The Brewery, Melmerby Green Road, Melmerby, Ripon, N Yorks, HG4 5NB
Shareholders: Sally Elizabeth Stafford; Nicholas Rowland Stafford
Officers: Ben Alexander Harrison [1983] Director; Rachel Clare Harrison [1983] Director; Hannah Jane Saunders [1981] Director; Nicholas Rowland Stafford [1958] Director; Sally Elizabeth Stafford [1956] Director

Hammerpot Brewery Limited
Incorporated: 26 April 2005
Net Worth Deficit: £95,526 *Total Assets:* £282,749
Registered Office: Unit 30 The Vinery, Arundel Road, Poling, W Sussex, BN18 9PY
Shareholder: Michael James Davis
Officers: Lee Mitchell, Secretary; Michael James Davis [1971] Director; Francis Phillips [1966] Director

The Hand Brewing Company Limited
Incorporated: 23 February 2016 *Employees:* 1
Net Worth Deficit: £22,325 *Total Assets:* £12,945
Registered Office: 33 Upper St James's Street, Brighton, BN2 1JN
Shareholders: Clark Left; Jennifer Kate Dalby
Officers: Jennifer Kate Dalby [1984] Director/Brewery; Clark Left [1979] Director/Brewery; Jack Tavare [1990] Director/Head Brewer

The Handyman Brewery Ltd
Incorporated: 9 January 2017
Net Worth: £2,190 *Total Assets:* £5,954
Registered Office: The Green Room, 13 Hope Street, Liverpool, L1 9BQ
Officers: Luke Kenneth Cooper [1980] Director/Architect; Andrew David James [1980] Director/Architect; Kevin James McArthur [1980] Director/Public House Landlord; Patricia O'Callaghan [1982] Director/Public House Manager [Irish]; Susan O'Neill [1980] Director/Brewer [Irish]; Colin Peter Stronge [1980] Director/Brewer [Irish]; Toby Richard Hamilton Wallis [1981] Director/Architect

Harbour Brewery Tenby Limited
Incorporated: 24 November 2014 *Employees:* 3
Net Worth Deficit: £66,449 *Total Assets:* £394,236
Registered Office: Alexander Partnership, Barclays Bank Chambers, 18 High Street, Tenby, Pembrokeshire, SA70 7HD
Major Shareholder: Michael Llewellyn Evans
Officers: Julie Griffiths Jones, Secretary; Michael Llewellyn Evans [1965] Director/Property Developer; Julie Griffiths Jones [1969] Director/Solicitor

The Harbour Brewing Company Limited
Incorporated: 16 August 2011 *Employees:* 13
Net Worth Deficit: £834,095 *Total Assets:* £2,073,234
Registered Office: 4 St Mary's Arcade, Wallingford, Oxon, OX10 0EY
Officers: Edward Lofthouse [1976] Director/General Manager; Richard Montague Rowse [1948] Director/Retailer

Hardknott UK Ltd
Incorporated: 9 March 2012 *Employees:* 2
Net Worth Deficit: £95,579 *Total Assets:* £126,678
Registered Office: Unit 10c Devonshire Road Industrial Estate, Millom, Cumbria, LA18 4JS
Shareholders: David William Bailey; Ann Maureen Wedgwood
Officers: David William Bailey [1965] Director/Brewer; Ann Maureen Wedgwood [1966] Director/Sales Executive

Hardstate Limited
Incorporated: 25 July 2003 *Employees:* 1
Net Worth: £68,444 *Total Assets:* £136,233
Registered Office: Roughacre, The Green, Castle Camps, Cambridge, CB21 4TA
Shareholders: Sarah Jane Hide; Mark Somerville Jackson
Officers: Henry Hide, Secretary; Sarah Hide [1970] Director/IT Consultant; Mark Somerville Jackson [1970] Director/IT Consultant

Thomas Hardy Burtonwood Limited
Incorporated: 10 July 1998 *Employees:* 43
Net Worth: £468,000 *Total Assets:* £6,525,000
Registered Office: Bold Lane, Burtonwood, Warrington, Cheshire, WA5 4TH
Officers: Gary Alexander Todd [1966] Site Director; Neil Mark Voss [1969] Director; Jonathan Christopher Ward [1978] Director; Margaret Rae Ward [1944] Director

Thomas Hardy Holdings Limited
Incorporated: 27 December 1996 *Employees:* 114
Net Worth: £12,852,000 *Total Assets:* £19,423,000
Registered Office: Bold Lane, Burtonwood, Warrington, Cheshire, WA5 4TH
Officers: Neil Mark Voss [1969] Director; Jonathan Christopher Ward [1978] Director; Margaret Rae Ward [1944] Director

Thomas Hardy Kendal Limited
Incorporated: 29 December 1998 *Employees:* 64
Net Worth: £6,922,000 *Total Assets:* £9,162,000
Registered Office: Bold Lane, Burtonwood, Warrington, Cheshire, WA5 4TH
Officers: Peter Michael Armstrong [1965] Site Director; Neil Mark Voss [1969] Director; Jonathan Christopher Ward [1978] Director; Margaret Rae Ward [1944] Director

Haresfoot Storage & Distribution Company Limited
Incorporated: 14 February 2014 *Employees:* 3
Net Worth: £35,765 *Total Assets:* £70,392
Registered Office: 271 High Street, Berkhamsted, Herts, HP4 1AA
Officers: Scott Raymond Carter [1958] Director; George Martin Harvey [1962] Director; Trevor Jones [1961] Director; Anthony Peter Laurenson [1958] Director; Simon Spurling [1955] Director

Harr Engineering Limited
Incorporated: 20 February 2018
Registered Office: Flat 5, 11 Clifton Road, London, SE25 6NJ
Major Shareholder: Nathan Harris
Officers: Nathan Harris, Secretary; Nathan Harris [1978] Director/Manager

Harrison's Brewery Ltd
Incorporated: 28 January 2019
Registered Office: 5 Fairway, Retford, Notts, DN22 7SQ
Shareholders: Christopher Lloyd Harrison-Hawkes; Gemma Elisheva Lane; Stuart Joseph Harrison
Officers: Gemma Eleshiva Lane, Secretary; Stuart Joseph Harrison [1986] Director; Christopher Lloyd Harrison-Hawkes [1981] Director

Harrogate Brewing Company Limited
Incorporated: 5 March 2014
Net Worth: £4,900 *Total Assets:* £17,400
Registered Office: 18 West Lea Avenue, Harrogate, N Yorks, HG2 0AT
Major Shareholder: Anton Stark
Officers: Anton Stark [1972] Director/Professional Photographer

Hart Family Brewers Limited
Incorporated: 14 December 2011 *Employees:* 3
Net Worth: £30,527 *Total Assets:* £62,164
Registered Office: 21 Nene Court, The Embankment, Wellingborough, Northants, NN8 1LD
Shareholders: Robert Hart; Sarah Helen Hart
Officers: Robert Hart [1971] Director/Brewer; Sarah Helen Hart [1975] Director

The Hartlebury Brewing Company Ltd
Incorporated: 18 September 2018
Registered Office: Station Park, Station Road, Hartlebury, Worcs, DY11 7YJ
Major Shareholder: David Edwin Higgs
Officers: David Edwin Higgs [1962] Director

Harvey & Son (Lewes) Limited
Incorporated: 24 November 1928 *Employees:* 228
Net Worth: £42,178,352 *Total Assets:* £47,975,480
Registered Office: 6 Cliffe High Street, Lewes, E Sussex, BN7 2AH
Officers: Hamish Carlyon Rundle Elder [1959] Director; Miles Anthony Jenner [1952] Director/Head Brewer; Julia Margaret Harvey Prescott [1957] Director; Adele MacKenzie Smith [1970] Director

Harvey Elizabeth Limited
Incorporated: 2 March 2018
Registered Office: 21 George Street, Montrose, Angus, DD10 8EW
Shareholders: David Coates; Katherine Nepute
Officers: David Coates [1980] Director/Publican; Katherine Nepute [1984] Director/Teacher [American]

Harviestoun Brewery (Holdings) Limited
Incorporated: 26 November 2007
Net Worth: £229,316 *Total Assets:* £1,800,046
Registered Office: Harviestoun Brewery, Alva Industrial Estate, Alva, Clackmannanshire, FK12 5DQ
Officers: Ian James Snodgrass, Secretary; Angus Donald Mackintosh Macdonald [1939] Director/Accountant; James Alexander MacConnell Orr [1939] Director/Solicitor

Harviestoun Brewery Limited
Incorporated: 5 October 1983 *Employees:* 20
Net Worth: £1,930,541 *Total Assets:* £3,420,250
Registered Office: Alva Industrial Estate, Alva, Clackmannanshire, FK12 5DQ
Officers: Ian James Snodgrass, Secretary; Ian Stuart Cail [1962] Director/Master Brewer; Angus Donald Mackintosh Macdonald [1939] Director/Accountant; Catherine Anne MacDonald [1978] Director/Fund Manager; Caroline Rosemary Orr [1957] Director; James Alexander MacConnell Orr [1939] Director/Solicitor

Hastings Brewery Ltd
Incorporated: 11 August 2010
Net Worth Deficit: £21,466 *Total Assets:* £37,351
Registered Office: 33a Manor Road, Bexhill on Sea, E Sussex, TN40 1SP
Shareholder: Peter Matthew Mason
Officers: Andrew Roy Mason [1950] Director/Teacher; Peter Matthew Mason [1978] Director/Web Developer

Hattie Brown's Brewery Ltd
Incorporated: 19 May 2015
Net Worth: £8,791 *Total Assets:* £88,605
Registered Office: Unit 1 The Sidings, Victoria Avenue Industrial Estate, Swanage, Dorset, BH19 1AU
Shareholders: Kevin Paul Hunt; Jean Elizabeth Young
Officers: Kevin Paul Hunt [1955] Director/Brewer; Jean Elizabeth Young [1967] Director/Brewer

Hawkins Drinks Limited
Incorporated: 15 January 2018
Registered Office: 3 All Saints Croft, Burton on Trent, Staffs, DE14 3EA
Major Shareholder: Martin John Hawkins
Officers: Martin John Hawkins [1957] Director

Hawkshead Brewery Limited
Incorporated: 7 June 1996 *Employees:* 41
Net Worth: £416,000 *Total Assets:* £1,481,000
Registered Office: Staveley Mill Yard, Staveley, Cumbria, LA8 9LR
Parent: Halewood International Limited
Officers: John Andrew Bradbury [1971] Managing Director; Nigel Ronald Campbell [1972] Commercial Director; Stewart Andrew Hainsworth [1969] Director; Alan William Robinson [1965] Director

The Hay Rake Brewery Ltd
Incorporated: 7 June 2012 *Employees:* 1
Net Worth Deficit: £4,160 *Total Assets:* £16,881
Registered Office: 6 Blackstone Edge Old Road, Littleborough, Rochdale, Lancs, OL15 0JX
Shareholders: Mark Paul Wickham; Ian Wickham
Officers: Mark Paul Wickham [1962] Director

Head Thirst Ltd
Incorporated: 13 April 2018
Registered Office: 19 George Street East, Sunderland, Tyne & Wear, SR3 1HG
Shareholders: Neil Anthony; Aaron Bate
Officers: Neil Anthony [1988] Director/Brewer

Headstocks Brewery Ltd Ltd
Incorporated: 16 February 2016
Previous: Prussia Food and Beverages Limited
Registered Office: Prussia Food and Beverages Limited Meden Road, Boughton, Newark, Notts, NG22 9ZD

Heaney Brewing Company Limited
Incorporated: 15 June 2016 *Employees:* 1
Net Worth: £267,088 *Total Assets:* £313,546
Registered Office: 96 Ballymacombs Road, Bellaghy, Magherafelt, Co Londonderry, BT45 8JP
Shareholder: Suzanne McCay
Officers: Jason Joseph McCay [1969] Director/Investment Manager; Malcolm Peter McCay [1978] Director/Brewer; Suzanne McCay [1981] Director/Supply Chain Coordinator

Heathen Brewers Limited
Incorporated: 11 June 2016
Registered Office: c/o Grape & Grain, 51 The Broadway, Haywards Heath, W Sussex, RH16 3AS
Officers: Mark Durant, Secretary; Mark Harvey Durant [1960] Director/Brewer; Stuart Hibling [1973] Director/Brewer; Graham Paul Hole [1955] Director/Brewer; Maria-Angelica Laricchiuta [1979] Director/Brewster [Italian]; Edward Perfect [1977] Director/Brewer

Heather Ale Limited
Incorporated: 19 April 1994 *Employees:* 62
Net Worth: £2,378,768 *Total Assets:* £5,044,741
Registered Office: Eglinton Store, Kelliebank, Alloa, Clackmannanshire, FK10 1NT
Major Shareholder: Scott John Williams
Officers: Scott John Williams, Secretary; Bruce Andrew Williams [1960] Director/Brewing Supplies; Scott John Williams [1964] Director/Brewer

Heavy Industry Brewing Limited
Incorporated: 31 January 2011 *Employees:* 4
Net Worth Deficit: £15,091 *Total Assets:* £96,619
Registered Office: The Old Slaughter House, Bryn Llyfanen, Henllan, Denbigh, Clwyd, LL16 5AR
Shareholders: Andrew Littlewood; Thomas Alistair McNeill
Officers: Thomas Alistair McNeill [1965] Director/Brewer

Hedgedog Brewing Ltd
Incorporated: 9 July 2013
Net Worth: £40,516 *Total Assets:* £65,080
Registered Office: Unit 5 Stroude Farm, Stroude Road, Virginia Water, Surrey, GU25 4BY
Shareholders: Marc Robert Sage; Sheila Joy Sage
Officers: Sheila Sage, Secretary; Marc Sage [1987] Director/Brewer

Heineken UK Limited
Incorporated: 31 July 1978 *Employees:* 2,013
Net Worth: £890,000,000 *Total Assets:* £6,296,000,000
Registered Office: 3-4 Broadway Park, South Gyle Broadway, Edinburgh, EH12 9JZ
Parent: Scottish & Newcastle Limited
Officers: Lynsey Jane Nicoll, Secretary; Simon Paul Amor [1972] Director: Off Trade; Jane Scott Brydon [1968] HR Director; Matthew John Callan [1975] Brewing Operations Director; Alexander Elberg [1968] Customer Service and Logistics Director; David Michael Forde [1968] Managing Director [Irish]; Christopher Michael Jowsey [1965] Trading Director; Lawson John Wembridge Mountstevens [1968] Director; Lynsey Jane Nicoll [1980] Director/Solicitor; David George Paterson [1977] Corporate Relations Director; Radovan Sikorsky [1967] Finance Director [Slovak]; Cindy Tervoort [1970] Marketing Director [Dutch]

Hepworth & Company Brewers Limited
Incorporated: 13 September 2000 *Employees:* 39
Net Worth: £768,475 *Total Assets:* £4,448,623
Registered Office: The New Brewery, Stane Street, North Heath, Pulborough, W Sussex, RH20 1DJ
Shareholders: Gary Lee; Andrew Charles Hamilton Hepworth; Margot Christie Price
Officers: Andrew Charles Hamilton Hepworth [1954] Director; Roger John Paterson [1941] Brewery Director; Dr Margot Christie Price [1952] Director/Teacher

Hercules Brewing & Co. Limited
Incorporated: 5 December 2012 *Employees:* 4
Net Worth Deficit: £32,238 *Total Assets:* £159,691
Registered Office: 100 Shore Road, Greenisland, Carrickfergus, Co Antrim, BT38 8UE
Shareholders: Niall Martin McMullan; Gavan McGill
Officers: Niall McMullan, Secretary; Niall Martin McMullan [1968] Director [Irish]

Heroic Brew Co Ltd
Incorporated: 14 January 2019
Registered Office: 20-22 Wenlock Road, London, N1 7GU
Shareholders: Christopher Mark Stansfield; Nick Paul Stansfield
Officers: Christopher Mark Stansfield [1981] Director; Nick Paul Stansfield [1983] Director

Hexad Brewing Ltd
Incorporated: 12 September 2017
Registered Office: 54 Sandhurst Street, Aigburth, Liverpool, L17 7BX
Officers: Maeve Elizabeth McMahon [1989] Director [American]

HFBC Ltd
Incorporated: 3 December 2014
Net Worth Deficit: £30,903 *Total Assets:* £92,037
Registered Office: 128 Glebe Road, Randalstown, Co Antrim, BT41 3DT
Shareholder: Deborah Elizabeth Mitchell
Officers: Nigel Logan [1976] Managing Director; Deborah Mitchell [1981] Director

Hickbrew Limited
Incorporated: 28 July 2016
Net Worth Deficit: £2,121 *Total Assets:* £3,875
Registered Office: Stonebreck, Market Place, Longnor, Buxton, Derbys, SK17 0NT
Major Shareholder: Mark Adrian Travis
Officers: Julia Travis, Secretary; Mark Adrian Travis [1965] Director

Highland Brewing Company Limited
Incorporated: 11 February 2004 *Employees:* 6
Net Worth: £168,844 *Total Assets:* £657,957
Registered Office: Swannay Brewery, Evie, Orkney, KW17 2NP
Shareholders: Carole Michelle Hill; Robert Joseph Hill
Officers: Carole Michelle Hill, Secretary; Carole Michelle Hill [1961] Director; Lewis Oliver Hill [1987] Director/Brewery Manager; Robert Joseph Hill [1961] Director/Head Brewer/Manager

Higsons 1780 Limited
Incorporated: 15 October 2015
Net Worth: £4,328,133 *Total Assets:* £4,386,360
Registered Office: 62-64 Bridgewater Street, Liverpool, L1 0AY
Officers: Anthony John Carson [1956] Director/Marketeer; Stephen Thomas Crawley [1962] Director; Campbell Doull Laird [1957] Director; Jonathan Christopher Ward [1978] Director

Hilden Brewery Limited
Incorporated: 7 June 2016
Registered Office: Hilden House, Grand Street, Hilden, Lisburn, Co Antrim, BT27 4TY
Officers: Frances Maguire [1970] Director; Ann Scullion [1946] Director; James Scullion [1942] Director; Owen Scullion [1978] Director; Siobhan Scullion [1971] Director

The Hildenborough Brewery Ltd
Incorporated: 24 October 2017
Registered Office: 8 Birch Close, Hildenborough, Tonbridge, Kent, TN11 9DU
Major Shareholder: Gregg Ellar
Officers: Catherine Leona Ellar, Secretary; Gregg Ellar [1981] Director

Hill House Inns Limited
Incorporated: 7 February 2014
Net Worth: £4,229 *Total Assets:* £396,760
Registered Office: The Hill House, Happisburgh, Norwich, NR12 0PW
Shareholders: Eric Clive Stockton; Susan Stockton
Officers: Eric Clive Stockton, Secretary; Adrian Charles Hillier [1964] Director; Eric Clive Stockton [1949] Director; Sam Alun Stockton [1975] Director/Chef; Susan Stockton [1948] Director

Hillfire Limited
Incorporated: 20 December 2012 *Employees:* 1
Net Worth Deficit: £37,738 *Total Assets:* £18,276
Registered Office: 6 Stevenson Road, Slough, Berks, SL2 3YE
Major Shareholder: Richard Neil Coxhead
Officers: Richard Neil Coxhead [1967] Director/Project Management

Hillside Brewery Limited
Incorporated: 7 May 2013 *Employees:* 8
Net Worth Deficit: £355,955 *Total Assets:* £646,493
Registered Office: Hedgebank, Old Church Road, Colwall, Malvern, Worcs, WR13 6EZ
Major Shareholder: Peter John Williamson
Officers: Paul David Williamson [1989] Director; Peter John Williamson [1959] Director

Hilltop Brewing Company Limited
Incorporated: 8 August 2015 *Employees:* 2
Net Worth: £6,268 *Total Assets:* £20,521
Registered Office: Hilltop Hotel, Sheffield Road, Conisbrough, Doncaster, S Yorks, DN12 2AY
Major Shareholder: John Bulcroft
Officers: John Bulcroft [1964] Director/Publican; David Luke Sheriff [1999] Director/Brewer

Himalayan Traders UK Ltd
Incorporated: 8 July 2009
Previous: Gurkha Beer Limited
Net Worth: £12,807 *Total Assets:* £14,819
Registered Office: 30 Shaftesbury Avenue, Southall, Middlesex, UB2 4HH
Major Shareholder: Satvir Singh Judge
Officers: Satvir Singh Judge [1961] Director/Businessman

Hindsight Collective Ltd
Incorporated: 20 January 2017
Net Worth Deficit: £788 *Total Assets:* £1,711
Registered Office: 37 Chelsfield Grove, Chorlton, Manchester, M21 7SU
Shareholders: Marcus James Baxendale; Jess James Hutchinson
Officers: Marcus James Baxendale [1990] Director; Jess James Hutchinson [1991] Director

Hip Hop Brewery Limited
Incorporated: 23 November 2018
Registered Office: 123 Mortimer Road, London, NW10 5TN
Officers: Guy Scott Templeton [1969] Director

Hitchin Brewery Ltd
Incorporated: 6 October 2017
Registered Office: 16 Thatchers End, Hitchin, Herts, SG4 0PD
Shareholder: Carl Robert Paddison
Officers: Carl Robert Paddison [1977] Director/Paramedic

Hiver Beers Ltd
Incorporated: 26 April 2013 *Employees:* 9
Net Worth: £250,559 *Total Assets:* £457,204
Registered Office: Arch 56 Stanworth Street, London, SE1 3NY
Major Shareholder: Hannah Louise Rhodes
Officers: Polly Elizabeth Dean, Secretary; Hannah Louise Rhodes [1983] Director/Sales and Marketing

Hobsons Brewery and Company Limited
Incorporated: 10 March 1997 *Employees:* 29
Net Worth: £1,725,156 *Total Assets:* £2,274,040
Registered Office: Britannia Court, 5 Moor Street, Worcester, WR1 3DB
Officers: Susan Mary Davis, Secretary; Paul Anthony Albini [1958] Director/Brewer; Martin John Churchward [1958] Director; Patricia Beatrice Churchward [1958] Director; Nicholas Edward James Davis [1965] Director/Brewer

Hoggshead Brewhouse Limited
Incorporated: 12 December 2014 *Employees:* 13
Net Worth: £253,521 *Total Assets:* £375,236
Registered Office: 3 Upper Nook, Sowerby Bridge, W Yorks, HX6 3RY
Major Shareholder: Christopher Michael Smith
Officers: Christopher Michael Smith [1967] Director

Hogs Back Brewery Limited
Incorporated: 24 July 1995 *Employees:* 34
Net Worth: £359,567 *Total Assets:* £1,992,264
Registered Office: Manor Farm, The Street, Tongham, Surrey, GU10 1DE
Shareholders: Rupert Geoffrey Ryland Thompson; Rupert Geoffrey Ryland Thompson
Officers: Rupert Thompson, Secretary; Miles Robert William Chesterman [1976] Director/Brewer; Nick Brian Miller [1965] Director; Martin Thatcher [1968] Director; Rupert Geoffrey Ryland Thompson [1958] Director

Holcot Hop-Craft Ltd
Incorporated: 14 January 2015
Net Worth Deficit: £3,371 *Total Assets:* £4,737
Registered Office: Chequers Row, Main Street, Holcot, Northants, NN6 9SP
Officers: Maureen Cooke, Secretary; David Carr Ashworth [1954] Director/Businessman; David Thomas Cooke [1947] Director/Retired; Roger Henry Gunnett [1944] Director; Martin Leslie Wilson [1946] Director/Retired

Holdens Brewery Limited
Incorporated: 3 July 1964
Net Worth: £4,093,158 *Total Assets:* £6,144,029
Registered Office: Hopden Brewery, George Street, Wood Setton, Dudley, W Midlands, DY1 4LN
Major Shareholder: Therese Victoria Holden
Officers: Therese Victoria Holden, Secretary; Jonathan Edwin Holden [1971] Director; Therese Victoria Holden [1947] Director/Secretary; Abigail Blanche Kemp [1980] Director

Holler Brewery Limited
Incorporated: 21 December 2017
Registered Office: 19-23 Elder Place, Brighton, BN1 4GF
Parent: Ironstone Brewery Ltd
Officers: Steve James Keegan [1982] Director; Davinder Singh Sahota [1975] Director

Holley Paquette Brewers Ltd
Incorporated: 8 September 2017
Net Worth Deficit: £6,114
Registered Office: The Brewery at Eagle Works, 90 Stevenson Road, Sheffield, S9 3XG
Shareholders: Martha Rosalind Simpson-Holley; Daniel Paul Paquette
Officers: Daniel Paul Paquette [1968] Director [American]; Dr Martha Rosalind Simpson-Holley [1977] Director

Hollow Tree Brewing Co. Ltd
Incorporated: 10 April 2018
Registered Office: 3 Glen Road, Whatstandwell, Matlock, Derbys, DE4 5EH
Major Shareholder: Stephen Sydney McKnight
Officers: Stephen Sydney McKnight [1986] Director

Joseph Holt Group Limited
Incorporated: 19 January 2000 *Employees:* 922
Net Worth: £77,161,888 *Total Assets:* £105,466,624
Registered Office: The Brewery, Empire Street, Manchester, M3 1JD
Shareholders: Richard Peter Kershaw; Maxwell Mark Rushbroke; Rosemary Sarah Adams; Timothy Guy Page; David John Tully
Officers: Philip Adrian Rowan, Secretary; Thomas Leo Dempsey [1952] Director; Richard Peter Kershaw [1955] Director; Richard Neil Frederick Lee [1959] Director/Solicitor; Frank Nicholson [1954] Director; Philip Adrian Rowan [1961] Director/Chartered Accountant; Maxwell Mark Rushbrooke [1942] Director/Farmer

Joseph Holt Limited
Incorporated: 28 June 1922 *Employees:* 896
Net Worth: £95,358,392 *Total Assets:* £111,061,576
Registered Office: The Brewery, Empire Street, Cheetham, Manchester, M3 1JD
Parent: Joseph Holt Group Limited
Officers: Philip Adrian Rowan, Secretary; Thomas Leo Dempsey [1952] Director/Administration Manager; Richard Peter Kershaw [1955] Director/Brewer; Philip Adrian Rowan [1961] Director/Chartered Accountant

Holy Well Brewing Ltd
Incorporated: 31 October 2014
Net Worth Deficit: £5,353 *Total Assets:* £2,196
Registered Office: 4 Barnfield Close, Egerton, Bolton, Lancs, BL7 9UP
Shareholders: Christopher John Fielding; Philip Wyatt
Officers: Chrsitopher Fielding [1969] Director/Brewer; Philip Wyatt [1967] Director/Brewer

Honest Brew Ltd
Incorporated: 1 November 2012 *Employees:* 11
Net Worth: £737,317 *Total Assets:* £1,289,386
Registered Office: OGC, Leroy House, 436 Essex Road, London, N1 3QP
Officers: Annabel Sarah Causer [1988] Director/Founder; Keith Nicholas Foreman [1959] Director; Sean Blair Justin Henry [1961] Director; Andrew Reeve [1988] Director/Founder

Hook Norton Brewery Company,Limited (The)
Incorporated: 12 July 1900 *Employees:* 60
Net Worth: £11,771,134 *Total Assets:* £15,070,130
Registered Office: The Brewery, Hook Norton, Banbury, Oxon, OX15 5NY
Shareholder: Fiona Elisabeth Williams
Officers: David Nigel Vardon Churton, Secretary; David Nigel Vardon Churton [1949] Director; James William Clarke [1971] Managing Director; Dr Jonathan David Paveley [1963] Director; Charles Henry Williams [1957] Director/Estate Owner; Fiona Elisabeth Williams [1954] Director/Housewife

Hop & Stagger Brewery Ltd
Incorporated: 31 January 2012 *Employees:* 1
Net Worth Deficit: £29,978 *Total Assets:* £32,809
Registered Office: Unit 1 Astol Farm, Norton, Salop, TF11 9EW
Shareholders: Robert William John Hayes; Samantha Hayes
Officers: Robert William John Hayes [1961] Director/Brewer/Publican; Samantha Hayes [1968] Director/Publican

Hop and Pray Ltd
Incorporated: 17 September 2018
Registered Office: 41 Wrenbeck Drive, Otley, W Yorks, LS21 2BP
Major Shareholder: Rachel Mary Morrison
Officers: Rachel Mary Morrison [1973] Director/Doctor

Hop Back Brewery Public Limited Company
Incorporated: 29 October 1991 *Employees:* 64
Net Worth: £2,740,485 *Total Assets:* £3,561,344
Registered Office: Hop Back Brewery, 23 Batten Road Industrial Estate, Downton, Salisbury, Wilts, SP5 3HU
Major Shareholder: John Michael Gilbert
Officers: Alison Judith Freezer, Secretary; John Michael Gilbert [1952] Director/Brewer; Simon James Jackson [1957] Director/Brewer; Steven Andrew Wright [1955] Director/Brewer

Hop Forward Ltd
Incorporated: 2 October 2018
Registered Office: 70 Cromwell Street, Sheffield, S6 3RN
Major Shareholder: Nicholas William Law
Officers: Nicholas William Law [1982] Director

Hop Fuzz Ltd
Incorporated: 10 May 2011 *Employees:* 3
Net Worth Deficit: £85,734 *Total Assets:* £11,266
Registered Office: Unit 8 Riverside Industrial Estate, West Hythe, Hythe, Kent, CT21 4NB
Shareholders: Martyn Playford; Daryl Stanford
Officers: Martyn Playford [1988] Marketing Director; Daryl Stanford [1988] Director/Head Brewer

Hop King Brewery Ltd
Incorporated: 12 September 2016 *Employees:* 4
Net Worth: £24,762 *Total Assets:* £44,940
Registered Office: East Lodge, Bedlars Green, Great Hallingbury, Bishop's Stortford, Herts, CM22 7TL
Major Shareholder: Benjamin John Hopkinson
Officers: Andrew John Hopkinson [1957] Commercial Director; Benjamin John Hopkinson [1990] Managing Director; Ludovic Hopkinson [1993] Sales and Marketing Director; Marcia Hopkinson [1954] Director

Hop Monster Brewing Company Ltd.
Incorporated: 14 February 2011
Registered Office: 198 Shoebury Road, Southend-on-Sea, Essex, SS1 3RQ
Major Shareholder: Mark Adam Mawson
Officers: Mark Adam Mawson [1963] Director/Brewer

The Hop Studio Limited
Incorporated: 30 November 2011 *Employees:* 4
Net Worth Deficit: £57,739 *Total Assets:* £107,904
Registered Office: Unit 3 Handley Park, Elvington Industrial Estate, York Road Elvington, York, YO41 4AR
Shareholders: David Geoffrey Shaw; Dawn Shaw; Colin Shaw
Officers: David Geoffrey Shaw [1960] Director; Dawn Shaw [1972] Director/Accounting Technician; Tracy Shaw [1962] Director

Hop Stuff Brewery Limited
Incorporated: 3 April 2013 *Employees:* 7
Net Worth: £379,299 *Total Assets:* £558,434
Registered Office: 35.9 Cobalt, White Hart Avenue, London, SE28 0GU
Major Shareholder: Nicholas James Yeomans
Officers: Emma Edwina Yeomans [1985] Director/Banker; Nicholas James Yeomans [1989] Director/Brewer

Hopdaemon Brewery Company Limited
Incorporated: 11 May 2000
Net Worth: £189 *Total Assets:* £30,881
Registered Office: 2 Mulberry Cottages, Mulberry Hill, Chilham, Kent, CT4 8AJ
Officers: Antonius Johannes Bernardus Prins, Secretary; Gail Maree O'Connor [1965] Director/Solicitor [New Zealander]; Antonius Johannes Bernardus Prins [1967] Director/Brewer [New Zealander]

Hope Brewery Ltd
Incorporated: 29 October 2014 *Employees:* 1
Net Worth Deficit: £19,144 *Total Assets:* £4,434
Registered Office: 29 Grampian Flats, Balmoral Road, Westcliff on Sea, Essex, SS0 7DH
Officers: Philip John Evans [1968] Director; Michelle Thomas [1972] Director

Hopforge Ltd
Incorporated: 10 March 2014
Net Worth Deficit: £4,226 *Total Assets:* £1,965
Registered Office: 32 Queens Road, Aberystwyth, Ceredigion, SY23 2HN
Major Shareholder: Alexander John Vokes
Officers: Alexander John Vokes [1979] Director

Hophurst Brewery Ltd
Incorporated: 3 February 2014
Net Worth: £12,146 *Total Assets:* £34,768
Registered Office: Unit 8 Hindley Business Centre, Platt Lane, Hindley, Wigan, Lancs, WN2 3PA
Major Shareholder: Stuart Darren Hurst
Officers: Stuart Darren Hurst [1976] Director/Master Brewer

Hopjacker Brewery Ltd
Incorporated: 17 June 2015
Net Worth: £4,561 *Total Assets:* £38,411
Registered Office: c/o Cairns Accountants, 102 Snape Hill Lane, Dronfield, Derbys, S18 2GP
Shareholders: Edward John Entwistle; Christopher Ian Sinclair
Officers: Edward John Entwistle [1983] Director/Brewer; Christopher Ian Sinclair [1975] Director

Hopper House Brew Farm Ltd
Incorporated: 7 January 2019
Registered Office: Hopper House, Brew Farm, Racecourse Road, Sedgefield, Co Durham, TS21 2HL
Shareholders: Stephen Brown; Ian Grieve
Officers: Stephen Brown [1969] Director/Farmer; Ian Grieve [1962] Director/Retired

Hops and Dots Brewing Company Ltd
Incorporated: 28 June 2018
Registered Office: 8 Orchard Road, Middlesbrough, Cleveland, TS5 5PW
Shareholders: John Chester; Hugh Grime
Officers: John Chester [1982] Director/Teacher; Hugh Grime [1981] Director/Lawyer

Hopscotch Craft Brewers Limited
Incorporated: 20 March 2018
Registered Office: 442 Manchester Road, Sheffield, S10 5DR
Officers: Joseph William Bentley [1983] Director/Administrator; Mark Booth [1983] Director/Health & Safety Consultant

Hopshackle Brewery Limited
Incorporated: 6 February 2006
Net Worth Deficit: £37,581 *Total Assets:* £45,368
Registered Office: 7 Millfield Road, Market Deeping, Lincs, PE6 8AD
Officers: Valerie Wright, Secretary; Nigel Wright [1963] Director/Brewer

The Hopsmith Brewing Company Ltd
Incorporated: 20 March 2015
Registered Office: 20-22 Wenlock Road, London, N1 7GU
Major Shareholder: James Edward Cheverton
Officers: James Edward Cheverton [1979] Director

Hopsox Brewing Company Ltd
Incorporated: 3 February 2017
Registered Office: The Barn, Bell Lane, Broadheath, Tenbury Wells, Worcester, WR15 8QX
Shareholders: Ben Joseph Bridges; Jamie Bates; Alexander Charles Brazier
Officers: Jamie Bates [1990] Director; Alexander Charles Brazier [1990] Director; Ben Joseph Bridges [1991] Director

The Hoptimistic Brewery Limited
Incorporated: 5 September 2017
Registered Office: 67 Etruria Old Road, Stoke on Trent, Staffs, ST1 5PE
Major Shareholder: Paul Cope
Officers: Paul Michael Cope [1964] Director

Horbury Ales Limited
Incorporated: 19 October 2015
Net Worth Deficit: £881 *Total Assets:* £53,776
Registered Office: The Toppits, Healey Road, Ossett, W Yorks, WF5 8LN
Shareholders: Richard Barry Hemingway; Jonathan Mark Hemingway
Officers: Jonathan Mark Hemingway, Secretary; Jonathan Mark Hemingway [1966] Director/Financial Advisor; Richard Barry Hemingway [1960] Director/Retired

Hornes Brewery Ltd
Incorporated: 13 January 2015
Net Worth: £3,240 *Total Assets:* £79,805
Registered Office: 19b Station Road, Bow Brickhill, Milton Keynes, Bucks, MK17 9JU
Shareholders: Ryan James Horne; Colette Elizabeth Morris
Officers: Colette Morris, Secretary; Ryan James Horne [1977] Director/Manager

Horse Box Brewing Ltd
Incorporated: 17 July 2017
Registered Office: 78 Lisburn Road, Ballynahinch, Co Down, BT24 8TT
Major Shareholder: Eamonn Murphy
Officers: Eamonn Murphy [1971] Director

Howard Town Brewery Limited
Incorporated: 7 April 2005
Net Worth: £38,668 *Total Assets:* £283,207
Registered Office: Hawkshead Mill, Hope Street, Glossop, Derbys, SK13 7SS
Shareholders: Stuart James Christian Swann; Emma Jane Swann
Officers: Emma Jane Swann, Secretary; John Hampshire [1973] Director/Oilfield Engineer; David Stowell [1969] Director/IT Architect; Emma Jane Swann [1976] Director/Brewer; Stuart James Christian Swann [1975] Director/Brewer

Howardian Hills Brewing Company Limited
Incorporated: 6 August 2018
Registered Office: Church View Farmhouse, The Square, Terrington, York, YO60 6PT
Shareholders: Chester James Hoy; Tina Hoy
Officers: Chester James Hoy [1967] Director/Chartered Engineer

Howe Capital Limited
Incorporated: 21 May 2018
Registered Office: 44 Moss Lane, Bramhall, Stockport, Cheshire, SK7 1EH
Major Shareholder: James Bonser
Officers: James Bonser, Secretary; James Bonser [1974] Director

HU Caret 4 Limited
Incorporated: 7 September 2018
Registered Office: Leigh House, 28-32 St Paul's Street, Leeds, LS1 2JT
Major Shareholder: David Mark Hunter
Officers: David Mark Hunter [1962] Director

Hubsters Brewery Ltd
Incorporated: 18 July 2016
Net Worth Deficit: £18,547 *Total Assets:* £17,238
Registered Office: Unit 9 Gough Lane, Bamber Bridge, Preston, Lancs, PR5 6AR
Shareholders: Michael Andrew Hubberstey; Peter Mark Edge
Officers: Sian Louise Andrew, Secretary; Peter Mark Edge [1971] Director/Brewer; Michael Andrew Hubberstey [1981] Director/Brewer

Hull Brewing Company Ltd
Incorporated: 2 June 2011
Registered Office: 23 North Bar Without, Beverley, E Yorks, HU17 7AG
Shareholders: Guy Stuart Falkingham; Susan Falkingham
Officers: Susan Falkingham, Secretary; Guy Stuart Falkingham [1960] Director; Susan Falkingham [1953] Director

Humber Brewery Ltd
Incorporated: 28 February 2011
Registered Office: 23 North Bar Without, Beverley, E Yorks, HU17 7AG
Major Shareholder: Guy Stuart Falkingham
Officers: Susan Falkingham, Secretary; Guy Stuart Falkingham [1960] Director/Consultant; Susan Falkingham [1953] Director/Teacher

Humber Doucy Brewing Company Ltd
Incorporated: 29 June 2018
Registered Office: Foxtails Church Lane, Little Stonham, Stowmarket, Suffolk, IP14 5JL
Shareholders: John David Ridealgh; Alan Ridealgh
Officers: Alan Ridealgh [1956] Director; John David Ridealgh [1987] Director

Humberside Properties [UK] Limited
Incorporated: 15 February 2013
Net Worth Deficit: £2,741 *Total Assets:* £28,157
Registered Office: Connoisseur Ales, Wolverhampton House, 121-125 Church Street, St Helens, Merseyside, WA10 1AJ
Major Shareholder: Kevin John Yates
Officers: Kevin Yates [1984] Director

The Hunter Brewing Company Limited
Incorporated: 8 January 2018
Registered Office: 5 Marleen Court, Heaton, Newcastle upon Tyne, NE6 5DW
Major Shareholder: Andrew James Robert Hunter
Officers: Andrew James Robert Hunter [1966] Managing Director

Hurly Burly Brewery Ltd
Incorporated: 17 October 2014 *Employees:* 2
Net Worth Deficit: £1,882 *Total Assets:* £3,708
Registered Office: 15 Glenorchy Road, North Berwick, E Lothian, EH39 4PE
Shareholders: Peter Lyle McNaught; Louise Allen McNaught
Officers: Louise Allen McNaught [1963] Director/Project Manager; Peter Lyle McNaught [1960] Director - Software Developer

Hurns Brewing Company Ltd.
Incorporated: 20 February 2002 *Employees:* 6
Net Worth: £468,521 *Total Assets:* £3,508,960
Registered Office: Hurns House, Kingsway Business Centre, Fforestfach, Swansea, SA5 4DL
Shareholders: Constance Patricia Parry; Claire Frances Parry
Officers: Constance Patricia Parry, Secretary/Manager; Claire Frances Parry [1967] Director; Constance Patricia Parry [1957] Director/Manager; William Thomas Parry [1959] Director/Solicitor

Hurst Brewery Ltd
Incorporated: 25 July 2017
Registered Office: Highfields Farm, College Lane, Hurstpierpoint, Hassocks, W Sussex, BN6 9JT
Shareholders: Duncan James Lane; Fleur Lane
Officers: Duncan James Lane [1974] Director/Head Brewer; Fleur Lane [1977] Director [New Zealander]

Hush Brewing Co. Ltd
Incorporated: 4 October 2018
Registered Office: 4 St Michaels Close, Little Leigh, Northwich, Cheshire, CW8 4SA
Shareholders: Christopher Robert Birtwistle; Simon Appleton
Officers: Simon Appleton [1980] Director/Electrician; Christopher Robert Birtwistle [1983] Director/Laboratory Manager

Husk Brewing Limited
Incorporated: 9 September 2015
Net Worth Deficit: £60,382 *Total Assets:* £19,539
Registered Office: Unit 58a Railway Arches, North Woolwich Road, London, E16 2AA
Major Shareholder: Christiaan van der Vyver
Officers: Christiaan Van Der Vyver [1976] Director/Bartender [South African]; Marta Aldona Van Der Vyver [1977] Director/Database Quality Officer [Polish]

Hybrid Brewing Ltd
Incorporated: 25 April 2016
Net Worth Deficit: £26,755 *Total Assets:* £56,096
Registered Office: 14c Abbots Inch Road, Grangemouth, Stirlingshire, FK3 9UX
Shareholders: James Wallace Gilbert; Robin Lee
Officers: James Gilbert [1987] Director; Robin Lee [1975] Director

Hyde & Wills Limited
Incorporated: 17 October 2013
Registered Office: 21 King Edward Street, Whitstable, Kent, CT5 1JU
Major Shareholder: Ashley William Hyde
Officers: Ashley William Hyde [1979] Director/Accountant [Australian]

Hydes' Brewery Limited
Incorporated: 27 December 1912 *Employees:* 623
Net Worth: £19,511,056 *Total Assets:* £38,585,184
Registered Office: The Beer Studio, 30 Kansas Avenue, Salford, M50 2GL
Officers: Charles Adam Hyde, Secretary; Brian Bagnall [1961] Director; Christopher Thomas Howard Hopkins [1961] Director/Chief Executive; Charles Adam Hyde [1954] Director/Chartered Accountant; Paul David Jefferies [1965] Director/Brewer; Peter Johnson [1942] Director/Chartered Accountant; Richard Mainon [1973] Director/Financial Adviser; Adam James Mayers [1975] Finance Director

I.T's Brewing Company Ltd
Incorporated: 22 February 2018
Registered Office: 14 Palmer Road, Devizes, Wilts, SN10 2FJ
Major Shareholder: Ian Matthew Johnson
Officers: Ian Matthew Johnson [1987] Director/Brewer

The Icecream Factory Limited
Incorporated: 10 June 2009
Net Worth: £13,048 *Total Assets:* £38,857
Registered Office: 21 Fetter Lane, York, YO1 6EH
Shareholders: Sarah Ann Lakin; Michael Baden Lakin
Officers: Sheila Elizabeth Ann Lakin, Secretary; Michael Baden Lakin [1972] Director/IT Project Manager; Sarah Ann Lakin [1965] Director/Bar Owner

Iceni Brewery Limited
Incorporated: 18 March 2009
Net Worth: £3,072 *Total Assets:* £3,372
Registered Office: 70 Risbygate Street, Bury St Edmunds, Suffolk, IP33 3AZ
Major Shareholder: Brendan Joseph Moore
Officers: Brendan Joseph Moore [1954] Director/Brewer

Icon Brewery Limited
Incorporated: 7 March 2018
Registered Office: 4 Brown Street East, Colne, Lancs, BB8 9BB
Major Shareholder: Frazer Troy Lowley
Officers: Frazer Troy Lowley [1976] Director/Builder

Ignition Brewery Limited
Incorporated: 17 August 2015
Net Worth: £10,697 *Total Assets:* £18,136
Registered Office: 44a Sydenham Road, London, SE26 5QF
Officers: William Peter Amery Evans [1984] Director; Terence Joseph McGuinness [1983] Director/Barrister [Irish]; Nicholas Martin O'Shea [1978] Director/Economist

The Ilkley Brewery Company Limited
Incorporated: 8 January 2009 *Employees:* 16
Net Worth: £147,279 *Total Assets:* £623,302
Registered Office: 83-85 Shambles Street, Barnsley, S Yorks, S70 2SB
Parent: Half Full Beer Co Limited
Officers: Luke Thomas Raven, Secretary; Ian Johnson [1957] Director; Simon Robert Ord [1963] Director; Luke Thomas Raven [1981] Director; Richard Shelton [1971] Director

Imaginary Friends Brewing Limited
Incorporated: 9 July 2018
Registered Office: Pressex Cottage Lower Street, Upton Noble, Shepton Mallet, Somerset, BA4 6BB
Parent: Brewed Boy Tap Houses Limited
Officers: George Isaac White [1996] Director

Impavive Ltd
Incorporated: 8 June 2018
Registered Office: 546 Chorley Old Road, Bolton, Lancs, BL1 6AB
Shareholders: Minie Grace Macale; Darrell Brannagan
Officers: Minie Grace Macale [1971] Director [Filipino]

The Inadequate Brewery Limited
Incorporated: 2 July 2014
Registered Office: 67 Etruria Old Road, Stoke on Trent, Staffs, ST1 5PE
Major Shareholder: Paul Michael Cope
Officers: Paul Michael Cope [1964] Director

Incapico Inc Limited
Incorporated: 12 November 2018
Registered Office: 11 Penrhyd Road, Wirral, Merseyside, CH61 2XJ
Major Shareholder: Max Leon Furlong
Officers: Max Leon Furlong [1996] Managing Director

The Indian Brewery Company Birmingham Ltd
Incorporated: 30 October 2014 *Employees:* 45
Net Worth: £66,739 *Total Assets:* £237,103
Registered Office: Unit 5 Aston Express Way Industrial Estate, Pritchett Street, Birmingham, B6 4EX
Major Shareholder: Jaspal Liam Singh Purewal
Officers: Jaspal Liam Singh Purewal [1994] Director/Sales Manager

Indian Summer Brewing Co. Limited
Incorporated: 11 October 2011 *Employees:* 1
Net Worth Deficit: £72,857 *Total Assets:* £4,307
Registered Office: 8th Floor, Elizabeth House, 54-58 High Street, Edgware, Middlesex, HA8 7EJ
Major Shareholder: Julian Edmund Hales
Officers: Julian Edmund Hales [1963] Director/Brewer

Inferno Brewery Limited
Incorporated: 10 April 2018
Registered Office: 17 Station Street, Tewkesbury, Glos, GL20 5NJ
Officers: Chris Bowley [1978] Director/Brewer

Infinite Session Ltd
Incorporated: 1 November 2017
Registered Office: 32 Chroma Mansions, 14 Penny Brookes Street, London, E20 1BP
Shareholders: Christopher John Hannaway; Thomas Eamon Hannaway
Officers: Christopher John Hannaway [1989] Director; Thomas Eamon Hannaway [1987] Director

Inkerman Ales Limited
Incorporated: 14 July 1998
Previous: Hall-Graham Consultancy Limited
Net Worth Deficit: £520 *Total Assets:* £1,123
Registered Office: Raglan House, Inkerman Cottages, Ashgate Road, Chesterfield, Derbys, S40 4BP
Major Shareholder: Charles Darcy Richard Hall
Officers: Charles Darcy Richard Hall, Secretary; Charles Darcy Richard Hall [1962] Director

The Inkspot Brewery Limited
Incorporated: 12 March 2014
Net Worth Deficit: £28,501 *Total Assets:* £119,119
Registered Office: 40 Streatham Common South, London, SW16 3BX
Shareholders: Thomas James Talbot; Bradley Aaron Ridge
Officers: Bradley Aaron Ridge, Secretary; Bradley Aaron Ridge [1978] Director/Manager; Thomas James Talbot [1970] Director/Brewer

The Inlaw Brewing Company Ltd
Incorporated: 23 October 2017
Registered Office: 96 Forest Road, Loughborough, Leics, LE11 3NR
Officers: Dr Richard James Ball [1976] Director/Teacher; James Sebastian Edward Busby [1982] Director/Solicitor; Michael Jude Murphy [1950] Director/Retired [Irish]

Inner Bay Brewery Limited
Incorporated: 28 April 2014 *Employees:* 2
Net Worth Deficit: £12,245 *Total Assets:* £8,856
Registered Office: Seacliffe Villa, Hill Street, Inverkeithing, Fife, KY11 1AB
Shareholders: Katherine Margaret Russell; Jed Martens
Officers: Jed Martens [1975] Director/Business Executive; Katherine Margaret Russell [1976] Director/Business Executive

The Innis & Gunn Brewing Company Limited
Incorporated: 1 October 2002 *Employees:* 43
Net Worth: £3,545,000 *Total Assets:* £12,160,000
Registered Office: 6 Randolph Crescent, Edinburgh, EH3 7TH
Parent: Innis & Gunn Holdings Limited
Officers: Esther Binnie [1976] Director; James Arthur Coyle [1967] Deputy Managing Director; Anthony Leonard Hunt [1946] Director/Consultant; Dougal Gunn Sharp [1972] Director/Brewer; Crawford McGowan Sinclair [1968] Sales Director

Innis & Gunn Holdings Limited
Incorporated: 14 December 2007 *Employees:* 120
Net Worth: £9,396,000 *Total Assets:* £19,979,000
Registered Office: 6 Randolph Crescent, Edinburgh, EH3 7TH
Major Shareholder: Dougal Gunn Sharp
Officers: Jean-Philippe Pierre Paul Barade [1973] Director/Partner in Private Equity [French]; Esther Binnie [1976] Director; James Arthur Coyle [1967] Deputy Managing Director; Caroline Folleas [1977] Investment Director [French]; Anthony Leonard Hunt [1946] Director/Consultant; Dougal Gunn Sharp [1972] Director; Crawford McGowan Sinclair [1968] Sales Director

The Innis & Gunn Inveralmond Brewery Limited
Incorporated: 19 November 1996 *Employees:* 11
Previous: The Inveralmond Brewery Limited
Net Worth: £1,230,000 *Total Assets:* £2,129,000
Registered Office: 6 Randolph Crescent, Edinburgh, EH3 7TH
Parent: Innis & Gunn Holdings Limited
Officers: Esther Binnie [1976] Director; Fergus Sydney Clark [1967] Director/Brewer; Kenneth Duncan [1960] Director/Head Brewer; Anthony Leonard Hunt [1946] Director; Dougal Gunn Sharp [1972] Director

Insight Driven Innovation Limited
Incorporated: 9 December 2003 *Employees:* 6
Net Worth Deficit: £48,399 *Total Assets:* £156,039
Registered Office: 14 Queen Square, Bath, BA1 2HN
Shareholders: Paul Geoffrey Nash; Melanie Anne Nash
Officers: Melanie Anne Nash, Secretary; Melanie Anne Nash [1965] Director/Secretary; Paul Geoffrey Nash [1964] Director/Consultant

The Instant Karma Brewing Company Ltd
Incorporated: 15 August 2012
Net Worth: £31,507 *Total Assets:* £155,918
Registered Office: 119a High Street, Clay Cross, Derbys, S45 9DZ
Major Shareholder: Glynn Owen Clarke
Officers: Glyn Clarke [1972] Director/Telecoms Consultant

Interstate Craft Brewing Company Limited
Incorporated: 9 March 2016
Registered Office: 10 Wren Walk, St Neots, Cambs, PE19 2GE
Major Shareholder: Paul John Wilson
Officers: Paul John Wilson [1971] Director/Risk Manager

Intrepid Brewing Company Limited
Incorporated: 17 March 2014
Net Worth: £27,693 *Total Assets:* £63,513
Registered Office: 51 Clarkegrove Road, Sheffield, S10 2NH
Major Shareholder: Benjamin Millner
Officers: Benjamin Millner [1990] Director/Brewer and Speleological Interpreter

Inverbrewery Limited
Incorporated: 19 March 2018
Registered Office: 5 Conglass Avenue, Inverurie, Aberdeenshire, AB51 4LE
Major Shareholder: Stewart Robert Birnie
Officers: Stewart Robert Birnie [1974] Director

Ipbridge Limited
Incorporated: 29 August 2017
Registered Office: Great Revel End Farm, Gaddesden Lane, Redbourn, St Albans, Herts, AL3 7AR
Major Shareholder: William Stanbridge
Officers: Ka Tung IP, Secretary; William Stanbridge [1983] Director/TV Producer

Ironstone Brewery JVW Ltd
Incorporated: 7 January 2019
Registered Office: 145699 York House, Green Lane West, Preston, Lancs, PR3 1NJ
Major Shareholder: Jonathan Victor Walker
Officers: Jonathan Victor Walker [1960] Director

Ironstone Brewery Ltd
Incorporated: 25 July 2016
Net Worth Deficit: £14,545 *Total Assets:* £46,941
Registered Office: 19-23 Elder Place, Brighton, BN1 4GF
Major Shareholder: Steven James Keegan
Officers: Steven James Keegan [1982] Director; Davinder Singh Sahota [1975] Director

Irving & Co. Brewers Limited
Incorporated: 26 April 2007 *Employees:* 3
Net Worth: £82,662 *Total Assets:* £96,810
Registered Office: Unit G1, Railway Triangle, Walton Road, Portsmouth, PO6 1TQ
Shareholders: Malcolm Gregor Linton Irving; Isobel Foulds Irving
Officers: Malcolm Gregor Linton Irving [1972] Director/Brewer

Irwell Works Brewery Ltd
Incorporated: 19 October 2009
Net Worth: £403,982 *Total Assets:* £616,797
Registered Office: Irwell Works, Irwell Street, Ramsbottom, Bury, Lancs, BL0 9YQ
Officers: Sara D'Arcy [1959] Director/Project Manager; Keith Powell [1944] Director/Retired

Isca Ales Limited
Incorporated: 17 October 2009
Net Worth Deficit: £61,327 *Total Assets:* £12,573
Registered Office: Gargoyles Brewery, Court Farm Barn, Holcombe Village, Dawlish, Devon, EX7 0JT
Major Shareholder: Andrew Brian Oakes
Officers: Andrew Brian Oakes [1964] Director/Engineer

Island Hamlet Brewing Company Limited
Incorporated: 30 August 2014
Net Worth Deficit: £23,323 *Total Assets:* £13,677
Registered Office: 19 Church Lane, Isleham, Ely, Cambs, CB7 5SQ
Shareholders: Mark James Borley; Fiona Caroline Borley
Officers: Fiona Caroline Borley, Secretary; Fiona Caroline Borley [1966] Director/Solicitor; Mark James Borley [1960] Director/IT Project Manager

Islay Ales Company Limited
Incorporated: 13 February 2003
Net Worth: £21,769 *Total Assets:* £56,543
Registered Office: The Brewery, Islay House Square, Bridgend, Islay, Argyll, PA44 7NZ
Officers: Donald MacKenzie [1962] Director/Brand Ambassador; Jason McGuire MacKay Smith [1969] Director

Isle of Ely Brewing Company Ltd.
Incorporated: 23 October 2014
Registered Office: Warren House, High Street, Wilburton, Ely, Cambs, CB6 3RA
Officers: James Lambert [1985] Director/Owner

Isle of Mull Brewing Company Limited
Incorporated: 21 June 2004
Net Worth: £19,929 *Total Assets:* £19,929
Registered Office: Unit 8a Baliscate Industrial Estate, Tobermory, Isle of Mull, PA75 6QA
Shareholders: Allan MacLean; Calum Eoghann MacLachlainn; Derwyn Hewitt
Officers: Derwyn Hewitt, Secretary; Derwyn Hewitt [1978] Director/Clerical; Calum Eoghann MacLachlainn [1963] Director; Allan MacLean [1953] Director

The Isle of Skye Brewing Company (Leann An Eilein) Ltd.
Incorporated: 21 January 1998 *Employees:* 15
Net Worth: £337,045 *Total Assets:* £636,642
Registered Office: The Pier, Uig, Isle of Skye, IV51 9XP
Major Shareholder: Kenneth Webster
Officers: Kenneth Webster [1963] Director

Isle-of-Cumbrae Brewing Company Ltd
Incorporated: 19 January 2010
Registered Office: 20 Balloch Crescent, Millport, Isle of Cumbrae, Ayrshire, KA28 0BY
Shareholders: Steven Batty; Graeme Schreiber; John Edgar Horn
Officers: Steven Batty [1978] Director/Marine Engineer; John Horn [1958] Director/Project Manager; Graeme Schreiber [1958] Director/Chartered Engineer

It's Braw Limited
Incorporated: 18 August 2016 *Employees:* 2
Net Worth Deficit: £6,513 *Total Assets:* £5,921
Registered Office: 33 Leslie Street, Blairgowrie, Perthshire, PH10 6AW
Shareholders: Conall Niall Iain Low; John McLeary Thomson
Officers: Conall Niall Iain Low [1992] Director; John McLeary Thomson [1957] Director

Itchen Valley Brewery Limited
Incorporated: 26 July 1999 *Employees:* 3
Net Worth Deficit: £267,700 *Total Assets:* £108,810
Registered Office: Unit D, Prospect Commercial Park, Prospect Road, New Alresford, Hants, SO24 9QF
Major Shareholder: Richard Steven Robinson
Officers: Richard Steven Robinson [1977] Director

Ivybridge Brewing Company Ltd
Incorporated: 17 December 2018
Registered Office: 41 Rue St Pierre, Ivybridge, Devon, PL21 0HZ
Officers: Simon David Rundle [1963] Director/University Professor

Jabru Bevco Ltd
Incorporated: 10 November 2016
Net Worth Deficit: £17,846 *Total Assets:* £17,036
Registered Office: 4 Waterside Mews, Stoughton Road, Guildford, Surrey, GU1 1LA
Officers: James Andrew Thomas Van Der Watt [1977] Director/Founder [Irish]

Jackrabbit Brewing Co. Ltd
Incorporated: 29 January 2019
Registered Office: 198 Berechurch Hall Road, Colchester, Essex, CO2 9PN
Shareholders: Amir William Anbouche; Spencer Aaron Gilbert
Officers: Amir William Anbouche [1992] Director

Jacobite Brewery Limited
Incorporated: 21 March 2018
Registered Office: International House, 38 Thistle Street, Edinburgh, EH2 1EN
Officers: Simon Yann Dominique Delvaux [1986] Director [Belgian]

Jarr Kombucha Ltd
Incorporated: 15 May 2015 *Employees:* 6
Net Worth Deficit: £88,839 *Total Assets:* £120,629
Registered Office: 1 Worsley Court, High Street, Worsley, Manchester, M28 3NJ
Parent: Duvel Moortgat N.V.
Officers: Gilles Aron Buchmann [1981] Director [Belgian]; Seraf de Smedt [1974] Director [Belgian]; Neil Robert Hinchley [1973] Director; Anouk Sophie Lagae [1975] Finance Director [Belgian]; Michel Luc Jozef Moortgat [1967] Director [Belgian]; Jessica Holly Seaton [1984] Director; Thomas Roger Seaton [1981] Director

Jarrow Innovations Ltd
Incorporated: 23 September 2014
Registered Office: 88 The Rise, Ponteland, Northumberland, NE20 9LG
Major Shareholder: Paul Minnikin
Officers: Paul Minnikin [1957] Director; Alan Minnikn [1959] Director

Jaw Brew Ltd
Incorporated: 17 June 2014
Registered Office: The Jaw, Baldernock, Milngavie, Glasgow, G62 6HD
Major Shareholder: Simon Mark Hazell
Officers: Alison Hazell [1960] Director/Brewery; Simon Mark Hazell [1960] Director/Brewer

The Jaw Brewery Ltd
Incorporated: 18 February 2014
Net Worth Deficit: £206,236 *Total Assets:* £73,876
Registered Office: The Jaw, Baldernock, Milngavie, Glasgow, G62 6HD
Shareholders: Simon Mark Hazell; Helen Alison Hazell
Officers: Helen Alison Hazell [1960] Director/Chartered Surveyor; Simon Mark Hazell [1960] Director/Brewer

Jawbone Brewing Ltd
Incorporated: 15 January 2019
Registered Office: 1 Isabel Hill Close, Hampton, Surrey, TW12 2FE
Shareholders: Ben Hughes; Emma Sheppard
Officers: Ben Hughes [1979] Director; Emma Sheppard [1984] Director

Jimbrew Ltd
Incorporated: 25 October 2018
Registered Office: 243-245 Clifton Drive South, Lytham St Annes, Lancs, FY8 1HW
Shareholders: James David Cuffe; Jennifer Hazel Cuffe
Officers: James David Cuffe [1990] Director

Jocks and Peers Brewing Company Limited
Incorporated: 24 July 2018
Registered Office: 180 St Pauls Road, London, N1 2LL
Shareholders: Akshit Raj Gupta; Ashwin Balivada; Aditya Nigudkar
Officers: Ashwin Balivada [1988] Sales Director [Indian]; Akshit Raj Gupta [1988] Director/Operations Manager [Indian]; Aditya Nigudkar [1983] Marketing Director [Indian]

John O'Groats Brewery Ltd
Incorporated: 22 May 2012
Net Worth Deficit: £9,492 *Total Assets:* £37,889
Registered Office: Seaview Hotel, John O'Groats, Wick, Caithness, Sutherland, KW1 4YR
Shareholder: Simon Garth Cottam
Officers: Simon Garth Cottam [1978] Director/Operator; Allan Farquhar [1960] Director/Operator; John Barrington Mainprize [1965] Director/Operator; Andrew Walter Mowat [1977] Director/Hotelier

The Jolly Boys Brewery Ltd
Incorporated: 28 November 2014 *Employees:* 4
Net Worth Deficit: £92,281 *Total Assets:* £63,265
Registered Office: Unit 16A, Redbrook Business Park, Wilthorpe Road, Barnsley, S Yorks, S75 1JN
Officers: Paul Michael Kennedy [1967] Director/Teacher; Ondrie Mann [1977] Director/Teacher; Hywel Eilian Wyn Roberts [1970] Director/Teacher; David John Whitaker [1970] Director/Teacher

Jolly Sailor Brewery Limited
Incorporated: 13 April 2017 *Employees:* 12
Net Worth Deficit: £7,433 *Total Assets:* £62,377
Registered Office: Olympia Hotel, 77 Barlby Road, Selby, N Yorks, YO8 5AB
Major Shareholder: David William Welsh
Officers: Dr David William Welsh [1961] Director

Jollyboat Brewery (Bideford) Limited
Incorporated: 18 May 2000
Net Worth: £1,038 *Total Assets:* £13,453
Registered Office: The Coach House, Buttgarden Street, Bideford, Devon, EX39 2AU
Major Shareholder: Hugh Lawrence Parry
Officers: Hugh Lawrence Parry [1943] Director/Brewer

Jon's Brewery Limited
Incorporated: 25 July 2012
Net Worth Deficit: £123,858 *Total Assets:* £136,845
Registered Office: 3 Hill Court, Hillhead, Colyton, Devon, EX24 6NJ
Shareholders: Jonathan David Hosking; Amanda Claire Edwards
Officers: Amanda Claire Edwards [1959] Director; Jonathan David Hosking [1959] Director

Jordan's Car Review Ltd
Incorporated: 17 February 2015
Previous: Ruddy's Brewery & Bar Ltd
Registered Office: Flat 4, 19 Newerne Street, Lydney, Glos, GL15 5RA
Major Shareholder: Jordan Conall Smith
Officers: Jordan Smith [1992] Director

Joules Brewery Limited
Incorporated: 4 February 2008 *Employees:* 50
Net Worth: £7,872,230 *Total Assets:* £14,329,697
Registered Office: The Brewery, Great Hales Street, Market Drayton, Salop, TF9 1JP
Shareholder: Steve Nuttall
Officers: Christine Elizabeth Nuttall, Secretary; Christine Elizabeth Nuttall [1965] Director; Hedley Stephen Nuttall [1966] Director/Business Executive

JP Brew Limited
Incorporated: 28 April 2017
Net Worth Deficit: £6,212 *Total Assets:* £1,643
Registered Office: First Floor, 85 Great Portland Street, London, W1W 7LT
Shareholders: Paul Michael Bartlett; Julian Geraint Draper
Officers: Paul Michael Bartlett [1979] Director/Manager; Julian Geraint Draper [1977] Director/Finance

The K L Brewery Limited
Incorporated: 16 April 2018
Registered Office: Bumbles, Lady Meadow, Kings Langley, Herts, WD4 9NF
Major Shareholder: Peter Hadden Timmis
Officers: Peter Hadden Timmis [1943] Director

K1 Beer PLC
Incorporated: 10 July 2012
Net Worth Deficit: £245,872 *Total Assets:* £12,046
Registered Office: Building 3, Chiswick Park, 566 Chiswick High Road, London, W4 5YA
Major Shareholder: Keyvan Foroshani
Officers: Keyvan Foroshani [1963] Director/Chief Executive

Kairos Solutions Ltd
Incorporated: 23 March 2017 *Employees:* 1
Net Worth: £2,289 *Total Assets:* £17,630
Registered Office: St Madoc Christian Youth Camp, Llanmadoc, Swansea, SA3 1DE
Shareholders: Alison Holland; Martin Holland
Officers: Alison Holland [1961] Director/Centre Manager; Martin Holland [1960] Sales Director

Kall Brand Ltd
Incorporated: 29 June 2015 *Employees:* 4
Net Worth: £11,494 *Total Assets:* £13,121
Registered Office: MacDonald House, 108 Commercial Street, Leith, Edinburgh, EH6 6NF
Shareholders: Michaela Berselius Kitchin; Thomas William Kitchin
Officers: Veronica Southcott, Secretary; Michaela Berselius Kitchin [1975] Director/Restaurateur [Swedish]; Ronald John McLellan Kitchin [1947] Director/Property Developer; Thomas William Kitchin [1977] Director/Chef; Veronica Southcott [1966] Director/Accountant

Kathmandu Link Limited
Incorporated: 3 July 2012
Net Worth: £17,819 *Total Assets:* £31,338
Registered Office: 273 Stag Lane, London, NW9 0EF
Officers: Gokul Prasad Dhungana [1974] Director/Accountant [Nepalese]; Shyam Mani Gautam [1973] Director [Nepalese]

Keep Brewing Ltd
Incorporated: 12 May 2016
Net Worth Deficit: £1,444 *Total Assets:* £2,590
Registered Office: The Village Inn, Bath Road, Nailsworth, Stroud, Glos, GL6 0HH
Shareholders: Paul Sugden; Deborah Anne Rogan; Jessica Sugden
Officers: Deborah Anne Rogan [1986] Director; Jessica Sugden [1991] Director; Paul Sugden [1987] Director

Keith Brewery Limited
Incorporated: 28 May 2012 *Employees:* 9
Previous: Brewmeister Ltd
Net Worth: £303,351 *Total Assets:* £784,487
Registered Office: Spalding House, 90-92 Queen Street, Broughty Ferry, Dundee, DD5 1AJ
Officers: James Derek Scott Carnegie [1961] Director; Graeme Hay [1966] Director; Anthony Schofield [1959] Managing Director; Donald John Smith [1968] Director

Kelburn Brewing Company Limited
Incorporated: 12 October 2001 *Employees:* 7
Net Worth: £75,740 *Total Assets:* £152,174
Registered Office: 10 Muriel Lane, Barrhead, Glasgow, G78 1QB
Major Shareholder: Derek James Moore
Officers: Derek James Moore [1951] Director

Kelchner Ltd
Incorporated: 2 November 2017
Registered Office: Unit D, The Sidings, Station Road, Ampthill, Bedford, MK45 2QY
Officers: Marisa Riette Kirchner [1978] Director [British/South African]

The Kelham Island Brewery Limited
Incorporated: 6 June 1997 *Employees:* 20
Net Worth: £247,272 *Total Assets:* £502,624
Registered Office: 23 Alma Street, Sheffield, S3 8SA
Major Shareholder: Helen Joan Wickett
Officers: Edward Michael Mark Wickett [1990] Managing Director; Helen Joan Wickett [1952] Director/Nurse

Kellentay Beers Ltd
Incorporated: 5 August 2014
Registered Office: 16 Hamilton Road, Derby, DE23 6RT
Major Shareholder: Alexandra Mills-Bell
Officers: Alexandra Mills-Bell [1979] Director

Keltek Cornish Brewery Limited
Incorporated: 27 March 1997 *Employees:* 12
Net Worth Deficit: £70,024 *Total Assets:* £550,492
Registered Office: 3 Chapel Street, Redruth, Cornwall, TR15 2BY
Parent: The Optoelectronic Manufacturing Corporation (UK) Ltd
Officers: Richard Stuart Heath [1986] Director/Business Development; Stuart Heath [1953] Director; William General Charles Heath [1983] Director/Business Development

Kendal Brewery Ltd
Incorporated: 19 September 2017
Registered Office: Masons Yard 24, 22 Stramongate, Kendal, Cumbria, LA9 4BN
Shareholders: Jonathan Gillis Ritson; Darren Lincoln
Officers: Darren Lincoln [1968] Director/Joiner

Kendal Brewing Company Limited
Incorporated: 4 January 2013
Net Worth: £2,962 *Total Assets:* £6,878
Registered Office: 19 Lowther Street, Kendal, Cumbria, LA9 4DH
Major Shareholder: Michael Andrew Pennington
Officers: Michael Andrew Pennington [1956] Director

Kent Brewery Ltd
Incorporated: 4 June 2010 *Employees:* 6
Net Worth: £1,113 *Total Assets:* £184,825
Registered Office: 50 Seymour Street, London, W1H 7JG
Shareholders: Paul Roy Herbert; Tobias Andrew Simmonds
Officers: Paul Roy Herbert, Secretary; Paul Roy Herbert [1956] Director; Tobias Andrew Simmonds [1970] Director

Kentish Town Brewery Limited
Incorporated: 30 September 2016
Net Worth Deficit: £7,039 *Total Assets:* £2,961
Registered Office: 1 Burghley Court, Ingestre Road, London, NW5 1UF
Major Shareholder: Mark William Drayton
Officers: Mark William Drayton [1974] Director

The Kernel Brewery Ltd
Incorporated: 25 January 2012
Net Worth: £1,467,334 *Total Assets:* £1,937,845
Registered Office: 01 Spa Business Park, Spa Road, London, SE16 4QT
Shareholder: Evin Tuck O'Riordain
Officers: Evin Tuck O'Riordain [1974] Director/Brewer [Irish]

Keswick Brewing Company Limited
Incorporated: 7 June 2018
Registered Office: 14 Clifford Court Cooper Way, Parkhouse Business Park, Carlisle, Cumbria, CA3 0JG
Major Shareholder: Susan Claire Jefferson
Officers: Susan Claire Jefferson [1969] Director

Kettle Green Brewing Ltd
Incorporated: 6 September 2018
Registered Office: Gainsborough House, Sheering Lower Road, Sawbridgeworth, Herts, CM21 9RG
Shareholders: Christopher Nicola; Nicholas Nicola
Officers: Christopher Nicola [1973] Director; Nicholas Nicola [1975] Director

Kettlesmith Brewing Company Limited
Incorporated: 5 May 2015 *Employees:* 3
Net Worth Deficit: £16,170 *Total Assets:* £89,279
Registered Office: 26 Palairet Close, Bradford on Avon, Wilts, BA15 1US
Major Shareholder: Antony Malcolm Field
Officers: Antony Malcolm Field [1972] Director; Caroline Julie Field [1972] Director

Kew Brewery Limited
Incorporated: 21 October 2014 *Employees:* 2
Net Worth: £8,142 *Total Assets:* £32,343
Registered Office: 648 Gateway House, Tollgate, Chandler's Ford, Eastleigh, Hants, SO50 0ND
Parent: Ampersand SG Ltd
Officers: Jonathan Timothy George Sumner [1963] Marketing Director

Khukuri Beer (UK) Limited
Incorporated: 8 June 2007
Net Worth Deficit: £31,537 *Total Assets:* £177,859
Registered Office: 17 Gainsborough Gardens, Greenford, Middlesex, UB6 0JG
Major Shareholder: Mahanta Bahadur Shrestha
Officers: Amika Shrestha, Secretary; Mahanta Bahadur Shrestha [1950] Director/Restaurateur

Killer Hop Brew Co Ltd
Incorporated: 11 April 2018
Registered Office: 27 Connaught Road, Newbury, Berks, RG14 5SP
Officers: Rebekah Emily Giles [1991] Director/Manager; Georgia Elisabeth Painting [1994] Director/Manager

The Kiln Brewery Ltd
Incorporated: 25 March 2014 *Employees:* 2
Net Worth Deficit: £27,379 *Total Assets:* £18,737
Registered Office: 1st Floor, 30 Church Road, Burgess Hill, W Sussex, RH15 9AE
Shareholders: Andrew Swaisland; Craig David Walter Wilson
Officers: Andrew Swaisland [1976] Director/Brewery; Craig David Walter Wilson [1975] Director/Brewery

Kimberley Brewery Limited
Incorporated: 9 July 2012
Registered Office: 26 Sidney Road, Beeston, Nottingham, NG9 1AN
Major Shareholder: Gary John Franks
Officers: Gary Franks, Secretary; Gary John Franks [1968] Director/HGV Driver

Kimberley Brewing Company Limited
Incorporated: 9 July 2012
Registered Office: 26 Sidney Road, Beeston, Nottingham, NG9 1AN
Major Shareholder: Gary John Franks
Officers: Gary Franks, Secretary; Gary John Franks [1968] Director/HGV Driver

Kimbland Distillery Ltd
Incorporated: 16 August 2017
Registered Office: 53a Hertford Road, Stevenage, Herts, SG2 8SA
Shareholder: Sebastian James Anthony Aiden Hadfield-Hyde
Officers: Sebastian James Anthony Aiden Hadfield-Hyde [1985] Overseas Director

Kindeace Ales Limited
Incorporated: 6 February 2019
Registered Office: Beinn-An-Oir, Invergordon, Ross-shire, IV18 0LL
Major Shareholder: Fergus Stanley Scott
Officers: Fergus Stanley Scott [1965] Director

The Kingdom Brewery Limited
Incorporated: 15 January 2016
Net Worth Deficit: £20,837 Total Assets: £4,725
Registered Office: 12 Jutland Street, Rosyth, Dunfermline, Fife, KY11 2ZL
Shareholder: Lois Helen Vettese
Officers: Lois Helen Vettese [1976] Director

Kingstone Brewery Limited
Incorporated: 1 May 2015 Employees: 1
Net Worth Deficit: £6,174 Total Assets: £112,074
Registered Office: Kingstone Brewery, Tintern, Chepstow, Gwent, NP16 7NX
Shareholders: Edward Biggs; Edward Popham-Holloway
Officers: Edward Biggs [1962] Director/Brewer; Edward Popham-Holloway [1976] Director

Kinkell Brewery Ltd
Incorporated: 9 November 2016
Net Worth Deficit: £2,814 Total Assets: £10,684
Registered Office: Kinkell House, St Andrews, Fife, KY16 8PN
Shareholders: Camilla Fyfe; Rory Fyfe
Officers: Camilla Fyfe [1977] Director/Teacher; Rory John Fyfe [1976] Director/Entrepreneur

The Kinross Brewery Limited
Incorporated: 24 May 2016 Employees: 11
Net Worth: £169,482 Total Assets: £202,786
Registered Office: The Windlestrae, The Muirs, Kinross, KY13 8AS
Major Shareholder: James David Keith Montgomery
Officers: Gareth Derek Lee [1954] Director/Brewing Consultant; Anthony Gerard McGrath [1956] Director/Investor; Thomas Dodds Moffat [1967] Director/Marketing; James David Keith Montgomery [1957] Director/Hotelier; Alan John Roy [1951] Director; Daniel Christie Slater [1961] Director

Kintyre Ales Limited
Incorporated: 18 January 2017
Registered Office: The Old Surgery, School Road, Tarbert, Argyll, PA29 6UL
Major Shareholder: John William Beveridge
Officers: John William Beveridge [1956] Director

The Kinver Brewery Limited
Incorporated: 18 June 2009
Net Worth: £52,289 Total Assets: £86,358
Registered Office: 1 Franchise Street, Kidderminster, Worcs, DY11 6RE
Shareholder: David Kelly
Officers: Carol Elizabeth Kelly [1957] Director; David Kelly [1957] Director; Robert James Kelly [1987] Director; Stephanie Louise Kelly [1992] Director; Thomas Gregory Kelly [1990] Director

Kirkstall Brewery Company Limited
Incorporated: 10 March 2009 Employees: 7
Net Worth: £137,353 Total Assets: £367,555
Registered Office: 423 Otley Road, Adel, Leeds, LS16 6AL
Parent: Kirkstall Yorkshire Limited
Officers: Lisa Dawn Ardron, Secretary; Stephen Anthony Holt [1955] Director

Kirton Fen Brewery Limited
Incorporated: 24 July 2017
Registered Office: 11 Lenton Way, Frampton, Boston, Lincs, PE20 1AU
Shareholders: Ian Robert Wagstaff; David Edward Wagstaff; Johnathan Michael Mitcham
Officers: Johnathan Michael Mitcham [1989] Director; David Edward Wagstaff [1988] Director; Ian Robert Wagstaff [1964] Managing Director

Knoydart Brewery Limited
Incorporated: 6 November 2015 Employees: 2
Net Worth Deficit: £35,695 Total Assets: £31,571
Registered Office: White Hart House, High Street, Limpsfield, Oxted, Surrey, RH8 0DT
Shareholders: Matthew Lewis Humphrey; Samantha Durston Humphrey
Officers: Matthew Lewis Humphrey [1966] Director; Samantha Durston Humphrey [1966] Director

Konigsberg Limited
Incorporated: 24 February 2016
Registered Office: Konigsberg Limited, Meden Road, Boughton, Newark, Notts, NG22 9ZD

Konigsberg Seven Bridges Breweries Ltd
Incorporated: 12 August 2014 Employees: 4
Net Worth Deficit: £342,854 Total Assets: £342,764
Registered Office: Konigsberg Seven Bridges Breweries Ltd, Meden Road, Boughton, Newark, Notts, NG22 9ZD
Shareholders: Richard Andrew Smyth; Graham Roy Lawrence
Officers: Graham Lawrence, Secretary; Robert Mark Handy [1988] Director/Brewer; Graham Roy Lawrence [1946] Director; Richard Andrew Smyth [1962] Director

Koomor Brewing Company Ltd
Incorporated: 21 November 2017
Registered Office: 8 Awliscombe Road, Welling, Kent, DA16 3JT
Shareholders: Joshua Michael Morrin; Kevin Koo
Officers: Kevin Koo, Secretary; Kevin Koo [1989] Director; Joshua Michael Morrin [1989] Director/IT Administrator

Korca Brewery St Andrews Limited
Incorporated: 3 May 2017
Registered Office: 59 Bonnygate, Cupar, Fife, KY15 4BY
Parent: Divino Incanto Wine & Spirits Group UK Ltd
Officers: Giorgio Cozzolino [1964] Director [Italian]

The Krafty Braumeister Ltd
Incorporated: 24 August 2016 Employees: 3
Net Worth Deficit: £17,432 Total Assets: £63,801
Registered Office: Unit 4A Eastlands Industrial Estate, Leiston, Suffolk, IP16 4LL
Shareholders: Ulrich Hans Schiefelbein; Victoria Phyllis Handevidt
Officers: Victoria Phyllis Handevidt [1958] Director/Brewer [American]; Ulrich Hans Schiefelbein [1958] Director/Brewer [German]; Auriol Frances Lilias Thomson [1968] Director/Certified Chartered Accountant

Kuwa Trading Ltd
Incorporated: 7 February 2019
Registered Office: 20 Westlands Way, Oxted, Surrey, RH8 0ND
Shareholders: The Mooli Restaurant Ltd; Didi London Ltd
Officers: Pamela Manster, Secretary; Purna Gurung [1973] Director/Restaurateur; Sirish Gurung [1976] Administrative Director

L1 Brewer Ltd
Incorporated: 9 August 2012
Registered Office: 2 Lakeland Close, Liverpool, L1 5HY
Major Shareholder: Gary Peter Rice
Officers: Gary Rice, Secretary; Kevin Paul Flynn [1954] Director/Police Sergeant (Retired); Carl Paul Rice [1980] Director/Publican; Gary Peter Rice [1980] Director/Brewer

Lads & Dads Brewing Limited
Incorporated: 28 December 2018
Registered Office: 9 Ethelbert Road, Orpington, Kent, BR5 3JN
Major Shareholder: Luke Francis Rossi
Officers: Luke Francis Rossi [1985] Director/Civil Servant

Laid Back Brewing Limited
Incorporated: 14 May 2014
Registered Office: Church House Farm, 108 Crewe Road, Haslington, Crewe, Cheshire, CW1 5RD
Shareholders: Frank Neil Jackson; Samantha Jackson
Officers: Frank Neil Jackson [1972] Director/Engineer; Samantha Jackson [1974] Director/Solicitor

Laiho Limited
Incorporated: 14 March 2018
Registered Office: 47 Abercairney Place, Blackford, Auchterarder, Perth & Kinross, PH4 1QB
Major Shareholder: Nisse-Thomas Tapio Laiho-Murdoch
Officers: Nisse-Thomas Tapio Laiho-Murdoch [1993] Director/General Manager [Finnish]; Courtney Speirs [1992] Director/Brewer/FOH Manager

The Lake District Brewery Limited
Incorporated: 26 March 2018
Registered Office: 92 Greenbank Drive, Sunderland, Tyne & Wear, SR4 0JX
Major Shareholder: Stephen Anthony Brace
Officers: Stephen Anthony Brace [1991] Director/Business Development

Lake View Country House Ltd
Incorporated: 26 May 2016 *Employees:* 10
Net Worth Deficit: £119,268 *Total Assets:* £222,571
Registered Office: Lake View Country House, Lake View Drive, Grasmere, Ambleside, Cumbria, LA22 9TD
Shareholder: Richard Abbott
Officers: Beth Abbott [1986] Director/Project Manager; Paul Thomas Abbott [1986] Associate Director; Richard Bruce Abbott [1959] Director/QA Manager

Lakehouse Brewing Company Limited
Incorporated: 15 March 2016
Net Worth: £2,479 *Total Assets:* £55,483
Registered Office: Lake House, Peachfield Road, Malvern, Worcs, WR14 3LE
Officers: Faith Jane Frost, Secretary; Dan Adrian Frost [1991] Director

Lam Brewing Limited
Incorporated: 6 October 2014
Net Worth Deficit: £135,274 *Total Assets:* £97,543
Registered Office: 68 Sandford Lane Industrial Estate, Kennington, Oxford, OX1 5RP
Major Shareholder: Kurt Moxley
Officers: Kurt Moxley [1961] Director/Manager

Lancar Limited
Incorporated: 27 March 2009
Net Worth: £9,972 *Total Assets:* £218,353
Registered Office: Horizon House, 2 Whiting Street, Sheffield, S8 9QR
Shareholder: Mark Steer
Officers: Andrea Jayne Steer [1963] Director/Secretary; Mark Steer [1960] Director/Management Consultant; Matthew John Steer [1982] Director/Manager

Lancaster Brewery Company Limited
Incorporated: 19 January 2005 *Employees:* 23
Net Worth Deficit: £255,234 *Total Assets:* £1,606,139
Registered Office: Lancaster Leisure Park, Wyresdale Road, Lancaster, LA1 3LA
Officers: Matthew Scott Jackson [1972] Director; Phillip Anthony Simpson [1971] Director

Lancaster Brewery Holdings Limited
Incorporated: 6 April 2017
Registered Office: Lancaster Leisure Park, Wyresdale Road, Lancaster, LA1 3LA
Shareholders: Phillip Anthony Simpson; Matthew Scott Jackson
Officers: Matthew Scott Jackson [1972] Director; Phillip Anthony Simpson [1971] Director

Landlocked Brewing Company Limited
Incorporated: 4 March 2014
Net Worth: £1,477 *Total Assets:* £16,618
Registered Office: 51 Queen Street, Waingroves, Ripley, Derbys, DE5 9TJ
Major Shareholder: Michael Godfrey James
Officers: Alison Jane James, Secretary; Michael Godfrey James [1962] Director/Brewer; Andrew Timothy Pardoe [1958] Director/Race Car Instructor

The Langford Brewing Co. Limited
Incorporated: 17 October 2012
Registered Office: Brigade House, Brigade Street, London, SE3 0TW
Major Shareholder: Timothy Richard Charles Wayman Francis
Officers: Timothy Richard Charles Wayman Francis [1984] Director

Langham Brewing Company Limited
Incorporated: 29 February 2016 *Employees:* 4
Net Worth: £13,809 *Total Assets:* £317,991
Registered Office: The Granary, Langham Lane, Lodsworth, Petworth, W Sussex, GU28 9BU
Shareholders: James Peter Berrow; Lesley Stephens Foulkes
Officers: James Peter Berrow [1961] Director/Electrician; Lesley Stephens Foulkes [1959] Director/Consultant

Langton Brewery Ltd
Incorporated: 5 January 2012
Net Worth: £71,218 Total Assets: £116,418
Registered Office: The Langton Brewery, Grange Farm, Welham Road, Thorpe Langton, Market Harborough, Leics, LE16 7TU
Major Shareholder: Sion Francis Roberts
Officers: Duncan Andrew Rawson, Secretary; Duncan Andrew Rawson [1970] Director/Management Consultant; Sion Francis Roberts [1966] Director/Management Consultant

Larkins Brewery Limited
Incorporated: 18 December 1986 Employees: 5
Net Worth: £180,771 Total Assets: £236,863
Registered Office: 4 Britannia House, Roberts Mews, Orpington, Kent, BR6 0JP
Major Shareholder: Robert Edward Dockerty
Officers: Karah Templeton, Secretary; Robert Edward Dockerty [1943] Director/Farmer Brewer; Karah Templeton [1945] Director/Housewife

Last Sign Brewing Company Ltd
Incorporated: 5 February 2018
Registered Office: 1 Bluebell Way, Worlingham, Beccles, Suffolk, NR34 7BT
Major Shareholder: Matthew James Caton
Officers: Matthew James Caton [1977] Director/Brewer

Lastonser Ltd
Incorporated: 23 July 2018
Registered Office: Suite 1, Fielden House, 41 Rochdale Road, Todmorden, Lancs, OL14 6LD
Major Shareholder: Michelle Kilcourse
Officers: Ruth Villacencio [1978] Director [Filipino]

Latimer Ales Ltd
Incorporated: 29 June 2012 Employees: 1
Net Worth: £21,738 Total Assets: £50,251
Registered Office: 13 South Folds Road, Oakley Hay, Corby, Northants, NN18 9EU
Shareholders: James Alexander Trent; Jane Ruth Trent
Officers: James Trent [1971] Director; Lorraine Trent [1945] Director

Laughing Ass Brewery Ltd
Incorporated: 20 February 2018
Registered Office: 49 Thorn Road, Hedon, E Yorks, HU12 8HN
Shareholders: Simon Paul North; Kelvin Hurd
Officers: Kelvin Hurd [1971] Director; Simon Paul North [1970] Director

The Laughing Pug Ltd
Incorporated: 10 October 2018
Registered Office: 7 King Edward Close, Shanklin, Isle of Wight, PO37 7DW
Major Shareholder: Barrie Wade
Officers: Barrie Wade [1967] Director

Law and Disorder Brew Co Ltd
Incorporated: 20 February 2019
Registered Office: Kitchens Bridge Cottage, Polesworth Road, Grendon, Atherstone, Warwicks, CV9 3DW
Shareholders: Simon David Watson-Burge; Alison Jayne Watson-Burge
Officers: Alison Jayne Watson-Burge [1977] Director/Publican; Simon David Watson-Burge [1983] Director/Project Manager

Lawman Brewing Company, Ltd.
Incorporated: 20 October 2015
Net Worth: £19,829 Total Assets: £40,464
Registered Office: 31 Kelvin Road North, Lenziemill, Cumbernauld, N Lanarks, G67 2BD
Major Shareholder: Craig Gordon Laurie
Officers: Thomas Gardiner [1965] Director/Whisky Auctioneer; Paul McDonagh [1959] Director/Publican

Peter Laws Brewing Limited
Incorporated: 11 October 2006
Net Worth: £1,375 Total Assets: £3,522
Registered Office: Low House, Setmurthy, Cockermouth, Cumbria, CA13 9SL
Officers: Nicola Jean Laws, Secretary; Peter Laws [1941] Director

Lazy Bay Brewery Ltd
Incorporated: 28 April 2018
Registered Office: 89 Julian Road, West Bridgford, Nottingham, NG2 5AL
Major Shareholder: Brett Phillips
Officers: Brett Phillips [1978] Director/Teacher

Lazy Turtle Brewing Co Ltd
Incorporated: 11 April 2018
Registered Office: Meadowbeck, Barnside Lane, Hepworth, Holmfirth, W Yorks, HD9 1TN
Officers: David Bore [1968] Director/Lazy Turtle Brewing Co

Leadmill Brewery Limited
Incorporated: 8 August 2003
Net Worth: £32,849 Total Assets: £51,271
Registered Office: Unit 3 Heanor Small Business Centre, Adams Close, Heanor, Derbys, DE75 7SW
Officers: Richard John Creighton, Secretary; Richard John Creighton [1965] Director/Brewer; Julie Weaving [1967] Director/Housewife

Leatherbritches Brewery Limited
Incorporated: 14 March 2007 Employees: 4
Net Worth: £19,935 Total Assets: £69,998
Registered Office: 41 St John Street, Ashbourne, Derbys, DE6 1GP
Shareholder: Edward William David Allingham
Officers: Sandra Allingham, Secretary; Edward William David Allingham [1967] Director/Brewer

Lecale Brewery Limited
Incorporated: 13 February 2017
Net Worth: £100 Total Assets: £20,000
Registered Office: 3 High Street, Ardglass, Downpatrick, Co Down, BT30 7TU
Major Shareholder: Michael Mary Howland
Officers: Sean Mark Brennan, Secretary; Michael Mary Howland [1963] Director

Ledbury Real Ales Ltd
Incorporated: 21 September 2011
Net Worth Deficit: £87,330 Total Assets: £91,310
Registered Office: Gazerdine House, Hereford Road, Ledbury, Herefords, HR8 2PZ
Major Shareholder: Katherine Alice Stevens
Officers: Katherine Alice Stevens [1974] Director

The Leeds Brewery Company Limited
Incorporated: 14 March 2006
Net Worth Deficit: £437,916 *Total Assets:* £1,774,296
Registered Office: 3 Sydenham Road, Leeds, LS11 9RU
Parent: LBC Holding Company Limited
Officers: Michael Alan Brothwell, Secretary/Director; Michael Alan Brothwell [1983] Director; Samuel Andrew Holbrook Moss [1984] Director

J.W.Lees & Co.(Brewers) Limited
Incorporated: 11 November 1955 *Employees:* 1,227
Net Worth: £82,299,600 *Total Assets:* £115,451,720
Registered Office: Greengate Brewery, Middleton Junction, Manchester, M24 2AX
Officers: Simon Cross, Secretary; Simon Cross [1972] Director; Anna Elizabeth Clare Griffin [1970] Director; Michael Christopher Lees Jones [1971] Director of Beer Quality; Simon Christopher Lees Jones [1966] Director; William George Richard Lees Jones [1964] Director/Manager; William Richard Lees Jones [1933] Director; Christina Francis Lees-Jones [1969] Director/Catering Manager; Christopher Peter Lees-Jones [1936] Director

Left Handed Giant Brewing Limited
Incorporated: 28 January 2015
Net Worth: £1,795 *Total Assets:* £28,268
Registered Office: Unit 9 Wadehurst Industrial Park, St Philips Road, Bristol, BS2 0JE
Major Shareholder: Bruce Gray
Officers: Bruce Gray, Secretary; Jack William Granger [1988] Operations Director; Bruce Gray [1981] Director/Distribution; Richard Michael Poole [1976] Director/Head Brewer

Left Handed Giant Ltd.
Incorporated: 27 June 2013 *Employees:* 9
Previous: Big Beer Distribution Ltd
Net Worth: £27,277 *Total Assets:* £246,169
Registered Office: Unit 8 and 9, Wadehurst Industrial Park, St Philips Road, Bristol, BS2 0JE
Major Shareholder: Bruce Gray
Officers: Jack William Granger [1988] Director [Australian]; Bruce Gray [1981] Director; Richard Michael Poole [1976] Director

Legenderry Brewing Company Limited
Incorporated: 15 May 2014 *Employees:* 16
Net Worth Deficit: £17,537 *Total Assets:* £143,997
Registered Office: 27 Hawkin Street, Londonderry, BT48 6RE
Major Shareholder: James Huey
Officers: James Huey [1977] Director/Brewer [Irish]; Louise Huey [1977] Director [Irish]

Legless Brewing Ltd
Incorporated: 23 October 2018
Registered Office: 3 Station Road, Wressle, Selby, N Yorks, YO8 6ES
Major Shareholder: Thomas Davies
Officers: Thomas Davies [1982] Director/Operator

The Leighton Buzzard Brewing Company Limited
Incorporated: 12 February 2014
Net Worth: £42,983 *Total Assets:* £124,276
Registered Office: Unit 23 Harmill Industrial Estate, Grovebury Road, Leighton Buzzard, Beds, LU7 4FF
Shareholders: Jonathan D'Este-Hoare; Amber Joy D'Este-Hoare
Officers: Brendan Daniel O'Donnell, Secretary; Amber Joy D'Este-Hoare [1983] Director/Operations Manager; Jonathan D'Este-Hoare [1978] Director/Brewer

The Leith Brewing Company Limited
Incorporated: 5 June 2017
Registered Office: 14/2 Dicksonfield, Edinburgh, EH7 5NE
Officers: Moyra Little [1971] Director; Nancy Little [1969] Director; James McLaughlin [1976] Director; Scott Richards [1969] Director

Lekker Days Ltd
Incorporated: 23 October 2017
Registered Office: Apartment 14, 12 Duke Street, Liverpool, L1 5GA
Officers: Harry Jonathan Brice [1989] Director/Project Manager; Jared Elvin [1986] Director/Supply Chain Manager [Irish]; James Thomas David McMullen [1987] Director/Supply Chain Manager

Lennox Brewery Limited
Incorporated: 12 December 2017
Registered Office: 62 Glencairn Road, Dumbarton, W Dunbartonshire, G82 4DW
Shareholders: Iain Ferguson McLaren; Andrew Samuel Jarvis
Officers: Andrew Samuel Jarvis [1980] Director; Iain Ferguson McLaren [1973] Director

The Lerwick Brewery Limited
Incorporated: 30 July 2013
Registered Office: Hamepark, Reawick, Shetland, ZE2 9NJ
Shareholders: John Charles Mercer; James Cowie Mercer; Roderick Graham Mercer
Officers: James Cowie Mercer [1967] Director; John Charles Mercer [1965] Director; Roderick Graham Mercer [1969] Director

Letterpress Brewery Ltd
Incorporated: 12 April 2018
Registered Office: 50 Carrington Road, Urmston, Manchester, M41 6HX
Officers: Andrew Bernard Clarke, Secretary; Andrew Bernard Clarke [1978] Director/Brewer

Leviathan Brewing Ltd
Incorporated: 29 January 2018
Registered Office: 221 Chester Road, Boldmere, Sutton Coldfield, W Midlands, B73 5BE
Major Shareholder: Christopher Darren Hodgetts
Officers: Christopher Darren Hodgetts, Secretary; Christopher Darren Hodgetts [1970] Managing Director

Lewanbrew Limited
Incorporated: 20 November 2017
Registered Office: 5 Carden Place, Aberdeen, AB10 1UT
Shareholders: Lewis Vorenkamp; Ewan Vorenkamp
Officers: Ewan Vorenkamp [1978] Director; Lewis Vorenkamp [1986] Director

LF Brewery Holdings Limited
Incorporated: 27 February 2017 *Employees:* 12
Total Assets: £4,017,000
Registered Office: Jacobsen House, 140 Bridge Street, Northampton, NN1 1PZ
Parent: Carlsberg UK Limited
Officers: Jeremy Robert Brown, Secretary; Julian Akhtar Karim Momen [1963] Director; Adam Stubbs [1972] Director

Lincoln Green Brewing Company Limited
Incorporated: 29 November 2011 *Employees:* 7
Net Worth: £54,837 *Total Assets:* £164,382
Registered Office: Unit E5, Enterprise Park, Wigwam Lane, Hucknall, Nottingham, NG15 7SZ
Shareholders: Anthony John Hughes; Lynette Justine Hughes
Officers: Philip John Daykin [1961] Director; Anthony John Hughes [1969] Director; Lynette Justine Hughes [1972] Director

Lincolnshire Brewing Company Limited
Incorporated: 28 December 2006
Net Worth Deficit: £14,559 *Total Assets:* £30,289
Registered Office: 15 Main Road, Langworth, Lincoln, LN3 5BJ
Major Shareholder: Claire Louise Brown
Officers: Claire Louise Brown [1972] Director

Lincolnshire Craft Beers Limited
Incorporated: 16 May 2017
Net Worth Deficit: £23,284 *Total Assets:* £46,903
Registered Office: 19 Helene Grove, Grimsby, N E Lincs, DN32 8JX
Officers: Mark Smith [1965] Director/Manager

Linear Brewing Company Limited
Incorporated: 17 August 2015
Net Worth Deficit: £1,001 *Total Assets:* £1,364
Registered Office: 2 Chaworth Road, Bingham, Nottingham, NG13 8EU
Major Shareholder: Marc Anthony Williamson
Officers: Marc Anthony Williamson [1974] Director

The Lingfield Brewing Company Ltd
Incorporated: 28 October 2011
Net Worth Deficit: £4,541 *Total Assets:* £130
Registered Office: 63 Lincolns Mead, Lingfield, Surrey, RH7 6TA
Officers: Stephen Marshall Curtis [1965] Director/Brewing Technical Manager; Ivan Edward Ericsson [1972] Director/IT Consultant; Peter Nicholas Goodbody [1960] Director; Stephen Alan Wiltshire [1969] Director

Lion Brewery Co. Limited
Incorporated: 13 January 2017
Registered Office: 3rd Floor, 207 Regent Street, London, W1B 3HH
Major Shareholder: Benjamin James Hendry-Prior
Officers: Benjamin James Hendry-Prior [1982] Director

Lion Craft Brewery Ltd
Incorporated: 25 March 2013 *Employees:* 8
Net Worth Deficit: £168,243 *Total Assets:* £64,914
Registered Office: New Lion Brewery, Station Road, Totnes, Devon, TQ9 5JR
Major Shareholder: Ann Monroe Howe
Officers: Ann Monroe Howe, Secretary; Kathryn Alexander [1959] Director/Tour Guide; Robert Alexander [1967] Director/Publican [Australian]; Robert John Hopkins [1968] Director/Catalyst and Outreach Manager, Transition Network; Ann Monroe Howe [1943] Director/Writer [American]; Josh W Howe [1974] Director/Professional Services Consultant [American]

Lion-Beer, Spirits & Wine (UK) Ltd
Incorporated: 15 November 2017
Registered Office: One Wood Street, London, EC2V 7WS
Parent: Kirin Holdings Co Ltd.
Officers: Elizabeth Mary Fay Davidson, Secretary; Stephanie Louise Nixon [1972] Director [Australian]; Matthew John Purcell Tapper [1969] Director [New Zealander]

Lions Den Beers Limited
Incorporated: 18 June 2012 *Employees:* 2
Net Worth: £2 *Total Assets:* £37,266
Registered Office: 11 Sowerby Way, Durham Lane Industrial Park, Eaglescliffe, Stockton on Tees, Cleveland, TS16 0RB
Major Shareholder: Samantha Marsden
Officers: Samantha Marsden [1972] Director

Liquid Light Brewing Company Limited
Incorporated: 30 November 2016
Net Worth Deficit: £4,050 *Total Assets:* £2,122
Registered Office: 125 Sneinton Boulevard, Nottingham, NG2 4FN
Shareholders: Thomas James David Stone; Grace Maisie Copley
Officers: Grace Maisie Copley [1995] Director/Sales and Brand Manager; Thomas Stone [1988] Director/Head Brewer

Liquid Revolution Ltd
Incorporated: 3 April 2017
Registered Office: 35 Lemon Street, Truro, Cornwall, TR1 2NR
Shareholders: Gary Gary Watts; Thomas Hannon
Officers: Thomas Hannon [1984] Director; Gary Stephen Watts [1973] Director

Lithic Brewing Limited
Incorporated: 6 May 2016
Net Worth Deficit: £20,027 *Total Assets:* £20,596
Registered Office: 2 Chapel Mead, Penperlleni, Pontypool, Monmouthshire, NP4 0BR
Major Shareholder: David James Drabble
Officers: David James Drabble [1986] Director

The Little Beer Corporation Ltd
Incorporated: 8 November 2011 *Employees:* 2
Net Worth: £5,972 *Total Assets:* £134,567
Registered Office: 9 Abbots Close, Onslow Village, Guildford, Surrey, GU2 7RW
Shareholder: James Andrew Taylor
Officers: Alison Mary Taylor [1969] Director; James Andrew Taylor [1964] Director; Martin Stephen West [1965] Director

Little Black Dog Beer Company Ltd
Incorporated: 19 July 2016
Net Worth Deficit: £11,042 *Total Assets:* £22,637
Registered Office: The Carlton Towers Brewery, Carlton Towers, Carlton, N Yorks, DN14 9LZ
Shareholder: Jordan Joseph Kot
Officers: Emily Maggie Kot [1989] Finance Director; Jordan Joseph Kot [1991] Director/Master Brewer; Nigel Joseph Kot [1959] Director/Brewing Master

Little Critters Brewing Company Limited
Incorporated: 28 August 2015
Net Worth: £14,935 *Total Assets:* £27,158
Registered Office: 2 Horizon House, Whiting Street, Sheffield, S8 9QR
Major Shareholder: Mark Steer
Officers: Andrea Jayne Steer [1963] Director; Mark Steer [1960] Director

Little Crosby Village Brewing Company Ltd
Incorporated: 10 February 2015
Net Worth: £22,479 *Total Assets:* £61,785
Registered Office: Little Crosby Village Brewing Co Ltd, 6 Little Crosby Village, Liverpool, L23 4TS
Major Shareholder: David Clive Barker
Officers: David Clive Barker [1960] Director/Brewer

Little Dragon Brewery Limited
Incorporated: 5 July 2012
Net Worth Deficit: £44,481 *Total Assets:* £12,931
Registered Office: 24 Rectory Road, Llangwm, Haverfordwest, Dyfed, SA62 4JA
Major Shareholder: Morgan Coe
Officers: Morgan Coe, Secretary; Morgan Coe [1971] Marketing Director

The Little Eaton Brewery Company Limited
Incorporated: 30 November 2017
Registered Office: The Mills, Canal Street, Derby, DE1 2RJ
Shareholders: Mark David Edmond; Carl Andrew Haspel
Officers: Mark David Edmond [1961] Director; Carl Andrew Haspel [1959] Director

Little London Brewery Limited
Incorporated: 23 July 2015
Net Worth Deficit: £59,393 *Total Assets:* £48,981
Registered Office: Unit 6b Ash Park Business Centre, Ash Lane, Little London, Hants, RG26 5FL
Shareholders: Andrew Watts; Joan Rosina Watts
Officers: Andrew Watts [1954] Director

Little Monster Brewing Company Limited
Incorporated: 27 February 2018
Registered Office: Metherell Gard, Burn View, Bude, Cornwall, EX23 8BX
Officers: Brenden Quinn [1972] Director/Brewer

Little Ox Brewery Limited
Incorporated: 3 March 2015
Net Worth Deficit: £85,720 *Total Assets:* £25,722
Registered Office: 25 Castle Road, Wootton, Woodstock, Oxon, OX20 1EQ
Major Shareholder: Ian Keith Hemingway
Officers: Ian Keith Hemingway [1966] Director

Little Rotters Limited
Incorporated: 30 August 2016
Net Worth Deficit: £9,332 *Total Assets:* £4,370
Registered Office: 47 Cambridge Road, Ely, Cambs, CB7 4HJ
Major Shareholder: Emily Trotter
Officers: Emily Charlotte Trotter [1975] Director

Little Teapot Ltd
Incorporated: 18 September 2018
Registered Office: 5 Kingsley Grove, Audenshaw, Manchester, M34 5GT
Major Shareholder: James Robert Whewell
Officers: James Robert Whewell [1980] Director

Little Valley Brewery Limited
Incorporated: 15 September 2004 *Employees:* 4
Net Worth: £36,034 *Total Assets:* £498,736
Registered Office: Turkey Lodge, New Road, Cragg Vale, Hebden Bridge, W Yorks, HX7 5TT
Shareholders: Willem Pieter van der Spek; Susan Cooper
Officers: Susan Cooper, Secretary; Susan Cooper [1966] Director; Willem Pieter Van Der Spek [1965] Director [Dutch]

Little Wolf Brewing Limited
Incorporated: 23 April 2018
Registered Office: 5 Bangholm Park, Edinburgh, EH5 3BA
Major Shareholder: Sean Woelfell Fleming
Officers: Sean Woelfell Fleming [1989] Director/Brewer

Littleover Brewery Limited
Incorporated: 7 May 2015
Net Worth Deficit: £1,226 *Total Assets:* £56,453
Registered Office: Unit 9 Robinsons Industrial Estate, Shaftesbury Street, Derby, DE23 8NL
Major Shareholder: Timothy John Dorrington
Officers: Timothy John Dorrington [1962] Director/Brewer

Littondale Brewing Company Limited
Incorporated: 17 January 2018
Registered Office: The Queens Arms, Litton, Skipton, N Yorks, BD23 5QJ
Major Shareholder: Stephen Gregson
Officers: Stephen Gregson [1971] Director

Live Brew Company Ltd
Incorporated: 25 May 2018
Registered Office: Unit 2 Reeth Dales Centre Silver Street, Reeth, Richmond, N Yorks, DL11 6SP
Major Shareholder: Stuart Oliver Miller
Officers: Melissa Ruth Marie Miller [1980] Director/Certified Chartered Accountant; Stuart Oliver Miller [1979] Director/Self Employed

Liverpool Brewery Limited
Incorporated: 20 July 2017
Registered Office: 38 Brasenose Road, Bootle, Merseyside, L20 8HG
Major Shareholder: William Mark Hensby
Officers: William Mark Hensby [1953] Director/Management Consultant

The Liverpool Craft Beer Company Limited
Incorporated: 1 November 2010 *Employees:* 10
Net Worth Deficit: £1,126,828 *Total Assets:* £4,015,029
Registered Office: 62-64 Bridgewater Street, Liverpool, L1 0AY
Parent: Higsons 1780 Limited
Officers: Stephen Thomas Crawley [1962] Director

Liverpool Craft Holdings Limited
Incorporated: 24 April 2018
Registered Office: 62-64 Bridgewater Street, Liverpool, L1 0AY
Officers: Stephen Thomas Crawley [1962] Director

Liverpool Craft Limited
Incorporated: 24 April 2018
Registered Office: 62-64 Bridgewater Street, Liverpool, L1 0AY
Officers: Stephen Thomas Crawley [1962] Director

Lizard Ales Limited
Incorporated: 9 July 2001
Net Worth: £12,108 *Total Assets:* £22,152
Registered Office: The Old Nuclear Bunker, Pednavounder, Coverack, Helston, Cornwall, TR12 6SE
Shareholder: Mark Stephen Nattrass
Officers: Dr Mark Stephen Nattrass, Secretary; Dr Mark Stephen Nattrass [1966] Director/Self Employed

Llangollen Brewery Ltd
Incorporated: 29 March 2012 *Employees:* 1
Net Worth: £4,530 *Total Assets:* £15,002
Registered Office: Abbey Grange Hotel, Llantysilio, Llangollen, Denbighshire, LL20 8DD
Major Shareholder: Steven Vaughan Evans
Officers: Steven Evans [1977] Director/Farmer

Loane Brothers Limited
Incorporated: 14 May 2015
Registered Office: 35 Roscah View Rosscah View, Rosscolban, Kesh, Enniskillen, Co Fermanagh, BT93 1WA
Shareholders: Brian Loane; Kris Loane
Officers: Brian Loane [1991] Director/Fleet Manager; Kris Loane [1988] Director/Account Manager

Loch Earn Brewery Ltd
Incorporated: 27 June 2003
Net Worth Deficit: £11,413 Total Assets: £69
Registered Office: 100 Wellington Street, Glasgow, G2 6DH
Major Shareholder: Gerald Robert Michaluk
Officers: Generald Robert Michaluk [1960] Director/Consultant; Veronica Michaluk [1989] Director/Student

Loch Lomond Brewery Limited
Incorporated: 26 October 2009
Net Worth: £62,041 Total Assets: £203,536
Registered Office: Carn-Dearg, Glen Luss, Luss, Argyll & Bute, G83 8NY
Shareholders: Fiona Anne MacEachern; Euan Duncan MacEachern
Officers: Euan MacEachern [1975] Director/Project Manager; Fiona MacEachern [1975] Director/Brewster

Lock 34 Brew Co. Limited
Incorporated: 31 March 2016
Net Worth Deficit: £515 Total Assets: £1,285
Registered Office: Bucket Lock Cottage, Yarningale Lane, Yarningale Common, Warwick, CV35 8HW
Shareholder: Sean Higginbotham
Officers: Paul Higginbotham [1969] Director/Consultant; Sean Higginbotham [1966] Director/Project Manager

Lock 81 Brewery Limited
Incorporated: 26 February 2018
Registered Office: 22 The Spinney, Chesham, Bucks, HP5 3HY
Shareholders: Henry Winter; Caroline Cummings Winter
Officers: Henry Winter [1982] Director

The Lockside Brewery Ltd.
Incorporated: 12 December 2011
Net Worth Deficit: £6,944 Total Assets: £3,348
Registered Office: 117 Arlington Road, London, NW1 7ET
Shareholders: Lewis Ward Thorne; Donald Bell
Officers: Dr Donald McI Bell [1971] Director/Brewer; Dr Lewis Ward Thorne [1971] Director/Brewer

The Loddon Brewery Ltd
Incorporated: 15 August 2002
Net Worth: £6,829 Total Assets: £234,714
Registered Office: 175 Wokingham Road, Reading, Berks, RG6 1LT
Shareholders: Christopher Hearn; Vanessa Ann Hearn
Officers: Vanessa Ann Hearn, Secretary/Nursery Nurse; Christopher Hearn [1957] Brewer Managing Director; Vanessa Ann Hearn [1962] Director/Marketing

Loka Polly Ltd
Incorporated: 5 April 2018
Registered Office: Holland Farm, Rhyd Y Goleu, Black Brook, Mold, Flintshire, CH7 6LU
Major Shareholder: Sean Robert Wheldon
Officers: Sean Robert Wheldon [1992] Director

London Ale UK Ltd
Incorporated: 27 October 2017
Registered Office: c/o Furuichoi & Co, Winchester House, 259-269 Old Marylebone Road, London, NW1 5RA
Parent: London Ale and Co.
Officers: Jee Young Ra [1987] Director [South Korean]

The London Beer Company Limited
Incorporated: 7 August 1992
Net Worth: £146,296 Total Assets: £438,913
Registered Office: Suite 215, Waterhouse Business Centre, Cromar Way, Chelmsford, Essex, CM1 2QE
Major Shareholder: Martin Kemp
Officers: Martin Kemp, Secretary/Business Executive; Martin Kemp [1957] Director/Business Executive

The London Beer Factory Ltd.
Incorporated: 4 October 2011 Employees: 10
Net Worth: £68,333 Total Assets: £876,032
Registered Office: Unit 4 Hamilton Road Industrial Estate, 160 Hamilton Road, London, SE27 9SF
Shareholders: Edward Dermot Cotton; Simon Charles Cotton
Officers: Edward Dermot Cotton [1983] Director/Manager; Neil Charles Cotton [1952] Director; Simon Charles Cotton [1986] Director/Manager

London Beer Lab Ltd
Incorporated: 6 June 2012 Employees: 9
Net Worth Deficit: £5,004 Total Assets: £113,870
Registered Office: Arch 41X, Nursery Road, London, SW9 8BP
Shareholders: Bruno Alajouanine; Karl Michael Robert Durand O'Connor; Tadhg McMahon
Officers: Bruno Alajouanine [1982] Director [French]; Karl Michael Robert Durand O'Connor [1981] Director/Brewery Manager [Irish]

London Brewery Limited
Incorporated: 2 July 2018
Registered Office: 55 Oakdale, London, N14 5RG
Major Shareholder: Ilyas Demirci
Officers: Ilyas Demirci [1990] Director

London Brewing Company Limited
Incorporated: 7 June 2010 Employees: 28
Net Worth: £148,093 Total Assets: £373,787
Registered Office: The Bohemia, 762-764 High Road, London, N12 9QH
Shareholders: Simon John Sexton; Nick Campregher
Officers: Dr Nick Campregher, Secretary; Dr Nick Campregher [1982] Director/Finance [Italian]; Simon John Sexton [1973] Director/Pub Manager [Irish]

London Cosmopolitan Drinks Limited
Incorporated: 3 September 2003
Previous: The Gourmet Jerk Company Limited
Net Worth Deficit: £38,384 Total Assets: £376
Registered Office: 41 East Stour Way, South Willesborough, Ashford, Kent, TN24 0SX
Major Shareholder: Silburn Augustus Daure
Officers: Catherine Cryer, Secretary; Catherine Cryer [1961] Director/Administrator; Silburn Augustus Daure [1961] Director/Manager

London Fields Brewery Opco Limited
Incorporated: 29 June 2017
Net Worth Deficit: £161,718 Total Assets: £365,636
Registered Office: 365-366 Warburton Street, London, E8 3RR
Parent: Carlsberg A/S
Officers: Paul Thomas Davies [1972] Director/Vice President; Joakim Kenneth Losin [1972] Managing Director [Swedish]; Julian Akhtar Karim Momen [1963] Managing Director; Liam Newton [1966] Marketing Director; Eric Blackburne Ottaway [1968] Director [American]

Long Arm Brewing Co Limited
Incorporated: 7 October 2014 Employees: 2
Net Worth Deficit: £499,178 Total Assets: £126,815
Registered Office: 10 Queen Street Place, London, EC4R 1AG
Parent: ETM Group Limited
Officers: Edward William Joseph Martin [1979] Director; Thomas Richard Eliot Martin [1971] Director; Landen Robert Prescott-Brann [1967] Director

The Long Ashton Cider Company Limited
Incorporated: 11 February 2004
Registered Office: Cox's Green, Wrington, Bristol, BS40 5PA
Parent: Butcombe Brewing Company Limited
Officers: Richard Stuart Grainger [1960] Director; Timothy Hubert [1962] Commercial Director; Nigel Richard Osborne [1966] Director

Long Man Brewery Limited
Incorporated: 1 June 2011 Employees: 13
Net Worth: £273,990 Total Assets: £525,815
Registered Office: Church Farm, Litlington, Polegate, E Sussex, BN26 5RA
Officers: Duncan Ellis [1977] Director; Stephen Colin Lees [1967] Director; Jamie Simm [1984] Director of Brewing

Longdog Brewery Limited
Incorporated: 8 February 2011
Net Worth: £18,110 Total Assets: £40,171
Registered Office: Unit A1, Moniton Estate, West Ham Lane, Basingstoke, Hants, RG22 6NQ
Shareholders: Philip Brian Robins; Lisa Marie Robins
Officers: Lisa Marie Robins [1968] Director; Philip Brian Robins [1972] Director

Longhill Garage Limited
Incorporated: 13 March 2012 Employees: 1
Net Worth: £206 Total Assets: £52,672
Registered Office: Wyvols Court, Basingstoke Road, Swallowfield, Reading, Berks, RG7 1WY
Shareholders: Suzanne Faye Melia; Paul Melia
Officers: Paul Melia [1954] Director; Suzanne Faye Melia [1966] Director

Loomshed Hebrides Ltd
Incorporated: 19 December 2017
Registered Office: Mann Judd Gordon, 26 Lewis Street, Stornoway, Isle of Lewis, HS1 2JF
Shareholders: Robert Finlay MacKinnon; James McGowan
Officers: Robert Finlay MacKinnon [1967] Director/Consultant; James McGowan [1973] Director/Business Owner

Loopland Brewing Company Ltd
Incorporated: 9 February 2017
Registered Office: Flat 1, 120a Orby Drive, Castlereagh, Co Down, BT5 6BB
Shareholders: Martin Briggs; Robert Murphy
Officers: Martin Briggs [1976] Director; Robert Murphy [1968] Director

The Loose Cannon Brewing Company Limited
Incorporated: 11 December 2007 Employees: 12
Net Worth Deficit: £650,163 Total Assets: £266,679
Registered Office: Unit 6 Suffolk Way, Abingdon, Oxon, OX14 5JX
Major Shareholder: William Wilson Laithwaite
Officers: Barbara Anne Laithwaite, Secretary; Barbara Anne Laithwaite [1946] Director/Chairman; William Wilson Laithwaite [1982] Director/Brewer

Lord Randalls Brewery Ltd
Incorporated: 15 August 2018
Registered Office: Kemp House, 160 City Road, London, EC1V 2NX
Officers: Abigail Haigh [1993] Director/Sales

Lords Brewing Company Ltd
Incorporated: 22 September 2015 Employees: 3
Net Worth Deficit: £937 Total Assets: £37,663
Registered Office: 15 Heath House Mill, Heath House Lane, Golcar, Huddersfield, W Yorks, HD7 4JW
Major Shareholder: Grace Miriam Pegg
Officers: Timothy Melvyn Pegg [1976] Director/Company Secretary; Benjamin Martyn Ruddlesden [1983] Director/Chairman; John Leslie Slumbers [1980] Director/Salesman

Lorimers Ales (1919) Limited
Incorporated: 19 February 2013
Net Worth: £60 Total Assets: £520
Registered Office: 6 Burns Drive, Baxenden, Accrington, Lancs, BB5 2PY
Major Shareholder: Hassan Webb
Officers: Hassan Webb [1973] Director/Accountant

Lorsho Limited
Incorporated: 6 March 2013 Employees: 2
Net Worth: £100 Total Assets: £535,472
Registered Office: 2 Thor Drive, Whitworth, Rochdale, Lancs, OL12 8EU
Major Shareholder: Paul Robert Wesley
Officers: Cheryl Jane Wesley [1973] Director; Paul Robert Wesley [1972] Director

Los Perros Sueltos Brewing Co Ltd
Incorporated: 19 February 2019
Registered Office: 20 South Mill Court, Southmill Road, Bishop's Stortford, Herts, CM23 3DA
Shareholders: Dominick Chad Hollinshead; Marco Biga; Francesco Lo Bue
Officers: Dominick Chad Hollinshead [1979] Director; Francesco Lo Bue [1992] Director/Brewer [Italian]

Lost and Grounded Brewers Ltd
Incorporated: 6 October 2015 Employees: 7
Net Worth: £393,575 Total Assets: £869,701
Registered Office: 91 Whitby Road, Bristol, BS4 4AR
Officers: Howard Davies Cearns [1960] Director [Australian]; Brent Pollard [1961] Director; Alejandro Troncoso [1974] Director/Brewer [Australian]

Lost at Sea Brewing Limited
Incorporated: 8 June 2018
Registered Office: Cross York Studios, Cross York Street, Leeds, LS2 7EE
Major Shareholder: Michael Holmes
Officers: Michael Holmes [1989] Director; Oliver Holmes [1995] Director; Charles Alexander Philip Pryce [1988] Director

Lost Boys Brewery Ltd
Incorporated: 30 January 2017
Net Worth: £4 Total Assets: £4
Registered Office: Tillbrook Cottage, 153b High Street, London Colney, St Albans, Herts, AL2 1RP
Officers: Mark Hamilton Howarth, Secretary; Jonathan Hamilton Howarth [1993] Director/Warehouse Assistant; Joshua James Kitt [1994] Director/Carpenter; Jordan Manfre [1993] Director/Community Support Officer; George Sanderson [1993] Director/Recruitment Consultant

Lost Industry Brewing Limited
Incorporated: 6 August 2013
Net Worth Deficit: £13,484 *Total Assets:* £25,969
Registered Office: Lloyd Chambers, 139 Carlton Road, Worksop, Notts, S81 7AD
Major Shareholder: Lesley Hazel Elizabeth Seaton
Officers: Lesley Hazel Elizabeth Seaton [1957] Director

Lost Roots Limited
Incorporated: 26 January 2017
Registered Office: 3rd Floor, 86-90 Paul Street, London, EC2A 4NE
Shareholders: Jack Calderwood; Alexander Maximilian Carlton Heal
Officers: Jack Calderwood [1992] Director/Consultant; Alexander Maximilian Carlton Heal [1992] Director/Analyst

Lost Skulls Brewing Company Limited
Incorporated: 22 March 2018
Registered Office: 8 Chalford Road, London, SE21 8BX
Major Shareholder: Richard Martin
Officers: Richard Martin [1979] Director/Marketing Consultant

Loud Shirt Brewing Co Ltd
Incorporated: 29 February 2016
Net Worth Deficit: £50,816 *Total Assets:* £175,436
Registered Office: Unit 5 Bell Tower Industrial Estate, Roedean Road, Brighton, BN2 5RU
Shareholders: Martyn Kenneth Batchelor; Michael Robert Thomson
Officers: Martyn Kenneth Bachelor [1957] Director/Brewer; Michael Robert Thomson [1963] Director/Brewer

Lough Neagh Distillers - 1837 Ltd
Incorporated: 26 November 2018
Registered Office: Inverlodge, 51 Bannfoot Road, Derrytrasna, Co Armagh, BT66 6PH
Major Shareholder: Vernon Fox
Officers: Vernon Fox [1973] Director [Irish]

Loyal City Brewing Company Ltd
Incorporated: 25 April 2017 *Employees:* 5
Net Worth Deficit: £9,292 *Total Assets:* £12,013
Registered Office: Suite 1a, Shire Business Park, Wainwright Road, Worcester, WR4 9FA
Officers: Steven Michael Bradley [1967] Director/Retired Emergency Service Worker; Miranda Caroline Coles [1966] Director/Accountant; Melvyn John Langford [1961] Director/Retired; Keith Lawrence [1964] Director; Stephen Paul Overall [1968] Director/Computer Programmer

Luckie Drinks Ltd
Incorporated: 20 June 2018
Registered Office: Unit 24 Fife Renewables and Innovation Centre Ajax Way, Leven, Fife, KY8 3RS
Major Shareholder: Lee Murray
Officers: Lee Murray [1969] Director

Lucky 7 Beer Co Ltd
Incorporated: 10 January 2014 *Employees:* 1
Net Worth Deficit: £22,412 *Total Assets:* £25,098
Registered Office: Brooklands, Albion Terrace, Hay on Wye, Hereford, HR3 5AP
Major Shareholder: Luke Llewellyn Manifold
Officers: Luke Llewellyn Manifold [1978] Director

Lucky Cat Brewery Limited
Incorporated: 23 August 2018
Registered Office: 305 Elmsleigh Drive, Leigh on Sea, Essex, SS9 4JP
Major Shareholder: William Frederick Evans
Officers: William Frederick Evans [1987] Director/Actuary

Lucky Shaman Limited
Incorporated: 22 March 2018
Registered Office: 52b Stirling Close, Stevenage, Herts, SG2 8TQ
Officers: Kennzo Eddy Thomas Southwell, Secretary; Kennzo Eddy Thomas Southwell [1988] Director/Nurseryman

Luddite Brewing Company Limited
Incorporated: 13 February 2017
Registered Office: Calder Vale Hotel, Millfield Road, Horbury, W Yorks, WF4 5EB
Parent: Luddite Industries Limited
Officers: Timothy James Murphy [1961] Director; Gary Portman [1962] Director; Ian Sizer [1961] Director

Luddites Revenge Ltd
Incorporated: 31 May 2016
Registered Office: 7 Rock Edge, Liversedge, W Yorks, WF15 6DY
Major Shareholder: Albert Richard Tyas
Officers: Albert Richard Tyas [1985] Director/Engineer

Ludlow Brewing Company Limited
Incorporated: 11 January 2006 *Employees:* 32
Net Worth: £1,137,569 *Total Assets:* £1,654,475
Registered Office: The Railway Shed, Station Drive, Ludlow, Salop, SY8 2PQ
Shareholders: Gary Edward Walters; Alison Marie Walters
Officers: Alison Marie Walters, Secretary/Administrator; Alison Marie Walters [1971] Director/Administrator; Gary Edward Walters [1971] Director/Brewer

Luxbev Limited
Incorporated: 4 October 2017
Registered Office: 71-75 Shelton Street, Covent Garden, London, WC2H 9JQ
Major Shareholder: Hernando Ramirez
Officers: Hernando Ramirez, Secretary; Hernando Ramirez [1969] Director [French]

LVS Bottling Limited
Incorporated: 10 January 2013
Net Worth Deficit: £455,770 *Total Assets:* £211,197
Registered Office: Unit 1A Townfoot Industrial Estate, Brampton, Cumbria, CA8 1SW
Major Shareholder: Navinder Kaur Gill
Officers: Navinder Kaur Gill [1977] Director/Computer Analyst

Lyme Bay Brewing Limited
Incorporated: 18 January 2007
Net Worth: £53,803 *Total Assets:* £84,308
Registered Office: Malt House, Mill Lane, Lyme Regis, Dorset, DT7 3PU
Officers: Wesley Thomas Dowell [1985] Director/General Manager; Elliot William Herbert [1979] Director/Manager; Daniel Peter Smith [1974] Director/Manager

Lymestone Brewery Limited
Incorporated: 13 June 2008 *Employees:* 21
Net Worth: £28,668 *Total Assets:* £309,822
Registered Office: Unit 5 Mount Industrial Estate, Mount Road, Stone, Staffs, ST15 8LL
Major Shareholder: Ian James Bradford
Officers: Ian James Bradford [1961] Director; Vivienne Mary Bradford [1963] Director

Macclesfield Brewing Company Ltd
Incorporated: 29 July 2015
Net Worth: £450 *Total Assets:* £931
Registered Office: 76 Brown Street, Macclesfield, Cheshire, SK11 6RY
Shareholder: David Harrison-Ward
Officers: Joanne Harrison-Ward, Secretary; David Harrison-Ward [1976] Director/Brewer

Mad Cat Brewery Limited
Incorporated: 11 May 2012
Net Worth Deficit: £35,760 *Total Assets:* £36,878
Registered Office: 20 Marigold Drive, Sittingbourne, Kent, ME10 4BZ
Major Shareholder: Peter Anthony Meaney
Officers: Peter Anthony Meaney [1961] Director

Mad Dog Brewing Co Ltd
Incorporated: 7 April 2014
Net Worth Deficit: £9,074 *Total Assets:* £42,374
Registered Office: Shed 4 Unit 9 Park Farm Plough Road, Penperlleni, Pontypool, Monmouthshire, NP4 0AL
Major Shareholder: Alexis Morgan Jones
Officers: Lee Nicholas Dunning [1967] Finance Director; Alexis Morgan Jones [1976] Director/Head Brewer

Mad Scientists Pty. Ltd
Incorporated: 14 June 2016
Registered Office: 125 Wood Street, London, EC2V 7AW
Major Shareholder: Shane Welch
Officers: Shane Welch [1979] Director/Craft Brewer [American]

The Mad Yank Brewery Ltd
Incorporated: 15 December 2017
Registered Office: Tad Accountancy Services, 106 The Avenue, Pinner, Middlesex, HA5 5BJ
Shareholders: Grant Kelly Graeber; Larissa Michelle Graeber
Officers: Grant Kelly Graeber [1978] Director/Chief Executive [American]; Larissa Michelle Graeber [1979] Director/Chief Executive [German]

The Madchester Brewing Company Limited
Incorporated: 24 February 2016
Registered Office: 122 Irlam Road, Urmston, Manchester, M41 6NA
Shareholder: Thomas Michael Slee
Officers: Russell Otterwell [1957] Director; Thomas Michael Slee [1975] Director

Maestro Brew Ltd
Incorporated: 8 May 2017
Registered Office: 12 John Princes Street, London, W1G 0JR
Major Shareholder: Ken Phong Lau
Officers: Ken Phong Lau [1981] Director

Magee,Marshall and Company,Limited
Incorporated: 22 March 1888
Net Worth: £1,000 *Total Assets:* £1,000
Registered Office: 8 Rushlake Drive, Halliwell, Bolton, Lancs, BL1 3RL
Officers: Edward Ian Mather [1976] Director/Brewer

Magic Rock Brewing Company Ltd
Incorporated: 9 September 2010 *Employees:* 32
Net Worth: £1,477,245 *Total Assets:* £2,827,454
Registered Office: Willow Park Business Centre, Willow Lane, Huddersfield, W Yorks, HD1 5EB
Major Shareholder: Richard Oliver Burhouse
Officers: Adam Lee Bamforth [1970] Director/Chartered Accountant; Richard Oliver Burhouse [1975] Creative Director; Justin St Clair Maitland [1967] Director/Sales Co-ordinator [Swedish]

Magna Bottling Limited
Incorporated: 19 January 2004
Net Worth: £23,653 *Total Assets:* £134,738
Registered Office: 31 Princess Drive, Sawston, Cambridge, CB22 3DL
Major Shareholder: Roger Dennis Chetwynd Jay
Officers: Roger Dennis Chetwynd Jay [1949] Director/Brewer

Magna Brewery Limited
Incorporated: 16 January 2004
Net Worth: £22,442 *Total Assets:* £133,486
Registered Office: 31 Princess Drive, Sawston, Cambridge, CB22 3DL
Major Shareholder: Roger Dennis Chetwynd Jay
Officers: Roger Dennis Chetwynd Jay [1949] Director/Brewer

Makemake Beer Ltd
Incorporated: 15 March 2018
Registered Office: Inglenook, Main Road, Chichester, W Sussex, PO18 8RR
Major Shareholder: Marc Renouf
Officers: Marc Renouf [1987] Director

Makeshift Brewing Company Limited
Incorporated: 12 September 2017
Registered Office: 2 Oak Avenue, Ormskirk, Lancs, L39 3PA
Shareholders: Neil Smith; Michelle Smith
Officers: Michelle Smith [1978] Director; Neil Smith [1971] Director

Maldon Brewing Company Limited
Incorporated: 15 April 2002
Net Worth: £78,663 *Total Assets:* £132,765
Registered Office: The Stable Brewery, Silver Street, Maldon, Essex, CM9 4QE
Shareholders: Michael Frederick Farmer; Jessica Elizabeth Farmer; Nigel Alfred Farmer; Christine Mary Farmer
Officers: Christine Mary Farmer, Secretary/Tourist Information Officer; Christine Mary Farmer [1956] Director/Tourist Information Officer; Nigel Alfred Farmer [1953] Director/Brewer

Malt, The Brewery Limited
Incorporated: 25 July 2011 *Employees:* 9
Net Worth Deficit: £19,041 *Total Assets:* £143,162
Registered Office: The Mill House, Boundary Road, Loudwater, High Wycombe, Bucks, HP10 9QN
Shareholders: Nicholas Paul Watson; Jenny Watson
Officers: Jenny Watson [1974] Director; Nicholas Paul Watson [1971] Director

Malts & Hops Brewing Limited
Incorporated: 16 February 2018
Registered Office: 10 King Charles House, Wandon Road, London, SW6 2JH
Officers: Madelaine Grace Fox [1976] Director; Paul Geoffrey Goodhew [1977] Director

Malvern Hills Brewery Limited
Incorporated: 6 July 1998
Net Worth: £29,420 *Total Assets:* £58,650
Registered Office: 15 West Malvern Road, Malvern, Worcs, WR14 4ND
Major Shareholder: Julian Mark Hawthornthwaite
Officers: Frances Casey, Secretary; Frances Caroline Casey [1957] Company Secretary/Director [Irish]; Julian Mark Hawthornthwaite [1960] Director/Brewer

Manchester Union Brewery Limited
Incorporated: 14 November 2016
Net Worth Deficit: £16,677 *Total Assets:* £11,241
Registered Office: 96d North Western Street, Manchester, M12 6JL
Officers: William Evans [1979] Director; Dr Ian Johnson [1972] Director/Software Engineer; Simon Pogson [1971] Director; Jamie Mathew Scahill [1973] Director/Marketing Manager

Manning Brewers Ltd
Incorporated: 26 July 2013 *Employees:* 5
Net Worth: £186,210 *Total Assets:* £340,175
Registered Office: Bromley House, Spindle Street, Congleton, Cheshire, CW12 1QN
Officers: Mark David Greaves [1962] Director; Amanda Manning [1953] Director; David John Manning [1951] Director/Chemist; Joseph Vincent Manning [1984] Director/General Manager; Michael Jan Manning [1990] Director; Michael William Potts [1991] Sales Director; Edward David Whitehead [1974] Director

Mansfield Brewery Trading Limited
Incorporated: 27 November 1947
Registered Office: Marston's House, Brewery Road, Wolverhampton, W Midlands, WV1 4JT
Parent: Mansfield Brewery Limited
Officers: Anne Marie Brennan, Secretary; Andrew Andonis Andrea [1969] Managing Director; Ralph Graham Findlay [1961] Director; Richard James Westwood [1952] Director

Mantle Brewery Limited
Incorporated: 5 July 2011
Net Worth: £25,422 *Total Assets:* £206,162
Registered Office: Unit 16 Pentood Industrial Estate, Cardigan, Dyfed, SA43 3AG
Shareholders: Dominique Kimber; Ian Kimber
Officers: Ian Kimber [1972] Director/Mechanical Engineer

Many Hands Brewery Ltd
Incorporated: 10 October 2017
Registered Office: The Airfield, Dunkeswell, Honiton, Devon, EX14 4LF
Shareholders: Richard Thomas Alston Charlton; Simon Alexander Pitts
Officers: Simon Alexander Pitts [1977] Director

Map Kernow Ltd.
Incorporated: 26 April 2002
Net Worth: £62 *Total Assets:* £62
Registered Office: 6 Wolfe Crescent, Rotherhithe, London, SE16 6SF
Major Shareholder: Roger Alan Courtenay
Officers: Shaun Foran Courtenay, Secretary; Dr. Roger Alan Courtenay [1970] Director/Economist

Marble Beers Limited
Incorporated: 29 December 1995 *Employees:* 46
Net Worth: £355,336 *Total Assets:* £1,096,277
Registered Office: Richard House, Winckley Square, Preston, Lancs, PR1 3HP
Major Shareholder: Janet Alison Rogers
Officers: Matthew James Williams, Secretary; Janet Alison Rogers [1963] Director

The Marches Brewery Limited
Incorporated: 15 January 2015
Registered Office: Shoreside, Warren Road, Rhosneigr, Anglesey, LL64 5QT
Major Shareholder: Adam Crickmore
Officers: Adam Crickmore [1984] Director

Marchingtons Ltd
Incorporated: 26 June 2017
Net Worth Deficit: £5,373 *Total Assets:* £5,931
Registered Office: Unit 10965 Chynoweth House, Trevissome Park, Truro, Cornwall, TR4 8UN
Major Shareholder: Robert Frank Marchington
Officers: Dr Robert Frank Marchington [1983] Director

Maregade Brew Co. Ltd.
Incorporated: 8 June 2015
Net Worth Deficit: £979 *Total Assets:* £4,780
Registered Office: 331J Mare Street, London, E8 1HY
Major Shareholder: Ian John Morton
Officers: Ian Morton [1975] Director

The Margate Brewery Limited
Incorporated: 10 July 2015
Net Worth Deficit: £2,563 *Total Assets:* £71,619
Registered Office: 1 Fairfield Mansions, Fifth Avenue, Cliftonville, Margate, Kent, CT9 2JL
Major Shareholder: David John Gorton
Officers: David John Gorton [1955] Director/Fire Officer (Retired)

Market Bosworth Brewery Ltd
Incorporated: 29 March 2017
Net Worth Deficit: £1,700 *Total Assets:* £5,964
Registered Office: T03 The Atkins Building, Lower Bond Street, Hinckley, Leics, LE10 1QU
Shareholders: Jonathan Skinner; Richard John Brine
Officers: Richard John Brine [1969] Director/IT Consultant; Jonathan Skinner [1976] Director

The Marlpool Brewing Company Limited
Incorporated: 21 April 2010 *Employees:* 2
Net Worth: £5,285 *Total Assets:* £22,637
Registered Office: 5 Breach Road, Heanor, Derbys, DE75 7NJ
Shareholders: Daniel Christopher McAuley; Francesca Annette McAuley; James Andrew McAuley
Officers: Daniel Christopher McAuley [1958] Director/Printer; James Andrew McAuley [1961] Director/Printer

Marourde Limited
Incorporated: 17 January 2017
Registered Office: Suite 5, 10 Churchill Square, West Malling, Kent, ME19 4YU
Major Shareholder: Evelyn George William Boscawen
Officers: Evelyn George William Boscawen [1979] Director

Marston's Acquisitions Limited
Incorporated: 20 July 1887
Net Worth: £32,300,000 *Total Assets:* £44,600,000
Registered Office: Marston's House, Brewery Road, Wolverhampton, W Midlands, WV1 4JT
Parent: Marston's Corporate Holdings Limited
Officers: Anne Marie Brennan, Secretary; Andrew Andonis Andrea [1969] Director; Ralph Graham Findlay [1961] Director/Chief Executive; Edward Hancock [1975] Director; Iain Kenneth Jackson [1969] Director/Chartered Surveyor; William Whittaker [1958] Director

Marston's PLC
Incorporated: 14 May 1890 *Employees:* 14,298
Net Worth: £957,600,000 *Total Assets:* £3,031,200,000
Registered Office: Marston's House, Brewery Road, Wolverhampton, W Midlands, WV1 4JT
Officers: Anne Marie Brennan, Secretary; Andrew Andonis Andrea [1969] Director; Carolyn Jane Bradley [1964] Director; Ralph Graham Findlay [1961] Director; Catherine Janet Glickman [1957] HR Director; Edward Matthew Giles Roberts [1963] Director; Robin Rowland [1961] Director; William John Rucker [1963] Director

Mart's Brewing Company Ltd
Incorporated: 11 December 2014
Net Worth Deficit: £6,398 *Total Assets:* £4,895
Registered Office: 56 Barthomley Road, Birches Head, Stoke on Trent, Staffs, ST1 6NJ
Shareholders: Jason Barlow; Susan Mary Grocott; Will Robert Haywood
Officers: Jason Barlow [1969] Director/Publican; Susan Mary Grocott [1958] Director/Publican; William Robert Haywood [1979] Director

Martland Mill Brewery Limited
Incorporated: 21 February 2014
Net Worth: £9,122 *Total Assets:* £88,921
Registered Office: Unit 5 Otterwood Square, Martland Mill, Wigan, Lancs, WN5 0LF
Major Shareholder: Paul Nicholas Wood
Officers: Mary Delia Wood [1974] Director; Paul Nicholas Wood [1965] Director

Mash Brewery Limited
Incorporated: 20 August 2012
Net Worth Deficit: £114,694 *Total Assets:* £33,184
Registered Office: Ravenswood, Park Road, Winchester, Hants, SO22 6AA
Shareholders: Graham Mark Turner; Andrew Ian Wythes; John Anthony Willmore
Officers: Doctor Graham Mark Turner [1964] Director/Brewer; John Anthony Willmore [1952] Director/Project Manager; Andrew Ian Wythes [1967] Director/Marketing Manager

Mashdown Brewery Ltd.
Incorporated: 26 March 2014
Net Worth Deficit: £3,637 *Total Assets:* £1,577
Registered Office: 58 Castlewellan Road, Banbridge, Co Down, BT32 4JF
Major Shareholder: Christopher Barrie Todd
Officers: Dr. Christopher Barrie Todd [1982] Director/Research Chemist [Irish]; Dr. Moira Helen Todd [1982] Director/Consultant Chemical Engineer [Irish]

Mashionistas Brewing Company Limited
Incorporated: 2 January 2018
Registered Office: 45 Rochester Road, Coventry, Warwicks, CV5 6AF
Shareholders: Fiona Isabelle Swann; Simon David Harper; Jonathan Richard Cook
Officers: Jonathan Richard Cook [1972] Director/Design Sculptor; Simon David Harper [1969] Director/IT Manager; Fiona Isabelle Swann [1970] Director/Marketer

Matheson Brewers Ltd
Incorporated: 27 November 2018
Registered Office: Burns Cottage, Cornhill, Banff, Aberdeenshire, AB45 2DL
Shareholders: Angus Iain Matheson; Meg Walker Matheson
Officers: Angus Iain Matheson [1988] Director/Master Brewer

Matlock Brewing Company Limited
Incorporated: 5 March 2015
Net Worth Deficit: £18,442 *Total Assets:* £47,865
Registered Office: South Barn, Farm Lane, Matlock, Derbys, DE4 3GZ
Major Shareholder: Robert Atkin
Officers: Robert Atkin [1957] Director/Entrepreneur

Matterdale Brewery Limited
Incorporated: 29 November 2017
Registered Office: Rushgill House, Dockray, Penrith, Cumbria, CA11 0JY
Shareholders: Helen Louise Ratcliffe; Nicholas Ratcliffe
Officers: Helen Louise Ratcliffe [1965] Director; Nicholas Ratcliffe [1965] Director

Matthews Brewing Company Ltd
Incorporated: 12 May 2005
Net Worth Deficit: £20,915 *Total Assets:* £37,096
Registered Office: 2 Woodborough Hill, Peasedown St John, Bath, BA2 8LN
Shareholders: Susan Mary Appleby; Stuart Richard Matthews
Officers: Susan Appleby, Secretary; Stuart Richard Matthews [1963] Director

Mauldon's Limited
Incorporated: 13 January 2000 *Employees:* 12
Net Worth: £54,785 *Total Assets:* £521,032
Registered Office: 13 Churchfield Road, Sudbury, Suffolk, CO10 2YA
Shareholder: Alison Joy Sims
Officers: Alison Joy Sims, Secretary; Alison Joy Sims [1954] Director; Stephen Sims [1954] Managing Director

Maverick Brewing Company Ltd
Incorporated: 11 February 2019
Registered Office: 2 Laurel Cottages, Longmoor Road, Greatham, Hants, GU33 6AQ
Major Shareholder: Martin James Charles Hoddinott
Officers: Martin James Charles Hoddinott [1976] Director/Head of Mayhem

Maxim Brewery Limited
Incorporated: 6 March 2010
Registered Office: 1 Gadwall Road, Houghton-le-Spring, Co Durham, DH4 5NL
Major Shareholder: Mark Anderson
Officers: Mark Anderson [1962] Director; Susan Anderson [1958] Director/Accounts Manager; Glen Andrew Whale [1974] Director/Brewer

Mayflower Brewery Ltd
Incorporated: 19 June 2013
Previous: Terra Trader Ltd
Net Worth Deficit: £15,162 *Total Assets:* £26,604
Registered Office: 2 Woodford Street, Hindley, Wigan, Lancs, WN2 4UR
Officers: Peter Haslam, Secretary; Peter Haslam [1960] Director

Maypole Brewery Limited
Incorporated: 2 February 2005
Net Worth Deficit: £39,497 *Total Assets:* £7,988
Registered Office: North Laithes Farm, Wellow Road, Eakring, Newark, Notts, NG22 0AN
Shareholders: Robert John Neil; Sandra Dawn Neil
Officers: Robert John Neil, Secretary/Brewer; Robert John Neil [1958] Director/Brewer; Sandra Dawn Neil [1969] Director/Creche Manager

MB Collective Limited
Incorporated: 8 February 2018
Registered Office: 62 Appledore Drive, Harwood, Bolton, Lancs, BL2 4HH
Major Shareholder: Cameron McKenzie-Wilde
Officers: Cameron McKenzie-Wilde [1990] Director

MBH Tap & Shop Limited
Incorporated: 14 March 2017 *Employees:* 2
Net Worth Deficit: £2,630 *Total Assets:* £7,790
Registered Office: Willow House, Davenport Lane, Mobberley, Knutsford, Cheshire, WA16 7NB
Shareholder: Philip John Roberts
Officers: James Philip Roberts [1991] Director; Philip John Roberts [1960] Director

MBJW Brewing Limited
Incorporated: 26 July 2016
Net Worth: £5 *Total Assets:* £7,627
Registered Office: 41 Steeple Grange, Wirksworth, Matlock, Derbys, DE4 4FS
Shareholders: Mark Walters; Mark Bernhardt James Walters
Officers: Mark Bernhardt James Walters [1967] Director/Brewer

MC & P Engineering Limited
Incorporated: 24 April 2017
Net Worth: £199 *Total Assets:* £11,461
Registered Office: Flat 3, 15 Chesham Place, Brighton, BN2 1FB
Shareholder: Michael Connelly
Officers: Helen Connelly, Secretary; Michael Connelly [1986] Director/Engineering

McColl's Brewery Limited
Incorporated: 1 September 2016 *Employees:* 4
Net Worth Deficit: £140,245 *Total Assets:* £112,433
Registered Office: Unit 4 Randolph Industrial Estate, Evenwood, Bishop Auckland, Co Durham, DL14 9SJ
Shareholders: Daniel John McColl; Gemma Jayne McColl; Michael Stephenson
Officers: Daniel John McColl [1982] Director/Brewer; Gemma Jayne McColl [1978] Director/Self Employed

McGrath Davies Public Houses Limited
Incorporated: 18 July 2013 *Employees:* 8
Previous: Camden Daughter Limited
Net Worth Deficit: £1,205,330 *Total Assets:* £427,181
Registered Office: Bath House, 6-8 Bath Street, Redcliffe, Bristol, BS1 6HL
Parent: McGrath Davies Property Services Limited
Officers: Paul Davies [1955] Director; James Kirk McGrath [1964] Director

McGrath's Brewing Limited
Incorporated: 5 January 2018
Registered Office: 155-157 Donegall Pass, Belfast, BT7 1DT
Parent: Kirker Greer (Holdings) Limited
Officers: Steven Clark Pattison [1979] Director; Richard Ryan [1977] Director

McMullen & Sons, Limited
Incorporated: 1 March 1897 *Employees:* 1,129
Net Worth: £150,388,000 *Total Assets:* £171,648,000
Registered Office: 26 Old Cross, Hertford, SG14 1RD
Officers: Alison Penfold, Secretary; Charles David Brims [1950] Director/Chairman; Steven Gill [1957] Commercial Director; Alexander Brodie McMullen [1981] Director/Chartered Accountant; David Shaun McMullen [1945] Director; Fergus John McMullen [1958] Director; Thomas Peter McMullen [1976] Director; Heydon Mizon [1974] Director; Andrew Wayne Newbury [1955] Property Director; Jenny Strathern [1964] Property Director

Meantime Brewing Company Limited
Incorporated: 8 April 1999
Net Worth: £11,617,000 *Total Assets:* £20,091,000
Registered Office: One Forge End, Woking, Surrey, GU21 6DB
Parent: Asahi Europe Ltd
Officers: James Smith, Secretary; Rohan Cummings [1975] Director/Chief Financial Officer; Hector Gorosabel [1960] Director/MD Western Europe [Canadian]; Alastair Frederick Hook [1963] Managing Director; Yusuke Naritsuka [1972] Director [Japanese]

The Meanwood Brewery Ltd
Incorporated: 2 December 2016 *Employees:* 2
Net Worth Deficit: £5,977 *Total Assets:* £4,372
Registered Office: 8a Stonegate Road, Meanwood, Leeds, LS6 4YH
Shareholders: Graeme Phillips; Barry Jon Phillips
Officers: Barry Jon Phillips [1984] Director/Advisor; Graeme Phillips [1981] Director

The Mechanic Brewing Company Ltd
Incorporated: 23 January 2018
Registered Office: Railway Arch, 22a Cudworth Street, London, E1 5QU
Major Shareholder: Olga Natalia Zubrzycka
Officers: Olga Natalia Zubrzycka, Secretary; Olga Natalia Zubrzycka [1983] Director [Polish]

The Medieval Bread and Ale Company Limited
Incorporated: 19 September 2016
Registered Office: Flat 3, 14 Vanbrugh Hill, London, SE3 7UF
Shareholders: Stephen Mark McQueen; David McQueen
Officers: David McQueen [1965] Director/Lecturer; Stephen Mark McQueen [1973] Director

Melin Tap Brewhouse Limited
Incorporated: 14 December 2015
Net Worth Deficit: £810 *Total Assets:* £164
Registered Office: The Old Stables adjacent to Halfway House, Berthon Road, Little Mill, Monmouthshire, NP4 0HL
Officers: Ian Jeffrey Blacker [1958] Director/Events Manager; Peter Stanley Davies [1950] Director/Retired; Robert Michael Kenneth John James [1950] Director

Melville's Fruit Beers Limited
Incorporated: 10 May 2011
Registered Office: 6 Randolph Crescent, Edinburgh, EH3 7TH
Parent: Innis & Gunn Holdings Limited
Officers: Dougal Gunn Sharp [1972] Director

The UK Brewing Industry

Merchant City Brewing Company Limited
Incorporated: 23 November 2016 *Employees:* 2
Net Worth Deficit: £102,972 *Total Assets:* £153,921
Registered Office: Pavilion 1, Finnieston Business Park, Minerva Way, Glasgow, G3 8AU
Shareholders: Allan Douglas Rimmer; Douglas Gordon Wheatley
Officers: Allan Douglas Rimmer [1982] Director

Meridian Brewery Limited
Incorporated: 15 March 2016 *Employees:* 1
Net Worth: £100,000 *Total Assets:* £100,000
Registered Office: 12 Hatherley Road, Sidcup, Kent, DA14 4DT
Major Shareholder: William Keith O'Prey
Officers: William Keith O'Prey [1988] Director/Brewery

Merlin Brewing Company Ltd
Incorporated: 9 December 2009 *Employees:* 2
Net Worth: £88,977 *Total Assets:* £158,333
Registered Office: 52 Bessancourt, Holmes Chapel, Cheshire, CW4 7NB
Shareholders: David Peart; Susan Lesley Peart
Officers: Mark Gavin Peart, Secretary; Susan Lesley Peart, Secretary; David Peart [1960] Director; Susan Lesley Peart [1963] Director

Merrimans Brewery Ltd
Incorporated: 22 April 2015
Registered Office: 1 Brown Avenue, Leeds, LS11 0DS
Major Shareholder: Peter Winterbottom
Officers: Peter Winterbottom [1964] Director

Merrimen Brewery Limited
Incorporated: 16 April 2018
Registered Office: Unit 12 Litchborough Trading Estate, Northampton Road, Litchborough, Northants, NN12 8JB
Officers: Richard James Bustin, Secretary; Janice Anne Bustin [1960] Director; Richard James Bustin [1975] Director

Merry Miner Brewery Ltd
Incorporated: 19 October 2010 *Employees:* 2
Net Worth: £3,384 *Total Assets:* £10,003
Registered Office: Unit 2 Grendon House Farm, Grendon, Atherstone, Warwicks, CV9 3DT
Shareholders: Alan Wood; Anita Pauline Wood; Anita Pauline Wood; Alan Wood
Officers: Alan Wood [1965] Director/Brewer; Anita Pauline Wood [1969] Director/Administrator

Mersea Island Brewery & Vineyard Ltd
Incorporated: 22 May 2018
Registered Office: Mersea Vineyard, Rewsalls Lane, East Mersea, Colchester, Essex, CO5 8SX
Shareholders: Charlotte Barber; Mark Barber
Officers: Charlotte Barber [1987] Director; Jacqueline Barber [1951] Director; Mark Barber [1977] Director; Roger George William Barber [1949] Director

The Mersey Gin Company Limited
Incorporated: 24 December 2018
Registered Office: 49 Sycamore Crescent, Macclesfield, Cheshire, SK11 8LW
Major Shareholder: Gary Stuart Crosbie
Officers: Gary Stuart Crosbie [1964] Director

Metcalfe & Metcalfe Company Ltd
Incorporated: 14 September 2006
Net Worth Deficit: £22,485 *Total Assets:* £39,253
Registered Office: Amicable House, 252 Union Street, Aberdeen, AB10 1TN
Shareholders: Steven Perry Lewis; Gary Gibb
Officers: Gary Gibb [1989] Director; Steven Perry Lewis [1989] Director [American]; Margo-Rose Felicity MacNab [1990] Director

Microcosm Brewing Ltd.
Incorporated: 21 November 2014
Registered Office: 6 Milton Close, St Ives, Cambs, PE27 6TX
Major Shareholder: Sam Robert Wise
Officers: Sam Robert Wise [1993] Director

Mid-Cheshire Brewing Ltd
Incorporated: 8 October 2015 *Employees:* 1
Net Worth Deficit: £9,460 *Total Assets:* £23,950
Registered Office: 114 Grange Lane, Winsford, Cheshire, CW7 2BX
Major Shareholder: Michael Thomas Hill
Officers: Michael Thomas Hill [1956] Director/Brewer

Middle Earth Brewing Company Limited
Incorporated: 23 May 2011
Registered Office: 53 Springfield Road, Etwall, Derby, DE65 6JZ
Major Shareholder: Stephen Andrew Twells
Officers: Stephen Andrew Twells [1963] Director/Engineer

C J Middleton Limited
Incorporated: 8 November 2000 *Employees:* 8
Net Worth: £282,844 *Total Assets:* £637,332
Registered Office: Glencora, Davidston, Cromarty, Ross-shire, IV11 8XD
Major Shareholder: Jonathan Maclaren Middleton
Officers: Jennifer Cranston Middleton, Secretary; Jonathan Maclaren Middleton [1960] Director/Engineer

Midmart Limited
Incorporated: 21 January 2004
Registered Office: 13 Lussielaw Road, Edinburgh, EH9 3BX
Major Shareholder: Martin Joseph Crompton Richards
Officers: Ruth Margaret Hill Richards, Secretary; Martin Joseph Crompton Richards [1952] Director/Lecturer; Ruth Margaret Hill Richards [1958] Director/Secretary

Midshires Brewery Limited
Incorporated: 10 September 2018
Registered Office: 42 Derby Road, Lower Kilburn, Belper, Derbys, DE56 0NG
Shareholders: David William Sidley; Helen Stephens
Officers: David William Sidley [1981] Director/Head Brewer

Mighty Medicine Brewing Company Ltd
Incorporated: 10 April 2015
Net Worth Deficit: £50,055 *Total Assets:* £85,492
Registered Office: Corner House, 28 Huddersfield Road, Milnrow, Rochdale, Lancs, OL16 3QF
Major Shareholder: John Harold Stoner
Officers: John Harold Stoner [1973] Director

The Mighty Oak Brewing Co. Limited
Incorporated: 14 August 1995 *Employees:* 17
Net Worth: £619,697 *Total Assets:* £1,241,703
Registered Office: 14b West Station Yard, Spital Road, Maldon, Essex, CM9 6TW
Shareholders: John James Boyce; Ruth Elizabeth O'Neill
Officers: Ruth Elizabeth O'Neill, Secretary; John James Boyce [1952] Director/Engineer; Ruth Elizabeth O'Neill [1951] Director/Secretary

Mile Tree Brewery Limited
Incorporated: 16 December 2011
Net Worth Deficit: £85,292 *Total Assets:* £29,142
Registered Office: Brandon House, 90 The Broadway, Chesham, Bucks, HP5 1EG
Major Shareholder: Richard Alan Matthews
Officers: Richard Alan Matthews [1962] Director

Mill Lane Brewing Company Limited
Incorporated: 5 May 2017
Registered Office: 5 The Old Chapel, Mill Lane, Stebbing, Dunmow, Essex, CM6 3SN
Officers: Bernard Ivan Bazley [1958] IT Director; Peter Parkinson [1965] Director/Retired

Mill Valley Brewery Limited
Incorporated: 5 January 2016
Net Worth Deficit: £689 *Total Assets:* £15,323
Registered Office: Unit 3 Woodroyd Mills, South Parade, Cleckheaton, W Yorks, BD19 3AF
Major Shareholder: Stephen John Hemingway
Officers: Stephen John Hemingway [1961] Director/Sales Manager

The Millis Brewing Company Limited
Incorporated: 11 July 2002
Net Worth Deficit: £35,137 *Total Assets:* £69,023
Registered Office: 48 Vigilant Way, Riverview Park, Gravesend, Kent, DA12 4PP
Officers: Miriam Marjorie Audrey Millis, Secretary/Housewife; John Eric William Millis [1947] Director/Retired; Miriam Marjorie Audrey Millis [1943] Director/Housewife

The Millstone Brewery Limited
Incorporated: 22 May 2002
Net Worth: £7,605 *Total Assets:* £61,587
Registered Office: Unit 4 Vale Mill, Micklehurst Road, Mossley, Ashton under Lyne, Lancs, OL5 9JL
Shareholders: Nicholas John Boughton; Jonathan Hunt
Officers: Nicholas John Boughton, Secretary/Director; Nicholas John Boughton [1961] Director; Jonathan Hunt [1964] Director

Milltown Brewing Co. Ltd
Incorporated: 13 January 2011 *Employees:* 1
Net Worth: £56,403 *Total Assets:* £136,264
Registered Office: 31 Haigh House Hill, Lindley Moor, Huddersfield, W Yorks, HD3 3SZ
Major Shareholder: Neil Moorhouse
Officers: Neil Moorhouse [1963] Director/Brewer

Milton and Mortimer Ltd
Incorporated: 22 July 2016
Net Worth Deficit: £21,788 *Total Assets:* £30,168
Registered Office: Hillside House East, Church Road, Todmorden, Lancs, OL14 8HP
Shareholders: Christopher Milton; David Mortimer
Officers: Christopher Paul Milton [1959] Director/IT Consultant; David Mortimer [1961] Director/University Lecturer

The Milton Brewery Cambridge Limited
Incorporated: 10 June 1999
Net Worth: £278,776 *Total Assets:* £1,008,562
Registered Office: Pegasus House, Pembroke Avenue, Waterbeach, Cambridge, CB25 9PY
Shareholders: Richard Tom Naisby; Michael Edward Morley
Officers: Richard Tom Naisby, Secretary/Director; Timothy John Cowper [1974] Director/Brewer; Clive Fussell [1972] Director/Chartered Structural Engineer; Dr Michael Edward Morley [1973] Director/Doctor of Medicine; Richard Tom Naisby [1973] Director; Helen Margaret Parham [1970] Director/Lighting Designer

Missing Link Brewing Ltd
Incorporated: 2 May 2017 *Employees:* 3
Net Worth Deficit: £12,286 *Total Assets:* £11,439
Registered Office: Suite 6, 141-143 South Road, Haywards Heath, W Sussex, RH16 4LZ
Major Shareholder: Jeremy Mark Cook
Officers: Jeremy Mark Cook [1974] Director/Business Owner

Mister A's Beer Company Limited
Incorporated: 28 March 2018
Registered Office: 9 Hillbrow Close, Rowland's Castle, Hants, PO9 6DJ
Shareholders: Simon Adey; Miles Harding
Officers: Simon Adey [1968] Director; Miles Harding [1967] Director

Miswell Brewery Ltd
Incorporated: 3 February 2017
Registered Office: Miswell House, Miswell, Tring, Herts, HP23 4JT
Major Shareholder: Geoff Owen Peppiatt
Officers: Geoff Peppiatt, Secretary; Geoff Owen Peppiatt [1953] Director; Jonathan Peppiatt [1990] Director/Client Relationship Manager

Mitchell Ward Limited
Incorporated: 19 June 2013
Net Worth Deficit: £18,516 *Total Assets:* £844
Registered Office: 104 Whitby Road, Ellesmere Port, Cheshire, CH65 0AB
Shareholders: Leslie Ward; Julie Perkins
Officers: Julie Ann Perkins, Secretary; Leslie Robert Ward [1955] Director/Manufacturing

The Mobberley Brewhouse Limited
Incorporated: 17 May 2011 *Employees:* 9
Previous: Mobberley Fine Ales Limited
Net Worth Deficit: £132,157 *Total Assets:* £299,698
Registered Office: Willow House, Davenport Lane, Mobberley, Knutsford, Cheshire, WA16 7NB
Shareholders: Philip John Roberts; James Philip Roberts
Officers: James Philip Roberts [1991] Director; Philip John Roberts [1960] Director

Modha Ales Ltd
Incorporated: 9 April 2014
Net Worth Deficit: £53,404 *Total Assets:* £2,959
Registered Office: 188 Uppingham Road, Leicester, LE5 0QG
Major Shareholder: Bhaveshchandra Modha
Officers: Bhaveshchandra Modha [1983] Director

Molson Coors Brewing Company (UK) Limited
Incorporated: 3 March 1888 *Employees:* 1,993
Net Worth: £332,433,984 *Total Assets:* £878,267,008
Registered Office: 137 High Street, Burton on Trent, Staffs, DE14 1JZ
Parent: Molson Coors Holdings Limited
Officers: Kristin Wolfe, Secretary; Simon Kerry [1970] Director; James Christian Shearer [1980] Marketing Director; Philip Mark Whitehead [1977] Director

Monachis Ltd
Incorporated: 23 January 2019
Registered Office: Opus @ Pyramid, Palmyra Square South, Warrington, Cheshire, WA1 1BL
Shareholders: William James Carr; Rob John Griffiths
Officers: William James Carr [1977] Director

Moncada Brewery Limited
Incorporated: 2 July 2010
Net Worth Deficit: £1,609,035 *Total Assets:* £1,065,707
Registered Office: Ground Floor, 45 Pall Mall, London, SW1Y 5JG
Shareholders: Eleonora Eliasco; Julio Guillermo Moncada
Officers: Julio Guillermo Moncada [1977] Director [Argentinian]

Mondo Brewing Company Limited
Incorporated: 9 September 2014 *Employees:* 9
Net Worth: £120,911 *Total Assets:* £1,243,654
Registered Office: 86 Stewarts Road, Battersea, London, SW8 4UG
Major Shareholder: James Keith Matteson
Officers: James Keith Matteson [1945] Director [American]; Todd Matteson [1980] Director/Brewer [American]; Thomas Arthur Palmer III [1973] Director/Brewer [American]

Monkey Shed Estate Brewing Co Ltd
Incorporated: 9 June 2017
Registered Office: Beaumont, Woodbury Lane, Norton, Worcester, WR5 2PT
Major Shareholder: Richard Bakewell Phillips
Officers: Richard Bakewell Phillips [1966] Director/Farmer

Monks Bridge Brewery Ltd
Incorporated: 3 December 2014
Registered Office: Chandos House, School Lane, Buckingham, MK18 1HD
Shareholders: Julian Mark Piercey; Kim Piercey
Officers: Christopher Dunn [1981] Director; Julian Piercey [1959] Director; Kim Piercey [1960] Director

The Monks Well Brewing Company Limited
Incorporated: 15 August 2017
Registered Office: Chilkoot, Stotfield Road, Lossiemouth, Moray, IV31 6QS
Major Shareholder: Harry Watt Halkett
Officers: Harry Watt Halkett [1954] Director

Monty's Brewery Limited
Incorporated: 17 June 2008 *Employees:* 10
Net Worth: £30,984 *Total Assets:* £420,498
Registered Office: Unit 1 Castle Works, Hendomen, Montgomery, Powys, SY15 6EZ
Shareholders: Pamela Honeyman; Russell James Honeyman
Officers: Russell James Honeyman, Secretary; Pamela Honeyman [1970] Director; Russell James Honeyman [1959] Director

Moo Brewing Company Limited
Incorporated: 7 October 2015
Registered Office: Charlton Farm Cottage, Lower Farm Road, Maidstone, Kent, ME17 4DB
Major Shareholder: John William Murdoch
Officers: John William Murdoch [1985] Director/Engineer

Moody Fox Ltd.
Incorporated: 2 December 2016
Net Worth Deficit: £4,938 *Total Assets:* £8,975
Registered Office: Hilcote Country Club, Hilcote Lane, Hilcote, Alfreton, Derbys, DE55 5HR
Officers: Jody Nicholas Fox [1980] Director/Master Brewer; Daniel Moody [1981] Director/Master Brewer

Moody Goose Brewery Limited
Incorporated: 13 November 2014
Net Worth Deficit: £3,575 *Total Assets:* £14,306
Registered Office: 114 London Road, Braintree, Essex, CM77 7PU
Shareholders: Marian Sophia Dennison; Angus John Hicks
Officers: Angus John Hicks, Secretary; Marian Sophia Dennison [1963] Director/Publican

Moody Stag Limited
Incorporated: 2 May 2018
Registered Office: Unit 3, 175 Woodville Street, Glasgow, G51 2RQ
Shareholders: Davide Angeletti; Ovenbird Coffee Roasters Ltd
Officers: Davide Angeletti [1970] Director/Owner [Italian]

Moogbrew Ltd
Incorporated: 28 August 2014
Net Worth Deficit: £4,285 *Total Assets:* £11,315
Registered Office: Meads End, Ye Meads, Taplow, Maidenhead, Berks, SL6 0DH
Major Shareholder: Margaret Doris Cornelia Williams
Officers: David Idwal Williams [1963] Director/Chief Executive; Margaret Doris Cornelia Williams [1971] Director/Engagement Manager

Moon Cartel Limited
Incorporated: 24 December 2018
Registered Office: Flat 6, 14 Mayfield Road, Whalley Range, Manchester, M16 8FT
Shareholders: Bernadette Leearna Snell; Catherine Sabrina Snell
Officers: Bernadette Leearna Snell [1989] Director/Software Engineer

Moonshine Drinks Limited
Incorporated: 17 January 2011 *Employees:* 1
Net Worth Deficit: £23,266 *Total Assets:* £63,937
Registered Office: Grafton House, 67 Loughborough Road, West Bridgford, Nottingham, NG2 7LA
Major Shareholder: Ian Hamilton Walker
Officers: Robert Constable-Maxwell [1933] Director; Christopher James Lightbody [1969] Director; Ian Hamilton Walker [1956] Director

Moor Beer Company Limited
Incorporated: 24 November 2005 *Employees:* 19
Net Worth: £694,090 *Total Assets:* £1,256,542
Registered Office: Ground Floor, Blackbrook Gate 1, Blackbrook Business Park, Taunton, Somerset, TA1 2PX
Shareholders: Justin Hawke; Maryann Hawke
Officers: Maryann Min-Yen Hawke, Secretary/Director [British/American]; Justin Craig Hawke [1971] Director [British/American]; Maryann Min-Yen Hawke [1971] Director [British/American]

Moorhouse's Brewery Ltd
Incorporated: 13 November 1985 *Employees:* 35
Previous: Moorhouses Brewery (Burnley) Limited
Net Worth: £13,300 *Total Assets:* £5,641,973
Registered Office: The Brewery, 250 Accrington Road, Burnley, Lancs, BB11 5EN
Officers: Ian William Parkinson [1965] Director; William Barry Parkinson [1940] Director; David Lee Williams [1967] Director

Moorside Brewery Ltd
Incorporated: 14 April 2014
Net Worth Deficit: £2,731 *Total Assets:* £2,370
Registered Office: 34 Dove Way, Kirkby Mills Industrial Estate, Kirkbymoorside, N Yorks, YO62 6QR
Major Shareholder: Helen Sheard
Officers: Helen Elizabeth Sheard, Secretary; Helen Elizabeth Sheard [1951] Director/Occupational Therapist

The Moot Oak Brewing Company Limited
Incorporated: 13 December 2017
Registered Office: Red Lion Inn, Matlock Green, Matlock, Derbys, DE4 3BT
Shareholders: Lee Mews; Philip Mews
Officers: Lee Mews [1976] Director; Philip Mews [1949] Director

Morecambe Bay Wines Limited
Incorporated: 25 January 2013 *Employees:* 28
Net Worth: £521,594 *Total Assets:* £1,638,859
Registered Office: Morecambe Bay Wines, Newgate, White Lund Industrial Estate, Morecambe, Lancs, LA3 3PT
Major Shareholder: Peter Michael Cross
Officers: Qi [1986] Director [Chinese]; Peter Michael Cross [1958] Director; Malcolm John Savage [1955] Director

Mortimer Brewing Company Ltd
Incorporated: 11 January 2018
Registered Office: 23 Reading Road, Cholsey, Wallingford, Oxon, OX10 9HL
Shareholders: Jonathan David Carroll; Michael Jon Udale-Clarke
Officers: Jonathan David Carroll [1968] Director; Michael Jon Udale-Clarke [1969] Director

Mortlake Brewery Ltd
Incorporated: 4 March 2013
Registered Office: 21 Glebe Road, London, SW13 0DR
Major Shareholder: Scott Douglas Brown
Officers: Jamie Adams [1968] Director; Scott Douglas Brown [1968] Director [Australian]

Morton Collins Brewing Company Ltd
Incorporated: 11 September 2015 *Employees:* 2
Net Worth: £3,374 *Total Assets:* £8,185
Registered Office: The Star, 42 Standbridge Lane, Wakefield, W Yorks, WF2 7DY
Officers: Sam William Brian Collins [1977] Director/Engineer; General Morton [1963] Director/Builder

Moseley Beer Company Limited
Incorporated: 2 June 2014
Net Worth: £4,356 *Total Assets:* £4,356
Registered Office: 14 Cleveland Court, St Agnes Road, Birmingham, B13 9PR
Shareholder: Christopher Murtagh
Officers: Paul McNally [1980] Director/Sales/Purchasing/Brewer; Christopher Murtagh [1981] Director/Brewer; Matthew Shaun Murtagh [1980] Director/Teaching Assistant

Motley Hog Brewery Limited
Incorporated: 28 November 2018
Registered Office: The Tap House, 1 Millpond Street, Ross on Wye, Herefords, HR9 2AP
Officers: Christine Susan Ree, Secretary; Christine Susan Ree [1961] Director/Landlady; Nigel Leonard Ree [1958] Director/Landlord

Mourne Mountains Brewery Limited
Incorporated: 23 May 2006 *Employees:* 2
Net Worth Deficit: £172,590 *Total Assets:* £54,829
Registered Office: Unit 2 Milltown East Industrial Estate, Upper Dromore Road, Warrenpoint, Co Down, BT34 3PN
Major Shareholder: Connaire Thomas Stephen McGreevy
Officers: Connaire McGreevy, Secretary; Connaire McGreevy [1982] Director [Irish]

Mousehole Brewery Limited
Incorporated: 19 March 2018
Registered Office: Jamies Wheal Whidden, Carbis Bay, St Ives, Cornwall, TR26 2QX
Major Shareholder: Joanne Michell
Officers: Joanne Michell [1974] Director/Home Keeper

Mr Bees Brewery Ltd
Incorporated: 2 December 2016
Net Worth Deficit: £19,641 *Total Assets:* £17,885
Registered Office: 21 Cavendish Road, Felixstowe, Suffolk, IP11 2AR
Major Shareholder: Timothy Berni
Officers: Timothy Berni [1971] Director; Michelle Halligan [1977] Director/Nurse

Muckle Brewing Ltd
Incorporated: 7 April 2016
Net Worth Deficit: £1,024 *Total Assets:* £29,574
Registered Office: 3 Bellister Close, Park Village, Haltwhistle, Northumberland, NE49 0HA
Shareholders: Thomas William Smith; Nicola Jane Smith
Officers: Nicola Jane Smith [1964] Director/Brewer; Thomas William Smith [1967] Director/Brewer

Mudlark Investments Ltd
Incorporated: 20 December 2017
Registered Office: 5 Newcroft Road, Woolton, Liverpool, L25 6EP
Major Shareholder: Dougal Freeman
Officers: Dougal Freeman [1970] Director/Accountant

Muirhouse Brewery Limited
Incorporated: 12 June 2012
Net Worth: £13,898 *Total Assets:* £44,958
Registered Office: 16 Queen Street, Ilkeston, Derbys, DE7 5GT
Shareholders: Richard Jamieson Muir; Mandy Marie Muir
Officers: Mandy Marie Muir [1975] Director; Richard Jamieson Muir [1971] Director

Mumbles Brewery Ltd
Incorporated: 19 September 2011 *Employees:* 5
Net Worth: £17,097 *Total Assets:* £93,326
Registered Office: 23 Oakland Road, Mumbles, Swansea, SA3 4AQ
Shareholders: Robert Stephen Turner; Peter Graham Turner
Officers: Peter Graham Turner [1955] Director; Robert Stephen Turner [1956] Director

Mumbles Brewing Company Limited
Incorporated: 24 March 2014
Registered Office: Mumbles Brewing Company, 726 Mumbles Road, Mumbles, Swansea, SA3 4EL
Major Shareholder: Richard Kenric Bennett
Officers: Richard Kenric Bennett [1966] Director

Munro Ventures Limited
Incorporated: 12 November 2009 Employees: 8
Net Worth: £75,850 Total Assets: £382,261
Registered Office: Milestone Brewery, Great North Road, Cromwell, Newark, Notts, NG23 6JE
Shareholders: Kenneth Patrick Munro; Frances Simone Munro
Officers: Frances Simone Munro [1967] Director/Brewer; Kenneth Patrick Munro [1964] Director/Brewer

Murree Breweries (UK) Limited
Incorporated: 9 July 1996
Registered Office: T-Shirts Etc!, Whippendell Spinney, Chipperfield Road, Kings Langley, Herts, WD4 9JE
Officers: Laurence Hamilton Hesse, Secretary/Director; Isphanyar Bhandara [1972] Director [Pakistani]; Laurence Hamilton Hesse [1960] Director

Musket Brewery Limited
Incorporated: 17 April 2013 Employees: 3
Net Worth: £40,330 Total Assets: £236,270
Registered Office: 3-4 Bower Terrace, Tonbridge Road, Maidstone, Kent, ME16 8RY
Shareholders: Rhys Harrison Williams; Antony John Williams
Officers: Linda Susan Pizani Williams [1947] Director; Antony John Williams [1953] Director; Rhys Harrison Williams [1985] Director/Brewer

Muswell Hillbilly Brewers Ltd
Incorporated: 2 September 2016 Employees: 3
Net Worth Deficit: £324 Total Assets: £2,253
Registered Office: 24-26 Avenue Mews, London, N10 3NP
Shareholders: Peter Syratt; Bob Hanson; Martin Christopher Hodgson
Officers: Peter Syratt, Secretary; Bob Hanson [1967] Director/Graphic Designer; Martin Christopher Hodgson [1964] Director/Teacher; Peter Syratt [1973] Director/Account Manager

Mybrewpub Limited
Incorporated: 30 September 2015
Net Worth: £1 Total Assets: £1
Registered Office: 151 Cleveland Street, London, W1T 6QN
Major Shareholder: Angelo Bernardo
Officers: Angelo Bernardo [1957] Director [Italian]

Myrlex Southend Limited
Incorporated: 8 February 2016 Employees: 1
Net Worth: £57,645 Total Assets: £186,872
Registered Office: The Mechanics Workshop, New Lanark, Lanark, ML11 9DB
Major Shareholder: Alexander John Adamson Wilson
Officers: Alexander John Adamson Wilson, Secretary; Alexander John Adamson Wilson [1975] Director/Chartered Surveyor

Nailmaker Brewing Company Ltd
Incorporated: 27 April 2017
Net Worth: £3,377 Total Assets: £74,478
Registered Office: Hodroyd Cottage, Felkirk, South Hiendley, Barnsley, S Yorks, S72 9DQ
Major Shareholder: David Jonathan Lockwood
Officers: David Jonathan Lockwood [1973] Director/Publican

Nameless Brewing Limited
Incorporated: 12 October 2015
Net Worth: £100 Total Assets: £19,300
Registered Office: 40 Holberton Road, Reading, Berks, RG2 8NH
Shareholders: Matthew James Piska; Karl Alexander Michael Bingham
Officers: Karl Alexander Michael Bingham [1985] Director; Matthew James Piska [1986] Director

Nansen Street Holdings Ltd
Incorporated: 17 October 2017
Registered Office: Oakmount House, 2 Queens Road, Lisburn, Co Antrim, BT27 4TZ
Officers: Ann Scullion [1946] Director; James Scullion [1942] Director

Narugelia Ltd
Incorporated: 20 August 2018
Registered Office: 15 Sunnymead Road, Burntwood, Staffs, WS7 2LL
Major Shareholder: Emma Louise Bishop
Officers: Emma Louise Bishop [1989] Director/Consultant

Nauticales Ltd
Incorporated: 8 August 2015
Net Worth Deficit: £4,744
Registered Office: 1st Floor Office, Aspen House, West Terrace, Folkestone, Kent, CT20 1TH
Officers: James Greenfield [1949] Director; Michael Rush [1957] Director

Naylor's Brewery Ltd
Incorporated: 31 October 2012 Employees: 7
Net Worth: £13,230 Total Assets: £284,477
Registered Office: Unit 10 Midland Mills Station Road, Crosshills, Keighley, W Yorks, BD20 7DT
Shareholders: Robert Andrew Naylor; Stephen Naylor
Officers: Stephen Naylor, Secretary; Robert Andrew Naylor [1980] Director; Stephen Naylor [1975] Director

The Near Beer Brewing Co. Ltd
Incorporated: 30 August 2018
Registered Office: 91 Nunhead Lane, London, SE15 3QE
Officers: Thomas Joseph Blackwood [1986] Director; Berin Chesney Bowen-Thomas [1982] Director; Gregory Paul Farrington [1985] Director; Suneil Steven Paul Saraf [1980] Director

Neepsend Brewery Ltd
Incorporated: 15 April 2015 Employees: 3
Net Worth: £97,041 Total Assets: £201,173
Registered Office: 283 South Road, Sheffield, S6 3TA
Officers: James Jolyon Birkett [1962] Director

Nellyd Limited
Incorporated: 6 February 2017 Employees: 1
Net Worth Deficit: £1,859 Total Assets: £3,526
Registered Office: 3 Kensworth Gate, 200-204 High Street South, Dunstable, Beds, LU6 3HS
Major Shareholder: Neal Durrant
Officers: Neal Durrant [1966] Director

Nelson Brewing Co.Uk Ltd.
Incorporated: 29 June 2006 Employees: 2
Net Worth: £6,321 Total Assets: £117,719
Registered Office: 1a St Luke's Avenue, Maidstone, Kent, ME14 5AL
Shareholder: Piers James MacDonald
Officers: Alan John MacDonald, Secretary; Piers James MacDonald [1966] Director/Licensee

Nene Valley Brewery Limited
Incorporated: 22 November 2011 *Employees:* 5
Net Worth: £598,773 *Total Assets:* £696,100
Registered Office: Oundle Wharf, Station Road, Oundle, Peterborough, Cambs, PE8 4DE
Shareholders: Richard William George Simpson; David John Stuart Burnett
Officers: Richard William George Simpson, Secretary; David John Stuart Burnett [1958] Director/Brewer; Richard William George Simpson [1957] Director/Brewer; Paul Stephen Woodcock [1988] Director/Brewer

Neon Raptor Brewing Company Ltd.
Incorporated: 16 October 2015
Net Worth Deficit: £19,100 *Total Assets:* £63,669
Registered Office: Unit 14 Avenue A, Sneinton Market, Nottingham, NG1 1DT
Major Shareholder: Adam Roderick Henderson
Officers: Thomas Ainsley [1982] Director; Adam Roderick Henderson [1989] Director/Brewer/Engineer; Joshua David Mellor [1990] Director

Neptune Brewery Ltd
Incorporated: 7 April 2015 *Employees:* 1
Net Worth Deficit: £7,749 *Total Assets:* £56,495
Registered Office: Unit 1 Sefton Lane Industrial Estate, Maghull, Merseyside, L31 8BX
Officers: Dr Geoff Wainwright, Secretary; Leslie Roy O'Grady [1968] Director; Dr Geoffrey Wainwright [1968] Director

Nethergate Brewery Co Ltd
Incorporated: 7 April 2014 *Employees:* 16
Net Worth: £1,036,637 *Total Assets:* £1,409,286
Registered Office: Rodbridge Corner Rodbridge Corner, Long Melford, Sudbury, Suffolk, CO10 9HJ
Shareholders: Gary John Burlison; John Holberry
Officers: Richard Burge [1935] Director/Business Owner; Gary John Burlison [1958] Director/Business Owner; Charles Frederic Eaton [1964] Director/Business Owner; Justin Grainger [1968] Director; John Simon Holberry [1958] Director/Business Owner

Nevis Brewery Ltd
Incorporated: 19 December 2013
Registered Office: Cawdor Tavern, Cawdor, Nairn, IV12 5XP
Major Shareholder: Norman James Anderson Sinclair
Officers: Norman James Sinclair, Secretary; Norman James Anderson Sinclair [1961] Director

New Bristol Brewery School Ltd
Incorporated: 25 April 2017
Net Worth: £13,302 *Total Assets:* £107,553
Registered Office: 1 Church Road, Severn Beach, Bristol, BS35 4PW
Shareholders: Noel Christian David James; Maria Kisten Knowles
Officers: Noel Christian David James [1971] Director; Maria Kisten Knowles [1974] Director

New Cross Ales Ltd
Incorporated: 10 July 2017
Registered Office: The Old Forge, New Cross, South Petherton, Somerset, TA13 5HD
Shareholder: Stephen John Burnell
Officers: Alison Louise Burnell, Secretary; Stephen John Burnell [1963] Managing Director

New Devon Brewing Ltd
Incorporated: 17 March 2016
Net Worth Deficit: £692 *Total Assets:* £7,838
Registered Office: Froginwell Vineyard, Woodbury Salterton, Exeter, EX5 1EP
Officers: Katherine May Howard Jenkins [1978] Director

New Forest Beer Company Limited
Incorporated: 7 July 2017
Registered Office: Balmer Lawn Hotel, Lyndhurst Road, Brockenhurst, Hants, SO42 7ZB
Shareholders: Christopher Edwin Wilson; Trevor Victor Madden
Officers: Christopher Edwin Wilson [1960] Director

New Invention Brewery Ltd
Incorporated: 2 November 2018
Registered Office: Unit 2 Pinfold Industrial Estate, Field Close, Bloxwich, Walsall, W Midlands, WS3 3JS
Shareholders: Nicholas David Wootton; Karol Krzysztof Kawecki
Officers: Marlena Magdalena Kawulka, Secretary; Karol Krzysztof Kawecki [1990] Director [Polish]; Nicholas David Wootton [1987] Director

New Lion Totnes Ltd
Incorporated: 14 October 2018
Registered Office: New Lion, Station Road, Totnes, Devon, TQ9 5JR
Major Shareholder: Robert John Hopkins
Officers: Robert John Hopkins [1968] Director/Consultant

New River Brewery Ltd
Incorporated: 11 August 2014 *Employees:* 4
Net Worth: £39,140 *Total Assets:* £187,083
Registered Office: Unit 47 Hoddesdon Industrial Centre, Pindar Road, Hoddesdon, Herts, EN11 0FF
Shareholders: John Stephen Bourdeaux; Jeremy Steven Alter
Officers: John Stephen Bourdeaux, Secretary; Jeremy Steven Alter [1969] Director/Stockbroker; John Stephen Bourdeaux [1963] Director/Accountant

The New Union Brewing Company Limited
Incorporated: 31 January 2019
Registered Office: 159 Stricklandgate, Kendal, Cumbria, LA9 4RF
Officers: Martin James Boyd [1968] Director/Architectural Technician; Philip Lawrence John Walker [1986] Director/Publican

New Wharf Brewing Company Limited
Incorporated: 15 February 2016
Registered Office: Suite 1, Unit A1 Tectonic Place, Holyport Road, Maidenhead, Berks, SL6 2YE
Shareholders: Ciaran McNulty; Ryan McNulty
Officers: Ciaran McNulty [1969] Director; Ryan McNulty [1992] Director

Newark Brewery Ltd
Incorporated: 8 February 2012
Net Worth Deficit: £74,724 *Total Assets:* £39,247
Registered Office: 77 William Street, Newark, Notts, NG24 1QU
Shareholder: Daniel Ironmonger Derry
Officers: Daniel Ironmonger Derry [1974] Director/Surveyor; William Ironmonger Derry [1948] Director; William McKeon [1964] Director/Web Consultant

Newcastle Brewing Ltd
Incorporated: 2 April 2015
Net Worth Deficit: £12,647 *Total Assets:* £78,333
Registered Office: 6 Peony Place, Newcastle upon Tyne, NE6 1LU
Shareholders: Michael Bell; Leo Bell
Officers: Mike Bell, Secretary; Leo Bell [1979] Director/Brewer; Mike Bell [1952] Director

Newcastle Eden Bottling Company Limited
Incorporated: 25 May 2018
Registered Office: Unit D, Contract House, Wellington Road, Dunston, Gateshead, Tyne & Wear, NE11 9HS
Major Shareholder: Paul Minnikin
Officers: Paul Minnikin [1957] Director/Financial Consultant

Newquay Brewing Company Limited
Incorporated: 14 March 2017
Registered Office: Unit D2, Southgate Commerce Park, Frome, Somerset, BA11 2RY
Officers: Richard John Lyall, Secretary; Richard John Lyall [1969] Director/Brewer

Newt Brew Ltd
Incorporated: 29 May 2018
Registered Office: 7/7 Cornwallis Place, Edinburgh, EH3 6NG
Major Shareholder: Michael Kenneth Clark
Officers: Michael Kenneth Clark [1968] Director/Accountant

Nexus Engineering Limited
Incorporated: 29 March 1993 *Employees:* 9
Net Worth: £80,589 *Total Assets:* £169,527
Registered Office: Unit 11 Diamond Business Park, Sandwash Close, Rainford, St Helens, Merseyside, WA11 8LY
Major Shareholder: Atif Mahmood
Officers: Atif Mahmood [1997] Director/Businessman

Nicol Brewery Ltd.
Incorporated: 8 September 2017
Registered Office: 121 Tryst Road, Larbert, Stirlingshire, FK5 4QJ
Officers: Ricky Nicol [1987] Director/Contract Manager

Nightcap Beer Company Limited
Incorporated: 11 February 2015 *Employees:* 1
Net Worth Deficit: £28,114 *Total Assets:* £14,717
Registered Office: Ship Canal House, 98 King Street, Manchester, M2 4WU
Major Shareholder: Declan Gabriel John Holmes
Officers: Declan Gabriel John Holmes [1989] Managing Director

Nightjar Brew Company Limited
Incorporated: 14 May 2015
Previous: The Slightly Foxed Brewing Company Limited
Net Worth: £10,309 *Total Assets:* £60,689
Registered Office: Higher Underbank House, Charlestown, Hebden Bridge, W Yorks, HX7 6PS
Major Shareholder: Matthew Robert Bell
Officers: Matthew Robert Bell [1968] Director/Manager

Nightowl Brewing Company Ltd
Incorporated: 24 June 2015
Registered Office: 1 Windsor Grove, Oakworth, Keighley, W Yorks, BD22 7PG
Officers: Andrew Bailey [1981] Director/Brewer; Matthew Dodd [1981] Director/Brewer

Nine Standards Brewery Limited
Incorporated: 30 March 2011
Net Worth: £5,604 *Total Assets:* £7,141
Registered Office: 39 Northgate, White Lund Industrial Estate, Morecambe, Lancs, LA3 3PA
Officers: Patricia Anne Lord [1957] Director

No Abode Brew Co Ltd
Incorporated: 22 January 2018
Registered Office: 20-22 Wenlock Road, London, N1 7GU
Shareholders: Thomas David Glenton Greensmith; Daniel Kenneth Gordon Cowley
Officers: Thomas David Glenton Greensmith [1986] Director

No Comply Ltd
Incorporated: 25 February 2019
Registered Office: 117 Boverton Road, Llantwit Major, Vale of Glamorgan, CF61 1YA
Major Shareholder: Robert Charles Byron Lilford
Officers: Robert Charles Byron Lilford [1972] Director/Brewer

Noah Beers Limited
Incorporated: 20 December 2007 *Employees:* 62
Net Worth: £855,433 *Total Assets:* £1,634,380
Registered Office: Suite 204, Templeton Business Centre, Binnie Place, Glasgow, G40 1AW
Parent: Noah Beers Holdings Limited
Officers: Petra Margareta Wetzel [1974] Director [German]

Nobby's Brewing Company Limited
Incorporated: 8 October 2014 *Employees:* 5
Net Worth: £756 *Total Assets:* £81,208
Registered Office: Unit 2 Cottingham Way, Thrapston, Northants, NN14 4PL
Major Shareholder: Paul David Mulliner
Officers: Paul David Mulliner [1967] Director

Nomadic Brewing Company Ltd
Incorporated: 15 December 2016
Net Worth Deficit: £10,354 *Total Assets:* £24,342
Registered Office: Unit 11, 15 Sheepscar Street, Leeds, LS7 1AD
Major Shareholder: Katie Elizabeth Rose Marriott
Officers: Dr Katie Elizabeth Rose Marriott [1986] Director/Brewer

Norn Iron Brew Company Limited
Incorporated: 3 June 2016
Net Worth: £15,728 *Total Assets:* £15,728
Registered Office: 87 Priory Park, Belfast, BT10 0AG
Shareholders: Aaron Craven; Paul McMullan
Officers: Aaron Craven [1986] Director/Brewer; Paul McMullan [1973] Director

North Brewing Company Limited
Incorporated: 10 May 2011 *Employees:* 14
Net Worth Deficit: £25,943 *Total Assets:* £397,713
Registered Office: Regents Court, 39a Harrogate Road, Leeds, LS7 3PD
Parent: North Brewing Group Limited
Officers: Steven Ballard [1972] Director; John Christopher Gyngell [1972] Director; Christian Townsley [1975] Director; Joanne Wilkinson [1986] Finance Director

North Cotswold Brewery Limited
Incorporated: 15 September 2011
Net Worth: £120,347   Total Assets: £215,485
Registered Office: Unit 3 Ditchford Farm, Stretton on Fosse, Moreton in Marsh, Warwicks, GL56 9RD
Major Shareholder: Guy Alexander Holiday
Officers: Guy Alexander Holiday [1963] Director; Terence David Welton Liggins [1943] Director; Neil Guest Wilson [1958] Director

North Country Ales Limited
Incorporated: 15 April 2014   Employees: 2
Net Worth: £2,584   Total Assets: £22,718
Registered Office: Brackenrigg Inn, Watermillock, Penrith, Cumbria, CA11 0LP
Shareholders: John Welch; John Welch Snr; Garry Smith
Officers: Garry Smith, Secretary; Garry Smith [1962] Director/Partner; John Welch Snr [1951] Director/Partner

North East Brewing Company Limited
Incorporated: 25 January 2008
Net Worth: £219,233   Total Assets: £605,460
Registered Office: Units D1 & D2 Narvik Way, Tyne Tunnel Trading Estate, North Shields, Tyne & Wear, NE29 7XJ
Shareholders: Garry Nathan Fawson; Matthew Allan Fawson
Officers: Matthew Allan Fawson, Secretary; Garry Nathan Fawson [1963] Sales Director; Matthew Allan Fawson [1974] Director/Brewer

North Riding Brewery Limited
Incorporated: 26 June 2014
Net Worth: £58,472   Total Assets: £191,911
Registered Office: 8a Pavilion Square, Scarborough, N Yorks, YO11 2JT
Officers: Paula Amelia Hornby [1968] Director; Karen Neilson [1969] Director; Stuart Neilson [1975] Director; Adrian Michael Tonge [1970] Director

North Yorkshire Brewing Company Limited
Incorporated: 6 July 2017
Net Worth Deficit: £4,725   Total Assets: £55,675
Registered Office: 47 Grassington Road, Middlesbrough, Cleveland, TS4 3DD
Shareholder: Razvan Ovidiu Oltianu
Officers: Razvan Ovidiu Oltianu [1979] Director/Brewer [Romanian]

Northern Alchemy Limited
Incorporated: 4 February 2014   Employees: 3
Net Worth Deficit: £13,909   Total Assets: £43,717
Registered Office: 66 Cartington Terrace, Newcastle upon Tyne, NE6 5SE
Shareholders: Carl Wayne Kennedy; Andrew Robert Aitchison
Officers: Andrew Robert Aitchison [1978] Director; Joanne Sarah Hodson [1976] Director; Carl Wayne Kennedy [1977] Director

Northern Craft Brewers Limited
Incorporated: 10 March 2016
Net Worth: £3,795   Total Assets: £77,405
Registered Office: The Granary, Haggs Road, Follifoot, Harrogate, N Yorks, HG3 1EQ
Shareholders: Tim Butler; Deborah Clayton
Officers: Deborah May Clayton, Secretary; Tim Butler [1974] Director; Deborah May Clayton [1981] Director and Company Secretary

Northern Monk Brewing Co. Ltd
Incorporated: 15 August 2013
Net Worth: £57,729   Total Assets: £1,191,657
Registered Office: The Old Flax Store, Marshalls Mills, Holbeck, Leeds, LS11 9YJ
Shareholders: Russell Anesu Bisset; David Terry Seymour
Officers: Russell Bisset [1985] Director; Brian Robert Dickson [1987] Director; Geoffrey Walters [1970] Director

Northern Monkey Brew Co. Ltd
Incorporated: 5 April 2017
Net Worth: £6,478   Total Assets: £30,247
Registered Office: Northern Monkey Brew Co Ltd Pack Horse, Nelson Square, Bolton, Lancs, BL1 1JT
Shareholders: David Thomas Cookson; Ryan Bailey; Liam Convey
Officers: Ryan Bailey [1986] Director; Kevin Barber [1969] Director; Liam Convey [1985] Director

Northern Whisper Brewing Company Limited
Incorporated: 14 March 2017   Employees: 11
Net Worth: £18,349   Total Assets: £588,992
Registered Office: Hill End Mill, Hill End Lane, Cloughfold, Rossendale, Lancs, BB4 7RN
Officers: Barnaby Michael Vines, Secretary; Carmelo Pillitteri [1984] Director; Barnaby Michael Vines [1988] Director; Joshua Albert Vines [1992] Director; Timothy Albert Vines [1957] Director/Farmer

Nothing Bound Brewing Co Ltd
Incorporated: 21 June 2018
Registered Office: Meadowside, Habberley Road, Bewdley, Worcs, DY12 1JA
Major Shareholder: David Anthony Hares
Officers: David Anthony Hares [1977] Director

Now Then Brewery Ltd
Incorporated: 10 September 2018
Registered Office: 2 Cliffe Crest, Horbury, Wakefield, W Yorks, WF4 6NL
Major Shareholder: Jonathan Mark Howard
Officers: Eva Louise Howard [1972] Director/Physiotherapist; Joe Harry Howard [1994] Director/Accountant; Jonathan Mark Howard [1966] Director/Professional Athlete; Lucy Anne Howard [1998] Director/Nurse

Nuglyfe Ltd
Incorporated: 25 April 2017
Registered Office: Flat 14, 4 Westport Street, London, E1 0RA
Major Shareholder: Rachel Elizabeth Rosser
Officers: Rachel Elizabeth Rosser [1988] Director/Account Manager

The Nungate Brewery Company Limited
Incorporated: 7 June 2018
Registered Office: 7/3 Rosevale Terrace, Edinburgh, EH6 8AR
Major Shareholder: Glen Dawkins
Officers: Glen Dawkins [1971] Director

Nutbrook Brewery Ltd
Incorporated: 5 April 2008   Employees: 1
Net Worth: £455   Total Assets: £5,622
Registered Office: 6 Hallam Way, West Hallam, Ilkeston, Derbys, DE7 6LA
Shareholders: Christopher Peter Richards; Dean Timothy Richards
Officers: Dean Timothy Richards, Secretary; Christopher Peter Richards [1984] Director/Brewer; Dean Timothy Richards [1953] Director/Business Trainer

Chris O'Connor and Associates Limited
Incorporated: 5 September 2001
Net Worth: £207,757 *Total Assets:* £309,543
Registered Office: Common Lodge, Moss Lane, St Michaels, Preston, Lancs, PR3 0TY
Major Shareholder: Christopher Joseph O'Connor
Officers: Christopher Joseph O'Connor [1966] Director/Manager

O'Neill's Brewing Company Limited
Incorporated: 22 March 2018
Registered Office: The Barn, Wood Farm, Coal Pit Lane, Willey, Warwicks, CV23 0SL
Officers: Mark Joseph O'Neill, Secretary; Mark Joseph O'Neill [1980] Managing Director

Oak Brewing Company Limited
Incorporated: 6 April 1990 *Employees:* 8
Net Worth: £894,769 *Total Assets:* £1,087,852
Registered Office: Phoenix Brewery, Green Lane, Heywood, Lancs, OL10 2EP
Major Shareholder: Anthony John Allen
Officers: Anthony John Allen, Secretary; Anthony John Allen [1952] Managing Director

Oakhill Brewery Limited
Incorporated: 28 February 2002
Registered Office: Ground Floor, Gate 1, Blackbrook Business Park, Taunton, Somerset, TA1 2PX
Major Shareholder: Colin George Keevil
Officers: Daniel Roy Newton, Secretary; Kevin Roy Newton [1965] Director

Oakland Brewing Company Ltd
Incorporated: 19 October 2018
Registered Office: Oakland House, Oaklands Terrace, Ty Coch, Cwmbran, NP44 7AJ
Major Shareholder: Lee Nicholas Dunning
Officers: Lee Nicholas Dunning [1967] Director/Engineer; Alexis Morgan Jones [1976] Director/Head Brewer

The Oaks Brewing Company Ltd
Incorporated: 9 August 2017
Registered Office: 6 Stanney Mill Industrial Estate, Dutton Green, Chester, CH2 4SA
Major Shareholder: Stephen John Ball
Officers: Stephen John Ball [1958] Director

Oast & Tread Brewing Ltd
Incorporated: 3 January 2019
Registered Office: 99 Argyle Gardens, Upminster, Essex, RM14 3EX
Major Shareholder: Scott Steven Treadwell
Officers: Scott Steven Treadwell [1993] Director

Oast House Breweries Cyf
Incorporated: 8 November 2012
Net Worth Deficit: £10,179 *Total Assets:* £7,162
Registered Office: 32 Brynystwyth, Penparcau, Aberystwyth, Ceredigion, SY23 1SS
Shareholders: Stephanie Louise Reveley; John Bodrick Dyer
Officers: John Bodrick Dyer [1990] Director/Head Brewer; Stephanie Louise Reveley [1989] Director/Brewster

Octagon Brewery Limited
Incorporated: 2 September 2010
Registered Office: 14 Warren Park, Plymouth, PL6 7QR
Shareholder: Clive David Beech
Officers: Clive David Beech [1957] Director/Physicist

Oddly Limited
Incorporated: 9 June 2015
Net Worth Deficit: £41,941 *Total Assets:* £21,097
Registered Office: Galla House, 695 High Road, North Finchley, London, N12 0BT
Major Shareholder: Brian Watson
Officers: Brian Watson [1965] Director/Brewer

Odyssey Brew Co Ltd
Incorporated: 28 January 2016 *Employees:* 2
Net Worth: £1,809 *Total Assets:* £43,817
Registered Office: 41 Epsom Walk, Hereford, HR4 0NJ
Shareholders: Mitchell David Evans; Alison Frances Evans
Officers: Alison Frances Evans [1980] Director; Mitchell David Evans [1980] Director

Offbeat Brewery Ltd
Incorporated: 20 March 2008
Net Worth Deficit: £112,745 *Total Assets:* £9,694
Registered Office: KFH Network, 3 Chantry Court, Forge Street, Crewe, Cheshire, CW1 2DL
Major Shareholder: Michelle Susan Shipman
Officers: Michelle Susan Shipman, Secretary; Michelle Susan Shipman [1976] Director

Ol Brewery Limited
Incorporated: 26 September 2017
Net Worth: £9,620 *Total Assets:* £33,104
Registered Office: 50 Nicolas Road, Chorlton Cum Hardy, Manchester, M21 9LR
Shareholders: David Michael McCall; Philip Francis Hannaway
Officers: Philip Francis Hannaway [1976] Managing Director; David Michael McCall [1969] Managing Director

Old Dairy Brewery Limited
Incorporated: 6 October 2009 *Employees:* 8
Net Worth: £87,312 *Total Assets:* £710,788
Registered Office: Old Dairy Brewery Limited, Station Road, Tenterden, Kent, TN30 6HE
Officers: Sean William Calnan [1968] Director/General Manager; Richard John Roberts [1957] Director

Old Farmhouse Brewery Ltd.
Incorporated: 7 February 2019
Registered Office: Upper Harglodd, St Davids, Haverfordwest, Pembrokeshire, SA62 6BX
Shareholders: Mark Wyn Raymond Evans; Emma Sarah Evans
Officers: Emma Sarah Evans [1981] Director/Planning Officer; Mark Wyn Raymond Evans [1979] Director/Farmer

Old Friends Brewery Ltd
Incorporated: 4 March 2015
Net Worth: £1,692 *Total Assets:* £16,907
Registered Office: 130 High Street, Cambridge, CB24 8RX
Shareholders: Jonathan Cockley; Timothy George Edward Pheasant
Officers: Jonathan William Cockley [1979] Director; Timothy George Edward Pheasant [1980] Director

Old Pie Factory Brewery Limited
Incorporated: 9 May 2011
Net Worth Deficit: £63,528 *Total Assets:* £33,106
Registered Office: The Old Pie Factory, Montague Road, Warwick, CV34 5LW
Officers: John Roland Kay, Secretary; John Senan Brew [1956] Director [Irish]; John Roland Kay [1957] Director; Timothy Morris Underwood [1958] Director; Charles Philip Willacy [1953] Director

The Old Prentonian Brewing Company Ltd.
Incorporated: 16 April 2015
Net Worth Deficit: £27,448 *Total Assets:* £6,944
Registered Office: Amelia House, Crescent Road, Worthing, W Sussex, BN11 1QR
Major Shareholder: Alan Paul Mearns
Officers: Alan Paul Mearns [1980] Director/Brewing

Old School Brewery Limited
Incorporated: 3 March 2011
Net Worth Deficit: £117,641 *Total Assets:* £167,079
Registered Office: Holly Bank Barn, Crag Road, Warton, Carnforth, Lancs, LA5 9PL
Shareholders: Ian Christopher Walsh; Renard Barry Wallbank
Officers: Ian Christopher Walsh, Secretary; Renard Barry Wallbank [1965] Director/Builder; Ian Christopher Walsh [1973] Director/Dentist

Old Spot Brewery Limited
Incorporated: 7 March 2005
Net Worth: £13,772 *Total Assets:* £40,444
Registered Office: Manor Farm, Station Road, Cullingworth, Bradford, BD13 5HN
Major Shareholder: Christopher John Thompson
Officers: Christopher John Thompson [1966] Director/Engineer; John Robert Thompson [1946] Director/Farmer

Old Street Brewery Ltd
Incorporated: 1 September 2016
Net Worth: £20 *Total Assets:* £20
Registered Office: Arch 11 Gales Gardens, London, E2 0EJ
Major Shareholder: Adam Green
Officers: Adam Green [1986] Director/Owner, Head Brewer; Andreas Wegelius [1990] Director/Computer Genius/Brewer [Finnish]

Old Thistle Company Limited
Incorporated: 26 September 2018
Registered Office: 7 Howe Street, Edinburgh, EH3 6TE
Major Shareholder: James Alexander Kerr
Officers: James Alexander Kerr [1987] Director/Brewing Consultant

Old Town Brewery Ltd.
Incorporated: 8 April 2013
Net Worth Deficit: £9,346 *Total Assets:* £9,611
Registered Office: 25 Goddard Avenue, Swindon, Wilts, SN1 4HR
Major Shareholder: David Michael Bugg
Officers: Clare Bugg, Secretary; David Michael Bugg [1980] Director/Head Brewer

Old Tree Brewery Ltd
Incorporated: 6 February 2018
Registered Office: Yacht Werks, 28-29 Richmond Place, Brighton, BN2 9NA
Major Shareholder: Thomas Charles Averell Daniell
Officers: Harold Abel [1992] Director; Thomas Charles Averell Daniell [1987] Director; Eve Beryl Jones [1991] Director and Company Secretary; Matthew Stuart Nash [1981] Director

The Old Vault Brewing Company Limited
Incorporated: 12 May 2017
Registered Office: 33-35 Thorne Road, Doncaster, S Yorks, DN1 2HD
Major Shareholder: Vicky Ailean Clark
Officers: Vicky Ailean Clark [1990] Director

Old Windsor Brewery Ltd
Incorporated: 24 May 2016
Net Worth Deficit: £2,669
Registered Office: 68 Straight Road, Old Windsor, Berks, SL4 2RX
Major Shareholder: Robert James Kilburn
Officers: Robert Kilburn, Secretary; Robert James Kilburn [1976] Director/IT Manager

Old Worthy Brewing Company Ltd
Incorporated: 21 July 2011 *Employees:* 1
Net Worth Deficit: £6,899 *Total Assets:* £49,015
Registered Office: 24a Ainslie Place, Edinburgh, EH3 6AJ
Shareholders: Nicholas Charles Ravenhall; Lee Cameron McCrohan
Officers: Lee Cameron McCrohan [1981] Director/Accountant [Australian]

Oldershaw Brewery Ltd
Incorporated: 12 February 2015
Net Worth: £100 *Total Assets:* £100
Registered Office: The Old Mushroom Farm Heath Lane, Barkston Heath, Grantham, Lincs, NG32 2DE
Shareholders: Kathy Britton; Tim Britton
Officers: Kathy Britton [1968] Managing Director; Tim John Britton [1968] Director

OM Food Corp Ltd
Incorporated: 13 April 2018
Registered Office: 63 Circus Drive, Cambridge, CB4 2BT
Major Shareholder: Naveen Kumar Nanjappan
Officers: Mathivanan Subramaniam, Secretary; Kavitha Lakshmy Mathivanan [1977] Director/Manager; Naveen Kumar Nanjappan [1986] Director/Manager [Indian]; Mathivanan Subramaniam [1977] Director/Manager

Omnebonum Ltd
Incorporated: 27 September 2017
Registered Office: Ysgubor Ysgubor, Velindre, Llandysul, Carmarthenshire, SA44 5XS
Major Shareholder: Jason Wray Neale
Officers: Jason Wray Neale [1987] Director

One Swan Ltd
Incorporated: 23 February 2018
Registered Office: 29 Josephine Avenue, Limavady, Co Londonderry, BT49 9BA
Major Shareholder: Conor McKay
Officers: Lauren Hutton, Secretary; Conor McKay [1997] Director/Consultancy [Irish]

Onebeer Brewing Ltd
Incorporated: 2 July 2018
Registered Office: 5 The Mall, London, W5 2PJ
Major Shareholder: Ireneusz Tomecki
Officers: Ireneusz Tomecki [1978] Director [Polish]

Orbit Brewing Limited
Incorporated: 19 November 2013 *Employees:* 4
Net Worth Deficit: £28,882 *Total Assets:* £239,623
Registered Office: Railway Arches 225 & 228, Fielding Street, London, SE17 3HD
Major Shareholder: Robert Campbell Middleton
Officers: Robert Campbell Middleton [1962] Director/Brewing

Orchard Road Brewery Limited
Incorporated: 13 April 2017
Net Worth Deficit: £10,546 *Total Assets:* £30,730
Registered Office: 81 Orchard Road, Darlington, Co Durham, DL3 6HR
Major Shareholder: David Ian Clough
Officers: David Ian Clough [1961] Director

Organic Laundry Limited
Incorporated: 6 July 2018
Registered Office: The Ca'D'Oro, 45 Gordon Street, Glasgow, G1 3PE
Shareholders: Jonathan Engels; Graham Kenneth Suttle
Officers: Rachel Marjory Irene Suttle [1984] Director

Origami Brewing Company Ltd.
Incorporated: 5 July 2016
Net Worth Deficit: £775 *Total Assets:* £1,305
Registered Office: 83 Ducie Street, Manchester, M1 2JQ
Shareholders: Erin Tickle; Simon Tierney-Wigg; Lauren Guy
Officers: Simon Tierney-Wigg, Secretary; Lauren Guy [1984] Director/Brewer; Erin Tickle [1982] Director/Brewer; Pamela Louise Tierney-Wigg [1980] Finance Director; Simon Tierney-Wigg [1976] Director/Brewery

Original Brewers Limited
Incorporated: 15 June 2018
Registered Office: 1 Union Court, Liverpool, L2 4SJ
Shareholders: Alan David Middleton; Sebastian Machado; Aidan Middleton; GSCM Investments Limited
Officers: Sebastian Machado [1983] Director; Nicholas Manning [1985] Director; Alan David Middleton [1956] Director/Solicitor

The Original Goole Brewery Company Limited
Incorporated: 25 January 2016
Registered Office: 15 Hobgate, York, YO24 4HE
Major Shareholder: Howard Mark Duckworth
Officers: Howard Mark Duckworth [1956] Director/Hotelier

Ossett Brewing Company Limited
Incorporated: 17 January 1997 *Employees:* 30
Net Worth: £943,943 *Total Assets:* £2,491,694
Registered Office: Kings Yard, Low Mill Road, Ossett, W Yorks, WF5 8ND
Parent: Ossett Brewery Group Holdings Limited
Officers: David Mark Hunter [1962] Director; James Robert Lawson [1972] Director; Sarah Marie Lawson [1985] Director; Jamie Andrew Merrill [1982] Finance Director

Ostlers Ales Ltd
Incorporated: 18 February 2013
Net Worth Deficit: £1,003 *Total Assets:* £20,523
Registered Office: White Horse, 2 York Street, Harborne, Birmingham, B17 0HG
Shareholders: Glyn Preece; Colin Raymond Marlow
Officers: Nigel Philip Beecroft [1965] Director/Programme Manager; Colin Raymond Marlow [1955] Director/Publican; Glyn Preece [1949] Director/Accountant

OTL Brew Co Ltd
Incorporated: 6 September 2018
Registered Office: 78 Harborough Road, London, SW16 2XW
Major Shareholder: Daniel Lee Paul Smith
Officers: Daniel Lee Paul Smith, Secretary; Daniel Lee Paul Smith [1988] Director

Otter Brewery Limited
Incorporated: 23 December 1998 *Employees:* 36
Net Worth: £807,875 *Total Assets:* £3,135,846
Registered Office: Mathayes Luppitt, Honiton, Devon, EX14 4SA
Shareholder: David Francis Anderson McCaig
Officers: Mary Ann McCaig, Secretary; David Francis Anderson McCaig [1946] Director/Brewer; Mary Ann McCaig [1941] Director/Company Secretary; Patrick McCaig [1965] Director/Brewer

Out of the Woods Brew Co Ltd
Incorporated: 20 August 2018
Registered Office: 173-175 London Road, Camberley, Surrey, GU15 3JS
Officers: William John Frazer Thomas Longmire [1993] Director; Thomas William Roe [1986] Director; Luke Connor Lyon Smith [1994] Director; Mark Justin Smith [1975] Director

Out of Town Brewing Limited
Incorporated: 21 March 2016
Net Worth: £21,132 *Total Assets:* £21,882
Registered Office: 11 Yarrow Gardens Lane, Glasgow, G20 6RZ
Shareholders: Owen Robert Kerr Sheerins; Richard O'Brien; James Patrick Bowie Morton
Officers: Dr James Patrick Bowie Morton [1991] Director/Brewer; Richard O'Brien [1979] Sales Director; Dr Owen Robert Kerr Sheerins [1988] Director/Doctor

Outgang Brewery Ltd
Incorporated: 10 March 2009
Net Worth: £100 *Total Assets:* £100
Registered Office: Finlayson & Co, Whitby Court, Abbey Road, Shepley, W Yorks, HD8 8EL
Major Shareholder: Gordon Peter Mair
Officers: Beverley Ann Radford, Secretary; Gordon Peter Mair [1963] Director; Beverley Ann Radford [1963] Director

Outhouse Brewing Ltd
Incorporated: 14 September 2017
Registered Office: Henry Morgan House, Industry Road, Carlton, Barnsley, S Yorks, S71 3PQ
Major Shareholder: Andrew Oliver Jones
Officers: Andrew Oliver Jones [1980] Director/Brewer

The Outstanding Brewing Company Ltd
Incorporated: 14 May 2007
Net Worth: £157,971 *Total Assets:* £477,993
Registered Office: Unit 2 Foundry Business Park, Ordsall Lane, Salford, M5 3AN
Shareholder: David Arthur Porter
Officers: David Arthur Porter, Secretary; Alexei Christopher Lord [1978] Director; David Arthur Porter [1959] Director; Paul David Sandiford [1972] Director; Glen Woodcock [1959] Director

Ovenstone 109 Limited
Incorporated: 13 February 2017
Net Worth Deficit: £23,654 *Total Assets:* £49,303
Registered Office: Ovenstone Works, Ovenstone, Anstruther, Fife, KY10 2RR
Major Shareholder: Nick Fleming
Officers: Nicholas Cain Kinrade Fleming [1976] Director

Over The Hill Brewery Ltd
Incorporated: 6 November 2014
Registered Office: 32 Mill Road, Over, Cambridge, CB24 5PY
Shareholder: David George Gilbey
Officers: David George Gilbey [1960] Director

Overtone Brewing Ltd
Incorporated: 6 February 2017
Net Worth Deficit: £56,480 Total Assets: £112,528
Registered Office: Unit 19 Halley Street, New Albion Industrial Estate, Glasgow, G13 4DJ
Major Shareholder: Bowei Wang
Officers: Bowei Wang [1982] Director/Brewer

Overworks Limited
Incorporated: 26 October 2017
Registered Office: Brewdog, Balmacassie Drive, Balmacassie Commercial Park, Ellon, Aberdeenshire, AB41 8BX
Parent: Brewdog PLC
Officers: Alan Martin Dickie [1982] Director; James Bruce Watt [1982] Director

Owlcrab Limited
Incorporated: 20 March 2018
Registered Office: c/o The Accountancy Partnership, Suite 1, 5th Floor, City Reach, 5 Greenwich View Place, London, E14 9NN
Major Shareholder: Sanna-Maarit Ratilainen
Officers: Sanna-Maarit Ratilainen [1973] Director/Homemaker [Finnish]

Oxbrew Ltd
Incorporated: 5 March 2015
Net Worth Deficit: £4,462 Total Assets: £46,064
Registered Office: Unit 4d Enstone Airfield, Enstone, Chipping Norton, Oxon, OX7 4NP
Shareholder: Aaron Thomas Baldwin
Officers: Aaron Thomas Baldwin [1987] Director; Simon Paul Scamp [1955] Director

Oxford Brewery Limited
Incorporated: 20 December 2018
Registered Office: Mount Manor House, 16 The Mount, Guildford, Surrey, GU2 4HN
Major Shareholder: Moira Allan Ross
Officers: Moira Allan Ross [1953] Director

The Oxford Brewing Company Limited
Incorporated: 24 August 2017
Registered Office: Mount Manor House, 16 The Mount, Guildford, Surrey, GU2 4HN
Major Shareholder: Moira Allan Ross
Officers: Moira Allan Ross [1953] Director

The Oxted Brewery Ltd
Incorporated: 1 October 2015
Net Worth: £15,886 Total Assets: £22,953
Registered Office: 24 Peter Avenue, Oxted, Surrey, RH8 9LG
Shareholders: Charlene Louise Gardner; David James Gardner
Officers: Charlene Gardner, Secretary; Charlene Louise Gardner [1976] Director; David James Gardner [1973] Director/Accountant

Paddy's Clover Ltd
Incorporated: 12 November 2013
Registered Office: 16d Castle Street, Lisburn, Co Antrim, BT27 4XD
Shareholders: Simon John Bruce; Michael John McCaughan
Officers: William Linden Allen [1946] Director; Simon John Bruce [1966] Director [Irish]; Michael John McCaughan [1954] Director

Padlock Brewery Ltd.
Incorporated: 4 January 2019
Registered Office: 247 Burton Road, Manchester, M20 2WA
Shareholders: Patrick Joseph Madigan; Nathan Boyes
Officers: Nathan Boyes [1993] Director; Patrick Joseph Madigan [1992] Director

Padstow Brewing Company (2013) Ltd
Incorporated: 4 October 1999 Employees: 2
Previous: Precise Consulting Limited
Net Worth: £24,371 Total Assets: £26,362
Registered Office: 62 Wilson Street, London, EC2A 2BU
Shareholders: Desmond John Archer; Caron Patricia Archer
Officers: Caron Patricia Archer [1960] Director/Customer Manager; Desmond John Archer [1958] Director

Thomas Paine Brewery Limited
Incorporated: 1 November 2016
Registered Office: Woodview, Hanby Lane, Welton-le-Marsh, Lincs, PE23 5TH
Officers: Kerry Lancaster, Secretary; David Albert Lancaster [1953] Director/Industrial Designer

J.C. & R.H. Palmer Limited
Incorporated: 17 November 1975 Employees: 55
Net Worth: £34,099,496 Total Assets: £37,139,700
Registered Office: Old Brewery, Bridport, Dorset, DT6 4JA
Shareholders: Anthony John Cleeves Palmer; Cleeves William Robert Palmer
Officers: Gary George Adcock, Secretary; Gary George Adcock [1963] Director/Accountant; Anthony John Cleeves Palmer [1951] Brewery Director; Cleeves William Robert Palmer [1962] Brewery Director; Emily Grace Palmer [1991] Director/Banker

Paper Fort Brew Co Ltd.
Incorporated: 21 February 2018
Registered Office: 11 Hemingway Close, Castleford, W Yorks, WF10 3PT
Officers: Louis-Anton Robert Green [1991] Director; Gareth Mann [1986] Director

Papworth Brewery Limited
Incorporated: 29 October 2014
Net Worth Deficit: £35,608 Total Assets: £69,899
Registered Office: 7 Byfield Road, Papworth Everard, Cambridge, CB23 3UQ
Shareholders: Christopher Jones; Sharon Ann Jones
Officers: Richard Willoughby Harrison [1961] Director; Dr Christopher Jones [1966] Director/Software Engineer

Paradigm Brewery Ltd
Incorporated: 12 May 2014
Net Worth Deficit: £29,603 Total Assets: £34,842
Registered Office: The Old Vicarage, 10 Church Street, Rickmansworth, Herts, WD3 1BS
Shareholder: Neil Robert Hodges
Officers: Robert Atkinson, Secretary; Neil Robert Hodges [1962] Director/Brewer

The Parbold Bottle Limited
Incorporated: 26 July 2018
Registered Office: c/o Holden Associates, V12, Merlin Park, Ringtail Road, Burscough, Lancs, L40 8JY
Major Shareholder: Richard Trevor Hale
Officers: Richard Trevor Hale [1957] Director

The Park Brewery Ltd
Incorporated: 11 June 2014 Employees: 2
Net Worth: £5,170 Total Assets: £32,834
Registered Office: 38 St Georges Road, Kingston upon Thames, Surrey, KT2 6DN
Shareholders: Frances Kearns; Joshuah Kearns
Officers: Frances Kearns [1973] Director; Joshuah Kearns [1977] Director

Parkway Brewing Company Ltd
Incorporated: 12 October 2018
Registered Office: Unit 11 Wessex Park, Somerton Business Park, Bancombe Road, Somerton, Somerset, TA11 6SB
Shareholders: Zina Clare French; Mark Dearman
Officers: Zina Clare French [1984] Director

Partizan Brewing Limited
Incorporated: 16 July 2012 *Employees:* 7
Net Worth: £181,151 *Total Assets:* £326,775
Registered Office: 34 Raymouth Road, London, SE16 2DB
Major Shareholder: Andrew Mark Smith
Officers: Andrew Mark Smith [1982] Director/Brewer

Partners Brewery Limited
Incorporated: 9 May 2011
Net Worth Deficit: £21,605 *Total Assets:* £75,637
Registered Office: c/o Phoenix Whirlpools Ltd Unit 8 Bruntcliffe Avenue, Morley, Leeds, LS27 0LL
Major Shareholder: Richard Dean Sharp
Officers: Nicholas Paul Sharp, Secretary; Richard Dean Sharp [1985] Director

Partridge Brewing Company Limited
Incorporated: 29 March 2016
Net Worth Deficit: £3,318 *Total Assets:* £10,666
Registered Office: Dog and Partridge Dog and Partridge, Hesketh Lane, Preston, Lancs, PR3 2TH
Shareholders: Andrew Barr; Rodrigo Brandim-Howson
Officers: Andrew Peter Barr [1990] Director/Investment Analyst; Rodrigo Brandim-Howson [1990] Director/Teacher

Pastore Brewing and Blending Limited
Incorporated: 19 September 2018
Registered Office: Unit 2 Convent Drive, Waterbeach, Cambridge, CB25 9QT
Shareholder: Benjamin Charles Demetrios Shepherd
Officers: Benjamin Charles Demetrios Shepherd [1995] Director

The Patriot Brewery Limited
Incorporated: 11 February 2009
Net Worth Deficit: £32,017 *Total Assets:* £25,053
Registered Office: c/o DP Associates, Unit 81 Basepoint Business Centre, Yeoford Way, Exeter, EX2 8LB
Shareholder: Timothy Young
Officers: Timothy Stephen Young [1971] Director

Pawed Brewery Ltd
Incorporated: 4 February 2019
Registered Office: 39 Ridgewood Drive, Harpenden, Herts, AL5 3LJ
Major Shareholder: Ian Nicholas Hubbard
Officers: Ian Nicholas Hubbard [1965] Director/Business Development

Peak Ales Limited
Incorporated: 11 March 2015
Net Worth Deficit: £33,043 *Total Assets:* £290,746
Registered Office: The Barn Brewery, Chatsworth, Bakewell, Derbys, DE45 1EX
Shareholders: Robert Graham Evans; Debra Evans
Officers: Debra Evans [1963] Director; Robert Graham Evans [1962] Director

Peakstones Rock Brewing Co Ltd
Incorporated: 15 July 2011 *Employees:* 2
Net Worth: £1,337 *Total Assets:* £21,384
Registered Office: 1 Tape Street, Cheadle, Stoke on Trent, Staffs, ST10 1BB
Shareholders: David Francis Edwards; Susan Mary Edwards
Officers: Susan Mary Edwards, Secretary; David Francis Edwards [1961] Director; James Francis Edwards [1994] Director; Susan Mary Edwards [1962] Director

Pedal Power Harrogate Limited
Incorporated: 16 August 2013
Net Worth Deficit: £387 *Total Assets:* £4,608
Registered Office: 3 Greengate, Cardale Park, Harrogate, N Yorks, HG3 1GY
Major Shareholder: Anthony Robert John Nelson
Officers: Anthony Robert John Nelson [1955] Director; Andrew Vernon Wild [1970] Director

Peerless Brewing Company Limited
Incorporated: 26 October 2009 *Employees:* 4
Net Worth: £72,753 *Total Assets:* £253,807
Registered Office: Barnston House, Beacon Lane, Heswall, Wirral, Merseyside, CH60 0EE
Shareholders: Steven Alan Briscoe; Rosemary Theresa Briscoe
Officers: Rosemary Theresa Briscoe [1959] Director; Steven Alan Briscoe [1961] Director

Penistone Brewers Limited
Incorporated: 23 May 2017
Registered Office: Thirteen77 Gate Bridge Street, Penistone, Sheffield, S36 7AH
Shareholders: Gillian Ward; Christopher Ward
Officers: Christopher Ward, Secretary; Christopher Ward [1959] Director; Gillian Ward [1965] Director

Penistone Brewing (Penistone) Limited
Incorporated: 11 September 2017
Registered Office: Thirteen77 Gate Bridge Street, Penistone, Sheffield, S36 7AH
Shareholders: Gillian Ward; Christopher Ward
Officers: Christopher Ward [1959] Director; Gillian Ward [1965] Director

Penton Park Brewery Limited
Incorporated: 15 April 2014 *Employees:* 2
Previous: Pentafra Limited
Net Worth: £27 *Total Assets:* £153,757
Registered Office: Midland House, 2 Poole Road, Bournemouth, BH2 5QY
Shareholders: Danielle Marie Rolfe; Guy William Rolfe
Officers: Danielle Marie Rolfe [1981] Director/Self Employed; Guy William Rolfe [1981] Director/Self Employed

Pentrich Brewing Co. Ltd
Incorporated: 27 November 2015 *Employees:* 4
Net Worth: £20,969 *Total Assets:* £57,517
Registered Office: Unit B, Asher Lane Business Park, Asher Lane, Pentrich, Ripley, Derbys, DE5 3RE
Major Shareholder: Joe Noble
Officers: Ryan Andrew Cummings [1990] Director/Brewing; Joe Adam Noble [1990] Director/Brewing

Penzance Brewing Co Ltd
Incorporated: 18 July 2008
Net Worth: £37,497 *Total Assets:* £95,852
Registered Office: The Star Inn, Crowlas, Penzance, Cornwall, TR20 8DX
Shareholders: Tracey Jayne Cornelius; Peter Elvin
Officers: Tracey Jayne Cornelius [1965] Director/Brewery; Peter Elvin [1958] Director/Brewery

Pershore Brewery Limited
Incorporated: 22 June 2015 *Employees:* 2
Net Worth Deficit: £4,759 *Total Assets:* £15,356
Registered Office: Unit 5 Lyttleton Road, Pershore, Worcs, WR10 2DF
Shareholders: Elizabeth Barnett; Sean Neil Barnett
Officers: Elizabeth Barnett [1974] Director/Micro Brewery; Sean Neil Barnett [1971] Director/Micro Brewery

Phaded World Ltd
Incorporated: 29 June 2017
Registered Office: Flat 2, 85 Ladbroke Grove, London, W11 2HB
Major Shareholder: Francesca Sandra Marotta
Officers: Francesca Sandra Marotta [1973] Director/Food [Italian]

Phantom Brewing Co. Limited
Incorporated: 23 November 2017
Registered Office: Halstead, Old Bath Road, Sonning, Reading, Berks, RG4 6TQ
Shareholders: Dominic Gemski; Dane White
Officers: Dominic Gemski [1991] Director; Dane White [1990] Director

Philsters Limited
Incorporated: 27 May 2014
Net Worth Deficit: £8,118 *Total Assets:* £1,943
Registered Office: Beehive Cottage, Little Haseley, Oxford, OX44 7LH
Major Shareholder: Philip Mark Lynn
Officers: Philip Mark Lynn [1959] Director

Phipps Northampton Brewery Company Limited
Incorporated: 7 October 2004 *Employees:* 17
Net Worth: £376,153 *Total Assets:* £485,990
Registered Office: 54 Kingswell Street, Northampton, NN1 1PR
Shareholder: Alaric James Neville
Officers: Alaric James Neville, Secretary; Roy Crutchley [1954] Director/Brewer; Alaric James Neville [1961] Director; Quentin John Neville [1963] Director; Jeremy Phipps [1963] Director

Phonymick Ltd
Incorporated: 24 August 2018
Registered Office: 24 Willow Avenue, Carlton in Lindrick, Worksop, Notts, S81 9HT
Major Shareholder: Jade Tizzard
Officers: Jade Tizzard [1994] Director/Consultant

Pictish Brewing Co Limited
Incorporated: 21 August 2002 *Employees:* 2
Net Worth: £422,562 *Total Assets:* £481,509
Registered Office: 2 Thor Drive, Whitworth, Rochdale, Lancs, OL12 8EU
Parent: Lorsho Limited
Officers: Cheryl Jane Wesley [1973] Director; Paul Robert Wesley [1972] Director

Piddle Brewery Limited
Incorporated: 30 July 2014
Net Worth Deficit: £16,796 *Total Assets:* £147,663
Registered Office: Unit 24 Enterprise Park, Piddlehinton, Dorchester, DT2 7UA
Major Shareholder: Ian Alan Siddall
Officers: Jonathan Lavers [1971] Sales Director; Ian Alan Siddall [1957] Director/Consultant

Pig and Porter Limited
Incorporated: 18 September 2012 *Employees:* 6
Net Worth Deficit: £61,654 *Total Assets:* £163,689
Registered Office: 5 Funtley Court, Funtley Hill, Fareham, Hants, PO16 7UY
Shareholders: Robin Paul Dalton Wright; Sean Edward Ayling
Officers: Juliette Myra Wright [1955] Director; Robin Paul Dalton Wright [1970] Director/Manufacture of Beer

Pig Iron Brewing Company Limited
Incorporated: 12 February 2014 *Employees:* 1
Net Worth: £941 *Total Assets:* £2,563
Registered Office: Polymer Court, Hope Street, Dudley, W Midlands, DY2 8RS
Major Shareholder: Dean William Cartwright
Officers: Justine Amanda Cartwright, Secretary; Dean William Cartwright [1967] Director/Brewery

Pig Iron Brewing Limited
Incorporated: 20 May 2014
Registered Office: Polymer Court, Hope Street, Dudley, W Midlands, DY2 8RS
Major Shareholder: Dean William Cartwright
Officers: Justine Amanda Cartwright, Secretary; Dean William Cartwright [1967] Director

The Pigeon Fishers Craft Brewery Limited
Incorporated: 2 December 2013
Net Worth Deficit: £27,013 *Total Assets:* £6,724
Registered Office: Unit B1, The Devonshire Buildings, Works Road Hollingwood, Chesterfield, Derbys, S43 2PE
Major Shareholder: Adrian Cole
Officers: Kathy Alina Chadwick [1980] Director/Licensee; Adrian Cole [1976] Director/Brewer and Marketing Consultant; Dale Barry Milburn [1973] Director/Builder

Piglove Brewing Co Limited
Incorporated: 23 March 2017
Registered Office: Companies House, Default Address, Cardiff, CF14 8LH
Officers: Jesus Moreno [1980] Director/Brewer Technician [Spanish]; Marcos Ramirez [1985] Director/Manufacturing Engineer [Venezuelan]

Pilgrim Brewery (Reigate) Limited
Incorporated: 19 April 2017
Net Worth: £2 *Total Assets:* £2
Registered Office: Pilgrim Brewery, 11 West Street, Reigate, Surrey, RH2 9BL
Officers: Adrian Neil Rothera, Secretary; Rory Fry-Stone [1966] Sales Director; Adrian Neil Rothera [1966] Director/Accountant

Pilot Beer Limited
Incorporated: 7 June 2012 *Employees:* 4
Net Worth: £40,917 *Total Assets:* £197,592
Registered Office: 4b Stewartfield, Edinburgh, EH6 5RQ
Shareholders: Patrick Matthew Jones; Matthew Roger Johnson
Officers: Matthew Roger Johnson [1979] Director; Patrick Matthew Jones [1980] Director

The Pilot Brewery Limited
Incorporated: 2 June 2014
Net Worth: £5,255 *Total Assets:* £5,255
Registered Office: Courtland House, 13 Gower Place, Mumbles, Swansea, SA3 4AB
Parent: J & R (Mumbles) Limited
Officers: Richard Kenric Bennett [1966] Director/Brewer

Pilot Wharf Limited
Incorporated: 21 March 2017
Net Worth Deficit: £42,227 *Total Assets:* £175,625
Registered Office: Courtland House, 13 Gower Place, Mumbles, Swansea, SA3 4AB
Shareholders: Joanna Elizabeth Bennett; Richard Kenric Bennett; Rhys Anthony Pillai
Officers: Joanna Elizabeth Bennett [1967] Director/Publican; Richard Kenric Bennett [1966] Director/Brewer; Rhys Anthony Pillai [1987] Director/Brewer

Pin-Up Beers Ltd.
Incorporated: 14 April 2011 *Employees:* 2
Net Worth: £24,344 *Total Assets:* £45,473
Registered Office: ASM House, 103a Keymer Road, Hassocks, W Sussex, BN6 8QL
Major Shareholder: Jonathan Booth
Officers: Jonathan Booth, Secretary; Jonathan Booth [1979] Director; Laurie Simon Vella [1974] Commercial Director

The Pink Ferry Ltd
Incorporated: 10 June 2015
Net Worth: £193,520 *Total Assets:* £197,060
Registered Office: The Old Casino, 28 Fourth Avenue, Hove, E Sussex, BN3 2PJ
Shareholders: Nicola Ruth Deighton; Justin Lance Deighton
Officers: Justin Lance Deighton [1970] Director/Business Owner; Nicola Ruth Deighton [1970] Director/Businesswoman; Paul William Frederick Kempe [1957] Director; Michael James Penkethman [1964] Director

Pink Moon Brewery Limited
Incorporated: 11 April 2016
Registered Office: 87 Northfield Road, Harborne, Birmingham, B17 0ST
Officers: Paul Michael Cook [1965] Director/Brewery

Pinnora Ltd
Incorporated: 25 April 2014
Previous: Pembroke Park Ltd
Registered Office: Unit 2 rear of Jubilee Parade, West End Avenue, Pinner, Middlesex, HA5 1BB
Shareholders: Gareth Cox; Gawain Cox
Officers: Gareth Cox [1977] Director/Site Manager; Gawain Cox [1980] Director/Entrepreneur

Pivo Beverages Ltd
Incorporated: 12 June 2018
Registered Office: Suite 10, Sheepscar Court, Northside Business Park, Leeds, LS7 2BB
Major Shareholder: Mandeep Singh
Officers: Jasdeep Singh [1981] Director; Mandeep Singh [1978] Director

Pivo-UK Limited
Incorporated: 22 November 2016 *Employees:* 2
Net Worth Deficit: £14,441 *Total Assets:* £20,922
Registered Office: 2 Old Bath Road, Newbury, Berks, RG14 1QL
Shareholders: Vit Rozehnal; Christopher Woodroffe
Officers: Vit Rozehnal [1982] Director [Czech]; Christopher Woodroffe [1986] Director

Pixie Spring Brewing Company Limited
Incorporated: 9 March 2012 *Employees:* 2
Net Worth: £84,912 *Total Assets:* £147,553
Registered Office: 9 Thomasville, Caerphilly, Gwent, CF83 2RE
Shareholders: Stephen Peter Lewis; Gary Prescott; Thomas William James Barlow
Officers: Stephen Lewis, Secretary; Thomas William James Barlow [1981] Director/Brewer; Stephen Peter Lewis [1968] Director/Manager; Gary Prescott [1970] Director/Brewer

Plain Ales Brewery Ltd
Incorporated: 3 January 2014 *Employees:* 3
Net Worth Deficit: £84,796 *Total Assets:* £60,276
Registered Office: Unit 17c Deverill Road, Sutton Veny, Warminster, Wilts, BA12 7BZ
Major Shareholder: Maureen Stokes
Officers: Robert Timoney [1950] Director/Self Employed

Plan B Brewing Company Ltd
Incorporated: 16 December 2015
Net Worth Deficit: £36,206 *Total Assets:* £7,131
Registered Office: Unit 10a Audley Avenue Enterprise Park, Newport, Salop, TF10 7DW
Major Shareholder: Jayne Margaret Charman
Officers: Jayne Margaret Chairman [1985] Director/Consultant

Platform 5 Brewing Company Ltd
Incorporated: 17 January 2013
Net Worth: £22,989 *Total Assets:* £41,661
Registered Office: 20 Fore Street, St Marychurch, Torquay, Devon, TQ1 4LY
Officers: Sally Anne Molloy, Secretary; Margaret Molloy [1948] Director/Publican; Richard Jeffery Molloy [1946] Director/Publican; Richard Michael Molloy [1974] Director/Publican; Sally Anne Molloy [1972] Director/Administrator; Helen Margaret West [1970] Director

Play Limited
Incorporated: 11 November 2016
Net Worth Deficit: £15,416 *Total Assets:* £13,843
Registered Office: 10 Mill Hill, Leeds, LS1 5DQ
Major Shareholder: Philip Layton
Officers: Philip Layton [1979] Director

PLS Special Projects Limited
Incorporated: 24 April 2007 *Employees:* 2
Net Worth: £170 *Total Assets:* £3,866
Registered Office: Northgate, 118 North Street, Leeds, LS2 7PN
Shareholders: Jason Edward Salvin; Sarah Louise Buckmaster
Officers: Sarah Louise Buckmaster, Secretary/Technical Manager; Sarah Louise Buckmaster [1979] Director/Technical Manager; Jason Edward Salvin [1972] Director

Isaac Poad Brewing Ltd
Incorporated: 29 February 2016 *Employees:* 3
Net Worth Deficit: £71,860 *Total Assets:* £53,848
Registered Office: Axholme, Cattal, York, YO26 8DY
Shareholders: Simon Rupert Mark Cockerill; Danielle Cockerill
Officers: Danielle Cockerill [1971] Director; Simon Rupert Mark Cockerill [1968] Director

Pointeer Ltd
Incorporated: 18 September 2018
Registered Office: 43 The Calls, St Peters House, Leeds, LS2 7EY
Shareholders: David John Rushton; Stefan Amato
Officers: Stefan Amato, Secretary; Stefan Amato [1987] Director; Henry Robert Brighton Crofts [1989] Director; David John Rushton [1987] Director

Pokertree Brewing Company Ltd
Incorporated: 9 July 2012
Net Worth Deficit: £13,549 *Total Assets:* £46,725
Registered Office: 357b Drumnakilly Road, Drumnakilly Road Carrickmore, Omagh, Co Tyrone, BT79 9JY
Shareholders: Peter McBride; Darren Paul Nugent
Officers: Darren Paul Nugent [1979] Director/Brewing [Irish]; Emma-Jayne Nugent [1980] Director/Healthcare

Polarity Brewing Ltd
Incorporated: 28 June 2016
Net Worth Deficit: £409 *Total Assets:* £3,516
Registered Office: 5 Abbotts Close, Worthing, W Sussex, BN11 1JB
Officers: Lee Tweed, Secretary; Matheau Hicks [1985] Director/Brewer; Lee Tweed [1989] Director/Brewer

Pomona Island Brew Co Ltd
Incorporated: 31 July 2017
Registered Office: 1 Shawcroft Hill, Hebden Bridge, W Yorks, HX7 8TD
Shareholders: Nicholas Anthony Greenhalgh; Ryan Thompson; Gareth Richard Bee
Officers: Gareth Richard Bee [1982] Director; Nicholas Anthony Greenhalgh [1981] Director; Ryan Thompson [1978] Director

Pongolo Ltd
Incorporated: 12 September 2018
Registered Office: Flat 2, 1-6 Rowhill Mansions, Rowhill Road, London, E5 8ED
Shareholders: Alexander Michael Woods; Henry John Magoveny Pescod
Officers: Henry John Magoveny Pescod [1983] Director/Chartered Surveyor; Alexander Michael Woods [1982] Director/Businessman

Popes Yard Brewery Limited
Incorporated: 29 August 2012 *Employees:* 2
Net Worth Deficit: £81,057 *Total Assets:* £9,199
Registered Office: Frogmore Mill, Fourdrinier Way, Hemel Hempstead, Herts, HP3 9RY
Shareholders: Geoffrey David Latham; Barbara Leenen
Officers: Geoffrey Latham [1971] Director; Barbara Leenen [1967] Director/Graphic Designer [German]

Portishead Brewing Co Ltd
Incorporated: 10 April 2018
Registered Office: 1 St Marys Park Road, Portishead, Bristol, BS20 6SN
Shareholders: Aleksandar Vladimirov Grigorov; Yavor Kostadinchev
Officers: Lyubomira Kostadincheva, Secretary; Aleksandar Vladimirov Grigorov [1980] Director [Bulgarian]; Yavor Kostadinchev [1981] Director [Bulgarian]

Portobello Brewing Company Ltd
Incorporated: 25 October 2011 *Employees:* 9
Net Worth: £2,882 *Total Assets:* £627,950
Registered Office: Unit 6 Mitre Bridge Industrial Park, Mitre Way, London, W10 6AU
Shareholder: Robert Huw Jenkins
Officers: Robert Jenkins [1967] Director/Sales; Farooq Khalid [1972] Brewing and Operations Director; Joseph Vivian Laventure [1954] Director/Sales and Marketing Star

The Portpatrick Brewery Ltd
Incorporated: 2 September 2014
Registered Office: The Neuk, Stoneykirk, Stranraer, Dumfries & Galloway, DG9 9EF
Major Shareholder: Keith Stebbens
Officers: Keith Stebbens, Secretary; Keith Stebbens [1968] Director/Bookkeeper

Posh Boys Brewery Limited
Incorporated: 21 July 2017
Net Worth Deficit: £2,791 *Total Assets:* £7,973
Registered Office: 36 Carlton Road, Wickford, Essex, SS11 7NB
Shareholder: Ian Giles
Officers: Ian Giles [1965] Director; Andrew Scates [1967] Director

Postlethwaites Brewery Ltd
Incorporated: 16 May 2018
Registered Office: 14 Haydock Road, Lancaster, LA1 4ND
Major Shareholder: Andrew Thomas Postlethwaite
Officers: Andrew Thomas Postlethwaite [1992] Director/Engineer

Potbelly Brewery Limited
Incorporated: 21 June 2004 *Employees:* 3
Net Worth: £46,622 *Total Assets:* £227,311
Registered Office: 3 Pine Close, Desborough, Kettering, Northants, NN14 2UQ
Officers: Gregory Lawrence Johnson [1969] Director; Ian James Loasby [1965] Director

Potton Brewing Company Ltd
Incorporated: 4 May 2017
Net Worth Deficit: £9,053 *Total Assets:* £42,487
Registered Office: 12 Festival Road, Potton, Sandy, Beds, SG19 2QN
Major Shareholder: Richard Haigh
Officers: Dr Joanna Haigh [1976] Director/Teacher; Richard Haigh [1976] Director/Brewer

Powderkeg Brewery Ltd
Incorporated: 3 April 2014
Net Worth: £101,487 *Total Assets:* £253,112
Registered Office: 32 Ashford Road, Topsham, Exeter, EX3 0LA
Officers: John Frederick Magill [1976] Managing Director

Pressure Drop Brewing Limited
Incorporated: 1 October 2012
Net Worth: £215,349 *Total Assets:* £792,590
Registered Office: 45 Elfort Road, London, N5 1AX
Shareholders: Sam Smith; Ben Freeman; Graham Patrick O'Brien
Officers: Benjamin Jack Freeman [1981] Director; Graham Patrick O'Brien [1972] Director; Sam Smith [1971] Director

The Pretty Decent Beer Company Ltd
Incorporated: 30 June 2016
Net Worth: £5,280 *Total Assets:* £25,702
Registered Office: Arch 338 Sheridan Road, London, E7 9EF
Officers: James David Nida [1988] Director

Priest Town Brewing Company Ltd
Incorporated: 28 July 2014 *Employees:* 1
Net Worth: £100 *Total Assets:* £20,549
Registered Office: 139 Ribbleton Avenue, Ribbleton, Preston, Lancs, PR2 6YS
Major Shareholder: Ian Stezaker
Officers: Ian Stezaker [1968] Director/Retail Manager

Priors Well Brewery Limited
Incorporated: 23 October 2015 *Employees:* 2
Net Worth Deficit: £26,077 *Total Assets:* £8,381
Registered Office: Unit 8 Block 21 Old Mill Lane Industrial Estate, Mansfield, Notts, NG19 9BQ
Major Shareholder: David John Vann
Officers: Philip Scotney [1959] Director/Manager; David John Vann [1953] Director/Brewer

Project Brewery Ltd
Incorporated: 15 June 2017
Registered Office: Flat 5, 42 The Gardens, London, SE22 9QG
Major Shareholder: Christopher Roberts
Officers: Christopher Roberts [1976] Director/Brewer

Project X Brewing Company Limited
Incorporated: 7 May 2015
Registered Office: Unit 29-30 Old Jamaica Business Estate, 24 Old Jamaica Road, London, SE16 4AW
Shareholder: David John Ackerley
Officers: David John Ackerley [1961] Director/Consultant; Alan Leslie Mead [1960] Director/Consultant

The Proper Beer Company Limited
Incorporated: 10 April 2012
Registered Office: 17 St Marks Road, Teddington, Middlesex, TW11 9DE
Shareholder: Nicholas John Eaton
Officers: Nick Eaton [1963] Director/Consultant; Daniel Lyus [1971] Director/Business Development Manager

The Proper Brewing Company Limited
Incorporated: 21 January 2014
Registered Office: 33 High Street, Welbourn, Lincoln, LN5 0NH
Officers: Andrew Burton [1967] Director; James Michael Colman [1970] Director; Adrian Cowell [1970] Director; Daymon Logan Nicolson [1970] Director

Prospect Brewery Limited
Incorporated: 29 January 2007
Net Worth: £40,615 *Total Assets:* £126,827
Registered Office: 10a Great George Street, Wigan, Lancs, WN3 4DL
Shareholders: Helen Patricia Slevin; John Francis Slevin
Officers: John Francis Slevin, Secretary; Helen Patricia Slevin [1964] Director

The Proud Peacock Limited
Incorporated: 7 February 2014
Registered Office: The Peacock, Fen Road, Ruskington, Sleaford, Lincs, NG34 9EA
Shareholders: Christopher James Astill; Emma Clare Donovan
Officers: Christopher James Astill [1967] Director/Craft Brewing, Artisanal Foods & Workshops; Emma Clare Donovan [1968] Director/Craft Brewing, Artisanal Foods & Workshops

Prussia 1701 Limited
Incorporated: 16 February 2016
Registered Office: Prussia 1701 Limited, Meden Road, Boughton, Newark, Notts, NG22 9ZD
Shareholder: Graham Roy Lawrence

Prussia Bier Limited
Incorporated: 16 February 2016
Registered Office: Prussia Bier Limited, Meden Road, Boughton, Newark, Notts, NG22 9ZD

Pryor Reid & Co Limited
Incorporated: 31 March 2014
Registered Office: 10 The Ryde, Hatfield, Herts, AL9 5DH
Major Shareholder: Jonathan Edwin Brindle
Officers: Jonathan Edwin Brindle [1954] Director

Pumphouse Brewing Company Limited
Incorporated: 18 April 2016 *Employees:* 4
Previous: The Beer Works Ltd
Net Worth Deficit: £52,685 *Total Assets:* £24,716
Registered Office: Unit 10 D Twydale Business Park, Skerne Road, Driffield, E Yorks, YO25 6JX
Shareholders: Zsolt Hangrad; David Jonathan Braysmith
Officers: David Jonathan Braysmith [1962] Director; Joanne Louise Hangrad [1971] Director; Zsolt Hangrad [1970] Director/Head Brewer [Hungarian]; Sarah Lorrain Hatfield [1971] Director/Community Development Worker; Carl Skelton [1969] Director

Punchbowl Brewery Limited
Incorporated: 16 April 2018
Registered Office: 453 Blackburn Road, Turton, Bolton, Lancs, BL7 0PW
Major Shareholder: Ian Brown
Officers: Ian Brown [1953] Director/Retired; Simon Brown [1983] Director/Self Employed

Punchline Brewery Limited
Incorporated: 7 April 2017
Net Worth: £17,128 *Total Assets:* £20,239
Registered Office: Unit 13 Stowheath Industrial Estate, Monmore Road, Wolverhampton, W Midlands, WV1 2TZ
Officers: Andrew Mark Bates [1965] Director/Technical Architect; James Plant [1976] Director; Louise Rowan [1970] Director/Communications Consultant; Lisa Shackleton [1972] Director/Administration Assistant; Richard William Shackleton [1971] Director

Punjabi Ltd
Incorporated: 9 May 2018
Registered Office: 71-75 Shelton Street, London, WC2H 9JQ
Major Shareholder: Manjit Singh Hanjra
Officers: Manjit Singh Hanjra, Secretary; Manjit Singh Hanjra [1966] Director/Engineer

Purity Brewing Company Limited
Incorporated: 27 August 2003 *Employees:* 40
Net Worth: £2,430,198 *Total Assets:* £5,428,463
Registered Office: The Brewery, Upper Spernall Farm, Spernall Lane, Great Alne, Alcester, Warwicks, B49 6JF
Parent: Purity Brewing Group Limited
Officers: James Philip Minkin, Secretary; Paul Halsey [1962] Director/Self Employed; James Philip Minkin [1966] Director/Accountant

Purple Moose Brewery Ltd
Incorporated: 11 January 2002 *Employees:* 34
Net Worth: £616,644 *Total Assets:* £1,037,016
Registered Office: Union Buildings, Madoc Street, Porthmadog, Gwynedd, LL49 9DB
Major Shareholder: Lawrence John Washington
Officers: Lawrence John Washington, Secretary; Jennifer Katherine Washington [1974] Director; Lawrence John Washington [1971] Director/Brewer

Quad Brewing Company Limited
Incorporated: 23 January 2015
Net Worth Deficit: £10,683 *Total Assets:* £55
Registered Office: 16 Park Avenue, Houghton Regis, Dunstable, Beds, LU5 5EA
Shareholders: Edward Button; Katherine Button
Officers: Edward Button [1981] Director; Katherine Button [1982] Director

Quantock Brewery Limited
Incorporated: 20 November 2018
Registered Office: Melbury House, Southborough Road, Bromley, Kent, BR1 2EB
Major Shareholder: Philip Owen Padgham
Officers: Philip Owen Padgham [1965] Director

Quartz Brewing Limited
Incorporated: 5 February 2005 *Employees:* 3
Net Worth Deficit: £362,255 *Total Assets:* £48,247
Registered Office: 4 Mill Court, Shenstone, Lichfield, Staffs, WS14 0DE
Shareholders: Scott William Pert Barnett; Julia Barnett
Officers: Julia Barnett, Secretary; Julia Barnett [1968] Director/Master Brewer; Scott William Pert Barnett [1969] Director

The Queer Brewing Project Ltd
Incorporated: 25 February 2019
Registered Office: Oakley Lodge, Oakley Road, Cheltenham, Glos, GL52 6NZ
Officers: Lilith Grace Hayward Waite [1994] Director

Quirky Ales Ltd
Incorporated: 9 May 2015 *Employees:* 3
Net Worth: £40,943 *Total Assets:* £77,851
Registered Office: Unit 3 Ash Lane, Garforth, Leeds, LS25 2HG
Major Shareholder: Michael Quirk
Officers: Michael Quirk [1962] Director; Richard James Scott [1963] Director

M Rackstraws Ltd
Incorporated: 24 April 2016 *Employees:* 2
Net Worth Deficit: £98,383 *Total Assets:* £141,231
Registered Office: Handsome Brewery, Bowston Bridge, Bowston, Kendal, Cumbria, LA8 9HD
Shareholders: Matthew James Laws Sanderson; Matthew James Laws Sanderson
Officers: Richard Stuart Colvill [1977] Director/Graphic Designer; Matthew James Laws Sanderson [1963] Director/Engineer; Marcin Kazimierz Serwatka [1978] Director/Head Brewer [Polish]

Radio City Beer Works Limited
Incorporated: 30 October 2017
Registered Office: Peartree Farm, Mole Hill Green,= Felsted, Dunmow, Essex, CM6 3JP
Major Shareholder: Daniel Harvey
Officers: William Bishop [1982] Director/Gardener; Daniel Harvey [1988] Director

Radlett Beer Company Limited
Incorporated: 14 April 2015
Net Worth Deficit: £31,581 *Total Assets:* £30,545
Registered Office: 34a Watling Street, Radlett, Herts, WD7 7NN
Shareholder: Rudi Keyser
Officers: Rudi Arthur Keyser [1977] Director [South African]

Ralphs Ruin Ltd
Incorporated: 8 July 2016
Net Worth Deficit: £1,048 *Total Assets:* £16,039
Registered Office: The Royal Oak, Lower Bristol Road, Bath, BA2 3BW
Major Shareholder: Christopher John Powell
Officers: Christopher John Powell [1980] Director/Landlord

The Ramsbury Brewing and Distilling Company Limited
Incorporated: 4 March 2013 *Employees:* 7
Net Worth Deficit: £1,902,932 *Total Assets:* £3,085,206
Registered Office: The Estate Office, Priory Farm, Axford, Marlborough, Wilts, SN8 2HA
Major Shareholder: Carl Stefan Erling Persson
Officers: Alistair Edward Stuart Ewing, Secretary; Carl Stefan Erling Persson [1947] Director [Swedish]

Ramsgate Brewery Limited
Incorporated: 4 November 2004 *Employees:* 11
Net Worth: £266,495 *Total Assets:* £433,045
Registered Office: Unit 1 Hornet Close, Pysons Rd Industrial Estate, Broadstairs, Kent, CT10 2YD
Officers: Lois Elizabeth Gadd, Secretary; George Edward Charles Gadd [1967] Director/Manager; Lois Elizabeth Gadd [1969] Director/Sales Manager; David Green [1945] Director/Retired

Range Ales Brewery Limited
Incorporated: 20 May 2013
Registered Office: Unit N4, Lympne Industrial Estate, Lympne, Hythe, Kent, CT21 4LR
Shareholders: David William Wood; James Charles Dempster
Officers: James Charles Dempster [1966] Director/Police Officer; David William Wood [1953] Director

Raven Hill Brewery Limited
Incorporated: 28 March 2018
Registered Office: Raven Hill Farm, Kilham, Driffield, E Yorks, YO25 4EG
Major Shareholder: Mark William Savile
Officers: Mark William Savile [1985] Director

The Real Crafty Brewing Company Ltd
Incorporated: 11 April 2016
Registered Office: Thatched House Farm, Dunsfold Road, Loxhill, Godalming, Surrey, GU8 4BW
Major Shareholder: Luke Arthur John Herman
Officers: Luke Arthur John Herman [1988] Director/The Crafty Brewing Company

Reality Brewing Limited
Incorporated: 3 December 2009
Net Worth Deficit: £23,347 *Total Assets:* £61
Registered Office: 8 Bramcote Road, Beeston, Nottingham, NG9 1AG
Major Shareholder: Alan Denis Monaghan
Officers: Alan Denis Monaghan [1947] Director/Manager

Rebellion Beer Company Limited
Incorporated: 10 September 1997 *Employees:* 53
Net Worth: £234,843 *Total Assets:* £2,536,358
Registered Office: Bencombe Farm, Marlow Bottom, Marlow, Bucks, SL7 3LT
Shareholders: Mark Ashley Gloyens; Timothy Coombes
Officers: Timothy Coombes, Secretary; John Andrew Coombes [1956] Finance Director; Timothy Coombes [1962] Director/Brewer; Mark Ashley Gloyens [1963] Director/Brewer; Paul Russell Gloyens [1961] Engineering & Projects Director; Andy James Rolstone [1971] Operation Director

Recognise Limited
Incorporated: 20 January 2009
Net Worth Deficit: £168,982 *Total Assets:* £72,133
Registered Office: 23 Twizel Close, Stonebridge, Milton Keynes, Bucks, MK13 0DX
Major Shareholder: Datis Gol-Shecan
Officers: Datis Gol-Shecan [1981] Director/Consultant

Recoil Brewing Company Ltd
Incorporated: 19 October 2016 *Employees:* 3
Net Worth Deficit: £56,318 *Total Assets:* £177,720
Registered Office: 3rd Floor, Ivy Mill, Crown Street, Failsworth, Manchester, M35 9BG
Major Shareholder: Matthew Steven Taylor
Officers: Matthew Steven Taylor [1984] Director/Brewery

Rectory Ales Limited
Incorporated: 7 November 1995
Net Worth: £22,381 *Total Assets:* £22,381
Registered Office: The Rectory, Station Road, Plumpton Green, Lewes, E Sussex, BN7 3BU
Officers: Godfrey David Broster, Secretary; Colin Hill [1937] Director/Retired; Nigel Ernest Riches [1931] Director/Retired [Australian]

Red Bay Brewing Company Limited
Incorporated: 31 July 2018
Registered Office: 9 Bellisk Park, Cushendall, Ballymena, Co Antrim, BT44 0AF
Shareholders: Fergus Oliver Wheeler; Emmet Patrick Connon
Officers: Fergus Oliver Wheeler, Secretary; Emmet Patrick Connon [1982] Director/Electrical Engineer; Fergus Oliver Wheeler [1978] Director/Lawyer

Red Cat Brewing Limited
Incorporated: 26 March 2013
Net Worth Deficit: £4,030 *Total Assets:* £208,840
Registered Office: Unit 10 Sun Valley Business Park, Winnall Close, Winchester, Hants, SO23 0LB
Major Shareholder: Andrew James Mansell
Officers: Andrew James Mansell [1989] Director/Brewer

Red Fox Brewery Limited
Incorporated: 29 April 2008
Net Worth: £3,935 *Total Assets:* £47,155
Registered Office: Scrips Farm Cottage, Cut Hedge Lane, Coggeshall, Essex, CO6 1RL
Shareholder: Russell Barnes
Officers: Russell Antony Barnes, Secretary; Russell Antony Barnes [1967] Director; Alison Mary Elizabeth Byrne [1967] Director

Red Moon Brewery Limited
Incorporated: 18 February 2019
Registered Office: 18-22 Stoney Lane, Yardley, Birmingham, B25 8YP
Shareholders: James Steven Hewitt; Mark Thompson
Officers: James Steven Hewitt [1978] Director; Mark Thompson [1970] Director

Red Rock Brewery Limited
Incorporated: 31 March 2006 *Employees:* 9
Net Worth Deficit: £33,273 *Total Assets:* £168,055
Registered Office: Red Rock Brewery Ltd, Higher Humber Farm, Humber, Teignmouth, Devon, TQ14 9TD
Major Shareholder: John Kirk Parkes
Officers: John Kirk Parkes, Secretary; Hollie Sian Lang [1986] Director/Brewer; John Kirk Parkes [1952] Director/Brewer; Lewis Iain Parkes [1984] Director/Brewer

Red Rose Brewery Ltd
Incorporated: 9 April 2013
Registered Office: 2 Hameldon View, Great Harwood, Lancs, BB6 7BL
Shareholders: Peter Booth; Luke Ashburne
Officers: Peter Booth [1963] Director/Engineer

Red Squirrel Brewery Limited
Incorporated: 1 December 2010
Net Worth Deficit: £192,338 *Total Assets:* £574,906
Registered Office: Unit 18 Boxted Farm, Berkhamsted Road, Hemel Hempstead, Herts, HP1 2SG
Parent: Red Squirrel Group Limited
Officers: Gregory Francis Blesson [1966] Director; Jason Duncan Duncan-Anderson [1975] Director

Red Star Brewery (Formby) Limited
Incorporated: 6 January 2015 *Employees:* 2
Net Worth: £1,319 *Total Assets:* £78,635
Registered Office: 54b Stephenson Way, Formby Business Park, Formby, Merseyside, L37 8EG
Major Shareholder: David Edward Blanchard
Officers: David Edward Blanchard [1959] Director; Raymond Glen Monaghan [1964] Director

The Redchurch Brewery Limited
Incorporated: 28 August 2009 *Employees:* 15
Net Worth Deficit: £100,702 *Total Assets:* £1,341,027
Registered Office: 275-276 Poyser Street, London, E2 9RF
Shareholders: Gary David Ward; Tracey Louise Cleland
Officers: Tracey Cleland [1973] Director; Gary David Ward [1965] Director/Solicitor

Redemption Brewing Company Limited
Incorporated: 6 February 2009
Net Worth Deficit: £87,891 *Total Assets:* £747,696
Registered Office: Unit 16 Compass West Industrial Estate, 33 West Road, Tottenham, London, N17 0XL
Shareholders: Andrew Moffat; Samantha Rigby
Officers: Andrew Moffat [1973] Director/Brewer; Samantha Rigby [1975] Director

Redruth Brewery Limited
Incorporated: 7 December 2016
Registered Office: Kernow House, Gas Hill, Newham, Truro, Cornwall, TR1 2XP
Major Shareholder: Rolf Hugo Munding
Officers: Rolf Hugo Munding [1953] Director

Reds Beer Co Ltd
Incorporated: 30 May 2014
Previous: Patara Wines Ltd
Net Worth: £116 *Total Assets:* £1,315
Registered Office: 352a Bearwood Road, Bearwood, Smethwick, W Midlands, B66 4ET
Parent: Patara Group Ltd
Officers: Kamaljit Kaur Bhamra [1973] Director

Redwillow Brewery Ltd
Incorporated: 15 July 2010 *Employees:* 9
Net Worth: £192,901 *Total Assets:* £400,283
Registered Office: The Lodge, Byrons Lane, Macclesfield, Cheshire, SK11 7JW
Shareholders: Toby Christopher James McKenzie; Caroline Lesley McKenzie
Officers: Caroline Lesley McKenzie [1972] Operations Director; Toby Christopher James McKenzie [1971] Managing Director

Reids Gold Brewing Company Ltd
Incorporated: 31 January 2017 *Employees:* 1
Net Worth Deficit: £3,305 *Total Assets:* £5,305
Registered Office: 61 Provost Barclay Drive, Stonehaven, Aberdeenshire, AB39 2GE
Major Shareholder: Barry Reid
Officers: Barry Reid [1977] Director/Brewer

Religious Ales Ltd
Incorporated: 18 June 2018
Registered Office: Blaen Y Nant, Nant Peris, Caernarfon, Gwynedd, LL55 4UL
Shareholders: Dominic Charles Knights; Joanne Todd
Officers: Dominic Charles Knights [1966] Director/Dental Surgeon; Joanne Todd [1964] Director/Art Tutor

The Renegade Pub Co 2 Limited
Incorporated: 21 July 2014
Previous: The Royal County of Berkshire Brewery Company Limited
Registered Office: 8th Floor, South Reading Bridge House, George Street, Reading, Berks, RG1 8LS
Parent: The West Berkshire Brewery PLC
Officers: Alexander David Michael Bruce [1948] Director; Tom Lucas [1980] Director

Republic of Beer Ltd
Incorporated: 15 January 2016
Registered Office: 151 Capstone Road, Bournemouth, BH8 8RZ
Major Shareholder: James Martin Hunt
Officers: Sara Hunt, Secretary; Steven Michael Hammond [1982] Director/Sales; James Martin Hunt [1983] Director/Brewer; Matthew Robert Waterman [1984] Director/Brewer

Reunion Ales Limited
Incorporated: 18 June 2015
Net Worth: £313,423 *Total Assets:* £318,016
Registered Office: Unit 17 Vector Park, Forest Road, London, TW13 7EJ
Shareholders: Nicholas Andrew Millar; Francis Gabriel Smedley
Officers: Francis Gabriel Smedley [1975] Director/Entrepreneur

Revelry Brewing & Distilling Ltd
Incorporated: 4 September 2018
Registered Office: Coldred Place, Church Road, Coldred, Dover, Kent, CT15 5AQ
Officers: Christian Maurice Peck [1973] Director/General Manager; Melanie Helen Peck [1981] Director/Receptionist; Benjamin Toms [1975] Director/Photographer; Cassandra Jane Toms [1977] Director/Human Resources

The Revolutions Brewing Company Limited
Incorporated: 1 October 2010
Net Worth: £3,022 *Total Assets:* £92,091
Registered Office: Hedley Court, Boothferry Road, Goole, E Yorks, DN14 6AA
Shareholders: Mark Allan Seaman; Andrew Paul Helm
Officers: Andrew Paul Helm, Secretary; Andrew Paul Helm [1968] Director; Mark Allan Seaman [1962] Director

Rhymney Brewery Ltd
Incorporated: 9 October 2002 *Employees:* 77
Net Worth: £2,179,131 *Total Assets:* £4,413,558
Registered Office: Gilchrist Thomas Industrial Estate, Blaenavon, Pontypool, Torfaen, NP4 9RL
Major Shareholder: Stephen Mark Evans
Officers: Cherril Lorraine Evans, Secretary; Marc Evans [1977] Director/Brewer; Stephen Mark Evans [1956] Director/Brewer

Richmond Brewing Company Limited
Incorporated: 4 September 2007 *Employees:* 2
Net Worth Deficit: £130,217 *Total Assets:* £42,174
Registered Office: Unit 3e Enterprise House, Valley Street North, Darlington, Co Durham, DL1 1GY
Parent: Waggies Limited
Officers: Peter Robert Loft, Secretary; Christopher James Wallace [1962] Director/Brewer

Ride Industrys Limited
Incorporated: 25 July 2016
Registered Office: 121 Herries Road, Glasgow, G41 4AN
Major Shareholder: Dave Lannigan
Officers: Dave Lannigan [1980] Director/Brewer

The Ridgeside Brewing Company Ltd
Incorporated: 20 January 2010 *Employees:* 3
Net Worth: £71,525 *Total Assets:* £111,189
Registered Office: Unit 24 Penraevon 2 Industrial Estate, Meanwood, Leeds, LS7 2AW
Shareholders: Jorge Gabriel Gonzalez Moore; Matthew Lovatt
Officers: Jorge Gabriel Gonzalez Moore [1974] Director/Industrial Engineer MBA [Colombian]; Matthew John Lovatt [1983] Director/Brewer

Ripple Steam Brewery Limited
Incorporated: 28 July 2011
Net Worth Deficit: £71,548 *Total Assets:* £135,355
Registered Office: First Floor, 47 Marylebone Lane, London, W1U 2NT
Major Shareholder: Paul Norris
Officers: David Peter Cliff [1953] Director; Paul Norris [1970] Director; Peter John Norris [1968] Director

Rival Brewing Co Limited
Incorporated: 23 March 2017
Net Worth Deficit: £7,783 *Total Assets:* £9,230
Registered Office: 60 Theobald Road, Cardiff, CF5 1LQ
Shareholders: Samuel Duncan Higgitt; Duncan Laurence Higgitt
Officers: Duncan Laurence Higgitt, Secretary; Duncan Laurence Higgitt [1968] Director/Press and Political Officer; Samuel Duncan Higgitt [1995] Director/Bar Manager

River Widow Brewery Ltd
Incorporated: 25 January 2017
Registered Office: 15 Huxley Road, London, E10 5QT
Officers: Andrew Adwick [1984] Director/Accountant; Edmund Bussey [1983] Director/Professional Musician; Marcus Hibbert [1984] Director/Teacher

Riverside Brewery Ltd
Incorporated: 27 July 2015
Net Worth: £30,000 *Total Assets:* £50,180
Registered Office: 13 Henderson Walk, Steyning, W Sussex, BN44 3SG
Shareholders: Michael Anthony Rice; Roger John Paxton; Keith Michael Kempton
Officers: Keith Michael Kempton [1958] Director; Roger Paxton [1946] Director; Michael Anthony Rice [1952] Director

Riviera Brewing Company Limited
Incorporated: 28 August 2014
Net Worth: £103 *Total Assets:* £8,854
Registered Office: 4 Yonder Meadow, Stoke Gabriel, Totnes, Devon, TQ9 6QE
Major Shareholder: Alan David Waldron
Officers: Alan David Waldron [1963] Director/Head Brewer

Rivington Brewing Co Limited
Incorporated: 8 December 2014
Net Worth: £694 *Total Assets:* £20,731
Registered Office: Cunliffe Farm, New Road, Anderton, Chorley, Lancs, PR6 9EY
Shareholders: Ben Stubbs; John Richardson
Officers: John Richardson [1981] Director/Farmer; Ben Stubbs [1986] Director/Sales

Roam Brewing Company Ltd
Incorporated: 7 July 2015
Previous: Tavy Brewing Company Limited
Net Worth: £28,891 *Total Assets:* £56,364
Registered Office: 9 Porsham Close, Roborough, Plymouth, PL6 7DB
Shareholders: Jonathan Stuart Clargo; Victoria Elizabeth Clargo
Officers: Brian Clargo [1949] Director; Jonathan Stuart Clargo [1983] Director; Victoria Elizabeth Clargo [1986] Director; Yolanda Mariea Clargo [1960] Director

Roath Brewery Ltd
Incorporated: 14 April 2016
Net Worth Deficit: £1,360 *Total Assets:* £4,439
Registered Office: 38 Colchester Avenue, Penylan, Cardiff, CF23 9BP
Shareholders: Tom Leo Lyons; Matthew Stephen Appleby
Officers: Tom Leo Lyons, Secretary; Matthew Stephen Appleby [1973] Director; Tom Leo Lyons [1977] Director

Robel Pawlos Ltd
Incorporated: 8 May 2018
Registered Office: 92 Crome House, Parkfied Drive, Northolt, Middlesex, UB5 5NU
Major Shareholder: Pawlos Habtezghi
Officers: Pawlos Habtezghi [1978] Director/Manager

John Roberts Brewing Co Ltd
Incorporated: 9 December 2002 *Employees:* 12
Net Worth: £1,087,036 *Total Assets:* £1,444,884
Registered Office: Office 8, Three Tuns Brewery, Enterprise House, Station Street, Bishops Castle, Salop, SY9 5AQ
Shareholder: John Phillip Russell
Officers: David Charles Russell, Secretary; Samantha Mary Edwards [1981] Director/Accountant; John Phillip Russell [1962] Director; Stephen Sinclair Willmer [1954] Director/Head Brewer

Frederic Robinson Limited
Incorporated: 7 October 1920 *Employees:* 517
Net Worth: £83,431,000 *Total Assets:* £98,526,000
Registered Office: Unicorn Brewery, Lower Hillgate, Stockport, Cheshire, SK1 1JJ
Shareholders: Oliver John Robinson; Dennis William Robinson; Peter Bryan Robinson
Officers: Sara Xanthe Robinson, Secretary; John Edwards [1957] Director; Stephen John Oliver [1958] Director; David John Robinson [1937] Director; Dennis William Robinson [1933] Director; Oliver John Robinson [1971] Director; Paul Andrew Robinson [1969] Director; Peter Bryan Robinson [1931] Director; Veronica Helen Robinson [1969] Director; William Joseph Robinson [1971] Director; Neil Robinson-Stanier [1966] Director

Rock & Roll Brewhouse Ltd
Incorporated: 21 July 2011
Registered Office: 1 Conway Road, Shirley, Solihull, W Midlands, B90 4RE
Major Shareholder: Mark William Shepherd
Officers: Mark William Shepherd [1958] Director/Brewery Services

Rock A Brew Ltd
Incorporated: 5 February 2018
Net Worth: £1 *Total Assets:* £1
Registered Office: 225 Western Road, Leigh on Sea, Essex, SS9 2PQ
Shareholders: James Royston Lord; Raymond Charles Knight
Officers: Raymond Charles Knight [1983] Director/Technician; James Royston Lord [1979] Director/Engineer

Rock Leopard Brewing Co Limited
Incorporated: 11 August 2017
Registered Office: 1 Kingfisher Close, London, SE28 8ES
Major Shareholder: Stacey Ayeh
Officers: Stacey Akwasi Ayeh [1972] Director

Rock Solid Brewing Company Limited
Incorporated: 27 April 2017
Net Worth Deficit: £1,040 *Total Assets:* £1,090
Registered Office: 36 Forest Gate, Blackpool, Lancs, FY3 9AW
Major Shareholder: Vincent Hamer
Officers: Vincent Hamer [1965] Director/Brewery Business Owner

Rock Springs Brewing Ltd
Incorporated: 23 December 2015
Net Worth: £465 *Total Assets:* £1,678
Registered Office: 43 Heckenhurst Avenue, Burnley, Lancs, BB10 3JN
Major Shareholder: Gary Williams
Officers: Gary Williams [1965] Director/Brewer

Rocket Ales Limited
Incorporated: 28 January 2016
Net Worth Deficit: £9,107 *Total Assets:* £27,260
Registered Office: c/o Coles Accounting (Cambridge) Ltd, 33 Newton Hall, Town Street, Newton, Cambridge, CB22 7ZE
Shareholders: Michael Blakesley; David Turner Smith
Officers: Michael Blakesley [1957] Director/IT Manager; David Turner Smith [1957] Director/Development Consultant

Rockhopper Brewing Company Limited
Incorporated: 17 August 2015
Net Worth Deficit: £15,702 *Total Assets:* £15,451
Registered Office: 1 Forrest Crescent, Luton, Beds, LU2 9AR
Major Shareholder: Darren James Oakley
Officers: Dr Darren James Oakley [1978] Director/Software Developer

Rockin Robin Brewery Ltd
Incorporated: 18 November 2013
Net Worth: £11,979 *Total Assets:* £83,159
Registered Office: 6 Pickering Street, Maidstone, Kent, ME15 9RS
Shareholders: Robin Christopher Smallbone; Stuart John Osgood
Officers: Robin Christopher Smallbone [1966] Director/Quality Engineer

Rocksnarl Ltd
Incorporated: 20 August 2018
Registered Office: 11 North View, Stakeford, Choppington, Northumberland, NE62 5JJ
Major Shareholder: Louise Bunn
Officers: Louise Bunn [1977] Director/Consultant

Roddenloft Brewery Ltd
Incorporated: 14 January 2014
Net Worth: £47,675 *Total Assets:* £134,701
Registered Office: Roddenloft House, Roddenloft, Mauchline, E Ayrshire, KA5 5HH
Major Shareholder: George Douglas Hammersley
Officers: Amanda Jane Hammersley, Secretary; George Douglas Hammersley [1952] Director

The Roebuck Brewing Company Limited
Incorporated: 8 June 2016
Net Worth: £199,694 *Total Assets:* £199,694
Registered Office: The Roebuck Brewing Company, Toby's Hill, Draycott in the Clay, Ashbourne, Derbys, DE6 5BT
Shareholders: Anne Topliss; Rosemary Clare Hardwick
Officers: Rosemary Clare Hardwick [1970] Director/Homemaker; Anne Topliss [1951] Director/Homemaker; Stephen Topliss [1951] Director/Brewer

Rogue Elephant Brewery Limited
Incorporated: 21 February 2017
Net Worth: £2,502 *Total Assets:* £2,502
Registered Office: 142 Werrington Road, Stoke on Trent, Staffs, ST2 9AJ
Officers: Katy Gough [1970] Director/Radiographer; Mick Gough [1965] Director

The Romford Brewery Company Limited
Incorporated: 20 March 2017
Registered Office: 13 Dover Close, Romford, Essex, RM5 3AX
Shareholder: Jason David Frost
Officers: Jason David Frost, Secretary; David Frost [1963] Director/Retired; Jason David Frost [1988] Director/Researcher; Richard Sean Tully [1963] Director/Business Owner

Romney Marsh Brewery Limited
Incorporated: 16 October 2014 *Employees:* 2
Net Worth: £68,121 *Total Assets:* £249,197
Registered Office: 10 Littlebourne Road, Maidstone, Kent, ME14 5QP
Shareholder: Matthew Calais
Officers: Cathy Koester, Secretary; Matthew Calais [1973] Director

Roosters Brewery Limited
Incorporated: 11 November 2011 *Employees:* 13
Net Worth: £672,765 *Total Assets:* £911,019
Registered Office: The Old Brewhouse, 8a Waterside, Knaresborough, N Yorks, HG5 9AZ
Major Shareholder: Ian Fozard
Officers: Ian Fozard, Secretary; Ian Fozard [1953] Director; Oliver Edward Fozard [1982] Director/Brewer; Thomas Martin Fozard [1982] Director/Commercial Manager

Roosters Brewing Company Limited
Incorporated: 22 March 2000
Net Worth: £100 *Total Assets:* £100
Registered Office: The Old Brewhouse, 8a Waterside, Knaresborough, N Yorks, HG5 9AZ
Parent: Roosters Brewery Ltd
Officers: Ian Fozard, Secretary; Ian Fozard [1953] Director/Chartered Accountant; Oliver Edward Fozard [1982] Director/Brewer; Thomas Martin Fozard [1982] Director/Sales Manager

Rosebank Brewery Camelon Limited
Incorporated: 27 November 2012
Registered Office: Atrium House, Callendar Business Park, Callendar Road, Falkirk, Stirlingshire, FK1 1XR
Major Shareholder: George Danskin Stewart
Officers: George Danskin Stewart [1945] Director/Engineer

Rosebank Brewery Limited
Incorporated: 27 November 2012
Registered Office: Atrium House, Callendar Business Park, Callendar Road, Falkirk, Stirlingshire, FK1 1XR
Major Shareholder: George Danskin Stewart
Officers: George Danskin Stewart [1945] Director/Engineer

Roseland Brewery Limited
Incorporated: 7 June 2009
Net Worth Deficit: £3,831 *Total Assets:* £3,237
Registered Office: The Roseland Inn, Philleigh, Truro, Cornwall, TR2 5NB
Shareholder: Philip Andrew Heslip
Officers: Philip Andrew Heslip [1966] Director/Publican

Rossendale Brew Co Ltd
Incorporated: 27 February 2019
Registered Office: Suite G1 (E), Adelphi Mill, Grimshaw Lane, Bollington, Cheshire, SK10 5JB
Major Shareholder: Luke John Williams
Officers: John Richard Williams [1947] Director/Bus Driver

Rough Brothers Brewing Limited
Incorporated: 4 October 2018
Registered Office: 42 Lower Ballyartan Road, Killaloo, Co Londonderry, BT47 3SY
Major Shareholder: Andrew Rough
Officers: Andrew Rough [1967] Director

Round Corner Brewing Ltd
Incorporated: 8 June 2017
Net Worth: £2 *Total Assets:* £200
Registered Office: 26 Southey Road, Wimbledon, London, SW19 1NS
Shareholders: Thomas Columba Cryan; Colin Paige
Officers: Thomas Columba Cryan [1974] Director/Sales [Irish]; Charles Erskine Howard [1981] Director/Communications; Colin Paige [1974] Director/Brewer

Round Tower Brewery (Chelmsford) Limited
Incorporated: 11 July 2018
Registered Office: 26 Heycroft Way, Chelmsford, Essex, CM2 8JG
Major Shareholder: John Edward Prior
Officers: John Edward Prior [1962] Director

Round Tower Brewery Ltd
Incorporated: 29 July 2013 *Employees:* 3
Net Worth Deficit: £3,327 *Total Assets:* £15,858
Registered Office: Unit 11-11a Robjohns House, Navigation Road, Chelmsford, Essex, CM2 6ND
Shareholders: Simon Tippler; Hannah Tippler
Officers: Hannah Tippler [1976] Director; Simon Tippler [1974] Director

Roundhill Brewery Limited
Incorporated: 21 July 2016 *Employees:* 1
Net Worth Deficit: £16,162 *Total Assets:* £40,899
Registered Office: 9 Trevine Gardens, Ingleby Barwick, Stockton on Tees, Cleveland, TS17 5HD
Major Shareholder: Russell Allen
Officers: Angela Christina Allen [1963] Director; Russell Allen [1964] Director

Rowton Brewery Ltd
Incorporated: 27 November 2008 *Employees:* 1
Net Worth: £16,537 *Total Assets:* £70,485
Registered Office: Stone House, Rowton, Telford, Salop, TF6 6QX
Shareholders: James Preston; Susan Helen Preston
Officers: Susan Helen Preston, Secretary; James Preston [1955] Director; Stephen David Preston [1989] Director

RPM Brewery Ltd
Incorporated: 22 May 2015
Registered Office: 19 Orchard Street, Weston-Super-Mare, Somerset, BS23 1RG
Shareholder: Christopher Cureton
Officers: Christopher Cureton [1952] Director/Publican; Samuel Cureton [1990] Director/Publican

Rude Mechanicals Limited
Incorporated: 10 May 2018
Registered Office: Boundary House, Cheadle Point, Cheadle, Cheshire, SK8 2GG
Shareholders: Michael Joseph Moriarty; Dennis Whiteley
Officers: Michael Joseph Moriarty [1965] Director and Company Secretary; Dennis Whiteley [1961] Director; Matthew Whiteley [1989] Director; Thomas Whiteley [1987] Director

Rudgate Brewery Limited
Incorporated: 2 July 1992 *Employees:* 13
Net Worth: £37,828 *Total Assets:* £792,284
Registered Office: 2 Centre Park, Marston Moor Business Park, Tockwith, York, YO26 7QF
Major Shareholder: Craig Anthony Lee
Officers: Victoria Louise Lee, Secretary; Craig Anthony Lee [1975] Director/Brewer

Rufford Abbey Brewery Ltd
Incorporated: 16 February 2016
Previous: Prussia Breweries Limited
Registered Office: Prussia Breweries Limited, Meden Road, Boughton, Newark, Notts, NG22 9ZD
Officers: Graham Lawrence, Secretary

The Runaway Brewery Limited
Incorporated: 30 October 2013 *Employees:* 5
Net Worth: £6,774 *Total Assets:* £112,340
Registered Office: 1 Billing Road, Northampton, NN1 5AL
Major Shareholder: Mark Stewart Welsby
Officers: Mark Stewart Welsby [1979] Director

Saeburh Brewery Ltd
Incorporated: 18 December 2018
Registered Office: 43 Melton Close, Clacton on Sea, Essex, CO16 8XZ
Shareholders: David Simon Warner; Chris Clark
Officers: Adriana Georgiana Filip, Secretary; Chris Clark [1974] Director/Brewer; David Simon Warner [1987] Director/Brewer

Saffron Brewery (Henham) Limited
Incorporated: 25 September 2012
Net Worth: £2,982 *Total Assets:* £136,747
Registered Office: The Cartshed, Church End, Henham, Bishop's Stortford, Herts, CM22 6AN
Shareholder: Peter Lisney Hoskins
Officers: James Anthony Lisney Hoskins, Secretary; Peter Lisney Hoskins [1951] Director/Farmer

The Saint Brewing Co Limited
Incorporated: 11 August 2011
Net Worth Deficit: £803,472 *Total Assets:* £13,614
Registered Office: 4 Market Square Building, 85 High Street, Manchester, M4 1BD
Shareholders: Christian Peter Barton; Kieron Mark Barton; Gareth Andrew Whittle
Officers: Kieron Mark Barton [1975] Managing Director; Gareth Andrew Whittle [1976] Managing Director

Saints Row Brewing Co. Ltd.
Incorporated: 24 November 2016
Net Worth: £17,490 *Total Assets:* £17,490
Registered Office: 18 Maude Street, Darlington, Co Durham, DL3 7PW
Major Shareholder: Michal Czubak
Officers: Michal Czubak [1992] Brewer/Director [Polish]

Saison 86 Limited
Incorporated: 27 May 2016
Net Worth: £13,994 *Total Assets:* £131,201
Registered Office: 71-75 Shelton Street, Covent Garden, London, WC2H 9JQ
Shareholders: Andrew Charles MacLeod; Julia Annette MacLeod
Officers: Andrew MacLeod, Secretary; Andrew Charles MacLeod [1963] Director/Engineer; Julia Annette MacLeod [1962] Director/Consultant

Salamander Brewing Company Limited
Incorporated: 2 December 1999
Net Worth: £64,539 *Total Assets:* £102,597
Registered Office: 22 Harry Street, Bradford, W Yorks, BD4 9PH
Major Shareholder: Daniel Peter Gent
Officers: Daniel Peter Gent [1968] Director/Brewer; Laurence Larroche [1967] Director/Translator [French]

The Salcombe Brewery Co. Limited
Incorporated: 16 September 2013 *Employees:* 10
Previous: The Salcombe Brewery Limited
Net Worth: £1,333,962 *Total Assets:* £1,524,242
Registered Office: Estuary View, Ledstone, Kingsbridge, Devon, TQ7 4BL
Shareholder: John Ivan Tiner
Officers: Michael MacKenzie George [1950] Director/Retired; Timothy Shaun McCord [1958] Director/Consultant; Generaldine Marion Alison Tiner [1957] Director; John Ivan Tiner [1957] Director

Salisbury Brewery Limited
Incorporated: 9 May 2016
Registered Office: 94 The Borough, Downton, Salisbury, Wilts, SP5 3LY
Officers: Dene Martyn Gentle [1961] Director/Civil Servant; Charles David Penny [1990] Director

Salopian Brewing Company Ltd.
Incorporated: 10 December 1997 *Employees:* 15
Net Worth: £1,051,251 *Total Assets:* £1,937,880
Registered Office: Old Station Yard, Station Road, Hadnall, Shrewsbury, Salop, SY4 3DD
Shareholder: Mark Adrian Bryan Hill
Officers: Dr Katherine Vanessa Anderson, Secretary; Jason Henry Douglas [1969] Director; Mark Adrian Bryan Hill [1968] Director/Sole Proprietor; William Frank Nelson [1963] Director/Brewer

Saltaire Brewery Limited
Incorporated: 11 June 2003 *Employees:* 30
Net Worth: £63,033 *Total Assets:* £3,133,189
Registered Office: 103 Dockfield Road, Shipley, W Yorks, BD17 7AR
Major Shareholder: Anthony Gartland
Officers: Anthony Gartland, Secretary; Andrew John Shackleton, Secretary; Anthony Gartland [1956] Director; Ewen James Gordon [1978] Director; Nicholas James Helliwell [1977] Sales Director; Daniel Henry James Spampinato [1978] Operations Director; Janet Anna Rita Wojtkow [1960] Director/Retired

Saltdean Brewing Company Limited
Incorporated: 8 May 2018
Registered Office: 11 Coombe Rise, Saltdean, Brighton, BN2 8QN
Officers: Richard Moss [1966] Director/Brewer; Robert Julian Skitmore [1976] Director/Brewer

Saltrock Brewing Company Limited
Incorporated: 30 January 2019
Registered Office: 70 Porterfield, Comrie, Dunfermline, Fife, KY12 9XG
Major Shareholder: Peter Daniel Rossborough
Officers: Peter Daniel Rossborough [1979] Director/Businessman

Sambrook's Brewery Limited
Incorporated: 12 June 2008
Net Worth: £389,577 *Total Assets:* £1,188,926
Registered Office: Unit 1 & 2 Yelverton Road, London, SW11 3QG
Officers: Paul Ian Nunny [1949] Managing Director; Duncan James Sambrook [1978] Director/Accountant

George Samuel Brewing Company Ltd.
Incorporated: 18 May 2015
Net Worth Deficit: £1,285
Registered Office: 6 Tangmere, Spennymoor, Co Durham, DL16 6TY
Major Shareholder: Andrew Ferriman
Officers: Andrew Ferriman [1981] Director/Brewer

Samuels Brewing Company Ltd
Incorporated: 14 June 2017 *Employees:* 2
Net Worth Deficit: £13,111 *Total Assets:* £12,933
Registered Office: Blick Studios, 46 Hill Street, Belfast, BT1 2LB
Major Shareholder: Gary Clarke
Officers: Gary Clarke [1974] Director [Irish]; Sean Clarke [1968] Director [Irish]

Sandbanks Brewery Limited
Incorporated: 31 January 2018
Registered Office: Unit 6, 4-6 Abingdon Road, Poole, Dorset, BH17 0UG
Shareholders: Iain Alexander Potter; Kim Patrick Rawson
Officers: Iain Alexander Potter [1964] Director; Kim Patrick Rawson [1955] Director

Sandstone Brewery Ltd
Incorporated: 5 September 2013
Net Worth Deficit: £92,882 *Total Assets:* £24,249
Registered Office: Unit 5a Wrexham Enterprise Park, Preston Road, off Ash Road North, Wrexham, Clwyd, LL13 9JT
Major Shareholder: William Stuart Deeley
Officers: William Stuart Deeley [1954] Brewery Director

Sativa Brewing Company Limited
Incorporated: 8 October 2018
Registered Office: Langham Brewery Langham Lane, Lodsworth, Petworth, W Sussex, GU28 9BU
Major Shareholder: Lesley Stephens Foulkes
Officers: Lesley Stephens Foulkes [1959] Director/Self Employed

Scarborough Brewery Limited
Incorporated: 26 April 2010
Net Worth Deficit: £129,022 *Total Assets:* £86,113
Registered Office: 21b Barrys Lane, Scarborough, N Yorks, YO12 4HA
Major Shareholder: James Alexander Soden
Officers: James Alexander Soden [1988] Director

Scariosa Ltd
Incorporated: 20 August 2018
Registered Office: 1 Hanbury Road, Liverpool, L4 8TR
Major Shareholder: Natalie Kilcourse
Officers: Natalie Kilcourse [1991] Director/Consultant

SchoolHouseBrewery Ltd
Incorporated: 3 June 2013
Net Worth Deficit: £100,972 *Total Assets:* £54,511
Registered Office: 3 Croft Meadows, Croft Road, Darlington, Co Durham, DL2 2SD
Officers: Helen Gannaway, Secretary; Graham John Gannaway [1957] Director/Brewer

Scot Brew Limited
Incorporated: 11 September 2017
Registered Office: 2nd Floor, Blenheim House, Fountainhall Road, Aberdeen, AB15 4DT
Parent: Signature Pubs Limited
Officers: Rory George Forrest [1982] Director; Nicholas John MacRae Wood [1973] Director

Scottish Borders Brewery Limited
Incorporated: 25 March 2008 *Employees:* 22
Net Worth Deficit: £506,855 *Total Assets:* £1,481,119
Registered Office: Chesters, Ancrum, Jedburgh, Roxburghshire, TD8 6UL
Parent: Chesters Stables Ltd
Officers: Ellen Henderson, Secretary; John Ronald Ogilvie Henderson [1973] Director/Copywriter

Scribbler's Ales Limited
Incorporated: 15 June 2015 *Employees:* 8
Net Worth Deficit: £20,500 *Total Assets:* £45,305
Registered Office: 9 Lime Grove, Stapleford, Nottingham, NG9 7GF
Shareholders: Christopher Richard Nettleton; Christopher Richard Nettleton
Officers: Roger Denis Frost [1954] Director; Christopher Richard Nettleton [1955] Director

Sea Brewing Company Limited
Incorporated: 2 August 2018
Registered Office: The Castle, The Village, Castle Eden, Co Durham, TS27 4SL
Major Shareholder: Stephen John Davis
Officers: Stephen John Davis [1966] Director

Seafire Brewing Co. Ltd
Incorporated: 22 February 2019
Registered Office: 10 Seafire Place, Dalgety Bay, Dunfermline, Fife, KY11 9GY
Major Shareholder: Kiera Browne
Officers: Kiera Browne [1982] Director/Chief Executive

Seal Bay Brewery Sel Bragdy Bae Ltd
Incorporated: 23 May 2014
Net Worth Deficit: £7,021 *Total Assets:* £7,224
Registered Office: Mayfield, Spring Gardens, St Dogmaels Road, Cardigan, Ceredigion, SA43 3AU
Shareholders: Timothy Tagg; Colin Thomas Mathew
Officers: Colin Thomas Mathew [1971] Director/Brewer; Timothy Tagg [1965] Director/Brewer

Second Wave Brewing Ltd
Incorporated: 29 June 2018
Registered Office: 71-75 Shelton Street, London, WC2H 9JQ
Major Shareholder: Ian Hewitt
Officers: Ian Hewitt, Secretary; Ian Hewitt [1982] Director/Engineer

Selby (Middlebrough) Brewery, Limited
Incorporated: 10 September 1945 *Employees:* 1
Net Worth Deficit: £22,208 *Total Assets:* £76,770
Registered Office: 131 Millgate, Selby, N Yorks, YO8 3LL
Shareholders: Martin Howard Sykes; Lynda Anne Sykes
Officers: Lynda Anne Sykes, Secretary; Andrew Francis Sykes [1981] Director; Katharine Louise Sykes [1979] Director; Lynda Anne Sykes [1953] Director/Secretary; Martin Howard Sykes [1946] Director/Lecturer

Sentinel Brewery Holdings Limited
Incorporated: 4 April 2017
Registered Office: Sentinel Brewhouse, 178 Shoreham Street, Sheffield, S1 4SQ
Officers: Alex Gavin Barlow [1965] Director/Brewer; Mark Gibson [1972] Sales Director; Jim Muirhead [1965] Ecommerce Director; Dave Walker [1956] Director/Technology Consultant

Seren Brewing Company Ltd
Incorporated: 8 January 2016
Registered Office: Syfnau House, Rosebush, Clynderwen, Dyfed, SA66 7QY
Major Shareholder: Alastair Matthew Kocho-Williams
Officers: Dr Alastair Matthew Kocho-Williams [1978] Director/Brewer

Serious Brewing Company Ltd
Incorporated: 28 April 2015 *Employees:* 1
Net Worth Deficit: £97,643 *Total Assets:* £77,774
Registered Office: Unit C5, Fieldhouse Industrial Estate, Fieldhouse Road, Rochdale, Lancs, OL12 0AA
Shareholders: Jennifer Frances Lynch; Kenneth Edward Lynch
Officers: Jennifer Frances Lynch [1975] Director; Kenneth Edward Lynch [1973] Director

Serpent Brew Co Ltd
Incorporated: 15 June 2018
Registered Office: 99 Woodland Avenue, Hutton, Brentwood, Essex, CM13 1HH
Shareholders: Matthew Tondziel; Simon John Davis
Officers: Simon John Davis [1981] Director; Matthew Tondziel [1979] Director

Session Brewing Co. Limited
Incorporated: 19 June 2017
Registered Office: Mount Noddy, Church Lane, Danehill, Haywards Heath, W Sussex, RH17 7EY
Major Shareholder: Rufus Wilkinson
Officers: Rufus Giles Wilkinson [1995] Director/Student

Seven Brothers Ancoats Ltd
Incorporated: 12 March 2015
Previous: Seven Brothers Bars Limited
Net Worth Deficit: £53,702 *Total Assets:* £157,003
Registered Office: 63 Waybridge Industrial Estate, Daniel Adamson Road, Salford, M50 1DS
Officers: Christopher McAvoy [1971] Director; Daniel McAvoy [1975] Director; Gregory McAvoy [1983] Director; Guy Richard McAvoy [1962] Director; Luke Philip McAvoy [1973] Director; Nathan McAvoy [1976] Director

Seven Brothers Brewery Limited
Incorporated: 12 November 2013 *Employees:* 6
Net Worth: £103,645 *Total Assets:* £392,828
Registered Office: Unit 63 Waybridge Industrial Estate, Daniel Adamson Road, Salford, M50 1DS
Officers: Christopher McAvoy [1981] Director; Daniel McAvoy [1975] Director; Gregory McAvoy [1983] Director; Luke Philip McAvoy [1973] Director; Nathan McAvoy [1976] Director

Sevenoaks Brewery Limited
Incorporated: 14 January 2014
Registered Office: 8 Plymouth Park, Sevenoaks, Kent, TN13 3RR
Shareholders: Paul David Shelley; Jason Edward Symonds
Officers: Paul David Shelley [1974] Director/Engineer; Jason Edward Symonds [1972] Director/Engineer

Severn Brewing Limited
Incorporated: 13 January 2014 *Employees:* 3
Previous: Nightshade Cider Company Limited
Net Worth Deficit: £25,703 *Total Assets:* £128,815
Registered Office: Pillar House, 113-115 Bath Road, Cheltenham, Glos, GL53 7LS
Parent: Foxstead Limited
Officers: Iain James Crockett [1965] Director

SF Brew Co Ltd
Incorporated: 16 October 2015
Previous: Stoney Ford Brew Co. Ltd
Net Worth: £21,926 *Total Assets:* £56,118
Registered Office: 22 St Georges Street, Stamford, Lincs, PE9 2BU
Major Shareholder: Simon Anthony Watson
Officers: Timothy John Nicol [1956] Director/Management Consultant; Simon Anthony Watson [1971] Director/Brewer

Shadow Brewing Ltd
Incorporated: 28 June 2018
Registered Office: 44 Whiteley Croft Rise, Otley, W Yorks, LS21 3NR
Major Shareholder: Ian Michael Shutt
Officers: Ian Michael Shutt [1978] Director/Entrepreneur

Shady Shed Brewery Limited
Incorporated: 16 April 2018
Registered Office: 144 Ship Lane, Farnborough, Hants, GU14 8BJ
Major Shareholder: Andrew Lutton
Officers: Andrew Lutton, Secretary; Andrew Lutton [1979] Director

Shandy Shack Ltd
Incorporated: 14 August 2018
Registered Office: 18 The Parkway, Southampton, SO16 3PQ
Shareholders: Frederick Joseph York Gleadowe; Edward Stapleton; Thomas Peter Stevens
Officers: Dr Frederick Joseph York Gleadowe [1991] Managing Director; Edward Stapleton [1992] Managing Director; Dr Thomas Peter Stevens [1991] Managing Director

Shardlow Brewing Company Limited
Incorporated: 5 August 1999 *Employees:* 3
Net Worth: £105,530 *Total Assets:* £203,741
Registered Office: Holywell Farm, Smisby Road, Smisby, Ashby De La Zouch, Leics, LE65 2UG
Major Shareholder: Audrey Joyce Morgan
Officers: Audrey Joyce Morgan, Secretary; Audrey Joyce Morgan [1937] Director/Company Secretary; Kevin Morgan [1959] Director/Brewer

Sharp's Brewery Limited
Incorporated: 10 April 2003 *Employees:* 114
Net Worth: £20,769,196 *Total Assets:* £29,014,440
Registered Office: Pityme Industrial Estate, Rock, Wadebridge, Cornwall, PL27 6NU
Parent: Molson Coors Brewing Company (UK) Limited
Officers: Gemma Louise Wisniewski, Secretary; Simon Kerry [1970] Finance Director; James Christian Shearer [1980] Marketing Director; Philip Mark Whitehead [1977] Director

Shed35 Ltd
Incorporated: 15 November 2016
Net Worth Deficit: £4,086 *Total Assets:* £6,435
Registered Office: 51 Chapman Drive, Carnoustie, Angus, DD7 6DX
Shareholders: John Wilson; Gary Mellon
Officers: Gary Mellon [1963] Director; John Wilson [1971] Director

Sheeptown Brewery Limited
Incorporated: 22 September 2017
Registered Office: White House Farm, White Hills Lane, Stirton, Skipton, N Yorks, BD23 3LH
Shareholders: Robert Kenneth Andrews; Jenny Ann Andrews
Officers: Jenny Andrews, Secretary; Robert Kenneth Andrews [1963] Director

Sheffield Brewers Collective
Incorporated: 13 March 2017
Registered Office: Office 209, J C Albyn Complex, Burton Road, Neepsend, Sheffield, S3 8BZ
Officers: Peter Andrew Rawlinson [1964] Director/Solicitor; Peter John Roberts [1969] Director; Andrew Neil Stephens [1978] Director/Publican

The Sheffield Brewery Company Limited
Incorporated: 15 February 2006 *Employees:* 8
Net Worth Deficit: £64,897 *Total Assets:* £42,493
Registered Office: Unit 111 JC Albyn Complex, Percy Street, Neepsend, Sheffield, S3 8BT
Major Shareholder: Peter Andrew Rawlinson
Officers: Peter Rawlinson, Secretary; Peter Andrew Rawlinson [1964] Director/Solicitor

The Shefford Brewery Co. Limited
Incorporated: 3 May 1990 *Employees:* 2
Net Worth Deficit: £3,588
Registered Office: 43 Manchester Street, London, W1U 7LP
Shareholder: Angela Ellis Ayres
Officers: Benjamin Leigh Ayres, Secretary; Benjamin Leigh Ayres [1976] Director; Doreen Desquesnes [1926] Director/Retired

Shelsley Brewing Company Ltd
Incorporated: 31 January 2019
Registered Office: Lilac Cottage, Camp Lane, Shelsley Beauchamp, Worcester, WR6 6RL
Shareholders: James Allen; Ruth Elliker
Officers: James Allen [1966] Director; Ruth Elliker [1974] Director

Shepherd Neame Limited
Incorporated: 9 November 1914 *Employees:* 1,569
Net Worth: £201,052,000 *Total Assets:* £334,227,008
Registered Office: 17 Court Street, Faversham, Kent, ME13 7AX
Officers: Robin Neil Duncan, Secretary; George Harold Abbott Barnes [1954] Director; William John Brett [1965] Director; Nigel James Bunting [1967] Retail Director; Jonathan Beale Neame [1964] Director; Richard John Oldfield [1955] Director; Mark John Rider [1976] Finance Director; Hilary Susan Riva [1957] Director; Miles Howard Templeman [1947] Director/Consultant

Sherborne Brewery Limited
Incorporated: 27 June 1997
Registered Office: 6 The Linen Yard, South Street, Crewkerne, Somerset, TA18 8AB
Shareholders: Martin Walsh; Stephen Christopher Walsh
Officers: Martin Walsh, Secretary; Stephen Christopher Walsh [1968] Director

Shere Brewery Ltd
Incorporated: 13 October 2011
Registered Office: 5 Jardine House, Harrovian Business Village, Bessborough Road, Harrow, Middlesex, HA1 3EX
Shareholder: Lee John Cary Nicholls
Officers: Stephen John Dodd [1965] Director/Brewer; Lee John Cary Nicholls [1965] Director/Brewer

Sherfield Village Brewery Limited
Incorporated: 25 October 2010
Net Worth Deficit: £9,481 *Total Assets:* £14,165
Registered Office: Goddards Farm, Goddards Lane, Sherfield on Loddon, Hook, Hants, RG27 0EL
Shareholder: Peter Cook
Officers: Bruce Batting [1949] Director; Peter Cook [1966] Director

David Sheriff Brewing Services Limited
Incorporated: 7 March 2017 *Employees:* 1
Net Worth Deficit: £239
Registered Office: 294 Askern Road, Toll Bar, Doncaster, S Yorks, DN5 0QN
Major Shareholder: David Luke Sheriff
Officers: David Luke Sheriff [1999] Director/Brewer

Sherwood Forest Brewing Company Limited
Incorporated: 5 February 2008
Registered Office: Avocet House, Bittern Way, Riverside Industrial Estate, Boston, Lincs, PE21 7NX
Shareholders: Kym Christopher Ellington; John Nicholas Gorensweigh
Officers: Kym Christopher Ellington, Secretary; John Nicholas Gorensweigh [1964] Director

Shetland Refreshments Limited
Incorporated: 5 November 1998
Net Worth Deficit: £18,532 *Total Assets:* £142,633
Registered Office: 31 Kalliness, Weisdale, Shetland, ZE2 9LR
Major Shareholder: John Henry Priest
Officers: Yvette Carnell, Secretary; John Henry Priest [1955] Director/Brewer

Shiny Brewing Company Ltd
Incorporated: 13 February 2012 *Employees:* 13
Net Worth: £21,172 *Total Assets:* £469,555
Registered Office: Furnace Inn, 9 Duke Street, Derby, DE1 3BX
Shareholder: Darren Menon
Officers: Darren Menon [1980] Brewer Director

Shipstones Beer Company Ltd
Incorporated: 5 April 2013 *Employees:* 3
Net Worth Deficit: £15,863 *Total Assets:* £71,013
Registered Office: 27 Grace Drive, Nottingham, NG8 5AG
Major Shareholder: Richard Neale
Officers: Richard James Neale [1971] Managing Director

Shoreditch Brewing Company Ltd
Incorporated: 20 February 2018
Registered Office: Arch 355 Westgate Street, London, E8 3RL
Officers: Peter Maclin Brown [1985] Director/Brewer [American]

The Shotover Brewing Company Ltd
Incorporated: 19 May 2009 *Employees:* 5
Net Worth: £10,631 *Total Assets:* £101,947
Registered Office: Mount Manor House, 16 The Mount, Guildford, Surrey, GU2 4HN
Parent: The Borthwick Group Limited
Officers: Moira Allan Ross, Secretary; Alastair Borthwick Ross [1953] Director; Caitlin Alexandra Ross [1985] Director; Moira Allan Ross [1953] Director

Shottle Farm Brewery Ltd
Incorporated: 17 May 2011
Net Worth Deficit: £31,620 *Total Assets:* £28,545
Registered Office: Handley Farm, Shottle, Belper, Derbys, DE56 2DT
Shareholder: Anthony John Laven
Officers: Susan Bridget Cowan [1962] Director/Hairdresser; Anthony John Laven [1958] Director/Farmer

Shropshire Beers Limited
Incorporated: 12 May 2018
Registered Office: St Annes Chruch, Lea Cross, Shrewsbury, Salop, SY5 8JE
Major Shareholder: Christopher Julius Jones
Officers: Christopher Julius Jones [1963] Director/Entrepreneur

The Shropshire Brewer Limited
Incorporated: 27 November 2012 *Employees:* 2
Previous: The Longden Brewing Company Ltd
Net Worth Deficit: £40,405 *Total Assets:* £16,597
Registered Office: Oakridge, Hookagate, Shrewsbury, Salop, SY5 8BE
Shareholders: Timothy Michael Wakeley; Oliver Waring
Officers: Dr Timothy Michael Wakeley [1965] Director; Oliver Waring [1983] Director/Licensee

Sibley Brewing Co Ltd.
Incorporated: 3 August 2016 *Employees:* 5
Net Worth: £12,729 *Total Assets:* £49,484
Registered Office: Basement, 11 St Marys Place, Newcastle upon Tyne, NE1 7PG
Major Shareholder: Jon Sibley
Officers: Jon Sibley [1985] Director

Signal Brewery Limited
Incorporated: 19 August 2014 *Employees:* 4
Net Worth Deficit: £588,269 *Total Assets:* £144,199
Registered Office: Unit 8 Stirling Way, Beddington Farm Road, Croydon, Surrey, CR0 4XN
Shareholders: Murray Daniel Remarque Roos; Catharine Mary Roos
Officers: Charles William Raker Luckin [1973] Director; Catharine Mary Roos [1978] Director [Australian]; Murray Daniel Remarque Roos [1975] Director [Zimbabwean]

Signature Brew Ltd
Incorporated: 26 October 2011 *Employees:* 8
Net Worth: £135,947 *Total Assets:* £471,671
Registered Office: Unit 25 Leyton Business Centre, Etloe Road, London, E10 7BT
Shareholders: Thomas Bott; Sam Alistair McGregor
Officers: Tom Bott [1988] Director; Sam Alistair McGregor [1985] Director

Signpost Brewery Ltd
Incorporated: 13 September 2018
Registered Office: 71-75 Shelton Street, London, WC2H 9JQ
Shareholders: David Berkeley Buchanan Kenning; Tobias Edward Burney Kenning
Officers: David Berkeley Buchanan Kenning [1951] Director; Tobias Edward Burney Kenning [1988] Director

Silks Brewery Limited
Incorporated: 27 March 2015
Net Worth Deficit: £39,651 *Total Assets:* £51,498
Registered Office: Enterprise House, Rippers Court, Sible Hedingham, Halstead, Essex, CO9 3PY
Major Shareholder: Ross Foggo
Officers: Ross Foggo [1971] Director/Brewer

Silktown Brewery Ltd
Incorporated: 21 May 2014
Registered Office: 30 Bedford Road, Macclesfield, Cheshire, SK11 8JQ
Major Shareholder: Andrew Kenneth Chatwood
Officers: Andrew Kenneth Chatwood [1967] Director/Nurse

Silver Brewhouse Limited
Incorporated: 1 June 2018
Registered Office: Unit 4 Adelphi Way, Staveley, Chesterfield, Derbys, S43 3LJ
Shareholders: Malcolm Watts; Richard Waddington
Officers: Richard Waddington [1970] Director; Malcolm Watts [1950] Director

Silver Rocket Brewing Ltd
Incorporated: 17 January 2018
Registered Office: 6 Meadows, Hassocks, W Sussex, BN6 8EH
Shareholders: Matthew Christopher McGuire; Ben McCully
Officers: Ben McCully [1976] Director; Matthew Christopher McGuire [1974] Director and Company Secretary

Silver Street Brewery Limited
Incorporated: 18 November 2015 *Employees:* 3
Net Worth Deficit: £16,976 *Total Assets:* £92,683
Registered Office: The Clarence, 2 Silver Street, Bury, Lancs, BL9 0EX
Major Shareholder: Lee Hollinworth
Officers: Lee Hollingworth [1970] Director

The Silverstone Brewing Co Limited
Incorporated: 29 January 2016
Net Worth: £100 *Total Assets:* £100
Registered Office: 18 Market Place, Brackley, Northants, NN13 7DP
Major Shareholder: Morris David Jones
Officers: Morris David Jones [1959] Director/Accountant

The Silverstone Real Ale Company Limited
Incorporated: 2 December 2014 *Employees:* 2
Net Worth: £3,922 *Total Assets:* £71,617
Registered Office: Silverstone Business Park, Silverstone, Northants, NN12 8TB
Shareholders: Morris David Jones; Robert Nigel Jackson
Officers: Simon Burn [1961] Director; Glenn Coffey [1952] Director; Brian David Hayward [1959] Director; Robert Nigel Jackson [1959] Marketing Director; Morris David Jones [1959] Director/Chartered Accountant

The Silvertown Brewery and Distillery Company Limited
Incorporated: 26 May 2017
Registered Office: H6 Sloane Avenue Mansions, Sloane Avenue, London, SW3 3JW
Major Shareholder: Bruce Kenneth McRobie
Officers: Bruce Kenneth McRobie [1962] Director/Chartered Surveyor

Sinclair Breweries Limited
Incorporated: 23 May 2006
Net Worth: £618,640 *Total Assets:* £3,310,000
Registered Office: Cawdor, Nairn, IV12 5XP
Major Shareholder: Norman James Sinclair
Officers: Christine Sinclair, Secretary; Norman James Anderson Sinclair [1961] Director/Restaurateur

Siren Craft Brew Limited
Incorporated: 16 August 2012 *Employees:* 23
Previous: Anley Ales Limited
Net Worth: £332,113 *Total Assets:* £2,008,344
Registered Office: HJS Chartered Accountants, 12-14 Carlton Place, Southampton, SO15 2EA
Shareholders: Darron John Anley; Joanne Anley
Officers: Darron John Anley [1970] Director; Joanne Anley [1974] Director

Six Towns Brewery Limited
Incorporated: 3 October 2018
Registered Office: 4-5 Boothen Old Road, Stoke on Trent, Staffs, ST4 4EE
Major Shareholder: Jonathan Murdo MacLeod Bate
Officers: Jonathan Murdo MacLeod Bate [1966] Director/Publican

Sixty Shilling Brewing Ltd
Incorporated: 20 January 2006
Net Worth: £90,411 *Total Assets:* £130,549
Registered Office: The Cottage, 2 Jessops Lane, Gedling, Nottingham, NG4 4BQ
Shareholder: Robert Owen Douglas
Officers: Robert Owen Douglas, Secretary/Civil Servant; Gavin Kenneth Morrison [1980] Director/Production Manager; Nicholas James Henry Sewter [1947] Director/Retired Teacher

SK Brew Ltd
Incorporated: 19 July 2017
Registered Office: Flat 3, 143 Kennington Park Road, London, SE11 4JJ
Officers: Ryan Hess [1985] Director [American]

Skelpers Ltd
Incorporated: 4 September 2018
Registered Office: 9 Harwich Close, Manchester, M19 3EZ
Major Shareholder: Valerie Roberts
Officers: Valerie Roberts [1954] Director/Consultant

Skinner's Brewing Co. Limited
Incorporated: 27 July 2002 *Employees:* 61
Net Worth: £637,057 *Total Assets:* £1,923,524
Registered Office: c/o Bishop Fleming, Chy Nyverow, Newham Road, Truro, Cornwall, TR1 2DP
Parent: Pritchmor Holdings Ltd
Officers: Sarah Jane Skinner, Secretary; Alun David Morgan [1967] Director; Michael Brian Pritchard [1968] Director; Steven John Skinner [1956] Director/Brewer

Skinnybrands Ltd
Incorporated: 2 September 2015 *Employees:* 3
Net Worth: £1,375,318 *Total Assets:* £1,702,059
Registered Office: Ashton Old Baths, Stamford Street West, Ashton under Lyne, Lancs, OL6 7FW
Shareholders: Thomas Neale Bell; Gary Nicholas Conway
Officers: Mihai Albu [1962] Director [Romanian]; Thomas Neale Bell [1989] Director/Alcohol Manufacturer; Gary Nicholas Conway [1971] Director [Irish]

Sky Pirate Ltd
Incorporated: 26 September 2018
Registered Office: 71-75 Shelton Street, London, WC2H 9JQ
Major Shareholder: Michael Bentley
Officers: Michael Bentley [1964] Director

The Slaughterhouse Brewery Limited
Incorporated: 31 March 2003 *Employees:* 3
Net Worth: £26,749 *Total Assets:* £53,806
Registered Office: The Slaughterhouse Brewery, Bridge Street, Warwick, CV34 5PD
Shareholders: Stepehn Ridgway; Alex Ridgway
Officers: Alex Ridgway [1981] Director; Stephen Ridgway [1951] Director/Brewer

Slice & Brew Ltd
Incorporated: 15 February 2019
Registered Office: 9 Brook Road, Prescot, Merseyside, L34 1BF
Shareholders: Andrew John Stovin; Lisa Vallance
Officers: Andrew John Stovin [1969] Director

Sloane Home Ltd
Incorporated: 14 November 2013
Net Worth Deficit: £19,094 *Total Assets:* £31,948
Registered Office: The Rectory, Llandow, Cowbridge, Vale of Glamorgan, CF71 7NT
Major Shareholder: Leanne Peta Johns
Officers: Leanne Peta Johns [1971] Director

Slopemeister Brewing Company Limited
Incorporated: 24 August 2018
Registered Office: Oak House, Airth Castle Estate, Airth, Falkirk, FK2 8JF
Shareholders: Thomas Hendrie Sloper; Karen McLean
Officers: Karen McLean [1980] Marketing Director; Thomas Hendrie Sloper [1977] Managing Director

Slow Beer Ltd
Incorporated: 20 September 2013
Registered Office: Royal Mail Cottage, Main Road, Thorngumbald, E Yorks, HU12 9NF
Major Shareholder: Michael Anthony Ferrier
Officers: Michael Anthony Ferrier [1958] Director

Sly Fox Brewery Ltd
Incorporated: 22 May 2009
Registered Office: 165b Rossmore Road, Parkstone, Poole, Dorset, BH12 2HG
Shareholder: Dean Sylvester Fox
Officers: Dean Sylvester Fox, Secretary; Dean Sylvester Fox [1977] Director

Small Beer Brew Co. Ltd
Incorporated: 18 May 2016
Net Worth: £467,090 *Total Assets:* £467,090
Registered Office: The Rivendell Centre, White Horse Lane, Maldon, Essex, CM9 5QP
Shareholders: Felix Trewartha James; James John Grundy
Officers: James John Grundy [1988] Director; Felix Trewartha James [1987] Director/Brewer

The Small Beer Brewing Company Limited
Incorporated: 29 March 2016
Net Worth Deficit: £7,663 *Total Assets:* £344
Registered Office: 13 Pavilion Terrace, Wood Lane, London, W12 0HT
Major Shareholder: Steven Conway Smith
Officers: Steven Conway Smith [1964] Director/Brewer

Small World Beers Ltd
Incorporated: 6 August 2013 Employees: 4
Net Worth Deficit: £136,504 Total Assets: £157,732
Registered Office: Unit 10 Barncliffe Business Park, nr Bank, Shelley, W Yorks, HD8 8LU
Major Shareholder: David Hill
Officers: David Hill [1965] Director/Brewer

Smith and Jones Brewery Ltd
Incorporated: 10 February 2011
Registered Office: Unit 13a Dunscar Industrial Estate, Blackburn Road Egerton, Bolton, Lancs, BL7 9PQ
Major Shareholder: Jeremy Mark Jones
Officers: Peter Haslam, Secretary; Peter Haslam [1960] Director/Accountant; Jeremy Mark Jones [1964] Director

Samuel Smith Old Brewery (Tadcaster)
Incorporated: 22 February 1923
Registered Office: The Old Brewery, Tadcaster, N Yorks, LS24 9SB
Officers: Mark Richard Butler, Secretary; Humphrey Richard Woollcombe Smith [1944] Director/Company Chairman; Oliver Geoffrey Woollcombe Smith [1947] Director; Samuel Geoffrey Gladstone Smith [1988] Director/Area Manager

Smokin Barrels Brewery Ltd
Incorporated: 16 July 2018
Registered Office: 114 Stonewell Crescent, Nuneaton, Warwicks, CV11 4TB
Major Shareholder: Mark John Rollason
Officers: Mark John Rollason [1976] Managing Director

Smoky Dragon Brewery & Preservas Limited
Incorporated: 12 December 2018
Registered Office: 15b The Grove, Rumney, Cardiff, CF3 3HG
Officers: Ian George [1962] Director/Coach Driver

Snakestorm Limited
Incorporated: 21 June 2018
Registered Office: 2 Drake House, Cook Way, Taunton, Somerset, TA2 6BJ
Shareholders: Stoirm Cesare Billy Arnold; Jake Maximilian Barrett
Officers: Stoirm Cesare Billy Arnold [1993] Director; Jake Maximilian Barrett [1990] Director

Sneaky Peacock Ltd
Incorporated: 9 October 2017
Registered Office: 59 Broadgate Lane, Deeping St James's, Peterborough, PE6 8NN
Major Shareholder: David Peacock
Officers: Anna Peacock [1977] Director/Brewer; David Peacock [1978] Director/Brewer

Snowdon Craft Beer Limited
Incorporated: 1 October 2018
Registered Office: Commodore House, 51 Conway Road, Colwyn Bay, Conwy, LL29 7AW
Major Shareholder: Jonathan Roger Hughes
Officers: Lorna Hughes, Secretary; Tristian Greenfield [1973] Director; Jonathan Roger Hughes [1972] Director

The Sociable Beer Company Ltd.
Incorporated: 24 February 2015
Registered Office: 6-8 Britannia Road, Worcester, WR1 3BQ
Shareholders: Jason Peter Clines; Steven Jeffery Tromans; Steven Jeffery Tromans
Officers: Jason Peter Clines [1966] Director/Chartered Surveyor; Steven Jeffery Tromans [1964] Director/Surveyor

Soham Brewery Ltd
Incorporated: 26 May 2018
Registered Office: Quantum House, The Shade, Soham, Ely, Cambs, CB7 5DE
Shareholders: Alastair Ian Anderson; Lexaris Ltd
Officers: Lord Alastair Ian Anderson [1984] Director

Soho Brewing Ltd
Incorporated: 11 September 2013
Previous: Soho Brewery Limited
Registered Office: Sovereign House, Shaftesbury Avenue, London, WC2H 8HQ
Major Shareholder: Michael Anthony Breen
Officers: Michael Breen [1965] Director/Procurement Manager [Irish]; Kevin Joseph Gallen [1961] Director/Chartered Accountant [Irish]

Solvay Brewing Ltd
Incorporated: 27 November 2015 Employees: 3
Net Worth Deficit: £39,267 Total Assets: £63,510
Registered Office: 21 Dorset Court, Hertford Road, London, N1 4SD
Major Shareholder: Roman Hochuli
Officers: Dr. Roman Hochuli [1989] Director/Student [Dutch]; John Paul Hussey [1975] Director/Engineer [Irish]

Solway Spirits Ltd
Incorporated: 4 May 2018
Registered Office: 1 Railway Cottage, Cummertrees, Annan, Dumfries & Galloway, DG12 5QG
Major Shareholder: Andrew Emmerson
Officers: Kathryn Edith Rimmer, Secretary; Andrew Emmerson [1968] Director/Brewer and Distiller

Somerset Ales Limited
Incorporated: 22 November 2016
Net Worth Deficit: £199,183 Total Assets: £98,263
Registered Office: Unit 5 Westridge Way, Bishops Lydeard, Taunton, Somerset, TA4 3RU
Shareholders: Richard Battersby; David Cass
Officers: James Beck, Secretary; Cheryl Denise Ford [1968] Managing Director; Philip Owen Padgham [1965] Director; Robert Rainey [1950] Director/Chairman

Sonder Brewing Company Ltd.
Incorporated: 1 December 2017
Registered Office: 16 Richmond Road, Worcester, WR5 1DH
Shareholders: Alex Wilcox; Thomas Hunt
Officers: Thomas Hunt [1992] Director/Engineer; Alex Wilcox [1992] Director/Consultant

Sonnet 43 Brewery Ltd
Incorporated: 12 October 2016
Registered Office: Cottage rear of Roker Hotel, Roker Terrace, Sunderland, Tyne & Wear, SR6 9ND
Major Shareholder: Mark Hird
Officers: Mark Hird [1973] Director

Soul Brewing Company Ltd
Incorporated: 12 October 2017
Registered Office: 18 Broomfield Road, Stockport, Cheshire, SK4 4ND
Major Shareholder: Bill Neagle
Officers: Dr Bill Neagle [1958] Director/Brewer

Soul Doubt Brewing Company Ltd
Incorporated: 15 October 2015
Net Worth: £421 *Total Assets:* £421
Registered Office: 20 Berkley Avenue, Levenshulme, Manchester, M19 2ED
Shareholders: Christopher Alan Buxton; Graham Harkis
Officers: Christopher Alan Buxton [1984] Director/Audio Visual Engineer; Graham Harkis [1985] Director/Business Development Manager

South Hams Brewery Ltd
Incorporated: 26 April 2017
Registered Office: Stokeley Barton, Stokenham, Kingsbridge, Devon, TQ7 2SE
Shareholder: Mark Brooking
Officers: Brenda Brooking, Secretary; Brenda Brooking [1963] Director/Company Secretary; Mark Brooking [1965] Director/Farmer; Samuel Brooking [1992] Director/Brewer

Southbourne Ales Limited
Incorporated: 16 August 2013
Net Worth Deficit: £76,875 *Total Assets:* £104,672
Registered Office: 40 Clingan Road, Bournemouth, BH6 5PZ
Officers: Jennifer Alison Tingay [1976] Director/Brewer; Sheldon Ashley Young [1969] Director/Architectural Technologist

Southbourne Brewing Limited
Incorporated: 15 August 2013
Net Worth: £208,576 *Total Assets:* £219,633
Registered Office: 40 Clingan Road, Bournemouth, BH6 5PZ
Shareholders: Jennifer Alison Tingay; Sheldon Ashley Young
Officers: George William Arthur West, Secretary; Paul Richard Ryder [1962] New Business Director; Jennifer Alison Tingay [1976] Director/Brewer; George William Arthur West [1991] Director/Teacher; Sheldon Ashley Young [1969] Director/Architectural Technologist

Southbrew Company Ltd
Incorporated: 23 July 2018
Registered Office: 13 Penlands Way, Steyning, W Sussex, BN44 3PN
Shareholders: Paul Michael Robertson; Christopher Stephen Bowen
Officers: Christopher Stephen Bowen [1976] Director/Platform Product Manager; Paul Michael Robertson [1977] Director/Management Accountant

The Southdown Brewery Limited
Incorporated: 20 September 2011
Net Worth Deficit: £8,248 *Total Assets:* £104,529
Registered Office: 254 Upper Shoreham Road, Shoreham-by-Sea, W Sussex, BN43 6BF
Shareholders: Geoffrey Paul Moseley; Andrew John Mars
Officers: Andrew John Mars [1971] Director/Operations Manager

The Southey Brewing Company Limited
Incorporated: 15 August 2016
Net Worth Deficit: £8,345 *Total Assets:* £30,692
Registered Office: East Lodge, Bedlars Green, Great Hallingbury, Bishop's Stortford, Herts, CM22 7TL
Shareholder: Propstock Community Pubs Limited
Officers: Samuel Jonathan Barber [1986] Director/Brewer; Darren MacRae [1989] Director/Bars Manager

Southport Brewery Limited
Incorporated: 6 March 2012
Net Worth: £10,681 *Total Assets:* £29,278
Registered Office: 233 Wigan Road, Ashton in Makerfield, Wigan, Lancs, WN4 9SL
Shareholders: Paul Bardsley; Elaine Bardsley
Officers: Paul Bardsley [1961] Director/Brewer

Southport Brewing Limited
Incorporated: 16 November 2018
Registered Office: Suite 64, 334 Kennington Lane, London, SE11 5HY
Shareholders: Chieh-Jen Tsai; Ting-I Chang
Officers: Ting-I Chang [1992] Director [Taiwanese]; Chieh-Jen Tsai [1992] Director

The Southsea Brewing Company Ltd
Incorporated: 13 November 2014
Net Worth: £1,015 *Total Assets:* £29,791
Registered Office: 216 Devonshire Avenue, Southsea, Hants, PO4 9EH
Shareholders: Daniel Frederick Tonkin; David George Eastwood; Lorna Elizabeth Eastwood
Officers: Lorna Eastwood, Secretary; David George Eastwood [1985] Director/Brewer; Lorna Elizabeth Eastwood [1986] Director/Local Government; Daniel Tonkin [1982] Director

Southside Brewing Ltd
Incorporated: 12 December 2018
Registered Office: 3a Dalrymple Crescent, Edinburgh, EH9 2NU
Major Shareholder: Sonja Christina Mitchell
Officers: Sonja Christina Mitchell [1978] Managing Director

Southwark Brewing Company Limited
Incorporated: 19 November 2013 *Employees:* 7
Net Worth: £115,268 *Total Assets:* £149,270
Registered Office: 5 Argosy Court Scimitar Way, Whitley Business Park, Coventry, Warwicks, CV3 4GA
Shareholder: Peter William Jackson
Officers: Peter William Jackson [1959] Director; Andrew Nichol [1956] Director; Alison O'Neill [1962] Director

Space Trash Brewing Ltd
Incorporated: 16 January 2017
Registered Office: 54 Eastmoor Park, Harpenden, Herts, AL5 1BW
Major Shareholder: Daniel Martin Blake
Officers: Daniel Martin Blake [1983] Director

Spartan Brewery Ltd
Incorporated: 2 November 2016
Net Worth Deficit: £9,275 *Total Assets:* £41,550
Registered Office: 3 Lewis Mews, Chislehurst, Kent, BR7 5FJ
Shareholders: Colin Brooks; Michael Willetts
Officers: Colin Brooks [1984] Director/Software Engineer; Michael Willetts [1985] Director/Brewer

Spencer Panacea Limited
Incorporated: 1 April 2008
Net Worth: £3,865 *Total Assets:* £7,662
Registered Office: Drayton Court, Drayton Road, Solihull, W Midlands, B90 4NG
Major Shareholder: Matthew James Spencer
Officers: Sally Margaret Spencer, Secretary; Matthew James Spencer [1977] Director/Pharmacist; Sally Margaret Spencer [1977] Director/HR Consultant

Sperrin Brewery Ltd
Incorporated: 22 August 2011 *Employees:* 2
Net Worth: £37,861 *Total Assets:* £78,762
Registered Office: Lord Nelson Inn, Birmingham Road, Ansley, Nuneaton, Warwicks, CV10 9PQ
Shareholders: Nicola Sperrin; Treeve Sperrin; Warren Paul Sperrin
Officers: Treeve Sperrin [1968] Director; Warren Paul Sperrin [1964] Director

Spey Valley Brewery Limited
Incorporated: 8 January 2007 *Employees:* 3
Previous: The Finest Brewery of Speyside Limited
Net Worth: £130,187 *Total Assets:* £513,372
Registered Office: Spalding House, 90-92 Queen Street, Broughty Ferry, Dundee, DD5 1AJ
Parent: Keith Brewery Holdings Limited
Officers: James Derek Scott Carnegie [1961] Director; Graeme Hay [1966] Director; David Alastair MacDonald [1977] Director; Anthony Schofield [1959] Managing Director; Donald John Smith [1968] Director

Speyside Craft Brewery Limited
Incorporated: 16 January 2012 *Employees:* 7
Net Worth: £31,500 *Total Assets:* £189,355
Registered Office: Ty Crwn, East Grange, Kinloss, Forres, Moray, IV36 2UD
Shareholder: Sebastian Pettit Jones
Officers: Sebastian Pettit Jones [1986] Director/Brewer

Spitting Feathers Limited
Incorporated: 1 June 2009 *Employees:* 70
Net Worth: £107,618 *Total Assets:* £393,052
Registered Office: Common Farm, Common Lane, Waverton, Chester, CH3 7QT
Major Shareholder: Matthew Walley
Officers: Matthew Walley [1971] Director

Splott Brewery Ltd
Incorporated: 15 June 2018
Registered Office: 47 Splott Road, Cardiff, CF24 2BW
Shareholders: Samuel Albert Hughes Farnfield; Gavin MacGregor Cleaver
Officers: Dr Gavin MacGregor Cleaver [1984] Director/Editor; Samuel Albert Hughes Farnfield [1983] Director/Charity Worker

Spotlight Brewing Ltd
Incorporated: 6 October 2017
Registered Office: The Goddards, Goole Road, West Cowick, E Yorks, DN14 9DJ
Major Shareholder: Richard J Womersley
Officers: Richard J Womersley [1992] Director/Head Brewer

Spotty Dog Brewery Limited
Incorporated: 6 August 2014
Net Worth: £1,243 *Total Assets:* £9,348
Registered Office: 16 Drayton Park, Daventry, Northants, NN11 8TB
Shareholder: Susan Elizabeth Lowe
Officers: Brian Godfrey Lowe [1955] Director/Brewer; Susan Elizabeth Lowe [1959] Director/Strategic Analysis Manager

Spyglass Brewing Company Ltd
Incorporated: 16 October 2018
Registered Office: The Cadbury Richmond Road, Montpelier, Bristol, BS6 5EW
Shareholders: Julian Brodie McLauchlan; Richard Alexander Neilson
Officers: Julian Brodie McLauchlan [1969] Managing Director; Richard Alexander Neilson [1983] Managing Director

Square Street Distillery Ltd
Incorporated: 27 June 2008
Previous: Bespoke Ale Limited
Net Worth: £3,171 *Total Assets:* £12,258
Registered Office: The Old Brewery, Back Square Street, Ramsbottom, Bury, Lancs, BL0 9FZ
Major Shareholder: Peter Booth
Officers: Peter Booth [1963] Director/Consultant

Squawk Brewing Company Limited
Incorporated: 17 May 2013 *Employees:* 1
Net Worth Deficit: £18,876 *Total Assets:* £87,213
Registered Office: 46 Dean Brook Road, Netherthong, Holmfirth, W Yorks, HD9 3UF
Officers: Oliver Ward Turton [1982] Director/Brewery

SRA Brewery Limited
Incorporated: 29 January 2019
Registered Office: 22 Scythe Road, Daventry, Northants, NN11 0WN
Major Shareholder: Timothy Coleman
Officers: Timothy Coleman [1987] Director/Quantity Surveyor

St Andrews Brewers Limited
Incorporated: 23 January 2012 *Employees:* 49
Net Worth Deficit: £3,316,901 *Total Assets:* £2,329,965
Registered Office: Eden Mill, Main Street, Guardbridge, St Andrews, Fife, KY16 0US
Major Shareholder: Anthony Kelly
Officers: Anthony Gerard Kelly, Secretary; Anthony Gerard Kelly [1991] Company Secretary/Director; Anthony Kelly [1963] Director [Irish]; Paul Miller [1961] Director

St Andrews Brewing Company Holdings Limited
Incorporated: 27 May 2015
Net Worth Deficit: £2,955 *Total Assets:* £19,406
Registered Office: Unit 9 Bassaguard Business Park, St Andrews, Fife, KY16 8AL
Shareholders: Patrick Philip Mackey; Timothy George Edward Butler
Officers: Timothy George Edward Butler [1972] Director; Kevin Gawn Grainger [1958] Director; Patrick Columba Mackey [1946] Director [Irish]; Patrick Philip Mackey [1974] Director; Tony Rodgers [1967] Director; Niall Fraser Stirling [1957] Director/Financial Consultant

St Andrews Brewing Company Limited
Incorporated: 28 May 2015 *Employees:* 7
Net Worth Deficit: £106,093 *Total Assets:* £108,702
Registered Office: Unit 9 Bassaguard Business Park, St Andrews, Fife, KY16 8AL
Officers: Timothy George Edward Butler [1972] Director; Patrick Philip Mackey [1974] Director

St Andrews Old Brewing Company Limited
Incorporated: 29 September 2008
Previous: St Andrews Brewing Company Limited
Net Worth: £12,235 *Total Assets:* £12,748
Registered Office: 7 Peterborough Close, Sheffield, S10 4JA
Officers: Timothy George Edward Butler [1972] Director/Restaurateur; Patrick Philip Mackey [1974] Director

St Davids Farm Brewery Ltd
Incorporated: 1 February 2019
Registered Office: Upper Harglodd, St Davids, Haverfordwest, Pembrokeshire, SA62 6BX
Shareholders: Mark Wyn Raymond Evans; Emma Sarah Evans
Officers: Emma Sarah Evans [1981] Director/Local Government Officer; Mark Wyn Raymond Evans [1979] Director/Farmer

St Ives Brewery Limited
Incorporated: 2 September 2010 *Employees:* 13
Net Worth Deficit: £14,221 *Total Assets:* £120,001
Registered Office: The Old School, The Stennack, St Ives, Cornwall, TR26 1QU
Major Shareholder: Marco Gervasio Amura
Officers: Gervasio Amura [1950] Director [Italian]; Marco Gervasio Amura [1981] Director; Yvonne Amura [1951] Director

St Mary's Brewery Ltd
Incorporated: 15 March 2016
Net Worth Deficit: £12,392 *Total Assets:* £4,104
Registered Office: 61 Quickswood, Primrose Hill, London, NW3 3SA
Shareholders: Roderick William James Monroe; Stephen Roy Reynolds
Officers: Roderick William James Monroe [1961] Director/Economist; Stephen Roy Reynolds [1962] Director

St. Peter's Brewery Co. Limited
Incorporated: 2 February 1995 *Employees:* 49
Net Worth: £1,677,873 *Total Assets:* £3,317,448
Registered Office: St Peter's Hall, South Elmham, Bungay, Suffolk, NR35 1NQ
Parent: St. Peter's Brewery Group PLC
Officers: John Matthew Murphy, Secretary/Director; Hayley Louise Oakes, Secretary; Janet Diane Fogg [1952] Retail Director; John Anthony Hadingham [1969] Managing Director; Julie Hinsley [1971] Finance Director; John Matthew Murphy [1944] Director; Hayley Louise Oakes [1986] Director and Company Secretary

St. Peter's Brewery Group Public Limited Company
Incorporated: 22 April 1997
Net Worth: £2,452,857 *Total Assets:* £2,502,368
Registered Office: St Peters Hall, St Peter, South Elmham, Bungay, Suffolk, NR35 1NQ
Shareholders: John Matthew Murphy; Janet Diane Fogg
Officers: David John James, Secretary; Janet Diane Fogg [1952] Retail Director; John Anthony Hadingham [1969] Managing Director; Julie Hinsley [1971] Finance Director; John Matthew Murphy [1944] Director

St. Peter's Trading Co. Limited
Incorporated: 25 June 1997
Net Worth Deficit: £8,691 *Total Assets:* £2
Registered Office: St Peters Hall, St Peter, South Elmham, Bungay, Suffolk, NR35 1NQ
Parent: St. Peter's Brewery Group PLC
Officers: John Matthew Murphy, Secretary/Director; Janet Diane Fogg [1952] Retail Director; John Anthony Hadingham [1969] Managing Director; John Matthew Murphy [1944] Director

St.Austell Brewery Company Limited
Incorporated: 17 January 1910 *Employees:* 1,553
Net Worth: £100,660,000 *Total Assets:* £188,327,008
Registered Office: 63 Trevarthian Road, St Austell, Cornwall, PL25 4BY
Officers: Colin John Stratton, Secretary; Gerard Hugh Barnes [1968] Director; Gillian Caseberry [1965] Director; Kevin Roger Georgel [1970] Director/Chief Executive; Thomas Adam Luck [1956] Director; William Franck Michelmore [1959] Director; Simon James Staughton [1959] Director; Colin John Stratton [1965] Director/Chartered Accountant; Piers Michael Thompson [1971] Director/Regional National Sales Manager; Stephen John Worrall [1969] Director

Staff Beer Ltd
Incorporated: 18 October 2017
Registered Office: Beer Office 166, 8 Shepherd Market, London, W1J 7JY
Major Shareholder: Scott Haspineall
Officers: Scott Haspineall [1971] Director/MD

The Staffordshire Brewery Limited
Incorporated: 29 June 2002 *Employees:* 23
Net Worth: £221,134 *Total Assets:* £963,800
Registered Office: Alexandra House, Queen Street, Leek, Staffs, ST13 6LP
Shareholders: Nigel Ilchester Cope; Adrian Corke; Susan Carline
Officers: Susan Carline, Secretary; Susan Carline [1953] Director; Lucy Clough [1968] Director; Nigel Ilchester Cope [1948] Director; Adrian Corke [1965] Director/Publican; Thomas Green [1980] Director

Staffordshire Spirits Company Limited
Incorporated: 12 July 2016
Net Worth Deficit: £8,282 *Total Assets:* £39,271
Registered Office: 1 Rolt Close, Stone, Staffs, ST15 8YX
Major Shareholder: Dominic Harvey
Officers: Dominic Harvey [1972] Director

Stag Ales Ltd
Incorporated: 15 August 2018
Registered Office: 2 Gibb Avenue, Darlington, Co Durham, DL1 1NQ
Major Shareholder: Andrew Trevor William Danby-Knight
Officers: Andrew Trevor William Danby-Knight [1992] Director/Entrepreneur

Stag Brewery Ltd
Incorporated: 6 January 2017
Net Worth: £9,000 *Total Assets:* £9,000
Registered Office: Little Engeham Farm, Woodchurch, Ashford, Kent, TN26 3QY
Officers: Jolian Robert McErlean [1971] Director/Brewer

Staggeringly Good Ltd
Incorporated: 28 April 2015 *Employees:* 4
Net Worth Deficit: £30,048 *Total Assets:* £109,919
Registered Office: Maria House, 35 Millers Road, Brighton, BN1 5NP
Shareholders: Jonathan Michael Chapman; Russell Cox; Josephus Ross
Officers: Jonathan Michael Chapman [1980] Director; Russell Cox [1985] Director; Josephus Ross [1979] Director

Stamford Ales Limited
Incorporated: 7 November 2016
Registered Office: 12 Conduit Road, Stamford, Lincs, PE9 1QQ
Major Shareholder: Anthony Leonard Riley
Officers: Anthony Leonard Riley [1957] Director/Trade Adviser

Stamps Brewery Limited
Incorporated: 11 October 2016 *Employees:* 1
Net Worth Deficit: £4,885 *Total Assets:* £26,895
Registered Office: St Mary's Complex, Waverley Street, Bootle, Merseyside, L20 4AP
Shareholder: Anthony Rothwell
Officers: Anthony Rothwell [1952] Director; Michael Rothwell [1979] Director

Stancill Brewery Limited
Incorporated: 8 August 2013 Employees: 8
Net Worth: £66,862 Total Assets: £196,192
Registered Office: 12 Victoria Road, Barnsley, S Yorks, S70 2BB
Shareholders: Thomas Edward Gill; Adam Gary Hague
Officers: Thomas Edward Gill [1989] Director; Dr Adam Gary Hague [1988] Director/Doctor

Staneyhill Brewery Limited
Incorporated: 21 April 2011
Net Worth Deficit: £706,359 Total Assets: £254,406
Registered Office: Hamepark, Reawick, Shetland, ZE2 9NJ
Shareholders: James Cowie Mercer; John Charles Mercer; Roderick Graham Mercer
Officers: James Cowie Mercer [1967] Director; John Charles Mercer [1965] Director; Roderick Graham Mercer [1969] Director

Stannary Brewing Company Ltd.
Incorporated: 29 October 2015
Net Worth Deficit: £12,003 Total Assets: £9,498
Registered Office: Unit 6 Pixon Trading Centre, Pixon Lane, Tavistock, Devon, PL19 8DH
Officers: Christopher Steven John [1975] Managing Director; Garry Michael White [1975] Director/Accounts

Stannington Brewery Ltd
Incorporated: 3 April 2018
Registered Office: 19 Oldfield Avenue, Stannington, Sheffield, S6 6DQ
Officers: Craig Beachell [1966] Director/Network Consultant Banking

Star Wing Brewery Ltd
Incorporated: 30 June 2015
Net Worth Deficit: £152,925 Total Assets: £45,678
Registered Office: 10 Wellington Street, Cambridge, CB1 1HW
Shareholders: Mark Steven Duxon; Neil Upton
Officers: Mark Steven Duxon [1972] Director; Dr Neil Upton [1958] Director

Stardust Brewery Ltd
Incorporated: 4 April 2016
Net Worth Deficit: £76,112 Total Assets: £68,258
Registered Office: Unit 5 How Lane Farm Estate Howe Lane, White Waltham, Maidenhead, Berks, SL6 3JP
Shareholders: Benjamin Roland Ebbetts; Martin Roland Ebbetts
Officers: Ben Ebbetts [1989] Director; Martin Roland Ebbetts [1957] Director

Station 119 Ltd
Incorporated: 28 January 2014 Employees: 4
Net Worth Deficit: £116,608 Total Assets: £227,857
Registered Office: Unit 4 Progress Way, Mid Suffolk Business Park, Eye, Suffolk, IP23 7HU
Shareholders: Marc Oliver Medland; Steven Matsell; Elliott James Norris
Officers: Steven Matsell [1965] Director; Marc Oliver Medland [1980] Director; Elliott James Norris [1979] Director

Stay Gold Beer Company Ltd
Incorporated: 28 September 2018
Registered Office: Flat 31, Drake Court, Tylney Avenue, London, SE19 1LW
Shareholders: Thomas Ewing; Harry Ewing
Officers: Harry Ewing [1994] Director; Thomas Ewing [1988] Director

Stealth Brew Co Limited
Incorporated: 7 December 2012
Previous: The Kennet & Avon Brewery Limited
Net Worth Deficit: £139,111 Total Assets: £120,446
Registered Office: Unit A, Lewin House, The Street, Radstock, Somerset, BA3 3FJ
Major Shareholder: Malcolm Trevor Shipp
Officers: Malcolm Trevor Shipp [1967] Director

The Steam Brewing Co Limited
Incorporated: 20 March 2018
Registered Office: 15c Elsecar Heritage Centre, Wath Road, Elsecar, Barnsley, S Yorks, S74 8HJ
Major Shareholder: Nigel Mount
Officers: Nigel Mount [1964] Director/Retail

Steam Machine Brewing Company Ltd
Incorporated: 12 January 2015 Employees: 3
Net Worth: £5,695 Total Assets: £59,622
Registered Office: Unit 14 IES Centre, Horndale Avenue, Aycliffe Business Park, Newton Aycliffe, Co Durham, DL5 6DS
Shareholders: Nicholas Andrew Smith; Gulen Ozmeral Smith
Officers: Gulen Ozmeral Smith [1981] Director [Turkish]; Nicholas Andrew Smith [1985] Director/Brewery

Steam Town Brewco Limited
Incorporated: 16 January 2017 Employees: 19
Net Worth: £165,550 Total Assets: £262,723
Registered Office: 1 Bishopstoke Road, Eastleigh, Hants, SO50 6AD
Major Shareholder: David Mackie
Officers: Andrew Graham Dyer, Secretary; Rebecca Leanne Holdsworth [1974] Director/Child Protection Team Manager; David Mackie [1971] Director/Brewer

Steel City Brewing Ltd
Incorporated: 4 February 2010
Net Worth: £8,933 Total Assets: £8,956
Registered Office: 33 Rockingham Lane, Sheffield, S1 4FW
Major Shareholder: David Alistair Szwejkowski
Officers: Gary Prescott [1970] Director/IT; David Alistair Szwejkowski [1979] Director/Accountant

Steel Coulson Ltd
Incorporated: 10 October 2016
Net Worth: £9,333 Total Assets: £9,333
Registered Office: First Floor, 85 Kingsdown Parade, Bristol, BS6 5UJ
Shareholders: Jane Dutson; Glen Dawkins
Officers: Glen Dawkins [1971] Director

Steel River Drinks Ltd
Incorporated: 15 May 2017
Registered Office: East Durham Business Centre, Station Town, Wingate, Cleveland, TS28 5HD
Officers: Jason Byers [1972] Director/Entrepreneur

Stenroth Limited
Incorporated: 11 September 2014 Employees: 1
Net Worth: £9,132 Total Assets: £29,719
Registered Office: 265 Cowley Road, Oxford, OX4 1XQ
Shareholders: Jimmy Mehtala; Kathryn Drinnan
Officers: Kathryn Drinnan [1988] Director/Financial Services Consultancy; Jimmy Mehtala [1986] Director [Swedish]

Stewart Brewing Limited
Incorporated: 13 January 2004 *Employees:* 56
Net Worth: £906,317 *Total Assets:* £1,899,475
Registered Office: 3 Braid Mount Crest, Edinburgh, EH10 6JN
Major Shareholder: Steven John Stewart
Officers: Joanne Stewart, Secretary; Edward Mauger Granville [1971] Director/Entrepreneur; Steven John Stewart [1971] Director/Brewer

Stoatcraft Revolutionary Beers Limited
Incorporated: 3 July 2017
Registered Office: Greenburn Cottage, Stoneywood, Aberdeen, AB21 9UA
Major Shareholder: Kieran Graeme Wall
Officers: Kieran Graeme Wall [1987] Director/Owner and Brewmaster

Stocklinch Ales Ltd
Incorporated: 26 April 2012 *Employees:* 1
Net Worth Deficit: £35,085 *Total Assets:* £16,665
Registered Office: Gerrards, Stocklinch, Ilminster, Somerset, TA19 9JF
Officers: Kevn Llewellyn Jones, Secretary; Kevn Llewellyn Jones [1960] Director

The Stockport Brewing Company Ltd
Incorporated: 4 February 2014
Net Worth: £7,001 *Total Assets:* £37,996
Registered Office: Unit 16 The Gate Centre, Bredbury Park Way, Bredbury Park Industrial Estate, Bredbury, Stockport, Cheshire, SK6 2SN
Major Shareholder: Andrew Leslie Pass
Officers: Andrew Leslie Pass [1966] Director/Brewer

Stocks Brewing Company Ltd
Incorporated: 22 May 2018
Registered Office: Hall Cross Pub, 33-34 Hallgate, Doncaster, S Yorks, DN1 3NL
Major Shareholder: David Mark Johnson
Officers: David Mark Johnson [1973] Director

Stod Fold Brewing Limited
Incorporated: 8 September 2017
Registered Office: Barclays Bank Chambers, Market Street, Hebden Bridge, W Yorks, HX7 6AD
Major Shareholder: Charles Angus Wood
Officers: Paul James Harris [1978] Director; Charles Angus Wood [1977] Director

Stokes Brewing Company Limited
Incorporated: 26 March 2018
Registered Office: 2nd Floor, Unit 7 Riverside Court, Bath, BA2 3DZ
Officers: Jonarthan Benedict Stokes [1964] Managing Director; Theodore Benedict Stokes [1997] Director/Brewer

Stokesley Brewing Company Ltd
Incorporated: 26 January 2018
Registered Office: Second Floor, 30 Heath Road, Twickenham, Middlesex, TW1 4DD
Shareholders: Gwendolyn Mary Savage Toovey; Stuart James Toovey
Officers: Gwendolyn Mary Savage Toovey [1949] Director; John Toovey [1949] Managing Director; Stuart James Toovey [1975] Director

Stone Cold Brewery Limited
Incorporated: 10 May 2018
Registered Office: CCF Accountancy, 30 Victoria Avenue, Harrogate, N Yorks, HG1 5PR
Shareholder: Hannah Lucy Kendrick
Officers: Alec Kendrick [1970] Operations Director

Stonehenge Ales Limited
Incorporated: 3 August 1998 *Employees:* 5
Net Worth: £42,927 *Total Assets:* £191,539
Registered Office: The Old Mill, Netheravon, Salisbury, Wilts, SP4 9QB
Shareholders: Stig Anker Andersen; Anna Marie Andersen
Officers: Anna Marie Andersen, Secretary; Stig Anker Andersen [1958] Director/Master Brewer [Danish]

Stoney Ford Brew Co. Ltd
Incorporated: 25 April 2018
Registered Office: 110 Regent Road, Leicester, LE1 7LT
Parent: Spidercrab Limited
Officers: Peter David Atkinson [1972] Director; William Anthony Davis [1974] Director

Storm Brewing Company Ltd
Incorporated: 11 January 2006 *Employees:* 3
Net Worth: £21,885 *Total Assets:* £60,967
Registered Office: 6 Jennings Court, Derby Range, Stockport, Cheshire, SK4 4AB
Shareholders: Thomas David Stebbings; David John Stebbings
Officers: David John Stebbings, Secretary/Brewer; Alice Stebbings [1993] Director; David John Stebbings [1958] Director/Brewer; Thomas David Stebbings [1989] Director

Stornoway Brewers Limited
Incorporated: 7 February 2019
Registered Office: 10 Shell Street, Stornoway, Isle of Lewis, HS1 2BS
Major Shareholder: Andrew Murdo Ribbens
Officers: Andrew Murdo Ribbens [1966] Director

Stowey Brewery Limited
Incorporated: 28 November 2005
Net Worth: £8,075 *Total Assets:* £8,096
Registered Office: 25 Castle Street, Nether Stowey, Bridgwater, Somerset, TA5 1LN
Major Shareholder: Ian Pearson
Officers: Ian Pearson, Secretary/Brewer; Lynne Michelle Abbott [1962] Director/Hotelier; Ian Pearson [1963] Director/Brewer

Strands Brewery Ltd
Incorporated: 20 December 2010
Net Worth: £39,053 *Total Assets:* £129,929
Registered Office: Strands Inn, Wasdale, Seascale, Cumbria, CA20 1ET
Shareholders: Mark Edwin Corr; Lesley Ann Corr
Officers: Lesley Ann Corr [1961] Director/Publican; Mark Edwin Corr [1963] Director/Publican

Stratford upon Avon Brewery Limited
Incorporated: 7 May 2014 *Employees:* 2
Net Worth Deficit: £208,290 *Total Assets:* £81,727
Registered Office: Bank Gallery, High Street, Kenilworth, Warwicks, CV8 1LY
Shareholders: Mark David Williams; Richard Michael Williams
Officers: Deborah Jane Mary Williams [1962] Director; Mark David Williams [1960] Director; Richard Michael Williams [1988] Director/Brewer

Strathaven Ales Limited
Incorporated: 15 September 1998
Net Worth Deficit: £28,993 *Total Assets:* £64,401
Registered Office: Craigmill, Strathaven, S Lanarks, ML10 6PB
Shareholder: Craig Buchanan
Officers: Craig Douglas Buchanan [1964] Director/General Manager

Strathmore Brewery Limited
Incorporated: 2 November 2016
Net Worth: £2,400 *Total Assets:* £2,400
Registered Office: Mansfield House, Kinnettles, Forfar, Angus, DD8 1TQ
Shareholder: Nicholas Graham Smith
Officers: Nicholas Graham Smith [1985] Director/Engineer; Russell Joseph Williams [1967] Director/Lecturer

Stratton Lane Ltd
Incorporated: 18 January 2019
Registered Office: South Building, Upper Farm, Wootton St Lawrence, Basingstoke, Hants, RG23 8PE
Shareholders: Barnaby Wheller; Bernadette Wheller
Officers: Barnaby Wheller [1967] Director; Bernadette Wheller [1972] Director

Strong House Brewery Ltd
Incorporated: 1 April 2016
Net Worth: £1,939 *Total Assets:* £638,400
Registered Office: Mercury House, Shipstones Business Center, North Gate, Nottingham, NG7 7FN
Officers: Peter Robson, Secretary; Peter Robson [1959] Director

Stroud Brewery Development Limited
Incorporated: 13 October 2017
Registered Office: Kingfisher Business Park, London Road, Thrupp, Stroud, Glos, GL5 2BY
Parent: Howard Tenens Limited
Officers: Benjamin John Morris [1972] Director; Daniel Peter Morris [1977] Director; Carl David Mark Waterer [1967] Director/Accountant

The Stroud Brewery Limited
Incorporated: 29 June 2004 *Employees:* 30
Net Worth: £203,840 *Total Assets:* £349,108
Registered Office: 141 Thrupp Lane, Thrupp, Stroud, Glos, GL5 2DQ
Shareholders: Greg Mitchell Pilley; Jade Lisa Bashford
Officers: Jade Lisa Bashford [1968] Director/Local Food Promoter; Adam James Starkey [1965] Managing Director

Stubborn Mule Brewery Limited
Incorporated: 5 May 2016
Net Worth: £27 *Total Assets:* £64,026
Registered Office: Unit 2 Radium House, Bridgewater Road, Altrincham, Cheshire, WA14 1LZ
Shareholders: Edward Bright; Swan Elizabeth Cheng
Officers: Edward Bright [1978] Director/Owner; Swan Elizabeth Cheng [1983] Financial Director

Sugar Pine Brewing Company Limited
Incorporated: 5 April 2002
Net Worth: £35,008 *Total Assets:* £47,799
Registered Office: EH20 Business Centre, 6 Dryden Road, Loanhead, Midlothian, EH20 9LZ
Shareholder: Russell Sharp
Officers: Russell Sharp [1942] Director

Sulwath Brewers Limited
Incorporated: 13 February 1996
Net Worth Deficit: £87,523 *Total Assets:* £74,525
Registered Office: The Brewery, 209 King Street, Castle Douglas, Kirkcudbrightshire, DG7 1DT
Shareholders: James Allen Henderson; James Henderson
Officers: Julie Yvette Henderson, Secretary; James Allen Henderson [1969] Managing Director

Summer Wine Brewery Limited
Incorporated: 20 October 2003 *Employees:* 6
Net Worth Deficit: £77,475 *Total Assets:* £115,610
Registered Office: New Court, Abbey Road North, Shepley, Huddersfield, W Yorks, HD8 8BJ
Shareholders: Andrew James Baker; James Francis Farran
Officers: James Francis Farran, Secretary; Andrew James Baker [1985] Director; James Francis Farran [1983] Director; Meyrick Nicholas Kirk [1970] Director

Summerhall Brewing Limited
Incorporated: 28 February 2012
Registered Office: Springfield House, Laurelhill Business Park, Stirling, FK7 9JQ
Major Shareholder: Andrew Roger Barnett
Officers: Andrew Roger Barnett [1966] Director/Brewer

Summershed Brewery Limited
Incorporated: 6 June 2017
Registered Office: Brew Cottage, The Bit, Wigginton, Tring, Herts, HP23 6EQ
Shareholders: Simon Crichton; Clare Crichton
Officers: Clare Crichton [1962] Director; Simon Patrick Crichton [1961] Director

Surrey Hills Brewery Ltd
Incorporated: 22 March 2004 *Employees:* 6
Net Worth: £937,536 *Total Assets:* £1,043,051
Registered Office: Station House, Station Approach, East Horsley, Surrey, KT24 6QX
Major Shareholder: Ross William Hunter
Officers: Penelope Jane Ainsworth, Secretary; Penelope Jane Ainsworth [1964] Director/Accountant; Ross William James Hunter [1966] Director/Brewer

The Sussex Beer Company Ltd
Incorporated: 24 May 2010
Net Worth: £659,665 *Total Assets:* £700,807
Registered Office: The Old Casino, 28 Fourth Avenue, Hove, E Sussex, BN3 2PJ
Shareholders: Justin Lance Deighton; Nicola Ruth Deighton
Officers: Justin Lance Deighton [1970] Director/Business Owner; Nicola Ruth Deighton [1970] Director/Businesswoman; Paul William Frederick Kempe [1957] Director; Michael James Penkethman [1964] Director

Swaddle Micro Brewery Limited
Incorporated: 19 April 2017 *Employees:* 3
Net Worth Deficit: £71,598 *Total Assets:* £49,069
Registered Office: 32 Portland Terrace, Newcastle upon Tyne, NE2 1QP
Shareholders: Anthony Nicholas Swaddle; Jennifer Susan Swaddle; Paul Hughes
Officers: Paul Hughes [1983] Director/Manager; Anthony Nicholas Swaddle [1955] Director/Manager; Jennifer Susan Swaddle [1949] Director/Manageress

Swift Half Collective Ltd
Incorporated: 2 May 2017
Registered Office: Hamlet Cottage, St Michaels Church Road, Liverpool, L17 7BD
Shareholder: Conor Foley
Officers: Conor Foley [1985] Managing Director [Irish]; Peter Michael John Hunter [1987] Marketing & Sales Director; Danny McCay [1985] Artistic Director [Irish]

Symmetry Brewing Co Ltd
Incorporated: 2 August 2018
Registered Office: 198 Ford Lane, Crewe, Cheshire, CW1 3TN
Major Shareholder: Edmund Joseph Francis Razzall
Officers: Edmund Joseph Francis Razzall [1989] Director/Brewer

Taddington Brewery Limited
Incorporated: 25 May 2006 *Employees:* 4
Net Worth: £84,290 *Total Assets:* £166,963
Registered Office: Blackwell Hall, Blackwell, Buxton, Derbys, SK17 9TQ
Shareholders: Richard Michael Hand; Mary Megan Hand
Officers: John Michael Hand, Secretary; Richard Michael Hand [1963] Director

Tally Ho! Brewery Limited
Incorporated: 4 March 2015
Net Worth Deficit: £6,440 *Total Assets:* £9,276
Registered Office: Tally Ho! Brewery, Market Street, Hatherleigh, Okehampton, Devon, EX20 3JN
Officers: Benjamin James Bailey [1988] Director/Brewing; Peter Cosgrove [1956] Director/Brewing; Peter John Embling [1952] Director/Brewing; Bradley Horn [1964] Director/Accountant; Robert Southwick [1957] Director/Brewing

Tamar Valley Brewing Company Limited
Incorporated: 1 February 2016
Registered Office: The Old Barn, Chilsworthy, Gunnislake, Cornwall, PL18 9PB
Officers: Gareth Gwyn Davies [1961] Director; Robert Keith Field [1952] Director; David Jerome Irons [1954] Director; Mark Robert Wash [1964] Director

Tankley's Brewery Limited
Incorporated: 22 January 2015
Registered Office: 33 Beech Avenue, Sidcup, Kent, DA15 8NH
Shareholders: Glenn Heinzel; Martin Hemmings
Officers: Glenn Heinzel [1975] Director/Master Brewer [Australian]; Martin Hemmings [1976] Director/Sales

Tanners Ales Ltd
Incorporated: 2 July 2015
Net Worth Deficit: £3,132 *Total Assets:* £43,383
Registered Office: 118 High Street, Staple Hill, Bristol, BS16 5HH
Shareholders: Jennifer Claire Tanner; Simon Ashley Tanner
Officers: Jennifer Claire Tanner [1969] Director; Simon Ashley Tanner [1965] Director/Hotel Manager

Tantum Brewing Limited
Incorporated: 28 February 2019
Registered Office: 205a Nantwich Road, Crewe, Cheshire, CW2 6DD
Shareholders: Michael Heaher; Charles Alistair Holt
Officers: Michael Heaher [1960] Director; Charles Alistair Holt [1963] Director

Tap Social Movement Limited
Incorporated: 11 July 2016
Net Worth Deficit: £54,563 *Total Assets:* £96,350
Registered Office: 27 Curtis Industrial Estate, North Hinksey Lane, Oxford, OX2 0LX
Shareholders: Paul Gareth Humpherson; Amy Rachel Taylor; Hannah Grace Taylor
Officers: Paul Gareth Humpherson, Secretary; Paul Gareth Humpherson [1986] Director/Lawyer; Amy Rachel Taylor [1987] Director/Civil Servant [British/Canadian]; Hannah Grace Taylor [1991] Director/Hospitality [British/Canadian]

Tapstone Brewing Company Ltd
Incorporated: 7 March 2013
Net Worth: £16,125 *Total Assets:* £17,580
Registered Office: 11 Bartlett Park, Millfield, Chard, Somerset, TA20 2BB
Major Shareholder: James Ashley Elliott Davies
Officers: James Davies [1983] Director

Target Brewery Limited
Incorporated: 20 January 2014 *Employees:* 1
Net Worth Deficit: £81,456 *Total Assets:* £20,074
Registered Office: 144 Burton Road, Melton Mowbray, Leics, LE13 1DL
Major Shareholder: Mark Stefan Nadany
Officers: Mark Nadany [1976] Director/Brewer

Tarn Hows Brewery Limited
Incorporated: 18 September 2013 *Employees:* 1
Net Worth Deficit: £13,406 *Total Assets:* £2,977
Registered Office: Low Bield, Knipe Fold, Ambleside, Cumbria, LA22 0PU
Major Shareholder: Alastair Francis Kirk
Officers: Alastair Francis Kirk [1965] Director

Tarn51 Brewing Company Limited
Incorporated: 26 February 2015
Net Worth Deficit: £642 *Total Assets:* £210
Registered Office: 10 Church Road, Normanton, W Yorks, WF6 2NJ
Officers: Hayley Joy Lumb [1988] Director/Brewer; Robin Duncan Turton [1966] Director/Brewer

Tatton Brewery Limited
Incorporated: 26 September 2006
Net Worth: £20,980 *Total Assets:* £196,437
Registered Office: Unit 7 Longridge Trading Estate, Knutsford, Cheshire, WA16 8PR
Major Shareholder: Gregg Anthony John Sawyer
Officers: Gregg Anthony John Sawyer, Secretary; Gregg Anthony John Sawyer [1962] Director

Taw Valley Brewery Limited
Incorporated: 21 February 2017
Net Worth Deficit: £11,031 *Total Assets:* £31,981
Registered Office: Westacott Barton, Westacott Lane, North Tawton, Devon, EX20 2BS
Shareholders: Marc Andrew Whiteside; Amy Elizabeth Louise Powell
Officers: Amy Elizabeth Louise Powell [1976] Director/Administrator; Marc Andrew Whiteside [1975] Director

Timothy Taylor & Co., Limited
Incorporated: 16 November 1929 *Employees:* 123
Net Worth: £31,732,548 *Total Assets:* £35,537,816
Registered Office: Knowle Spring Brewery, Keighley, W Yorks, BD21 1AW
Officers: John Edward Thomas Varley, Secretary; Michael Lloyd Bramley [1951] Director; Timothy Clarke [1957] Director; Benjamin Thomas Dent [1984] Director/Partner; Sarah Louise Dent [1984] Director/Advertising & Sponsorship Manager; Timothy William Dewey [1958] Director/Chief Executive; Claire Hodgson [1985] Director/Marketing Manager; James Clive Orrock Simpson [1965] Director/Wine Shipper; John Edward Thomas Varley [1966] Director/Chartered Accountant; John Philip Tempest Walsh [1960] Director

Taylor Illingworth Brewing Company Limited
Incorporated: 8 March 2018
Registered Office: 21 Harwood Court, Middlesbrough, Cleveland, TS2 1PU
Shareholders: Leslie Illingworth; Martin Illingworth
Officers: Leslie Illingworth [1959] Director; Martin Illingworth [1968] Director; Benjamin Taylor [1993] Director

Taylors Blackbeck Brewery Limited
Incorporated: 25 November 2014 *Employees:* 2
Net Worth: £28,250 *Total Assets:* £106,632
Registered Office: Carleton House, 136 Gray Street, Workington, Cumbria, CA14 2LU
Shareholders: Kenneth O'Hara; Kate Taylor
Officers: Kenneth William O'Hara [1958] Director; Kate Belinda Taylor [1963] Director

Tealby Brewing Company Limited
Incorporated: 13 October 2015
Registered Office: 13 Arnold Close, Laceby, N E Lincs, LN11 0LQ
Shareholder: Geoffrey Lloyd John Melton
Officers: Geoffrey Lloyd John Melton [1957] Director; Sarah Jane Parsons [1966] Director

The Team Toxic Ltd
Incorporated: 30 October 2018
Registered Office: Offices A13-A14 Champions Business Park, Arrowe Brook Road, Wirral, Merseyside, CH49 0AB
Shareholders: Susan Jane Hayward; Gary Prescott
Officers: Susan Jane Hayward [1966] Director/Brewer; Gary Prescott [1970] Director/Brewer

Teignworthy Brewery Limited
Incorporated: 24 March 2003 *Employees:* 7
Net Worth: £8,354 *Total Assets:* £139,603
Registered Office: Sigma House, Oak View Close, Edginswell Park, Torquay, Devon, TQ2 7FF
Shareholders: John Gregory Lawton; Rachel Helen Lawton
Officers: Rachel Helen Lawton, Secretary; John Gregory Lawton [1964] Director/Brewer; Rachel Helen Lawton [1968] Director

The Teller Lager Company Limited
Incorporated: 20 February 2002
Registered Office: Enterprise House, The Courtyard, Old Court House Road, Bromborough, Wirral, Merseyside, CH62 4UE
Officers: Ramonde Terrence Newell, Secretary; Shaun Mark Newell [1970] Director

Temperance Brewing Company Limited
Incorporated: 11 September 2015
Net Worth: £35,063 *Total Assets:* £35,063
Registered Office: 197 Rochdale Road, Shaw, Oldham, Lancs, OL2 7JN
Shareholder: Paul Robert Mellor
Officers: John Mellor, Secretary; Paul Robert Mellor [1980] Director/Brewer

Tempest Brewing Co Limited
Incorporated: 6 September 2013 *Employees:* 15
Net Worth: £577,593 *Total Assets:* £1,142,723
Registered Office: Block 11, Units 1 & 2 Tweedbank Industrial Estate, Tweedbank, Galashiels, Selkirkshire, TD1 3RS
Shareholders: Gavin John Meiklejohn; Annika Gabrielle Meiklejohn
Officers: Annika Gabrielle Meiklejohn [1977] Director [New Zealander]; Gavin John Meiklejohn [1976] Director

Temple Road Brewing Company Limited
Incorporated: 21 January 2016
Registered Office: 26 Littleham Road, Exmouth, Devon, EX8 2QQ
Major Shareholder: Bruce Robert Vogt
Officers: Dr Bruce Robert Vogt, Secretary; Dr Bruce Robert Vogt [1980] Director/Medical Doctor

Ten Tors Brewery Ltd
Incorporated: 5 February 2018
Registered Office: 71-75 Shelton Street, Covent Garden, London, WC2H 9JQ
Major Shareholder: Daryl Hall
Officers: Daryl Hall [1984] Director/HGV Driver

Tenby Brewing Co. Limited
Incorporated: 20 October 2014
Net Worth: £124,466 *Total Assets:* £293,537
Registered Office: Unit 15 Tenby Brewing Co, The Salterns, Tenby, Pembrokeshire, SA70 8EQ
Shareholder: Robert Faulkner
Officers: Hilary Dowdall, Secretary; James Alexander Beaven [1985] Director/Business Development Manager; Robert Faulkner [1981] Director/Licensee

Test Brewing Ltd
Incorporated: 15 July 2016
Registered Office: Fleming Court, Leigh Road, Eastleigh, Southampton, SO50 9PD
Officers: Timothy John Abram [1969] Director; Christopher Roman Brown [1972] Director; Jonathon Nelson Deacon [1969] Director; Neil Palmer [1976] Director

Tewkesbury Brewery Ltd
Incorporated: 20 November 2013
Registered Office: 35 Gravel Walk, Tewkesbury, Glos, GL20 5NH
Officers: James Hamilton Blockley [1973] Director/Brewery

T.& R. Theakston Limited
Incorporated: 6 August 2003 *Employees:* 31
Net Worth: £2,422,000 *Total Assets:* £4,944,000
Registered Office: The Brewery, Masham, Ripon, N Yorks, HG4 4YD
Shareholder: Heineken UK Limited
Officers: Simon Francis Owen Theakston, Secretary/Director; Richard Anthony Bradbury [1963] Director; Christopher Michael Jowsey [1965] Director; Edward David Theakston [1962] Director; Nicholas Robert Theakston [1955] Director; Simon Francis Owen Theakston [1957] Director; Timothy James Owen Theakston [1957] Director/Surveyor; William James Collin Wood [1953] Director

Thesis Brewing Co. Ltd
Incorporated: 24 January 2019
Registered Office: 27 Tower Way, Canterbury, Kent, CT1 2DP
Major Shareholder: Stuart Morrison
Officers: Dr. Stuart Morrison [1990] Director/Barman

The Thetford Brewery Limited
Incorporated: 19 May 2017
Registered Office: Unit 1.01, 9 Brighton Terrace, London, SW9 8DJ
Major Shareholder: Tobias Thomas Bidwell
Officers: Dominic Edward Charles Bidwell [1965] Director; Stephen James John Bidwell [1964] Director; Tobias Thomas Bidwell [1971] Director

Thirst Class Ale Limited
Incorporated: 29 July 2014
Net Worth Deficit: £19,410 *Total Assets:* £39,065
Registered Office: Unit 16 Station Road Industrial Estate, Reddish, Stockport, Cheshire, SK5 6ND
Major Shareholder: Richard Conway
Officers: Richard Conway [1979] Director/Head Brewer/Owner

Thirsty Pioneers Brewing Company Ltd
Incorporated: 21 June 2018
Registered Office: 46 Vine Lane, Warwick, CV34 5BE
Shareholders: Archie James Skelcher; Joseph Lawrence Skelcher
Officers: Archie James Skelcher [1992] Director; Joseph Lawrence Skelcher [1995] Director

Thirsty Smile Ltd
Incorporated: 1 March 2017
Net Worth: £1,554 *Total Assets:* £1,554
Registered Office: Crown House, 27 Old Gloucester Street, London, WC1N 3AX
Shareholders: Matthew Daniel Trim; David Reginald Childs; Andrew Henderson
Officers: Matthew Daniel Trim [1966] Director

Thistlerock Enterprises UK Limited
Incorporated: 26 July 2017
Registered Office: 3 Pool Road, Hartley Wintney, Hook, Hants, RG27 8RD
Shareholder: James Francis Turley
Officers: James Francis Turley, Secretary; Kevin John Conroy [1985] Director; Andrew John Seward [1987] Director [Irish]; James Francis Turley [1989] Director

The Thornbridge Hall Country House Brewing Company Limited
Incorporated: 1 June 2004 *Employees:* 49
Net Worth: £120,980 *Total Assets:* £4,227,784
Registered Office: Riverside Brewery, Buxton Road, Bakewell, Derbys, DE45 1GS
Parent: Thornbridge Brewery Holdings Limited
Officers: James Robert Harrison, Secretary/Director; James Robert Harrison [1959] Director; Simon David Webster [1968] Director

Three Acre Brewery Limited
Incorporated: 24 September 2018
Registered Office: Little Woodbine Farm, Fir Grove Road, Cross in Hand, E Sussex, TN21 0SU
Shareholders: Peter James Mayhew; Chester Patrick Broad; James Mathew, Albert Newton
Officers: Peter James Mayhew [1996] Director; James Mathew Albert Newton [1996] Director

Three Arches Brewing Limited
Incorporated: 29 November 2017
Registered Office: 7 The Arches, Bracondale, Norwich, NR1 2EF
Parent: Unicorn Craft Brewing Co Limited
Officers: Ben Dawson Handford [1977] Marketing Director; Benjamin Luke Hopkins [1977] Director

Three Brothers Brewing Company Limited
Incorporated: 4 March 2016 *Employees:* 4
Net Worth Deficit: £133,369 *Total Assets:* £134,467
Registered Office: 4 Clayton Court, Bowesfield Crescent, Stockton on Tees, Cleveland, TS18 3QX
Shareholders: Christopher Edward Dodd; Christopher David Wright; David William Dodd
Officers: Christopher Edward Dodd [1989] Director; David William Dodd [1985] Director; Christopher David Wright [1976] Director

Three Castles Brewery Limited
Incorporated: 27 April 2006
Net Worth Deficit: £74,297 *Total Assets:* £59,901
Registered Office: Unit 12 Salisbury Road Business Park, Pewsey, Wilts, SN9 5PZ
Officers: Roger Johnston, Secretary; Ian Johnston [1973] Director/Insurance Business Manager; Roger Johnston [1947] Director/Business Consultant; Antony Craig Mulcock [1974] Director/Brewer; Lyn Mulcock [1975] Director

The Three Counties Brewery Limited
Incorporated: 19 January 2011
Net Worth Deficit: £18,804 *Total Assets:* £4,713
Registered Office: Building 5B, The Mousery, Beeches Road, Battlesbridge, Essex, SS11 8TJ
Shareholder: George Gledhill
Officers: Dr Kevin Charles Carr [1969] Director; Michael Coverdale [1976] Director; George Gledhill [1945] Director/Surveyor; David Snaith [1962] Director

Three Engineers Brewery Ltd
Incorporated: 21 September 2015
Net Worth Deficit: £1,137 *Total Assets:* £4,388
Registered Office: Court Farm, Church Lane, Winterbourne, Bristol, BS36 1SE
Officers: Daniel Matthew Gillians [1974] Director; Keith Andrew Lewis [1961] Director/Engineer; Greg Shipton [1993] Director/Engineer

Three Geezers Brewing Limited
Incorporated: 23 April 2018
Registered Office: 28 Laurel Gardens, Greenham, Thatcham, Berks, RG19 8XU
Shareholders: Terence Harry Weatherill; Kevin John Wilkins; Mark Walsingham
Officers: Terence Harry Weatherill, Secretary; Mark Walsingham [1960] Director/Supply Chain Manager; Terence Harry Weatherill [1962] Director/Principal Solution Architect; Kevin John Wilkins [1966] Director/Airport Senior Manager

Three Hills Brewing Ltd
Incorporated: 16 August 2018
Registered Office: 4 Thrapston Road, Woodford, Kettering, Northants, NN14 4HY
Major Shareholder: Andrew Andrew Catherall
Officers: Andrew Osborne Catherall [1987] Director

Three Kings Brewery Limited
Incorporated: 4 April 2012 Employees: 5
Net Worth Deficit: £914 Total Assets: £35,619
Registered Office: 14-15 Prospect Terrace, North Shields, Tyne & Wear, NE30 1DX
Major Shareholder: Ewan Andrew McCann
Officers: Ewan McCann, Secretary; Ewan Andrew McCann [1973] Director

The Three Legs Brewing Company Limited
Incorporated: 22 April 2014 Employees: 4
Net Worth: £1,693 Total Assets: £180,583
Registered Office: Unit 1 Burnt House Farm, Udimore Road, Broad Oak, Rye, E Sussex, TN31 6BX
Shareholder: Samuel Peter Trenham Chamier
Officers: Samuel Peter Trenham Chamier, Secretary; Samuel Peter Trenham Chamier [1987] Director/Brewer; Benjamin David Murray [1978] Director/Brewer

Three Lions Brewery Ltd
Incorporated: 20 August 2018
Registered Office: 56 Manor Road South, Esher, Surrey, KT10 0QQ
Shareholders: Anthony Richard Powell; Anthony Richard Powell
Officers: Anthony Richard Powell [1968] Director/Engineer

Three Shires Brewery Ltd
Incorporated: 6 October 2014 Employees: 2
Net Worth Deficit: £41,281 Total Assets: £44,763
Registered Office: 7 Copenhagen Street, Worcester, WR1 2HB
Major Shareholder: Robert Wintrip
Officers: Robert Charles Wintrip [1984] Director/Micro-Brewery

Thunder and Little Ltd
Incorporated: 2 January 2019
Registered Office: 93 Brinkley Road, Worcester Park, Surrey, KT4 8JE
Major Shareholder: Justin Gregory
Officers: Justin Gregory [1969] Director/Train Driver

Thurstons Horsell Brewery Company Limited
Incorporated: 2 November 2012 Employees: 2
Net Worth: £4,284 Total Assets: £51,028
Registered Office: 102c High Street, Horsell, Woking, Surrey, GU21 4ST
Officers: John Mintram, Secretary; John Fraser Mintram [1963] Director/Brewer; Frank Leonard Pawley [1947] Director; George Adams Smith [1956] Director/Brewer; Edward Wray [1971] Director

Daniel Thwaites Public Limited Company
Incorporated: 17 March 1897 Employees: 819
Net Worth: £174,200,000 Total Assets: £308,600,000
Registered Office: Myerscough Road, Mellor Brook, Blackburn, Lancs, BB2 7LB
Officers: Susan Irene Woodward, Secretary; Richard Anthony John Bailey [1973] Director/Investment Banker; Nicholas Stephen MacKenzie [1968] Director; Richard Andrew Stothert [1957] Director; Kevin David Wood [1966] Finance Director; Ann Jean Mary Yerburgh [1947] Director; Oscar Guy Hamlyn Yerburgh [1983] Director

Ticketytap Ltd
Incorporated: 11 May 2016
Registered Office: Unit 6 Waterloo Court, Waterloo Road, Stalybridge, Cheshire, SK15 2AU
Shareholders: Keri Louise Barton; Duncan Barton
Officers: Duncan Barton [1982] Director/Brewery Tap; Keri Louise Barton [1981] Director/Brewery Tap

Tidal London Ltd
Incorporated: 19 May 2017
Net Worth: £75 Total Assets: £1,096
Registered Office: 17 North Worple Way, London, SW14 8QA
Major Shareholder: Paul Young
Officers: Paul Young [1984] Director

Tillingbourne Brewery Ltd
Incorporated: 22 August 2011 Employees: 3
Net Worth: £16,787 Total Assets: £106,651
Registered Office: 5 Jardine House, Harrovian Business Village, Bessborough Road, Harrow, Middlesex, HA1 3EX
Officers: Stephen John Dodd [1965] Director/Brewer; Lee John Cary Nicholls [1965] Director/Brewer

Emma J Tilston Ltd
Incorporated: 10 March 2017
Net Worth: £227 Total Assets: £8,550
Registered Office: Tenby Place, 102 Selby Road, West Bridgford, Nottingham, NG2 7BA
Officers: Emma Jane Tilston [1966] Director/Contractor

Time & Tide Brewing Limited
Incorporated: 29 August 2013 Employees: 3
Net Worth Deficit: £50,235 Total Assets: £178,562
Registered Office: Statenborough Farm, Felderland Lane, Worth, Deal, Kent, CT14 0BX
Shareholders: Samuel Robert Gordon Weller; Kerry Alicia Campling
Officers: Kerry Alicia Campling [1977] Director/HR Manager

Tintagel Brewery Limited
Incorporated: 4 October 2006 Employees: 4
Net Worth: £360,863 Total Assets: £497,841
Registered Office: 5 West Street, Okehampton, Devon, EX20 1HQ
Shareholders: Elizabeth Anne Heard; John Reford Heard
Officers: John Reford Heard, Secretary/Fencing Contractor; Elizabeth Anne Heard [1969] Director/Holiday Cottage Owner; John Reford Heard [1962] Director/Fencing Contractor

Tinworks Brewing Company Ltd.
Incorporated: 18 April 2017
Net Worth Deficit: £7,665 Total Assets: £14,462
Registered Office: Llys Cerdd, Heol Gelli Fawr, Five Roads, Llanelli, Dyfed, SA15 5EQ
Major Shareholder: Matthew David Stevenson
Officers: Matthew David Stevenson [1987] Director

Tiny Vessel Brewing Company Limited
Incorporated: 2 August 2006
Previous: Exquisite Essentials Ltd
Net Worth Deficit: £23,181 Total Assets: £3,599
Registered Office: Unit 505 Platts Eyot, Lower Sunbury Road, Hampton, Surrey, TW12 2HF
Major Shareholder: Ivailo Penchev Penev
Officers: Ivailo Penchev Penev [1979] Director [Bulgarian]

Tipsy Angel Brewery Ltd
Incorporated: 15 December 2015
Registered Office: Unit 20 Manor Industrial Estate, Lower Wash Lane, Latchford, Warrington, Cheshire, WA4 1PL
Officers: Aidan Grannell [1947] Director/Brewer; John Robinson [1950] Director/Retired

The Tiptree Brewing Company Limited
Incorporated: 14 October 2016
Registered Office: The Old Grange, Warren Estate Lordship Road, Writtle, Chelmsford, Essex, CM1 3WT
Major Shareholder: Mark Lyndon Acketts
Officers: Mark Lyndon Acketts [1965] Director/Salesman

Tirindrish Trading Company Limited
Incorporated: 25 January 2017
Net Worth: £100 *Total Assets:* £29,274
Registered Office: Tirindrish House, Spean Bridge, Inverness-shire, PH34 4EU
Shareholder: Ian Peter MacDonald
Officers: Lucy Alexandra Hicks [1976] Director/B & B Proprietor; James Fraser Leggett [1970] Director/B & B Proprietor; Ian Peter MacDonald [1961] Director

Tirril Brewery Limited
Incorporated: 28 November 2001
Net Worth Deficit: £83,612 *Total Assets:* £253,237
Registered Office: Red House, Long Marton, Appleby in Westmorland, Cumbria, CA16 6BN
Shareholders: Christopher James Tomlinson; Christopher James Tomlinson; Alison Tomlinson
Officers: Alison Tomlinson, Secretary; Alison Tomlinson [1970] Director; Christopher James Tomlinson [1969] Director/Publican/Hotelier

Titanic Brewery Co Limited
Incorporated: 20 May 2003 *Employees:* 100
Net Worth: £793,260 *Total Assets:* £2,652,566
Registered Office: Unit 5 Callender Place, Lingard Street, Burslem, Stoke on Trent, Staffs, ST6 1JL
Shareholders: David Antony Bott; Keith Andrew Bott
Officers: Thomas William Bebb, Secretary/Consultant; David Antony Bott [1958] Director/Manager; Keith Andrew Bott [1967] Director/Owner Manager of Brewery; Andrew Peter Slee [1965] Director/Management Consultant

Titsey Brewing Co. Limited
Incorporated: 19 January 2018
Registered Office: Stables Cottage, Hayes Lane, Slinfold, Horsham, W Sussex, RH13 0RF
Major Shareholder: Craig Vroom
Officers: Craig Vroom [1983] Director/Brewer [South African]

TKS Brewing Limited
Incorporated: 3 February 2017
Net Worth: £2 *Total Assets:* £2
Registered Office: 10 Essex Road, London, E17 8AN
Officers: Daniel Joseph Cain [1990] Director/Head Brewer; Michael John Cave [1985] Director/Head Brewer; Andrew John Matthews [1985] Director/Research and Development; Charlie John Waites [1991] Director/Head of Sales

To The Moon Brewery Ltd
Incorporated: 29 May 2018
Registered Office: 3 Woodcote Avenue, Bramhall, Cheshire, SK7 3ND
Major Shareholder: Matthew Alan Haley
Officers: Matthew Alan Haley [1986] Director/Accounts Manager

Tollgate Brewery Limited
Incorporated: 26 July 2011 *Employees:* 18
Net Worth Deficit: £16,984 *Total Assets:* £99,453
Registered Office: Unit 1 Southwood House Farm, Staunton Lane, Calke, Ashby De La Zouch, Leics, LE65 1RG
Major Shareholder: Kevin Elliott
Officers: Kevin Paul Elliott [1963] Director

Tom's Tap and Brewhouse Ltd
Incorporated: 15 March 2018
Registered Office: 4-5 Thomas Street, Crewe, Cheshire, CW1 2BD
Officers: Jacqui Ayling, Secretary; Jacqui Ayling [1962] Director/Bar Manager; Sean Edward Ayling [1967] Director/Brewer; Thomas Andrew Farmer [1985] Director/Insurance Professional

Tombstone Brewery Limited
Incorporated: 7 November 2014
Net Worth: £10,434 *Total Assets:* £11,626
Registered Office: 6 George Street, Great Yarmouth, Norfolk, NR30 1HR
Major Shareholder: Paul Hodgson
Officers: Paul Hodgson [1965] Director

Tomos & Lilford Holdings Limited
Incorporated: 1 December 2015 *Employees:* 1
Net Worth Deficit: £7,145 *Total Assets:* £11,896
Registered Office: 117 Boverton Road, Llantwit Major, S Glamorgan, CF61 1YA
Shareholders: Robert Charles Byron Lilford; Rolant Tomos
Officers: James Lilford [1975] Director/Brewery; Robert Charles Byron Lilford [1972] Director/Brewery; Rolant Tomos [1974] Director/Brewery

Tomson & Wotton Limited
Incorporated: 14 December 2005
Registered Office: Engine Bank Farm, Moulton Chapel, Spalding, Lincs, PE12 0XX
Officers: Peter Marcus Mandell [1953] Director/Civil Engineer

Tonbridge Brewery Limited
Incorporated: 11 February 2013 *Employees:* 7
Net Worth: £80,537 *Total Assets:* £193,405
Registered Office: Whiteoaks, Tudeley Road, Tonbridge, Kent, TN11 0NW
Shareholders: Mark Wotton Gardner; Paul Geoffrey Bournazian
Officers: Lynne Bournazian [1956] Director/Administrator; Paul Geoffrey Bournazian [1956] Director/Brewery Operator; Laura Elizabeth Gardner [1965] Director/TV Production Manager; Mark Wotton Gardner [1960] Director

Toolmakers Brewery Limited
Incorporated: 20 June 2012 *Employees:* 2
Net Worth Deficit: £58,725 *Total Assets:* £13,662
Registered Office: 6-8 Botsford Street, Sheffield, S3 9PF
Shareholders: Marion Anne Ferns; Oliver Peter Ferns
Officers: Marion Ferns [1964] Director; Oliver Ferns [1955] Director

Top Rope Brewing Limited
Incorporated: 6 April 2017
Net Worth Deficit: £1,320 *Total Assets:* £57,899
Registered Office: 17 Bampton Road, Liverpool, L16 6AX
Shareholders: Ben Jackson; Neil Rothwell
Officers: Ben Jackson [1988] Director; Neil Rothwell [1990] Director

The Top-Notch Brewing Company Ltd
Incorporated: 5 March 2018
Registered Office: 60 Wickham Way, Haywards Heath, W Sussex, RH16 1UQ
Major Shareholder: Alistair Duncan Charles Maddock
Officers: Alistair Duncan Charles Maddock [1969] Director/Airline Pilot

Topcat Brewery Limited
Incorporated: 16 January 2018
Registered Office: 42 Glebe Street, Loughborough, Leics, LE11 1JR
Shareholders: Christopher Willacy; R & M Industries Limited
Officers: Rachel Hunt [1991] Director; Ricky John Hunt [1959] Director/Engineer; Michael William Rogers [1960] Director/Operations Manager; Christopher Willacy [1988] Director/Brewer

Topsham Brewery Ltd
Incorporated: 17 January 2018
Registered Office: The Old Stables, Countess Wear Road, Exeter, EX2 6LR
Shareholders: Declan Elliott Beeson; Jason Virok; Eric Courtney Julian Eveleigh
Officers: Declan Elliott Beeson [1991] Director; Eric Courtney Julian Eveleigh [1969] Director/Head Brewer; Jason Virok [1978] Director/Brewer [American]

Torrside Brewing Ltd
Incorporated: 21 October 2014
Net Worth: £40,247 Total Assets: £145,313
Registered Office: The Warehouse, New Mills Marina Hibbert Street, New Mills, High Peak, Derbys, SK22 3JJ
Shareholders: Peter Christopher Sidwell; Christopher Roger Clough; Nicholas Marshall Rothko-Wright
Officers: Chris Roger Clough [1979] Director/Translator; Nicholas Marshall Rothko-Wright [1978] Director/IT Developer; Peter Christopher Sidwell [1974] Director/Accountant

Totally Brewed Limited
Incorporated: 6 December 2012
Net Worth: £16,740 Total Assets: £62,335
Registered Office: 13 Blenheim Drive, Beeston, Nottingham, NG9 5ES
Shareholders: Robert John Witt; Virginia Claire Witt
Officers: Virginia Claire Witt, Secretary; Robert John Witt [1982] Director; Virginia Claire Witt [1978] Director

Totnes Brewing Co Limited
Incorporated: 19 June 2015 Employees: 15
Net Worth: £15,553 Total Assets: £141,845
Registered Office: 28 Alexandra Terrace, Exmouth, Devon, EX8 1BD
Shareholders: Sarah Louise Kidd; Richard John Kidd
Officers: Barbara Ann Everatt [1943] Director; Richard John Kidd [1968] Director; Sarah Louise Kidd [1970] Director

Towcester Mill Brewery Limited
Incorporated: 10 June 2009 Employees: 3
Net Worth: £51,134 Total Assets: £121,709
Registered Office: The Mill, Pury Hill Business Park, Alderton Road, Towcester, Northants, NN12 7LS
Officers: John Lawrence Evans [1960] Director; Raymond Paul Hunt [1959] Director

Tower Brewery Limited
Incorporated: 24 March 2006
Net Worth: £9,811 Total Assets: £339,839
Registered Office: Tower Brewery, Glensyl Way, Burton on Trent, Staffs, DE14 1LX
Shareholder: John Geoffrey Mills
Officers: Karen Anne Mills, Secretary; John Geoffrey Mills [1965] Director/Brewer Retailer

Towler and Webb Limited
Incorporated: 5 December 2016 Employees: 15
Net Worth Deficit: £38,562 Total Assets: £66,690
Registered Office: Mad O'Rourkes Pie Factory, Hurst Lane, Tipton, W Midlands, DY4 9AB
Shareholders: Peter Charles Towler; Oliver John Webb
Officers: Peter Charles Towler [1959] Director; Oliver John Webb [1992] Director

Townes Brewery Limited
Incorporated: 21 October 2013 Employees: 5
Net Worth: £5,966 Total Assets: £143,197
Registered Office: Speedwell Inn, Lowgates, Staveley, Chesterfield, Derbys, S43 3TT
Shareholders: Charles Lawrie Evans; Nicoleta Lenuta Evans
Officers: Charles Lawrie Evans [1960] Director/Brewer; Nicoleta Lenuta Evans [1968] Director [Romanian]

Track Brewing Company Ltd
Incorporated: 18 February 2014
Net Worth: £83,680 Total Assets: £267,451
Registered Office: Unit 5 Sheffield Street, Manchester, M1 2ND
Major Shareholder: Sam Dyson
Officers: Sam Dyson [1978] Director

Traditional Scottish Ales Limited
Incorporated: 15 September 2005 Employees: 8
Net Worth Deficit: £427,062 Total Assets: £526,805
Registered Office: 7c Bandeath Industrial Estate, Throsk, Stirling, FK7 7NP
Shareholder: Andrew John Richardson
Officers: Alexander Douglas Moffat, Secretary; Andrew John Richardson [1962] Director; Carlo Louis Valente [1962] Director

Trailhead Brew Company Ltd
Incorporated: 25 February 2019
Registered Office: Three Brooms, Hoe Lane, Abinger Hammer, Dorking, Surrey, RH5 6RH
Major Shareholder: Richard Malcolm Keay Wallace
Officers: Richard Malcolm Keay Wallace [1974] Director

Trale Brewing Company Ltd
Incorporated: 9 February 2018
Registered Office: 242/242a Farnham Road, Slough, Berks, SL1 4XE
Major Shareholder: Thomas Michael Ross
Officers: Edmund Joseph Michael Ross, Secretary; Edmund Joseph Michael Ross [1959] Director; Thomas Michael Ross [1991] Managing Director

Traquair House Brewery Limited
Incorporated: 7 February 1997 Employees: 3
Net Worth Deficit: £40,689 Total Assets: £150,336
Registered Office: Traquair House, Innerleithen, Peebles-shire, EH44 6PW
Major Shareholder: Catherine Margaret Mary Maxwell Stuart
Officers: Catherine Margaret Mary Maxwell Stuart, Secretary/Estate Administrator; Catherine Margaret Mary Maxwell Stuart [1964] Director/Estate Administrator; Mark Oliver Benjamin Muller [1964] Director/Barrister

Treboom Limited
Incorporated: 27 May 2011 Employees: 5
Net Worth: £37,057 Total Assets: £70,537
Registered Office: Club Chambers, Museum Street, York, YO1 7DN
Shareholders: John Llewelyn Lewis; Jane Blackman
Officers: Jane Blackman [1965] Director; Dr John Llewelyn Lewis [1960] Director

Treen's Brewery Ltd.
Incorporated: 29 February 2016
Net Worth Deficit: £70,190 Total Assets: £78,090
Registered Office: 18 St Michaels Road, Ponsanooth, Truro, Cornwall, TR3 7EA
Shareholders: Simon James Treen; Sarah Michele Treen
Officers: Sarah Michele Treen [1980] Director; Simon James Treen [1980] Director

Tres Bien Brewery Ltd
Incorporated: 22 August 2017
Registered Office: 54 Adderley Road, Leicester, LE2 1WB
Officers: David McLean Canning [1984] Director/Brewer

The Tring Brewery Company Limited
Incorporated: 19 May 1992
Net Worth: £1,014,476 Total Assets: £1,279,175
Registered Office: Dunsley Farm, London Road, Tring, Herts, HP23 6HA
Officers: Edith Jane Shardlow, Secretary; Dr Andrew Conan Jackson [1967] Director/Sales & Marketing; Richard Peter Shardlow [1957] Director

Trinity Ales Limited
Incorporated: 12 February 2015 Employees: 2
Net Worth Deficit: £6,751 Total Assets: £9,332
Registered Office: Wild Hearts Cottage, Church Road, Gisleham, Lowestoft, Suffolk, NR33 8DS
Major Shareholder: Graham Hunt
Officers: Graham Hunt [1964] Director

Triple Point Brewing Ltd
Incorporated: 15 November 2018
Registered Office: 178 Shoreham Street, Sheffield, S1 4SQ
Major Shareholder: Michael Jonathan Brook
Officers: Michael Jonathan Brook [1961] Director

True North Brew Co Limited
Incorporated: 9 July 2002 Employees: 305
Previous: Forum Cafe Bars Limited
Net Worth: £2,182,204 Total Assets: £5,119,779
Registered Office: 13-17 Paradise Square, Sheffield, S1 2DE
Major Shareholder: Kane Steven Yeardley
Officers: Sean Francis Kelly, Finance Director; Sean Francis Kelly [1982] Finance Director; Alex David Liddle [1976] Operations Director; Kane Steven Yeardley [1961] Director

Trumark Properties Limited
Incorporated: 9 September 2008 Employees: 95
Net Worth: £2,743,431 Total Assets: £5,902,612
Registered Office: Roker Terrace, Sunderland, Tyne & Wear, SR6 9ND
Shareholders: Mark Hird; Nicola Foster Hird
Officers: Steven Andrew Akers [1981] Finance Director; Nicola Jane Foster-Hird [1972] Director; Jonathan Graham [1974] Operations Director; Mark Hird [1973] Director

Tuckers Ales Limited
Incorporated: 24 August 2016
Registered Office: Unit 1 Tweed Road Industrial Estate, Tweed Road, Clevedon, Somerset, BS21 6RR
Major Shareholder: Howard James Tucker
Officers: Howard James Tucker [1964] Director

Tumanny Albion Brewing Company Limited
Incorporated: 4 September 2012
Net Worth: £11,440 Total Assets: £27,260
Registered Office: 85 Great Portland Street, London, W1W 7LT
Major Shareholder: Alex Klaos
Officers: Alex Klaos [1965] Director [Estonian]

Tunnel Brewery Limited
Incorporated: 9 July 2004 Employees: 1
Net Worth Deficit: £16,145 Total Assets: £50,045
Registered Office: 13 Swinburne Close, Galley Common, Nuneaton, Warwicks, CV10 9RX
Shareholder: Robert Anthony Yates
Officers: Robert Anthony Yates, Secretary; Robert Anthony Yates [1957] Director/Designer

Turing Complete Solutions Ltd
Incorporated: 12 August 2010 Employees: 24
Net Worth: £25,850 Total Assets: £77,736
Registered Office: 125 Putnoe Lane, Bedford, MK41 8LB
Major Shareholder: Alan Kelly
Officers: Alan Kelly [1972] Director

Turner & Shaw Glasgow Brewing Company Limited
Incorporated: 17 October 2016 Employees: 2
Net Worth Deficit: £50,263 Total Assets: £7,386
Registered Office: Unit 17 Andrew Court, South Douglas Street, Clydebank, W Dunbartonshire, G81 1PD
Shareholders: Michael Shaw; Samuel Sam Turner
Officers: Michael Shaw [1981] Director; Samuel Sam Turner [1989] Director

Turning Point Brewing Company Limited
Incorporated: 16 January 2017
Net Worth: £13,817 Total Assets: £101,334
Registered Office: Unit 34 Kirby Mills Industrial Estate, Kirkbymoorside, N Yorks, YO62 6QR
Shareholders: Aron Michael McMahon; Cameron James Brown
Officers: Cameron James Brown [1993] Director; Aron Michael McMahon [1977] Director

TW@ Limited
Incorporated: 22 July 2018
Registered Office: 57a Harold Road, Margate, Kent, CT9 2HS
Officers: Shaun Faraday [1966] Director/Engineer

Tweed Brewing Ltd
Incorporated: 1 February 2016
Net Worth: £3,180 Total Assets: £24,432
Registered Office: Phoenix House, 2 Huddersfield Road, Stalybridge, Cheshire, SK15 2QA
Major Shareholder: Anthony Lewis
Officers: Anthony Lewis [1969] Director/Company Manager

Twickenham Fine Ales Limited
Incorporated: 15 March 2004
Net Worth: £639,472 Total Assets: £1,028,140
Registered Office: 8 Kenilworth Court, Hampton Road, Twickenham, Middlesex, TW2 5QL
Major Shareholder: Stephen James Brown
Officers: Graeme Edward Neat, Secretary; Stephen James Brown [1958] Managing Director; Benedict John Norman [1972] Sales Director

Twin Barrel Brewery Limited
Incorporated: 24 December 2018
Registered Office: 45 Whitecross Avenue, Bristol, BS14 9JF
Shareholders: Brett John Williams; ABW Global Limited
Officers: Brett John Williams [1993] Director/Co-Founder

Twinshock Brewery Ltd
Incorporated: 10 November 2017
Registered Office: 428 Manchester Road, Tyldesley, Manchester, M29 7BT
Shareholder: Dayle Seddon Roberts
Officers: Craig Thomas Reynolds [1989] Director/Builder; Dayle Seddon Roberts [1985] Director/Project Manager

Twisted Barrel Ale Limited
Incorporated: 22 July 2013
Net Worth Deficit: £46,791 *Total Assets:* £153,837
Registered Office: Unit 11 Fargo Village, Far Gosford Street, Coventry, Warwicks, CV1 5ED
Officers: Jennifer Michelle Bosworth [1983] Director/Training Administration; Ritchie Darren Bosworth [1979] Director/Accountant; Ann-Marie Olivia Cooper [1982] Director/Purchasing Coordinator; Christopher James Cooper [1980] Director/IT Manager; Martin Stephen Paul Leape [1980] Director/Businessman; Michael Christopher Leape [1969] Director/Businessman

The Twisted Brewing Company Limited
Incorporated: 11 December 2013
Net Worth Deficit: £42,252 *Total Assets:* £43,689
Registered Office: Unit 8 Commerce Business Centre, Commerce Close, West Wilts Trading Estate, Westbury, Wilts, BA13 4LS
Major Shareholder: Andrew John Murray
Officers: Andrew John Murray [1964] Director

Twisted Oak Brewery Ltd
Incorporated: 13 October 2010 *Employees:* 14
Net Worth: £761 *Total Assets:* £39,420
Registered Office: Edinburgh House, 1-5 Bellevue Road, Clevedon, Somerset, BS21 7NP
Shareholders: Simon Rhodri Gait; Debra Sarah Hayles; Keith Anthony Hayles
Officers: Simon Rhodri Gait [1970] Director/Brewer; Debra Sarah Hayles [1967] Director; Keith Anthony Hayles [1967] Director/Brewer

Two Beach Brewing Co Limited
Incorporated: 19 November 2012 *Employees:* 1
Net Worth Deficit: £13,293 *Total Assets:* £17,515
Registered Office: Ness Cove, Ness Drive, Shaldon, Teignmouth, Devon, TQ14 0HP
Major Shareholder: Andrew Martin Cope
Officers: Andrew Martin Cope [1969] Director

Two Bears Brewery Ltd
Incorporated: 14 March 2017
Registered Office: 19 Brook Road, Rubery, Birmingham, B45 9UH
Officers: Daniel James Wilson [1982] Director; Ryan Wilson [1982] Director

The Two Bob Brewing Company Ltd
Incorporated: 7 February 2019
Registered Office: 10 Abbots Close, Datchworth, Knebworth, Herts, SG3 6TA
Shareholders: Robert Arthur Clarke; Robert Underwood; John Stuart Thurlow
Officers: Robert Arthur Clarke [1965] Director/Brewer; John Stuart Thurlow [1966] Director/Brewer; Robert Underwood [1966] Director/Brewer

Two By Two Brewing Ltd
Incorporated: 10 October 2013
Net Worth: £13,589 *Total Assets:* £93,088
Registered Office: 14 Albany Gardens, Whitley Bay, Tyne & Wear, NE26 2DY
Shareholders: Robert John MacLeod; Roderick MacLeod
Officers: Roderick MacLeod, Secretary; Claire Amy MacLeod [1982] Director/Teacher; Dylis MacLeod [1948] Director/Retired; Robert John MacLeod [1982] Director/Brewery; Roderick MacLeod [1948] Director/Retired

Two Cocks Farm Limited
Incorporated: 15 November 2016 *Employees:* 2
Net Worth Deficit: £32,107 *Total Assets:* £162,234
Registered Office: Orwell House, 50 High Street, Hungerford, Berks, RG17 0NE
Officers: Caroline Davenport [1953] Farm Director; Shelley Maree Logan [1982] Director/Psychologist [New Zealander]

Two Drifters Brewery Ltd
Incorporated: 4 May 2017
Net Worth Deficit: £6,053 *Total Assets:* £1,863
Registered Office: 1 Perriams, Old Ebford Lane, Ebford, Exeter, EX3 0QB
Officers: Roger Charles Scoble [1949] Director/Retired; Gemma Clare Wakeham [1982] Director/Social Media Manager; Dr Russell Jon Wakeham [1983] Director/Scientist

Two Fathoms Distillery Ltd.
Incorporated: 17 November 2017
Registered Office: Hollytree House, Croquet Gardens, Wivenhoe, Colchester, Essex, CO7 9PQ
Officers: Godwin Girth Baron [1962] Director/Distillery Founder

Two Finches Brewery Ltd.
Incorporated: 24 December 2015
Net Worth: £1,110 *Total Assets:* £1,400
Registered Office: 1 Arden Cottages, 33-45 East End Road, London, N3 2TA
Shareholder: Jake Milton
Officers: Jake Milton [1979] Director; William Munford [1991] Director

Two Fools Brewery Ltd
Incorporated: 5 June 2017
Registered Office: 76 Nevendon Road, Wickford, Essex, SS12 0NE
Officers: Paul Richard Kaufman [1972] Director/Brewer; Jason Peall [1970] Director/Brewer

Two Happy Captains Ltd
Incorporated: 16 March 2016
Registered Office: Holly House, Cross Street, Bury St Edmunds, Suffolk, IP30 9TP
Shareholders: David Michael Prior; Alison Margaret Prior
Officers: Alison Margaret Prior [1966] Director; David Michael Prior [1957] Director

Two Rabbit Brewing Company Ltd
Incorporated: 17 March 2017
Net Worth Deficit: £1,141 *Total Assets:* £58
Registered Office: Unit 62, 22 Notting Hill Gate, London, W11 3JE
Major Shareholder: Jeremy John Gazmararian
Officers: Jeremy John Gazmararian [1984] Director

Two Roses Brewery Ltd
Incorporated: 22 October 2010
Registered Office: Unit 9 Darton Business Park, Barnsley Road, Darton, Barnsley, S Yorks, S75 5QX
Major Shareholder: James Taylor
Officers: James Taylor [1956] Director

Two Thirsty Men Ltd
Incorporated: 7 December 2015 Employees: 2
Net Worth Deficit: £13,161 Total Assets: £49,711
Registered Office: 14 City Quay, Camperdown Street, Dundee, DD1 3JA
Major Shareholder: Gordon Whyte

The Two Towers Brewery Ltd
Incorporated: 22 February 2010
Net Worth Deficit: £103,914 Total Assets: £77,854
Registered Office: 29 Shadwell Street, Birmingham, B4 6HB
Major Shareholder: Mark John Arnott-Job
Officers: Mark John Arnott-Job [1957] Director/Brewer/Business Person

Two Towns Down Brewing Ltd
Incorporated: 14 February 2019
Registered Office: 1 Stravaig Path, Paisley, Renfrewshire, PA2 0RZ
Major Shareholder: Sandy Thomas McKelvie
Officers: Sandy Thomas McKelvie [1991] Director/Brewer

Two Tribes Brewing Ltd
Incorporated: 13 October 1999 Employees: 5
Previous: King Beer Limited
Net Worth Deficit: £5,449 Total Assets: £647,627
Registered Office: The Old Casino, 28 Fourth Avenue, Hove, E Sussex, BN3 2PJ
Parent: Sussex Beer Company Limited
Officers: Justin Lance Deighton [1970] Director/Businessman; Nicola Ruth Deighton [1970] Director/Businesswoman; Paul William Frederick Kempe [1957] Director; Michael James Penkethman [1964] Director

TwT Lol Cyf
Incorporated: 3 December 2014 Employees: 2
Net Worth Deficit: £2,412 Total Assets: £59,329
Registered Office: 1 Heol Llanwynno, Ynyshir, Porth, Rhondda Cynon Taf, CF39 0HU
Major Shareholder: Philip Mark Thomas
Officers: Philip Mark Thomas [1982] Director/Owner

Tyne Bank Brewery Limited
Incorporated: 15 February 2011
Net Worth: £40,049 Total Assets: £383,024
Registered Office: 375 Walker Road, Newcastle upon Tyne, NE6 2AB
Major Shareholder: Julia Helen Austin
Officers: Julia Helen Austin [1971] Director

Tynemill Limited
Incorporated: 7 May 1975 Employees: 220
Net Worth: £5,002,969 Total Assets: £11,375,271
Registered Office: Castle Rock Brewery, Queens Bridge Road, Nottingham, NG2 1NB
Major Shareholder: Christopher Roger Holmes
Officers: Neil Kellett, Secretary; Peter Robert Brettell [1943] Director; Anthony William Eastwood [1948] Director/Wholesaler; Geoffrey David Newton [1964] Director/Consultancy; Vicki Louise Saxby [1978] Finance & Administration Director; Colin Francis Wilde [1971] Commercial Director; Peter John Wilde [1944] Director/Wholesaler

UBrewCC Limited
Incorporated: 30 July 2014 Employees: 10
Net Worth: £47,288 Total Assets: £154,889
Registered Office: c/o Matthew Denham 24 Old Jamaica Road, Arch 29-30 Old Jamaica Road, London, SE16 4AW
Shareholders: Matthew Denham; Wilf Horsfall
Officers: Matthew Denham, Secretary; Matthew Denham [1984] Director

UK Camra Beer Co., Ltd
Incorporated: 26 October 2012
Registered Office: Chase Business Centre, 39-41 Chase Side, London, N14 5BP
Shareholders: Ai Yi; Yuanyi Tang; Tuo Lu
Officers: Yuanyi Tang [1972] Director [Chinese]

Uley Ales Limited
Incorporated: 21 February 2007
Net Worth: £146,369 Total Assets: £162,671
Registered Office: 31 The Street, Uley, Dursley, Glos, GL11 5TB
Shareholders: John Charles Wright; Mary Phillipa Wright
Officers: Martin Robert Brooks [1952] Director; Mary Phillipa Wright [1947] Director

Ullage Ale Ltd
Incorporated: 21 July 2016
Registered Office: 9 Spencer Close, Hedon, Hull, HU12 8HE
Major Shareholder: Daniel Rutter
Officers: Daniel Rutter [1980] Director/Brewer

Ultimate Maltgold Limited
Incorporated: 5 April 2017
Net Worth: £188 Total Assets: £10,247
Registered Office: 38 Dunsmore Road, Walton on Thames, Surrey, KT12 2LJ
Major Shareholder: Ideletta Katharina Meijering
Officers: Hendrik Meijering [1953] Director/Retired [Dutch]; Ideletta Katharina Meijering [1952] Director/Consultant Barley and Malt [Dutch]

Ulverston Brewing Company Limited
Incorporated: 2 February 2005
Net Worth: £75,555 Total Assets: £206,688
Registered Office: The Old Auction Mart, Lightburn Road, Ulverston, Cumbria, LA12 0AU
Major Shareholder: Anita Garnett
Officers: Paul Murray Swann, Secretary; Anita Garnett [1960] Director/Hairdresser

Umbrella Brewing Limited
Incorporated: 28 July 2015 Employees: 4
Net Worth Deficit: £70,034 Total Assets: £115,512
Registered Office: 626a Holloway Road, London, N19 3PA
Shareholders: Alastair Charles Tatton; Stephen Robert Thompson; Andrew James Kerr; Matthew Graham Armitage
Officers: Matthew Graham Armitage [1984] Director; Andrew James Kerr [1979] Director; Alastair Charles Tatton [1982] Director; Stephen Robert Thompson [1987] Director

Unbarred Brewery Limited
Incorporated: 24 April 2017
Net Worth: £3,968 Total Assets: £28,050
Registered Office: 4 Dukes Court, Bognor Road, Chichester, W Sussex, PO19 8FX
Major Shareholder: Jordan Christopher Mower
Officers: Jordan Christopher Mower [1984] Director/Head Brewer

Uncanny Valley Brewing Company Limited
Incorporated: 11 July 2017
Registered Office: 16 Balmoral Way, Prescot, Merseyside, L34 1QB
Major Shareholder: Gerard Courtney
Officers: Gerard Courtney [1988] Director/Brewer

Under The Stairs Brewery Ltd
Incorporated: 17 December 2013
Net Worth: £1,753 *Total Assets:* £1,753
Registered Office: 12 Thornwood Court, Thurnscoe, Rotherham, S Yorks, S63 0LL
Shareholders: Philip Smith; Daniel Woodhead
Officers: Philip Smith [1985] Director/Brewer; Daniel Woodhead [1985] Director/Brewer

Unicorn Craft Brewing Co Limited
Incorporated: 24 November 2017
Registered Office: 7 The Arches, Bracondale, Norwich, NR1 2EF
Officers: Ben Dawson Handford [1977] Marketing Director; Benjamin Luke Hopkins [1977] Director

Unity Brewing Ltd
Incorporated: 21 August 2014 *Employees:* 3
Net Worth: £46,235 *Total Assets:* £52,018
Registered Office: 88 Church Street, Southampton, SO15 5LU
Major Shareholder: James William Hatherley
Officers: James William Hatherley [1985] Managing Director

Universal Robo Innovations Limited
Incorporated: 24 May 2018
Registered Office: 71-75 Shelton Street, London, WC2H 9JQ
Officers: Ankit Mehta [1981] Director [Indian]

Unsworth's Yard Brewery Ltd
Incorporated: 13 June 2011 *Employees:* 2
Net Worth: £32,266 *Total Assets:* £117,766
Registered Office: Unit 4 Unsworth's Yard, Cartmel, Grange Over Sands, Cumbria, LA11 6PN
Shareholder: Peter John Unsworth
Officers: Mark Eugino Grunnill [1958] Director/Shop Proprietor; David Ernest Unsworth [1969] Director/Commercial Landlord; Peter John Unsworth [1965] Director/Technical Sales

The Untapped Brewing Co Ltd
Incorporated: 12 March 2013 *Employees:* 3
Net Worth: £30,617 *Total Assets:* £81,761
Registered Office: Unit 2 Wyevale Way, Stretton Sugwas, Hereford, HR4 7BS
Shareholders: Martyn James Darby; Owen Thomas Davies
Officers: Martyn James Darby [1968] Director/Brewer; Owen Thomas Davies [1969] Director/Brewer

Upper Harglodd Farm Ltd
Incorporated: 13 June 2018
Registered Office: Upper Harglodd, St Davids, Haverfordwest, Pembrokeshire, SA62 6BX
Shareholders: Mark Wyn Raymond Evans; Emma Sarah Evans
Officers: Emma Sarah Evans [1981] Director/Local Government Officer; Mark Wyn Raymond Evans [1979] Director/Farmer

Uppingham Brewery Limited
Incorporated: 9 November 2017
Registered Office: Aston House, York Road, Maidenhead, Berks, SL6 1SF
Parent: Wills Inns Limited
Officers: Roger David Mortimer [1960] Director; James David Torbell [1987] Director; Robert Hugo Weyl Wills [1949] Director

Uppingham Brewhouse Limited
Incorporated: 9 November 2017
Registered Office: Aston House, York Road, Maidenhead, Berks, SL6 1SF
Parent: Wills Inns Limited
Officers: Roger David Mortimer [1960] Director; James David Torbell [1987] Director; Robert Hugo Weyl Wills [1949] Director

Upstart Brewing Ltd
Incorporated: 17 June 2013
Net Worth Deficit: £7,524 *Total Assets:* £4,003
Registered Office: 5 Oak Hall Road, London, E11 2JT
Major Shareholder: James Foster Weir
Officers: James Weir [1976] Director/Brewer

Urban Alchemy Brewing Company Limited
Incorporated: 17 May 2018
Registered Office: 14 York Road, Barnet, Herts, EN5 1LJ
Shareholders: Simon James John Morley; Matthew Simon Javes
Officers: David Christopher Boldrin [1987] Director/Research Chemist; Neill Stuart Boscoe [1982] Director/Engineer/Builder; Ian Harper [1978] Director/Chairman; Matthew Simon Javes [1978] Director; Simon James John Morley [1979] Director

The Urban Brewery Ltd
Incorporated: 30 August 2018
Registered Office: 33 Liverpool Road North, Maghull, Merseyside, L31 2HB
Shareholders: Peter Michael Darlington; Matthew David Day
Officers: Peter Michael Darlington [1972] Director; Matthew David Day [1971] Company Secretary/Director

Urban Island Brewing Co. Limited
Incorporated: 7 July 2014
Net Worth Deficit: £114 *Total Assets:* £2,286
Registered Office: Unit 28 Limberline Spur, Portsmouth, PO3 5DZ
Major Shareholder: Guy Edward Lymn
Officers: Guy Edward Lymn [1970] Director/Consultant; Hayley Jane Wise [1974] Director/Consultant

Urbeer Ltd
Incorporated: 23 April 2018
Registered Office: Kemp House, 160 City Road, London, EC1V 2NX
Major Shareholder: Yen-Kai Lee
Officers: Yen-Kai Lee [1993] Director/Student [Taiwanese]

Utopian Brewing Limited
Incorporated: 16 May 2017
Net Worth: £65,683 *Total Assets:* £77,583
Registered Office: 2nd Floor, 100 Cannon Street, London, EC4N 6EU
Shareholder: Richard Archer
Officers: Richard Archer [1960] Director; Stephen Cox [1971] Director; Steve Hanlon [1980] Director/Accountant

Uttoxeter Brewing Company Ltd
Incorporated: 15 April 2016
Net Worth Deficit: £1,800 *Total Assets:* £8,478
Registered Office: 7 Faraday Court, First Avenue, Burton on Trent, Staffs, DE14 2WX
Shareholders: Thomas Abbott; Robert Andrew Ockleton
Officers: Thomas Abbott [1956] Director; Robert Andrew Ockleton [1967] Director

Vadum Brewery Ltd
Incorporated: 30 July 2018
Registered Office: 27 Burman Road, Wath upon Dearne, Rotherham, S Yorks, S63 7NE
Major Shareholder: Roy Lomax
Officers: Roy Lomax [1952] Director/Landlord

Vale Brewery Company Ltd.
Incorporated: 6 September 2013 *Employees:* 8
Net Worth: £438,725 *Total Assets:* £921,900
Registered Office: Tramway Business Park, Ludgershall Road, Brill, Aylesbury, Bucks, HP18 9TY
Shareholders: Phillip James Stevens; Mark Timothy Stevens
Officers: Anne Stevens [1961] Director; Jennifer Helen Stevens [1958] Director/Financial Analyst; Mark Timothy Stevens [1961] Joint Managing Director; Phillip James Stevens [1963] Joint Managing Director

Vale of Glamorgan Brewery Limited
Incorporated: 30 November 2004
Net Worth: £48,451 *Total Assets:* £167,632
Registered Office: Vale of Glamorgan Brewery, Atlantic Trading Estate, Barry, Vale of Glamorgan, CF63 3RF
Officers: Serge Andre Rene Luceau [1976] Director [French]; Sean Murphy [1973] Director; Philip John Newbould [1988] Director; Joseph Evan Roach [1990] Director

Valve Brewing Company Ltd.
Incorporated: 5 January 2015
Registered Office: 1 Burnside Way, Stow, Galashiels, Selkirkshire, TD1 2RS
Officers: Paul David Marshall [1976] Director/Brewer

Van Pur UK Ltd
Incorporated: 15 January 2018
Registered Office: 6th Floor, First Central 200, 2 Lakeside Drive, London, NW10 7FQ
Major Shareholder: Zbigniew Wantusiak
Officers: Nicholas Jaksic, Secretary; Ryszard Czopik [1967] Director/Vice-President [Polish]; Nicholas Jaksic [1984] Director/Entrepreneur

Vandal Brewing Company Limited
Incorporated: 11 April 2018
Registered Office: Calder & Co, 16 Charles II Street, London, SW1Y 4NW
Major Shareholder: Jeremy Ziggy Sidney Harris
Officers: Jeremy Ziggy Sidney Harris [1985] Director

Vault City Brewing Ltd.
Incorporated: 11 January 2018
Registered Office: 111 Corstorphine Road, Edinburgh, EH12 5PZ
Shareholders: Steven Robert Smith-Hay; Jonathan Horn
Officers: Jonathan Horn [1988] Director/Brewer; Steven Robert Smith-Hay [1991] Accounts Director - IT

Vaux Beers Ltd
Incorporated: 9 March 2006
Net Worth Deficit: £5,840 *Total Assets:* £155
Registered Office: 6 Burns Drive, Accrington, Lancs, BB5 2PY
Major Shareholder: Hassan Webb
Officers: Hassan Webb [1973] Director/Accountant

Vaux Brewery Ltd
Incorporated: 18 May 2012
Previous: VSES Projects Limited
Net Worth: £150,001 *Total Assets:* £150,001
Registered Office: North East Business and Innovation Centre (BIC), Wearfield, Sunderland Enterprise Park, Sunderland, Tyne & Wear, SR5 2TA
Major Shareholder: Steven James Smith
Officers: Steven James Smith [1981] Director; Michael William Thompson [1981] Director

The Velvet Owl Brewing Company Ltd.
Incorporated: 11 April 2016
Net Worth Deficit: £3,144 *Total Assets:* £24,503
Registered Office: 5 Latham Avenue, Ormskirk, Lancs, L39 2EU
Shareholders: Duncan Illsley; Richie Joseph Lesbirel; Richie Joseph Lesbirel
Officers: Richie Joseph LesbIreland [1988] Director

Vendetta Brewing Company Limited
Incorporated: 10 March 2017
Net Worth: £5,967 *Total Assets:* £54,395
Registered Office: 28 Usk Road, Aveley, South Ockendon, Essex, RM15 4PB
Shareholders: James Daniel King; Richard James Venour
Officers: James Daniel King [1984] Director/Brewer; Richard James Venour [1980] Director/Brewer

Verdant Brewing Company Limited
Incorporated: 30 September 2014 *Employees:* 3
Net Worth: £79,457 *Total Assets:* £210,865
Registered Office: The Peloton, The Warehouse, Anchor Quay, Penryn, Cornwall, TR10 8GZ
Shareholders: Adam Robertson; James Robert Heffron
Officers: James Robert Heffron [1979] Director/Brewer; Adam Robertson [1974] Director/Brewer; Richard Garry White [1981] Director/Electrician

Vertical Stack Ltd
Incorporated: 5 October 2016
Net Worth: £20,096 *Total Assets:* £28,225
Registered Office: 58 Nethercote Road, Tackley, Kidlington, Oxon, OX5 3AT
Major Shareholder: Brian Collins
Officers: Brian Collins [1977] Director/Entrepreneur [American]

The Verulam Brewery Limited
Incorporated: 8 April 2010
Registered Office: 59 Union Street, Dunstable, Beds, LU6 1EX
Shareholders: Douglas Andrew Atenyi Kintu; Rosalind Elizabeth Kintu
Officers: Douglas Andrew Ateyni Kintu, Secretary; Douglas Andrew Atenyi Kintu [1966] Director; Rosalind Elizabeth Kintu [1953] Director

Veterans Brewing (South East) Ltd
Incorporated: 16 March 2018
Registered Office: 35 Carden Hill, Brighton, BN1 8AA
Shareholder: William Albert Farmer
Officers: William Albert Farmer [1989] Director

Veterans Brewing Ltd
Incorporated: 11 November 2014 *Employees:* 4
Net Worth Deficit: £27,109 *Total Assets:* £63,615
Registered Office: Unit O, 16 Dundyvan Enterprise Park, Coatbridge, N Lanarks, ML5 4AQ
Major Shareholder: Alexander McDivitt
Officers: Alex McDivitt [1962] Sales Director; Thomas McIntyre Watt [1959] Director/Brewer

Veterans Brewing Sussex Ltd
Incorporated: 8 January 2018
Registered Office: Unit O, 16 Dundyvan Enterprise Park, Coatbridge, N Lanarks, ML5 4AQ
Shareholders: Alex McDivitt; Thomas McIntyre Watt; William Albert Farmer
Officers: William Albert Farmer [1989] Director; Alex McDivitt [1962] Director; Thomas McIntyre Watt [1959] Director

Via Academia Vocatus Ltd
Incorporated: 10 August 2018
Registered Office: 272 Bath Street, Glasgow, G2 4JR
Major Shareholder: David Matthew Hughes
Officers: David Matthew Hughes [1978] Director/Entrepreneur

Vibrant Forest Brewery Limited
Incorporated: 14 August 2013 *Employees:* 5
Net Worth: £99,446 *Total Assets:* £264,729
Registered Office: Unit 3 Gordleton Industrial Park, Hannah Way Pennington, Lymington, Hants, SO41 8JD
Major Shareholder: Kevin James Robinson
Officers: Kevin James Robinson [1973] Director/Brewer

Victor's Drinks Limited
Incorporated: 6 April 2010 *Employees:* 14
Net Worth Deficit: £2,110,609 *Total Assets:* £557,301
Registered Office: Unit 308, E1 Business Studios, 7 Whitechapel Road, London, E1 1DU
Shareholders: Ralph Thierry Broadbent; Alex Paul Dixon
Officers: Cecelia Broadbent [1991] Commercial Director; Ralph Thierry Broadbent [1986] Director; Alex Paul Dixon [1986] Director

The Village Inn Pub Company Ltd
Incorporated: 11 January 2011
Net Worth Deficit: £5,792 *Total Assets:* £10,337
Registered Office: Unit E, Hawkhill Industrial Park, Lesbury, Alnwick, Northumberland, NE66 3PG
Shareholders: The Alnwick Brewery Company Limited; Philip Bell
Officers: Philip James Bell [1990] Director/Manager; Ian Booth Robinson [1947] Director; Keith Caville Stephenson [1954] Director; Christopher Darryl Walwyn-James [1952] Director

Villages Brewery Limited
Incorporated: 22 January 2016
Net Worth: £110,539 *Total Assets:* £191,112
Registered Office: Fuzz Cottage Buxton Road, Ashford in The-Water, Bakewell, Derbys, DE45 1QP
Shareholders: Archie Jevremov Village; Louis Jevremov Village
Officers: Archie Jevremov Village [1986] Director/Founder; Louis Jevremov Village [1987] Director/Founder

The Vine Inn Brewery 2016 Limited
Incorporated: 22 December 2015
Net Worth Deficit: £9,870 *Total Assets:* £30,953
Registered Office: 6 Parkside Court, Greenhough Road, Litchfield, Staffs, WS13 7AU
Officers: Oliver Westwood [1983] Director/Manager

Vinifera Limited
Incorporated: 28 April 2004 *Employees:* 2
Net Worth: £21,582 *Total Assets:* £55,120
Registered Office: The Stables, Hall Farm, London Road, Newmarket, Suffolk, CB8 0TY
Shareholders: Rachael Jane Beardsmore; Robert Horatio Beardsmore
Officers: Rachael Jane Beardsmore, Secretary; Rachael Jane Beardsmore [1970] Director; Robert Horatio Beardsmore [1971] Director

Violet Cottage Brewing Company Ltd
Incorporated: 14 February 2012
Net Worth Deficit: £6,741 *Total Assets:* £11,682
Registered Office: Gwaelod Y Garth Inn, Main Road, Gwaelod Y Garth, Cardiff, CF15 9HH
Shareholders: Richard Angell; Barbara Angell
Officers: Barbara Angell [1960] Director/Landlord; Richard Angell [1949] Director/Carpenter

Vision Brewing Co Ltd
Incorporated: 15 July 2016
Registered Office: 33 Laburnum Avenue, Garden Village, Hull, HU8 8PF
Major Shareholder: Shaun Harrison
Officers: Shaun Harrison [1971] Director/Owner

Vitosha Wine Ltd
Incorporated: 10 January 2019
Registered Office: 7 Victoria Road, Alton, Hants, GU34 2DH
Shareholders: Umesh Prasad; Neelesh Prasad
Officers: Umesh Prasad [1965] Director

Vocation Brewery Limited
Incorporated: 25 February 2014 *Employees:* 10
Net Worth: £473,301 *Total Assets:* £1,523,819
Registered Office: Barclays Bank Chambers, Market Street, Hebden Bridge, W Yorks, HX7 6AD
Major Shareholder: John Hickling
Officers: John Hickling [1975] Director; Richard Allen Stenson [1986] Director

Vodaso Limited
Incorporated: 17 July 2018
Registered Office: Fernhills House, Todd Street, Bury, Lancs, BL9 5BJ
Officers: Thomas William Lordan [1982] Director

Volden Brewing Limited
Incorporated: 24 May 2016 *Employees:* 3
Net Worth: £2,311 *Total Assets:* £163,706
Registered Office: 77 Malham Road, Forest Hill, London, SE23 1AH
Major Shareholder: Anthony James Thomas
Officers: Anthony James Thomas [1970] Director

Volden Limited
Incorporated: 5 November 2014
Net Worth Deficit: £61,906 *Total Assets:* £144,603
Registered Office: 77 Malham Road, London, SE23 1AH
Officers: Anthony James Thomas [1970] Director

Vovin Ltd
Incorporated: 29 November 2017
Registered Office: 607 Green Lane, Maghull, Merseyside, L31 2JD
Shareholders: Susan Waring; Nadene Eksteen
Officers: Kevin Murray, Secretary; Nadene Eksteen [1982] Director [South African]; Susan Waring [1982] Director [South African]

Vyrnwy Developments Limited
Incorporated: 24 May 2004 *Employees:* 2
Net Worth: £42,794 *Total Assets:* £326,647
Registered Office: Inglewood, Llanwddyn, Oswestry, Salop, SY10 0LX
Major Shareholder: Brian Douglas Bisiker
Officers: Brian Douglas Bisiker [1959] Director; Edward James Rees Bisiker [1986] Director; Susan Bisiker [1965] Director; Timothy John Dunning [1961] Director

W & W Drinks Ltd
Incorporated: 9 January 2019
Registered Office: Unit 2 Broadview Farm, The Ridge, Cold Ash, Thatcham, Berks, RG18 9HX
Shareholders: Gary Christopher Wickens; Richard Anthony Wyatt
Officers: Gary Christopher Wickens [1977] Director; Richard Anthony Wyatt [1977] Director

W.L.B.C Ltd
Incorporated: 20 May 2011 *Employees:* 10
Net Worth Deficit: £60,770 *Total Assets:* £226,640
Registered Office: The White Lion, No 352 Tamworth Road, Long Eaton, Nottingham, NG10 3AT
Major Shareholder: James Douglas Maxwell Bryce
Officers: James Douglas Maxwell Bryce [1965] Director

Wadworth and Company Limited
Incorporated: 18 November 1889 *Employees:* 1,043
Net Worth: £83,381,000 *Total Assets:* £152,864,992
Registered Office: Northgate Brewery, Devizes, Wilts, SN10 1JW
Officers: Alison Jane Skedd, Secretary; Nigel John Bewley Atkinson [1953] Director; Rupert Bagnall [1970] Operations Director - Managed Houses; Charles John Eric Bartholomew [1951] Managing Director/Chairman; John Edward Beard [1962] Director; Edward Scandrett Harford [1948] Director/Computer Consultant; Alison Jane Skedd [1963] Director/Accountant; Nicola Claire Stenhouse [1979] Director; Lloyd John Stephens [1957] Tenanted Trade Director; Jonathan Thomas [1964] Sales Director; Christopher Welham [1970] Director/Chief Executive Officer

Walsall Brewing Company Limited
Incorporated: 20 November 2017
Registered Office: 8a-10a, Gatehouse Trading Estate, Lichfield Road, Brownhills, Walsall, W Midlands, WS8 6JZ
Shareholders: Austen Morgan; Michael Bates
Officers: Lisa Bates [1977] Director/Teaching Assistant

Wanderlust Bar Limited
Incorporated: 17 October 2017
Registered Office: 79 Baxter Mews, Sheffield, S6 1LG
Officers: Kyle Houldsworth [1989] Director/Master Scheduler

WantsumBrewery Ltd
Incorporated: 9 February 2009 *Employees:* 5
Net Worth: £26,348 *Total Assets:* £139,437
Registered Office: The Kent Barn, St Nicholas Court Farm, Court Road, St Nicholas at Wade, Kent, CT7 0PT
Shareholders: James William Sandy; Ingvild Leslyn Hindmarch
Officers: John Martin Burrows [1958] Director; Mr Mark John Hart Grimsdale [1959] Director; Ingvild Leslyn Hindmarch [1963] Director/Housewife; James William Sandy [1964] Director/Pharmaceuticals; Simon Torkil Sandy-Hindmarch [1990] Director/Brewer

Watling Street Brewery Limited
Incorporated: 2 December 2015
Net Worth: £58,331 *Total Assets:* £107,534
Registered Office: Flat 1, 15 Highbury Grange, London, N5 2QB
Major Shareholder: Reece Wood
Officers: Reece Wood [1985] Director/Brewery

Watts & Co. Ltd.
Incorporated: 1 February 2016
Net Worth: £13,868 *Total Assets:* £13,868
Registered Office: 57 Gardeners Road, Debenham, Stowmarket, Suffolk, IP14 6RX
Major Shareholder: Oliver James Watts
Officers: Oliver James Watts [1984] Director

Wayland's Sixpenny Brewery Ltd
Incorporated: 24 March 2009
Net Worth: £77,287 *Total Assets:* £118,424
Registered Office: The Old Dairy, Holwell Farm, Holwell, Cranborne, Dorset, BH21 5QP
Major Shareholder: Scott Wayland
Officers: Lorraine Gillian Wayland [1969] Director; Scott Wayland [1968] Director/Micro Brewery Consultant

WBC (Norfolk) Limited
Incorporated: 9 February 2005 *Employees:* 17
Net Worth: £184,592 *Total Assets:* £525,378
Registered Office: Decoy Farm, Norwich Road, Besthorpe, Attleborough, Norfolk, NR17 2LA
Major Shareholder: John Stanley Edwards
Officers: Kay Edwards, Secretary; John Stanley Edwards [1951] Director/Landlord; Kay Diane Edwards [1960] Director/Administrator

Weal Ales Brewery Limited
Incorporated: 17 March 2014
Net Worth Deficit: £16,498 *Total Assets:* £40,025
Registered Office: Unit 6 London Road, Chesterton, Newcastle, Staffs, ST5 7HT
Shareholders: Andrea Kate Wealleans; Paul John Wealleans
Officers: Andrea Kate Wealleans [1970] Director/Microbrewery; Paul John Wealleans [1956] Director

Weatheroak Brewery Ltd
Incorporated: 16 July 2002 *Employees:* 3
Net Worth: £640 *Total Assets:* £58,404
Registered Office: 21a-21b High Street, Studley, Warwicks, B80 7HN
Major Shareholder: David Bertram Smith
Officers: Patricia Susan Smith, Secretary; David Bertram Smith [1953] Director/Brewer; Patricia Susan Smith [1948] Director/Secretary; Tobias David Smith [1978] Director/Manufacturer of Beer

Weatheroak Hill Brewery Limited
Incorporated: 29 October 2008 *Employees:* 1
Net Worth: £2,247 *Total Assets:* £18,375
Registered Office: Unit 3 Waterside Business Park, 1649 Pershore Road, Kings Norton, Birmingham, B30 3DR
Shareholders: Philip Gough Meads; Sheila Ann Meads
Officers: Gary Philip Meads, Secretary; Gary Philip Meads [1969] Director; Philip Gough Meads [1937] Director; Sheila Ann Meads [1948] Director

WeBrew4U Ltd
Incorporated: 19 July 2017
Registered Office: Fowler Cottage, Chance Inn, Fife, KY15 5QJ
Officers: Cheryl Rennie, Secretary; Colin Rennie [1958] Director/Brewing Beer

Webru4u Ltd
Incorporated: 19 July 2017
Registered Office: Fowler Cottage, Chance Inn, Fife, KY15 5QJ
Officers: Cheryl Rennie, Secretary; Colin Rennie [1958] Director/Brewing Beer

Samuel Webster & Sons Limited
Incorporated: 20 March 2006
Net Worth Deficit: £4,175 *Total Assets:* £122,887
Registered Office: 17 Lansdowne Crescent, Edinburgh, EH12 5EH
Major Shareholder: William James Collin Wood
Officers: William James Collin Wood [1953] Director

Websters Brewery Ltd.
Incorporated: 26 January 2016
Registered Office: 15 Hobgate, York, YO24 4HE
Major Shareholder: Howard Duckworth
Officers: Howard Mark Duckworth [1956] Director/Hotelier

Wedmore Ales Ltd
Incorporated: 7 June 2018
Registered Office: Field House, Quab Lane, Wedmore, Somerset, BS28 4AR
Major Shareholder: Stephen John De-Gay
Officers: Stephen John De-Gay [1960] Director/Manager

Weetwood Ales Limited
Incorporated: 19 February 1992 *Employees:* 13
Net Worth: £862,353 *Total Assets:* £1,200,384
Registered Office: The Brewery, Common Lane, Kelsall, Tarporley, Cheshire, CW6 0PY
Parent: Cheshire Cat Management Limited
Officers: Laura Jane Humby [1971] Director/Chartered Accountant; Philip Robert McLaughlin [1974] Sales Director; Robert McLaughlin [1944] Director

Weird Beard Brew Co Ltd
Incorporated: 26 October 2011 *Employees:* 8
Net Worth: £82,001 *Total Assets:* £307,311
Registered Office: Unit 5 Boston Business Park, Trumpers Way, London, W7 2QA
Shareholders: Jonathan Samuel Gregg Irwin; Bryan Martyn Spooner
Officers: Bryan Martyn Spooner [1978] Director/Engineer

Welbeck Abbey Brewery Limited
Incorporated: 21 October 2009 *Employees:* 12
Net Worth: £87,354 *Total Assets:* £219,922
Registered Office: Portland Estate Office, Cavendish House, Welbeck, Whitwell, Worksop, Notts, S80 3LL
Parent: The Welbeck Estates Company Limited
Officers: Ian Goodwin [1961] Director/Chief Executive; Henry Joseph Parente [1983] Director; Claire Elizabeth Roe [1986] Director/Brewer

Well Drawn Brewing Company Limited
Incorporated: 23 January 2017
Net Worth: £33,440 *Total Assets:* £33,440
Registered Office: 5 Greenway Workshops, Bedwas House Industrial Estate, Bedwas, Caerphilly, Gwent, CF83 8HW
Major Shareholder: Andrew David Millar
Officers: Andrew David Millar [1987] Director/Brewer; Matthew Shannon [1985] Director/Banker

Welland Brewery Ltd
Incorporated: 3 July 2018
Registered Office: Welland House, Cradge Bank, Spalding, Lincs, PE11 3AN
Shareholders: Thomas James Bradshaw; David Peter Jackson; Charles Richard Neavy Rawlings
Officers: Thomas James Bradshaw [1985] Director; David Peter Jackson [1988] Director; Charles Richard Neavy Rawlings [1966] Director

Charles Wells Brewery Limited
Incorporated: 24 February 2006 *Employees:* 204
Previous: Wells & Young's Brewing Company Limited
Net Worth: £7,753,000 *Total Assets:* £65,067,000
Registered Office: The Brewery, Havelock Street, Bedford, MK40 4LU
Parent: Charles Wells Limited
Officers: Anthony Robert Fryer [1973] Finance Director; William Andrew Justin Phillimore [1962] Director; Paul Richard Wells [1958] Director

Charles Wells,Limited
Incorporated: 7 January 1910 *Employees:* 365
Net Worth: £75,246,000 *Total Assets:* £141,250,000
Registered Office: Eagle Brewery, Havelock Street, Bedford, MK40 4LU
Officers: Anthony Robert Fryer [1973] Finance Director; Robert Lewis Ivell [1952] Director; William Andrew Justin Phillimore [1962] Director/Chief Executive; Paul Stephen Rawlinson [1959] Director; Geoffrey Charles Vaughan Wells [1970] Director/Lawyer [Canadian]; Paul Richard Wells [1958] Director; Peter John Wells [1970] Director

Weltons Limited
Incorporated: 11 April 1995
Net Worth: £5,920 *Total Assets:* £85,450
Registered Office: 1 Rangers Lodge, Oakhill Road, Horsham, W Sussex, RH13 5LF
Major Shareholder: Raymond Allen Welton
Officers: James Leslie Sargent, Secretary; Katja Welton [1964] Director/Administrator [German]; Raymond Allen Welton [1950] Director/Brewer

Wensleydale Brewery (2013) Limited
Incorporated: 7 January 2013
Net Worth: £150,447 *Total Assets:* £235,650
Registered Office: Unit 4 Badger Court, Leyburn, N Yorks, DL8 5BF
Shareholders: Carl Gehrman; Geoff Southgate
Officers: Carl Gehrman [1990] Director/Brewer; Geoff Southgate [1989] Director/Brewer

Wentworth Brewery Ltd
Incorporated: 2 May 2018
Registered Office: 6 Shepcote Office Village, 333 Shepcote Lane, Sheffield, S9 1TG
Officers: David John David Richards, Secretary; David John David Richards [1974] Director; David Generald Richards [1943] Director/Company Chairman

The Wessex Brewery Limited
Incorporated: 4 September 2000
Registered Office: Farm Cottage, Norton Ferris, Warminster, Wilts, BA12 7HT
Officers: Louise Natalie Hobden, Secretary; Charles Frederick Hobden [1958] Director/Brewer; Louise Natalie Hobden [1960] Director/Forester

Wessex Brewing & Pub Company Limited
Incorporated: 23 May 2014
Registered Office: Freshford House, Redcliffe Way, Bristol, BS1 6NL
Major Shareholder: Michael Samuel Thomas Watts
Officers: Michael Samuel Thomas Watts [1949] Director

West Belfast Real Ale Limited
Incorporated: 29 October 2012
Registered Office: 44 Glen Road, Andersonstown, Belfast, BT11 8BG
Major Shareholder: Joseph Quinn
Officers: Joseph Quinn [1954] Director [Irish]

The West Berkshire Brewery PLC
Incorporated: 16 November 1998 Employees: 46
Net Worth: £6,959,743 Total Assets: £10,169,723
Registered Office: 8th Floor, South Reading Bridge House, George Street, Reading, Berks, RG1 8LS
Officers: Thomas Alexander Richard Lucas, Secretary; Alexander David Michael Bruce [1948] Director; Andrew William Dickson [1980] Director; Sarah Louise Herriman [1975] Director/Chartered Accountant; Thomas Alexander Richard Lucas [1980] Director; Simon Gesto Robertson-MacLeod [1953] Director

West By Three Limited
Incorporated: 30 April 2016 Employees: 4
Net Worth Deficit: £23,166 Total Assets: £111,457
Registered Office: 20 Clevedon Court, Uplands, Swansea, SA2 0RG
Shareholders: Richard Richard Axon; Hamish Stewart Thain
Officers: Richard Axon [1982] Sales Director; Hamish Stewart Thain [1981] Marketing Director

West Highland Breweries Limited
Incorporated: 10 February 2017
Total Assets: £51,343
Registered Office: Tirindrish House, Spean Bridge, Inverness-shire, PH34 4EU
Parent: Tirindrish Trading Company Limited
Officers: Lucy Alexandra Hicks [1976] Director/B&B Proprietor; James Fraser Leggett [1970] Director/B&B Proprietor; Ian Peter MacDonald [1961] Director

Westbournia Brewing Company Limited
Incorporated: 5 September 2013
Net Worth Deficit: £106,120 Total Assets: £100,552
Registered Office: 178 Towcester Road, Northampton, NN4 8LW
Shareholders: Steven John Maule; Thomas Steven Maule; Joel William Maule
Officers: Joel William Maule [1985] Director/Brewer; Steven John Maule [1956] Director/Brewer; Thomas Maule [1979] Director/Brewer

Westerham Brewery Company Limited
Incorporated: 3 July 2003 Employees: 15
Net Worth: £502,696 Total Assets: £1,073,934
Registered Office: Beggars Lane, Westerham, Kent, TN16 1QP
Shareholders: Elizabeth Ann Wicks; Robert Wicks
Officers: Raymond Malcolm James Lowe, Secretary; Nicholas John Ewen Naismith [1961] Director; Robert James Cairns Wicks [1965] Managing Director

Westley Brewing Company Ltd.
Incorporated: 29 October 2015
Registered Office: 64 Sutton Road, Rochford, Essex, SS4 1HL
Major Shareholder: Michael Westley
Officers: Michael Westley [1956] Director/Brewer

Westmoor Botanicals Limited
Incorporated: 22 November 2018
Registered Office: 132 Ravenstone Drive, Greetland, Halifax, W Yorks, HX4 8DY
Shareholder: Philip George Scoley
Officers: Helen Rose-Marie Scoley [1966] Director/Teacher; Philip George Scoley [1962] Director/Management Consultant

Wetherby Brew Co Limited
Incorporated: 26 July 2017
Registered Office: Wetherby Brew Co, York Road Estate, York Road, Wetherby, W Yorks, LS22 7SU
Shareholders: John David Frgusson; Richard Ivan Roberts
Officers: John David Fergusson [1971] Director; Richard Ivan Roberts [1957] Director; Thomas Gwilym Roberts [1990] Director

Wetherells Contracts Limited
Incorporated: 10 August 1922 Employees: 34
Net Worth: £5,211,642 Total Assets: £6,314,174
Registered Office: 9 The Crescent, Selby, N Yorks, YO8 4PD
Major Shareholder: Paul Russell Lucas Wetherell
Officers: Paul Russell Lucas Wetherell, Secretary; Gladys Margaret Wetherell [1934] Director/Married Woman; Mark Lucas Wetherell [1965] Director; Paul Russell Lucas Wetherell [1935] Director/Furnishing Contractor

Weymouth Brewery Limited
Incorporated: 8 May 2018
Registered Office: 1721b Wimborne Road, Bournemouth, BH11 9AS
Major Shareholder: Matthew James Hobby
Officers: Matthew James Hobby [1971] Director/Brewer

Wharf Beers Ltd
Incorporated: 24 January 2018
Registered Office: 1 Vicarage Lane, Stratford, London, E15 4HF
Major Shareholder: Mark Middleton
Officers: Mark Middleton [1976] Director

Wharf Brewing Company Limited
Incorporated: 26 May 2016
Registered Office: Gardeners Cottage, Gustard Wood, Wheathampstead, Herts, AL4 8RN
Shareholders: Ian Donald Robertson Stewart; Alexander John Adamson Wilson
Officers: Ian Donald Robertson Stewart [1970] Business Director; Alexander John Adamson Wilson [1975] Director/Chartered Surveyor

Wharfedale Brewery Limited
Incorporated: 16 October 2012
Net Worth: £13,918 Total Assets: £45,448
Registered Office: c/o The Flying Duck, 16 Church Street, Ilkley, W Yorks, LS29 9DS
Officers: William John Eddison [1954] Director/Estate Agent; Dr Robin Bryan Oldfield [1964] Director/Project Manager; Jonathan Anthony David Shepherd [1970] Director/Entrepreneur

Whim Ales Limited
Incorporated: 29 January 1999 Employees: 7
Net Worth: £21,197 Total Assets: £77,598
Registered Office: Ford House, Market Street, Leek, Staffs, ST13 6JA
Shareolders: William Giles Litchfield; Emma Louise Litchfield
Officers: William Giles Litchfield, Secretary; Emma Louise Litchfield [1964] Director/Consultant; William Giles Litchfield [1962] Director/Brewer

Whitby Brewery Ltd
Incorporated: 17 May 2012 Employees: 6
Net Worth Deficit: £25,718 Total Assets: £161,533
Registered Office: Whitby Brewery, East Cliff, Whitby, N Yorks, YO22 4JR
Major Shareholder: Richard Thomas Wells
Officers: Richard Wells [1988] Director

White Boar Brewing Company Ltd
Incorporated: 2 March 2012
Registered Office: 27 Stanmore Place, Leeds, LS4 2RR
Officers: Wayne Hodgin [1973] Director/Project Manager; Robin Michael Phelan [1967] Director/Governance & Control Manager

White Hart Halstead Limited
Incorporated: 1 November 2012 Employees: 10
Net Worth Deficit: £93,422 Total Assets: £94,906
Registered Office: The White Hart Inn, 15 High Street, Halstead, Essex, CO9 2AA
Officers: Charles Peter Townsend [1949] Director/Businessman

White Horse Brewery Company Limited
Incorporated: 5 May 2004 Employees: 12
Net Worth: £2,105 Total Assets: £225,353
Registered Office: White Horse Business Park, 3 Ware Road, Stanford in the Vale, Faringdon, Oxon, SN7 8NY
Shareholders: Thomas William Bebb; Titanic Brewery Co Ltd
Officers: Thomas William Bebb, Secretary; Thomas William Bebb [1955] Director/Consultant; Keith Andrew Bott [1967] Director/Brewer; Andrew Paul Wilson [1963] Director/Sales Marketing

White Park Brewery Limited
Incorporated: 28 December 2018
Registered Office: The Three Cups, 45 Newnham Street, Bedford, MK40 3JR
Shareholders: Benjamin Thomas Herrick Cave; Turing Complete Solutions Limited
Officers: Anna Kelly, Secretary; Benjamin Thomas Herrick Cave [1964] Director/Brewer

White Rose Brewery Limited
Incorporated: 2 November 2007 Employees: 2
Net Worth: £2,387 Total Assets: £7,395
Registered Office: 119 Chapel Road, Chapeltown, Sheffield, S35 1QL
Shareholder: Eric Butcher
Officers: Eric Butcher, Secretary; Gary Sheriff [1954] Director/Brewer

White Wolf Brewery Ltd
Incorporated: 14 September 2017
Registered Office: 36 Stocker Way, Eynesbury Manor, St Neots, Cambs, PE19 2HA
Major Shareholder: Gregory Daren Peddell-Grant
Officers: Gregory Daren Peddell-Grant, Secretary; Gregory Daren Peddell-Grant [1970] Director/Facilities Delivery Manager

White's Brewery Limited
Incorporated: 3 February 2010 Employees: 1
Net Worth Deficit: £152,804 Total Assets: £98,659
Registered Office: Franklins Brewing Co, Highfields Farm, The Broyle, Ringmer, E Sussex, BN8 5AR
Major Shareholder: Steven Andrew Medniuk
Officers: Steven Andrew Medniuk [1971] Director/Head Brewer

Whitechapel Industries Ltd
Incorporated: 4 August 2017
Registered Office: 22 Newbold Cottages, Sidney Street, London, E1 2HJ
Major Shareholder: Sarah Louise King
Officers: Sarah Louise King [1990] Joint Managing Director

Whitefaced Ltd
Incorporated: 15 May 2017
Net Worth: £2,953 Total Assets: £3,008
Registered Office: 24 Ashfield Close, Penistone, Sheffield, S36 6EY
Shareholder: David Hampshaw
Officers: David Hampshaw [1979] Director/Teacher; Sarah Louise Hampshaw [1982] Director/Teacher

Whitewater Brewing Co. Ltd
Incorporated: 6 July 2001 Employees: 7
Net Worth: £539,635 Total Assets: £1,493,683
Registered Office: Lakeside Brae, Castlewellan, Co Down, BT31 9RH
Shareholders: Bernard Sloan; Kerry Ann Sloan
Officers: Bernard Sloan, Secretary [Irish]; Patrick McMahon [1980] Director [Irish]; Bernard Sloan [1967] Managing Director [Irish]; Kerry Ann Sloan [1969] Director/Brewer [Irish]

Whitley Bay Brewing Company Ltd
Incorporated: 13 April 2016
Net Worth Deficit: £4,556 Total Assets: £34,805
Registered Office: 1 East Parade, Whitley Bay, Tyne & Wear, NE26 1AW
Shareholders: Stuart Scrafton; Gavin John Hattrick; Gary Harding
Officers: Gary Harding [1978] Director; Gavin John Hattrick [1979] Director; Stuart Scrafton [1954] Director

The Whitstable Brewery Company Limited
Incorporated: 23 January 2007 Employees: 7
Net Worth: £192,409 Total Assets: £426,611
Registered Office: The East Quay, The Harbour, Whitstable, Kent, CT5 1AB
Officers: James Daniel Watts Green, Secretary; Rafik Abidi [1973] Director; George Barrie Green [1934] Director; James Daniel Watts Green [1968] Director; Richard Watts Green [1965] Director/Restaurateur; David Knight [1983] Director

Whyte Bar Brewing Company Limited
Incorporated: 12 January 2018
Registered Office: 32 Roxburgh Avenue, Upminster, Essex, RM14 3BA
Shareholders: Joel Lewis Bernard; Andrew Henry Whyte
Officers: Joel Lewis Barnard [1993] Director; Andrew Henry Whyte [1994] Director

Whyte BR Brewing Company Limited
Incorporated: 11 January 2018
Registered Office: 32 Roxburgh Avenue, Upminster, Essex, RM14 3BA
Shareholders: Andrew Henry Whyte; Joel Lewis Barnard
Officers: Joel Lewis Barnard [1993] Director; Andrew Henry Whyte [1994] Director

Wibblers Brewery (Farms) Limited
Incorporated: 13 May 2010
Net Worth: £23,970 Total Assets: £187,463
Registered Office: Wibblers Brewery, Goldsands Road, Southminster, Essex, CM0 7JW
Shareholders: Philip John Wilcox; Abigayle Margaret Wilcox; Jeremy John Wilcox
Officers: Abigayle Wilcox [1980] Director; Jeremy John Wilcox [1942] Director/Retired; Philip John Wilcox [1973] Director

Wicked Hathern Brewery Limited
Incorporated: 17 May 1999
Net Worth: £30,258 *Total Assets:* £32,413
Registered Office: 17 Nixon Walk, East Leake, Loughborough, Leics, LE12 6HL
Officers: Sean Joseph O'Neill, Secretary; Sean Joseph O'Neill [1965] Director/General Manager; John Howard Worsfold [1943] Director/Retired

The Wicked Hog Brewery Ltd
Incorporated: 2 July 2018
Registered Office: 83 Coningswath Road, Carlton, Nottingham, NG4 3SG
Shareholders: Benjamin Nicholas Harwood; Sally Jane Harwood
Officers: Benjamin Nicholas Harwood [1974] Director; Sally Jane Harwood [1982] Director

Wickwar Craft Taverns Limited
Incorporated: 23 May 2014
Registered Office: Freshford House, Redcliffe Way, Bristol, BS1 6NL
Major Shareholder: Michael Samuel Thomas Watts
Officers: Michael Samuel Thomas Watts [1949] Director

Wickwar Town Taverns Ltd
Incorporated: 9 May 2014
Registered Office: Freshford House, Redcliffe Way, Bristol, BS1 6NL
Major Shareholder: Michael Samuel Thomas Watts
Officers: Michael Samuel Thomas Watts [1949] Director

Wickwar Wessex Brewing Company Limited
Incorporated: 30 January 2001 *Employees:* 10
Previous: Wickwar Brewing Company Limited
Net Worth: £603,210 *Total Assets:* £1,291,132
Registered Office: c/o Prydis, Senate Court, Southernhay Gardens, Exeter, EX1 1NT
Officers: Michael Samuel Thomas Watts, Secretary; Michael Anthony Flavin [1959] Director; Ian Tinsley Frost [1957] Director; Michael Samuel Thomas Watts [1949] Director

Wigan Brew House Ltd
Incorporated: 6 September 2017
Registered Office: Colmart House, Stephens Way, Warrington Road Industrial Estate, Wigan, Lancs, WN3 6PH
Major Shareholder: Martin Blythe
Officers: Martin Blythe [1972] Managing Director

The Wild Beer Co Ltd
Incorporated: 1 June 2012 *Employees:* 75
Net Worth: £2,688,291 *Total Assets:* £5,741,497
Registered Office: Lower Westcombe Farm, Evercreech, Shepton Mallet, Somerset, BA4 6ER
Shareholder: Andrew James Cooper
Officers: Andrew James Cooper [1978] Director; Brett Joel Ellis [1984] Director/Brewer [American]; Martin Fink [1964] Director [Canadian]; Richard John Owen [1958] Director; William Thomas Anthony Simmons [1977] Director/Financial Adviser

Wild Card Brewery Limited
Incorporated: 24 July 2012 *Employees:* 20
Net Worth: £37,394 *Total Assets:* £312,674
Registered Office: Unit 2 Lockwood Way, London, E17 5RB
Shareholders: Andrew John Birkby; William John Harris
Officers: Andrew John Birkby [1985] Director; William John Harris [1988] Director

Wild Horse Brewing Company Limited
Incorporated: 30 August 2014 *Employees:* 5
Net Worth Deficit: £1,733 *Total Assets:* £604,829
Registered Office: Unit 4 Cae Bach, Builder Street, Llandudno, Conwy, LL30 1DR
Shareholders: David Richard Faragher; Emma Ruth Faragher; Dylan Arthur Southern
Officers: David Richard Faragher [1981] Director; Emma Ruth Faragher [1983] Director/Accountant; Dylan Arthur Southern [1959] Director/Business Angel

Wild Weather Ales Ltd
Incorporated: 5 March 2012 *Employees:* 6
Net Worth: £37,426 *Total Assets:* £437,919
Registered Office: Unit 19 Easter Park, Benyon Road, Silchester, Reading, Berks, RG7 2PQ
Shareholder: Michael Andrew Tempest
Officers: Karen Tempest [1960] Director; Michael Andrew Tempest [1958] Director

Wildcraft Brewery Limited
Incorporated: 11 February 2016 *Employees:* 1
Net Worth Deficit: £28,512 *Total Assets:* £42,491
Registered Office: Foragers Rest, Coltishall Road, Buxton, Norwich, NR10 5JD
Shareholders: Micheal Roy Deal; Mark Goodman
Officers: Mike Deal [1978] Director/Teacher; Mark Goodman [1979] Director/Farmer

Wilde Child Brewing Co. Ltd.
Incorporated: 12 October 2017 *Employees:* 4
Net Worth: £43,716 *Total Assets:* £149,548
Registered Office: Unit 5 Armley Road, Leeds, LS12 2DR
Major Shareholder: Keir McAllister-Wilde
Officers: Christine McAllister-Wilde [1985] Director; Keir McAllister-Wilde [1985] Director

Wilderness Brewery Ltd
Incorporated: 20 March 2017
Net Worth Deficit: £15,868 *Total Assets:* £73,586
Registered Office: Unit 54 Mochdre Industrial Estate, Newtown, Powys, SY16 4LE
Major Shareholder: James Edward Godman
Officers: Dr James Edward Godman, Secretary; Dr James Edward Godman [1985] Director/Brewery Manager

Wily Fox Brewery Limited
Incorporated: 15 January 2015 *Employees:* 3
Net Worth Deficit: £52,012 *Total Assets:* £66,176
Registered Office: 15 Market Street, Standish, Wigan, Lancs, WN6 0HW
Major Shareholder: Andrea Sharon Cox
Officers: Andrea Sharon Cox [1968] Director; Beverley Jean Cox [1962] Director/Sales Manager; Michael William Cox [1967] Director/Warehouse Manager

The Wimbledon Brewery Company Limited
Incorporated: 4 February 2013 *Employees:* 15
Net Worth Deficit: £639,552 *Total Assets:* £1,095,844
Registered Office: 8 College Fields, Prince Georges Road, Wimbledon, London, SW19 2PT
Major Shareholder: Mark Charles Gordon
Officers: Mark Charles Gordon [1968] Director/Entrepreneur

Wimborne Beer Company Limited
Incorporated: 3 December 2013
Net Worth Deficit: £66,779 *Total Assets:* £101,159
Registered Office: 2 Albany Park, Cabot Lane, Poole, Dorset, BH17 7BX
Major Shareholder: Steven Charles Farrell
Officers: Steven Charles Farrell [1984] Director

Winchester Brewery Ltd
Incorporated: 25 August 2010
Registered Office: Hill View Farm, Hensting Lane, Owslebury, Winchester, Hants, SO21 1LE
Shareholder: Andrew James Rigg
Officers: Rebecca Anne Crawford [1966] Director/Brewer; Andrew James Rigg [1958] Director/Farmer; Stephen Leonard Sherlock [1957] Director/Electronic Engineer

Wincle Beer Company Limited
Incorporated: 23 June 2008
Net Worth: £468 *Total Assets:* £145,957
Registered Office: Tolls Barn, Barlow Hill, Wincle, Macclesfield, Cheshire, SK11 0QE
Major Shareholder: Giles Henry Meadows
Officers: Sonia Anderson, Secretary; Giles Henry Meadows [1972] Director/Brewer

Windermere Brewery Ltd
Incorporated: 20 April 2010
Registered Office: Watermiill Inn, Tweenbridges, Ings, Kendal, Cumbria, LA8 9PY
Major Shareholder: Brian Coulthwaite
Officers: Brian Coulthwaite [1964] Director/Publican

Windmill Hill Brewing Co. Ltd.
Incorporated: 16 February 2017 *Employees:* 2
Net Worth Deficit: £10,310 *Total Assets:* £28,524
Registered Office: Garage Unit, 11 Williams Road, Radford Semele, Leamington Spa, Warwicks, CV31 1UR
Officers: Gavin Raymond Leach [1988] Director; Robert Singleton [1984] Director

Windsor & Eton Brewing Company Limited
Incorporated: 7 November 2009
Net Worth: £439,948 *Total Assets:* £1,096,020
Registered Office: Unit 1 Vansittart Estate, Duke Street, Windsor, Berks, SL4 1SE
Officers: George William Calvert, Secretary; George William Calvert [1957] Director/Business Manager; Patrick William Johnson [1958] Director/Business Consultants; James John Morrison [1958] Director/Engineering Consultant; Robert Morrison [1962] Marketing Director

Windsor Castle Brewery Limited
Incorporated: 4 March 2004 *Employees:* 19
Net Worth: £442,999 *Total Assets:* £1,325,613
Registered Office: Unit 2 Conyers Trading Estate, Station Drive, Lye, Stourbridge, W Midlands, DY9 3EH
Parent: Halewood International Limited
Officers: John Andrew Bradbury [1971] Director; Stewart Andrew Hainsworth [1969] Director/Chief Executive; Alan William Robinson [1965] Financial Director; Aster Louise Sadler [1983] Director; Christopher John Sadler [1982] Director

Windswept Brewing Co Ltd
Incorporated: 27 January 2012 *Employees:* 8
Net Worth Deficit: £20,941 *Total Assets:* £283,572
Registered Office: Unit B, 13 Coulardbank Industrial Estate, Lossiemouth, Moray, IV31 6NG
Shareholders: Jeremy Nigel Tiddy; Alisdair John Read
Officers: Alisdair John Read [1971] Director/Brewery; Jeremy Nigel Tiddy [1968] Director/Microbrewery

Wingtip Brewing Company Limited
Incorporated: 9 February 2015
Net Worth Deficit: £58,846 *Total Assets:* £44,309
Registered Office: Suite Ff10, Brooklands House, 58 Marlborough Road, Lancing, W Sussex, BN15 8AF
Major Shareholder: Christopher Thomas John Tripp
Officers: Christopher Tripp [1952] Director; Simon Robert Tripp [1979] Director

Winton Brewery Limited
Incorporated: 12 February 2016
Net Worth Deficit: £7,220 *Total Assets:* £8,980
Registered Office: 4 Vinefields, Pencaitland, Tranent, E Lothian, EH34 5HD
Shareholders: David John MacKinnon; Steven Holligan
Officers: Steven Holligan [1978] Director/Brewer; David John MacKinnon [1984] Director/Brewer

Wiper & True Ltd.
Incorporated: 1 October 2012 *Employees:* 14
Net Worth Deficit: £102,966 *Total Assets:* £677,818
Registered Office: 2-8 York Street, St Werburghs, Bristol, BS2 9XT
Shareholders: Michael Henry Wiper; Francesca Elizabeth Lee Garton
Officers: Francesca Elizabeth Lee Garton [1982] Director; Martin James Saunders [1968] Director; Alexander James Edward True [1981] Director; Joan Mary Wiper [1953] Director; Michael Henry Wiper [1982] Director/Brewer; Philip Michael Wiper [1949] Director

Wishbone Brewery Limited
Incorporated: 28 August 2014
Net Worth Deficit: £49,034 *Total Assets:* £116,977
Registered Office: Elisa Brown, Central Place, Clayton, Bradford, W Yorks, BD14 6AZ
Shareholders: Adrian Daniel Chapman; Emma Chapman
Officers: Adrian Daniel Chapman, Secretary; Adrian Daniel Chapman [1974] Director/Brewer; Emma Chapman [1977] Director

Witch Craft Beers Limited
Incorporated: 21 March 2017
Net Worth Deficit: £223 *Total Assets:* £1,821
Registered Office: Unit 1 Scotch Park Trading Estate, Forge Lane, Armley, Leeds, LS12 2PY
Major Shareholder: David Andrew Longfellow
Officers: David Andrew Longfellow [1975] Director

Witchcraft Brewery Limited
Incorporated: 2 November 2017
Registered Office: No 1, 29 Jamaica Mews, New Town, Edinburgh, EH3 6HL
Major Shareholder: Andrew Michael Megginson
Officers: Andrew Michael Megginson [1990] Director

Withnell's Brewing Company Limited
Incorporated: 22 March 2016
Net Worth Deficit: £25,327 *Total Assets:* £21,346
Registered Office: Chapel House, 45a Bury Lane, Withnell, Chorley, Lancs, PR6 8SB
Shareholders: Paul Timothy Rowe; Thomas Bennett
Officers: Thomas Bennett [1984] Director/Manager; Paul Timothy Rowe [1985] Director/Manager

Wiveliscombe Breweries Limited
Incorporated: 5 April 2006 *Employees:* 2
Net Worth: £521,545 *Total Assets:* £1,241,768
Registered Office: Golden Hill Brewery, Old Brewery Road, Wiveliscombe, Somerset, TA4 2PW
Major Shareholder: Jonathan Price
Officers: Penelope Jane Price, Secretary; Jonathan Price [1951] Director; Robin Mark Dodgson Price [1956] Director/Chartered Accountant

The Wizard Brewing Company Combe Ltd
Incorporated: 7 September 2017
Registered Office: Unit 4 Lundy View, Mullacott Cross Industrial Estate, Ilfracombe, Devon, EX34 8PY
Major Shareholder: Carly Ellen O'Callaghan
Officers: Carly Ellen O'Callaghan [1979] Director/Brewer

The Wobbly Brewing Company Limited
Incorporated: 28 May 2013
Net Worth Deficit: £101,410 *Total Assets:* £132,296
Registered Office: Unit 22c Beech Business Park, Tillington Road, Holmer, Hereford, HR4 9QT
Major Shareholder: Andrew Gareth Hughes
Officers: Andrew Gareth Hughes [1972] Director; Jason Hughes [1974] Director

Wold Toppers Limited
Incorporated: 17 April 2000 *Employees:* 18
Net Worth: £407,383 *Total Assets:* £1,794,538
Registered Office: Hunmanby Grange, Wold Newton, Driffield, E Yorks, YO25 3HS
Shareholders: Thomas Leslie Mellor; Gillian Mary Mellor
Officers: Thomas Leslie Mellor, Secretary; Alexander David Balchin [1988] Director/Operations Manager; Katherine Emma Balchin [1987] Director/Accounts Manager; Gillian Mary Mellor [1960] Director/Farmer; Thomas Leslie Mellor [1959] Director/Farmer

The Wombourne Brewing Company Ltd
Incorporated: 4 May 2011
Registered Office: 28 Hatch Heath Close, Wombourne, Staffs, WV5 8DR
Shareholders: Stephen John Turner; Mark Beckett Freemantle
Officers: Mark Beckett Freemantle [1964] Director; Stephen John Turner [1969] Director

Wood Brewery Limited (The)
Incorporated: 9 June 1981 *Employees:* 12
Net Worth: £605,550 *Total Assets:* £779,520
Registered Office: Bradford Group, Stafford Business Village, Dyson Way, Stafford, ST18 0TW
Parent: Yerrawaddie Brands Limited
Officers: Patrick Generald McGuckian [1965] Director; Stephen Anthony O'Neill [1965] Director/Management Consultant

The Woodbridge Brewing Company Limited
Incorporated: 27 February 2016
Registered Office: 5a Woolnough Road, Woodbridge, Suffolk, IP12 1HJ
Major Shareholder: Christopher Sears
Officers: Jaydene Sears, Secretary; Chris Sears [1958] Director

Woodcote Manor Brewing Company Limited
Incorporated: 13 March 2015
Net Worth Deficit: £4,958 *Total Assets:* £9,030
Registered Office: Woodcote Manor, Kidderminster Road, Dodford, Bromsgrove, Worcs, B61 9DY
Shareholders: William Paul Taylor; Shirley Jean Taylor
Officers: Shirley Jean Taylor [1959] Director; William Paul Taylor [1957] Director

Woodforde's BPP Limited
Incorporated: 29 March 2016 *Employees:* 2
Net Worth: £6,097,420 *Total Assets:* £6,100,000
Registered Office: Broadland Brewery, Woodbastwick, Norwich, NR13 6SW
Officers: MOD Razali Bin Abdul Rahman [1947] Director [Malaysian]; Oh Chong Peng [1944] Director/Chartered Accountant [Malaysian]; Nicholas Joseph Dolan [1976] Director; Rupert Michael Fraser [1968] Director/Management Consultant; Duncan George Harvey [1979] Director [Australian/British]; James Edward Alexander Hughes [1974] Director

Woodforde's Limited
Incorporated: 17 June 1999 *Employees:* 70
Net Worth: £733,435 *Total Assets:* £1,612,566
Registered Office: Broadland Brewery, Woodbastwick, Norwich, NR13 6SW
Parent: Woodforde's BPP Limited
Officers: Stephanie Millsted, Secretary; Nicholas Joseph Dolan [1976] Director; Rupert Michael Fraser [1968] Director/Management Consultant; Duncan George Harvey [1979] Director [Australian/British]; James Edward Alexander Hughes [1974] Director; Mr Chong Peng Oh [1944] Director/Chartered Accountant [Malaysian]; Mond Razali Abdul Rahman [1947] Director/Executive Chairman [Malaysian]

Woodforde's Norfolk Ales Limited
Incorporated: 26 April 1983
Registered Office: CHARLES RUSSELL SPEECHLYS, 5 Fleet Place, London, EC4M 7RD
Officers: James Hughes, Secretary; Nicholas Joseph Dolan [1976] Director; James Edward Alexander Hughes [1974] Director

Woodhalls Brewery Limited
Incorporated: 16 August 2007
Net Worth Deficit: £15,377 *Total Assets:* £17,083
Registered Office: Dove Leys, Homer, Much Wenlock, Salop, TF13 6NF
Shareholder: Freya Alice Woodhall
Officers: Freya Alice Woodhall, Secretary/Director; Adam Edwin Barnes [1968] Director; Sandra Patricia Barnes [1962] Director [Argentinian]; Freya Alice Woodhall [1975] Director; Ross John Woodhall [1968] Director

Woodruff Brewing Ltd
Incorporated: 25 July 2017
Registered Office: 7 Hamilton Avenue, Harrogate, N Yorks, HG2 8JB
Major Shareholder: Jack Woodruff
Officers: Jack Woodruff [1987] Director/Duty Manager

Wooha Brewing Company Ltd
Incorporated: 16 June 2014
Net Worth Deficit: £129,453 *Total Assets:* £451,945
Registered Office: Suite 8, Dundee One, River Court, West Victoria Dock Road, Dundee, DD1 3JT
Shareholder: Heather Erin Kelly McDonald
Officers: Mark Bowers [1963] Director; Lauchlin Archibald Kelly III [1950] Director [American]; Heather Erin Kelly McDonald [1978] Director/Homemaker [American]

Worfield Brewery Limited
Incorporated: 12 September 2012
Net Worth: £83 *Total Assets:* £4,711
Registered Office: College House, St Leonards Close, Bridgnorth, Salop, WV16 4EJ
Officers: Michael John Handley [1948] Director/Brewer

Workshy Brewing Ltd
Incorporated: 9 October 2017
Registered Office: 1 Glendale House, Cardigan Road, London, TW10 6BW
Shareholders: Tom Paunic; Louis Salem
Officers: Tom Paunic [1979] Director; Louis Salem [1976] Director [Australian]

World Bier Huis Limited
Incorporated: 10 October 2016
Registered Office: 9-15 Grundy Street, Liverpool, L5 9SG
Major Shareholder: Keith Tomlinson
Officers: Keith Tomlinson [1959] Director

Worsthorne Brewing Co Ltd
Incorporated: 14 October 2010 *Employees:* 5
Net Worth: £1,323 *Total Assets:* £85,541
Registered Office: 5 Heckenhurst Ave, Worsthorne, Burnley, Lancs, BB10 3JN
Shareholder: Michael Vincent Whittaker
Officers: Michael Vincent Whittaker [1953] Director/Brewer

Wrexham Lager Beer Company Limited
Incorporated: 10 July 2009 *Employees:* 9
Net Worth: £680,612 *Total Assets:* £1,819,298
Registered Office: Park Lodge, Rhosddu Road, Wrexham, Clwyd, LL11 1NF
Officers: Christopher Vaughan Roberts, Secretary/Wholesaler; Janet Elaine Gaffey [1968] Director/Wholesaler; Christopher Vaughan Roberts [1963] Director/Wholesaler; Jonathan Gwyn Roberts [1972] Director/Wholesaler; Kevin Mark Roberts [1960] Director/Builder

The Wriggly Monkey Brewery Limited
Incorporated: 15 August 2016 *Employees:* 1
Net Worth Deficit: £9,598
Registered Office: Hill Cottage, The Hill, Souldern, Bicester, Oxon, OX27 7JE
Major Shareholder: Luke Roberts
Officers: Luke Roberts [1987] Director/Engineer

Wright & Spillane Limited
Incorporated: 15 February 2011
Net Worth Deficit: £34,824 *Total Assets:* £271,617
Registered Office: Red Barn - Office The Street, Stowlangtoft, Bury St Edmunds, Suffolk, IP31 3JX
Shareholders: Patrick Thomas Spillane; Paula Jane Wright
Officers: Patrick Thomas Spillane [1963] Director/Web Designer [Australian]; Paula Jane Wright [1967] Director/Web Designer

Wrytree Brewery Limited
Incorporated: 29 August 2014
Previous: Pit Top Brewery Limited
Net Worth Deficit: £9,792 *Total Assets:* £2,270
Registered Office: Unit 1 Wrytree Park, Greenhead, Brampton, Cumbria, CA8 7JA
Major Shareholder: John Deal
Officers: Fiona Deal [1964] Director/Steward; John Kenneth Deal [1963] Director/Engineer

The Wye Brewing Company Limited
Incorporated: 7 September 2015
Registered Office: 20 Church Street, Wye, Kent, TN25 5BJ
Major Shareholder: Andrew Graham
Officers: Andrew Graham [1979] Director/Product Manager

Wye Valley Brewery Limited
Incorporated: 24 June 1993 *Employees:* 53
Net Worth: £3,466,495 *Total Assets:* £5,867,068
Registered Office: The Brewery, Stoke Lacy, Herefords, HR7 4HG
Parent: Wye Valley Brewery Holdings Limited
Officers: Vernon Patrick Amor, Secretary; Peter William Amor [1946] Director/Publican & Brewer; Vernon Patrick Amor [1973] Director/Brewery Manager

Wylam Brewery Limited
Incorporated: 11 September 2000
Net Worth: £404,185 *Total Assets:* £928,179
Registered Office: Palace of Arts Exhibition Park, Claremont Road, Newcastle upon Tyne, NE2 4PZ
Officers: Matthew Dunstan Boyle [1973] Director/Business Development Manager; Robert Cameron [1968] Director; Carina Elena McKenzie Curry [1979] Director/Office Administrator; David Jonathan Stone [1963] Director

Wylde Sky Brewing Ltd
Incorporated: 17 November 2017
Registered Office: Unit 8a The Grip, Linton, Cambridge, CB21 4XN
Shareholders: Christopher Philip Heath; Paul Francis Elilio; Paulo Jose Hillhouse Figurelli
Officers: Paul Francis Elilio [1974] Director/Brewer; Christopher Philip Heath [1969] Director/Solicitor; Paulo Jose Hillhouse Figurelli [1977] Director/Brewer [Brazilian/British]

X-Ray Brewing Company Ltd
Incorporated: 20 April 2009
Registered Office: 26 Adwick Place, Leeds, LS4 2RA
Major Shareholder: Michael Christopher Wynnyczuk
Officers: Michael Christopher Wynnyczuk [1973] Director/Brewer

XL Brew Ltd
Incorporated: 14 February 2013
Net Worth Deficit: £4,256 *Total Assets:* £49
Registered Office: 159 Wroslyn Road, Freeland, Witney, Oxon, OX29 8AL
Major Shareholder: Gary Paul Exell
Officers: Gary Paul Exell [1967] Director

XT Brewing Company Limited
Incorporated: 28 June 2011 *Employees:* 12
Net Worth: £135,690 *Total Assets:* £507,090
Registered Office: XT Brewerym Notley Farm, Chearsley Road, Long Crendon, Bucks, HP18 9ER
Shareholders: Gareth Andrew Xifaras; Steven Russell Taylor
Officers: Steven Russell Taylor [1969] Director/Brewer; Gareth Andrew Xifaras [1972] Director/Brewer; Michael Xifaras [1969] Director/Financial Services

Xtraflow Limited
Incorporated: 7 May 2013
Net Worth Deficit: £6,190 *Total Assets:* £3,007
Registered Office: Flat 12, Mounts Court, Mounts Road, Greenhithe, Kent, DA9 9LX
Major Shareholder: Jacek Wolfart
Officers: Joanna Kostepski [1984] Director/Housewife [Polish]; Jacek Wolfart [1983] Director/Service Engineer [Polish]

Xtreme Ales Limited
Incorporated: 4 July 2013
Net Worth Deficit: £22,501 *Total Assets:* £15,364
Registered Office: 67 Red Barn, Turves, Whittlesey, Peterborough, Cambs, PE7 2DZ
Shareholders: Neil Morris Holmes; Michael Clifford Holmes
Officers: Michael Clifford Holmes [1949] Director/Production Planner; Neil Morris Holmes [1979] Director/Planning Engineer

Xylo Brewing Ltd
Incorporated: 3 September 2018
Registered Office: 583a Battersea Park Road, London, SW11 3BH
Shareholders: Ben Christopher Atkins; Neil Wright
Officers: Ben Christopher Atkins [1981] Director/Barman; Neil Wright [1981] Director

The Yard of Ale Brewing Company Limited
Incorporated: 1 April 2008
Net Worth: £16,615 *Total Assets:* £31,140
Registered Office: The Surtees Arms, Chilton Lane, Ferryhill Station, Ferryhill, Co Durham, DL17 0DH
Shareholders: Alan Hogg; Susan Debbie Hogg
Officers: Susan Debbie Hogg, Secretary; Alan Hogg [1972] Director/Licensee; Susan Debbie Hogg [1974] Director/Registered Nurse

Yardley Brothers Europe Ltd
Incorporated: 18 February 2016
Net Worth: £82,122 *Total Assets:* £83,196
Registered Office: St Wilfrid's House, Church Lane, South Muskham, Newark, Notts, NG23 6EQ
Shareholders: Luke Denton Yardley; Duncan Thomas Yardley
Officers: Duncan Thomas Yardley [1983] Director; Luke Denton Yardley [1986] Director; Thomas Yardley [1953] Director

Yarm Brewing and Distilling Co Ltd
Incorporated: 22 March 2018
Registered Office: 11 Sowerby Way, Durham Lane Industrial Park, Eaglescliffe, Stockton on Tees, Cleveland, TS16 0RB
Major Shareholder: Samantha Marsden
Officers: Samantha Marsden [1972] Director

Yates Iow Brewery Limited
Incorporated: 4 April 2005 *Employees:* 8
Net Worth: £206,726 *Total Assets:* £545,559
Registered Office: Unit 4 Langbridge Business Centre, Newchurch, Sandown, Isle of Wight, PO36 0NP
Shareholders: David Robert Yates; David Robert Yates
Officers: David Robert Yates [1973] Director/Wholesaler; David Stanley Yates [1942] Director/Brewer

YB Ventures (2018) Ltd
Incorporated: 21 November 2018
Registered Office: The Old Rectory, Ubbeston, Halesworth, Suffolk, IP19 0ET
Major Shareholder: Rupert John Alexander Farquharson
Officers: Rupert John Alexander Farquharson [1967] Director; Dennis Michael Nudd [1949] Director

Yeast Pod Ltd
Incorporated: 29 January 2007
Registered Office: 6 Randolph Crescent, Edinburgh, EH3 7TH
Parent: Innis & Gunn Holdings Limited
Officers: Anthony Leonard Hunt [1946] Director/Consultant; Dougal Sharp [1972] Managing Director

Yellow Hammer Brewing Limited
Incorporated: 11 November 2010 *Employees:* 7
Net Worth: £21,846 *Total Assets:* £349,229
Registered Office: Hill Farm, Half Moon Village, Newton St Cyres, Exeter, Devon, EX5 5AE
Major Shareholder: Daniel James Taylor
Officers: Daniel Taylor [1980] Director

Yellow Top Brewing Company Limited
Incorporated: 5 December 2017
Registered Office: 40 Highglen Drive, Plymouth, PL7 5LA
Officers: Barry Charles Pooley [1987] Managing Director

Yeovil Ales Limited
Incorporated: 15 October 1999 *Employees:* 6
Net Worth Deficit: £5,500 *Total Assets:* £148,679
Registered Office: 2 Forde Park, Yeovil, Somerset, BA21 3QR
Shareholders: David Thomas Sherwood; Robert Dean Sherwood
Officers: Sarah Sherwood, Secretary; David Thomas Sherwood [1943] Director; Robert Dean Sherwood [1971] Director

York Brewery Limited
Incorporated: 19 April 2018
Registered Office: 1 Park View Court, St Pauls Road, Shipley, W Yorks, BD18 3DZ
Major Shareholder: Andrew Barker
Officers: Andrew Barker [1970] Director

Yorkshire Brewhouse Limited
Incorporated: 10 March 2017 *Employees:* 2
Net Worth Deficit: £3,363 *Total Assets:* £15,522
Registered Office: Matrich House, Hatfield Hi-Tech Park, Goulton Street, Kingston upon Hull, HU3 4DD
Shareholders: Jonathan Paul Constable; Simon Cooke
Officers: Simon Cooke [1967] Director

Yorkshire Brewing Company Ltd
Incorporated: 14 January 2011
Net Worth Deficit: £87,646 *Total Assets:* £26,010
Registered Office: Brewery Wharf, 70 Humber Street, Hull, HU1 1TU
Shareholders: Guy Stuart Falkingham; Susan Falkingham
Officers: Susan Falkingham, Secretary; Guy Stuart Falkingham [1960] Director; Susan Falkingham [1953] Director

Yorkshire Dales Brewing Company Limited
Incorporated: 26 August 2005 *Employees:* 2
Net Worth: £1,182 *Total Assets:* £61,152
Registered Office: 80 Dale Grove, Leyburn, N Yorks, DL8 5GA
Shareholder: Anne Elizabeth Barlow-Wiltshire
Officers: Robert Wiltshire, Secretary; Anne Elizabeth Barlow-Wiltshire [1969] Director; Robert Wiltshire [1968] Director

Yorkshire Heart Limited
Incorporated: 17 March 2011
Net Worth Deficit: £163,425 *Total Assets:* £508,433
Registered Office: 22 Victoria Avenue, Harrogate, N Yorks, HG1 5PR
Shareholders: Christopher Spakouskas; Gillian Evelyn Spakouskas
Officers: Christopher Spakouskas [1953] Director; Gillian Evelyn Spakouskas [1954] Director

Youngs Beers Limited
Incorporated: 1 December 2014
Registered Office: Navigation House, 22a Navigation House, 22a Broad Street, Ramsgate, Kent, CT11 8QY
Major Shareholder: Graham Dougal Young
Officers: Graham Dougal Young [1943] Director/Communicator

YSTY Limited
Incorporated: 21 December 2018
Registered Office: 3 Osmand Gardens, Plymouth, PL7 1AA
Major Shareholder: Thomas Jackson
Officers: Thomas Jackson [1993] Director/Salesman

Zapato Brewery Ltd.
Incorporated: 24 April 2015
Net Worth: £7,071 *Total Assets:* £14,730
Registered Office: 3 Rock Lane, Slaithwaite, Huddersfield, W Yorks, HD7 5DA
Shareholder: Russell Edward Watson
Officers: Matthew Stefan Gorecki [1979] Managing Director; Russell Edward Watson [1979] Production Director

Zulu Alpha Brewing Limited
Incorporated: 25 October 2013
Previous: Castles Brewery Ltd
Net Worth Deficit: £49,748 *Total Assets:* £46,241
Registered Office: Unit 51b Symondscliffe Way, Portskewett, Caldicot, Monmouthshire, NP26 5PW
Shareholders: David Johns; Anthony Gillespie
Officers: Anthony Gillespie [1992] Director/Administrator; David Johns [1980] Director/Administrator

ZX Ventures Limited
Incorporated: 17 February 1995 *Employees:* 8
Previous: Pioneer Brewing Company Limited
Net Worth: £184,283,008 *Total Assets:* £281,748,992
Registered Office: Bureau, Fetter Lane, London, EC4A 1EN
Parent: ABI UK Holding 1 Limited
Officers: Terri Francis, Secretary; Ricardo Dos Santos Neves [1985] Director/Head of Finance [Portuguese]; Paul Willem Dufourne [1989] Brand Experience Director Europe [Dutch]; Terri Nicole Francis [1986] Director/Lawyer [Australian]; Rita Hallgato [1980] People Director [Hungarian]; Andrew Kenneith Logan [1985] E-Commerce Director; Adrien Pierre Bernard Frederic Mahieu [1985] Director/Head of Craft & Specialties [Belgian]

Zymurgorium Ltd
Incorporated: 13 September 2016 *Employees:* 3
Net Worth: £447,149 *Total Assets:* £765,763
Registered Office: Unit B6, Fairhills Road, Irlam, Manchester, M44 6BA
Major Shareholder: Aaron Ross Darke
Officers: Aaron Ross Darke [1991] Distiller/Brewer Managing Director; Callum Thomas Darke [1989] Director/Operations/Accounts Manager

This page is intentionally left blank

Index of Directorships

Abbott, Beth
Lake View Country House Ltd

Abbott, Lynne Michelle
Stowey Brewery Limited

Abbott, Paul Thomas
Lake View Country House Ltd

Abbott, Richard Bruce
Lake View Country House Ltd

Abbott, Thomas
Uttoxeter Brewing Co Ltd

Abel, Harold
Old Tree Brewery Ltd

Abidi, Rafik
The Whitstable Brewery Co Ltd

Abrahams, Roger William
Buffy's Brewery Limited

Abram, Timothy John
Test Brewing Ltd

Ackerley, David John
Project X Brewing Co Ltd

Acketts, Mark Lyndon
The Tiptree Brewing Co Ltd

Adams, Jamie
Mortlake Brewery Ltd

Adcock, Gary George
J.C. & R.H. Palmer Limited

Adedipe, Anthony
Eko Brewery Limited

Adedipe, Helena-Aude
Eko Brewery Limited

Adey, Simon
Mister A's Beer Co Ltd

Adnams, Jonathan
Adnams PLC

Adwick, Andrew
River Widow Brewery Ltd

Ainsley, Thomas
Neon Raptor Brewing Co Ltd.

Ainsworth, Penelope Jane
Surrey Hills Brewery Ltd

Aitcheson, Stephen
The East Yorkshire Beer Co Ltd

Aitchison, Andrew Robert
Northern Alchemy Limited

Akerlund, Jon Andreas
Grace Land Beer Limited

Akers, Steven Andrew
Trumark Properties Limited

Al-Khedheri, Adam
Degrees Plato Brewing Ltd.

Alajouanine, Bruno
London Beer Lab Ltd

Albini, Paul Anthony
Hobsons Brewery and Co Ltd

Albu, Mihai
Skinnybrands Ltd

Alden, Jeffrey Stephen Denton
The Burton Old Cottage Beer Co Ltd
Gloucestershire Old Cottage Beer Co Ltd
Greenwich Old Cottage Beer Co Ltd

Alexander, Duncan George
71 Brewing Limited

Alexander, Kathryn
Lion Craft Brewery Ltd

Alexander, Robert
Lion Craft Brewery Ltd

Alldis, Caroline
Brumaison Ltd

Alldis, Peter James
Brumaison Ltd

Allen McNaught, Louise
Hurly Burly Brewery Ltd

Allen, Angela Christina
Roundhill Brewery Limited

Allen, Anthony John
Oak Brewing Co Ltd

Allen, James
Shelsley Brewing Co Ltd

Allen, Nick Eric Leonard
Greyhound Brewery Limited

Allen, Nigel Geoffrey
Everards Brewery Limited

Allen, Richard
Bomb Shelter Brewing Limited

Allen, Russell
Roundhill Brewery Limited

Allen, Sarah Rebecca
Greyhound Brewery Limited

Allen, William Linden
Paddy's Clover Ltd

Allingham, Edward William David
Leatherbritches Brewery Ltd

Allingham, Keith
Fokof Limited

Allison, Steven
The Five Points Brewing Co Ltd

Allkin, Roy John George
Boss Brewing Co Ltd

Allott, Delia Robina
Binghams Brewery Limited

Allott, Ian David
Chequers Micropub Limited

Allott, Maria Yolanda
Chequers Micropub Limited

Allsopp, James Leonard
Samuel Allsopp & Sons Ltd

Alter, Jeremy Steven
New River Brewery Ltd

Amato, Stefan
Pointeer Ltd

Amor, Peter William
The Barrels Hereford Limited
Wye Valley Brewery Limited

Amor, Simon Paul
Heineken UK Limited

Amor, Vernon Patrick
Wye Valley Brewery Limited

Amura, Gervasio
St Ives Brewery Limited

Amura, Marco Gervasio
St Ives Brewery Limited

Amura, Yvonne
St Ives Brewery Limited

An, Qi
Morecambe Bay Wines Limited

Anand, Rooney
Greene King Brewing and Retailing

Anbouche, Amir William
4 Acre Brewing Co. Ltd
Jackrabbit Brewing Co. Ltd

Andersen, Stig Anker
Stonehenge Ales Limited

Anderson, Alastair Ian, Lord
Soham Brewery Ltd

Anderson, Mark
Double Maxim Beer Co Ltd
Maxim Brewery Limited

Anderson, Susan
Double Maxim Beer Co Ltd
Maxim Brewery Limited

Andrea, Andrew Andonis
Mansfield Brewery Trading Ltd
Marston's Acquisitions Limited
Marston's PLC

Andrews, Eileen
The Bosun's Brewing Co Ltd

Andrews, Grahame Francis
The Bosun's Brewing Co Ltd

Andrews, Robert Kenneth
Sheeptown Brewery Limited

Angeletti, Davide
Moody Stag Limited

Angell, Barbara
Violet Cottage Brewing Co Ltd

Angell, Richard
Violet Cottage Brewing Co Ltd

Anley, Darron
Anley Ales Limited

Anley, Darron John
Siren Craft Brew Limited

Anley, Joanne
Anley Ales Limited
Siren Craft Brew Limited

Anspach, Paul James
Anspach & Hobday Limited

Anthony, Neil
Head Thirst Ltd

Anwyl, Gwyn
Bragdy Mona Cyf

Ap Dafydd, Myrddin
Cwrw Llyn Cyf

Ap Llyfnwy, Iwan
Cwrw Llyn Cyf

Appleby, Matthew Stephen
Roath Brewery Ltd

Appleton, Simon
Hush Brewing Co. Ltd

Aqulin, Anders
AD Hop Brewing Ltd

Archer, Caron Patricia
Padstow Brewing Company (2013) Ltd

Archer, Desmond John
Padstow Brewing Company (2013) Ltd

Archer, Paul Duncan
Brewboard Limited

Archer, Richard
Utopian Brewing Limited

Archibald, James Leslie
32 Islands Brewery Ltd

Arkell, Alexander Thomas
Arkell's Brewery Limited

Arkell, George James
Arkell's Brewery Limited

Arkell, James Rixon
Arkell's Brewery Limited
Donnington Brewery Limited

Arkell, Lucy Ann
Equal Brewkery CIC

Arkell, Nicholas Henry
Arkell's Brewery Limited

Arkley, Alistair Grant
S.A.Brain & Co Ltd

Armitage, Matthew Graham
Umbrella Brewing Limited

Armstrong, Paul Benedict
Carlsberg Supply Company UK Ltd

Armstrong, Peter Michael
Thomas Hardy Kendal Limited

Arnese, Antony
Dawkins & Georges Ltd

Arnold, Stoirm Cesare Billy
Snakestorm Limited

Arnott-Job, Mark John
The Two Towers Brewery Ltd

Aschmann, Hudson John
Crooked Brewing Limited

Ashbridge-Thomlinson, Claire
East London Brewing Co Ltd

Ashcroft, Robert
The Cains Brewing Co Ltd

Ashley, Christopher
3's A Crowd Brewing Ltd

Ashley, Nicholas Vaughan, Dr
Angles Ales Limited

Ashworth, David Carr
Holcot Hop-Craft Ltd

Ashworth, Paul Michael
Four Kings Brewery Limited

Astal Stain, Paul Henry Oswald
The Company of Dead Brewers Ltd

Astill, Christopher James
The Proud Peacock Limited

Atherton, James Peter
The Beerblefish Brewing Co Ltd

Atkin, Robert
Matlock Brewing Co Ltd

Atkings, John David
Ellismuir Limited

Atkins, Ben Christopher
Xylo Brewing Ltd

Atkinson, Cameron Alan
Craft Life Brewing Ltd.

Atkinson, David
Goose Eye Brewery Limited

Atkinson, Jack
Goose Eye Brewery Limited

Atkinson, Nigel John Bewley
Wadworth and Co Ltd

Atkinson, Peter David
The Grainstore Brewery Limited
Stoney Ford Brew Co. Ltd

Atte La Crouche, Zak Joshua
Brew Locker Ltd

Austin, Julia Helen
Tyne Bank Brewery Limited

Avis, Michael
Brockley Brewing Co Ltd.

Axon, Richard
West By Three Limited

Ayeh, Stacey
Crafty Leopard Brewing Co Ltd

Ayeh, Stacey Akwasi
Rock Leopard Brewing Co Ltd

Ayling, Jacqui
Tom's Tap and Brewhouse Ltd

Ayling, Sean Edward
Tom's Tap and Brewhouse Ltd

Ayres, Benjamin Leigh
The Shefford Brewery Co. Ltd

Ayres, Martin Leigh
B & T Brewery Limited

Bachelor, Martyn Kenneth
Loud Shirt Brewing Co Ltd

Back, Samuel
Attic Brew Co. Ltd

Bacon, David
Hairy Brewers Ales Limited

Badwell, Lee
Badwells Brewery Ltd

Bagnall, Brian
Hydes' Brewery Limited

Bagnall, Rupert
Wadworth and Co Ltd

Bailey, Andrew
Nightowl Brewing Co Ltd

Bailey, Benjamin James
Tally Ho! Brewery Limited

Bailey, David William
Hardknott UK Ltd

Bailey, Jessica Lucy
Bad Joke Brew Co Ltd

Bailey, Martin Bryan
The Coach House Brewing Co Ltd

Bailey, Richard Anthony John
Daniel Thwaites PLC

Bailey, Ryan
Northern Monkey Brew Co. Ltd

Bain, Michael Alexander
Deeside Brewery Limited

Baker, Andrew James
Summer Wine Brewery Limited

Baker, Dean Matthew
Baker's Dozen Brewing Co Ltd

Baker, Keith John
Dynamite Valley Brewery Ltd

Baker, Neil Adam
Cheviot Brewery Ltd

Baker, Terence
Flack Manor Brewery Limited

Baker, Xavier Lee
Goddards Brewery Limited

Balchin, Alex
Agricola Bottling Limited

Balchin, Alexander David
Wold Toppers Limited

Balchin, Kate
Agricola Bottling Limited

Balchin, Katherine Emma
Wold Toppers Limited

Baldock, John
Derventio Brewery Limited

Baldwin, Aaron Thomas
Oxbrew Ltd

Balivada, Ashwin
3ABC Ltd
Jocks and Peers Brewing Co Ltd

Ball, Richard James, Dr
The Inlaw Brewing Co Ltd

Ball, Stephen John
The Oaks Brewing Co Ltd

Ballantyne, Andrew Charles
Ards Brewing Co Ltd

Ballard, Steven
North Brewing Co Ltd

Ballota, Teresa
Arran Brew Ltd.

Bamforth, Adam Lee
Magic Rock Brewing Co Ltd

Bamping, Jessica Anne
Candid Brewing Co. Limited

Bamping, Mark Christopher Carlton
Candid Brewing Co. Limited

Bannister, Christopher Peter
Bizzy Play Limited

Bannister, Sharon Jayne Galliers
Bizzy Play Limited

Barade, Jean-Philippe Pierre Paul
Innis & Gunn Holdings Limited

Barber, Charlotte
Mersea Island Brewery & Vineyard Ltd

Barber, Jacqueline
Mersea Island Brewery & Vineyard Ltd

Barber, Kevin
Northern Monkey Brew Co. Ltd

Barber, Mark
Mersea Island Brewery & Vineyard Ltd

Barber, Roger George William
Mersea Island Brewery & Vineyard Ltd

Barber, Samuel Jonathan
The Southey Brewing Co Ltd

Bardsley, Paul
Southport Brewery Limited

Barker, Alan Douglas
Daleside Brewery Limited
Daleside Holdings (Harrogate) Ltd

Barker, Andrew
York Brewery Limited

Barker, David Clive
Little Crosby Village Brewing Co Ltd

Barker, Simon Stanley, Dr
All Day Brewing Co Ltd

Barlow, Alex Gavin
Alex Barlow Brewing Consulting Ltd
Sentinel Brewery Holdings Ltd

Barlow, Jason
Mart's Brewing Co Ltd

Barlow, Kyle Russell
Crank Beers Limited

Barlow, Thomas William James
Pixie Spring Brewing Co Ltd

Barlow-Wiltshire, Anne Elizabeth
Yorkshire Dales Brewing Co Ltd

Barnard, Joel Lewis
Whyte BR Brewing Co Ltd
Whyte Bar Brewing Co Ltd

Barnes, Adam Edwin
Woodhalls Brewery Limited

Barnes, Andrew
Dolphin Brewery Limited

Barnes, George Harold Abbott
Shepherd Neame Limited

Barnes, Gerard Hugh
St.Austell Brewery Co Ltd

Barnes, Russell Antony
Red Fox Brewery Limited

Barnes, Sandra Patricia
Woodhalls Brewery Limited

Barnett, Andrew Roger
Barney's Beer Limited
Summerhall Brewing Limited

Barnett, Elizabeth
Pershore Brewery Limited

Barnett, Julia
Quartz Brewing Limited

Barnett, Scott William Pert
Quartz Brewing Limited

Barnett, Sean Neil
Pershore Brewery Limited

Baron, Godwin Girth
Two Fathoms Distillery Ltd.

Barr, Andrew Peter
Partridge Brewing Co Ltd

Barrell, Martin
Barrell & Sellers Limited

Barrett, Jake Maximilian
Snakestorm Limited

Bartholomew, Charles John Eric
Wadworth and Co Ltd

Bartlett, Paul Michael
JP Brew Limited

Bartlett, Simon John
Bristol Brewing Co Ltd

Barton, Duncan
Ticketytap Ltd

Barton, Keri Louise
Ticketytap Ltd

Barton, Kieron Mark
The Saint Brewing Co Limited

Barton, Stephanie Jane Henderson
Barngates Brewery Limited

Bashford, Jade Lisa
The Stroud Brewery Limited

Basquill, Michael Gerard John
Brockley Brewing Co Ltd.

Bate, Jonathan Murdo MacLeod
Six Towns Brewery Limited

Bateman, Jaclyn Carol
George Bateman & Son Limited

Bateman, Stuart George Carson
George Bateman & Son Limited

Bates, Andrew Mark
Punchline Brewery Limited

Bates, Derek Seth
Duration Brewing Ltd

Bates, Jamie
Hopsox Brewing Co Ltd

Bates, Lisa
Walsall Brewing Co Ltd

Bath, Gareth
Curious Drinks Limited

Batham, Dorothy Jean
Daniel Batham & Son Limited
Bathams (Delph) Limited

Batham, Matthew Daniel
Daniel Batham & Son Limited
Bathams (Delph) Limited

Batham, Timothy Arthur Joseph
Daniel Batham & Son Limited
Bathams (Delph) Limited

Batt, Rory
Camden Town Brewery Limited

Batteson, John Seymour
Gan Yam Brewing Co Ltd

Batting, Bruce
Sherfield Village Brewery Ltd

Batty, Steven
Isle-of-Cumbrae Brewing Co Ltd

Baxendale, Marcus James
Hindsight Collective Ltd

Baxendale, Paul
Baltic Beer Co Ltd

Baxter, Daniel James
Abbeydale Brewery Limited

Bayliffe, Jason
Broadtown Brewery Ltd

Bayliss, Robert
Fingerprint Brewing Co Ltd

Baynham, Henry Roland Atton
Baynhams Brewery Limited

Baynham, Lawrence Peter Stewart
Baynhams Brewery Limited

Baynham, Thomas Roland James
Baynhams Brewery Limited

Bazley, Bernard Ivan
Mill Lane Brewing Co Ltd

Beachell, Craig
Stannington Brewery Ltd

Bealby, Henry John
Brook House Brewery Limited

Beaman, Annabelle
Bridgnorth Brewing Co Ltd

Beard, John Edward
Wadworth and Co Ltd

Beardsmore, Rachael Jane
Vinifera Limited

Beardsmore, Robert Horatio
Vinifera Limited

Beaumont, Karen Linda
The Dove Street Brewery Ltd

Beaven, James Alexander
Tenby Brewing Co. Limited

Beaver, Neil
Fire Rock Brewing Co Ltd.

Bebb, Thomas William
White Horse Brewery Co Ltd

Bee, Gareth Richard
Pomona Island Brew Co Ltd

Beech, Clive David
Octagon Brewery Limited

Beecroft, Nigel Philip
Ostlers Ales Ltd

Beeley, Judith de Quincey
Dent Brewery Limited

Beeley, Paul, Dr
Dent Brewery Limited

Beeson, Declan Elliott
Topsham Brewery Ltd

Bekker, Danielle
Good Living Brew Co Limited

Belchier, Guy
BeerHug Ltd

Bell, Donald McI, Dr
The Lockside Brewery Ltd.

Bell, Eleanor Jayne
The Durham Brewery Limited

Bell, Leo
Newcastle Brewing Ltd

Bell, Matthew Robert
Nightjar Brew Co Ltd

Bell, Michael John
Beer Station Brewery Ltd

Bell, Mike
Newcastle Brewing Ltd

Bell, Philip James
The Village Inn Pub Co Ltd

Bell, Stewart Michael
Black Dragon Brewery Limited

Bell, Thomas Neale
Skinnybrands Ltd

Bennett, Graham Charles
Gleneagles Distillery Limited

Bennett, Joanna Elizabeth
Pilot Wharf Limited

Bennett, Richard Kenric
Mumbles Brewing Co Ltd
The Pilot Brewery Limited
Pilot Wharf Limited

Bennett, Richard Peter
Boutilliers Limited

Bennett, Thomas
Withnell's Brewing Co Ltd

Bennett, William John
Clavell & Hind Limited

Benson, Andrew James
Big Hand Brewing Co Ltd

Bent, Nigel James
Cellarhead Brewing Co Ltd

Bentley, Joseph William
Hopscotch Craft Brewers Ltd

Bentley, Michael
Sky Pirate Ltd

Beresford, Jacqueline Jane
Ashover Brewery Limited

Beresford, Kim Shaun
Ashover Brewery Limited

Beresford, Thomas
Bomb Shelter Brewing Limited

Berezowski, Robert John
Brew Club Limited

Bernardo, Angelo
Mybrewpub Limited

Berni, Timothy
Mr Bees Brewery Ltd

Berrow, James Peter
Langham Brewing Co Ltd

Berry, Mark Dominic Loxham
Gun Brewery Limited

Best, Andrew Gregory
Best Brewery Ltd

Beveridge, John William
Kintyre Ales Limited

Beverley, Russell
Empire Brewing Ltd

Bhamra, Kamaljit Kaur
Reds Beer Co Ltd

Bhandara, Isphanyar
Murree Breweries (UK) Limited

Bi, Qifen
Bib Brewing Ltd

Biddle, Haydn
George Bateman & Son Limited

Bidwell, Dominic Edward Charles
The Bidwell Brewery Co Ltd
The Thetford Brewery Limited

Bidwell, Stephen James John
The Bidwell Brewery Co Ltd
The Thetford Brewery Limited

Bidwell, Tobias
The Bidwell Brewery Co Ltd

Bidwell, Tobias Thomas
The Thetford Brewery Limited

Bigg, Michael
The Filo Brewing Co Ltd

Bigg, Sharon Ann
The Filo Brewing Co Ltd

Biggs, Edward
Kingstone Brewery Limited

Biggs, George Albert James
Boody Brewery Ltd.

Bilimoria, Karan Faridoon, Lord
Cobra Beer Partnership Limited

Bin Abdul Rahman, MOD Razali
Woodforde's BPP Limited

Bingham, Christopher
Binghams Brewery Limited

Bingham, Karl Alexander Michael
Nameless Brewing Limited

Bingham, Michelle Ann Joyce
Binghams Brewery Limited

Binnie, Esther
The Innis & Gunn Brewing Co Ltd
Innis & Gunn Holdings Limited
The Innis & Gunn Inveralmond Brewery

Bird, Joseph
Blackjack Beers Limited

Birkby, Andrew John
Wild Card Brewery Limited

Birkett, James Jolyon
Neepsend Brewery Ltd

Birnie, Stewart Robert
Inverbrewery Limited

Birtwistle, Christopher Robert
Hush Brewing Co. Ltd

Bishop, David James
Bishop's Crook Brewery Ltd.

Bishop, Emma Louise
Narugelia Ltd

Bishop, Trevor James
Aurora Ales Limited

Bishop, William
Radio City Beer Works Limited

Bisiker, Brian Douglas
Vyrnwy Developments Limited

Bisiker, Edward James Rees
Vyrnwy Developments Limited

Bisiker, Susan
Vyrnwy Developments Limited

Bisset, Russell
Northern Monk Brewing Co. Ltd

Bittleston, Timothy Steven
Ascot Ales Limited

Bjornson, John Stephen
Earl Soham Brewery Limited

Blacker, Ian Jeffrey
Melin Tap Brewhouse Limited

Blackman, Jane
Treboom Limited

Blackwood, Thomas Joseph
The Near Beer Brewing Co. Ltd

Blake, Alric Anthony
Cumberland Breweries Limited

Blake, Daniel Martin
Space Trash Brewing Ltd

Blakesley, Michael
Rocket Ales Limited

Blanchard, David Edward
Red Star Brewery (Formby) Ltd

Blanchard, Phillip
Exile Brewing Co Ltd
Hafod Brewing Co Ltd

Bland, Rhys
Birkenhead Brewery Co Ltd

Blaylock, Ian
Doncaster Brewery Limited

Blesson, Gregory Francis
Red Squirrel Brewery Limited

Blockley, James Hamilton
Tewkesbury Brewery Ltd

Blythe, Martin
Wigan Brew House Ltd

Bocking, Colin John
Crouch Vale Brewery Limited

Bocking, Fiona Michelle
Crouch Vale Brewery Limited

Boddy, Stephen
Chevin Brew Co Ltd

Boglione, Harry Luca
Gilt & Flint Ltd

Boldrin, David Christopher
Urban Alchemy Brewing Co Ltd

Bollen, Felix
German Kraft Brewing Limited

Boltman, Russell James
Fierce Beer Limited

Bond, Dean Earl
Bond Brews Ltd

Bond, William
Cullach Brewing Ltd

Bone, Anthony Charles Watney
Colchester Brewery Ltd

Bonnington, Keith
Colonsay Beverages Ltd.

Bonser, James
Howe Capital Limited

Boon, Carl Daniel
Green Times Brewing Limited

Booth, Jonathan
Pin-Up Beers Ltd.

Booth, Mark
Hopscotch Craft Brewers Ltd

Booth, Peter
Red Rose Brewery Ltd
Square Street Distillery Ltd

Bore, David
Lazy Turtle Brewing Co Ltd

Borkmann, Anton
German Kraft Brewing Limited

Borley, Fiona Caroline
Island Hamlet Brewing Co Ltd

Borley, Mark James
Island Hamlet Brewing Co Ltd

Boscawen, Evelyn George William
Marourde Limited

Boscoe, Neill Stuart
Urban Alchemy Brewing Co Ltd

Bosworth, Ian Leslie
Boot Town Brewery Ltd

Bosworth, Jennifer Michelle
Twisted Barrel Ale Limited

Bosworth, Ritchie Darren
Twisted Barrel Ale Limited

Bott, David Antony
Titanic Brewery Co Limited

Bott, Keith Andrew
Titanic Brewery Co Limited
White Horse Brewery Co Ltd

Bott, Tom
Signature Brew Ltd

Boughton, Nicholas John
The Millstone Brewery Limited

Bourdeaux, John Stephen
New River Brewery Ltd

Bournazian, Lynne
Tonbridge Brewery Limited

Bournazian, Paul Geoffrey
Tonbridge Brewery Limited

Bowden, Frederick James
Brew Toon Ltd.

Bowden, Shirley-Ann Gerrard
Brew Toon Ltd.

Bowen, Christopher Stephen
Southbrew Co Ltd

Bowen, Thomas Wyndham
Foghorn Brew Co Ltd

Bowen-Thomas, Berin Chesney
The Near Beer Brewing Co. Ltd

Bowers, Mark
Wooha Brewing Co Ltd

Bowley, Chris
Inferno Brewery Limited

Boyce, John James
The Mighty Oak Brewing Co. Ltd

Boyd, Martin James
The New Union Brewing Co Ltd

Boyes, Nathan
Padlock Brewery Ltd.

Boyle, Matthew Dunstan
Wylam Brewery Limited

Boyle, Stephen
Foxhat Beer Limited

Brace, Stephen Anthony
The Lake District Brewery Ltd

Bradbury, John Andrew
Hawkshead Brewery Limited
Windsor Castle Brewery Limited

Bradbury, Richard Anthony
T.& R. Theakston Limited

Bradford, Ian James
Lymestone Brewery Limited

Bradford, Reggie
Beersheba Ltd

Bradford, Vivienne Mary
Lymestone Brewery Limited

Bradley, Carolyn Jane
Marston's PLC

Bradley, Ian Stewart
The Coniston Brewing Co Ltd

Bradley, Steven Michael
Loyal City Brewing Co Ltd

Bradley, Susan Mary
The Coniston Brewing Co Ltd

Bradshaw, Thomas James
Welland Brewery Ltd

Brady, Carolyn Jayne
Forth Bridge Brewery and Distillery

Brady, James Stephen
Forth Bridge Brewery and Distillery

Braham, Malcolm Ernest Elihood
Enville Ales Limited

Brain, Charles Nicholas
S.A.Brain & Co Ltd

Bramley, Michael Lloyd
Timothy Taylor & Co.,Limited

Brandim-Howson, Rodrigo
Partridge Brewing Co Ltd

Brasher, Deborah Jayne
Fleabag Brewing Co Ltd

Brasher, Robert Alexander
Fleabag Brewing Co Ltd

Brauer, Crichton Peter
Beermats Brewing Co Ltd

Braysmith, David Jonathan
Pumphouse Brewing Co Ltd

Brazier, Alexander Charles
Hopsox Brewing Co Ltd

Breen, Michael
Soho Brewing Ltd

Brett, William John
Shepherd Neame Limited

Brettell, Peter Robert
Tynemill Limited

Brew, John Senan
Old Pie Factory Brewery Ltd

Brew, Peter Louis
Crooked Fish Ltd

Brewis, Christopher
Brewis Beer Co Ltd

Brewis, Maxine
Brewis Beer Co Ltd

Brice, Harry Jonathan
Lekker Days Ltd

Bridge, Andrew Daniel
Abyss Brewing Ltd

Bridge, Jonathan
S.A.Brain & Co Ltd

Bridges, Ben Joseph
Hopsox Brewing Co Ltd

Briggs, Martin
Loopland Brewing Co Ltd

Briggs, Peter
400 Software Limited

Bright, Edward
Stubborn Mule Brewery Limited

Bright, Jonathan
After The Harvest Brewing Ltd

Brims, Charles David
McMullen & Sons, Limited

Brind, David Leonard
H.B.Clark & Co.(Successors) Ltd

Brindle, Jonathan Edwin
Pryor Reid & Co Limited

Brine, Richard John
Market Bosworth Brewery Ltd

Briscoe, Rosemary Theresa
Peerless Brewing Co Ltd

Briscoe, Steven Alan
Peerless Brewing Co Ltd

Britton, Kathy
Oldershaw Brewery Ltd

Britton, Tim John
Oldershaw Brewery Ltd

Broad, James Cameron
Bad Seed Brewery Ltd

Broadbank, Thomas
Delphic Brewing Co Ltd

Broadbent, Cecelia
Victor's Drinks Limited

Broadbent, John Edward
Golcar Brewery Limited

Broadbent, Peter Howard
Golcar Brewery Limited

Broadbent, Ralph Thierry
Victor's Drinks Limited

Broderick, Eugene Pacelli
Block Brewery Limited

Bromley, Ian
Bromtec Limited

Brook, Michael Jonathan
Triple Point Brewing Ltd

Brooking, Brenda
South Hams Brewery Ltd

Brooking, Mark
South Hams Brewery Ltd

Brooking, Samuel
South Hams Brewery Ltd

Brooks, Colin
Spartan Brewery Ltd

Brooks, Martin Robert
Uley Ales Limited

Brooks, Robert Charles
Brooks Brewhouse Limited

Brothwell, Michael Alan
The Leeds Brewery Co Ltd

Brown, Alistair Sandford Burns
Bellfield Brewery Limited

Brown, Cameron James
Turning Point Brewing Co Ltd

Brown, Carola Jane
Ballard's Brewery Limited

Brown, Christopher Roman
Test Brewing Ltd

Brown, Claire Louise
Lincolnshire Brewing Co Ltd

Brown, Colin William
Belvoir Brewery Limited

Brown, Daniel John
Chapter Brewing Co Ltd

Brown, David Patrick
Brewing and Distilling Co Ltd

Brown, Eileen
Askham Brewery Limited

Brown, Ian
Askham Brewery Limited
Punchbowl Brewery Limited

Brown, James Ronald
Coast Beer Co Limited

Brown, Jared
Gloucester Brewery Ltd

Brown, Kevin Paul
Baird Brewing Co Ltd

Brown, Marie
Bellfield Brewery Limited

Brown, Michael Dennis
Church Farm Brewery Ltd

Brown, Peter Maclin
Shoreditch Brewing Co Ltd

Brown, Sam
Church Farm Brewery Ltd

Brown, Scott Douglas
Mortlake Brewery Ltd

Brown, Simon
Punchbowl Brewery Limited

Brown, Stephen
Hopper House Brew Farm Ltd

Brown, Stephen James
Twickenham Fine Ales Limited

Browne, Kiera
Seafire Brewing Co. Ltd

Bruce, Alexander David Michael
The Renegade Pub Co 2 Limited
The West Berkshire Brewery PLC

Bruce, Simon John
Paddy's Clover Ltd

Bryan, Adrian Keith
Blimey! Brewing Co Ltd

Bryan, Michelle Louise
Buccaneer Brewery Ltd

Bryant, Sharon Ann
Fixed Wheel Brewery Limited

Bryce, James Douglas Maxwell
W.L.B.C Ltd

Brydon, Jane Scott
Heineken UK Limited

Buchanan, Craig Douglas
Strathaven Ales Limited

Buchmann, Gilles Aron
Jarr Kombucha Ltd

Buckler, Niall Richard
Foghorn Brew Co Ltd

Buckley, Phil
Applecross Brewing Co Ltd

Buckmaster, Sarah Louise
PLS Special Projects Limited

Bugg, David Michael
Old Town Brewery Ltd.

Bulcroft, John
Hilltop Brewing Co Ltd

Bull, Alex
By The Horns Ltd

Bumagat, Richard
Casorho Ltd

Bunn, Louise
Rocksnarl Ltd

Bunting, Nigel James
Shepherd Neame Limited

Burchell, Neil Harper
Bluestone Brewing Co Ltd

Burden, Angela Margaret Constantine
Cartmel Valley Brewery Ltd

Burden, Ian Armstrong
Cartmel Valley Brewery Ltd

Burge, Richard
Nethergate Brewery Co Ltd

Burgess, William
Gan Yam Brewing Co Ltd

Burgis, Gillian
Broxbourne Brewery Ltd.

Burgis-Smith, Gillian Margaret
Fallen Angel Brewery Ltd

Burhouse, Richard Oliver
Magic Rock Brewing Co Ltd

Burke, Donncha
Ar Suil Brewing Project Ltd

Burke, Samantha Jane
Carnival Brewing Co Ltd

Burlison, Gary John
Nethergate Brewery Co Ltd

Burn, Simon
The Silverstone Real Ale Co Ltd

Burnell, Stephen John
New Cross Ales Ltd

Burnett, David John Stuart
Nene Valley Brewery Limited

Burrows, Andrew Stuart
Alnwick Ales Limited

Burrows, John Martin
WantsumBrewery Ltd

Burrows, Sam
Bristol Brewing Co Ltd

Burrows, Shona Patrine Jean
Alnwick Ales Limited

Burton, Andrew
The Proper Brewing Co Ltd

Burton, Andrew John
Bestens Brewery Limited

Burton, Mark Jonathan
Fellows Brewery Limited

Busby, James Sebastian Edward
The Inlaw Brewing Co Ltd

Bushell, Aaron Michael
Gander Brewing Co Ltd

Bushell, Lee Anthony
Gander Brewing Co Ltd

Bussey, Edmund
River Widow Brewery Ltd

Bustin, Janice Anne
Merrimen Brewery Limited

Bustin, Richard James
Merrimen Brewery Limited

Butchart, Duncan
3ways Brewing Co Limited

Butchart, James
3ways Brewing Co Limited

Butler, Craig
The Great Yorkshire Brewery Ltd

Butler, Tim
Northern Craft Brewers Limited

Butler, Timothy George Edward
St Andrews Brewing Co Holdings Ltd
St Andrews Brewing Co Ltd
St Andrews Old Brewing Co Ltd

Butt, Christopher Geoffrey
Butts Brewery Limited

Button, Edward
Quad Brewing Co Ltd

Button, Katherine
Quad Brewing Co Ltd

Buxton, Christopher Alan
Soul Doubt Brewing Co Ltd

Byatt, Lee Anthony
Byatt's Brewery Ltd

Byers, Jason
Steel River Drinks Ltd

Byram, Nicholas
Caveman Brewing Co Ltd

Byrne, Alison Mary Elizabeth
Red Fox Brewery Limited

Cail, Ian Stuart
Harviestoun Brewery Limited

Cain, Daniel Joseph
TKS Brewing Limited

Calais, Matthew
Romney Marsh Brewery Limited

Calderwood, Jack
Lost Roots Limited

Callan, Matthew John
Heineken UK Limited

Calnan, Sean William
Old Dairy Brewery Limited

Calver, Jonathan Charles
Branded Drinks Ltd

Calverley, Samuel Thomas
Calverley's Brewery Ltd

Calverley, Thomas George
Calverley's Brewery Ltd

Calvert, George William
Windsor & Eton Brewing Co Ltd

Cameron, Kevin
Copper Fox Brewery Ltd

Cameron, Reuben
Glesga Brewery Ltd.

Cameron, Robert
By The River Brewery Ltd
Wylam Brewery Limited

Campbell, Ian St Clair
Abernyte Brewery Limited

Campbell, James Douglas
JD Campbell Brewing Limited

Campbell, Murray Alasdair Lister
Campbells Brewery Ltd

Campbell, Nigel Ronald
Hawkshead Brewery Limited

Campling, Kerry Alicia
Time & Tide Brewing Limited

Campregher, Nick, Dr
London Brewing Co Ltd

Canavan, Aidan
Bute Brew Co Ltd

Canavan, Deborah Anne
Brockley Brewing Co Ltd.

Candler, Warren
Cygnus Brewing Co Limited

Canning, David McLean
Tres Bien Brewery Ltd

Carline, Susan
The Staffordshire Brewery Ltd

Carnegie, James Derek Scott
Alechemy Brewing Ltd
Keith Brewery Limited
Spey Valley Brewery Limited

Carr, David Edward
Bewdley Brewery Limited

Carr, Kevin Charles, Dr
The Three Counties Brewery Ltd

Carr, William James
Monachis Ltd

Carroll, Jonathan David
Mortimer Brewing Co Ltd

Carruthers, Justine Louise
Dowr Kammel Brewing Co Ltd

Carruthers, Simon James
Dowr Kammel Brewing Co Ltd

Carson, Anthony John
Higsons 1780 Limited

Carter, Scott Raymond
Haresfoot Storage & Distribution Co Ltd

Cartwright, Dean William
Pig Iron Brewing Co Ltd
Pig Iron Brewing Limited

Cartwright, James
Elemental Brew House Limited

Cartwright, Rachel Louise
Evensong Brewing Limited

Cary, Robert James
Good Chemistry Apparatus Ltd
Good Chemistry Brewing Limited

Caseberry, Gillian
St.Austell Brewery Co Ltd

Casey, Frances Caroline
Malvern Hills Brewery Limited

Cassin, Holly Beth
Calarta Ltd

Castle II, Earl Michael
Cumberland Breweries Limited

Catherall, Andrew Osborne
Three Hills Brewing Ltd

Caton, Matthew James
Last Sign Brewing Co Ltd

Causer, Annabel Sarah
Honest Brew Ltd

Cave, Benjamin Thomas Herrick
White Park Brewery Limited

Cave, Michael John
TKS Brewing Limited

Cearns, Howard Davies
Lost and Grounded Brewers Ltd

Chadwick, Karen Elizabeth
Anglesey Ales Ltd

Chadwick, Kathy Alina
The Pigeon Fishers Craft Brewery Ltd

Chairman, Jayne Margaret
Plan B Brewing Co Ltd

Challoner, Kevin
Cillenx Ltd

Chamberlain, Lloyd Francis
Blindmans Brewery Limited

Chambers, Raymond Stuart
Brewboard Limited

Chamier, Samuel Peter Trenham
The Three Legs Brewing Co Ltd

Chamley-Byatt, Shelley Ann
Byatt's Brewery Ltd

Chang, Ting-I
Southport Brewing Limited

Chapman, Adrian Daniel
Wishbone Brewery Limited

Chapman, Emma
Wishbone Brewery Limited

Chapman, Jonathan Michael
Staggeringly Good Ltd

Chapman, Robin
The East India Company India Pale Ale

Charlesworth, Jonathan
Dogtag Beer Co. Ltd

Chatwin, Anselm
Grace Land Beer Limited

Chatwood, Andrew Kenneth
Silktown Brewery Ltd

Cheng, Swan Elizabeth
Stubborn Mule Brewery Limited

Chester, John
Hops and Dots Brewing Co Ltd

Chesterman, Miles Robert William
Hogs Back Brewery Limited

Chetwynd Jay, Roger Dennis
Magna Bottling Limited
Magna Brewery Limited

Cheverton, James Edward
The Hopsmith Brewing Co Ltd

Chiappi, Sarah Jane
Creative Juices Brewing Co Ltd

Chillingworth, Tiernan Alexis
Fit Like Beer Limited

Chiverton, Paul Graham
Gower Brewery Co Limited

Chong Peng, Oh
Woodforde's BPP Limited

Churchward, Martin John
Hobsons Brewery and Co Ltd

Churchward, Patricia Beatrice
Hobsons Brewery and Co Ltd

Churton, David Nigel Vardon
Hook Norton Brewery Co Ltd

Clargo, Brian
Roam Brewing Co Ltd

Clargo, Jonathan Stuart
Roam Brewing Co Ltd

Clargo, Victoria Elizabeth
Roam Brewing Co Ltd

Clargo, Yolanda Mariea
Roam Brewing Co Ltd

Clark, Chris
Saeburh Brewery Ltd

Clark, Fergus Sydney
The Innis & Gunn Inveralmond Brewery

Clark, Garry John
Anglia Pub Co Ltd

Clark, Ian
Clarkshaws Brewing Co Ltd.

Clark, Matthew Jon
Coalition Brewing Co Ltd

Clark, Michael Kenneth
Newt Brew Ltd

Clark, Roger John
Colchester Brewery Ltd

Clark, Tony
Tony Clark Enterprises Ltd

Clark, Vicky Ailean
The Old Vault Brewing Co Ltd

Clarke, Andrea
Dovedale Brewing Co Ltd

Clarke, Andrew
Dark Tribe Brewery Limited

Clarke, Andrew Bernard
Letterpress Brewery Ltd

Clarke, Gary
Samuels Brewing Co Ltd

Clarke, Glyn
The Instant Karma Brewing Co Ltd

Clarke, James William
Hook Norton Brewery Co Ltd

Clarke, Jason Paul Sansom
Genius Brewing Limited

Clarke, Robert Arthur
The Two Bob Brewing Co Ltd

Clarke, Sean
Samuels Brewing Co Ltd

Clarke, Timothy
Hall & Woodhouse Limited
Timothy Taylor & Co.,Limited

Clayton, Deborah May
Northern Craft Brewers Limited

Clayton-Jones, Lucy Alice
Double Barrelled Brewery Ltd.

Clayton-Jones, Michael Alan
Double Barrelled Brewery Ltd.

Cleaver, Gavin MacGregor, Dr
Splott Brewery Ltd

Cleaver, Geoffrey John
The Burford Brewery Co Ltd

Cleland, Andrew James Edward
Archangel Brewing Ltd.

Cleland, Tracey
The Redchurch Brewery Limited

Cliff, David Peter
Ripple Steam Brewery Limited

Cliff, Peter Brian Maurice
Dartmoor Brewery Limited

Clifford, Rory
Clifford Brothers Brewery Ltd

Clifford, Seamus
Clifford Brothers Brewery Ltd

Clines, Jason Peter
The Sociable Beer Co Ltd.

Clinton, Marie-Claire
Bog Brew Beers Limited

Clinton, Paul
Bog Brew Beers Limited

Clough, Andrew
Bridge House Brewery Limited
The Bridgehouse Pub Co Ltd

Clough, Chris Roger
Torrside Brewing Ltd

Clough, David Ian
Orchard Road Brewery Limited

Clough, Lucy
The Staffordshire Brewery Ltd

Coates, David
Harvey Elizabeth Limited

Cobham, Ian
Dartmoor Brewery Limited

Cobley, Gareth
The Bears Den Brewery Limited

Cockerill, Danielle
Isaac Poad Brewing Ltd

Cockerill, Simon Rupert Mark
Isaac Poad Brewing Ltd

Cockley, Jonathan William
Old Friends Brewery Ltd

Coe, Morgan
Little Dragon Brewery Limited

Coetser, Joanne Leigh
The Craft Beer Cab Co Ltd

Coffey, Glenn
The Silverstone Real Ale Co Ltd

Coghill, Alexander James
Cuillin Brewery Limited

Coghill, Rachael MacLeod
Cuillin Brewery Limited

Cohen, Paul David
Hairy Dog Brewery Ltd

Colbourne, Toby
Four Kings Brewery Limited

Cole, Adrian
The Pigeon Fishers Craft Brewery Ltd

Coleman, Timothy
SRA Brewery Limited

Coles, Martin Anthony
Double Tap Brewery Ltd

Coles, Miranda Caroline
Loyal City Brewing Co Ltd

Colhoun, Adam
Baronscourt Brewing Co Ltd

Collings, Sandra
Caythorpe Brewery Limited

Collins, Brian
Vertical Stack Ltd

Collins, David John
Hadham Brewing Co Ltd

Collins, Mark Ainley
Genesis Craft Ales Limited

Collins, Sam William Brian
Morton Collins Brewing Co Ltd

Collyer, Alan Anthony
Avocet Ales Limited
The Exeter Brewery Limited

Colman, James Michael
The Proper Brewing Co Ltd

Colvill, Richard Stuart
M Rackstraws Ltd

Comer, Jonathan Hugh
Arbor Ales Ltd

Comonte, Dominic Sheridan Austell
The Fowey Brewery Ltd

Connelly, Michael
MC & P Engineering Limited

Connon, Emmet Patrick
Red Bay Brewing Co Ltd

Conroy, Jonathan Michael
Abbeydale Brewery Limited

Conroy, Kevin John
Thistlerock Enterprises UK Ltd

Constable, Stephen John
The Black Sheep Brewery PLC

Constable-Maxwell, Robert
Moonshine Drinks Limited

Conte, Vincenzo
Brewheadz Limited

Convey, Liam
Northern Monkey Brew Co. Ltd

Conway, Anthony Thomas
Droylsden Craft Limited

Conway, Gary Nicholas
Skinnybrands Ltd

Conway, Richard
Thirst Class Ale Limited

Cook, Jeremy Mark
Missing Link Brewing Ltd

Cook, Jonathan Richard
Mashionistas Brewing Co Ltd

Cook, Kathryn
Barearts Ltd

Cook, Paul Michael
Pink Moon Brewery Limited

Cook, Peter
Sherfield Village Brewery Ltd

Cooke, David Thomas
Holcot Hop-Craft Ltd

Cooke, Simon
Yorkshire Brewhouse Limited

Coombes, Charles Edward Hardy
Felinfoel Brewery Co Ltd

Coombes, John Andrew
Rebellion Beer Co Ltd

Coombes, Timothy
Rebellion Beer Co Ltd

Coombs, Charles Edward Hardy
Gustmain Limited

Coomes, Edward Alexander
Brightwater Brewery Limited

Cooper, Allan Roy
Elmtree Beers Ltd

Cooper, Andrew James
The Wild Beer Co Ltd

Cooper, Ann-Marie Olivia
Twisted Barrel Ale Limited

Cooper, Christopher James
Twisted Barrel Ale Limited

Cooper, Luke Kenneth
The Handyman Brewery Ltd

Cooper, Nicholas John, Dr
Bedlam Brewery Limited

Cooper, Susan
Little Valley Brewery Limited

Cooper, Thomas Albert
Barefaced Brewing Ltd

Cope, Andrew Martin
Two Beach Brewing Co Limited

Cope, Nigel Ilchester
The Staffordshire Brewery Ltd

Cope, Paul Michael
The Hoptimistic Brewery Ltd
The Inadequate Brewery Limited

Copley, Grace Maisie
Liquid Light Brewing Co Ltd

Corden, Matthew James
Drygate Brewing Co Ltd

Cordiner, George Ritchie
Bold Brewing Ltd

Cordrey, Lucy Catherine
Corinium Ales Ltd

Corke, Adrian
The Staffordshire Brewery Ltd

Cornelius, Tracey Jayne
Penzance Brewing Co Ltd

Corner, Raymond Jonathan
Brewit Microbrewery Ltd

Corr, Lesley Ann
Strands Brewery Ltd

Corr, Mark Edwin
Strands Brewery Ltd

Cosgrove, Peter
Tally Ho! Brewery Limited

Cottam, Simon Garth
John O'Groats Brewery Ltd

Cotton, Edward Dermot
The London Beer Factory Ltd.

Cotton, Neil Charles
The London Beer Factory Ltd.

Cotton, Simon Charles
The London Beer Factory Ltd.

Coulthwaite, Brian
Windermere Brewery Ltd

Courtenay, Roger Alan, Dr
Map Kernow Ltd.

Courtney, Gerard
Uncanny Valley Brewing Co Ltd

Coutts, Graeme Forbes
Devanha Brewery Holdings Ltd
Devanha Brewery Limited

Coventry, Ian Frederick
Bucket Brewing Co Ltd

Coverdale, Michael
The Three Counties Brewery Ltd

Cowan, Susan Bridget
Shottle Farm Brewery Ltd

Cowell, Adrian
The Proper Brewing Co Ltd

Cowell, Jamie Masters
Elements Brewing Co Ltd

Cowper, Timothy John
The Milton Brewery Cambridge Ltd

Cox, Andrea Sharon
Wily Fox Brewery Limited

Cox, Beverley Jean
Wily Fox Brewery Limited

Cox, Gareth
Pinnora Ltd

Cox, Gawain
Pinnora Ltd

Cox, Michael William
Wily Fox Brewery Limited

Cox, Russell
Staggeringly Good Ltd

Cox, Simon John
Cobra Beer Partnership Limited

Cox, Stephen
Utopian Brewing Limited

Cox, Tom
Boody Brewery Ltd.

Coxhead, Richard Neil
Hillfire Limited

Coyle, James Arthur
The Innis & Gunn Brewing Co Ltd
Innis & Gunn Holdings Limited

Cozzolino, Giorgio
Etrusca Brewery & Distillery in St. Andrews
Korca Brewery St Andrews Ltd

Cozzolino, Giorgio Cozzolino
A-Zero Energy Beer Limited
A & C Green Food and Beverage Ltd

Craig, Charles Thomas Garrioch
Genius Brewing Limited

Craig, Richard Andrew
Big Smoke Brew Co Limited

Craven, Aaron
Norn Iron Brew Co Ltd

Craven, Christopher John
The Dartmouth Brewing Co Ltd

Crawford, Rebecca Anne
Winchester Brewery Ltd

Crawley, Stephen Thomas
Higsons 1780 Limited
The Liverpool Craft Beer Co Ltd
Liverpool Craft Holdings Ltd
Liverpool Craft Limited

Creamer, Laurence James
Chichester Brewery Limited

Creighton, Richard John
Leadmill Brewery Limited

Crichton, Clare
Summershed Brewery Limited

Crichton, Simon Patrick
Summershed Brewery Limited

Crickmore, Adam
The Marches Brewery Limited

Cridland, David
Chevin Brew Co Ltd

Crocker, Christopher Robert
Good Kombucha Drinks Ltd

Crocker, Vincent
Ashley Down Brewery Limited

Crockett, Iain James
Severn Brewing Limited

Crockett, Michael Eric John
Ascent Location Solutions Ltd

Crockford, Alistair Martin
Elemental Brewing Ltd

Crofts, Henry Robert Brighton
Pointeer Ltd

Crosbie, Gary Stuart
The Mersey Gin Co Ltd

Cross, David
Avid Brewing Co. Ltd

Cross, James Phillip
Bad Joke Brew Co Ltd

Cross, Peter Michael
Cross Bay Brewery Limited
Morecambe Bay Wines Limited

Cross, Simon
J.W.Lees & Co.(Brewers) Ltd

Croston, Benjamin Thomas
Fuzzy Duck Brewery Limited

Crowley, Daniel Anthony
Abbey Ford Brewery Ltd

Crowther, Robert Alexander John
Bert and Chris Brew Beer Ltd

Crump, Jonathon Henry
Black Tor Brewery Ltd

Crump, Steve
Ghost Brewing Co Limited

Crutchley, Roy
Phipps Northampton Brewery Co Ltd

Cryan, Thomas Columba
Round Corner Brewing Ltd

Cryer, Catherine
London Cosmopolitan Drinks Ltd

Cuffe, James David
Jimbrew Ltd

Cullum, Timothy Edward
Bason Bridge Brewing Co Ltd

Cully, Richard Lewis
Burton Town Brewery Limited

Cummings, Rohan
Meantime Brewing Co Ltd

Cummings, Ryan Andrew
Pentrich Brewing Co. Ltd

Cunningham, Lea
888 Global Trade Ltd

Cunningham, Stephen
888 Global Trade Ltd

Cuppaidge, Jasper George
Camden Brewing Group Limited
Camden Town Brewery Limited

Curd, Matthew
Fallen Acorn Brewing Co. Ltd

Cureton, Christopher
The Bespoke Beer Co Ltd
RPM Brewery Ltd

Cureton, Samuel
RPM Brewery Ltd

Currie, Andrew
Chin Chin Brewing Co Ltd

Currie, David
Chin Chin Brewing Co Ltd

Curry, Carina Elena McKenzie
Wylam Brewery Limited

Curtis, Stephen Marshall
The Lingfield Brewing Co Ltd

Cussons, William John
Ferry Ales Brewery Limited

Cuthbertson, James Richard
The Dark Star Brewing Co Ltd

Czopik, Ryszard
Van Pur UK Ltd

Czubak, Michal
Saints Row Brewing Co Ltd

D'arcy, Sara
Irwell Works Brewery Ltd

D'elia, Giuseppe
Connecting Hops Ltd

D'este-Hoare, Amber Joy
The Leighton Buzzard Brewing Co Ltd

D'este-Hoare, Jonathan
The Leighton Buzzard Brewing Co Ltd

Dalby, Jennifer Kate
The Hand Brewing Co Ltd

Dale, Simon Christopher
The Cronx Brewery Limited

Dampney-Jay, Gail Joanna
Bestens Brewery Limited

Dampney-Jay, Steven Mark
Bestens Brewery Limited

Danby-Knight, Andrew Trevor William
Stag Ales Ltd

Daniell, Thomas Charles Averell
Old Tree Brewery Ltd

Darby, Alistair William
S.A.Brain & Co Ltd

Darby, Martyn James
The Untapped Brewing Co Ltd

Darke, Aaron Ross
Zymurgorium Ltd

Darke, Callum Thomas
Zymurgorium Ltd

Darlington, Peter Michael
The Urban Brewery Ltd

Daure, Silburn Augustus
London Cosmopolitan Drinks Ltd

Davenport, Caroline
Two Cocks Farm Limited

Davey, Giles Sinclair
Egghead Brewery Limited

Davey, Mark Charles
Epic Beers Limited

Davidson, John
The Great Glen Brewing Co Ltd

Davidson, Samuel
Halifax Steam Brewing Co Ltd

Davies, Anthony Raymond
Broadtown Brewery Ltd

Davies, Christopher
Ascot Ales Limited

Davies, Gareth Gwyn
Tamar Valley Brewing Co Ltd

Davies, James
Tapstone Brewing Co Ltd

Davies, James William, Dr
Alechemy Brewing Ltd

Davies, Owen Thomas
The Untapped Brewing Co Ltd

Davies, Paul
McGrath Davies Public Houses Ltd

Davies, Paul Thomas
London Fields Brewery Opco Ltd

Davies, Peter Stanley
Melin Tap Brewhouse Limited

Davies, Philip Glyn
Dartmoor Brewery Limited

Davies, Raymond Thomas
Grey Trees Brewery Limited

Davies, Thomas
Legless Brewing Ltd

Davis, Michael James
Hammerpot Brewery Limited

Davis, Nicholas Edward James
Hobsons Brewery and Co Ltd

Davis, Nicholas Paul
Brewboard Limited

Davis, Simon John
Serpent Brew Co Ltd

Davis, Stephen John
Sea Brewing Co Ltd

Davis, William Anthony
The Grainstore Brewery Limited
Stoney Ford Brew Co. Ltd

Dawkins, Glen
Dawkins & Georges Ltd
The Nungate Brewery Co Ltd
Steel Coulson Ltd

Dawson, Steven Joseph
Crooked Brewing Limited

Day, Matthew David
The Urban Brewery Ltd

Daykin, Philip John
Lincoln Green Brewing Co Ltd

Daykin, Robert
Bridlington Brewing Co. Ltd

Dayus, Christopher Jon
Bridgnorth Brewery Limited

De Silva, Nimmitha
Bear Brewery Co Ltd

De Smedt, Seraf
Jarr Kombucha Ltd

De-Gay, Stephen John
Wedmore Ales Ltd

Deacon, Jonathon Nelson
Test Brewing Ltd

Deal, Fiona
Wrytree Brewery Limited

Deal, John Kenneth
Wrytree Brewery Limited

Deal, Mike
Wildcraft Brewery Limited

Dean, Andrew Christopher
Coul Brewing Co Ltd

Deeley, William Stuart
Sandstone Brewery Ltd

Deighton, Justin Lance
The Beer Collective Limited
The Pink Ferry Ltd
The Sussex Beer Co Ltd
Two Tribes Brewing Ltd

Deighton, Nicola Ruth
The Beer Collective Limited
The Pink Ferry Ltd
The Sussex Beer Co Ltd
Two Tribes Brewing Ltd

Delap, Anastasia Diana
Fyne Ales Limited

Delap, James Robert Onslow
Fyne Ales Limited

Delap, Michael Jonathan Sinclair
Fyne Ales Limited

Delport, Anthony Michael
3 Bru's Brewing Co Ltd

Delvaux, Simon Yann Dominique
Jacobite Brewery Limited

Demirci, Ilyas
London Brewery Limited

Dempsey, James, Dr
Eyeball Brewing Ltd

Dempsey, Thomas Leo
Joseph Holt Group Limited
Joseph Holt Limited

Dempster, James Charles
Range Ales Brewery Limited

Denham, Matthew
UBrewCC Limited

Dennis, Thomas
Forest Hill Brewing Co Ltd

Dennison, Marian Sophia
Moody Goose Brewery Limited

Dent, Benjamin Thomas
Timothy Taylor & Co.,Limited

Dent, Sarah Louise
Timothy Taylor & Co.,Limited

Derbyshire, Mark Wayne
Aurora Ales Limited

Derry, Daniel Ironmonger
Newark Brewery Ltd

Derry, William Ironmonger
Newark Brewery Ltd

Desquesnes, Doreen
The Shefford Brewery Co. Ltd

Desquesnes, Michel Andre
B & T Brewery Limited

Deverell, Benjamin Robert
Deverell's Brewing Co Ltd

Deverell, Michael Robert
Deverell's Brewing Co Ltd

Devine, Jaime Clifford
Boozy Bods Ltd

Devon, Oliver James
AB InBev UK Limited
Camden Brewing Group Limited

Dewey, Timothy William
Timothy Taylor & Co.,Limited

Dhillon, Dalvinder Singh
Dhillons Brewery Ltd

Dhungana, Gokul Prasad
Kathmandu Link Limited

Diamond, Paul
Diamond Dicks Brewing Limited

Dickie, Alan Martin
Brewdog PLC
Overworks Limited

Dickinson, Paul Kenneth
Angles Ales Limited

Dickson, Andrew William
The West Berkshire Brewery PLC

Dickson, Brian Robert
Northern Monk Brewing Co. Ltd

Digby, Wilson
3SB Limited

Dimond, Paul Christopher
Branscombe Vale Brewery Ltd

Dineen, Leigh Andrew John
Gower Brewery Co Limited

Dixon, Alex Paul
Victor's Drinks Limited

Dobbin, Brendan Patrick
The Dobbins Guiltless Stout Co Ltd

Dobinson, Luke Ashley
Dovik Bast Ltd

Dobson, James Warren Diamond
Clavell & Hind Limited

Dobson, Nerys
Bragdy Nant Cyf

Dockerty, Robert Edward
Larkins Brewery Limited

Dodd, Christopher Edward
Three Brothers Brewing Co Ltd

Dodd, David William
Three Brothers Brewing Co Ltd

Dodd, Helen Louise
Dodd's Brewery Co. Limited

Dodd, Matthew
Nightowl Brewing Co Ltd

Dodd, Philip
Boutilliers Limited

Dodd, Simon Ray
The Dark Star Brewing Co Ltd

Dodd, Stephen John
Shere Brewery Ltd
Tillingbourne Brewery Ltd

Dodman-Edwards, Barry
Charlbury Brewing Co Ltd

Doherty, Damian John
Emperor's Brewery Ltd.

Doherty, Liam James
The Big Brewing Co Ltd

Doherty, Simon Thomas
Artisan Brewing Co Ltd

Dolan, Nicholas Joseph
Fulham Brewery Ltd
Woodforde's BPP Limited
Woodforde's Limited
Woodforde's Norfolk Ales Ltd

Dolphin, Laura
Dolphin Brewery Limited

Donald, Robert
Ellismuir Limited

Donaldson, Norman James
Fermanagh Beer Co Ltd

Donovan, Emma Clare
The Proud Peacock Limited

Dorber, Mark Lindsay
Dorber Brewing Limited

Dorrington, Timothy John
Littleover Brewery Limited

Dos Santos Neves, Ricardo
ZX Ventures Limited

Douglas, Jason Henry
Salopian Brewing Co Ltd.

Douglas, William
Axholme Brewing Co Ltd
Docks Beers Limited

Douws, Kevin Jean-Frederic
AB InBev UK Finance Co Ltd
AB InBev UK Investment Co Ltd
ABI SAB Group Holding Limited
ABI UK Holding 1 Limited
ALE Finance Services Limited
Anheuser-Busch Europe Limited

Dowell, Wesley Thomas
Lyme Bay Brewing Limited

Doyle, Simon Andrew
Birkenhead Brewery Co Ltd

Drabble, David James
Lithic Brewing Limited

Draper, Julian Geraint
JP Brew Limited

Drayton, Mark William
Kentish Town Brewery Limited

Drinnan, Kathryn
Stenroth Limited

Drummond, Christopher
Good Things Brewing Co Ltd

Drury, David
Black Market Brewery Limited

Duck, Ben
Gravity Well Brewing Co Ltd

Duckworth, Howard Mark
The Original Goole Brewery Co Ltd
Websters Brewery Ltd.

Dudman, Joanna
Battle Brewery Limited

Dudman, Robert William
Battle Brewery Limited

Duffy, Steven
Duffstar Brewing Limited

Dufourne, Paul Willem
ZX Ventures Limited

Dulieu, Nicola Joy
Adnams PLC

Dunbavan, Graham
Epic Beers Limited

Duncan - Dean, Robyn Christina Janet
Coul Brewing Co Ltd

Duncan, Kenneth
The Innis & Gunn Inveralmond Brewery

Duncan, Sandra Rowan
Coul Brewing Co Ltd

Duncan-Anderson, Jason Duncan
Red Squirrel Brewery Limited

Dunford, Timothy Richard
Green Jack Brewing Co Ltd

Dunkin, Margaret Susan
Flipside Brewing Ltd

Dunkley, Joshua Christian
Cornish Crown Limited

Dunlop, Alexander
Beltane Brewing Co Ltd

Dunn, Andrew
Black Angus Brewing Ltd

Dunn, Christopher
Monks Bridge Brewery Ltd

Dunning, Lee Nicholas
Mad Dog Brewing Co Ltd
Oakland Brewing Co Ltd

Dunning, Timothy John
Vyrnwy Developments Limited

Dunsmore, John Michael
The Edinburgh Beer Factory Ltd

Dunsmore, Lynne
The Edinburgh Beer Factory Ltd

Durand O'Connor, Karl Michael Robert
London Beer Lab Ltd

Durant, Mark Harvey
Heathen Brewers Limited

Durbridge, Kristy
Arcadian Brewing Co Ltd

Durrant, Neal
Nellyd Limited

Durritt, James Frederick
The Flying Fox Brewery Limited

Dusanj, Sudarghara Singh
Cains Limited

Duxon, Mark Steven
Star Wing Brewery Ltd

Dye, Giselle Jane Therese
Bellfield Brewery Limited

Dyer, John Bodrick
Oast House Breweries Cyf

Dyson, Sam
Track Brewing Co Ltd

Eardley, James Robert
The Ale Club Ltd

Eardley, Robert Carter
The Ale Club Ltd

Earley, Connor Declan
Bad Boy Brewing Ltd

Earnshaw, Paul David
Halifax Steam Brewing Co Ltd

Easterbrook, Beatrix Mary
Joseph Camm Farms Limited

Easterbrook, Mark
Joseph Camm Farms Limited

Eastwood, Anthony William
Tynemill Limited

Eastwood, David George
The Southsea Brewing Co Ltd

Eastwood, Lorna Elizabeth
The Southsea Brewing Co Ltd

Eaton, Charles Frederic
Nethergate Brewery Co Ltd

Eaton, Nick
The Proper Beer Co Ltd

Ebbetts, Ben
Stardust Brewery Ltd

Ebbetts, Martin Roland
Stardust Brewery Ltd

Eddison, Dominic
Boody Brewery Ltd.

Eddison, William John
Wharfedale Brewery Limited

Edge, Peter Mark
Hubsters Brewery Ltd

Edmond, Mark David
Black Hole Brewery Limited
The Little Eaton Brewery Co Ltd

Edmonds, Neil William
Bohem Brewery Ltd

Edney, Paul
Blindmans Brewery Limited

Edwards, Amanda Claire
Jon's Brewery Limited

Edwards, David Francis
Peakstones Rock Brewing Co Ltd

Edwards, James Francis
Peakstones Rock Brewing Co Ltd

Edwards, John
Frederic Robinson Limited

Edwards, John Stanley
WBC (Norfolk) Limited

Edwards, Kay Diane
Cambridge-Brewery Limited
WBC (Norfolk) Limited

Edwards, Robert Gwilym
Cwrw Llyn Cyf

Edwards, Samantha Mary
John Roberts Brewing Co Ltd

Edwards, Sion Morgan
Bragdy Mona Cyf

Edwards, Susan Mary
Peakstones Rock Brewing Co Ltd

Edwards, William George
Cambridge-Brewery Limited

Egan, Craig William
Egan & Martin Limited

Eksteen, Nadene
Vovin Ltd

Elberg, Alexander
Heineken UK Limited

Elder, Hamish Carlyon Rundle
Harvey & Son (Lewes) Limited

Elgood, Anne Mary
Elgood & Sons,Limited

Elgood, Nigel Stewart
Elgood & Sons,Limited

Elilio, Paul Francis
Wylde Sky Brewing Ltd

Ellar, Gregg
The Hildenborough Brewery Ltd

Ellenberg, Michael
Ellenberg's Brewery Ltd

Elliker, Ruth
Shelsley Brewing Co Ltd

Elliot, Nicholas Robertson
Greene King Brewing and Retailing

Elliott, Kevin Paul
Tollgate Brewery Limited

Elliott, Richard Mark
The Bears Den Brewery Limited

Elliott, Rosemary Ann
Church End Brewery Limited

Elliott, Samantha Jane
Evolution Brewing Ltd

Elliott, Stewart Martin
Church End Brewery Limited

Elliott-Berry, Clarice Bijou
Dowdeswell Brewery Limited

Ellis, Brett Joel
The Wild Beer Co Ltd

Ellis, Duncan
Long Man Brewery Limited

Ellis, James Douglas
Aston Manor Limited

Else, John Derek
George Bateman & Son Limited

Elvidge, Matthew
Farr Brew Ltd

Elvin, Jared
Lekker Days Ltd

Elvin, Peter
Penzance Brewing Co Ltd

Embling, Peter John
Tally Ho! Brewery Limited

Emeny, Simon
The Dark Star Brewing Co Ltd

Emirali, Cameron James
The Braybrooke Beer Co Ltd

Emmerson, Andrew
Solway Spirits Ltd

Emms, Robert Andrew
Bedlam Brewery Limited

Entwistle, Edward John
Hopjacker Brewery Ltd

Ericsson, Ivan Edward
The Lingfield Brewing Co Ltd

Ersando, Precious Anne
Alonaoracle Ltd

Erskine, Allan Robert
Colonsay Beverages Ltd.

Evans, Alison Frances
Odyssey Brew Co Ltd

Evans, Amy Ffion
Bluestone Brewing Co Ltd

Evans, Andrew John
Crooked Brewing Limited

Evans, Charles Lawrie
Townes Brewery Limited

Evans, Clare
Bullards Beers Limited

Evans, Debra
Peak Ales Limited

Evans, Emma Sarah
Old Farmhouse Brewery Ltd.
St Davids Farm Brewery Ltd
Upper Harglodd Farm Ltd

Evans, Gareth Alun
Faking Bad Brewery Limited

Evans, John Lawrence
Towcester Mill Brewery Limited

Evans, Julian Kendall
The Bushey Brewery Co Ltd

Evans, Marc
Rhymney Brewery Ltd

Evans, Mark Wyn Raymond
Old Farmhouse Brewery Ltd.
St Davids Farm Brewery Ltd
Upper Harglodd Farm Ltd

Evans, Michael
Bent Iron Brewing Co Ltd

Evans, Michael Llewellyn
Harbour Brewery Tenby Limited

Evans, Mitchell David
Odyssey Brew Co Ltd

Evans, Nicoleta Lenuta
Townes Brewery Limited

Evans, Philip John
Hope Brewery Ltd

Evans, Robat Rhys
Bragdy Mona Cyf

Evans, Robert Graham
Peak Ales Limited

Evans, Robin Wyn
Cwrw Ogwen Cyf

Evans, Russel Barrie
Bullards Beers Limited

Evans, Simon Ieuan
Dingbat Beer Ltd

Evans, Stephen Mark
Rhymney Brewery Ltd

Evans, Steven
Llangollen Brewery Ltd

Evans, Steven Vaughan
Abbey Grange Brewing Limited

Evans, William
Manchester Union Brewery Ltd

Evans, William Frederick
Lucky Cat Brewery Limited

Evans, William Peter Amery
Ignition Brewery Limited

Eveleigh, Eric Courtney Julian
Topsham Brewery Ltd

Everall, Jennifer Anne
Elgood & Sons,Limited

Everard, Julian William Spencer
Everards Brewery Limited

Everard, Richard Anthony Spencer
Everards Brewery Limited

Everatt, Barbara Ann
Totnes Brewing Co Limited

Ewing, Harry
Stay Gold Beer Co Ltd

Ewing, Thomas
Stay Gold Beer Co Ltd

Exell, Gary Paul
XL Brew Ltd

Faircliff, Samantha Jane
The Cairngorm Brewery Co Ltd

Fairpo, Charles Henry
The Angel Brewery Co Ltd

Falkingham, Guy Stuart
Anchor Brewery Ltd
Beverley Brewery Co Ltd
Hull Brewing Co Ltd
Humber Brewery Ltd
Yorkshire Brewing Co Ltd

Falkingham, Susan
Anchor Brewery Ltd
Beverley Brewery Co Ltd
Hull Brewing Co Ltd
Humber Brewery Ltd
Yorkshire Brewing Co Ltd

Fallen, Karen Belinda
Fallen Brewing Co Ltd

Fallen, Paul Raymond, Dr
Fallen Brewing Co Ltd

Fanner, Mark Ashley
The 3 Brewers Ltd

Faraday, Shaun
TW@ Limited

Faragher, David Richard
Wild Horse Brewing Co Ltd

Faragher, Emma Ruth
Wild Horse Brewing Co Ltd

Farmer, Christine Mary
Maldon Brewing Co Ltd

Farmer, Nigel Alfred
Maldon Brewing Co Ltd

Farmer, Thomas Andrew
Tom's Tap and Brewhouse Ltd

Farmer, William Albert
Veterans Brewing (South East) Ltd
Veterans Brewing Sussex Ltd

Farnfield, Samuel Albert Hughes
Splott Brewery Ltd

Farnworth, Frederick James
Blackdown Brewery Ltd
Brewbox Systems Ltd

Farquhar, Allan
John O'Groats Brewery Ltd

Farquharson, Rupert John Alexander
YB Ventures (2018) Ltd

Farr, Nick John
Farr Brew Ltd

Farran, James Francis
Summer Wine Brewery Limited

Farrell, Steven Charles
Wimborne Beer Co Ltd

Farrell, Susan
Equal Brewkery CIC

Farrington, Gregory Paul
The Near Beer Brewing Co. Ltd

Faulkner, Robert
Tenby Brewing Co. Limited

Fawcett, James
Another Beer Ltd

Fawson, Garry Nathan
North East Brewing Co Ltd

Fawson, Matthew Allan
North East Brewing Co Ltd

Fearnhead, Joseph Thomas
Alphabet Brewing Ltd

Fearon, Daren, Dr
Bellrock Brew Co. Ltd

Fegan, Kelly Shaun
Cornish Brewery Limited

Felce, Matthew John Walmsley
Cotton End Brewery Co Ltd

Fenton, Morris Hunter
Dead Fridge Farm Limited

Ferguson, George Robin Paget
Bristol Brewing Co Ltd

Fergusson, John David
Wetherby Brew Co Limited

Ferns, Marion
Toolmakers Brewery Limited

Ferns, Oliver
Toolmakers Brewery Limited

Ferrier, Michael Anthony
East Riding Brewery Ltd
Slow Beer Ltd

Ferriman, Andrew
George Samuel Brewing Co Ltd.

Field, Antony Malcolm
Kettlesmith Brewing Co Ltd

Field, Caroline Julie
Kettlesmith Brewing Co Ltd

Field, Robert Keith
Tamar Valley Brewing Co Ltd

Field-Gibson, Mark William
Crooked Brewing Limited

Fielding, Chrsitopher
Holy Well Brewing Ltd

Finch, Stephen William
Boxcar Brewery Limited

Findlay, Ralph Graham
Mansfield Brewery Trading Ltd
Marston's Acquisitions Limited
Marston's PLC

Fink, Martin
The Wild Beer Co Ltd

Fink, Robert
Big Drop Brewing Co Ltd

Finlay, Andrew Peter
Black Squirrel Brewing Limited

Finnerty, Antony Patrick
Finns (UK) Limited

Firth, Edward
Crazy Mountain Brewing Co UK Ltd

Fischer, Janet Ann Nichole
Beerfisch Brewery Limited

Fish, Gregory Michael
Compass Brewery Limited

Fisher, Hannah Magdaline
The Craft Soft Drinks Community Ltd

Fisher, Mike
Fisher's Brewing Co Ltd.

Fisher, Oliver
Brighton Bier Limited

Fitzpatrick, Daniel Paul
Gilt & Flint Ltd

Flavin, Michael Anthony
Wickwar Wessex Brewing Co Ltd

Fleming, Nicholas Cain Kinrade
Ovenstone 109 Limited

Fleming, Sean Woelfell
Little Wolf Brewing Limited

Florit, Thierry
Green Times Brewing Limited

Flynn, Kevin Paul
L1 Brewer Ltd

Foat, Kyle Edward
Gil's Brewery Ltd

Fogg, Janet Diane
St. Peter's Brewery Co. Ltd
St. Peter's Brewery Group PLC
St. Peter's Trading Co. Ltd

Foggo, Ross
Silks Brewery Limited

Foley, Conor
Swift Half Collective Ltd

Folkard, Nicholas John
FGW Brewery Limited

Folleas, Caroline
Innis & Gunn Holdings Limited

Foots, John Richard
Camerons Brewery Limited

Forbes, Andrew
Cotswold Lion Brewery Ltd
Festival Brewery Ltd.

Ford, Cheryl Denise
Somerset Ales Limited

Ford, Steven Robert
Dore Brewery Limited

Forde, David Michael
Caledonian Brewery Limited
Heineken UK Limited

Foreman, Keith Nicholas
Honest Brew Ltd

Foroshani, Keyvan
K1 Beer PLC

Forrest, Rory George
Scot Brew Limited

Foster, Adam Paul
3SB Limited

Foster-Hird, Nicola Jane
Trumark Properties Limited

Foulkes, Lesley Stephens
Langham Brewing Co Ltd
Sativa Brewing Co Ltd

Fowlestone, Mark Garry, Dr
71 Brewing Limited

Fownes, David Reginald
Fownes Brewing Co Ltd.

Fownes, James David
Fownes Brewing Co Ltd.

Fownes, Thomas David
Fownes Brewing Co Ltd.

Fox, Dean Sylvester
Sly Fox Brewery Ltd

Fox, Jody Nicholas
Moody Fox Ltd.

Fox, Madelaine Grace
Malts & Hops Brewing Limited

Fox, Vernon
Lough Neagh Distillers - 1837 Ltd

Fozard, Ian
Roosters Brewery Limited
Roosters Brewing Co Ltd

Fozard, Oliver Edward
Roosters Brewery Limited
Roosters Brewing Co Ltd

Fozard, Thomas Martin
Roosters Brewery Limited
Roosters Brewing Co Ltd

Francis, Stephen Edwin
Elland Brewery Limited

Francis, Terri Nicole
Camden Town Brewery Limited
ZX Ventures Limited

Francis, Timothy Richard Charles Wayman
The Langford Brewing Co. Ltd

Francis-Baum, Marc
Grace Land Beer Limited

Franks, Gary John
Kimberley Brewery Limited
Kimberley Brewing Co Ltd

Fraser, Leslie Peter
Fisher's Brewing Co Ltd.

Fraser, Rupert Michael
Woodforde's BPP Limited
Woodforde's Limited

Frederick, John Mario
Brampton Brewery Ltd

Freeland, William James Henry
Bays Brewery Limited

Freeman, Benjamin Jack
Pressure Drop Brewing Limited

Freeman, Dougal
Mudlark Investments Ltd

Freemantle, Mark Beckett
The Wombourne Brewing Co Ltd

Fremlin-Key, William George
Fremlins Limited

French, Ross David
Another Brewery Limited

French, Zina Clare
Parkway Brewing Co Ltd

Friedrich, Carley
Brightside Brewing Co Ltd

Friedrich, Lance
Brightside Brewing Co Ltd

Friedrich, Maxine Louise
Brightside Brewing Co Ltd

Friedrich, Neil
Brightside Brewing Co Ltd

Frost, Dan Adrian
Lakehouse Brewing Co Ltd

Frost, David
The Romford Brewery Co Ltd

Frost, Ian Tinsley
Wickwar Wessex Brewing Co Ltd

Frost, Jason David
The Romford Brewery Co Ltd

Frost, Roger Denis
Scribbler's Ales Limited

Fry-Stone, Rory
Pilgrim Brewery (Reigate) Ltd

Fryer, Anthony Robert
Charles Wells Brewery Limited
Charles Wells, Limited

Fuller, Richard Hamilton Fleetwood
The Dark Star Brewing Co Ltd

Furlong, Max Leon
Incapico Inc Limited

Furniss, Ian William
George Bateman & Son Limited

Fussell, Clive
The Milton Brewery Cambridge Ltd

Fussell, David
Floff UK Limited

Fyfe, Camilla
Kinkell Brewery Ltd

Fyfe, Rory John
Kinkell Brewery Ltd

Gadd, George Edward Charles
Ramsgate Brewery Limited

Gadd, Lois Elizabeth
Ramsgate Brewery Limited

Gaffey, Janet Elaine
Wrexham Lager Beer Co Ltd

Gait, Simon Rhodri
Twisted Oak Brewery Ltd

Galaun, Jeremy Daniel
Brixton Brewery Limited

Gale, Paul Antony
Gales Brewery Limited

Gallen, Kevin Joseph
Soho Brewing Ltd

Gannaway, Graham John
SchoolHouseBrewery Ltd

Gardiner, Thomas
Lawman Brewing Company, Ltd.

Gardner, Charlene Louise
The Oxted Brewery Ltd

Gardner, David James
The Oxted Brewery Ltd

Gardner, Laura Elizabeth
Tonbridge Brewery Limited

Gardner, Mark Wotton
Tonbridge Brewery Limited

Gargiulo, Pasquale
Gargiulo's Production Ltd

Garland, David George
Frontier Brewing Co Ltd

Garner, Philip John
Blue Bee Brewery Ltd

Garner, Richard
First Chop Brewing Arm Ltd

Garnett, Anita
Ulverston Brewing Co Ltd

Garrett, Michael William
Dolphin Brewery Poole Ltd

Garrett, Paul
Crafty Monkey Brewing Co Ltd

Gartland, Anthony
Saltaire Brewery Limited

Gartland, Tony
Bluestone Brewing Co Ltd

Garton, Francesca Elizabeth Lee
Wiper & True Ltd.

Garwood, Ben
Ground Hammer Beer Co Ltd

Gaughan, Felicity Jane
The Atlantic Craft Soda Co Ltd

Gaughan, Gerard Brendan
The Atlantic Craft Soda Co Ltd

Gautam, Shyam Mani
Kathmandu Link Limited

Gazmararian, Jeremy John
Two Rabbit Brewing Co Ltd

Geeves, Henry Hugo
Geeves Brewery Limited

Geeves, Peter Michael
Geeves Brewery Limited

Gehrman, Carl
Wensleydale Brewery (2013) Ltd

Geldard, Jack
Big Mountain Brewing Co Ltd

Gemski, Dominic
Phantom Brewing Co. Limited

Gent, Daniel Peter
Salamander Brewing Co Ltd

Gentle, Dene Martyn
Salisbury Brewery Limited

George, Ian
Smoky Dragon Brewery & Preservas

George, Michael MacKenzie
The Salcombe Brewery Co. Ltd

Georgel, Kevin Roger
St.Austell Brewery Co Ltd

Geupel, Erik Arnold
Geipel Brewing Limited

Ghulati, Tarun
1st Icon Ltd

Gibb, Gary
Metcalfe & Metcalfe Co Ltd

Gibbons, Andrew William
Amwell Springs Brewery Co Ltd

Gibbons, David Ernest
Amwell Springs Brewery Co Ltd

Gibbons, Michael David
Amwell Springs Brewery Co Ltd

Gibbs, Steven
The Durham Brewery Limited

Gibson, Catherine
Devon Ales Limited

Gibson, John
Devon Ales Limited

Gibson, Mark
Sentinel Brewery Holdings Ltd

Gibson, Paul Andrew
The Campervan Brewery Ltd

Gilbert, James
Hybrid Brewing Ltd

Gilbert, John Michael
Hop Back Brewery PLC

Gilbey, David George
Over The Hill Brewery Ltd

Gilbody, Lindsey Ann
Deva Craft Beer Ltd

Gilbody, Neil Adrian
Deva Craft Beer Ltd

Giles, Ian
Posh Boys Brewery Limited

Giles, Peter George
Broadway Brewery Ltd

Giles, Rebekah Emily
Killer Hop Brew Co Ltd

Gill, John Richard
Bradfield Brewery Limited

Gill, Leslie Allan
Donkeystone Brewing Co Ltd

Gill, Navinder Kaur
LVS Bottling Limited

Gill, Richard William
Bradfield Brewery Limited

Gill, Steven
McMullen & Sons, Limited

Gill, Susan
Bradfield Brewery Limited

Gill, Thomas Edward
Stancill Brewery Limited

Gillam, Matthew John
Faultline Brew Co. Ltd

Gillespie, Anthony
Zulu Alpha Brewing Limited

Gillians, Daniel Matthew
Three Engineers Brewery Ltd

Gillies, Ewen Alexander
Applecross Brewing Co Ltd

Gilligan, John
Drygate Brewing Co Ltd

Gilliland, Stewart Charles
Curious Drinks Limited

Gillingham, Valerie
Gemstone Ales Ltd.

Girdham, Ruth Margaret
Joseph Camm Farms Limited

Girvan, Catriona
Great Glen Trading Centre Ltd

Girvan, George Wilson
Great Glen Trading Centre Ltd

Girvan, Robbie James Macpherson
Great Glen Trading Centre Ltd

Gladwin, David John
Black Isle Brewing Co Ltd

Gladwin, Julia-Jane Kristen
Black Isle Brewing Co Ltd

Gleadowe, Frederick Joseph York, Dr
Shandy Shack Ltd

Gledhill, George
The Three Counties Brewery Ltd

Glickman, Catherine Janet
Marston's PLC

Gloyens, Mark Ashley
Rebellion Beer Co Ltd

Gloyens, Paul Russell
Rebellion Beer Co Ltd

Glyn, Richard Rufus Francis
Brewers Folly Brewery Ltd.

Goddard, Alix Ormond
Goddards Brewery Limited

Goddard, Anthony Howard
Goddards Brewery Limited

Goddard, Janet Margaret
Goddards Brewery Limited

Goddard, Marcus Garry Edward
3 Cities Brewing Co Ltd

Godman, James Edward, Dr
Wilderness Brewery Ltd

Goff, Marcus James
Goff's Brewery Limited

Gol-Shecan, Datis
Growler Swap Ltd
Recognise Limited

Gold, Simon
Boxcar Brewery Limited

Gomes, Carlos Eduardo Santos
Br3wery Ltd

Gonzalez Moore, Jorge Gabriel
The Ridgeside Brewing Co Ltd

Goodbody, Peter Nicholas
The Lingfield Brewing Co Ltd

Goode, Phillip John
Bear's Head Brewery Limited

Goodhew, Paul Geoffrey
Malts & Hops Brewing Limited

Goodliffe, Andrew Duncan
Framework Brewery Limited

Goodman, Mark
Wildcraft Brewery Limited

Goodwin, David Jonathan
Black Eagle Brewery Ltd

Goodwin, Ian
Welbeck Abbey Brewery Limited

Goody, Karen
Goody Ales Limited

Gopaul, Misha
Big Mountain Brewing Co Ltd

Gordon, Ewen James
Saltaire Brewery Limited

Gordon, Mark Charles
The Wimbledon Brewery Co Ltd

Gordon-Leaf, Jake Laurance
Allbeer Limited

Gorecki, Matthew Stefan
Zapato Brewery Ltd.

Gorensweigh, John Nicholas
Alcazar Brewing Co Ltd
Sherwood Forest Brewing Co Ltd

Gorna, Barbara Elizabeth
Bad Girls Brew Limited

Gorosabel, Hector
Meantime Brewing Co Ltd

Gorton, David John
The Margate Brewery Limited

Gough, Katy
Rogue Elephant Brewery Limited

Gough, Mick
Rogue Elephant Brewery Limited

Gould, Stephen
Everards Brewery Limited

Goulding, Lee
Big Lamp Brewers Limited

Grabham, Lee David
Brew York Limited

Grady, Mark David
360 Degree Brewing Co Ltd

Grae, Steven Phillip
Affinity Brewing Co Ltd

Graeber, Grant Kelly
The Mad Yank Brewery Ltd

Graeber, Larissa Michelle
The Mad Yank Brewery Ltd

Graham, Andrew
The Wye Brewing Co Ltd

Graham, Christopher
Blackhill Brewery Limited

Graham, Derrick John
Devon Ales Limited

Graham, Jonathan
Trumark Properties Limited

Graham, Michael
Credence Brewing Ltd

Grainger, Justin
Nethergate Brewery Co Ltd

Grainger, Kevin Gawn
St Andrews Brewing Co Holdings Ltd

Grainger, Richard Stuart
Butcombe Brewery Limited
Butcombe Brewing Co Ltd
Butcombe Pubco Limited
The Long Ashton Cider Co Ltd

Granger, Jack William
Left Handed Giant Brewing Ltd
Left Handed Giant Ltd.

Grannell, Aidan
Tipsy Angel Brewery Ltd

Grant, David
Fierce Beer Limited

Grant, Ian David
Bishop's Crook Brewery Ltd.

Grant, Niall Gordon Forrest
Foxhat Beer Limited

Granville, Edward Mauger
Stewart Brewing Limited

Grattidge, Toby David
Abbeydale Brewery Limited

Graves, Nicolas Kyle
Gan Yam Brewing Co Ltd

Gray, Bruce
Left Handed Giant Brewing Ltd
Left Handed Giant Ltd.

Gray, Lucinda Rachel
Hall & Woodhouse Limited

Gray, Nicholas
Box Brewery Ltd

Greaves, Mark David
Manning Brewers Ltd

Green, Adam
Old Street Brewery Ltd

Green, Allison Dawn
Brewdog PLC

Green, David
Ramsgate Brewery Limited

Green, David Benjamin
Epic Brewing Limited

Green, George Barrie
The Whitstable Brewery Co Ltd

Green, Harry Rupert
Burnt Hill Brewery Limited

Green, James Daniel Watts
The Whitstable Brewery Co Ltd

Green, Laura Aileen
Barefaced Brewing Ltd

Green, Louis-Anton Robert
Paper Fort Brew Co Ltd.

Green, Richard Watts
The Whitstable Brewery Co Ltd

Green, Thomas
The Staffordshire Brewery Ltd

Greenfield, James
Nauticales Ltd

Greenfield, Tristian
Snowdon Craft Beer Limited

Greenhalgh, Nicholas Anthony
Pomona Island Brew Co Ltd

Greensmith, Thomas David Glenton
No Abode Brew Co Ltd

Greetham, Paul William
Beatnikz Republic Brewing Co Ltd

Greggor, Charles Keith
Brewdog PLC

Gregory, Adam David
Beavertown Brewery Ltd

Gregory, Justin
Thunder and Little Ltd

Gregson, Stephen
Littondale Brewing Co Ltd

Greier, Patrick
Bavarian Gold Limited

Gretton, Rachel Lucy
Brockley Brewing Co Ltd.

Grieve, Ian
Hopper House Brew Farm Ltd

Griffin, Anna Elizabeth Clare
J.W.Lees & Co.(Brewers) Ltd

Griffith, Dyfed Wyn
Cwrw Llyn Cyf

Griffiths, Euron Wyn
Cwrw Llyn Cyf

Griffiths, Mark John
71 Brewing Limited

Griffiths, Paul David
Genesis Craft Ales Limited

Grigorov, Aleksandar Vladimirov
Portishead Brewing Co Ltd

Grime, Hugh
Hops and Dots Brewing Co Ltd

Grimsdale, Mark John Hart, Mr
WantsumBrewery Ltd

Grimshaw, Lucinda Celia, Dr
Clarkshaws Brewing Co Ltd.

Grocott, Susan Mary
Mart's Brewing Co Ltd

Grundy, James John
Small Beer Brew Co. Ltd

Grunnill, Mark Eugino
Unsworth's Yard Brewery Ltd

Gudgin, John
Bubble Works Brew Co Ltd

Guest, Katie Jayne
Brewery Z Ltd

Guest, Timothy Lawrence Peter
Brewery Z Ltd

Gunnarsson Lundgren, Anna Cecilia
Carlsberg UK Limited

Gunnett, Roger Henry
Holcot Hop-Craft Ltd

Gupta, Akshit Raj
3ABC Ltd
Jocks and Peers Brewing Co Ltd

Gurner, Christopher
The Gentleman Bear Brewing Co Ltd

Gurung, Purna
Kuwa Trading Ltd

Gurung, Sirish
Kuwa Trading Ltd

Guy, Lauren
Origami Brewing Co Ltd.

Guy, Martin Richard
Canterbrew Ltd

Gyngell, John Christopher
North Brewing Co Ltd

Gyuricza, Christian Matyas
Aquila Visum Ltd

Habtezghi, Pawlos
Robel Pawlos Ltd

Hadfield-Hyde, Sebastian James Anthony Aiden
Kimbland Distillery Ltd

Hadingham, John Anthony
St. Peter's Brewery Co. Ltd
St. Peter's Brewery Group PLC
St. Peter's Trading Co. Ltd

Hague, Adam Gary, Dr
Stancill Brewery Limited

Haigh, Abigail
Lord Randalls Brewery Ltd

Haigh, Joanna, Dr
Potton Brewing Co Ltd

Haigh, Richard
Potton Brewing Co Ltd

Hainsworth, Stewart Andrew
Hawkshead Brewery Limited
Windsor Castle Brewery Limited

Hale, Richard Trevor
The Parbold Bottle Limited

Hales, Julian Edmund
Indian Summer Brewing Co. Ltd

Haley, Matthew Alan
To The Moon Brewery Ltd

Halford, David Stuart
Donkeystone Brewing Co Ltd

Halkett, Harry Watt
The Monks Well Brewing Co Ltd

Hall, Benjamin David
Cotton End Brewery Co Ltd

Hall, Charles Darcy Richard
Inkerman Ales Limited

Hall, Christopher Randall
Deil's Heid Brewing Co Ltd

Hall, Daryl
Ten Tors Brewery Ltd

Hall, Jill
Breworks Ltd
Great British Breworks Ltd

Hall, Michael
The Gentleman Bear Brewing Co Ltd

Hall, Philip Robert
Breworks Ltd
Great British Breworks Ltd

Hall, Tristan
Great British Breworks Ltd

Hallam, Daniel
Fire Rock Brewing Co Ltd.

Hallgato, Rita
ZX Ventures Limited

Halliday, David John
The Bridgehouse Pub Co Ltd

Halliday, David Jonathan
Bridge House Brewery Limited

Halligan, Michelle
Mr Bees Brewery Ltd

Halls, Hilary Anne
Grain Brewery Limited

Halls, Phil
Grain Brewery Limited

Halsey, Paul
Purity Brewing Co Ltd

Ham, Jeremy Robert
Cheddar Ales Limited

Ham, Lucy
Cheddar Ales Limited

Hamer, Vincent
Rock Solid Brewing Co Ltd

Hamilton, Robert
Blackjack Beers Limited

Hamilton, Ross Robert
Beltane Brewing Co Ltd

Hamilton, Ross William
Edinbrew Ltd

Hammersley, George Douglas
Ethical Ales Limited
Roddenloft Brewery Ltd

Hammond, Peter Clark
Carlsberg Supply Company UK Ltd

Hammond, Steven Michael
Republic of Beer Ltd

Hammond, Thomas James
Amwell Springs Brewery Co Ltd

Hampshaw, David
Whitefaced Ltd

Hampshaw, Sarah Louise
Whitefaced Ltd

Hampshire, John
Howard Town Brewery Limited

Hancock, Darran
Copper Dragon Brewery Limited

Hancock, Edward
Marston's Acquisitions Limited

Hand, Richard Michael
Taddington Brewery Limited

Handevidt, Victoria Phyllis
The Krafty Braumeister Ltd

Handford, Ben Dawson
Three Arches Brewing Limited
Unicorn Craft Brewing Co Ltd

Handley, Michael John
Worfield Brewery Limited

Handy, Robert Mark
Konigsberg Seven Bridges Breweries Ltd

Hangrad, Joanne Louise
Pumphouse Brewing Co Ltd

Hangrad, Zsolt
Pumphouse Brewing Co Ltd

Hanjra, Manjit Singh
Punjabi Ltd

Hanlon, Steve
Utopian Brewing Limited

Hannah, Simon John
Clan Brewing Co Ltd

Hannaway, Christopher John
Infinite Session Ltd

Hannaway, Philip Francis
Ol Brewery Limited

Hannaway, Thomas Eamon
Infinite Session Ltd

Hannon, Thomas
Liquid Revolution Ltd

Hanson, Bob
Muswell Hillbilly Brewers Ltd

Harding, Gary
Whitley Bay Brewing Co Ltd

Harding, Miles
Mister A's Beer Co Ltd

Hardman, Michael
1533 Brewery Limited

Hardwick, Rosemary Clare
The Roebuck Brewing Co Ltd

Hardy, Philippa Alexis
Eyes Brewing Limited

Hares, David Anthony
Nothing Bound Brewing Co Ltd

Harford, Edward Scandrett
Wadworth and Co Ltd

Harkin, Nicholas Paul
Brewhouse Brewery Limited

Harkis, Graham
Soul Doubt Brewing Co Ltd

Harnischfeger, Christian Wilhelm Walter
Beersheba Ltd

Harper, Ian
Urban Alchemy Brewing Co Ltd

Harper, Simon David
Mashionistas Brewing Co Ltd

Harris, Dean Patrick
Brewers Folly Brewery Ltd.

Harris, Edward Barnaby
Barnaby's Brewhouse Ltd

Harris, Jeremy Ziggy Sidney
Vandal Brewing Co Ltd

Harris, Leanne
Derby Brewing Co Ltd

Harris, Linda Ann
Derby Brewing Co Ltd

Harris, Meg
Botley Brewery Ltd

Harris, Nathan
Harr Engineering Limited

Harris, Paul Andrew
Derby Brewing Co Ltd

Harris, Paul James
Stod Fold Brewing Limited

Harris, Stephen
Bucklebury Brewers Ltd

Harris, Trevor Andrew
Derby Brewing Co Ltd

Harris, William John
Wild Card Brewery Limited

Harrison, Adam Oliver
Damnation Breweries Limited
Damnation Limited

Harrison, Ben
Brew & Bottle Limited

Harrison, Ben Alexander
Hambleton Brewery Limited

Harrison, James Robert
The Thornbridge Hall Country House Brewing Co

Harrison, Rachel Clare
Hambleton Brewery Limited

Harrison, Richard Willoughby
Papworth Brewery Limited

Harrison, Shaun
Vision Brewing Co Ltd

Harrison, Stuart Joseph
Harrison's Brewery Ltd

Harrison-Hawkes, Christopher Lloyd
Harrison's Brewery Ltd

Harrison-Ward, David
Macclesfield Brewing Co Ltd

Harrop, Christopher Samuel
Bert and Chris Brew Beer Ltd

Harrow, Timothy James
Foghorn Brew Co Ltd

Hart, Robert
Cotton End Brewery Co Ltd
Hart Family Brewers Limited

Hart, Sarah Helen
Hart Family Brewers Limited

Hartley, Jonathan
Blackjack Beers Limited

Harvey, Daniel
Radio City Beer Works Limited

Harvey, Dominic
Staffordshire Spirits Co Ltd

Harvey, Duncan George
Woodforde's BPP Limited
Woodforde's Limited

Harvey, George Martin
Haresfoot Storage & Distribution Co Ltd

Harvey, Richard Charles
Goddards Brewery Limited

Harwood, Benjamin Nicholas
The Wicked Hog Brewery Ltd

Harwood, Paul
Birmingham Brewing Co Ltd

Harwood, Sally Jane
The Wicked Hog Brewery Ltd

Haslam, Paul
Bad Boy Brewing Ltd

Haslam, Peter
Mayflower Brewery Ltd
Smith and Jones Brewery Ltd

Haspel, Carl Andrew
Black Hole Brewery Limited
The Little Eaton Brewery Co Ltd

Haspineall, Scott
1936 Limited
Staff Beer Ltd

Hatch, John Vincent
1533 Brewery Limited

Hatfield, Sarah Lorrain
Pumphouse Brewing Co Ltd

Hatherley, James William
Unity Brewing Ltd

Hattersley, David John
Brampton Brewery Ltd

Hattrick, Gavin John
Whitley Bay Brewing Co Ltd

Hawes, Eimear Anthony
Fishponds Brewery Ltd

Hawes, Oisin Senan
Fishponds Brewery Ltd

Hawke, Justin Craig
Moor Beer Co Ltd

Hawke, Maryann Min-Yen
Moor Beer Co Ltd

Hawkins, Ian Mark
Bedlam Brewery Limited

Hawkins, Martin John
Hawkins Drinks Limited

Hawthornthwaite, Julian Mark
Malvern Hills Brewery Limited

Hay, Graeme
Keith Brewery Limited
Spey Valley Brewery Limited

Haycraft, Alexander Richard
Blueball Brewery Ltd

Hayes, Robert William John
Hop & Stagger Brewery Ltd

Hayes, Ryan
Chain House Brewing Co Ltd

Hayes, Samantha
Hop & Stagger Brewery Ltd

Hayles, Debra Sarah
Twisted Oak Brewery Ltd

Hayles, Keith Anthony
Twisted Oak Brewery Ltd

Haynes, Caoimhe
Delphic Brewing Co Ltd

Hayward, Brian David
The Silverstone Real Ale Co Ltd

Hayward, Susan Jane
The Team Toxic Ltd

Haywood, William Robert
Mart's Brewing Co Ltd

Hazeldene, Elizabeth Jane
The Boat Lane Brewery Limited

Hazeldene, Ian
The Boat Lane Brewery Limited

Hazell, Alison
Jaw Brew Ltd

Hazell, Helen Alison
The Jaw Brewery Ltd

Hazell, Simon Mark
Jaw Brew Ltd
The Jaw Brewery Ltd

Heaher, Michael
Tantum Brewing Limited

Heal, Alexander Maximilian Carlton
Lost Roots Limited

Heald, Michael Guy Hilliard
Adnams PLC

Heap, Malcolm Stuart Joseph
Black Eagle Brewery Ltd

Heard, Elizabeth Anne
Tintagel Brewery Limited

Heard, John Reford
Tintagel Brewery Limited

Hearle, Emma
Black Eagle Brewery Ltd

Hearn, Christopher
The Loddon Brewery Ltd

Hearn, Vanessa Ann
The Loddon Brewery Ltd

Heath, Christopher Philip
Wylde Sky Brewing Ltd

Heath, Richard Stuart
Keltek Cornish Brewery Limited

Heath, Stuart
Keltek Cornish Brewery Limited

Heath, William Generald Charles
Keltek Cornish Brewery Limited

Heaven, Charles Lewin
BAA Brewing Limited

Heaven, Sian Elizabeth
BAA Brewing Limited

Heffron, James Robert
Verdant Brewing Co Ltd

Heinzel, Glenn
Tankley's Brewery Limited

Helliwell, Nicholas James
Saltaire Brewery Limited

Helm, Andrew Paul
The Revolutions Brewing Co Ltd

Hely-Hutchinson Graves, Oliver
The Devil's Pleasure Limited

Hemingway, Ian Keith
Little Ox Brewery Limited

Hemingway, Jonathan Mark
Horbury Ales Limited

Hemingway, Richard Barry
Horbury Ales Limited

Hemingway, Stephen John
Mill Valley Brewery Limited

Hemmings, Martin
Tankley's Brewery Limited

Hemple, Bradley Charles
Bib Brewing Ltd

Hemus, Michael-George Carwardine
Black Eagle Brewery Ltd

Hender, Alison Jane
Castle Combe Brewery Limited

Hender, Martin William
The Flying Monk Brewery Ltd

Hender, Martin William
Castle Combe Brewery Limited

Hender, William Thomas
Castle Combe Brewery Limited

Henderson, Adam Roderick
Neon Raptor Brewing Co Ltd.

Henderson, Ian
The Bespoke Brewing Co. Ltd

Henderson, James Allen
Sulwath Brewers Limited

Henderson, John Ronald Ogilvie
Scottish Borders Brewery Ltd

Henderson, Sandra Louise Hague
The Bespoke Brewing Co. Ltd

Hendry-Prior, Benjamin James
Lion Brewery Co. Limited

Henry, Michael Gainford
3 Piers Brewery Limited

Henry, Sean Blair Justin
Honest Brew Ltd

Hensby, William Mark
Liverpool Brewery Limited

Heptinstall, Stephen Barry
Cotleigh Brewery Limited

Hepworth, Andrew Charles Hamilton
Hepworth & Company Brewers Ltd

Hepworth, Paul Anthony Charles
J. Church Brewing Co. Ltd

Herbert, Elliot William
Lyme Bay Brewing Limited

Herbert, Paul Roy
Kent Brewery Ltd

Herbert, Raymond Peter
Bucklebury Brewers Ltd

Herman, Ashley John
The Crafty Brewing Co. Limited

Herman, Luke Arthur John
The Crafty Brewing Co. Limited
The Crafty Brewing Co Ltd
The Real Crafty Brewing Co Ltd

Herriman, Sarah Louise
The West Berkshire Brewery PLC

Herrington, Andrew Mark
Ainsty Ales Limited

Hesketh-Crafts, Claire Louise
7 Reasons To Brew Ltd

Heslip, Philip Andrew
Roseland Brewery Limited

Hess, Ryan
SK Brew Ltd

Hesse, Laurence Hamilton
Murree Breweries (UK) Limited

Hester, Karen
Adnams PLC

Hewett, Keith Edward
Frome Brewing Co Ltd

Hewitt, Derwyn
Argyll Breweries Limited
Isle of Mull Brewing Co Ltd

Hewitt, Ian
Second Wave Brewing Ltd

Hewitt, James Steven
Red Moon Brewery Limited

Hibbard, Anthony David
The Flying Monk Brewery Ltd

Hibbert, Marcus
River Widow Brewery Ltd

Hibling, Stuart
Heathen Brewers Limited

Hick, Lucy Claire
Allendale Brew Co Ltd

Hick, Thomas James Augustine
Allendale Brew Co Ltd

Hickling, John
Vocation Brewery Limited

Hicks, Lucy Alexandra
The Glenfinnan Brewing Co Ltd
Tirindrish Trading Co Ltd
West Highland Breweries Ltd

Hicks, Matheau
Polarity Brewing Ltd

Hide, Sarah
Hardstate Limited

Hieghton-Jackson, Timothy
Clavell & Hind Limited

Higginbotham, Paul
Lock 34 Brew Co. Limited

Higginbotham, Sean
Lock 34 Brew Co. Limited

Higgitt, Duncan Laurence
Rival Brewing Co Limited

Higgitt, Samuel Duncan
Rival Brewing Co Limited

Higgs, David Edwin
The Hartlebury Brewing Co Ltd

Hill, Alex Edward
Green Duck Beer Co. Limited

Hill, Carole Michelle
Highland Brewing Co Ltd

Hill, Colin
Rectory Ales Limited

Hill, David
Small World Beers Ltd

Hill, Lewis Oliver
Highland Brewing Co Ltd

Hill, Mark Adrian Bryan
Salopian Brewing Co Ltd.

Hill, Michael Thomas
Mid-Cheshire Brewing Ltd

Hill, Robert Joseph
Highland Brewing Co Ltd

Hill, Rowan
The Bespoke Brewing Co. Ltd

Hill, Sharon
The Bespoke Brewing Co. Ltd

Hillhouse Figurelli, Paulo Jose
Wylde Sky Brewing Ltd

Hillier, Adrian Charles
Hill House Inns Limited

Hills, Peter John
Hackney Brewery Ltd

Hinchley, Neil Robert
Crate Bars Limited
Crate Brewery Limited
Jarr Kombucha Ltd

Hind, Jeffrey John
Consett Ale Works Limited

Hind, Lynn
Consett Ale Works Limited

Hindmarch, Ingvild Leslyn
WantsumBrewery Ltd

Hine, Lucy Catherine
East Neuk Organic Brewing & Distilling

Hinsley, Julie
St. Peter's Brewery Co. Ltd
St. Peter's Brewery Group PLC

Hipwell, Adrian Paul
Ampersand Brew Co Ltd

Hipwell, Andrew James
Ampersand Brew Co Ltd

Hird, Mark
Sonnet 43 Brewery Ltd
Trumark Properties Limited

Hirst, John
Brampton Brewery Ltd

Hiscock, Michael George
Elland Brewery Limited

Hislop, Mark
Hale Brewing Limited

Hoare, David Harry Christopher
Hall & Woodhouse Limited

Hobby, Matthew James
Weymouth Brewery Limited

Hobday, John Henly
Anspach & Hobday Limited

Hobden, Charles Frederick
The Wessex Brewery Limited

Hobden, Louise Natalie
The Wessex Brewery Limited

Hobson, Anthony Alexander
Fosse Way Brewing Co Ltd.

Hochuli, Roman, Dr
Biercafe Ltd
Solvay Brewing Ltd

Hoddinott, Martin James Charles
Maverick Brewing Co Ltd

Hodge, Peter Robert
Bowtie Brewers Limited

Hodges, Matthew Simon
3ways Brewing Co Limited

Hodges, Neil Robert
Paradigm Brewery Ltd

Hodges, Timothy Philip
3ways Brewing Co Limited

Hodgetts, Christopher Darren
Leviathan Brewing Ltd

Hodgin, Wayne
White Boar Brewing Co Ltd

Hodgson, Claire
Timothy Taylor & Co.,Limited

Hodgson, Jonathan
The Great Newsome Brewery Ltd

Hodgson, Jonathan Philip
Cheviot Brewery Ltd

Hodgson, Laurence
The Great Newsome Brewery Ltd

Hodgson, Martin Christopher
Muswell Hillbilly Brewers Ltd

Hodgson, Paul
Tombstone Brewery Limited

Hodson, Joanne Sarah
Northern Alchemy Limited

Hodson, Matthew
The Great Newsome Brewery Ltd

Hoffmann, Jens
AB InBev UK Limited

Hogg, Alan
The Yard of Ale Brewing Co Ltd

Hogg, Susan Debbie
The Yard of Ale Brewing Co Ltd

Holberry, John Simon
Nethergate Brewery Co Ltd

Holbrook, Tobie William
Ferox and Noble Limited

Holden, Jonothan Edwin
Holdens Brewery Limited

Holden, Therese Victoria
Holdens Brewery Limited

Holdsworth, Rebecca Leanne
Steam Town Brewco Limited

Hole, Graham Paul
Heathen Brewers Limited

Holiday, Guy Alexander
North Cotswold Brewery Limited

Holland, Alison
Kairos Solutions Ltd

Holland, David Graham
Bruin Beer Co Ltd

Holland, Martin
Kairos Solutions Ltd

Holland, Nicola Joy
Box Social Ltd

Holland, Stephen
Box Social Ltd

Holland, Stuart James
Brithop Brewing Co Ltd

Hollett, Garry
Equal Brewkery CIC

Holligan, Steven
Winton Brewery Limited

Hollingworth, Lee
Silver Street Brewery Limited

Hollinshead, Dominick Chad
Los Perros Sueltos Brewing Co Ltd

Holloway, Edward
Hair of The Frog Brewing Ltd

Holloway, Julian Edward
Asylum Harbour Brewing Co Ltd

Holman, Michael Stuart
Ferry Ales Brewery Limited

Holmes, Declan Gabriel John
Nightcap Beer Co Ltd

Holmes, Michael
Lost at Sea Brewing Limited

Holmes, Michael Clifford
Xtreme Ales Limited

Holmes, Neil Morris
Xtreme Ales Limited

Holmes, Oliver
Lost at Sea Brewing Limited

Holmes, Steven James
Farm Yard Ales Ltd

Holt, Charles Alistair
Tantum Brewing Limited

Holt, Simon Nicholas
Baltic Fleet Brewery Limited

Holt, Stephen Anthony
Kirkstall Brewery Co Ltd

Honeyman, Pamela
Monty's Brewery Limited

Honeyman, Russell James
Monty's Brewery Limited

Hook, Alastair Frederick
Meantime Brewing Co Ltd

Hooper, David Michael
Fisher's Brewing Co Ltd.

Hope, John Frederick
H.B.Clark & Co.(Successors) Ltd

Hope, Steven
Brew Shed Beers Limited
Brucehaven Brewery Ltd.

Hope-Smith, Dominic Stefan
Carnival Brewing Co Ltd

Hopkins, Benjamin Luke
Three Arches Brewing Limited
Unicorn Craft Brewing Co Ltd

Hopkins, Christopher Thomas Howard
Hydes' Brewery Limited

Hopkins, Robert John
Lion Craft Brewery Ltd
New Lion Totnes Ltd

Hopkinson, Andrew John
Hop King Brewery Ltd

Hopkinson, Benjamin John
Hop King Brewery Ltd

Hopkinson, Ludovic
Hop King Brewery Ltd

Hopkinson, Marcia
Hop King Brewery Ltd

Hopkinson, Neil Antony
Ainsty Ales Limited

Hopper, Sarah
Dancing Man Brewery Limited
Flat Cap Holding Co Ltd

Horn, Bradley
Tally Ho! Brewery Limited

Horn, John
Isle-of-Cumbrae Brewing Co Ltd

Horn, Jonathan
Vault City Brewing Ltd.

Hornby, Paula Amelia
North Riding Brewery Limited

Horne, Nicholas James
Barefaced Brewing Ltd

Horne, Ryan James
Hornes Brewery Ltd

Horner, Martin Richard
The Borough Brewery Limited

Horsley, Mark Robert
Applecross Brewing Co Ltd

Hosking, Jonathan David
Jon's Brewery Limited

Hoskins, Peter Lisney
Saffron Brewery (Henham) Ltd

Houldsworth, Kyle
Wanderlust Bar Limited

Hounsell, Elizabeth Jane
Amber Ales Limited

Hounsell, Peter Neil
Amber Ales Limited

Howard, Charles Erskine
Round Corner Brewing Ltd

Howard, Eva Louise
Now Then Brewery Ltd

Howard, Joe Harry
Now Then Brewery Ltd

Howard, Jonathan Mark
Now Then Brewery Ltd

Howard, Lucy Anne
Now Then Brewery Ltd

Howard, Martin
The Downton Brewery Co Ltd

Howarth, John Jason
Bay View Brewery Limited

Howarth, Jonathan Hamilton
Lost Boys Brewery Ltd

Howarth, Lisa Jane Angela
Bay View Brewery Limited

Howe, Ann Monroe
Lion Craft Brewery Ltd

Howe, Josh W
Lion Craft Brewery Ltd

Howell, Joseph James
Bowing Hound Brewing Co Ltd

Howland, Michael Mary
Lecale Brewery Limited

Hoy, Chester James
Howardian Hills Brewing Co Ltd

Hubbard, Ian Nicholas
Pawed Brewery Ltd

Hubberstey, Michael Andrew
Hubsters Brewery Ltd

Hubert, Timothy
Butcombe Brewery Limited
Butcombe Brewing Co Ltd
Butcombe Pubco Limited
The Long Ashton Cider Co Ltd

Hucker, Ben David
Cloak and Dagger Brewing Co Ltd

Hudson, Benjamin
Bubble Works Brew Co Ltd

Hudson, Carl
Coastal Brewing Co Ltd

Hudson, Miranda Lilian
Duration Brewing Ltd

Hudson, Paul Samual
Custom Head Brewing Ltd

Huey, James
Legenderry Brewing Co Ltd

Huey, Louise
Legenderry Brewing Co Ltd

Hughes, Amelia
The Bespoke Brewing Co. Ltd

Hughes, Andrew Gareth
The Wobbly Brewing Co Ltd

Hughes, Anthony John
Lincoln Green Brewing Co Ltd

Hughes, Ben
Jawbone Brewing Ltd

Hughes, Christy
Acorn Brewery of Barnsley Ltd

Hughes, David Matthew
Via Academia Vocatus Ltd

Hughes, David Stewart
Acorn Brewery of Barnsley Ltd

Hughes, Dominic Michael
DHBeers Ltd

Hughes, Ffion Haf
Cwrw Mon Cyf

Hughes, Gregory
Dark Revolution Ltd

Hughes, James Edward Alexander
Woodforde's BPP Limited
Woodforde's Limited
Woodforde's Norfolk Ales Ltd

Hughes, Jason
The Wobbly Brewing Co Ltd

Hughes, Joel
BeerHug Ltd

Hughes, Jonathan Roger
The Great Orme Brewery Limited
Snowdon Craft Beer Limited

Hughes, Joshua Andrew
Glasshouse Beer Co Ltd

Hughes, Lynette Justine
Lincoln Green Brewing Co Ltd

Hughes, Mark
The Big Bear Brewery Limited

Hughes, Matthew
The Bespoke Brewing Co. Ltd

Hughes, Paul
Swaddle Micro Brewery Limited

Hughes, Rhys
The Bespoke Brewing Co. Ltd

Hughes, Susan
The Bespoke Brewing Co. Ltd

Hughes, Tanya
Dark Revolution Ltd

Hughes-Jones, Gareth
Cwrw Llyn Cyf

Hugill, Reece
Donzoko Brewing Co Ltd

Hugill, Robert
Donzoko Brewing Co Ltd

Hull, Joel Charles Robert
Equal Brewkery CIC

Humby, Laura Jane
Weetwood Ales Limited

Humpherson, Paul Gareth
Tap Social Movement Limited

Humphrey, Matthew Lewis
Knoydart Brewery Limited

Humphrey, Samantha Durston
Knoydart Brewery Limited

Hunt, Anthony Leonard
The Edinburgh Brewing Co Ltd
The Innis & Gunn Brewing Co Ltd
Innis & Gunn Holdings Limited
The Innis & Gunn Inveralmond Brewery
Yeast Pod Ltd

Hunt, Graham
Trinity Ales Limited

Hunt, James Martin
Republic of Beer Ltd

Hunt, John Simon
Broughton Ales Limited
Greyhound Drinks Limited

Hunt, Jonathan
The Millstone Brewery Limited

Hunt, Kevin Paul
Hattie Brown's Brewery Ltd

Hunt, Linda
Greyhound Drinks Limited

Hunt, Rachel
Beat Ales Ltd.
Topcat Brewery Limited

Hunt, Raymond Paul
Towcester Mill Brewery Limited

Hunt, Ricky John
Beat Ales Ltd.
Topcat Brewery Limited

Hunt, Stephen Norris
360 Degree Brewing Co Ltd

Hunt, Thomas
Sonder Brewing Co Ltd.

Hunt, William James
Froth Blowers Brewing Co Ltd

Hunter, Andrew James Robert
The Hunter Brewing Co Ltd

Hunter, David Mark
HU Caret 4 Limited
Ossett Brewing Co Ltd

Hunter, Peter Michael John
Swift Half Collective Ltd

Hunter, Ross William James
Surrey Hills Brewery Ltd

Hurd, Kelvin
Laughing Ass Brewery Ltd

Hurlow, Oliver James
Attic Brew Co. Ltd

Hurst, Stuart Darren
Hophurst Brewery Ltd

Husbands, Richard Henry Charles
Appleby Brewery Ltd.
Bowness Bay Brewing Limited

Hussey, John Paul
Solvay Brewing Ltd

Hutchings, Richard John
Dartmoor Brewery Limited

Hutchings, Tom
Brew By Numbers Ltd.

Hutchinson, Jess James
Hindsight Collective Ltd

Hutchinson, Peter John
Clouded Minds Limited

Hyde, Ashley William
Hyde & Wills Limited

Hyde, Charles Adam
Hydes' Brewery Limited

Ijntema, Martin Evert
AB InBev UK Limited

Illingworth, Leslie
Taylor Illingworth Brewing Co Ltd

Illingworth, Martin
Taylor Illingworth Brewing Co Ltd

Ince, Andrew
Andys' Ales Limited

Ingham, Robert William Jacob
Beerkat Brewing Co Ltd

Inskip, Ruth Mary
Adshead's Ales Ltd

Irons, David Jerome
Tamar Valley Brewing Co Ltd

Irvine, David Andrew
Brute Brewing Co Ltd

Irvine, Victor Michael
Cerne Abbas Brewery Ltd

Irving, Malcolm Gregor Linton
Irving & Co. Brewers Limited

Italia, Dynshaw Fareed
Cobra Beer Partnership Limited

Ivell, Robert Lewis
Charles Wells,Limited

Jack, Frances Blythe
Brewdog PLC

Jackson, Andrew Conan, Dr
The Tring Brewery Co Ltd

Jackson, Ben
Top Rope Brewing Limited

Jackson, David Peter
Welland Brewery Ltd

Jackson, Frank Neil
Laid Back Brewing Limited

Jackson, Iain Kenneth
Marston's Acquisitions Limited

Jackson, Mark Somerville
Hardstate Limited

Jackson, Matthew Scott
Lancaster Brewery Co Ltd
Lancaster Brewery Holdings Ltd

Jackson, Peregrine Orr
The Friday Beer Co Ltd

Jackson, Peter William
Southwark Brewing Co Ltd

Jackson, Robert Nigel
The Silverstone Real Ale Co Ltd

Jackson, Samantha
Laid Back Brewing Limited

Jackson, Simon James
Hop Back Brewery PLC

Jackson, Susan
Farmageddon Brewing Limited

Jackson, Thomas
YSTY Limited

Jacobs, Yves
Aston Manor Limited

Jaksic, Nicholas
Van Pur UK Ltd

James, Andrew David
The Handyman Brewery Ltd

James, Felix Trewartha
Small Beer Brew Co. Ltd

James, Ian
Epic Brewing Limited

James, Mark
Hall & Woodhouse Limited

James, Michael Godfrey
Landlocked Brewing Co Ltd

James, Noel Christian David
New Bristol Brewery School Ltd

James, Robert Michael Kenneth John
Melin Tap Brewhouse Limited

James, Stephen Michael
Donkeystone Brewing Co Ltd

Janaway, Ben
Creative Juices Brewing Co Ltd

Jarvis, Andrew Samuel
Lennox Brewery Limited

Jarvis, Gary
GT Ales Limited

Javes, Matthew Simon
Urban Alchemy Brewing Co Ltd

Javinal, Jovelle
Adriyel Ltd

Jefferies, Paul David
Big Bog Brewing Co Ltd
Hydes' Brewery Limited

Jefferson, Susan Claire
Keswick Brewing Co Ltd

Jeffery, Anne Mairi
Billericay Brewing Co Ltd

Jeffery, Trevor Lawrence
Billericay Brewing Co Ltd

Jeffries, Lee Thomas
Brew & Bottle Limited

Jenkins, Gareth Edward
Dynamite Valley Brewery Ltd

Jenkins, Katherine May Howard
New Devon Brewing Ltd

Jenkins, Richard Dean
Agnate Limited

Jenkins, Robert
Portobello Brewing Co Ltd

Jenner, Miles Anthony
Harvey & Son (Lewes) Limited

Jepson, Joshua Michael
Blue Bee Brewery Ltd

Jiang, Sibil
AB InBev UK Finance Co Ltd
AB InBev UK Investment Co Ltd
ABI SAB Group Holding Limited
ABI UK Holding 1 Limited
ALE Finance Services Limited
Anheuser-Busch Europe Limited

Joannides, Dean Stratos
Hale Brewing Limited

John, Christopher Steven
Stannary Brewing Co Ltd.

John, Sarah
Boss Brewing Co Ltd

Johncox, Gordon Paul Hazell
Aston Manor Limited

Johns, David
Zulu Alpha Brewing Limited

Johns, Kelvin
Fairy Glen Brewery Ltd

Johns, Leanne Peta
Sloane Home Ltd

Johns, Simon
Fairy Glen Brewery Ltd

Johnson, Alex
Alphabet Brewing Ltd

Johnson, Connor William David
Bulletproof Brewing Ltd

Johnson, David Mark
Stocks Brewing Co Ltd

Johnson, David Richard
BCM Brewing Co Ltd

Johnson, Everoy
Samuel Adams (Beer) Ltd

Johnson, Gregory Lawrence
Potbelly Brewery Limited

Johnson, Ian
The Ilkley Brewery Co Ltd

Johnson, Ian Matthew
I.T's Brewing Co Ltd

Johnson, Ian, Dr
Manchester Union Brewery Ltd

Johnson, Leonard Anthony
Fearnought Brewery Ltd

Johnson, Matthew Roger
Pilot Beer Limited

Johnson, Patrick William
Windsor & Eton Brewing Co Ltd

Johnson, Peter
Hydes' Brewery Limited

Johnson, Rhys
Crosby Beverages Ltd

Johnston, Alison
Derwent Brewery Ltd

Johnston, David Melville Steele
Colonsay Beverages Ltd.
Colonsay Brewing Co Ltd

Johnston, Ian
Three Castles Brewery Limited

Johnston, Mark
Derwent Brewery Ltd

Johnston, Roger
Three Castles Brewery Limited

Johnstone, Denis Andrew
Buxton Brewery Co Ltd

Jones, Alexis Morgan
Mad Dog Brewing Co Ltd
Oakland Brewing Co Ltd

Jones, Andrew Oliver
Outhouse Brewing Ltd

Jones, Bleddyn Prys
Cwrw Llyn Cyf

Jones, Christopher Julius
Shropshire Beers Limited

Jones, Christopher, Dr
Papworth Brewery Limited

Jones, Dewi Arfon
Bragdy Nant Cyf

Jones, Dylan
Cwrw Llyn Cyf

Jones, Elwyn
Bragdy Lleu Cyf

Jones, Eve Beryl
Old Tree Brewery Ltd

Jones, Gareth Wyn
Bragdy Nant Cyf

Jones, Huw Gethin
Bragdy Mona Cyf

Jones, Jeremy Mark
Smith and Jones Brewery Ltd

Jones, John Llyfnwy
Cwrw Llyn Cyf

Jones, Julie Griffiths
Harbour Brewery Tenby Limited

Jones, Keith Robert
Gower Brewery Co Limited

Jones, Kevn Llewellyn
Stocklinch Ales Ltd

Jones, Meirion Tudor, Dr
Cwrw Ial Limited

Jones, Meurig Rhys
Bragdy Mona Cyf

Jones, Morris David
The Silverstone Brewing Co Ltd
The Silverstone Real Ale Co Ltd

Jones, Nicholas Richard
Fisher's Brewing Co Ltd.

Jones, Patrick Matthew
Pilot Beer Limited

Jones, Paul
Cloudwater Brew Co Ltd

Jones, Rhys Lloyd
Bragdy Mona Cyf

Jones, Robat Eifion
Bragdy Lleu Cyf

Jones, Sebastian Pettit
Speyside Craft Brewery Limited

Jones, Trevor
Haresfoot Storage & Distribution Co Ltd

Jonsson-Buttery, David
3SB Limited

Jopson, Jason Barry
Brentwood Brewing Co Ltd

Joslin, Matthew Richard Lewis
Gower Brewery Co Limited

Josserand, Antoine
Faultline Brew Co. Ltd

Jowsey, Christopher Michael
Heineken UK Limited
T.& R. Theakston Limited

Judd, Scott
The Four Bulls Brewing Co Ltd

Judge, Satvir Singh
Himalayan Traders UK Ltd

Juggins, Matthew
Bowtie Brewers Limited

Jupp, David Holroyd
French & Jupps Limited

Kane, Liam James
Anthology Brewing Co Ltd

Kannor, Roland Henry
Brentwood Brewing Co Ltd

Karjalainen, Kimmo Eerik
Bone Machine Brewing Co Ltd

Karjalainen, Marko Antero
Bone Machine Brewing Co Ltd

Kaufman, Paul Richard
Two Fools Brewery Ltd

Kawecki, Karol Krzysztof
New Invention Brewery Ltd

Kay, John Roland
Old Pie Factory Brewery Ltd

Kean, James Joseph Anthony
Fitbeer Ltd.

Kean, Rebecca Lucy Anne
Copper Tun Ltd
Fitbeer Ltd.

Kean, Susan Patricia
Fitbeer Ltd.

Kearns, Frances
The Park Brewery Ltd

Kearns, Joshuah
The Park Brewery Ltd

Kearsey, Matthew Richard
Hall & Woodhouse Limited

Keegan, Steve James
Holler Brewery Limited

Keegan, Steven James
Ironstone Brewery Ltd

Keene, Emma
The Cotswold Brewing Co Ltd

Keene, Richard Thomas
The Cotswold Brewing Co Ltd

Keir, Andrew
The Friday Beer Co Ltd

Kellett, Lee Arthur
Boot Town Brewery Ltd

Kelly III, Lauchlin Archibald
Wooha Brewing Co Ltd

Kelly, Alan
Turing Complete Solutions Ltd

Kelly, Anthony
Eden Mill Brewers Ltd
St Andrews Brewers Limited

Kelly, Anthony Gerard
Eden Brewery Limited
Eden Mill Brewers Ltd
St Andrews Brewers Limited

Kelly, Carol Elizabeth
The Kinver Brewery Limited

Kelly, Christopher John
Ampthill & Woburn Brewery Ltd

Kelly, David
The Kinver Brewery Limited

Kelly, Mark Anthony
Bridge House Brewery Limited
The Bridgehouse Pub Co Ltd

Kelly, Robert James
The Kinver Brewery Limited

Kelly, Sean Francis
True North Brew Co Limited

Kelly, Stephanie Louise
The Kinver Brewery Limited

Kelly, Thomas Gregory
The Kinver Brewery Limited

Kelly, Tony
Eden Brewery Limited

Kemp, Abigail Blanche
Holdens Brewery Limited

Kemp, Martin
The London Beer Co Ltd

Kempe, Paul William Frederick
The Beer Collective Limited
The Pink Ferry Ltd
The Sussex Beer Co Ltd
Two Tribes Brewing Ltd

Kempton, Keith Michael
Riverside Brewery Ltd

Kendrick, Alec
Stone Cold Brewery Limited

Kendrick, Andrew James
Beermats Brewing Co Ltd

Kennedy, Carl Wayne
Northern Alchemy Limited

Kennedy, Paul Michael
The Jolly Boys Brewery Ltd

Kenning, David Berkeley Buchanan
Signpost Brewery Ltd

Kenning, Tobias Edward Burney
Signpost Brewery Ltd

Kent, James
Oliver Chester Limited

Kent, Vanessa Ann
Canterbrew Ltd

Kerr, Andrew James
Umbrella Brewing Limited

Kerr, James Alexander
Old Thistle Co Ltd

Kerry, Simon
Molson Coors Brewing Co (UK) Ltd
Sharp's Brewery Limited

Kershaw, Richard Peter
Joseph Holt Group Limited
Joseph Holt Limited

Kerslake-Davies, Tracey
Grey Trees Brewery Limited

Keyser, Rudi Arthur
Radlett Beer Co Ltd

Khalid, Farooq
Portobello Brewing Co Ltd

Kidd, Gordon George
Faking Bad Brewery Limited

Kidd, Richard John
Totnes Brewing Co Limited

Kidd, Sarah Louise
Totnes Brewing Co Limited

Kilburn, Robert James
Old Windsor Brewery Ltd

Kilcourse, Natalie
Scariosa Ltd

Kimber, Ian
Mantle Brewery Limited

Kindred, James
Big Drop Brewing Co Ltd

King, James Daniel
Vendetta Brewing Co Ltd

King, Sarah Louise
Whitechapel Industries Ltd

King, Simon
Abstract Jungle Brewing Ltd

King, William James
Firebird Brewing Co Ltd

Kinghan, Anneka
Crai Cider Co Ltd

Kinghan, Stephen
Crai Cider Co Ltd

Kingsbury, Adrian
81artisan Limited

Kinsella, Roger
Darkplace Brewery Limited

Kintu, Douglas Andrew Atenyi
The Verulam Brewery Limited

Kintu, Rosalind Elizabeth
The Verulam Brewery Limited

Kirchner, Marisa Riette
Ampthill & Woburn Brewery Ltd
Kelchner Ltd

Kirk, Alastair Francis
Tarn Hows Brewery Limited

Kirk, Andreas Bernhard
Carlsberg UK Limited

Kirk, Andrew John
Angel Ales Limited

Kirk, Meyrick Nicholas
Summer Wine Brewery Limited

Kirk, Nicholas
Endure Brewing Co Ltd

Kirkham, Thomas
Big Hop Brewing Co Ltd

Kirkillari, Christalla
CFS Castus Test 001 Ltd

Kirrane, Jordan
3SB Limited

Kiszka, Curt Nathan
Green Duck Beer Co. Limited

Kitchin, Michaela Berselius
Kall Brand Ltd

Kitchin, Ronald John McLellan
Kall Brand Ltd

Kitchin, Thomas William
Kall Brand Ltd

Kitt, Joshua James
Lost Boys Brewery Ltd

Klaos, Alex
Baltic Beer Co Ltd
Tumanny Albion Brewing Co Ltd

Klawitter, Lars
Greyhound Brewery Limited

Kletta, Jan Andreas, Dr
Bont Brew Ltd

Knight, Colin
Corinium Ales Ltd

Knight, David
The Whitstable Brewery Co Ltd

Knight, Raymond Charles
Rock A Brew Ltd

Knights, Dominic Charles
Religious Ales Ltd

Knowles, Maria Kisten
New Bristol Brewery School Ltd

Knowles, Toby Jason Kelly
Fourpure Limited

Knox, Richard
Gower Pub Co Ltd

Knox, Sarah Gwen
Gower Pub Co Ltd

Knox, Thomas Kenyon
Colchester Brewery Ltd

Kocho-Williams, Alastair Matthew, Dr
Seren Brewing Co Ltd

Koo, Kevin
Koomor Brewing Co Ltd

Kostadinchev, Yavor
Bigla Brewing Co Ltd
Portishead Brewing Co Ltd

Kostepski, Joanna
Xtraflow Limited

Kot, Emily Maggie
Little Black Dog Beer Co Ltd

Kot, Jordan Joseph
Little Black Dog Beer Co Ltd

Kot, Nigel Joseph
Little Black Dog Beer Co Ltd

Kubinski, Pawel Michal
Fine Tuned Brewery Limited

Kudr, Zdenek
Bohem Brewery Ltd

Labeij, Jacobus
4 Mice Brewery Limited

Lacey-Cross, Mandy
Dancing Man Brewery Limited
Flat Cap Holding Co Ltd

Lagae, Anouk Sophie
Jarr Kombucha Ltd

Laiho-Murdoch, Nisse-Thomas Tapio
Laiho Limited

Laird, Campbell Doull
Higsons 1780 Limited

Laithwaite, Barbara Anne
The Loose Cannon Brewing Co Ltd

Laithwaite, William Wilson
The Loose Cannon Brewing Co Ltd

Lakin, Michael Baden
The Icecream Factory Limited

Lakin, Sarah Ann
The Icecream Factory Limited

Lambert, James
Isle of Ely Brewing Co Ltd.

Lamerton, Michael James
Arlingham Ales Limited

Lancaster, David Albert
Thomas Paine Brewery Limited

Lane, Duncan James
Hurst Brewery Ltd

Lane, Fleur
Hurst Brewery Ltd

Lang, Hollie Sian
Red Rock Brewery Limited

Langford, Melvyn John
Loyal City Brewing Co Ltd

Langworth, James Howard
BAA Brewing Limited

Langworth, Juliette
BAA Brewing Limited

Lannigan, Dave
Ride Industrys Limited

Laricchiuta, Maria-Angelica
Heathen Brewers Limited

Larroche, Laurence
Salamander Brewing Co Ltd

Lascelles, Stuart Francis
East London Brewing Co Ltd

Latham, Geoffrey
Popes Yard Brewery Limited

Lau, Ken Phong
Maestro Brew Ltd

Laurenson, Anthony Peter
Haresfoot Storage & Distribution Co Ltd

Laven, Anthony John
Shottle Farm Brewery Ltd

Laventure, Joseph Vivian
Portobello Brewing Co Ltd

Lavers, Jonathan
Piddle Brewery Limited

Lavin, Aidan
Dancing Man Brewery Limited
Flat Cap Holding Co Ltd

Law, Nicholas William
Hop Forward Ltd

Lawrence, Alistair William
Firebrick Brewery Limited

Lawrence, Benjamin James
Bulletproof Brewing Ltd

Lawrence, Darren
Bishop's Stortford Brewery Ltd

Lawrence, Graham Roy
Konigsberg Seven Bridges Breweries Ltd

Lawrence, Keith
Loyal City Brewing Co Ltd

Lawrence, Philip Patrick
Bulletproof Brewing Ltd

Laws, Peter
Peter Laws Brewing Limited

Lawson, James Robert
Ossett Brewing Co Ltd

Lawson, Sarah Marie
Ossett Brewing Co Ltd

Lawton, John Gregory
Teignworthy Brewery Limited

Lawton, Rachel Helen
Teignworthy Brewery Limited

Layton, Philip
Play Limited

Le Mare, Jonathan
Gan Yam Brewing Co Ltd

Leach, Gavin Raymond
Windmill Hill Brewing Co Ltd

Leape, Martin Stephen Paul
Twisted Barrel Ale Limited

Leape, Michael Christopher
Twisted Barrel Ale Limited

Leatherbarrow, John
The Brechin Park Brewing Co Ltd

Leck, Ian
Crooked Ship Brewery Ltd

Lee, Craig Anthony
Rudgate Brewery Limited

Lee, Gareth Derek
The Kinross Brewery Limited

Lee, Katharine Ann Dennes
Chapeau Brewing Limited

Lee, Philip Craig
The Great Yorkshire Brewery Ltd

Lee, Richard Neil Frederick
Joseph Holt Group Limited

Lee, Robin
Hybrid Brewing Ltd

Lee, Steven Robert
Christchurch Brewing Co. Ltd

Lee, Yen-Kai
Urbeer Ltd

Leeming, Jon Paul
Brampton Brewery Ltd

Leenen, Barbara
Popes Yard Brewery Limited

Lees Jones, Michael Christopher
J.W.Lees & Co.(Brewers) Ltd

Lees Jones, Simon Christopher
J.W.Lees & Co.(Brewers) Ltd

Lees Jones, William George Richard
J.W.Lees & Co.(Brewers) Ltd

Lees Jones, William Richard
J.W.Lees & Co.(Brewers) Ltd

Lees, Stephen Colin
Long Man Brewery Limited

Lees-Jones, Christina Francis
J.W.Lees & Co.(Brewers) Ltd

Lees-Jones, Christopher Peter
J.W.Lees & Co.(Brewers) Ltd

Left, Clark
The Hand Brewing Co Ltd

Leggett, James Fraser
The Glenfinnan Brewing Co Ltd
Tirindrish Trading Co Ltd
West Highland Breweries Ltd

Lehmann, Mark Wolfram
Goldmark Craft Beers Ltd

Lekman, Tobias Bror
Beta Pilot Brewing Ltd

Lemmens, Nik Leontine Maurice
Foamology Limited

LesbIreland, Richie Joseph
The Velvet Owl Brewing Co Ltd.

Lesch, Marc-Oliver
Deutschlond Brewery Limited

Lethem, Aidan Julius
Doromomo & Sons Ltd

Lewis, Alex
Earth Ale Ltd

Lewis, Anthony
Tweed Brewing Ltd

Lewis, Beryn Charles Martin
Felinfoel Brewery Co Ltd
Gustmain Limited

Lewis, Beryn Charles Martin, Captain
Blewin Trust Limited

Lewis, Christopher
Dead End Brew Machine Limited

Lewis, Christopher Adrian Rees
Electric Bear Brewing Co Ltd

Lewis, Jacqueline Ann
Electric Bear Brewing Co Ltd

Lewis, Jeremy John Cayley
Felinfoel Brewery Co Ltd

Lewis, John Llewelyn, Dr
Treboom Limited

Lewis, Joseph Brian
Brotherhood Brewery Ltd

Lewis, Keith Andrew
Three Engineers Brewery Ltd

Lewis, Philip John
Felinfoel Brewery Co Ltd
Gustmain Limited

Lewis, Richard
Greene King Brewing and Retailing

Lewis, Stephen Peter
Pixie Spring Brewing Co Ltd

Lewis, Steven Perry
Metcalfe & Metcalfe Co Ltd

Lewis, Thomas Owen Rhys
Five Clouds Brewing Co Ltd

Liddle, Alex David
True North Brew Co Limited

Liggins, Terence David Welton
North Cotswold Brewery Limited

Lightbody, Christopher James
Moonshine Drinks Limited

Lilford, James
Tomos & Lilford Holdings Ltd

Lilford, Robert Charles Byron
No Comply Ltd
Tomos & Lilford Holdings Ltd

Limond, John Michael Toby Clifford
The Clun Brewery Ltd.

Lincoln, Darren
Kendal Brewery Ltd

Lindenberg, Paula Nogueira
AB InBev UK Limited

Litchfield, Emma Louise
Whim Ales Limited

Litchfield, William Giles
Whim Ales Limited

Little, Moyra
The Leith Brewing Co Ltd

Little, Nancy
The Leith Brewing Co Ltd

Litton, Gavin Matthew
Four Pillars Brewery Limited

Livesey, Dean James
Hall & Woodhouse Limited

Livingstone, Peter
Cosmic Brewing Co Ltd

Llewellyn-Jones, Jonathan
Brew Club Limited

Lloyd, John Nicholas
Everards Brewery Limited

Lo Bue, Francesco
Los Perros Sueltos Brewing Co Ltd

Loane, Brian
Loane Brothers Limited

Loane, Kris
Loane Brothers Limited

Loasby, Ian James
Potbelly Brewery Limited

Lockhart, Paul Robert
BL Drinks Ltd

Lockwood, David Jonathan
Nailmaker Brewing Co Ltd

Lofthouse, Edward
The Harbour Brewing Co Ltd

Logan, Andrew Kenneith
ZX Ventures Limited

Logan, Daniel Jon
Eyes Brewing Limited

Logan, Nigel
HFBC Ltd

Logan, Shelley Maree
Two Cocks Farm Limited

Lomax, Roy
Vadum Brewery Ltd

Longfellow, David Andrew
Witch Craft Beers Limited

Longley, George Phillip
Dukeries Brewery Ltd.

Longmire, William John Frazer Thomas
Out of the Woods Brew Co Ltd

Lord, Alexei Christopher
The Outstanding Brewing Co Ltd

Lord, James Royston
Rock A Brew Ltd

Lord, Patricia Anne
Nine Standards Brewery Limited

Lord, Susan Margaret
4 Mice Brewery Limited

Lordan, Thomas William
Vodaso Limited

Losin, Joakim Kenneth
London Fields Brewery Opco Ltd

Lovatt, Matthew John
The Ridgeside Brewing Co Ltd

Low, Conall Niall Iain
It's Braw Limited

Lowe, Brian Godfrey
Spotty Dog Brewery Limited

Lowe, Susan Elizabeth
Spotty Dog Brewery Limited

Lowley, Frazer Troy
Icon Brewery Limited

Lucas, Eric
Daleside Brewery Limited
Daleside Holdings (Harrogate) Ltd

Lucas, Thomas Alexander Richard
The West Berkshire Brewery PLC

Lucas, Tom
The Renegade Pub Co 2 Limited

Luceau, Serge Andre Rene
Vale of Glamorgan Brewery Ltd

Luck, Thomas Adam
St.Austell Brewery Co Ltd

Luckin, Charles William Raker
Signal Brewery Limited

Ludlow, Robin Anthony
Brews of the World Limited

Lumb, Hayley Joy
Tarn51 Brewing Co Ltd

Lumley, Charles
Axholme Brewing Co Ltd

Lund, Emma Sarah
The Bosun's Brewing Co Ltd

Lutton, Andrew
Shady Shed Brewery Limited

Lyall, Richard John
Frome Brewery Limited
Newquay Brewing Co Ltd

Lymn, Guy Edward
Urban Island Brewing Co. Ltd

Lynch, Jennifer Frances
Serious Brewing Co Ltd

Lynch, Kenneth Edward
Serious Brewing Co Ltd

Lynn, Philip Mark
Philsters Limited

Lyons, Charlene
The Black Sheep Brewery PLC

Lyons, Mark Pearse
Cumberland Breweries Limited

Lyons, Tom Leo
Roath Brewery Ltd

Lyus, Daniel
The Proper Beer Co Ltd

Mabbett, Christopher John
Gower Brewery Co Limited

Mabe, Matthew Philip
Framework Brewery Limited

MacDonald, Angus Donald Mackintosh
Harviestoun Brewery (Holdings) Ltd
Harviestoun Brewery Limited

MacDonald, Catherine Anne
Harviestoun Brewery Limited

MacDonald, David Alastair
Spey Valley Brewery Limited

MacDonald, Ian Peter
The Glenfinnan Brewing Co Ltd
Tirindrish Trading Co Ltd
West Highland Breweries Ltd

MacDonald, Piers James
Nelson Brewing Co.Uk Ltd.

MacDonald, Roderick Read
Brightbeer Limited

MacEachern, Euan
Loch Lomond Brewery Limited

MacEachern, Fiona
Loch Lomond Brewery Limited

MacKay, Jay
H.B.Clark & Co.(Successors) Ltd

MacKenzie, Donald
Islay Ales Co Ltd

MacKenzie, Nicholas Stephen
Daniel Thwaites PLC

MacKinnon, David John
Winton Brewery Limited

MacKinnon, Robert Finlay
Loomshed Hebrides Ltd

MacLachlainn, Calum Eoghann
Argyll Breweries Limited
Isle of Mull Brewing Co Ltd

MacLean, Allan
Isle of Mull Brewing Co Ltd
Argyll Breweries Limited

MacLeod, Andrew Charles
Saison 86 Limited

MacLeod, Claire Amy
Two By Two Brewing Ltd

MacLeod, Dylis
Two By Two Brewing Ltd

MacLeod, Julia Annette
Saison 86 Limited

MacLeod, Robert John
Two By Two Brewing Ltd

MacLeod, Roderick
Two By Two Brewing Ltd

MacNab, Margo-Rose Felicity
Metcalfe & Metcalfe Co Ltd

MacRae, Darren
The Southey Brewing Co Ltd

Macale, Minie Grace
Impavive Ltd

Mace, Matthew Anthony
Bexar County Brewery Ltd

Machado, Sebastian
Original Brewers Limited

Mackey, Patrick Columba
St Andrews Brewing Co Holdings Ltd

Mackey, Patrick Philip
St Andrews Brewing Co Holdings Ltd
St Andrews Brewing Co Ltd
St Andrews Old Brewing Co Ltd

Mackie, Andrew James
Bullmastiff Brewery Limited

Mackie, David
Steam Town Brewco Limited

Macpherson, Douglas Rory
Cwrw Ial Limited

Maddock, Alistair Duncan Charles
The Top-Notch Brewing Co Ltd

Madigan, Patrick Joseph
Padlock Brewery Ltd.

Magill, John Frederick
Powderkeg Brewery Ltd

Maguire, Frances
Hilden Brewery Limited

Mahendran, Arjun Fyron
Beardyman Brewery Limited

Mahieu, Adrien
Camden Town Brewery Limited

Mahieu, Adrien Pierre Bernard Frederic
ZX Ventures Limited

Mahmood, Atif
Nexus Engineering Limited

Mahoney, Lisa Marie
City Vaults Real Ale Ltd

Mahoney, Richard
Comet Brewery Ltd

Mainon, Richard
Hydes' Brewery Limited

Mainprize, John Barrington
John O'Groats Brewery Ltd

Mair, Gordon Peter
Outgang Brewery Ltd

Maitland-Robinson, Joseph Charles
Blonde Brothers Limited

Maitland-Robinson, Samuel James
Blonde Brothers Limited

Makins, Matthew
Alter Ego Brewing Co Ltd

Malet, Charles Neville Wyndham
Force Brewery Limited

Mandell, Peter Marcus
Tomson & Wotton Limited

Manfre, Jordan
Lost Boys Brewery Ltd

Manifold, Luke Llewellyn
Lucky 7 Beer Co Ltd

Mann, Gareth
Paper Fort Brew Co Ltd.

Mann, Ondrie
The Jolly Boys Brewery Ltd

Mann, Steven
Greyfriars Brewery Ltd

Manney, Gwynth Alise
Dead Fridge Farm Limited

Manning, Amanda
Manning Brewers Ltd

Manning, David John
Manning Brewers Ltd

Manning, Joseph Vincent
Manning Brewers Ltd

Manning, Michael Jan
Manning Brewers Ltd

Manning, Nicholas
Original Brewers Limited

Mansell, Andrew James
Red Cat Brewing Limited

Mapp, Derek
The Collyfobble Brewery Ltd

Marchington, Robert Frank, Dr
Marchingtons Ltd

Marcus, Mike
Chorlton Brewing Co Ltd

Marczuk-Santiago, Joanna Malgorzata
Exiled Brewers Limited

Marjoram, David
Brewshed Ltd

Marks, Darren Paul
Bingley Brewery Limited

Marks, Michael Elliott
Beermondsey Limited

Marlow, Colin Raymond
Ostlers Ales Ltd

Marnock, Calum Robert
Glasshouse Beer Co Ltd

Marotta, Francesca Sandra
Phaded World Ltd

Marriott, Antony
Grasshopper Brewery Limited

Marriott, Katie Elizabeth Rose, Dr
Nomadic Brewing Co Ltd

Mars, Andrew John
The Southdown Brewery Limited

Marsden, Samantha
Lions Den Beers Limited
Yarm Brewing and Distilling Co Ltd

Marsh, Howard
Boothtown Brewery Co Ltd

Marsh, Lewis
The Four Bulls Brewing Co Ltd

Marsh, Nicholas Simon
Craft Beer Collective Limited

Marsh, Toby
GT Ales Limited

Marshall, Jason Keith
Brewdog PLC

Marshall, Jason Shaun
Fuddy Duck Limited

Marshall, Paul David
Valve Brewing Co Ltd.

Marshall, Stephen Joseph
East Neuk Organic Brewing & Distilling

Marten, Lewis Benedict Sinclair
Duration Brewing Ltd

Martens, Jed
Inner Bay Brewery Limited

Martin, Edward William Joseph
Long Arm Brewing Co Limited

Martin, James William George
Egan & Martin Limited

Martin, Richard
Lost Skulls Brewing Co Ltd

Martin, Richard Geoffrey
Andwell Brewing Co Ltd

Martin, Thomas Richard Eliot
Long Arm Brewing Co Limited

Maskalick, Gail
The Draycott Brewing Co Ltd

Maskalick, Gregory Kenneth
The Draycott Brewing Co Ltd

Mason, Andrew Roy
Hastings Brewery Ltd

Mason, Edward
The Five Points Brewing Co Ltd

Mason, Peter Matthew
Hastings Brewery Ltd

Massa, Giovanni
Brewheadz Limited

Masson, Robert Dougal
Dog Falls Brewing Co. Ltd

Mather, Edward Ian
Magee,Marshall and Co Ltd

Matheson, Angus Iain
Matheson Brewers Ltd

Mathew, Colin Thomas
Seal Bay Brewery Sel Bragdy Bae Ltd

Mathews, Richard James
Beer in the Blood Ltd

Mathews, Thomas Charles
Beer in the Blood Ltd

Mathivanan, Kavitha Lakshmy
OM Food Corp Ltd

Matsell, Steven
Station 119 Ltd

Matteson, James Keith
Mondo Brewing Co Ltd

Matteson, Todd
Mondo Brewing Co Ltd

Matthews, Andrew John
TKS Brewing Limited

Matthews, Gareth Michael John Kershaw, Dr
Gibberish Brewing Ltd

Matthews, Rachel Claire
Dancing Duck Beer Ltd
Dancing Duck Holdings Ltd

Matthews, Richard Alan
Mile Tree Brewery Limited

Matthews, Stuart Richard
Matthews Brewing Co Ltd

Maule, Joel William
Westbournia Brewing Co Ltd

Maule, Steven John
Westbournia Brewing Co Ltd

Maule, Thomas
Westbournia Brewing Co Ltd

Mawson, Mark Adam
George's Brewery Limited
Hop Monster Brewing Co Ltd.

Maxwell Stuart, Catherine Margaret Mary
Traquair House Brewery Limited

Mayers, Adam James
Hydes' Brewery Limited

Mayhew, Peter James
Three Acre Brewery Limited

Mayne, William David
Bullhouse Brewing Co Ltd

McAllister-Wilde, Christine
Wilde Child Brewing Co Ltd

McAllister-Wilde, Keir
Wilde Child Brewing Co Ltd

McArdle, Sara Louise
Brewster's Brewing Co Ltd

McArdle, Sean Peter
Brewster's Brewing Co Ltd

McArthur, Kevin James
The Handyman Brewery Ltd

McAuley, Daniel Christopher
The Marlpool Brewing Co Ltd

McAuley, James Andrew
The Marlpool Brewing Co Ltd

McAvoy, Christopher
Seven Brothers Ancoats Ltd

McAvoy, Christopher
Seven Brothers Brewery Limited

McAvoy, Daniel
Seven Brothers Ancoats Ltd
Seven Brothers Brewery Limited

McAvoy, Gregory
Seven Brothers Ancoats Ltd
Seven Brothers Brewery Limited

McAvoy, Guy Richard
Seven Brothers Ancoats Ltd

McAvoy, Luke Philip
Seven Brothers Ancoats Ltd
Seven Brothers Brewery Limited

McAvoy, Nathan
Seven Brothers Ancoats Ltd
Seven Brothers Brewery Limited

McBride, Andrew Alan
Beer Hut Brewing Co Ltd

McCabe, Peter
Goody Ales Limited

McCabe, Robert Joseph
Braemar Brewery Ltd

McCaig, David Francis Anderson
Otter Brewery Limited

McCaig, Mary Ann
Otter Brewery Limited

McCaig, Patrick
Otter Brewery Limited

McCall, David Michael
Ol Brewery Limited

McCann, Ewan Andrew
Three Kings Brewery Limited

McCarney, Stephen Lawrence
Broughton Ales Limited

McCarthy, Anna Katherine
The Beauty and The Beer Ltd

McCaughan, Michael John
Paddy's Clover Ltd

McCay, Danny
Swift Half Collective Ltd

McCay, Jason Joseph
Heaney Brewing Co Ltd

McCay, Malcolm Peter
Heaney Brewing Co Ltd

McCay, Suzanne
Heaney Brewing Co Ltd

McClellan, Alan Keith, Dr
Chapter Brewing Co Ltd

McClune, Christopher Mark
360 Degree Brewing Co Ltd

McColl, Daniel John
McColl's Brewery Limited

McColl, Gemma Jayne
McColl's Brewery Limited

McCord, Timothy Shaun
The Salcombe Brewery Co. Ltd

McCormack, Christopher
Brews of the World Limited

McCormick, Calum
Glen Affric Brewery Limited

McCoull, Russell
7grains Limited

McCrohan, Lee Cameron
Old Worthy Brewing Co Ltd

McCully, Ben
Silver Rocket Brewing Ltd

McDermott, Gregg Ivan
Beermats Brewing Co Ltd

McDivitt, Alex
Veterans Brewing Ltd
Veterans Brewing Sussex Ltd

McDonagh, Paul
Lawman Brewing Company, Ltd.

McDonald, Heather Erin Kelly
Wooha Brewing Co Ltd

McDonald, Stephen Paul
Frank and Otis Brewing Ltd

McDowall, David
Brewdog PLC

McErlean, Jolian Robert
Stag Brewery Ltd

McGarry, Mark
Almasty Brewing Co Ltd

McGeever, Caroline
Broken Bridge Brewing Ltd

McGeever, Katie
Broken Bridge Brewing Ltd

McGeever, Michael Dermot Patrick
Broken Bridge Brewing Ltd

McGill, Alasdair Iain
71 Brewing Limited

McGowan, David Andrew
Broughton Ales Limited

McGowan, James
Loomshed Hebrides Ltd

McGrath, Anthony Gerard
The Kinross Brewery Limited

McGrath, Ian Denis
Beathbrewing Ltd

McGrath, James Kirk
McGrath Davies Public Houses Ltd

McGreevy, Connaire
Mourne Mountains Brewery Ltd

McGregor, Sam Alistair
Signature Brew Ltd

McGuckian, Patrick Generald
Wood Brewery Limited

McGuinness, Terence Joseph
Ignition Brewery Limited

McGuinness-Smith, Mark Rowley
The Belleville Brewing Co Ltd

McGuire, Matthew Christopher
Silver Rocket Brewing Ltd

McHardy, David Charles
Fierce Beer Limited

McIntyre, Bridget Fiona
Adnams PLC

McKay, Conor
One Swan Ltd

McKay, Peter
Beckenham Brewery Ltd.

McKelvie, Sandy Thomas
Two Towns Down Brewing Ltd

McKenna, Stephen Charles
Clearsky Brewing Co Ltd

McKenzie, Caroline Lesley
Redwillow Brewery Ltd

McKenzie, Christopher Cromar
Cellarhead Brewing Co Ltd

McKenzie, Julia Caroline
Cellarhead Brewing Co Ltd

McKenzie, Toby Christopher James
Redwillow Brewery Ltd

McKenzie-Wilde, Cameron
MB Collective Limited

McKeon, William
Newark Brewery Ltd

McKnight, Stephen Sydney
Hollow Tree Brewing Co. Ltd

McLaren, Iain Ferguson
Lennox Brewery Limited

McLauchlan, Julian Brodie
Spyglass Brewing Co Ltd

McLaughlin, James
The Leith Brewing Co Ltd

McLaughlin, Philip Robert
Weetwood Ales Limited

McLaughlin, Robert
Weetwood Ales Limited

McLean, Karen
Slopemeister Brewing Co Ltd

McLean, Maria
Dark Tower Brewery Ltd

McLean, Paul
Black Angus Brewing Ltd

McLean, Raymond
Dark Tower Brewery Ltd

McLean, Ryan Francis
Bullfinch Brewery Limited

McLellan, Rory
AB InBev UK Limited

McLoughney, Kieran James
Blue Armadillo Brewing Co Ltd

McMackin, James Generald
Alcohol Beverages Co Ltd

McMahon, Aron Michael
Turning Point Brewing Co Ltd

McMahon, Maeve Elizabeth
Hexad Brewing Ltd

McMahon, Patrick
Whitewater Brewing Co. Ltd

McMeeking, Angus Gilchrist
Black Country Brewery Limited

McMullan, Niall Martin
Hercules Brewing & Co. Limited

McMullan, Paul
Norn Iron Brew Co Ltd

McMullen, Alexander Brodie
McMullen & Sons, Limited

McMullen, David Shaun
McMullen & Sons, Limited

McMullen, Fergus John
McMullen & Sons, Limited

McMullen, James Thomas David
Lekker Days Ltd

McMullen, Thomas Peter
McMullen & Sons, Limited

McNally, Paul
Moseley Beer Co Ltd

McNaught, Peter Lyle
Hurly Burly Brewery Ltd

McNeill, Thomas Alistair
Heavy Industry Brewing Limited

McNulty, Ciaran
New Wharf Brewing Co Ltd

McNulty, Ryan
New Wharf Brewing Co Ltd

McQueen, David
The Medieval Bread and Ale Co Ltd

McQueen, Stephen Mark
The Medieval Bread and Ale Co Ltd

McRobie, Bruce Kenneth
The Silvertown Brewery and Distillery Co

Mead, Alan Leslie
Project X Brewing Co Ltd

Meadows, Giles Henry
Wincle Beer Co Ltd

Meads, Gary Philip
Weatheroak Hill Brewery Ltd

Meads, Philip Gough
Weatheroak Hill Brewery Ltd

Meads, Sheila Ann
Weatheroak Hill Brewery Ltd

Meads, Thomas Oliver
Errant Ltd

Meagher, Sean St John
Cader Ales Limited

Meaney, Peter Anthony
Mad Cat Brewery Limited

Mearns, Alan Paul
The Old Prentonian Brewing Co Ltd.

Medland, Marc Oliver
Station 119 Ltd

Medlicott, Stephen Anthony
Altarnun Brewing Limited

Medniuk, Steven Andrew
White's Brewery Limited

Meese, Andrew Philip
Castle Gate Brewery Limited

Meeson, Lesley Edna
BCM Brewing Co Ltd

Megaw, Gareth William John
Drumgaw Holdings Ltd

Megginson, Andrew Michael
Witchcraft Brewery Limited

Mehta, Ankit
Universal Robo Innovations Ltd

Mehtala, Jimmy
Stenroth Limited

Meijering, Hendrik
Ultimate Maltgold Limited

Meijering, Ideletta Katharina
Ultimate Maltgold Limited

Meiklejohn, Annika Gabrielle
Tempest Brewing Co Limited

Meiklejohn, Gavin John
Tempest Brewing Co Limited

Meldrum, Stuart Donald
Abernyte Brewery Limited

Melia, Paul
Longhill Garage Limited

Melia, Suzanne Faye
Longhill Garage Limited

Mellon, Gary
Shed35 Ltd

Mellor, Andrew Peter
Abyss Brewing Ltd

Mellor, Gillian Mary
Agricola Bottling Limited
Wold Toppers Limited

Mellor, Joshua David
Neon Raptor Brewing Co Ltd.

Mellor, Paul Robert
Temperance Brewing Co Ltd

Mellor, Sophie
Dorber Brewing Limited

Mellor, Thomas Leslie
Agricola Bottling Limited
Wold Toppers Limited

Melton, Geoffrey Lloyd John
Tealby Brewing Co Ltd

Menon, Darren
Shiny Brewing Co Ltd

Mercer, James Cowie
The Lerwick Brewery Limited
Staneyhill Brewery Limited

Mercer, John Charles
The Lerwick Brewery Limited
Staneyhill Brewery Limited

Mercer, Roderick Graham
The Lerwick Brewery Limited
Staneyhill Brewery Limited

Merrick, Jenn
Earth Station Beers Ltd

Merrill, Jamie Andrew
Ossett Brewing Co Ltd

Mews, Lee
The Moot Oak Brewing Co Ltd

Mews, Philip
The Moot Oak Brewing Co Ltd

Michael, Andrew George
Cold Formd Ltd

Michael, Stephen Martin Pio
3 Bru's Brewing Co Ltd

Michaluk, Generall Robert
Arran Brew Ltd.
Arran Brewery PLC
Loch Earn Brewery Ltd

Michaluk, Malcolm Douglas
Arran Brew Ltd.

Michaluk, Veronica
Arran Brew Ltd.
Arran Brewery PLC
Loch Earn Brewery Ltd

Michell, Joanne
Mousehole Brewery Limited

Michelmore, William Franck
St.Austell Brewery Co Ltd

Micklewright, Simon
Crooked Ship Brewery Ltd

Middleton, Alan David
Original Brewers Limited

Middleton, Jonathan Maclaren
C J Middleton Limited

Middleton, Mark
Wharf Beers Ltd

Middleton, Robert Campbell
Orbit Brewing Limited

Mikhail, Andrew
The Cains Brewing Co Ltd

Milburn, Dale Barry
The Pigeon Fishers Craft Brewery Ltd

Mildenhall, Sarah Elisabeth
Another Brewery Limited

Miles, Dawn
Anarchy Brew Co. Limited

Miles, Simon
Anarchy Brew Co. Limited

Millar, Andrew David
Well Drawn Brewing Co Ltd

Miller, Christopher Stuart
Clan Brewing Co Ltd

Miller, Melissa Ruth Marie
Live Brew Co Ltd

Miller, Natasha Clare Arabella Elsbeth
Bristol Brewing Co Ltd

Miller, Nick Brian
Hogs Back Brewery Limited

Miller, Paul
Eden Brewery Limited
Eden Mill Brewers Ltd
St Andrews Brewers Limited

Miller, Stuart Oliver
Live Brew Co Ltd

Millett, Bethan
Arcadian Brewing Co Ltd

Millis, John Eric William
The Millis Brewing Co Ltd

Millis, Miriam Marjorie Audrey
The Millis Brewing Co Ltd

Millner, Benjamin
Intrepid Brewing Co Ltd

Mills, Christopher
By The Horns Ltd

Mills, John Geoffrey
Tower Brewery Limited

Mills-Bell, Alexandra
Kellentay Beers Ltd

Milton, Christopher Paul
Eagles Crag Brewery Ltd
Milton and Mortimer Ltd

Milton, Jake
Two Finches Brewery Ltd.

Minion, Michael John
Blackened Abbey Ltd

Minkin, James Philip
Purity Brewing Co Ltd

Minnikin, Paul
The Great North Eastern Brewing Co Ltd
Jarrow Innovations Ltd
Newcastle Eden Bottling Co Ltd

Minnikn, Alan
Jarrow Innovations Ltd

Minter, Andrew James
Black Eagle Brewery Ltd

Mintram, John Fraser
Thurstons Horsell Brewery Co Ltd

Mitcham, Johnathan Michael
Kirton Fen Brewery Limited

Mitchell, Deborah
HFBC Ltd

Mitchell, Sonja Christina
Southside Brewing Ltd

Mitchinson, Christopher Thomas
The Crossroads Brewery Limited

Mizon, Heydon
McMullen & Sons, Limited

Moat, Lisa
Bradfield Brewery Limited

Modha, Bhaveshchandra
Modha Ales Ltd

Mody, Kaushik Amritlal
Andwell Brewing Co Ltd
Bavarian Gold Limited

Moffat, Alexander Douglas
Black Wolf Brewery Limited

Moffat, Andrew
Redemption Brewing Co Ltd

Moffat, Thomas Dodds
The Kinross Brewery Limited

Moir, Iain Alexander
Battery Brewing Ltd

Moir, James Iain
Battery Brewing Ltd

Molloy, Margaret
Platform 5 Brewing Co Ltd

Molloy, Richard Jeffery
Platform 5 Brewing Co Ltd

Molloy, Richard Michael
Platform 5 Brewing Co Ltd

Molloy, Sally Anne
Platform 5 Brewing Co Ltd

Momen, Julian Akhtar Karim
Carlsberg UK Limited
LF Brewery Holdings Limited
London Fields Brewery Opco Ltd

Monaghan, Alan Denis
Reality Brewing Limited

Monaghan, Raymond Glen
Red Star Brewery (Formby) Ltd

Moncada, Julio Guillermo
Moncada Brewery Limited

Monroe, Roderick William James
St Mary's Brewery Ltd

Montague-Ebbs, Rachel
Curious Drinks Limited

Montgomery, James David Keith
The Kinross Brewery Limited

Moody, Daniel
Moody Fox Ltd.

Moon, Josh Paul
Bad Moon Brewery Ltd

Moore, Brendan Joseph
East Anglian Brewers Ltd.
Iceni Brewery Limited

Moore, David Neill
Clan Brewing Co Ltd

Moore, Derek James
Kelburn Brewing Co Ltd

Moore, Jeffrey Philip
George Bateman & Son Limited

Moore, Jodie Robert
Cerne Abbas Brewery Ltd

Moore, Richard
Brighton Brewery Ltd

Moorhouse, Neil
Milltown Brewing Co. Ltd

Moortgat, Michel Luc Jozef
Jarr Kombucha Ltd

Moran, Mark
The Ferry Brewery Co Ltd

Moreno, Jesus
Piglove Brewing Co Limited

Morgan, Alan Richard
Abbey Ales Limited

Morgan, Alun David
Skinner's Brewing Co. Limited

Morgan, Audrey Joyce
Shardlow Brewing Co Ltd

Morgan, Austen James
The Backyard Brewhouse Limited

Morgan, David Paul
Cross Inn (Maesteg) Limited

Morgan, Gareth Edward
The Dead Crafty Beer Co Ltd

Morgan, James Laurence
Big Smoke Brew Co Limited

Morgan, James William Heudebourck
Black Eagle Brewery Ltd

Morgan, Kevin
Shardlow Brewing Co Ltd

Morgan, Simon Lewis
Abbey Ales Limited

Morgan, Stuart David
Avitas Craft Beer Ltd

Morgan, Susan Elizabeth
Abbey Ales Limited

Morgan, Victoria
The Dead Crafty Beer Co Ltd

Moriarty, John Michael
Blimey! Brewing Co Ltd

Moriarty, Michael Joseph
Rude Mechanicals Limited

Morley, Michael Edward, Dr
The Milton Brewery Cambridge Ltd

Morley, Simon James John
Urban Alchemy Brewing Co Ltd

Morrell, Margaret Emily
Joseph Camm Farms Limited

Morrin, Joshua Michael
Koomor Brewing Co Ltd

Morris, Benjamin John
Stroud Brewery Development Ltd

Morris, Carly Ann
Bullfinch Brewery Limited

Morris, Daniel Peter
Stroud Brewery Development Ltd

Morris, Iwan Gwyn
Bragdy Lleu Cyf

Morrison, Gavin Kenneth
Sixty Shilling Brewing Ltd

Morrison, Iain Cameron
The Flying Monk Brewery Ltd

Morrison, James John
Windsor & Eton Brewing Co Ltd

Morrison, Rachel Mary
Hop and Pray Ltd

Morrison, Robert
Windsor & Eton Brewing Co Ltd

Morrison, Stuart, Dr
Thesis Brewing Co. Ltd

Morse, Gary David
Blackened Sun Brewing Co Ltd

Morse, Sharon Elaine
Blackened Sun Brewing Co Ltd

Mortensen, Christopher Matthew
Elemental Brew House Limited

Mortimer, David
Eagles Crag Brewery Ltd
Milton and Mortimer Ltd

Mortimer, Neal
Foresight Holdings Limited

Mortimer, Roger David
Uppingham Brewery Limited
Uppingham Brewhouse Limited

Mortimer, Timothy Martin John
3ways Brewing Co Limited

Morton, Eric Charles
Burnt Mill Brewery Ltd

Morton, Generald
Morton Collins Brewing Co Ltd

Morton, Ian
Maregade Brew Co Ltd

Morton, James Patrick Bowie, Dr
Out of Town Brewing Limited

Morton, Patrick Hugh
Abbeydale Brewery Limited

Morton, Sally Anne
Burnt Mill Brewery Ltd

Morton, Susan Ann
Abbeydale Brewery Limited

Moss, Jeremy
Earl Soham Brewery Limited

Moss, Richard
Saltdean Brewing Co Ltd

Moss, Samuel Andrew Holbrook
The Leeds Brewery Co Ltd

Mossman, James Raymond
Cold Bath Brewing Co Ltd

Mouat, Alastair
The Freewheelin' Brewery Co Ltd

Mount, Nigel
The Steam Brewing Co Limited

Mountstevens, Lawson John Wembridge
Heineken UK Limited

Mowat, Andrew Walter
John O'Groats Brewery Ltd

Mower, Jordan Christopher
Unbarred Brewery Limited

Moxham, Roger Timothy
Cold Bath Brewing Co Ltd

Moxley, Kurt
Lam Brewing Limited

Muir, Mandy Marie
Muirhouse Brewery Limited

Muir, Richard Jamieson
Muirhouse Brewery Limited

Muirhead, James Michael
Crafty Pales Ltd

Muirhead, Jim
Sentinel Brewery Holdings Ltd

Mulchandani, Rahul
Enfield Brewery Limited

Mulcock, Antony Craig
Three Castles Brewery Limited

Mulcock, Lyn
Three Castles Brewery Limited

Muller, Mark Oliver Benjamin
Traquair House Brewery Limited

Mulliner, Paul David
Nobby's Brewing Co Ltd

Mumford, Geoffrey Charles
Burton Bridge Brewery Limited

Munckton, Gary Daniel
Cross Borders Brewing Co Ltd

Munding, Rolf Hugo
The Cornwall and West Country Craft Brewing Co
Crafty Beer Seller Limited
Redruth Brewery Limited

Munford, William
Two Finches Brewery Ltd.

Munro, Frances Simone
Munro Ventures Limited

Munro, Kenneth Patrick
Munro Ventures Limited

Murdoch, John William
Moo Brewing Co Ltd

Murfin, Ian
Dancing Duck Holdings Ltd

Murfin, Ian James
Dancing Duck Beer Ltd

Murphy, Clifford Russell David
Bexley Brewery Limited

Murphy, Eamonn
Horse Box Brewing Ltd

Murphy, John Matthew
St. Peter's Brewery Co. Ltd
St. Peter's Brewery Group PLC
St. Peter's Trading Co. Ltd

Murphy, Michael Jude
The Inlaw Brewing Co Ltd

Murphy, Richard James
Burning Soul Brewing Ltd

Murphy, Robert
Loopland Brewing Co Ltd

Murphy, Sean
Vale of Glamorgan Brewery Ltd

Murphy, Timothy James
Luddite Brewing Co Ltd

Murray, Andrew John
The Twisted Brewing Co Ltd

Murray, Benjamin David
The Three Legs Brewing Co Ltd

Murray, Lee
Luckie Drinks Ltd

Murtagh, Christopher
Moseley Beer Co Ltd

Murtagh, Matthew Shaun
Moseley Beer Co Ltd

Mussell, Dino Sebastian
Cirencester Brewery Ltd

Nadany, Mark
Target Brewery Limited

Naisby, Richard Tom
The Milton Brewery Cambridge Ltd

Naish, Matthew Charles
Bartleby's Ltd

Naismith, Nicholas John Ewen
Westerham Brewery Co Ltd

Nanjappan, Naveen Kumar
OM Food Corp Ltd

Napier, Harry
The Ale Factory Ltd

Naritsuka, Yusuke
Meantime Brewing Co Ltd

Nash, Matthew Stuart
Old Tree Brewery Ltd

Nash, Melanie Anne
Insight Driven Innovation Ltd

Nash, Paul Geoffrey
The Glastonbury Brewing Co Ltd
Insight Driven Innovation Ltd

Nash, Peter Charles
Cheviot Brewery Ltd

Nash, Peter David
Derventio Brewery Limited

Nattrass, Mark Stephen, Dr
Lizard Ales Limited

Naylor, Robert Andrew
Naylor's Brewery Ltd

Naylor, Stephen
Naylor's Brewery Ltd

Neagle, Bill, Dr
Soul Brewing Co Ltd

Neal, Andy Philip
5hop Limited

Neale, Jason Wray
Omnebonum Ltd

Neale, Richard James
Shipstones Beer Co Ltd

Neame, Jonathan Beale
Shepherd Neame Limited

Neame, Michael John
Ascot Ales Limited

Neil, Robert John
Maypole Brewery Limited

Neil, Sandra Dawn
Maypole Brewery Limited

Neilson, Karen
North Riding Brewery Limited

Neilson, Richard Alexander
Spyglass Brewing Co Ltd

Neilson, Stuart
North Riding Brewery Limited

Nelmes, Jacqueline Claire
Elmtree Beers Ltd

Nelms, John Wesley
71 Brewing Limited

Nelson, Anthony Robert John
Pedal Power Harrogate Limited

Nelson, Eric Frank
Brewers Folly Brewery Ltd.

Nelson, William Frank
Salopian Brewing Co Ltd.

Nepute, Katherine
Harvey Elizabeth Limited

Nettleton, Christopher Richard
Scribbler's Ales Limited

Neville, Alaric James
Phipps Northampton Brewery Co Ltd

Neville, Quentin John
Phipps Northampton Brewery Co Ltd

New, Michael
Dogtag Beer Co. Ltd

Newbould, Philip John
Vale of Glamorgan Brewery Ltd

Newbury, Andrew Wayne
McMullen & Sons, Limited

Newell, Guy Barrington
Bristol Brewing Co Ltd

Newell, Rebecca Anne
Bristol Brewing Co Ltd

Newell, Shaun Mark
The Teller Lager Co Ltd

Newman, Richard Froude
Felday Limited

Newton, Geoffrey David
Tynemill Limited

Newton, James Mathew Albert
Three Acre Brewery Limited

Newton, Kevin Roy
Oakhill Brewery Limited

Newton, Liam
London Fields Brewery Opco Ltd

Newton, Maurice
Brew & Bottle Limited

Nichol, Andrew
Southwark Brewing Co Ltd

Nicholas, Michael John
The Five Points Brewing Co Ltd

Nicholls, Lee John Cary
Shere Brewery Ltd
Tillingbourne Brewery Ltd

Nicholson, Anthony
Finns (UK) Limited

Nicholson, Frank
Joseph Holt Group Limited

Nicol, Ricky
Nicol Brewery Ltd.

Nicol, Timothy John
SF Brew Co Ltd

Nicola, Christopher
Kettle Green Brewing Ltd

Nicola, Nicholas
Kettle Green Brewing Ltd

Nicoll, Lynsey Jane
Caledonian Brewery Limited
Heineken UK Limited

Nicolson, Daymon Logan
The Proper Brewing Co Ltd

Nida, James David
The Pretty Decent Beer Co Ltd

Nigudkar, Aditya
3ABC Ltd
Jocks and Peers Brewing Co Ltd

Nisbet, Christopher William
Colonsay Beverages Ltd.
Colonsay Brewing Co Ltd

Nixon, Stephanie Louise
Lion-Beer, Spirits & Wine (UK) Ltd

Noble, Joe Adam
Pentrich Brewing Co. Ltd

Nock, Paul Stuart
Ealing Brewing Ltd

Nockolds, Stephen Lindsay
The Battersea Brewery Co Ltd

Nolan, Isaac
Chasing Everest Brew Co Ltd

Nolan, James Peter
Hairy Dog Brewery Ltd

Nolan, Paul Richard
The Black Sheep Brewery PLC

Norman, Benedict John
Twickenham Fine Ales Limited

Norman, Helen Lesley
Bridlington Brewing Co. Ltd

Norris, Elliott James
Station 119 Ltd

Norris, Ian Anthony
J.B. Almond Ltd

Norris, Paul
Ripple Steam Brewery Limited

Norris, Peter John
Ripple Steam Brewery Limited

North, Andrew Stephen
Groovy Grains Brewery Limited

North, Simon Paul
Laughing Ass Brewery Ltd

Northam, Steven John
Brewkeepers Limited

Nudd, Dennis Michael
YB Ventures (2018) Ltd

Nugent, Darren Paul
Pokertree Brewing Co Ltd

Nugent, Emma-Jayne
Pokertree Brewing Co Ltd

Nugent, Michael John
Chapeau Brewing Limited

Nunny, Paul Ian
Sambrook's Brewery Limited

Nutt, Gregory James
Burner Drinks Limited

Nuttall, Christine Elizabeth
Joules Brewery Limited

Nuttall, Hedley Stephen
Joules Brewery Limited

Nye, James Owen Bradley
Brancaster Brewery Limited

O'Brien, Daniel Ryan
EFG International Ltd

O'Brien, Graham Patrick
Pressure Drop Brewing Limited

O'Brien, Richard
Out of Town Brewing Limited

O'Callaghan, Carly Ellen
The Wizard Brewing Company Combe Ltd

O'Callaghan, Patricia
The Handyman Brewery Ltd

O'Connor, Christopher Joseph
Chris O'Connor and Associates Ltd

O'Connor, Gail Maree
Hopdaemon Brewery Co Ltd

O'Connor, James
Bedlam Brewery Limited

O'Connor, Maryann
Common Rioters Beer Limited

O'Connor, Stephen James Granville
Common Rioters Beer Limited

O'Dowd, Beau
Grasshopper Brewery Limited

O'Grady, Leslie Roy
Neptune Brewery Ltd

O'Hara, James Lewis
Brewdog PLC

O'Hara, Kenneth William
Taylors Blackbeck Brewery Ltd

O'Kane, Brian Patrick
The Downton Brewery Co Ltd

O'Mahony, Alexander David
23-7 Brewing Ltd

O'Neill, Alison
Southwark Brewing Co Ltd

O'Neill, Mark Joseph
O'Neill's Brewing Co Ltd

O'Neill, Ruth Elizabeth
The Mighty Oak Brewing Co. Ltd

O'Neill, Sean Joseph
Wicked Hathern Brewery Limited

O'Neill, Stephen Anthony
Wood Brewery Limited

O'Neill, Susan
The Handyman Brewery Ltd

O'Prey, William Keith
Meridian Brewery Limited

O'Reilly, Charles
Burnt Mill Brewery Ltd

O'Reilly, Conor
Buzz Brewing Co Ltd

O'Reilly, David Terence, Dr
Burnt Mill Brewery Ltd

O'Reilly, Olivia
Burnt Mill Brewery Ltd

O'Riordain, Evin Tuck
The Kernel Brewery Ltd

O'Shea, Nicholas Martin
Ignition Brewery Limited

Oakes, Andrew Brian
Isca Ales Limited

Oakes, Hayley Louise
St. Peter's Brewery Co. Ltd

Oakley, Darren James, Dr
Rockhopper Brewing Co Ltd

Ockleton, Robert Andrew
Uttoxeter Brewing Co Ltd

Oelofse, Johannes Stephanus Albertus
Chelmsford Brewing Co Ltd.

Oh, Mr Chong Peng
Woodforde's Limited

Okeefe, Jack
Flash House Brewing Co Ltd

Olali, Odi
Crosby Beverages Ltd

Oldfield, Richard John
Shepherd Neame Limited

Oldfield, Robin Bryan, Dr
Wharfedale Brewery Limited

Oliver, Ishka Megan
Arbor Ales Ltd

Oliver, Stephen
Brighton Brewery Ltd

Oliver, Stephen John
George Bateman & Son Limited
Frederic Robinson Limited

Olliver, Gray Bensted
Branded Drinks Ltd

Oltianu, Razvan Ovidiu
North Yorkshire Brewing Co Ltd

Olvanhill, Gary
Crafty Monkey Brewing Co Ltd

Ord, Simon Robert
The Ilkley Brewery Co Ltd

Oreilly, Brendan James
Croft Ales Ltd

Orr, Caroline Rosemary
Harviestoun Brewery Limited

Orr, David William
Crasi Limited

Orr, James Alexander MacConnell
Harviestoun Brewery (Holdings) Ltd
Harviestoun Brewery Limited

Orr, Wilma Margaret
Crasi Limited

Osborne, Nigel Richard
Butcombe Brewery Limited
Butcombe Brewing Co Ltd
Butcombe Pubco Limited
The Long Ashton Cider Co Ltd

Osnowska-Evans, Rachel Dawn
The Bushey Brewery Co Ltd

Ottaway, Eric Blackburne
London Fields Brewery Opco Ltd

Otterwell, Russell
The Madchester Brewing Co Ltd

Overall, Stephen Paul
Loyal City Brewing Co Ltd

Owen, Jeremy
Arundel Brewery Limited

Owen, John Tudur
Cwrw Ogwen Cyf

Owen, Michael James
Badger Ales Limited
Hall & Woodhouse Limited

Owen, Richard John
The Wild Beer Co Ltd

Pacarada, Arber
Blithe Nook Brewery Ltd

Packer, John Edward
The Engineer Brewery Limited

Paddison, Carl Robert
Hitchin Brewery Ltd

Padgham, Philip Owen
Quantock Brewery Limited
Somerset Ales Limited

Page, Raymond Clifford
Bowman Ales Limited

Page, Sean Thomas
Chantry Brewery Ltd

Paginton, Jason
Brew Monster Limited

Paige, Colin
Round Corner Brewing Ltd

Painting, Georgia Elisabeth
Killer Hop Brew Co Ltd

Palewicz, Jan Peter
Cereal Technology Limited

Palmer III, Thomas Arthur
Mondo Brewing Co Ltd

Palmer, Anthony John Cleeves
J.C. & R.H. Palmer Limited

Palmer, Cleeves William Robert
J.C. & R.H. Palmer Limited

Palmer, Emily Grace
J.C. & R.H. Palmer Limited

Palmer, Neil
Test Brewing Ltd

Paquette, Daniel Paul
Holley Paquette Brewers Ltd

Pardoe, Andrew Timothy
Landlocked Brewing Co Ltd

Parente, Henry Joseph
Welbeck Abbey Brewery Limited

Parham, Helen Margaret
The Milton Brewery Cambridge Ltd

Parke, Jodi Ann
The Ennerdale Brewery Ltd

Parker, Andrew
Elusive Brewing Limited

Parker, Robert James
Frank and Otis Brewing Ltd

Parkes, John Kirk
Red Rock Brewery Limited

Parkes, Lewis Iain
Red Rock Brewery Limited

Parkes, William Roger
Coalition Brewing Co Ltd

Parkinson, Ian William
Moorhouse's Brewery Ltd

Parkinson, John
Abbeydale Brewery Limited

Parkinson, Peter
Mill Lane Brewing Co Ltd

Parkinson, William Barry
Moorhouse's Brewery Ltd

Parry, Claire Frances
Hurns Brewing Co Ltd.

Parry, Constance Patricia
Hurns Brewing Co Ltd.

Parry, Hugh Lawrence
Jollyboat Brewery (Bideford) Ltd

Parry, James Michael Paul
The Beer Belly Brewery Limited

Parry, William Thomas
Hurns Brewing Co Ltd.

Parsons, Andrew Philip
The Company of Dead Brewers Ltd
Eldridge, Pope & Co Ltd

Parsons, Sarah Jane
Tealby Brewing Co Ltd

Pascoe, Christopher John
Brews Brothers Brewery Ltd

Pascoe, Richard
Brews Brothers Brewery Ltd

Pass, Andrew Leslie
The Stockport Brewing Co Ltd

Paterson, David George
Heineken UK Limited

Paterson, Roger John
Hepworth & Company Brewers Ltd

Pattison, Steven
Clanconnel Brewing Co Ltd

Pattison, Steven Clark
McGrath's Brewing Limited

Patton, Antony David
The Dog and Rabbit Brewery Ltd

Patton, Julie
The Dog and Rabbit Brewery Ltd

Patton, Nigel
Bang The Elephant Brewing Co Ltd

Paul, Chris Nicholas
360 Degree Brewing Co Ltd

Paulson, John
Big Shed Brewery Limited

Paunic, Tom
Workshy Brewing Ltd

Paveley, Jonathan David, Dr
Hook Norton Brewery Co Ltd

Pavitt, Darren Rudkin
Amwell Springs Brewery Co Ltd

Pawley, Frank Leonard
Thurstons Horsell Brewery Co Ltd

Paxton, Roger
Riverside Brewery Ltd

Payze, Christopher
The Beer Engineer Ltd

Peacock, Anna
Sneaky Peacock Ltd

Peacock, David
Sneaky Peacock Ltd

Peall, Jason
Two Fools Brewery Ltd

Pearce, Leigh James
Cloak and Dagger Brewing Co Ltd

Pearce, Timothy
Big Mountain Brewing Co Ltd

Pearman, Georgina Elizabeth
Bobby Beer Co Ltd

Pearson, Ian
Stowey Brewery Limited

Pearson, Michael Edwin
The Freewheelin' Brewery Co Ltd

Pearson, Norman Mark
Clanconnel Brewing Co Ltd

Peart, David
Merlin Brewing Co Ltd

Peart, Susan Lesley
Merlin Brewing Co Ltd

Peck, Christian Maurice
Revelry Brewing & Distilling Ltd

Peck, Melanie Helen
Revelry Brewing & Distilling Ltd

Peddell-Grant, Gregory Daren
White Wolf Brewery Ltd

Pegg, Timothy Melvyn
Lords Brewing Co Ltd

Penev, Ivailo Penchev
Tiny Vessel Brewing Co Ltd

Penkethman, Michael James
The Beer Collective Limited
The Pink Ferry Ltd
The Sussex Beer Co Ltd
Two Tribes Brewing Ltd

Pennington, Michael Andrew
Kendal Brewing Co Ltd

Penny, Charles David
Salisbury Brewery Limited

Peppiatt, Geoff Owen
Miswell Brewery Ltd

Peppiatt, Jonathan
Miswell Brewery Ltd

Perfect, Edward
Heathen Brewers Limited

Perfect, Jayson Peter
Butcombe Brewery Limited

Perkins, Jill Frances
Baker's Dozen Brewing Co Ltd

Perkovic, Nicholas John
2731 Limited

Persson, Carl Stefan Erling
The Ramsbury Brewing and Distilling Co

Pescod, Henry John Magoveny
Pongolo Ltd

Peters, Kevin Russell
Double Tap Brewery Ltd

Peters, Richard David
Firebird Brewing Co Ltd

Pheasant, Timothy George Edward
Old Friends Brewery Ltd

Phelan, Robin Michael
White Boar Brewing Co Ltd

Phelps, Martin David Luther
Botley Brewery Ltd

Phillimore, William Andrew Justin
Charles Wells Brewery Limited
Charles Wells,Limited

Phillips, Barry Jon
The Meanwood Brewery Ltd

Phillips, Brett
Lazy Bay Brewery Ltd

Phillips, Francis
Hammerpot Brewery Limited

Phillips, Graeme
The Meanwood Brewery Ltd

Phillips, Richard Bakewell
Monkey Shed Estate Brewing Co Ltd

Phipps, Jeremy
Phipps Northampton Brewery Co Ltd

Pickering, James
Gun Dog Ales Ltd

Pickering, John Robert
Cheltenham Brewery Limited

Pickering, Sarah
Gun Dog Ales Ltd

Piercey, Julian
Monks Bridge Brewery Ltd

Piercey, Kim
Monks Bridge Brewery Ltd

Pillai, Rhys Anthony
Pilot Wharf Limited

Pilling, Steven
Dockyard Brewery Limited

Pillitteri, Carmelo
Northern Whisper Brewing Co Ltd

Pinder, Emma
Boudicca Brewing Co Ltd

Piska, Matthew James
Nameless Brewing Limited

Pitt, Harry George
Blackstar Brewery Ltd

Pitts, Simon Alexander
Many Hands Brewery Ltd

Pizani Williams, Linda Susan
Musket Brewery Limited

Plant, James
Punchline Brewery Limited

Plant, Logan Romero
Beavertown Brewery Ltd

Playford, Martyn
Hop Fuzz Ltd

Pogson, Simon
Manchester Union Brewery Ltd

Pollard, Alistair Richard
The Devil's Pleasure Limited

Pollard, Brent
Lost and Grounded Brewers Ltd

Poole, Richard Michael
Left Handed Giant Brewing Ltd
Left Handed Giant Ltd.

Pooley, Barry Charles
Yellow Top Brewing Co Ltd

Popham-Holloway, Edward
Kingstone Brewery Limited

Porteous, Adrian Brian
Ashen Clough Ales Ltd

Porter, David Arthur
The Outstanding Brewing Co Ltd

Porter, Rosalyn
BCM Brewing Co Ltd

Porter, Stephen John
BCM Brewing Co Ltd

Portman, Gary
Luddite Brewing Co Ltd

Postlethwaite, Andrew Thomas
Postlethwaites Brewery Ltd

Potter, Iain Alexander
Sandbanks Brewery Limited

Potter, Mark Daniel Colin
Cataclysm Brewing Limited

Potts, Michael William
Manning Brewers Ltd

Povey, Scott Kristian
Fixed Wheel Brewery Limited

Powell, Amy Elizabeth Louise
Taw Valley Brewery Limited

Powell, Anthony Richard
Three Lions Brewery Ltd

Powell, Christopher John
Ralphs Ruin Ltd

Powell, Julian Robert
BAA Brewing Limited

Powell, Keith
Irwell Works Brewery Ltd

Powell, Victoria
BAA Brewing Limited

Prasad, Umesh
Vitosha Wine Ltd

Preece, Alan James
Green Duck Beer Co. Limited

Preece, Glyn
Ostlers Ales Ltd

Preece, John
Green Duck Beer Co. Limited

Preece, Paul Graham
Blue Armadillo Brewing Co Ltd

Prescott, Gary
Pixie Spring Brewing Co Ltd
Steel City Brewing Ltd
The Team Toxic Ltd

Prescott, Julia Margaret Harvey
Harvey & Son (Lewes) Limited

Prescott-Brann, Landen Robert
Long Arm Brewing Co Limited

Preston, James
Rowton Brewery Ltd

Preston, Stephen David
Rowton Brewery Ltd

Price, Jonathan
Exmoor Ales Limited
Wiveliscombe Breweries Limited

Price, Margot Christie, Dr
Hepworth & Company Brewers Ltd

Price, Robin Mark Dodgson
Exmoor Ales Limited
Wiveliscombe Breweries Limited

Pride, Richard David
Dolphin Brewery Poole Ltd

Prideaux, James
The Barsham Brewery Limited

Priest, John Henry
Shetland Refreshments Limited

Prins, Antonius Johannes Bernardus
Hopdaemon Brewery Co Ltd

Prior, Alison Margaret
Two Happy Captains Ltd

Prior, David Michael
Two Happy Captains Ltd

Prior, John Edward
Round Tower Brewery (Chelmsford) Ltd

Pritchard, Michael Brian
Skinner's Brewing Co. Limited

Pryce, Charles Alexander Philip
Lost at Sea Brewing Limited

Pugh, Oliver Peter
Brewboard Limited

Pugh, Stephen Crommelin
Adnams PLC

Pulcinelli, Riccardo
Clouded Minds Limited

Purewal, Jaspal Liam Singh
The Indian Brewery Company Birmingham

Purves, Russell, Dr
Bellrock Brew Co. Ltd

Pye, Anthony Joseph
Greenfield Real Ale Brewery Ltd

Pye, Patricia Georgina
Greenfield Real Ale Brewery Ltd

Pyne, Nick Simon
Arran Brewery PLC

Queally, Joan Rosemary
Alpha State Limited

Queally, Jonathan Patrick
Alpha State Limited

Quinn, Brenden
Little Monster Brewing Co Ltd

Quinn, Deborah Kathleen
Buxton Brewery Co Ltd

Quinn, Geoff
Buxton Brewery Co Ltd

Quinn, Joseph
West Belfast Real Ale Limited

Quirk, Michael
Quirky Ales Ltd

Ra, Jee Young
London Ale UK Ltd

Radford, Beverley Ann
Outgang Brewery Ltd

Radford, Christopher Mark
Brampton Brewery Ltd

Rahman, Mond Razali Abdul
Woodforde's Limited

Rainey, Robert
Somerset Ales Limited

Rainford, Alan
Avid Brewing Co. Ltd

Rajbahak, Tulsi Das
Camden Beer Ltd

Ramirez, Hernando
Luxbev Limited

Ramirez, Marcos
Piglove Brewing Co Limited

Ramsay, Simon David, Lord
Angus Brewing Limited

Rana, Preeti
1st Icon Ltd

Randle, Neil Peter
Bang-On Brewery Limited

Ratcliffe, Helen Louise
Matterdale Brewery Limited

Ratcliffe, Nicholas
Matterdale Brewery Limited

Ratilainen, Sanna-Maarit
Owlcrab Limited

Ratsep, Jaan
Black Metal Brewery Ltd

Raven, Luke Thomas
The Ilkley Brewery Co Ltd

Rawlings, Charles Richard Neavy
Welland Brewery Ltd

Rawlinson, Paul Stephen
Charles Wells,Limited

Rawlinson, Peter Andrew
Sheffield Brewers Collective
The Sheffield Brewery Co Ltd

Rawson, Duncan Andrew
Langton Brewery Ltd

Rawson, Kim Patrick
Sandbanks Brewery Limited

Raynes, Barry George
Clearwater Brewery Ltd

Raynor, Yvonne
Feisty Caribbean Ltd

Razaq, Eamonn Muhammed
Four Pillars Brewery Limited

Razaq, Omar Andrew
Four Pillars Brewery Limited

Razaq, Samie Heider
Four Pillars Brewery Limited

Razzall, Edmund Joseph Francis
Symmetry Brewing Co Ltd

Read, Alisdair John
Windswept Brewing Co Ltd

Reade, John
Craft Origins Limited

Ree, Christine Susan
Motley Hog Brewery Limited

Ree, Nigel Leonard
Motley Hog Brewery Limited

Reece, David Elliot
Beer Brothers Ltd

Reed, Martin Stuart
S.A.Brain & Co Ltd

Reed, Nic
Cwrw Llyn Cyf

Rees, Stephen John
Gower Brewery Co Limited

Reeve, Andrew
Honest Brew Ltd

Reid, Barry
Reids Gold Brewing Co Ltd

Renforth, Lee Andrew, Dr
Brinkburn Street Brewery Ltd

Rennie, Colin
WeBrew4U Ltd
Webru4u Ltd

Renouf, Marc
Makemake Beer Ltd

Reveley, Stephanie Louise
Oast House Breweries Cyf

Revell, Henry Wallis
The Beer Necessities Limited

Reynolds, Andrew Paul
Church Farm Brewery Ltd

Reynolds, Craig Thomas
Twinshock Brewery Ltd

Reynolds, Joanna Lorraine
Church Farm Brewery Ltd

Reynolds, Shaun
Blackedge Brewing Co Ltd

Reynolds, Stephen Roy
St Mary's Brewery Ltd

Rhodes, Hannah Louise
Hiver Beers Ltd

Rhys, John Frederick William
S.A.Brain & Co Ltd

Riach, Gavin Duncan
Darkland Brewery Limited

Ribbens, Andrew Murdo
Stornoway Brewers Limited

Rice, Allan Edward
Atom Brewing Co Limited

Rice, Carl Paul
L1 Brewer Ltd

Rice, Gary Peter
L1 Brewer Ltd

Rice, Michael Anthony
Riverside Brewery Ltd

Rice, Patricia Ada
H.B.Clark & Co.(Successors) Ltd

Rich, Roger
Garagebrew Ltd

Richards, Christopher Peter
Nutbrook Brewery Ltd

Richards, Daniel Peter
Fallen Acorn Brewing Co. Ltd

Richards, David Generald
Wentworth Brewery Ltd

Richards, David John David
Wentworth Brewery Ltd

Richards, Dean Timothy
Nutbrook Brewery Ltd

Richards, Julie
Axholme Brewing Co Ltd

Richards, Martin Joseph Crompton
Midmart Limited

Richards, Michael
Axholme Brewing Co Ltd

Richards, Ruth Margaret Hill
Midmart Limited

Richards, Scott
The Leith Brewing Co Ltd

Richards, Serena Anne
Everards Brewery Limited

Richardson, Andrew John
Black Wolf Brewery Limited
Traditional Scottish Ales Ltd

Richardson, Claire Louise
AB InBev UK Limited
Camden Brewing Group Limited

Richardson, David Michael
Ground Hammer Beer Co Ltd

Richardson, John
Rivington Brewing Co Limited

Richardson, John Edward, Dr
Beeston Hop Ltd

Riches, Mark Stephen
Beeston Brewery Ltd

Riches, Nigel Ernest
Rectory Ales Limited

Ridealgh, Alan
Humber Doucy Brewing Co Ltd

Ridealgh, John David
Humber Doucy Brewing Co Ltd

Ridel, Mark
Fat Boi Brewery & Sauce Co Ltd

Rider, Mark John
Shepherd Neame Limited

Ridge, Bradley Aaron
The Inkspot Brewery Limited

Ridgway, Alex
The Slaughterhouse Brewery Ltd

Ridgway, Stephen
The Slaughterhouse Brewery Ltd

Ridley, Elizabeth Anne
Bishop Nick Limited

Ridley, Nelion Lorimer Edward
Bishop Nick Limited

Rigby, Samantha
Redemption Brewing Co Ltd

Rigg, Andrew James
Winchester Brewery Ltd

Riley, Anthony Leonard
Stamford Ales Limited

Riley, Martin John
The Cairngorm Brewery Co Ltd

Riley, Paul
Foresight Holdings Limited

Rimmer, Allan Douglas
Merchant City Brewing Co Ltd

Rippon, Matthew James
Annuity Ales Limited

Riva, Hilary Susan
Shepherd Neame Limited

Roach, Joseph Evan
Vale of Glamorgan Brewery Ltd

Robbins, Ryan
Beersheba Ltd

Roberts, Barrie
The Ennerdale Brewery Ltd

Roberts, Christopher
Project Brewery Ltd

Roberts, Christopher Vaughan
Wrexham Lager Beer Co Ltd

Roberts, Dayle Seddon
Twinshock Brewery Ltd

Roberts, Edward Matthew Giles
Marston's PLC

Roberts, Gwynedd
Cwrw Ogwen Cyf

Roberts, Hywel Eilian Wyn
The Jolly Boys Brewery Ltd

Roberts, James Philip
MBH Tap & Shop Limited
The Mobberley Brewhouse Ltd

Roberts, Jonathan Gwyn
Wrexham Lager Beer Co Ltd

Roberts, Kelvin
Bragdy Lleu Cyf

Roberts, Kevin Mark
Wrexham Lager Beer Co Ltd

Roberts, Luke
The Wriggly Monkey Brewery Ltd

Roberts, Martin Gilman
Bowman Ales Limited

Roberts, Peter John
Exit 33 Brewing Ltd
Sheffield Brewers Collective

Roberts, Philip John
MBH Tap & Shop Limited
The Mobberley Brewhouse Ltd

Roberts, Rhys
Bragdy Lleu Cyf

Roberts, Richard Ivan
Wetherby Brew Co Limited

Roberts, Richard John
Old Dairy Brewery Limited

Roberts, Sion Francis
Langton Brewery Ltd

Roberts, Thomas Gwilym
Wetherby Brew Co Limited

Roberts, Valerie
Skelpers Ltd

Robertson Goff, Alison
Goff's Brewery Limited

Robertson, Adam
Verdant Brewing Co Ltd

Robertson, Paul Michael
Southbrew Co Ltd

Robertson-MacLeod, Simon Gesto
The West Berkshire Brewery PLC

Robins, Lisa Marie
Longdog Brewery Limited

Robins, Philip Brian
Longdog Brewery Limited

Robinson, Alan William
Hawkshead Brewery Limited
Windsor Castle Brewery Limited

Robinson, David John
Frederic Robinson Limited

Robinson, Dennis William
Frederic Robinson Limited

Robinson, Ian Booth
The Alnwick Brewery Co Ltd
The Village Inn Pub Co Ltd

Robinson, Ian Edward
The Blue Bear Brewery (Worcester)

Robinson, John
Tipsy Angel Brewery Ltd

Robinson, Kevin James
Vibrant Forest Brewery Limited

Robinson, Oliver John
Frederic Robinson Limited

Robinson, Paul
Grafham Brewing Co Ltd

Robinson, Paul Andrew
Frederic Robinson Limited

Robinson, Peter Bryan
Frederic Robinson Limited

Robinson, Richard Steven
Itchen Valley Brewery Limited

Robinson, Sam Pallach
Good Things Brewing Co Ltd

Robinson, Tom Oakley
Bedlam Brewery Limited

Robinson, Veronica Helen
Frederic Robinson Limited

Robinson, William Joseph
Frederic Robinson Limited

Robinson-Stanier, Neil
Frederic Robinson Limited

Robson, Jamie
Fearless Brewing Ltd

Robson, Mark Fairfax
Genesis Craft Ales Limited

Robson, Peter
Strong House Brewery Ltd

Rodgers, Tony
St Andrews Brewing Co Holdings Ltd

Roe, Claire Elizabeth
Welbeck Abbey Brewery Limited

Roe, Thomas William
Out of the Woods Brew Co Ltd

Rogan, Deborah Anne
Keep Brewing Ltd

Rogers, Anthony George
Half Moon Brewery Ltd

Rogers, Jacqueline
Half Moon Brewery Ltd

Rogers, Janet Alison
Marble Beers Limited

Rogers, Michael William
Beat Ales Ltd.
Topcat Brewery Limited

Rolfe, Danielle Marie
Penton Park Brewery Limited

Rolfe, Guy William
Penton Park Brewery Limited

Rolfe, Holly-Anne Katherine Lydia
Garden City Brewery Limited

Rollason, Mark John
Smokin Barrels Brewery Ltd

Rolstone, Andy James
Rebellion Beer Co Ltd

Rooksby, Angela Mary Catherine
7 Reasons To Brew Ltd

Roos, Catharine Mary
Signal Brewery Limited

Roos, Murray Daniel Remarque
Signal Brewery Limited

Rooth-Geupel, Amanda
Geipel Brewing Limited

Roper, Rowena Rose
Blackedge Brewing Co Ltd

Roper, Wayne
Blackedge Brewing Co Ltd

Ross, Alastair Borthwick
The Shotover Brewing Co Ltd

Ross, Caitlin Alexandra
The Shotover Brewing Co Ltd

Ross, David Michael
Brixton Brewery Limited

Ross, Edmund Joseph Michael
Trale Brewing Co Ltd

Ross, Josephus
Staggeringly Good Ltd

Ross, Moira Allan
Oxford Brewery Limited
The Oxford Brewing Co Ltd
The Shotover Brewing Co Ltd

Ross, Thomas Michael
Trale Brewing Co Ltd

Rossborough, Peter Daniel
Saltrock Brewing Co Ltd

Rosser, Rachel Elizabeth
Nuglyfe Ltd

Rossi, Luke Francis
Lads & Dads Brewing Limited

Rothera, Adrian Neil
Pilgrim Brewery (Reigate) Ltd

Rothko-Wright, Nicholas Marshall
Torrside Brewing Ltd

Rothwell, Anthony
Stamps Brewery Limited

Rothwell, Michael
Stamps Brewery Limited

Rothwell, Neil
Top Rope Brewing Limited

Rotunno, Gianni
Brewheadz Limited

Rotunno, Stefano
Brewheadz Limited

Roubaud, Marc
Aston Manor Limited

Rough, Andrew
Rough Brothers Brewing Limited

Rowan, Louise
Punchline Brewery Limited

Rowan, Philip Adrian
Joseph Holt Group Limited
Joseph Holt Limited

Rowe, James Malcom
AB InBev UK Limited

Rowe, Paul Timothy
Withnell's Brewing Co Ltd

Rowland, Robin
Marston's PLC

Rowley, Neil Charles Leonard
Great Central Brewery Limited

Rowlinson, Mark Andrew
The Downton Brewery Co Ltd

Rowse, Richard Montague
The Harbour Brewing Co Ltd

Rowsell, Aaron Thomas
Boozehound Ltd
The Fresh Beer Co Ltd

Roy, Alan John
The Kinross Brewery Limited

Rozehnal, Vit
Pivo-UK Limited

Rucker, William John
Marston's PLC

Ruddlesden, Benjamin Martyn
Lords Brewing Co Ltd

Ruffinato, Adam Nicholas
Blackstar Brewery Ltd

Runcie, Hannah Elizabeth
Block Brewery Limited

Rundle, Simon David
Ivybridge Brewing Co Ltd

Rush, Melanie
Cygnus Brewing Co Limited

Rush, Michael
Nauticales Ltd

Rushbrooke, Maxwell Mark
Joseph Holt Group Limited

Rushton, David John
Pointeer Ltd

Rushton, James Peter
Bratch Beers Ltd

Russell, Barry John
Arkell's Brewery Limited

Russell, John Phillip
John Roberts Brewing Co Ltd

Russell, John William
Frontier Brewing Co Ltd

Russell, Katherine Margaret
Inner Bay Brewery Limited

Russell, Mark David
The Cronx Brewery Limited

Russell, William
Equal Brewkery CIC

Rutter, Daniel
Ullage Ale Ltd

Ryan, Richard
McGrath's Brewing Limited

Ryan, Richard Henderson
Clanconnel Brewing Co Ltd

Ryder, Paul Richard
Southbourne Brewing Limited

Sace, Anthony
Conferta Ltd

Sadler, Aster Louise
Windsor Castle Brewery Limited

Sadler, Christopher John
Windsor Castle Brewery Limited

Sadler, David Paul, Dr
Darkplace Brewery Limited

Sadler, Susi Elizabeth
Darkplace Brewery Limited

Sage, Marc
Hedgedog Brewing Ltd

Sahota, Davinder Singh
Holler Brewery Limited
Ironstone Brewery Ltd

Saint, Carl David
Frisky Bear Brewing Co Ltd

Saldana, Steven
Bexar County Brewery Ltd

Salem, Louis
Workshy Brewing Ltd

Sales, Benedict
Black Flag Brewery Ltd

Sales, Nicholas
Black Flag Brewery Ltd

Salmon, James Peter
The Brunswick Brewing Co Ltd

Salmon, Mark Stephen
Bays Brewery Limited

Salmon, Peter David James
Bays Brewery Limited

Saltonstall, Philip James Rous
Brass Castle Brewery Limited

Salvin, Jason Edward
PLS Special Projects Limited

Sam, Pearman
Bobby Beer Co Ltd

Sambrook, Duncan James
Sambrook's Brewery Limited

Samuel, Cureton
The Bespoke Beer Co Ltd

Sandbach, Merlin
The Cairngorm Brewery Co Ltd

Sanderson, George
Lost Boys Brewery Ltd

Sanderson, Glyn Paul
Barlow Brewery Limited

Sanderson, Matthew James Laws
M Rackstraws Ltd

Sanderson, Robert Steven
Botley Brewery Ltd

Sandhu, Paran Singh
The Blue Bear Brewery (Worcester)

Sandiford, Paul David
The Outstanding Brewing Co Ltd

Sandy, James William
WantsumBrewery Ltd

Sandy-Hindmarch, Simon Torkil
WantsumBrewery Ltd

Santiago, Daniel Alberto Chavez
Exiled Brewers Limited

Saraf, Suneil Steven Paul
The Near Beer Brewing Co. Ltd

Saunders, Brook
Brolly Brewing Limited

Saunders, Hannah Jane
Hambleton Brewery Limited

Saunders, Martin James
Wiper & True Ltd.

Savage, Malcolm John
Cross Bay Brewery Limited
Morecambe Bay Wines Limited

Savile, Mark William
Raven Hill Brewery Limited

Savory, Julie
Buffy's Brewery Limited

Sawyer, Gregg Anthony John
Tatton Brewery Limited

Saxby, Vicki Louise
Tynemill Limited

Scahill, Jamie Mathew
Manchester Union Brewery Ltd

Scamp, Simon Paul
Oxbrew Ltd

Scanlon, Luke Stephen
Beersheba Ltd

Scantlebury, Anna Ruth
Cullercoats Brewery Limited

Scantlebury, Jason William Jesse
Cullercoats Brewery Limited

Scates, Andrew
Posh Boys Brewery Limited

Schiefelbein, Ulrich Hans
The Krafty Braumeister Ltd

Schofield, Anthony
Alechemy Brewing Ltd
Keith Brewery Limited
Spey Valley Brewery Limited

Schreiber, Graeme
Isle-of-Cumbrae Brewing Co Ltd

Scoble, Roger Charles
Two Drifters Brewery Ltd

Scoley, Helen Rose-Marie
Westmoor Botanicals Limited

Scoley, Philip George
Westmoor Botanicals Limited

Scotney, Philip
Priors Well Brewery Limited

Scott Morgan, Gillian Christine
Cross Inn (Maesteg) Limited

Scott, Fergus Stanley
Kindeace Ales Limited

Scott, James Martin
Hall & Woodhouse Limited

Scott, Karl James
Foggie Beer Co Ltd

Scott, Richard James
Quirky Ales Ltd

Scott, Roderick
Argyll Breweries Limited

Scrafton, Stuart
Whitley Bay Brewing Co Ltd

Scullion, Ann
Hilden Brewery Limited
Nansen Street Holdings Ltd

Scullion, James
Hilden Brewery Limited
Nansen Street Holdings Ltd

Scullion, Owen
Hilden Brewery Limited

Scullion, Siobhan
Hilden Brewery Limited

Seaman, Mark Allan
The Revolutions Brewing Co Ltd

Sears, Chris
The Woodbridge Brewing Co Ltd

Seaton, Jessica Holly
Crate Bars Limited
Crate Brewery Limited
Jarr Kombucha Ltd

Seaton, Lesley Hazel Elizabeth
Lost Industry Brewing Limited

Seaton, Thomas Roger
Crate Bars Limited
Crate Brewery Limited
Jarr Kombucha Ltd

Sebaratnam, Sebajeevan
Ellismuir Limited

Seiffert, Paul Michael
Black Lodge Brewery Ltd

Sellers, Margaret Amanda
Barrell & Sellers Limited

Serwatka, Marcin Kazimierz
M Rackstraws Ltd

Seward, Andrew John
Thistlerock Enterprises UK Ltd

Seward, David John
Cloak and Dagger Brewing Co Ltd

Sewter, Nicholas James Henry
Sixty Shilling Brewing Ltd

Sexton, Simon John
London Brewing Co Ltd

Seymour, David
Brew By Numbers Ltd.

Shackleton, Lisa
Punchline Brewery Limited

Shackleton, Richard William
Punchline Brewery Limited

Shadan, Shahram Paul
Axholme Brewing Co Ltd

Shannon, Matthew
Well Drawn Brewing Co Ltd

Shardlow, Richard Peter
The Tring Brewery Co Ltd

Sharman, Jonathan Lewis
Dunfermline Brewery Limited

Sharp, Dougal
Yeast Pod Ltd

Sharp, Dougal Gunn
The Edinburgh Brewing Co Ltd
The Innis & Gunn Brewing Co Ltd
Innis & Gunn Holdings Limited
The Innis & Gunn Inveralmond Brewery
Melville's Fruit Beers Limited

Sharp, Richard Dean
Bob's Brewing Co Ltd
Partners Brewery Limited

Sharp, Russell
Sugar Pine Brewing Co Ltd

Sharp, Steven Michael, Dr
Adnams PLC

Sharples, Joshua Mark Alan
Five Clouds Brewing Co Ltd

Shaw, Andrew
Brewdog PLC

Shaw, David Andrew
A Northerly Brewing Ltd

Shaw, David Geoffrey
The Hop Studio Limited

Shaw, David Ian
Big Hand Brewing Co Ltd

Shaw, Dawn
The Hop Studio Limited

Shaw, Michael [1963]
The Craft Beer Society Ltd

Shaw, Michael [1981]
Turner & Shaw Glasgow Brewing Co Ltd

Shaw, Tracy
The Hop Studio Limited

Sheard, Helen Elizabeth
Moorside Brewery Ltd

Shearer, James Christian
Cobra Beer Partnership Limited
Molson Coors Brewing Co (UK) Ltd
Sharp's Brewery Limited

Sheens, Edward Murray
Golden Fox Brewing Ltd

Sheerins, Owen Robert Kerr, Dr
Out of Town Brewing Limited

Shelley, Paul David
Sevenoaks Brewery Limited

Shelton, Richard
The Ilkley Brewery Co Ltd

Shepherd, Benjamin Charles Demetrios
Pastore Brewing and Blending Ltd

Shepherd, John David
360 Degree Brewing Co Ltd

Shepherd, Jonathan Anthony David
Wharfedale Brewery Limited

Shepherd, Mark William
Rock & Roll Brewhouse Ltd

Shepherd, Philip David
360 Degree Brewing Co Ltd

Shepherd, Robert James
Bedlam Brewery Limited

Sheppard, Emma
Jawbone Brewing Ltd

Sheriff, David Luke
Hilltop Brewing Co Ltd
David Sheriff Brewing Services Ltd

Sheriff, Gary
White Rose Brewery Limited

Sherlock, Andrew John
Evensong Brewing Limited

Sherlock, Stephen Leonard
Winchester Brewery Ltd

Sherwood, David Thomas
Yeovil Ales Limited

Sherwood, Robert Dean
Yeovil Ales Limited

Shipman, Michael
Bang The Elephant Brewing Co Ltd

Shipman, Michelle Susan
Offbeat Brewery Ltd

Shipp, Malcolm Trevor
Stealth Brew Co Limited

Shipton, Greg
Three Engineers Brewery Ltd

Shone, Roger Barry
The Burton Old Cottage Beer Co Ltd
Gloucestershire Old Cottage Beer Co Ltd
Greenwich Old Cottage Beer Co Ltd

Shorrock, Janine
Ashover Brewery Limited

Shorrock, Roy David Alan
Ashover Brewery Limited

Shorting, Richard Carl
Clavell & Hind Limited

Shrestha, Mahanta Bahadur
Khukuri Beer (UK) Limited

Shurvinton, Wayne
Greene King Brewing and Retailing

Shutt, Ian Michael
Chevin Brew Co Ltd
Shadow Brewing Ltd

Sibley, Jon
Sibley Brewing Co Ltd.

Siddall, Ian Alan
Piddle Brewery Limited

Sidgwick, Kelly Anna
Good Chemistry Apparatus Ltd
Good Chemistry Brewing Limited

Sidley, David William
Midshires Brewery Limited

Sidwell, Peter Christopher
Torrside Brewing Ltd

Sikorsky, Radovan
Caledonian Brewery Limited
Heineken UK Limited

Sillence, Gary James
Brighton Bier Limited

Simkins, Ian Daniel
4 Ladies Brewery Ltd

Simm, Jamie
Long Man Brewery Limited

Simmonds, Tobias Andrew
Kent Brewery Ltd

Simmonite, Nicholas Brian
Dead Parrot Beer Co Ltd

Simmons, William Thomas Anthony
The Wild Beer Co Ltd

Simpson, Alison Louise
Arnold and Hancock Limited

Simpson, Claire Jane
Elgood & Sons,Limited

Simpson, David
Calside Brewery and Taste Room Ltd

Simpson, Ian Andrew
Gene Pool Brewing Ltd

Simpson, James Clive Orrock
Timothy Taylor & Co.,Limited

Simpson, Lindsey Michael
Gene Pool Brewing Ltd

Simpson, Manuela Alice
Buccaneer Brewery Ltd

Simpson, Neil Allan
Brewdog PLC

Simpson, Phillip Anthony
Lancaster Brewery Co Ltd
Lancaster Brewery Holdings Ltd

Simpson, Richard William George
Nene Valley Brewery Limited

Simpson, Thomas
Beckenham Brewery Ltd.

Simpson-Holley, Martha Rosalind, Dr
Holley Paquette Brewers Ltd

Sims, Alison Joy
Mauldon's Limited

Sims, Stephen
Mauldon's Limited

Sinclair, Christopher Ian
Hopjacker Brewery Ltd

Sinclair, Crawford McGowan
The Innis & Gunn Brewing Co Ltd
Innis & Gunn Holdings Limited

Sinclair, Norman James Anderson
Atlas Brewery Limited
Nevis Brewery Ltd
Sinclair Breweries Limited

Singh, Daman Raj
Dorking Brewery (2016) Limited

Singh, Jasdeep
Pivo Beverages Ltd

Singh, Mandeep
Pivo Beverages Ltd

Singh, Neel
Dorking Brewery (2016) Limited

Singleton, Robert
Windmill Hill Brewing Co Ltd

Sisson, Adam John
Burner Drinks Limited

Sizer, Ian
Luddite Brewing Co Ltd

Skedd, Alison Jane
Wadworth and Co Ltd

Skelcher, Archie James
Thirsty Pioneers Brewing Co Ltd

Skelcher, Joseph Lawrence
Thirsty Pioneers Brewing Co Ltd

Skelton, Carl
Pumphouse Brewing Co Ltd

Skene, Andrew Elliott
Dominion Brewery Co Ltd

Skinner, Jonathan
Market Bosworth Brewery Ltd

Skinner, Steven John
Skinner's Brewing Co. Limited

Skitmore, Robert Julian
Saltdean Brewing Co Ltd

Skocek, Petr
Bohem Brewery Ltd

Slack, Joseph David
Boody Brewery Ltd.

Slade, Jason Samuel
Gilt & Flint Ltd

Slater, Andrew Philip
The Eccleshall Brewing Co Ltd

Slater, Daniel Christie
The Kinross Brewery Limited

Slater, Moyra Jennifer
The Eccleshall Brewing Co Ltd

Slater, Victoria
The Eccleshall Brewing Co Ltd

Slee, Andrew Peter
The Black Sheep Brewery PLC
Titanic Brewery Co Limited

Slee, Thomas Michael
The Madchester Brewing Co Ltd

Slevin, Helen Patricia
Prospect Brewery Limited

Sloan, Bernard
Whitewater Brewing Co. Ltd

Sloan, Kerry Ann
Whitewater Brewing Co. Ltd

Sloan, Paul Gerard
Argyll Breweries Limited

Slocombe, David John
Barton House Brewing Co Ltd

Sloper, Thomas Hendrie
Slopemeister Brewing Co Ltd

Slumbers, John Leslie
Lords Brewing Co Ltd

Small, Christopher Richard Marvin
Burning Soul Brewing Ltd

Smallbone, Robin Christopher
Rockin Robin Brewery Ltd

Smallpeice, Toby John
Gun Brewery Limited

Smeath, Giles Nicholas
Dorset Brewing Co Ltd

Smedley, Francis Gabriel
Reunion Ales Limited

Smiles, Alan
Airborne Ales Ltd

Smith, Aaron
Beer Smiths Limited

Smith, Adele MacKenzie
Harvey & Son (Lewes) Limited

Smith, Adrian Nigel
The Dove Street Brewery Ltd

Smith, Andrew Mark
Partizan Brewing Limited

Smith, Christopher Michael
Hoggshead Brewhouse Limited

Smith, Colin
Devanha Brewery Holdings Ltd
Devanha Brewery Limited

Smith, Daniel Lee Paul
OTL Brew Co Ltd

Smith, Daniel Peter
Lyme Bay Brewing Limited

Smith, David Bertram
Weatheroak Brewery Ltd

Smith, David Turner
Rocket Ales Limited

Smith, Donald John
Alechemy Brewing Ltd
Keith Brewery Limited
Spey Valley Brewery Limited

Smith, Dorothy
Brewsmith Limited

Smith, Garry
North Country Ales Limited

Smith, Geoff Richard
Black Eagle Brewery Ltd

Smith, George Adams
Thurstons Horsell Brewery Co Ltd

Smith, Graeme Christopher Iain
Fisher's Brewing Co Ltd.

Smith, Gulen Ozmeral
Steam Machine Brewing Co Ltd

Smith, Holly Faye
Beckstones Brewery Limited

Smith, Humphrey Richard Woollcombe
Samuel Smith Old Brewery (Tadcaster)

Smith, James Edward
Brewsmith Beer Limited

Smith, Janice
Got 2 Bee Clean Ltd

Smith, Jason McGuire MacKay
Islay Ales Co Ltd

Smith, Jennifer Ellen
Brewsmith Beer Limited

Smith, Jordan
Jordan's Car Review Ltd

Smith, Luke Connor Lyon
Out of the Woods Brew Co Ltd

Smith, Mark
Lincolnshire Craft Beers Ltd

Smith, Mark Edward Charles
Crazy Mountain Brewing Co UK Ltd

Smith, Mark Justin
Out of the Woods Brew Co Ltd

Smith, Martin William
Broxbourne Brewery Ltd.
Fallen Angel Brewery Ltd

Smith, Michael John
Gil's Brewery Ltd

Smith, Michelle
Makeshift Brewing Co Ltd

Smith, Neil
Makeshift Brewing Co Ltd

Smith, Nicholas Andrew
Steam Machine Brewing Co Ltd

Smith, Nicholas Graham
Strathmore Brewery Limited

Smith, Nicola Jane
Muckle Brewing Ltd

Smith, Oliver Geoffrey Woollcombe
Samuel Smith Old Brewery (Tadcaster)

Smith, Patricia Susan
Weatheroak Brewery Ltd

Smith, Philip
Under The Stairs Brewery Ltd

Smith, Richard William
Dartmoor Brewery Limited

Smith, Roger, Dr
Asylum Harbour Brewing Co Ltd

Smith, Sam
Pressure Drop Brewing Limited

Smith, Samuel Geoffrey Gladstone
Samuel Smith Old Brewery (Tadcaster)

Smith, Steven Conway
The Small Beer Brewing Co Ltd

Smith, Steven James
Vaux Brewery Ltd

Smith, Thomas
Eskdale Brewery Ltd

Smith, Thomas William
Muckle Brewing Ltd

Smith, Tobias David
Weatheroak Brewery Ltd

Smith, Wayne Steven
Brew York Limited

Smith-Hay, Steven Robert
Vault City Brewing Ltd.

Smocowisk Miranda, Renata
Connecting Hops Ltd

Smothers, Richard
Belhaven Brewery Co Ltd
Greene King Brewing and Retailing

Smyth, Richard Andrew
Konigsberg Seven Bridges Breweries Ltd

Snaith, David
The Three Counties Brewery Ltd

Snaith, David Andrew
Crystalbrew Limited

Snell, Bernadette Leearna
Moon Cartel Limited

Soames, Archibald Christopher Winston
The Barsham Brewery Limited

Soames, Susanna
The Barsham Brewery Limited

Soden, James Alexander
Scarborough Brewery Limited

Soley, Christopher David
Camerons Brewery Limited

Soley, David John
Camerons Brewery Limited

Solley, Ian Peter
Cellarhead Brewing Co Ltd

Solomons, Luke Anthony
Fourpure Limited

Soper, Matthew Philip
Crafted Brewing Co. Ltd

Soper, Philip
Crafted Brewing Co. Ltd

Southall, Andrew Vincent
Blackened Abbey Ltd

Southcott, Veronica
Kall Brand Ltd

Southern, Dylan Arthur
Wild Horse Brewing Co Ltd

Southgate, Geoff
Wensleydale Brewery (2013) Ltd

Southwell, Kennzo Eddy Thomas
Lucky Shaman Limited

Southwick, Robert
Tally Ho! Brewery Limited

Spackman, Luke Joseph
Chubby Seal Ltd

Spackman, Roger William
Chubby Seal Ltd

Spakouskas, Christopher
Yorkshire Heart Limited

Spakouskas, Gillian Evelyn
Yorkshire Heart Limited

Spampinato, Daniel Henry James
Saltaire Brewery Limited

Speirs, Courtney
Laiho Limited

Spencer, Christopher James
The Great Yorkshire Brewery Ltd

Spencer, Matthew James
Spencer Panacea Limited

Spencer, Sally Margaret
Spencer Panacea Limited

Sperrin, Treeve
Sperrin Brewery Ltd

Sperrin, Warren Paul
Sperrin Brewery Ltd

Spiers, Ludovic
Aston Manor Limited

Spillane, Patrick Thomas
Wright & Spillane Limited

Spooner, Bryan Martyn
Weird Beard Brew Co Ltd

Spurling, Simon
Haresfoot Storage & Distribution Co Ltd

St Clair Maitland, Justin
Magic Rock Brewing Co Ltd

St Ruth, Helen
Boudicca Brewing Co Ltd

St Ruth, Simon
Boudicca Brewing Co Ltd

Stacey, Tim
Barnaby's Brewhouse Ltd

Stachura, John
Caythorpe Brewery Limited

Stack, Edward Charles Rowan
Decagram Art and Craft CIC

Stadukhina, Tatiana
AB InBev UK Limited

Stafford, Nicholas Rowland
Hambleton Brewery Limited

Stafford, Sally Elizabeth
Hambleton Brewery Limited

Stagg, George Randle William
Crossover Blendery Limited

Stanbridge, William
Ipbridge Limited

Stanford, Daryl
Hop Fuzz Ltd

Stansfield, Christopher Mark
Heroic Brew Co Ltd

Stansfield, Nick Paul
Heroic Brew Co Ltd

Stantiford, Ann Marie
Flack Manor Brewery Limited

Stapleton, Edward
Shandy Shack Ltd

Starbuck, Matthew Anthony
Greene King Brewing and Retailing

Stark, Anton
Harrogate Brewing Co Ltd

Stark, Eliot James
Foxhat Beer Limited

Starkey, Adam James
The Stroud Brewery Limited

Staughton, Simon James
St.Austell Brewery Co Ltd

Stebbens, Keith
The Portpatrick Brewery Ltd

Stebbings, Alice
Storm Brewing Co Ltd

Stebbings, David John
Storm Brewing Co Ltd

Stebbings, Thomas David
Storm Brewing Co Ltd

Steeple, David
Fuggle Bunny Brew House Ltd

Steer, Andrea Jayne
Lancar Limited
Little Critters Brewing Co Ltd

Steer, Mark
Lancar Limited
Little Critters Brewing Co Ltd

Steer, Matthew John
Lancar Limited

Stenhouse, Nicola Claire
Wadworth and Co Ltd

Stenson, Richard Allen
Vocation Brewery Limited

Stephens, Andrew Neil
Sheffield Brewers Collective

Stephens, Anthony Paul Fleming
Christopher Ellis and Son Ltd

Stephens, Christopher George
Christopher Ellis and Son Ltd

Stephens, Claire Louise
Christopher Ellis and Son Ltd

Stephens, Elaine Mary
Christopher Ellis and Son Ltd

Stephens, Lloyd John
Wadworth and Co Ltd

Stephens, Mark David
Blackstar Brewery Ltd

Stephenson, Keith Caville
The Alnwick Brewery Co Ltd
The Village Inn Pub Co Ltd

Stevens, Anne
Vale Brewery Co Ltd.

Stevens, Christopher Paul
Gower Brewery Co Limited
Gower Pub Co Ltd

Stevens, Jennifer Helen
Vale Brewery Co Ltd.

Stevens, Katherine Alice
Ledbury Real Ales Ltd

Stevens, Mark Timothy
Vale Brewery Co Ltd.

Stevens, Phillip James
Vale Brewery Co Ltd.

Stevens, Thomas Peter, Dr
Shandy Shack Ltd

Stevenson, Matthew David
Tinworks Brewing Co Ltd.

Stewart, Anne
Deeply Vale Brewery Ltd

Stewart, George Danskin
Rosebank Brewery Camelon Ltd
Rosebank Brewery Limited

Stewart, George Michael
Deeply Vale Brewery Ltd

Stewart, Ian Donald Robertson
Brick Brewery Ltd
Wharf Brewing Co Ltd

Stewart, James Michael
Deeply Vale Brewery Ltd

Stewart, Sally Lorraine
Brick Brewery Ltd

Stewart, Steven John
Stewart Brewing Limited

Stezaker, Ian
Priest Town Brewing Co Ltd

Stirling, Niall Fraser
St Andrews Brewing Co Holdings Ltd

Stockley, Martyn Eric
Errant Ltd

Stocks, David Ayrton
Bridge House Brewery Limited
The Bridgehouse Pub Co Ltd

Stockton, Eric Clive
Hill House Inns Limited

Stockton, Sam Alun
Hill House Inns Limited

Stockton, Susan
Hill House Inns Limited

Stokes, Elizabeth
Ardgour Ales Ltd

Stokes, Fergus Findlay
Ardgour Ales Ltd

Stokes, Jonarthan Benedict
Stokes Brewing Co Ltd

Stokes, Theodore Benedict
Stokes Brewing Co Ltd

Stone, Ashley Craig
Great Western Brewing Co Ltd

Stone, David Jonathan
By The River Brewery Ltd
Wylam Brewery Limited

Stone, Kevin Paul
Great Western Brewing Co Ltd

Stone, Leanne Jane
Great Western Brewing Co Ltd

Stone, Sandra
Great Western Brewing Co Ltd

Stone, Thomas
Liquid Light Brewing Co Ltd

Stoner, John Harold
Mighty Medicine Brewing Co Ltd

Stoppard, Diane Lesley
Beer Ink Limited

Stoppard, Ryan
Beer Ink Limited

Storey, George Kenneth
Big Lamp Brewers Limited

Stothert, Richard Andrew
Daniel Thwaites PLC

Stovin, Andrew John
Slice & Brew Ltd

Stowell, David
Howard Town Brewery Limited

Strachan, Craig Robert
The Craft Soft Drinks Community Ltd

Stradling, John David
BC Brewing & Pub Co Ltd

Stradling, Mary
BC Brewing & Pub Co Ltd

Strange, Tom Charles Fleming
Encoder Brewery Limited

Strange, William Peter Fleming
Encoder Brewery Limited

Strathern, Jenny
McMullen & Sons, Limited

Stratton, Colin John
St.Austell Brewery Co Ltd

Strawbridge, Katie Elizabeth
The Downton Brewery Co Ltd

Strawbridge, Martin David
The Downton Brewery Co Ltd

Street, Michael Anthony
Hall & Woodhouse Limited

Stringer, Stephen
Carlsberg UK Limited

Stronge, Colin Peter
The Handyman Brewery Ltd

Stuart, David Peter
Chapter Brewing Co Ltd

Stubbs, Adam
Carlsberg UK Limited
LF Brewery Holdings Limited

Stubbs, Ben
Rivington Brewing Co Limited

Subramaniam, Mathivanan
OM Food Corp Ltd

Sudbury, Daniel Patrick
Alphabet Brewing Ltd

Sugden, Jessica
Keep Brewing Ltd

Sugden, Paul
Keep Brewing Ltd

Sumner, Jonathan Timothy George
Kew Brewery Limited

Suttle, Rachel Marjory Irene
Organic Laundry Limited

Sutton, Belinda Mary
Elgood & Sons, Limited

Swaddle, Anthony Nicholas
Swaddle Micro Brewery Limited

Swaddle, Jennifer Susan
Swaddle Micro Brewery Limited

Swaffield, Paul Michael
Bestens Brewery Limited

Swaffield, William James
Bestens Brewery Limited

Swain, Jonathan
Hackney Brewery Ltd

Swaine, Jonathon David
The Dark Star Brewing Co Ltd

Swaisland, Andrew
The Kiln Brewery Ltd

Swann, Emma Jane
Howard Town Brewery Limited

Swann, Fiona Isabelle
Mashionistas Brewing Co Ltd

Swann, Stuart James Christian
Howard Town Brewery Limited

Swarbrick, David Francis
The Edenfield Brewery Limited

Sweeney, Angela
Bank Top Brewery Limited

Sweeney, Sharn David
Bank Top Brewery Limited

Swindells, Shane Robert
The Cheshire Brewhouse Ltd

Sykes, Andrew Francis
Selby (Middlebrough) Brewery, Limited

Sykes, Katharine Louise
Selby (Middlebrough) Brewery, Limited

Sykes, Lynda Anne
Selby (Middlebrough) Brewery, Limited

Sykes, Martin Howard
Selby (Middlebrough) Brewery, Limited

Symonds, Jason Edward
Sevenoaks Brewery Limited

Syms, Christa Jane
Endure Brewing Co Ltd

Syms, Gareth
Endure Brewing Co Ltd

Syratt, Peter
Muswell Hillbilly Brewers Ltd

Szabo, Derek William
Fierce Beer Limited

Sznerch, Antoni
The Erddig Brewing Co Ltd

Szwejkowski, David Alistair
Steel City Brewing Ltd

Tagg, Timothy
Seal Bay Brewery Sel Bragdy Bae Ltd

Talbot, Christopher Robert
Gan Yam Brewing Co Ltd

Talbot, Thomas James
The Inkspot Brewery Limited

Tang, Yuanyi
UK Camra Beer Co., Ltd

Tanner, Jennifer Claire
Tanners Ales Ltd

Tanner, Simon Ashley
Tanners Ales Ltd

Tapper, Daniel Alexander
The Beak Brewery Limited

Tapper, Matthew John Purcell
Lion-Beer, Spirits & Wine (UK) Ltd

Tatton, Alastair Charles
Umbrella Brewing Limited

Taub, Benjamin Ari
Deviant and Dandy Brewery Ltd

Tavare, Jack
Beercraft Brewery Limited
The Hand Brewing Co Ltd

Taylor, Alison Mary
The Little Beer Corporation Ltd

Taylor, Amy Rachel
Tap Social Movement Limited

Taylor, Andrew Robert
Born in a Brewery Ltd

Taylor, Benjamin
Taylor Illingworth Brewing Co Ltd

Taylor, Daniel
Yellow Hammer Brewing Limited

Taylor, David
Beckstones Brewery Limited

Taylor, Hannah Grace
Tap Social Movement Limited

Taylor, James
Two Roses Brewery Ltd

Taylor, James Andrew
The Little Beer Corporation Ltd

Taylor, Kate Belinda
Taylors Blackbeck Brewery Ltd

Taylor, Matthew Steven
Recoil Brewing Co Ltd

Taylor, Michael
Black Fen Brewery Ltd

Taylor, Robert Bruce
Black Eagle Brewery Ltd

Taylor, Shirley Jean
Woodcote Manor Brewing Co Ltd

Taylor, Steven
Copper Dragon Brewery Limited

Taylor, Steven Russell
XT Brewing Co Ltd

Taylor, William Paul
Woodcote Manor Brewing Co Ltd

Tear, Jason
Brixworth Brewery Co Ltd

Tempest, Karen
Wild Weather Ales Ltd

Tempest, Michael Andrew
Wild Weather Ales Ltd

Templeman, Greg
Battle Brewery Limited

Templeman, Miles Howard
Shepherd Neame Limited

Templeman, Rachel
Battle Brewery Limited

Templeton, Guy Scott
Hip Hop Brewery Limited

Templeton, Karah
Larkins Brewery Limited

Tennant, Alexandra Sara
Belfast Brewing Co Ltd

Tervoort, Cindy
Heineken UK Limited

Thackray, Christopher James
Craftwater Brewing Co Ltd

Thackray, Sarah, Dr
Atom Brewing Co Limited

Thain, Hamish Stewart
West By Three Limited

Thatcher, Martin
Hogs Back Brewery Limited

Theakson, Jonathan Francis
The Black Sheep Brewery PLC

Theakston, Edward David
T.& R. Theakston Limited

Theakston, Nicholas Robert
T.& R. Theakston Limited

Theakston, Robert Joseph
The Black Sheep Brewery PLC

Theakston, Simon Francis Owen
T.& R. Theakston Limited

Theakston, Timothy James Owen
T.& R. Theakston Limited

Theobalds, Estelle
Canopy Beer Co Ltd

Theobalds, Matthew James
Canopy Beer Co Ltd

Thomas, Adele
Conwy Brewery Limited

Thomas, Adrian
The Belleville Brewing Co Ltd

Thomas, Anthony James
Antic Brewing Limited
Volden Brewing Limited
Volden Limited

Thomas, Anwen
The Cardiff Brewing Co Ltd

Thomas, Gwynne Byron
Conwy Brewery Limited

Thomas, Jonathan
Wadworth and Co Ltd

Thomas, Keith Robert, Dr
Darwin Brewery Limited

Thomas, Michelle
Hope Brewery Ltd

Thomas, Neil John Allan
Allendale Brew Co Ltd

Thomas, Nicholas David
The Craft Beer Cab Co Ltd

Thomas, Philip Andrew
Greene King Brewing and Retailing

Thomas, Philip Mark
TwT Lol Cyf

Thomas, Samuel Fraser
Angry Coot Fermentation Co Ltd.

Thompson, Christopher
Black Bird Brewery Limited

Thompson, Christopher John
Old Spot Brewery Limited

Thompson, Frazer Douglas
Curious Drinks Limited

Thompson, James
Ghost Brewing Co Limited

Thompson, John Robert
Old Spot Brewery Limited

Thompson, Mark
Red Moon Brewery Limited

Thompson, Michael
Black Bird Brewery Limited

Thompson, Michael William
Vaux Brewery Ltd

Thompson, Nathan Edward
The Clandestine Distillery Ltd

Thompson, Piers Michael
St.Austell Brewery Co Ltd

Thompson, Rupert Geoffrey Ryland
Hogs Back Brewery Limited

Thompson, Ryan
Pomona Island Brew Co Ltd

Thompson, Sarah
The Boutique Cellar Limited

Thompson, Stephen Robert
Umbrella Brewing Limited

Thomson, Alan Rodger
The GKH Beer Co Ltd

Thomson, Auriol Frances Lilias
The Krafty Braumeister Ltd

Thomson, John McLeary
It's Braw Limited

Thomson, Joseph
Altarnun Brewing Limited

Thomson, Michael Robert
Loud Shirt Brewing Co Ltd

Thorne, Lewis Ward, Dr
The Lockside Brewery Ltd.

Thornton, Michael Edward Charles
Dorset Brewing Co Ltd

Thornton, Susan Valerie
Dorset Brewing Co Ltd

Thornton-Davidson, Robert
The Craft Brewery Limited

Thurlow, John Stuart
The Two Bob Brewing Co Ltd

Tickle, Erin
Origami Brewing Co Ltd.

Tidbury, Nigel Quentin
Cumberland Breweries Limited

Tiddy, Jeremy Nigel
Windswept Brewing Co Ltd

Tieghi, Michele
German Kraft Brewing Limited

Tierney-Wigg, Pamela Louise
Origami Brewing Co Ltd.

Tierney-Wigg, Simon
Origami Brewing Co Ltd.

Tiley, Peter Robert
The Ham Brewing Co Ltd

Tilston, Emma Jane
Emma J Tilston Ltd

Timmis, Peter Hadden
The K L Brewery Limited

Timoney, Robert
Plain Ales Brewery Ltd

Tindall, David
Chevin Brew Co Ltd

Tiner, Generaldine Marion Alison
The Salcombe Brewery Co. Ltd

Tiner, John Ivan
The Salcombe Brewery Co. Ltd

Tingay, Jennifer Alison
Southbourne Ales Limited
Southbourne Brewing Limited

Tippler, Hannah
Round Tower Brewery Ltd

Tippler, Simon
Round Tower Brewery Ltd

Tischler, Petr
Buzz Brewing Co Ltd

Tizzard, Jade
Phonymick Ltd

Todd, Christopher Barrie, Dr
Mashdown Brewery Ltd.

Todd, Gary Alexander
Thomas Hardy Burtonwood Ltd

Todd, Joanne
Religious Ales Ltd

Todd, Moira Helen, Dr
Mashdown Brewery Ltd.

Tomecki, Ireneusz
Onebeer Brewing Ltd

Tomlinson, Alison
Tirril Brewery Limited

Tomlinson, Christopher James
Tirril Brewery Limited

Tomlinson, Keith
World Bier Huis Limited

Tomos, Rolant
Tomos & Lilford Holdings Ltd

Toms, Benjamin
Revelry Brewing & Distilling Ltd

Toms, Cassandra Jane
Revelry Brewing & Distilling Ltd

Tondziel, Matthew
Serpent Brew Co Ltd

Tonge, Adrian Michael
North Riding Brewery Limited

Tonkin, Daniel
The Southsea Brewing Co Ltd

Toovey, Gwendolyn Mary Savage
Stokesley Brewing Co Ltd

Toovey, John
Stokesley Brewing Co Ltd

Toovey, Stuart James
Stokesley Brewing Co Ltd

Topliss, Anne
The Roebuck Brewing Co Ltd

Topliss, Stephen
The Roebuck Brewing Co Ltd

Torbell, James David
Uppingham Brewery Limited
Uppingham Brewhouse Limited

Torn, Noah
Chapter Brewing Co Ltd

Tosca, Edoardo
Connecting Hops Ltd

Tough, Michael Stuart
Galldachd Na H-Alba Brewing Ltd

Towler, Peter Charles
Towler and Webb Limited

Townsend, Charles Peter
White Hart Halstead Limited

Townsley, Christian
North Brewing Co Ltd

Tranter, Mark Crispin
Burning Sky Brewery Limited

Travis, Mark Adrian
Hickbrew Limited

Treadwell, Scott Steven
Oast & Tread Brewing Ltd

Treen, Sarah Michele
Treen's Brewery Ltd.

Treen, Simon James
Treen's Brewery Ltd.

Trent, James
Latimer Ales Ltd

Trent, Lorraine
Latimer Ales Ltd

Trim, Matthew Daniel
Thirsty Smile Ltd

Tripp, Christopher
Wingtip Brewing Co Ltd

Tripp, Simon Robert
Wingtip Brewing Co Ltd

Tromans, Steven Jeffery
The Sociable Beer Co Ltd.

Troncoso, Alejandro
Lost and Grounded Brewers Ltd

Trotman, Douglas Joseph
Double Maxim Beer Co Ltd

Trotter, Emily Charlotte
Little Rotters Limited

Troup, Geoff
The Fowey Brewery Ltd

Trower, Nicholas James
The Braybrooke Beer Co Ltd

True, Alexander James Edward
Wiper & True Ltd.

Tsai, Chieh-Jen
Southport Brewing Limited

Tucker, David
The Glastonbury Brewing Co Ltd

Tucker, Dawn
Glede Brewing Co Ltd

Tucker, Howard James
Glede Brewing Co Ltd
Tuckers Ales Limited

Tugwell, Adam
Black Horse Brewery Ltd

Tull, Andrew James
Dood and Frinks Ltd

Tullberg, Hayley Louise
Chubby Seal Ltd

Tully, Richard Sean
The Romford Brewery Co Ltd

Turley, James Francis
Thistlerock Enterprises UK Ltd

Turner, Christopher Paul
Halton Turner Brewing Co Ltd

Turner, David Allen
Epic Beers Limited

Turner, Graham Mark, Doctor
Mash Brewery Limited

Turner, Kenneth John
Evolution Brewing Ltd

Turner, Kerry Patricia
Bluestone Brewing Co Ltd

Turner, Peter Graham
Mumbles Brewery Ltd

Turner, Robert Stephen
Mumbles Brewery Ltd

Turner, Samuel Sam
Turner & Shaw Glasgow Brewing Co Ltd

Turner, Simon Robert
Bluestone Brewing Co Ltd

Turner, Stephen John [1969]
The Wombourne Brewing Co Ltd

Turner, Stephen John [1966]
AB InBev UK Finance Co Ltd
AB InBev UK Investment Co Ltd
ABI SAB Group Holding Limited
ABI UK Holding 1 Limited
ALE Finance Services Limited
Anheuser-Busch Europe Limited

Turpin, Marcus
Black Bess Limited

Turton, Oliver Ward
Squawk Brewing Co Ltd

Turton, Robin Duncan
Tarn51 Brewing Co Ltd

Tweed, Lee
Polarity Brewing Ltd

Tweedy, Kevin
Golden Triangle Brewery Ltd

Twells, Stephen Andrew
Middle Earth Brewing Co Ltd

Twist, Robin
Emprise Brewery Limited

Twort, Peter John
The Grumpy Git Brewery Limited

Tyas, Albert Richard
Luddites Revenge Ltd

Tyldsley, Nicholas James Thomas Snaith
Crystalbrew Limited

Udale-Clarke, Michael Jon
Mortimer Brewing Co Ltd

Underwood, Robert
The Two Bob Brewing Co Ltd

Underwood, Timothy Morris
Old Pie Factory Brewery Ltd

Unsworth, David Ernest
Unsworth's Yard Brewery Ltd

Unsworth, Peter John
Unsworth's Yard Brewery Ltd

Uprichard, Mark
Farmageddon Brewing Limited

Upton, Neil, Dr
Star Wing Brewery Ltd

Upward, Glen
Devitera Ltd

Vale, Sebastian
Brothers of Ale Limited

Valente, Carlo Louis
Black Wolf Brewery Limited
Traditional Scottish Ales Ltd

Vallance, Denzil William
Great Heck Brewing Co Ltd

Van Der Spek, Willem Pieter
Little Valley Brewery Limited

Van Der Vyver, Christiaan
Husk Brewing Limited

Van Der Vyver, Marta Aldona
Husk Brewing Limited

Van Der Watt, James Andrew Thomas
Jabru Bevco Ltd

Van Esch, Johannes Henricus Adrianus
Brixton Brewery Limited

Vann, David John
Priors Well Brewery Limited

Varin, Amelie Jeannine Marcelle
After The Harvest Brewing Ltd

Varley, John Edward Thomas
Timothy Taylor & Co.,Limited

Vart, Ian Terence
Beer Monkey Brew Co. Limited

Vella, Laurie Simon
Pin-Up Beers Ltd.

Venour, Richard James
Vendetta Brewing Co Ltd

Venter, Brett Jason
Good Living Brew Co Limited

Vettese, Lois Helen
The Kingdom Brewery Limited

Veverka, Radomir
Decagram Art and Craft CIC

Vickers, Elizabeth Ann
Blue Monkey Brewing Limited

Vickers, Thomas William
Blue Monkey Brewing Limited

Vickers, Trevor John
Blue Monkey Brewing Limited

Vickery, James Edgar Leigh
3ways Brewing Co Limited

Villacencio, Ruth
Lastonser Ltd

Village, Archie Jevremov
Villages Brewery Limited

Village, Louis Jevremov
Villages Brewery Limited

Vines, Barnaby Michael
Northern Whisper Brewing Co Ltd

Vines, Joshua Albert
Northern Whisper Brewing Co Ltd

Vines, Timothy Albert
Northern Whisper Brewing Co Ltd

Virok, Jason
Topsham Brewery Ltd

Vogt, Bruce Robert, Dr
Temple Road Brewing Co Ltd

Vokes, Alexander John
Hopforge Ltd

Vorenkamp, Ewan
Lewanbrew Limited

Vorenkamp, Lewis
Lewanbrew Limited

Voss, Neil Mark
Thomas Hardy Burtonwood Ltd
Thomas Hardy Holdings Limited
Thomas Hardy Kendal Limited

Vowles, Charlotte Ione
Everards Brewery Limited

Vroom, Craig
Titsey Brewing Co. Limited

Waddington, Richard
Silver Brewhouse Limited

Wade, Barrie
The Laughing Pug Ltd

Wagstaff, David Edward
Kirton Fen Brewery Limited

Wagstaff, Ian Robert
Kirton Fen Brewery Limited

Wainwright, Geoffrey, Dr
Neptune Brewery Ltd

Wainwright, Kirsten
Bollington Brewing Co. Limited

Wainwright, Lee Owen
Bollington Brewing Co. Limited

Waite, Lilith Grace Hayward
The Queer Brewing Project Ltd

Waites, Charlie John
TKS Brewing Limited

Wakefield, Scott
Dingbat Beer Ltd

Wakeham, Gemma Clare
Two Drifters Brewery Ltd

Wakeham, Russell Jon, Dr
Two Drifters Brewery Ltd

Wakeley, Timothy Michael, Dr
The Shropshire Brewer Limited

Waldron, Alan David
Riviera Brewing Co Ltd

Walker, Dave
Sentinel Brewery Holdings Ltd

Walker, Ian Hamilton
Moonshine Drinks Limited

Walker, Ian Robert
2 Bobs Brewing Co Ltd

Walker, Jonathan Victor
Ironstone Brewery JVW Ltd

Walker, Peter David
Equal Brewkery CIC

Walker, Philip Lawrence John
The New Union Brewing Co Ltd

Walker, Rory
The Borough Brewery Limited

Walker, Simon
Crooked Ship Brewery Ltd

Walker, Stuart Daniel
Arundel Brewery Limited

Wall, Kieran Graeme
Stoatcraft Revolutionary Beers Ltd

Wallace, Alastair Wyllie, Dr
The Company of Dead Brewers Ltd
Eldridge, Pope & Co Ltd

Wallace, Christopher James
Richmond Brewing Co Ltd

Wallace, Richard Malcolm Keay
Trailhead Brew Co Ltd

Wallace, Robert
The 1648 Brewing Co Limited

Wallace, Stuart
Creative Juices Brewing Co Ltd

Wallbank, Renard Barry
Old School Brewery Limited

Walley, Matthew
Spitting Feathers Limited

Wallis, Toby Richard Hamilton
The Handyman Brewery Ltd

Walsh, Cathy
Bakewell Road Brewery Ltd

Walsh, David Stuart
Bakewell Road Brewery Ltd

Walsh, Ian
Beer Station Brewery Ltd

Walsh, Ian Christopher
Old School Brewery Limited

Walsh, John Philip Tempest
Timothy Taylor & Co.,Limited

Walsh, Keir Edward
Beer Station Brewery Ltd

Walsh, Stephen Christopher
Sherborne Brewery Limited

Walsingham, Mark
Three Geezers Brewing Limited

Walters, Alison Marie
Ludlow Brewing Co Ltd

Walters, Gary Edward
Ludlow Brewing Co Ltd

Walters, Geoffrey
Northern Monk Brewing Co. Ltd

Walters, Mark Bernhardt James
MBJW Brewing Limited

Walwyn-James, Christopher Darryl
The Alnwick Brewery Co Ltd
The Village Inn Pub Co Ltd

Wang, Bowei
Overtone Brewing Ltd

Waplington, Christopher Michael
Bad Seed Brewery Ltd

Warburton, Andrew Robert
The Bowland Beer Co Ltd

Warburton, James Peter
The Bowland Beer Co Ltd

Warburton, Kevin
Chantry Brewery Ltd

Warburton, Michael
Chantry Brewery Ltd

Ward, Christopher
Penistone Brewers Limited
Penistone Brewing (Penistone) Ltd

Ward, Gary David
The Redchurch Brewery Limited

Ward, Gillian
Penistone Brewers Limited
Penistone Brewing (Penistone) Ltd

Ward, Jonathan Christopher
Thomas Hardy Burtonwood Ltd
Thomas Hardy Holdings Limited
Thomas Hardy Kendal Limited
Higsons 1780 Limited

Ward, Kenneth
Black Market Brewery Limited

Ward, Leslie Robert
Mitchell Ward Limited

Ward, Margaret Rae
Thomas Hardy Burtonwood Ltd
Thomas Hardy Holdings Limited
Thomas Hardy Kendal Limited

Ward, Mike
Garretts Green Garage Mikro Brewery Ltd

Ward, Steven
Cotton End Brewery Co Ltd

Ware, David John
Charles Cooper Limited

Waring, Oliver
The Shropshire Brewer Limited

Waring, Susan
Vovin Ltd

Warman, Richard
Broken Bridge Brewing Ltd

Warne, Desmond John
Beerkat Brewing Co Ltd

Warner, David Simon
Saeburh Brewery Ltd

Warnock, Alan Ian
71 Brewing Limited

Wash, Mark Robert
Tamar Valley Brewing Co Ltd

Washington, Jennifer Katherine
Purple Moose Brewery Ltd

Washington, Lawrence John
Purple Moose Brewery Ltd

Waterer, Carl David Mark
Stroud Brewery Development Ltd

Waterman, Matthew Robert
Republic of Beer Ltd

Watson, Brian
Oddly Limited

Watson, David Frank
French & Jupps Limited

Watson, Jenny
Malt, The Brewery Limited

Watson, Nicholas Paul
Malt, The Brewery Limited

Watson, Russell David
Aussie Brewing Co Ltd

Watson, Russell Edward
Zapato Brewery Ltd.

Watson, Simon Anthony
SF Brew Co Ltd

Watson-Burge, Alison Jayne
Law and Disorder Brew Co Ltd

Watson-Burge, Simon David
Law and Disorder Brew Co Ltd

Watt, James Bruce
Overworks Limited

Watt, Jamie Bruce
Brewdog PLC

Watt, Thomas McIntyre
Veterans Brewing Ltd
Veterans Brewing Sussex Ltd

Watts, Andrew
Little London Brewery Limited

Watts, Gary Stephen
Liquid Revolution Ltd

Watts, Malcolm
Silver Brewhouse Limited

Watts, Michael Samuel Thomas
Wessex Brewing & Pub Co Ltd
Wickwar Craft Taverns Limited
Wickwar Town Taverns Ltd
Wickwar Wessex Brewing Co Ltd

Watts, Oliver James
Watts & Co Ltd

Wauchob, Matthew John
Baronscourt Brewing Co Ltd

Wayland, Lorraine Gillian
Wayland's Sixpenny Brewery Ltd

Wayland, Scott
Wayland's Sixpenny Brewery Ltd

Wealleans, Andrea Kate
Weal Ales Brewery Limited

Wealleans, Paul John
Weal Ales Brewery Limited

Weatherill, Terence Harry
Three Geezers Brewing Limited

Weaving, Julie
Leadmill Brewery Limited

Webb, Hassan
Bentley's Yorkshire Breweries (1828)
Devenish & Co (Weymouth) Ltd
Thomas Dutton Ales Limited
Lorimers Ales (1919) Limited
Vaux Beers Ltd

Webb, Oliver John
Towler and Webb Limited

Webb, Russell
Dow Bridge Brewery Limited

Webster, Kenneth
The Isle of Skye Brewing Company (Leann An Eilein)

Webster, Simon David
The Thornbridge Hall Country House Brewing Co

Wedgwood, Ann Maureen
Hardknott UK Ltd

Wegelius, Andreas
Old Street Brewery Ltd

Wehmeier, Thomas Jan
3ways Brewing Co Limited

Weir, James
Upstart Brewing Ltd

Welch Snr, John
North Country Ales Limited

Welch, Darren
BL Drinks Ltd

Welch, Shane
Mad Scientists Pty. Ltd

Welham, Christopher
Wadworth and Co Ltd

Wells, Geoffrey Charles Vaughan
Charles Wells,Limited

Wells, Paul Richard
Charles Wells Brewery Limited
Charles Wells,Limited

Wells, Peter John
Charles Wells,Limited

Wells, Richard
Whitby Brewery Ltd

Wells, Stephen
Ascot Ales Limited

Welsby, Mark Stewart
The Runaway Brewery Limited

Welsh, David William, Dr
Jolly Sailor Brewery Limited

Welsh, Nigel Stead
Flack Manor Brewery Limited

Welton, Katja
Weltons Limited

Welton, Raymond Allen
Weltons Limited

Wesley, Cheryl Jane
Lorsho Limited
Pictish Brewing Co Limited

Wesley, Paul Robert
Lorsho Limited
Pictish Brewing Co Limited

West, George William Arthur
Southbourne Brewing Limited

West, Helen Margaret
Platform 5 Brewing Co Ltd

West, Martin Stephen
The Little Beer Corporation Ltd

Westley, Michael
Westley Brewing Co Ltd.

Weston, Adrian Robert
Everards Brewery Limited

Westwood, Oliver
The Vine Inn Brewery 2016 Ltd

Westwood, Richard James
Mansfield Brewery Trading Ltd

Wetherell, Gladys Margaret
Wetherells Contracts Limited

Wetherell, Mark Lucas
Wetherells Contracts Limited

Wetherell, Paul Russell Lucas
Wetherells Contracts Limited

Wetzel, Petra Margareta
Noah Beers Limited

Whale, Glen Andrew
Double Maxim Beer Co Ltd
Maxim Brewery Limited

Wheeler, Duncan Charles
Blackpit Brewery Ltd

Wheeler, Fergus Oliver
Red Bay Brewing Co Ltd

Wheldon, Sean Robert
Loka Polly Ltd

Wheller, Barnaby
Stratton Lane Ltd

Wheller, Bernadette
Stratton Lane Ltd

Whewell, James Robert
Little Teapot Ltd

Whitaker, David John
The Jolly Boys Brewery Ltd

White, Dane
Phantom Brewing Co. Limited

White, Fiona
The Chalk Stone Brewery Ltd

White, Garry Michael
Stannary Brewing Co Ltd.

White, George Isaac
Imaginary Friends Brewing Ltd

White, Linda
The Freewheelin' Brewery Co Ltd

White, Richard Charles
The Freewheelin' Brewery Co Ltd

White, Richard Garry
Verdant Brewing Co Ltd

White, Russell
The Chalk Stone Brewery Ltd

White, Stephen Glenn
Brew Monster Limited

Whitehead, Edward David
Manning Brewers Ltd

Whitehead, Liam
3's A Crowd Brewing Ltd

Whitehead, Philip Mark
Cobra Beer Partnership Limited
Molson Coors Brewing Co (UK) Ltd
Sharp's Brewery Limited

Whitehurst, Stephen
Brighton Bier Limited

Whiteley, Dennis
Rude Mechanicals Limited

Whiteley, Matthew
Rude Mechanicals Limited

Whiteley, Oliver Richard
Blackpit Brewery Ltd

Whiteley, Thomas
Rude Mechanicals Limited

Whiteside, Marc Andrew
Taw Valley Brewery Limited

Whiting, Andrew George
AB InBev UK Limited

Whittaker, Michael Vincent
Worsthorne Brewing Co Ltd

Whittaker, William
Marston's Acquisitions Limited

Whittle, Colin Douglas Richardson
The Cairngorm Brewery Co Ltd

Whittle, Gareth Andrew
The Saint Brewing Co Limited

Whitwell, Philip
Batch Brew Ltd

Whyatt, Joshua
Brews Brothers Brewery Ltd

Whyte, Andrew Henry
Whyte BR Brewing Co Ltd
Whyte Bar Brewing Co Ltd

Wickens, Gary Christopher
W & W Drinks Ltd

Wickett, Edward Michael Mark
The Kelham Island Brewery Ltd

Wickett, Helen Joan
The Kelham Island Brewery Ltd

Wickham, Mark Paul
The Hay Rake Brewery Ltd

Wicks, Robert James Cairns
Westerham Brewery Co Ltd

Wilcox, Abigayle
Wibblers Brewery (Farms) Ltd

Wilcox, Alex
Sonder Brewing Co Ltd.

Wilcox, Jeremy John
Wibblers Brewery (Farms) Ltd

Wilcox, Philip John
Wibblers Brewery (Farms) Ltd

Wild, Andrew Vernon
Pedal Power Harrogate Limited

Wilde, Colin Francis
Tynemill Limited

Wilde, Peter John
Tynemill Limited

Wilkins, Kevin John
Three Geezers Brewing Limited

Wilkins, Timothy Edward
Bewdley Brewery Limited

Wilkinson, David
The East Yorkshire Beer Co Ltd

Wilkinson, Gillian Margaret
Darlington Brewing and Distilling Co Ltd

Wilkinson, James Bruce
Burton Bridge Brewery Limited

Wilkinson, Joanne
North Brewing Co Ltd

Wilkinson, Jonathan Mark
Arlingham Ales Limited

Wilkinson, Ralph English
Darlington Brewing and Distilling Co Ltd

Wilkinson, Rufus Giles
Session Brewing Co. Limited

Wilkinson, William
Gan Yam Brewing Co Ltd

Willacy, Charles Philip
Old Pie Factory Brewery Ltd

Willacy, Christopher
Beat Ales Ltd.
Topcat Brewery Limited

Willetts, Michael
Spartan Brewery Ltd

Williams, Andrew James
Froth Blowers Brewing Co Ltd

Williams, Andrew Lee
Andys' Ales Limited

Williams, Antony John
Musket Brewery Limited

Williams, Benjamin John
Blackpit Brewery Ltd

Williams, Brett John
Twin Barrel Brewery Limited

Williams, Bruce Andrew
Heather Ale Limited

Williams, Charles Henry
Hook Norton Brewery Co Ltd

Williams, Dafydd Peredur
Cwrw Llyn Cyf

Williams, David Idwal
Moogbrew Ltd

Williams, David Lee
Moorhouse's Brewery Ltd

Williams, David Vaughn Alan
Getset Brew Co Ltd

Williams, Deborah Jane Mary
Stratford upon Avon Brewery Ltd

Williams, Fiona Elisabeth
Hook Norton Brewery Co Ltd

Williams, Frances
Granite Rock Brewery and Home Brew Supplies

Williams, Gary
Rock Springs Brewing Ltd

Williams, Generald Martin
The Friday Beer Co Ltd

Williams, Haydn David
Crankshaft Brewery Limited

Williams, Iorwerth Llywelyn
Cwrw Llyn Cyf

Williams, James Edward Campion
Campion Ale Limited

Williams, John Richard
Rossendale Brew Co Ltd

Williams, Laurence Orchard
Dawkins & Georges Ltd

Williams, Margaret Doris Cornelia
Moogbrew Ltd

Williams, Mark David
Stratford upon Avon Brewery Ltd

Williams, Michael John
Andys' Ales Limited

Williams, Myrddin
Bragdy Lleu Cyf

Williams, Neil Alan
Froth Blowers Brewing Co Ltd

Williams, Rhys Harrison
Musket Brewery Limited

Williams, Richard Derby
Diamond Dicks Brewing Limited

Williams, Richard Michael
Stratford upon Avon Brewery Ltd

Williams, Russell Joseph
Strathmore Brewery Limited

Williams, Scott John
Clan Brewing Co Ltd
Drygate Brewing Co Ltd
Heather Ale Limited

Williams, Thomas Daniel
Bragdy Mona Cyf

Williamson, Alec Philip
Calvors Brewery Limited

Williamson, James Andrew Thomas
3ways Brewing Co Limited

Williamson, Marc Anthony
Linear Brewing Co Ltd

Williamson, Matthew James Ian, Dr
The Clun Brewery Ltd.

Williamson, Paul David
Hillside Brewery Limited

Williamson, Peter John
Hillside Brewery Limited

Willis, David
Cwrw Ial Limited

Willis, James Thomas
Framework Brewery Limited

Willis, Michael Martin
Framework Brewery Limited

Willmer, Stephen Sinclair
John Roberts Brewing Co Ltd

Willmore, John Anthony
Mash Brewery Limited

Willmot, David Richard
Granite Rock Brewery and Home Brew Supplies

Wills, Robert Hugo Weyl
Uppingham Brewery Limited
Uppingham Brewhouse Limited

Willson, Matthew William
Freedom Brewery Ltd

Wilson, Alexander David
FGW Brewery Limited

Wilson, Alexander John Adamson
Myrlex Southend Limited
Wharf Brewing Co Ltd

Wilson, Andrew Paul
White Horse Brewery Co Ltd

Wilson, Christopher Edwin
Brockenhurst Brewery Limited
New Forest Beer Co Ltd

Wilson, Craig David Walter
The Kiln Brewery Ltd

Wilson, Daniel James
Two Bears Brewery Ltd

Wilson, Eoin
Farmageddon Brewing Limited

Wilson, John
Shed35 Ltd

Wilson, Jonathan William Edward
Cross Borders Brewing Co Ltd

Wilson, Luke Adam
The Braybrooke Beer Co Ltd

Wilson, Martin Leslie
Holcot Hop-Craft Ltd

Wilson, Matthew James
Bartleby's Ltd

Wilson, Neil Guest
North Cotswold Brewery Limited

Wilson, Paul John
Interstate Craft Brewing Co Ltd

Wilson, Peter John
S.A.Brain & Co Ltd

Wilson, Ryan
Two Bears Brewery Ltd

Wilson, Vivienne Gail
Beer Monkey Brew Co. Limited

Wiltshire, Robert
Yorkshire Dales Brewing Co Ltd

Wiltshire, Stephen Alan
The Lingfield Brewing Co Ltd

Windridge, Mark Antony
Bostin Brews Ltd

Wing, Alexander Daniel
Brazen Brewing Co. Ltd

Winter, Henry
Lock 81 Brewery Limited

Winterbottom, Peter
Merrimans Brewery Ltd

Wintrip, Robert Charles
Three Shires Brewery Ltd

Wiper, Joan Mary
Wiper & True Ltd.

Wiper, Michael Henry
Wiper & True Ltd.

Wiper, Philip Michael
Wiper & True Ltd.

Wise, Hayley Jane
Urban Island Brewing Co. Ltd

Wise, Sam Robert
Microcosm Brewing Ltd.

Witt, Robert John
Totally Brewed Limited

Witt, Virginia Claire
Totally Brewed Limited

Wojtkow, Janet Anna Rita
Saltaire Brewery Limited

Wolfart, Jacek
Xtraflow Limited

Womersley, Richard J
Spotlight Brewing Ltd

Wood, Alan
Merry Miner Brewery Ltd

Wood, Andrew Charles
Adnams PLC

Wood, Anita Pauline
Merry Miner Brewery Ltd

Wood, Charles Angus
Stod Fold Brewing Limited

Wood, Charles William
Crossover Blendery Limited

Wood, David William
Range Ales Brewery Limited

Wood, Kevin David
Daniel Thwaites PLC

Wood, Mary Delia
Martland Mill Brewery Limited

Wood, Nicholas John MacRae
Scot Brew Limited

Wood, Paul Nicholas
Martland Mill Brewery Limited

Wood, Reece
Watling Street Brewery Limited

Wood, William James Collin
T.& R. Theakston Limited
Samuel Webster & Sons Limited

Woodcock, Glen
The Outstanding Brewing Co Ltd

Woodcock, Paul Stephen
Nene Valley Brewery Limited

Woodhall, Freya Alice
Woodhalls Brewery Limited

Woodhall, Ross John
Woodhalls Brewery Limited

Woodhead, Daniel
Under The Stairs Brewery Ltd

Woodhead, David Leonard
Froth Blowers Brewing Co Ltd

Woodhouse, Anthony William
Badger Ales Limited
Hall & Woodhouse Limited

Woodhouse, Mark John Michael
Badger Ales Limited
Hall & Woodhouse Limited

Woodhouse, Richard Alexander Bruce
Curious Drinks Limited

Woodroffe, Christopher
Pivo-UK Limited

Woodruff, Jack
Woodruff Brewing Ltd

Woods, Alexander Michael
Pongolo Ltd

Wootton, Nicholas David
New Invention Brewery Ltd

Worrall, Dominic Christian
Bedlam Brewery Limited

Worrall, Stephen John
St.Austell Brewery Co Ltd

Worsfold, John Howard
Wicked Hathern Brewery Limited

Wratten, Kathryn Margaret Mary
Black Cat Brewery Limited

Wratten, Paul
Black Cat Brewery Limited

Wray, Edward
Thurstons Horsell Brewery Co Ltd

Wren, Michael
Cold Bath Brewing Co Ltd

Wright, Brian
The Great Glen Brewing Co Ltd

Wright, Christopher David
Three Brothers Brewing Co Ltd

Wright, Geoff
Grain Brewery Limited

Wright, Juliette Myra
Pig and Porter Limited

Wright, Mary Phillipa
Uley Ales Limited

Wright, Neil
Xylo Brewing Ltd

Wright, Nigel
Hopshackle Brewery Limited

Wright, Paula Jane
Wright & Spillane Limited

Wright, Robin Paul Dalton
Pig and Porter Limited

Wright, Steven Andrew
Hop Back Brewery PLC

Wright, Victoria Kate
Grain Brewery Limited

Wyatt, Philip
Holy Well Brewing Ltd

Wyatt, Richard Anthony
W & W Drinks Ltd

Wyn, Sion
Bragdy Nant Cyf

Wynnyczuk, Michael Christopher
X-Ray Brewing Co Ltd

Wythes, Andrew Ian
Mash Brewery Limited

Xifaras, Gareth Andrew
XT Brewing Co Ltd

Xifaras, Michael
XT Brewing Co Ltd

Yardley, Duncan Thomas
Yardley Brothers Europe Ltd

Yardley, Luke Denton
Yardley Brothers Europe Ltd

Yardley, Thomas
Yardley Brothers Europe Ltd

Yarnell, Mark David
Ealing Brewing Ltd

Yates, David Robert
Yates low Brewery Limited

Yates, David Stanley
Yates low Brewery Limited

Yates, Kevin
Humberside Properties [UK] Ltd

Yates, Robert Anthony
Tunnel Brewery Limited

Yeardley, Kane
Cocktails and Craft Beers Ltd

Yeardley, Kane Steven
True North Brew Co Limited

Yeomans, Emma Edwina
Hop Stuff Brewery Limited

Yeomans, Nicholas James
Hop Stuff Brewery Limited

Yerburgh, Ann Jean Mary
Daniel Thwaites PLC

Yerburgh, Oscar Guy Hamlyn
Daniel Thwaites PLC

Young, Benjamin John Matthew
Brimstage Brewing Co. Ltd

Young, Gareth, Dr
Epochal Barrel-Fermented Ales Ltd

Young, Graham Dougal
The Blighty Brewery Limited
Youngs Beers Limited

Young, Jean Elizabeth
Hattie Brown's Brewery Ltd

Young, Nathanial Joseph
Brimstage Brewing Co. Ltd

Young, Paul
Tidal London Ltd

Young, Paul Victor
H.B.Clark & Co.(Successors) Ltd

Young, Sheldon Ashley
Southbourne Ales Limited
Southbourne Brewing Limited

Young, Timothy Stephen
The Patriot Brewery Limited

Zanacchi, Emily Jane
The Ennerdale Brewery Ltd

Zanacchi, Paul
The Ennerdale Brewery Ltd

Zivkovic, Nicholas
The Brewery Limited

Zivkovic, Petar
The 3 Brewers Ltd

This page is intentionally left blank

Standard Industrial Classification
excluding
Manufacture of beer

01110 Growing of cereals (except rice), leguminous crops and oil seeds
Joseph Camm Farms Limited

01130 Growing of vegetables and melons, roots and tubers
Joseph Camm Farms Limited
Dead Fridge Farm Limited

01140 Growing of sugar cane
CFS Castus Test 001 Ltd

01230 Growing of citrus fruits
CFS Castus Test 001 Ltd
Crai Cider Co Ltd

01270 Growing of beverage crops
Crai Cider Co Ltd

01470 Raising of poultry
Dead Fridge Farm Limited

01500 Mixed farming
Everards Brewery Limited
Two Cocks Farm Limited
Wibblers Brewery (Farms) Ltd

02300 Gathering of wild growing non-wood products
Mudlark Investments Ltd

10130 Production of meat and poultry meat products
London Cosmopolitan Drinks Ltd

10320 Manufacture of fruit and vegetable juice
Crosby Beverages Ltd
Doromomo & Sons Ltd
Gilt & Flint Ltd
Little Teapot Ltd
W & W Drinks Ltd

10519 Manufacture of other milk products
Doromomo & Sons Ltd

10520 Manufacture of ice cream
London Cosmopolitan Drinks Ltd

10710 Manufacture of bread; manufacture of fresh pastry goods and cakes
Equal Brewkery CIC

10832 Production of coffee and coffee substitutes
OM Food Corp Ltd

10840 Manufacture of condiments and seasonings
Fat Boi Brewery & Sauce Co Ltd

10850 Manufacture of prepared meals and dishes
Slice & Brew Ltd

10860 Manufacture of homogenized food preparations and dietetic food
Sly Fox Brewery Ltd

10890 Manufacture of other food products n.e.c.
Cereal Technology Limited
A & C Green Food and Beverage Ltd
Whitechapel Industries Ltd

11010 Distilling, rectifying and blending of spirits [51]
Adnams PLC
Batch Brew Ltd
Black Cat Brewery Limited
Boutique Cellar Limited
Branscombe Vale Brewery Ltd
Broughton Ales Limited
Clandestine Distillery Limited
Colonsay Beverages Ltd.
Darlington Brewing and Distilling Co Ltd
Droylsden Craft Limited
Duration Brewing Ltd
East Neuk Organic Brewing & Distilling
Etrusca Brewery & Distillery in St. Andrews
Evolution Brewing Ltd
Forth Bridge Brewery and Distillery
Galldachd Na H-Alba Brewing Ltd
Gleneagles Distillery Limited
Halton Turner Brewing Co Ltd
Holler Brewery Limited
K1 Beer PLC
Kendal Brewery Ltd
Kimbland Distillery Ltd
Liquid Revolution Ltd
Little Rotters Limited
Loch Earn Brewery Ltd
London Brewery Limited
Lost Roots Limited
Lough Neagh Distillers - 1837 Ltd
Luxbev Limited
Mersey Gin Co Ltd
Mousehole Brewery Limited
Mudlark Investments Ltd
New Union Brewing Co Ltd
One Swan Ltd
Penton Park Brewery Limited
Ramsbury Brewing and Distilling Co Ltd
Revelry Brewing & Distilling Ltd
Silvertown Brewery and Distillery Co Ltd
Skinnybrands Ltd
Sky Pirate Ltd
Solway Spirits Ltd
Southey Brewing Co Ltd
Square Street Distillery Ltd
St Andrews Brewers Limited
Steel River Drinks Ltd
Swift Half Collective Ltd
True North Brew Co Limited
Two Fathoms Distillery Ltd.
Universal Robo Innovations Ltd
Yarm Brewing and Distilling Co Ltd
Zymurgorium Ltd

11020 Manufacture of wine from grape [12]
Alcohol Beverages Co Ltd
Amwell Springs Brewery Co Ltd
Boutique Cellar Limited
Clandestine Distillery Limited
K1 Beer PLC
Luxbev Limited
Mersea Island Brewery & Vineyard Ltd
Skinnybrands Ltd
Swift Half Collective Ltd
Universal Robo Innovations Ltd
Vitosha Wine Ltd
Yorkshire Heart Limited

11030 Manufacture of cider and other fruit wines [51]
Alcohol Beverages Co Ltd
Angry Coot Fermentation Co Ltd.
Aston Manor Limited
Boutique Cellar Limited
Branded Drinks Ltd
Brewers Folly Brewery Ltd.
Broughton Ales Limited
Broxbourne Brewery Ltd.
Brute Brewing Co Ltd
Clandestine Distillery Limited
Craftwater Brewing Co Ltd
Crai Cider Co Ltd
Crosby Beverages Ltd
Crossroads Brewery Limited
Thomas Hardy Burtonwood Ltd
Thomas Hardy Holdings Limited
Thomas Hardy Kendal Limited
Hawkins Drinks Limited
Holler Brewery Limited
Jordan's Car Review Ltd
Kendal Brewery Ltd
Kinross Brewery Limited
Last Sign Brewing Co Ltd
Laughing Ass Brewery Ltd
Little Teapot Ltd
Little Wolf Brewing Limited
London Beer Co Ltd
Long Ashton Cider Co Ltd
Lost Boys Brewery Ltd
Mad Yank Brewery Ltd
Marourde Limited
Meanwood Brewery Ltd
Missing Link Brewing Ltd
Monkey Shed Estate Brewing Co Ltd
New Union Brewing Co Ltd
Old Town Brewery Ltd.
Old Tree Brewery Ltd
One Swan Ltd
Overtone Brewing Ltd
Thomas Paine Brewery Limited
Penton Park Brewery Limited
Sky Pirate Ltd
Solway Spirits Ltd
Southey Brewing Co Ltd
Ten Tors Brewery Ltd
Twin Barrel Brewery Limited
Umbrella Brewing Limited
W & W Drinks Ltd
Westmoor Botanicals Limited
Wibblers Brewery (Farms) Ltd
Zymurgorium Ltd

11040 Manufacture of other non-distilled fermented beverages [24]
Amwell Springs Brewery Co Ltd
Black Horse Brewery Ltd
Crossroads Brewery Limited
Deil's Heid Brewing Co Ltd
Ealing Brewing Ltd
Ellismuir Limited
Good Kombucha Drinks Ltd
Good Living Brew Co Limited
Thomas Hardy Burtonwood Ltd
Thomas Hardy Holdings Limited
Thomas Hardy Kendal Limited
Hawkins Drinks Limited
Last Sign Brewing Co Ltd
Little Wolf Brewing Limited
Long Arm Brewing Co Limited
Old Tree Brewery Ltd
One Swan Ltd
Riverside Brewery Ltd
Sky Pirate Ltd
Sly Fox Brewery Ltd
Universal Robo Innovations Ltd
Westmoor Botanicals Limited
XL Brew Ltd
Zymurgorium Ltd

11060 Manufacture of malt
Brewers Folly Brewery Ltd.
Ultimate Maltgold Limited

11070 Manufacture of soft drinks; production of mineral waters and other bottled waters [24]
ABI SAB Group Holding Limited
Bad Girls Brew Limited
Bigla Brewing Co Ltd
Craft Soft Drinks Community Ltd
Crosby Beverages Ltd
A & C Green Food and Beverage Ltd
Thomas Hardy Burtonwood Ltd
Thomas Hardy Holdings Limited
Thomas Hardy Kendal Limited
Hawkins Drinks Limited
Heather Ale Limited
Infinite Session Ltd
Kendal Brewery Ltd
LVS Bottling Limited
Lough Neagh Distillers - 1837 Ltd
Luxbev Limited
Pointeer Ltd
Seafire Brewing Co. Ltd
Session Brewing Co. Limited
Shandy Shack Ltd
Signpost Brewery Ltd
Upper Harglodd Farm Ltd
Vitosha Wine Ltd
Westmoor Botanicals Limited

14131 Manufacture of other men's outerwear
Session Brewing Co. Limited

14190 Manufacture of other wearing apparel and accessories n.e.c.
Phaded World Ltd

17290 Manufacture of other articles of paper and paperboard n.e.c.
Phaded World Ltd

20420 Manufacture of perfumes and toilet preparations
Sloane Home Ltd

20590 Manufacture of other chemical products n.e.c.
Doromomo & Sons Ltd

28930 Manufacture of machinery for food, beverage and tobacco processing
Nicol Brewery Ltd.
Octagon Brewery Limited

31090 Manufacture of other furniture
Wetherells Contracts Limited

32120 Manufacture of jewellery and related articles
Little Rotters Limited

32990 Other manufacturing n.e.c.
Brockenhurst Brewery Limited
New Forest Beer Co Ltd

41100 Development of building projects
French & Jupps Limited
K1 Beer PLC
MC & P Engineering Limited

41201 Construction of commercial buildings
By The River Brewery Ltd

43220 Plumbing, heat and air-conditioning installation
Vertical Stack Ltd

43999 Other specialised construction activities n.e.c.
Wetherells Contracts Limited

45200 Maintenance and repair of motor vehicles
Longhill Garage Limited

46170 Agents involved in the sale of food, beverages and tobacco
Branded Drinks Ltd
Equal Brewkery CIC
Heather Ale Limited
Kairos Solutions Ltd
Konigsberg Seven Bridges Breweries Ltd
Whitechapel Industries Ltd

46190 Agents involved in the sale of a variety of goods
888 Global Trade Ltd
Bear Brewery Co Ltd
Tiny Vessel Brewing Co Ltd

46220 Wholesale of flowers and plants
Mudlark Investments Ltd

46341 Wholesale of fruit and vegetable juices, mineral water and soft drinks
Infinite Session Ltd
Seafire Brewing Co. Ltd

46342 Wholesale of wine, beer, spirits and other alcoholic beverages [145]
23-7 Brewing Ltd
3 Cities Brewing Co Ltd
3ABC Ltd
4 Acre Brewing Co. Ltd
888 Global Trade Ltd
Abyss Brewing Ltd
Adnams PLC
Amwell Springs Brewery Co Ltd
Arkell's Brewery Limited
Atlantic Craft Soda Co Ltd
Atom Brewing Co Limited
Aurora Ales Limited
BCM Brewing Co Ltd
BL Drinks Ltd
Bad Girls Brew Limited
Bad Joke Brew Co Ltd
Bakewell Road Brewery Ltd
Bang The Elephant Brewing Co Ltd
Belvoir Brewery Limited
Black Cat Brewery Limited
Blackedge Brewing Co Ltd
Bobby Beer Co Ltd
Bone Machine Brewing Co Ltd
S.A.Brain & Co Ltd
Branded Drinks Ltd
Brewis Beer Co Ltd
Bridgnorth Brewing Co Ltd
Broughton Ales Limited
Bucklebury Brewers Ltd
Canopy Beer Co Ltd
H.B.Clark & Co.(Successors) Ltd
Cobra Beer Partnership Limited
Cold Formd Ltd
Craftwater Brewing Co Ltd
Creative Juices Brewing Co Ltd
Crouch Vale Brewery Limited
Dark Revolution Ltd
Deutschlond Brewery Limited
Donnington Brewery Limited
Droylsden Craft Limited
Drumgaw Holdings Ltd
East London Brewing Co Ltd
Ellismuir Limited
Epic Beers Limited
Everards Brewery Limited
Faking Bad Brewery Limited
Force Brewery Limited
Forest Hill Brewing Co Ltd
Galldachd Na H-Alba Brewing Ltd
Gleneagles Distillery Limited
Good Living Brew Co Limited
Grafham Brewing Co Ltd
Great Newsome Brewery Limited
Hall & Woodhouse Limited
Halton Turner Brewing Co Ltd
Head Thirst Ltd
Hindsight Collective Ltd
Hitchin Brewery Ltd
Hopper House Brew Farm Ltd
Hops and Dots Brewing Co Ltd
Hydes' Brewery Limited
Incapico Inc Limited
Infinite Session Ltd
Jabru Bevco Ltd

Jackrabbit Brewing Co. Ltd
Jocks and Peers Brewing Co Ltd
Kairos Solutions Ltd
Keltek Cornish Brewery Limited
Kimbland Distillery Ltd
Kinkell Brewery Ltd
Konigsberg Seven Bridges Breweries Ltd
Koomor Brewing Co Ltd
Laughing Ass Brewery Ltd
Laughing Pug Ltd
Law and Disorder Brew Co Ltd
Lion-Beer, Spirits & Wine (UK) Ltd
London Ale UK Ltd
Loopland Brewing Co Ltd
Los Perros Sueltos Brewing Co Ltd
Lough Neagh Distillers - 1837 Ltd
Marston's Acquisitions Limited
Matheson Brewers Ltd
McGrath's Brewing Limited
Molson Coors Brewing Co (UK) Ltd
Monkey Shed Estate Brewing Co Ltd
Morecambe Bay Wines Limited
Mumbles Brewery Ltd
Myrlex Southend Limited
Near Beer Brewing Co. Ltd
Oxford Brewery Limited
Oxford Brewing Co Ltd
Padlock Brewery Ltd.
Padstow Brewing Company (2013) Ltd
Pivo Beverages Ltd
Play Limited
Pomona Island Brew Co Ltd
Pongolo Ltd
Punjabi Ltd
Purity Brewing Co Ltd
Raven Hill Brewery Limited
Red Bay Brewing Co Ltd
Red Squirrel Brewery Limited
Reids Gold Brewing Co Ltd
River Widow Brewery Ltd
Rockin Robin Brewery Ltd
Rossendale Brew Co Ltd
Rude Mechanicals Limited
Saints Row Brewing Co Ltd
Saltrock Brewing Co Ltd
Samuels Brewing Co Ltd
Seafire Brewing Co. Ltd
Shandy Shack Ltd
Sheffield Brewers Collective
Shelsley Brewing Co Ltd
Shepherd Neame Limited
Shropshire Beers Limited
Signature Brew Ltd
Silver Rocket Brewing Ltd
Sloane Home Ltd
Slopemeister Brewing Co Ltd
Solway Spirits Ltd
Southbourne Brewing Limited
Southbrew Co Ltd
St.Austell Brewery Co Ltd
Stag Ales Ltd
Stag Brewery Ltd
Stay Gold Beer Co Ltd
Steel Coulson Ltd
Time & Tide Brewing Limited
Tiny Vessel Brewing Co Ltd
Tom's Tap and Brewhouse Ltd
Triple Point Brewing Ltd
Urbeer Ltd
Van Pur UK Ltd
Via Academia Vocatus Ltd
Vitosha Wine Ltd

Wadworth and Co Ltd
Charles Wells Brewery Limited
Charles Wells,Limited
Wetherby Brew Co Limited
White Wolf Brewery Ltd
Wold Toppers Limited
Workshy Brewing Ltd
Xtraflow Limited
Yates Iow Brewery Limited

46380 Wholesale of other food, including fish, crustaceans and molluscs
Wold Toppers Limited

46390 Non-specialised wholesale of food, beverages and tobacco
Arkell's Brewery Limited

46450 Wholesale of perfume and cosmetics
Sloane Home Ltd

46690 Wholesale of other machinery and equipment
Haresfoot Storage & Distribution Co Ltd

46900 Non-specialised wholesale trade
888 Global Trade Ltd
Bear Brewery Co Ltd
Tiny Vessel Brewing Co Ltd

47110 Retail sale in non-specialised stores with food, beverages or tobacco predominating
Foresight Holdings Limited
Hunter Brewing Co Ltd
Play Limited

47250 Retail sale of beverages in specialised stores [24]
3's A Crowd Brewing Ltd
Adnams PLC
Bluestone Brewing Co Ltd
Craft Beer Collective Limited
Creative Juices Brewing Co Ltd
Crouch Vale Brewery Limited
Dorset Brewing Co Ltd
Eden Mill Brewers Ltd
Great Newsome Brewery Limited
Greene King Brewing and Retailing
Kinkell Brewery Ltd
Lion-Beer, Spirits & Wine (UK) Ltd
Marston's Acquisitions Limited
Owlcrab Limited
Oxford Brewery Limited
Play Limited
Rockin Robin Brewery Ltd
Sheffield Brewers Collective
Southbourne Ales Limited
Southbourne Brewing Limited
Towler and Webb Limited
Wetherby Brew Co Limited
Whitefaced Ltd
Wold Toppers Limited

47710 Retail sale of clothing in specialised stores
Moon Cartel Limited

47789 Other retail sale of new goods in specialised stores (not commercial art galleries and opticians)
Granite Rock Brewery and Home Brew Supplies

47810 Retail sale via stalls and markets of food, beverages and tobacco products [13]
Bobby Beer Co Ltd
Bohem Brewery Ltd
By The River Brewery Ltd
Creative Juices Brewing Co Ltd
Forest Hill Brewing Co Ltd
Hildenborough Brewery Ltd
Hunter Brewing Co Ltd
Old Thistle Co Ltd
Saltrock Brewing Co Ltd
Sheffield Brewers Collective
Wetherby Brew Co Limited
Whitechapel Industries Ltd
Whitefaced Ltd

47820 Retail sale via stalls and markets of textiles, clothing and footwear
Hunter Brewing Co Ltd

47910 Retail sale via mail order houses or via Internet
Craft Beer Collective Limited
Gleneagles Distillery Limited
Hildenborough Brewery Ltd
Honest Brew Ltd
Padstow Brewing Company (2013) Ltd
Quad Brewing Co Ltd
Reids Gold Brewing Co Ltd
Stag Brewery Ltd

47990 Other retail sale not in stores, stalls or markets
Craft Beer Collective Limited
Totnes Brewing Co Limited

49410 Freight transport by road
Sly Fox Brewery Ltd

52220 Service activities incidental to water transportation
2731 Limited

55100 Hotels and similar accommodation
S.A.Brain & Co Ltd
Breworks Ltd
Hill House Inns Limited
Lake View Country House Ltd
Shepherd Neame Limited
Daniel Thwaites PLC
Trumark Properties Limited
Vovin Ltd
White Hart Halstead Limited

55900 Other accommodation
Dead Fridge Farm Limited

56101 Licenced restaurants [19]
Arran Brew Ltd.
Charlbury Brewing Co Ltd
Chubby Seal Ltd
Dancing Man Brewery Limited
Duration Brewing Ltd
Flat Cap Holding Co Ltd
Hall & Woodhouse Limited
Harvey Elizabeth Limited
Hickbrew Limited
Hill House Inns Limited
Laiho Limited
Lake View Country House Ltd
Marston's PLC
OM Food Corp Ltd
Phaded World Ltd
Round Corner Brewing Ltd
Daniel Thwaites PLC
Trumark Properties Limited
Wanderlust Bar Limited

56102 Unlicenced restaurants and cafes
London Ale UK Ltd

56103 Take-away food shops and mobile food stands
Bib Brewing Ltd
Bigla Brewing Co Ltd
Nuglyfe Ltd
Round Corner Brewing Ltd
Slice & Brew Ltd

56210 Event catering activities [12]
Bang The Elephant Brewing Co Ltd
Barefaced Brewing Ltd
Bohem Brewery Ltd
Cold Formd Ltd
Craft Origins Limited
Harvey Elizabeth Limited
Hexad Brewing Ltd
Hickbrew Limited
Liquid Revolution Ltd
Meanwood Brewery Ltd
Missing Link Brewing Ltd
Near Beer Brewing Co. Ltd

56290 Other food services
Askham Brewery Limited

56301 Licenced clubs
Wanderlust Bar Limited

56302 Public houses and bars [114]
Anglia Pub Co Ltd
Anspach & Hobday Limited
Ar Suil Brewing Project Ltd
Arkell's Brewery Limited
Arran Brew Ltd.
Attic Brew Co. Ltd
BC Brewing & Pub Co Ltd
Bang The Elephant Brewing Co Ltd
Belvoir Brewery Limited
Bib Brewing Ltd
Biercafe Ltd
Bigla Brewing Co Ltd
Birmingham Brewing Co Ltd
Bohem Brewery Ltd
S.A.Brain & Co Ltd
Breworks Ltd

Brewsmith Limited
Bullfinch Brewery Limited
Butcombe Brewery Limited
Butcombe Brewing Co Ltd
Butcombe Pubco Limited
Cairngorm Brewery Co Ltd
Candid Brewing Co. Limited
Charlbury Brewing Co Ltd
Church End Brewery Limited
Cross Inn (Maesteg) Limited
Cullach Brewing Ltd
Dancing Man Brewery Limited
Dog and Rabbit Brewery Ltd
Donnington Brewery Limited
Duration Brewing Ltd
Everards Brewery Limited
Fearless Brewing Ltd
Filo Brewing Co Ltd
Fire Rock Brewing Co Ltd.
Flat Cap Holding Co Ltd
Foghorn Brew Co Ltd
Fulham Brewery Ltd
Garden City Brewery Limited
Greene King Brewing and Retailing
Hall & Woodhouse Limited
Halton Turner Brewing Co Ltd
Harvey & Son (Lewes) Limited
Harvey Elizabeth Limited
Hickbrew Limited
Hill House Inns Limited
Hoggshead Brewhouse Limited
Joseph Holt Group Limited
Joseph Holt Limited
Hop Back Brewery PLC
Hopper House Brew Farm Ltd
Hydes' Brewery Limited
Instant Karma Brewing Co Ltd
Ironstone Brewery Ltd
Joules Brewery Limited
Killer Hop Brew Co Ltd
Kinkell Brewery Ltd
Laiho Limited
Lancar Limited
Lancaster Brewery Holdings Ltd
Last Sign Brewing Co Ltd
Laughing Pug Ltd
Leeds Brewery Co Ltd
Lincolnshire Craft Beers Ltd
Liquid Revolution Ltd
London Ale UK Ltd
London Brewing Co Ltd
Mansfield Brewery Trading Ltd
Marble Beers Limited
Marston's PLC
Mart's Brewing Co Ltd
McMullen & Sons, Limited
Meanwood Brewery Ltd
Missing Link Brewing Ltd
Newcastle Brewing Ltd
Northern Monkey Brew Co. Ltd
Nungate Brewery Co Ltd
Ol Brewery Limited
Old Thistle Co Ltd
Orchard Road Brewery Limited
Postlethwaites Brewery Ltd
Rhymney Brewery Ltd
Round Corner Brewing Ltd
Sentinel Brewery Holdings Ltd
Shandy Shack Ltd
Shepherd Neame Limited
Shiny Brewing Co Ltd
Sibley Brewing Co Ltd.

St. Peter's Brewery Co. Ltd
St.Austell Brewery Co Ltd
Steam Town Brewco Limited
Steel Coulson Ltd
Symmetry Brewing Co Ltd
Three Counties Brewery Limited
Three Shires Brewery Ltd
Daniel Thwaites PLC
Tirril Brewery Limited
Tom's Tap and Brewhouse Ltd
Townes Brewery Limited
Triple Point Brewing Ltd
True North Brew Co Limited
Turing Complete Solutions Ltd
Two Bears Brewery Ltd
Tynemill Limited
Ullage Ale Ltd
Vovin Ltd
W.L.B.C Ltd
Wadworth and Co Ltd
Wanderlust Bar Limited
Charles Wells,Limited
Wetherells Contracts Limited
White Hart Halstead Limited
Woodruff Brewing Ltd
Wright & Spillane Limited

58110 Book publishing
Vinifera Limited

62012 Business and domestic software development
Turing Complete Solutions Ltd

62020 Information technology consultancy activities
Hardstate Limited
Inkerman Ales Limited
Lancar Limited
Turing Complete Solutions Ltd
Vertical Stack Ltd

62090 Other information technology service activities
Agnate Limited
Map Kernow Ltd.

63110 Data processing, hosting and related activities
Vertical Stack Ltd

63990 Other information service activities n.e.c.
Company of Dead Brewers Ltd
Eldridge, Pope & Co Ltd

64202 Activities of production holding companies
No Comply Ltd

64209 Activities of other holding companies n.e.c.
Devanha Brewery Holdings Ltd

64922 Activities of mortgage finance companies
Chris O'Connor and Associates Ltd

66220 Activities of insurance agents and brokers
Chris O'Connor and Associates Ltd

68100 Buying and selling of own real estate
Christopher Ellis and Son Ltd

68209 Other letting and operating of own or leased real estate
Colonsay Brewing Co Ltd
Greene King Brewing and Retailing
Hydes' Brewery Limited

70210 Public relations and communications activities
Lincolnshire Brewing Co Ltd

70229 Management consultancy activities other than financial management
Brightbeer Limited
Greyhound Drinks Limited
Insight Driven Innovation Ltd
Chris O'Connor and Associates Ltd
Religious Ales Ltd

71121 Engineering design activities for industrial process and production
Bone Machine Brewing Co Ltd

71122 Engineering related scientific and technical consulting activities
Drumgaw Holdings Ltd
Taylors Blackbeck Brewery Ltd

74100 Specialised design activities
Hop Forward Ltd
McGrath's Brewing Limited

74909 Other professional, scientific and technical activities n.e.c.
Company of Dead Brewers Ltd

74990 Non-trading company
Dobbins Guiltless Stout Co Ltd
London Beer Factory Ltd.

77210 Renting and leasing of recreational and sports goods
Vyrnwy Developments Limited

77390 Renting and leasing of other machinery, equipment and tangible goods n.e.c.
MBJW Brewing Limited
Saison 86 Limited
Sentinel Brewery Holdings Ltd
Vyrnwy Developments Limited

77400 Leasing of intellectual property and similar products, except copyright works
Reds Beer Co Ltd

80100 Private security activities
2731 Limited

81100 Combined facilities support activities
2731 Limited

81210 General cleaning of buildings
Got 2 Bee Clean Ltd

81299 Other cleaning services
Vyrnwy Developments Limited

82920 Packaging activities
Agricola Bottling Limited
Enfield Brewery Limited

82990 Other business support service activities n.e.c.
ALE Finance Services Limited
Crafty Leopard Brewing Co Ltd
Hop Forward Ltd

85520 Cultural education
Queer Brewing Project Ltd

86900 Other human health activities
Spencer Panacea Limited

90010 Performing arts
Decagram Art and Craft CIC

90020 Support activities to performing arts
Decagram Art and Craft CIC

90030 Artistic creation
Decagram Art and Craft CIC
Little Rotters Limited
PLS Special Projects Limited

91040 Botanical and zoological gardens and nature reserves activities
By The River Brewery Ltd

93290 Other amusement and recreation activities n.e.c.
Lekker Days Ltd

94110 Activities of business and employers membership organisations
Craft Soft Drinks Community Ltd

94910 Activities of religious organisations
Kairos Solutions Ltd

96090 Other service activities n.e.c.
Got 2 Bee Clean Ltd

99999 Dormant company
Two Roses Brewery Ltd

Printed in 8pt Nimbus Sans L

Designed by URW++ Design and Development GmbH

Dellam Publishing Limited

2 Heath Drive, Sutton, Surrey, SM2 5RP

Fax: 020 8770 7478   email: enquiries@dellam.com

SAN: 0177881   EAN/GLN: 5030670177882

www.ingramcontent.com/pod-product-compliance
Lightning Source LLC
Chambersburg PA
CBHW081106080526
44587CB00021B/3469